WILLS AND ADMINISTRATIONS

of

ACCOMACK COUNTY

V I R G I N I A

1663–1800

❧❦❧

Compiled and Edited by
Stratton Nottingham

HERITAGE BOOKS
2019

HERITAGE BOOKS
AN IMPRINT OF HERITAGE BOOKS, INC.

Books, Cds, and more—Worldwide

For our listing of thousands of titles see our website
at
www.HeritageBooks.com

A Facsimile Reprint
Published 2019 by
HERITAGE BOOKS, INC.
Publishing Division
5810 Ruatan Street
Berwyn Heights, Md. 20740

International Standard Book Numbers
Paperbound: 978-1-55613-405-0
Clothbound: 978-0-7884-8989-1

CONTENTS

PREFACE

I have been asked by Mr. Nottingham to write a preface for his ACCOMACK WILLS and ADMINISTRATIONS. I suppose I have been asked because I am almost as familiar with Accomack records as Mr. Nottingham, himself, at least I know their minute completeness and their great value. I have not, however, the advantage of being within daily reach of the Accomack office. Not only do I know the value of these records but from my research work in Virginia and the states further south, I know how very many people have gone inland to the "continent" of Virginia (as the quaint phrase goes) and to North and South Carolina, to Georgia, Alabama, Kentucky, Tennessee, and the more distant West.

Accomack is only twelve miles wide at its widest, and for generations it was an isolated section. Fortunately its sons and daughters did not stay there, otherwise, as they say of the Island of Aquidneck, Rhode Island, when the Friends hold their annual meeting there .... the peninsula might have tipped up with the excess population!

But they did move away following the urge which seems to be an inheritance of Americans, leaving behind them in the County Court their ancestral records. And many of them, for the County Court, though sadly careless as to their births and baptisms, recorded their cattle-marks (almost as soon as they were born!) set them down in orderly lists as they grew to tithable age, called them to jury duty, processioned their lands, recorded every mortgage and every demise of land, and above all, probated their wills and issued letters of administration on the estates of the intestates.

These wills and administrations are remarkably complete, and they are the only history (with the titles to land) that many southern families have.

Mr. Nottingham has compiled a most unusually comprehensive abstract of these records of what, in other states, is the Probate Court. And he is peculiarly fitted for this work, having a natural taste for antiquarian research, a wider reading than the average searcher, considerable association with and training in the forms of law, a familiarity with the families (several of whom are his own) and above all, a marked ability in reading the old script. These very early pages are Greek to many, and strange errors have been made by the inexperienced. Also, on account of the isolation of the Eastern Shore, equally strange traditions have arisen.

This is a volume of FACTS. I have never read of a testator having been accused of untruthful statements. The very naivete of the wills speaks for their truth and makes them fascinating reading.

We can ask but one question. Why did not the immigrant ancestor occasionally say from what English shire, Welsh, Irish or Scotch parish he hailed?

Washington, D. C.   Milnor Ljungstedt.

FOREWORD

The abstracts of wills and administrations contained in the compila-
tion now issued are drawn from a critical study of the records of
Accomack. There has been but one objective in the study: to find
every record of will and administration, to obtain the names of every
beneficiary of an estate, to discover the degree of relationship of the
beneficiary to the testator or intestate, and to find the nature of the
inheritance.

This has been done by carefully reading every page of the Accomack
County records of wills and administrations, between 1663 and 1800.
Special attention has been paid to the orders of probate, which often
contain the names of children and heirs not mentioned in the body of
the will, particularly the "heir at law." It was not unusual for a man
to give his eldest son his share of his estate before his death, and
when this was done, very often the eldest son is not mentioned in the
will, but when the will was probated the "heir at law" was cited to
appear and show cause, if any he could, why the will should not be
admitted to record. This order gives the name of the "heir at law,"
which is duly set forth in the order of probate. Again, a man frequent-
ly left property to his wife and made her his executrix, but did not
state her name; when the will was probated her name appears in the
order either as qualifying or as relinquishing her right to qualify.

Every effort has been made to avoid errors--after the wills and administration orders were abstracted they were all carefully gone over,
checked with the originals and verified.

In the wills the first date given is the date of the instrument, the
second the date of probate. Few abbreviations have been used, and
these are obvious. Witt: witness; Planta: Plantation; Bro. Brother;
Wid: widow &c.

As is the case with most publications of this character, this is more
than likely to prove to be a "labor of love," but the compiler will feel
fully repaid in making these records available to the public, and in
doing his modest bit toward preserving the records of Colonial Virginia.

The compiler wishes to acknowledge his sincere appreciation of the
courtesy and consideration shown him by Mr. John D. Grant, Jr.,

Clerk, Mr. Robert Oldham, Deputy, Miss Tabitha Grant, Miss Susan Grant, and Mrs. Harry Taylor, while making these abstracts, and also wishes to take this opportunity of expressing his appreciation of the interest shown by Mrs. H. D. Sheppard and Mrs. Milnor Ljungstedt, without whose encouragement and valuable advice it is doubtful if this volume would have ever been published.

INTRODUCTION

Stratton Nottingham's untimely death at age forty-five robbed Virginia of an indefatigable compiler of genealogical data. Born in 1887 at Eastville in Northampton County on Virginia's Eastern Shore, Nottingham as a young man served as deputy clerk of the Northampton court. About 1920, he removed to Onancock in the adjoining county of Accomack. There, Nottingham took up the full-time practice of genealogy and, as a byproduct of his professional research, began the publication of numerous genealogical compilations--marriage bonds, militia rolls, land causes, wills and administrations. His output was prolific. Between 1927 and 1931, he published thirteen volumes of abstracts from the court records of Accomack, Northampton, Lancaster, Mecklenburg, Northumberland, and Westmoreland counties. His work has enjoyed an enviable reputation for accuracy and has saved generations of genealogists countless hours of research. Stratton Nottingham surely would have accomplished more had not appendicitis occasioned a fatal attack of pneumonia. Nottingham died at the home of his parents on King Street, Onancock, on March 30, 1932.

Heritage Books' republication of Stratton Nottingham's work is most welcome. Many of Nottingham's books have long been unavailable, and all were originally printed on inferior paper, now rapidly deteriorating. *Wills and Administrations of Accomack County,* the second volume to be republished, has since its appearance in 1931 been considered essential for the study of Eastern Shore of Virginia genealogy. The volume includes abstracts of wills and administrations for the period 1663-1800. It greatly aids the genealogist and the historian in determining kinship patterns, holdings in real, personal, and slave properties, and the geographical location of tracts of land. Occasionally it provides the place of origin or prior residence of the testator. In its painstaking detail, *Wills and Administrations of Accomack County* is characteristic of Stratton Nottingham's dedication to his calling. In its length and in its depth of research, it is Nottingham's masterwork.

Brooks Miles Barnes
Onancock, Virginia
13 September 1990

VOLUME I

MAJOR, JOHN - Not dated - 18 July, 1774 - Bro. Richard Johnson. Cousin William Waller. Sister Elizabeth Johnson. Godson Owen Ocollena. Planta. to be divided between bro. Richard Johnson & William Waller, my mother loving [sic] upon the said planta. as long as she is in ye condition she is in. To my mother my servants, she maintaining my bro. Richard, reversion to bro. Richard Johnson. Bro. William Major & Andrew Finnie overseers over what is left unto the children. Witt: Owen Ocollena, Andrew Finnie, William Major - p. 70

BAKER, EDWARD, late of London - 19 Oct. 1664 - 16 Nov. 1664 - To Bro. in law Lt. Col. William Kendall. To Capt. Robert Pitt. Lt. Col. William Kendall & Robert Pitt Ex'rs. in trust of the goods I now have with me in the ship Mary of London upon her voyage for Virginia, whereof the said Robert Pitt is commander, to make the best of said goods with all convenient speed & return the net proceeds to my two friends Mr. George Clark "at ye signe of ye Shipp & Starr in Cheapside & Mr. Simon Hackett watchmaker in Cornehill in London" to be disposed of by them for the use of my two children, Edward & Elizabeth Baker. Witt: Devorax Browne, Hn. Jones, Will: Stevens - p. 79

DUNSTON, EDWARD - Adm. on his estate to Elizabeth Dunston, widow of said Edward. 18 Dec. 1665 - p. 106

RACKLIFF, CHARLES - Adm. his est. to Elizabeth Rackliff, wid. of Charles - 18 Dec. 1665 - p. 107

RODOLPHUS, WILLIAM - Adm. his est. to George Hamling as marrying the widow of said William - 18 Sept. 1666 - p. 124

DIE, JOHN - Adm. his est. to Lawrence Robinson - 18 Sept. 1666 - p. 125

SHERWOOD, FRANCIS - Adm. his est. to Joseph Newton - 16 Oct. 1666 - p. 1

JONES, HENRY - 8 Feb. 1664 - 16 Feb. 1664 - To mother Mary Harper mourning ring & 10 L in the hands of Mr. Anthony Joyner of Ramsdon in the County of Oxford. To Bro. James Jones 50 L when he hath served his apprenticeship. To sister Margaret Jones. To sister Elizabeth Jones. To Jane Hickman, Joan Hickman & Rachel Hickman, children of my dec. sister Jane Hickman. To half sister Sarah Harper & half bro. Robert Harper. To friends George Watson, Capt. Edm: Bowman & wife Elizabeth & his dau. Gertrude Bowman. Bro. in law Richard Bayley & sister Mary Bayley resid. Legatees & Ex'rs. Witt: Elizabeth Bowman, George Watson - p. 5

HACK, Dr. GEORGE - 5 Mar. 1664 - 17 Apr. 1665 - Maj. Goldsmith & Capt. Howell guardians of my three children. Should my wife marry she to have half my est. & the other half to my children, if she do not marry whole estate to remain in her possession. Wife Ann Exec. Maj. John Tilney, Hugh Yeo & James Weadon to assist her while she stays here & for her transportation up the Bay. Witt: Richard Buckland, Tobias Selvey - p. 11

HODCKINS, ANTHONY - 19 June 1665 - 16 Aug. 1665 - Eldest dau. Elizabeth (under 16) sole heir. Dau. Ann. Wife Joyce Exec. & to have the use of my planta. for life. To Ralph Dow, Jr. an iron pott in the possession of his father. I confirm my former gift to Hugh Partridge, being a two year old heifer, a sow & their increase. To my servant Dorothy Young. Father Capt. William Jones & friend Lt. Col. William Waters supervisors of my will & "I desire them for God sake to assist my wife & children". Witt: Tob: Selvey, Robert Hutchinson - p. 15

BALL, ALPHONSO - Adm. his est. to Lawrence Robinson - 18 Mar. 1666 - p. 16

FURLONG, EDMOND - Adm. his est. to John Fawsett, Attorney for the County - 16 July 1667 - p. 29

BONWELL, JAMES - Adm. his est. to Mary Bonwell, wid. of James - 16 July 1667 - p. 29

SHERWOOD, MARGARET - Nunc. 21 Sept. 1666 - 16 Feb. 1666 - Joseph Newton sole legatee - Proved by Robert Hutchinson & Daniell Owen - p. 36

COX, RICHARD - Adm. his est. to George Watson, His Maj's. Att'y. for the county of Accomack - 25 Oct. 1667 - p. 40

CRUMP, GEORGE - Adm. his est. to Thomas Tunnell - 19 Dec. 1667 - p. 44

SIMES, ROBERT - 11 July 1667 - 24 Oct. 1667 - To Robert Hewitt all my goods in Virginia. Witt: Christopher Stribling, Thomas Hall, Joseph Pitman, Roger Barker - p. 62

CRUMP, GEORGE - 12 Sept. 1667 - 24 Oct. 1667 - To Esther Littleton. To Thomas Tunnell, son of Thomas Tunnell. Friend Thomas Tunnell resid. legatee. & Ex'r. Witt: Edward Smalle, Richard Holland. - p. 64

BOOTE, NICHOLAS - 9 Jan. 1667 - 8 Apr. 1668 - To wife Ann all my land in Mobjack Bay in Gloucester County cont. by patent 150 A. & my interest in land at Pungotege in Accomack County. To wife proceeds of all goods sent home to Holland consigned to William Shive - Wife resid. legatee & Exec. Hugh Yeo & Charles Scarburgh to assist her in disposing of her affairs. Witt: Charles Scarburgh, George Nich: Hack - p. 68

WILLIAMS, JOHN, of Accomack, at ye upper end of Nusswadox Creek - 14 Feb. 1666 - 8 Apr. 1668 - Wife Frances sole legatee & Exec. Witt: Rowland Baugh, Phillip Fisher - p. 64

RUSSELL, CHARLES - 6 June 1668 - 16 June 1668 - To wife Sarah half my est. Remaining half to my 5 grandchildren (not named) Dau. Sarah Johnson. Gr. son John Johnson. Gr. son Bennett Remse. To Anthony Bell, son of Thomas Bell. Witt: Rich: Bally, Thomas Hedges. - p. 71

GOWERS, WILLIAM - 31 July 1668 - 5 Jan. 1668 - To Francis Ayres, son of John Ayres, 300 A. To John Arew 300 A., being the planta. where I now live in exchange for 300 A. belonging to the said John Arew lying in Hunting Creek & adj. the land where John Ayres now lives: which said 300 A., exchanged or not, I give to John Ayres, son of John Ayres. To Patience Ayres, dau. of John Ayres. To John Drummond & to his sons Richard & John Drummond. To Isaac Dix. To George Middleton & William Willet. To Dorothy Conder. To Mary Hewett, dau. of Robert Hewett. Capt. Richard Hill resid. legatee. Witt: Rich: Hill, John Drummond. - p. 91

WALFORD. JOHN - 20 Nov. 1667 - 16 Mar. 1668 - To Sarah Johnson, dau. of George Johnson of Muddy Creek. Wife Christian Walford Exec. Witt: Edward Moore, John White, Edward Moore, Jr. - p. 102

SEVERN, PETER, of Patuxent River in Calvert County, Md. 13 Jan. 1667 - 7 Nov. 1668 - To Arthur Ludford & Tobias Norton for drawing will, witnessing same &c. To John Holshott. Jane Severn resid. legatee - Uncle John Pott Ex'r. Witt: Arthur Loudford, Tobias Norton - p. 108

WHITE, HENRY - 2 Aug. 1669 - 24 Nov. 1669 - To Josias Cowdery 200 A. on Nusswadox Creek, being part of 950 A., said 950 A. being part of 1800 A. granted me by patent. To godson Henry Scott, son of Owen Scott, 100 A. out of said tract. To friend John Tankard, Gent. residue of said 950 A. John Tankard Ex'r. Witt: Benj: Cowdery, Mathew Patrick - p. 139

EVANS, JOHN - 19 Apr. 1667 - 16 Oct. 1670 - To Godson Tobias Pepergum & wife Joane whole estate. Wife Joane Exec., Edward Smith to assist her. Witt: Henry White, Nicholas Lawrence - p. 167

TREWETT, GEORGE - 10 July 1670 - 16 Oct. 1670 - To son Henry land at Onancock. To son James 200 A. at Mudey Creek & 50 A. marsh. To son George land adj. my son James & 50 A. marsh. To son John land at Mudey Creek & 50 A. marsh. To son Job 100 A. called Peninsula or Hills Choyce, 50 A, adj. my son John & 100 A. in marsh. To children Jane, Dorathy, James, Susanna, John, Elizabeth & Job Trewett cattle, household goods &c. to remain in control of my sons Henry & George, they to give each of my said children their equal portion as they come to age of 18. To my servant Robert Spencer. Sons Henry & George Exrs. - p. 168

PITT, ROBERT - "Upon intelligence of the death of Mr. Robert Pitt, Devoras Browne produced a will formerly made by the sd Pitt appointing him to be his executor" Browne willing to take charge of said estate for 9 months from this date, and if no other will appears the Court to grant adminstration upon the petition of sd: Browne, he in the meantime to take an inventory of the estate in this country & Mr. Richard Hill to be present - 16 June 1670 - p. 196

Orders 1666-1670(iii)

FINNE, ANDREW - Adm. his est. to Jane Finne, wid. of said Andrew - 17 May 1669 - p. 140

Orders 1671-1673(iv)

DOLBY, JOHN, Sr., of the Parish of Hungars in the County of Northampton - 29 Apr. 1671 - 27 June 1671 - To Margaret & Ann Dolby, daus. of my son Edward. To John, Margaret & Mary Major, children of William Major. To Thomas & Temperance Johnson, children of Obedience Johnson. To son Peter. To son John. To wife (no name) To son Peter & my wife all my land & mill jointly during her life, reversion to sons Edward & John equally, 100 A. to each & 250 A. to my son Peter, being the remainder of my plantation. Wife & children resid. legatees. Wife Exec. Edward Dolby, Obedience Johnson & William Major overseers - Witt: John Tilney, John White - p. 5

PARTRIDGE, HUGH, lying at the house of William Benston - Nunc. - 17 Oct. 1671 - 21 Nov. 1671 - Whole est. to Alexander Benston after William Benston is paid for his trouble. Proved by Thomas Leatherbury & Mary Benston - p. 35

SACKER, EDWARD - Adm. his est. to Frances Sacker, wid, of said Edward - 6 Mar. 1671 - p. 69

4

TAYLOR, WALTER - 12 Dec. 1671 - 17 Apr. 1672 - Wife Joan & friend John Drummond Ex'rs. To wife Joan 1/3 of personal est. with her choice of which planta. she shall live on during her single life, she to have use of whole est. for the benefit of my 4 sons during their minority provided she remain single. To eldest son John planta. known as Gabriells or Watts Island. To sons Walter & James Taylor planta. in Pocomoke River, Somersett County, Md., known as the Strand. Sons John, Walter, James & Gilbert (under 16) Witt: Henry Browne, Phillip___, Osmond Dering p. 83

MILBY, JOHN - 20 Jan. 1664 - 17 Apr. 1672 - To son John my thickett on the main bay. To son Joseph land adj. his brother John known as the Long Neck. To son Samuel land adj. his bro. Joseph. To son William the remainder of my land adj. his bro. Samuel. "And for my wife, seeing she hath been a very cruel wife unto me" - Wife to receive no part of est. owing to her behaviour subject to order of Court. Sons under 18. John Wise & John Rowles overseers - Witt: Southy Littleton, William Taitum - p. 90

PITT, ROBERT - Adm. his est. to Devoras Browne upon the petition of Tabitha Browne, wife of sd. Devorax, in accordance with an order dated 16 June, 1670 - 19 Oct. 1672 - p. 144

SCARBURGH, Col. EDMUND - Devoras Browne his administrator - No order of qualification - 1672 - p. 188

BROWNE, DEVORAS - Adm. his est. to Tabitha Browne, wid. of sd. Devoras; Charles Scarburgh & Capt. Daniel Jenifer sec. 17 June 1673 - p. 206
Will presented but the Court decided that there was not sufficient evidence and testimony that it was the real will and testament of the said decedent - p. 204

STOCKLY, JOHN - 3 Feb. 1670 - 18 Aug. 1673 - Planta. at Assawoman, being 2700 A. to be equally divided between such sons as shall survive me, they to receive their estates at 18, but should my wife remain a widow she to have use of said land until my sons are 21. To wife Elizabeth planta. where I now live during her widowhood, then to my son Thomas; should my sons all die land to be divided between my daughters Jane, Hanna, Ann & Elizabeth. Wife Elizabeth, William Custis & Edward Revell Ex'rs. Witt: William Custis, Thomas Bagwell - Memo: Having already given my 3 sons William, Woodman & John their shares of cows & chattels, they to have no share of cows at my dec., only mares & land, except one Neck of land to the Northward of Christopher Stanley's planta. which I give to my wife to be at her own disposing. dated 9 Apr. 1673 - p. 231

LEATHERBURY, THOMAS - 3 July 1673 - 19 Aug. 1673 - To eldest son Charlss Leatherbury planta. where I now live after the death of my wife Ellenor, reversion to my second son George Leatherbury. To my second son Perry Leatherbury (under 21) 600 acres at Onancock Creek, also 300 A. adjoining it & 1000 A. purchased of Capt. John West, reversion to son Charles - Wife Ellenor resid, legatee & Exec. Witt: Ja: Matts, John Jenkins, Daniell Byles - p. 234

Wills 1673-1676(v)

ROBINSON, LAWRENCE, of Muddy Creek - 23 Aug. 1673 - 16 Oct. 1673 - To wife Elizabeth planta. where I now live for life then to my son John Robinson (under 21), reversion to my other two children, George & Mary Robinson. To son George (under 21) 450 A., also 50 A. out of 200 A. the remainder of a patent for 1200 A. which I sold to George Trewett, reversion to John & Mary. To godchild Lawrence Rially. To Sarah & Margaret Dye. To William Freeman & John Betts. Wife Exec. Witt: Daniel Jenifer, Ann Jenifer, Jacob Jenifer, Richard Bundock - p. 3

FAWSETT, JOHN - 15 Aug. 1673 - 16 Oct. 1673 - To eldest son John Fawsett planta. where I now live - Wife Rodeah to have use of same until John arrives to 18 years. To son William (under 18) 1/2 of 500 A. & the other 1/2 to my son Charles (under 18). To son Thomas (under 18) & son Charles a tract of land called James Neck purchased of John Cropper, at the head of Occohannock Creek, being 245 A. To dau. Elizabeth. Wife Exec. Mr. Thomas Teackle & Mr. Southy Littleton to be assistants. Witt: Richard Kellam, Joseph Foxcroft. - p. 7

JOHNSON, RICHARD - 20 Nov. 1673 - 18 Feb. 1673 - To mother (no name) whole est. during her life. To bro. Thomas Johnson. To bro. William Major. To sister Elizabeth Johnson. Cousins William Finnie & Sarah Finnie. To the children of my bro. Obedience Johnson. To cousin Elizabeth Rowles. Witt: Peter Browne, John Bratton, Elizabeth Pitman - p. 97

FOWKES, THOMAS - 10 Sept. 1673 - 18 May 1674 - To "neafew" Mary Ryle, dau. of Ann, now Ann Miels, formerly in the possession of Henry Ryle, not in the custody of John Smally. To sister Ann Miells. To George, the eldest son of John & Amy Parker. To Amy, dau. of Robert & Temperance Mason. "To each and every grandchild of my wife's" To godchildren Rachel, dau. of Edward Revell, Thomas, son of John Savage, to _____ son of John Rogers, Thomas, son of Ruth Bundick. Remainder of land where I now live, being 400 acres, to George Parker after the death of my wife, should he die then to William, the third son of John & Amy Parker, & if he should die then to the heirs of William Anderson. Wife Amy Exec. Witt: William Anderson, Isack Henman, John Sturges. - p. 152

OBEN, FULLCART - 22 Mar. 1663 - 16 July 1674 - Son Obedience (under 18). Dau. Mary (under 16). Should my son die before the age of 18 my friend Obedience Johnson to take him into his custody, & should Obedience Johnson die then John Johnson to take him. Obedience Johnson & John Tomson overseers. Wife(no name) resid. lega-

6

tee. Witt: Obedience Johnson, Peter Dolby, Fra: Lord. - p. 160

SMITH, WILLIAM - I5 July 1671 - 23 Feb. 1674 - To eldest son
Thomas Smith land where I now live "now largely expresst by
Pattent". To each of my children - No names - All under age. Wife
Sarah resid, legatee & Exec. Thomas Browne & John Michaell, Jr.
overseers. Witt: John Michael, Jr. Thomas Browne - p. 183

PARKER,. GEORGE - __ Feb. 1673 - 10 Oct. 1674 - To son George
land where I now live on the North side of Onancock - Wife to have
use of same until son reaches 21 years. To son John land on South
side of Onancock. To son George all my land in England. All arreara-
gss of rents from said lands to my four sons now living. To two
youngest sons, Phillip & Charles my other lands. To dau. Abigall. To
bro. John Parker. To Thomas Teackle. Wife Florence resid. legatee
together with my 6 children, wife to have 1/3 and children 2/3 as they
arrive to age. Wife Exec. Charles Scarburgh & Thomas Teackle
overseers. Witt: Daniel Jenifer, Ann Jenifer, Frances Taler - p. 184

ROGERS, JOHN - Adm. his est. to Nich: Rogers & Mary Rogers - 11
Oct. 1674 - p. 200

BOWLES, THOMAS, of Ockahanock - 20 June 1674 - 9 Nov. 1674 -
"Whereas the Lord hath blessed me with many children, six whereof I
trust are living, three sons & three daughters, viz:" William, the
elder, Ann Bowles 2nd, Elizabeth 3rd, Jane Bowles 4th, Edward
Bowles 5th & Robert Bowles, the younger - To the first son or dau.
who shall first arrive & come into this county of Accomack in Virginia, 1/2 of a water mill at the head of Occahanock Creek, with all the
land & other appurnenances, being between Mr. Devorax Brown, dec. &
myself, land at the head of Occahanock Creek. Should two or more of
my children come into this country at the same shipping the eldest to
be possessed of the said estate. Richard Bayley of Cradock Creek &
Arthur Robins of Matchipongo Ex'rs. to take in hand the land & cattle
until the arrival of my children. Witt: John Cropper, Lawrence Pery -
p. 205

GOSSLING, JOHN - Adm. his sst. to Elizabeth Gossling, wid. of said
John - 16 Feb. 1674. p. 23_

WATSON, GEORGE - 4 Nov. 1674 - 7 Feb. 1674 - To Tabitha Whittington, dau. of William Whittington & Tabitha, his wife. To Henry
Edwards. To Tabitha Whittington, wife of William Whittington & to
William Whittington mourning rings. 600 A. at Long Love Branch to
be divided, 300 A. to Jon. & Thomas Bundick, sons of Ralph & Ruth
Bundick, the other 300 A. to Tabitha Browne, relict of Mr. Devoras
Browne. Tabitha Browne Exec. To Capt. Southy Littleton. After
payment of debts bal. of est. to be sent home to my dau. the next
year, 1675. Witt: Tobias Sellvey, Edm: Browne, Edith Robinson - p.
242

ROGERS, JOHN - 23 Sept. 1674 - 19 Mar. 1674 - Real & personal est. to be divided between sons Nicholas, Peter, Richard & William Rogers. Witt: Tobias Selvey, William Chase. William Chase & Tobias Selvey Ex'rs. & guardians of children. p. 259.

HAILL, HENRY - 18 Oct. 1675 - Date of probate not given - Cattle to be divided between Tobias Selvey, Ann White & James Ewell - Ann White Exec. Witt: William Fletcher, William_____. - p. 339

SMITH, EDWARD - 18 Aug. 1675 - 16 Feb. 1675 - To dau. Elizabeth 625 A., being the South-western half of my 1250 A. at Accocomson, reversion to unborn child; should said child die then to my wife Marie. The other 625 A. to my said wife for life then to my unborn child or children, reversion to my dau. Elizabeth, & should they all die without issue then to my wife forever. Wife & children resid. legatees. Wife Exec., dau. Elizabeth overseer, William Andrews overseer of my dau. Elizabeth. Witt: John Wallop, Rebecka Wallop - p. 380

Wills & Deeds 1676-1690(vi)

SCARBOROUGH, HENRY - Not dated - Rec, 26 May 1676 - To Grandmother Ann Charlton cattle & increase for life then to nephews Bennony & Jonathan West, sons of Maj. John West. To aunt, Mrs Matilda West. To nephew John West the younger. To nephew Scarburgh West. Uncle John West Ex'r. To Hatton Hill, son of Robert Hill. Witt: William Towers, Robert Watsone - p. 6

TRINIMAN, BENJAMIN - 1 May 1676 - 1 June 1676 - To sister Jane Juell & my 2 daus. Catherine & Elizabeth. Robert Watson & Susana Watson resid. legatees. Cousin Robert Watson Ex'r. Witt: Tobias Selvey, Elizabeth Selvey - p. 8

TRUIT, HENRY, of Muddy Creek - 5 Sept. 1676 - 19 Dec. 1676 - My only son George Truit sole heir to land & tenements, he to remain with his mother, Elizabeth, until he is 21, should he die then to my unborn child. Wife Elizabeth Exec. Witt: Baptis Nucom, Robert Barton, William Luis - p. 18

HUITT, ROBERT, of Choratock - 16 Mar. 1676 - 17 Apr. 1677 - To wife Micall planta. where I now live at Choratock for life then to my dau. Mary Huitt, reversion to my son in law Richard Jones, Jr. To son in law Richard Jones, Jr. 300 A. at Pungoteage where he now lives. To Rowland Savage 300 A. at Pungoteage where he now lives. To dau. Mary 200 acres at Pungoteage., reversion to Francis Savage son of Rowland Savage. To Mary Savage, dau. of Rowland Savage. To Richard Joanes, Sr. Wife & dau. Mary (under 16) resid. legatees. Wife Exec. Witt: Andrew Winder, William Littlehouse. - p. 35

BLACKLOCK, THOMAS - 29 Nov. 1676 - 13 Sept. 1677 - Wife Christian Exec. with the advice of my son Thomas Blacklock. To son

8

Thomas planta. where I now live. Maj. John West, Capt. Richard Hill & John Drummond to divide est. between wife & 3 children. Witt: John Drummond, Thomas Berrit. - p. 60

SMITH, JOHN, Taylor - 27 Oct. 1677 - 19 Feb. 1677 - To eldest son George Smith 200 A. where I now live, reversion to his brothers. Wife Joyce. To son James 150 A. adj. George's land. To son John 150 A. adj. the land of his bro. James, reversion to my youngest son Thomas. To dau. Ann Hammon. Son in law Edward Hamon. To my 5 youngest children, James, John, Thomas, Director & Joyce. Son in law Thomas Savage. To John Tomson & his wife Rebecca. John Tomson, George Smith & Thomas Savage overseers over my above named children. Sons to be at age at 18 & daus. at 15. Witt: John Booth, Alexander Addison. - p. 85

MASON, ROBERT - 12 Dec. 1677 - 24 Apr. 1678 - To dau. Amey planta. at Pungoteague on the seaside cont. 650 A. provided she confirm to my dau. Elizabeth (under 14) 100 A. given her by her grandfather Fookes, & if she refuse Elizabeth to have the 650 A. & Amey to have the planta. where I now live. I hereby confirm the said 100 A. to my dau. Elizabeth & she to have the planta. where I now live. Godson Robert Parker. Goddau. Mary Widgin. To Thomas White. Wife (no name) resid. legatee & Exec., Ambrose White to assist her and to see my land confirmed to my children. Witt: John Sturgis, William Nock - p. 86

HILL: ROBERT - 19 July 1678 - 19 Aug. 1678 - To son Robert. To son Richard. "To three of my smallest children". To dau. Prescilla. Wife Jane Exec. To my other children (no names) Witt: John Parker, Matapany, George Hope, John Richardson. p. 114 (Other children Ruth, Dorcus, Roger youngest son - son "huton hill" - p. 116)

FOWKES, AMY - Nunc. 20 Aug. 1678 - Rec. 23 Oct. 1678 - To grandson George, eldest son of John & Amy Parker. To Naomy & Comfort, daus. of my son William Anderson. To Ambrose, eldest son of Ambrose & Comfort White. To Amy & Elizabeth, daus. of Robert & Temperance Mason. To William Nock & his son William Nock. To John, the son of William & Patience Nock. To Richard Saywell. To Jane Paremaine & her youngest dau. To John & Edith Hancock & their son Arthur Hancock - Son William Anderson Exr. 1000 L of tobacco to be raised out of my estate by my Ex'r. to be laid out for the best advantage of Mary Right, dau. of Ann Myles & of Henry Right, dec. Proved by depositions of Susannah Johnson & Mary Dix (v. viii - p. 8) p. 117 - Amy Fowkes d. about 10 Apr. 1678

GORDING, JOHN - 9 Jan. 1677 - 17 Oct. 1678 - To 5 children living with me. Lenard to be at age & his own disposing if he will stay with his mother & aid & assist her. Nathaniel, John & George To be at age at 21 if they stay with their mother, & if she marry to be at age at 18. Dau. Margaret to be at age at 16. Wife (no name). Obedience Johnson Ex'r. Witt: Obodience Johnson: Thomas Marshall - p. 118

JACKSON, JONAH – 6 Feb. 1678 – 17 Mar. 1678 – To eldest son Nathaniel Jackson planta. at Occahanocke where I now live. To son Jonah Jackson planta. at Nickowamson. To son John Jackson land at Occahanocke. To dau. Jane Jackson silver cup marked IWA, spoons marked H & a stone ring that was my mother's. To friends Obedience Johnson, Robert Watson, Arthur Robins, John Tankred. Wife Lydia Jackson & children resid legatees. Wife Exec. Robort Watson & Arthur Robins overseers. Witt: John Tankred, John Booth. – p. 140

BOWEN, JOHN – 8 Feb. 1678 – 18 Mar. 1678 – To sons John & Richard Bowen. Wife Elizabeth Exec. To servant Thomas Jones. Daus. Elizabeth & Elliner – Children under ags. John Stockley, Woodman Stockley & Jonathan Owen to divide household goods – Witt: John Wallop, Jonathan Owen. – p. 141

DEVENISH, JOHN – 16 Jan. 1678 – 17 Mar. 1678 – To Rowland Savage my planta & all the land belonging to it as by patent will appear & all & every parcell of my est: he paying my debts. Rowland Savage Ex'r. Witt: Will: Stevens, John Terrey, John Charls. – p. 144

LITTLETON, SOUTHY – Dated in Albany, upon Hudson River, 16 Sept. 1679 – Rec. in Albany, N. Y. 12 Oct. 1679 – Probated in Accomack 17 Dec. 1679 – To eldest son Nataniel Littleton land on Magety Bay cont. 4050 A. in Northampton County for life remainder to his male heirs, & for want of such heirs to my heirs at common law. To dau. Ester a Neck of land at Jengotege called King's Neck on Swansicut Creek. To youngest son Southy Littleton for life 2270 acres at Nandua in Accomack County, remainder to his male heirs, & for want of such heirs to my heirs at common law. To John Rust 200 A. in Somerset County, Md., all the rest of the land on that neck I give to my dau. Gertrude Littleton. To Francis Williams 300 A. in Somerset County, Md. where he now lives provided he pays for it as shown by my books. The remainder of said Neck I give to my dau. Elizabeth Littleton. All the rest of my land at Jengotege in Somerset County to my son Bowman Littleton. To dau. Sarah Littleton 600 A. at Pokimoke in Accomack County. To Nathaniell Tunnell all my land at Occokonson in Accomack County. To Richard Jones, Jr. 200 A. in Accomack County as provided by deed, he paying accordingly. To William White, planter. 155 A. at the head of the beanches of Pungotege. Bal. of my land not disposed of to my four daus. Personal est. to be divided between my 7 children. Sons to be at age at 18 & daus. at 16. Ester to be kept at my sister Robins & dau. Sarah at Mrs Bridget Foxcroft's. Dau, Elizabeth at Mrs Ann Jenifer's & dau. Gertrude at Maj. Bowman's. Son Bowman to be kept at Richard Bally's & Southy Littleton to be kept 4 years with his nurse, Nicholas Tyler's wife. Thomas Teagle, Clerk, Col. William Kendall, Maj. Edmund Bowman, Capt. John Robins, Capt. Daniel Jenifer & Mr. Richard Bayly overseers of my will & to look after the education of my children. Witt: John Willett, Thomas Eares, Robert Livingstone – p. 171

MACKARTY, DANIEL - 10 Oct. 1678 - 18 Nov. 1600 - To godchild Charles White, son of William White. To William Dine, son of William Dine, dec. Capt. Edmund Scarburgh resid. legatee & Ex'r. Witt: George Ginne: Joseph Aymes - p. 230

SELVEY, TOBIAS - 14 Feb. 1681 - 16 Feb. 1681 - To dau. Matillda Harrison. To Joseph Harrison (under age) Daus. Climencye Elizabeth & Matillda 50 A. O. To William Allford, if he stays with me until I die & serves his time justly, 1000 L of tobacco - Three daus. resid. legatees & Executrices. Witt: John Smalley, William Alford. - p. 300

WAGGAMAN, HENDRICK - 8 June 1682 - 17 Aug.. 1682 - To the two first born children of my dau. Winniphree Myles. To wife Frances. To children Jacob, Ephrahim, Mary & Jonathan. Wife Exec. Witt: George Nich: Hack, John Rowles, Peter Hack, John Chase - p. 313

LAYLER, NICHOLAS - 16 July 1682 - 27 Dec. 1682 - To wife Jacominte Layler 1/3 of my land during her life & 1/3 of all my other est., the other 2/3 of my land to my sons Luke & Arthur & the other 2/3   of my other est. to be divided between my seven children. To son Mathew. To son John, To sons Joseph & Benjamin. To dau.   Jacoba. To godson William Hamerin,. Daniel Eshon & John White to see my will performed. 6 sons to be at age at 19 & dau. at 15. Wife Exec. Witt: Christopher Sadberrie, Sarah Sadberrie, George Dewey, William Littlehouse - p. 320

MEERS, BARTHOLOMEW - 16 Dec. 1682 - 28 Dec. 1682 - To godson John Rogers. To Samuel, the son of William Williams. To eldest son Bartholomew Mears planta. where I now live on the South side of the branch; privilege of timber on planta. on East side of Beaver Dam Branch. To son John all the land from the Small Branch Southerly to Richard Kellam's line. To son Richard land from that Little Branch Northwest. To sons Robert & William planta. at Occahannock, Robert to have 200 A. & William the remainder. Wife Mary Exec. Dau. Elizabeth, wife of George Freshwater to have no part of my est. Personal est. to remain as it is until my children come to age. William Nock & William Burton overseers. Sons to be at age at 18 & daus. at 16. Witt: John Washbourne, Susanna Washbourne, John Willis, Sr. - p. 323

WHITE, JOHN - 9 Sept. 1682 - 19 Feb. 1682 - To son John White, Jr., planta. where I now live & all other lands which I purchased of Col. Custis adj. where I now live; son to be at age at 17. To dau. Sary White (under 15) Wife Sarah Exec.   Obedience Johnson & Thomas Parramore overseers. Witt: Obedience Johnson & Thomas Parramore - p. 325

VAHAN, EDWARD - To dau. Elizabeth planta. where I now live, being 150 A. & for want of heirs to dau. Margaret. Wife Ann Exec.   William Stockley to see my will performed, Should wife die dau. Elizabeth to be with John Stratton & his wife & dau. Margaret with William Stockley & his wife. Witt: William Stockley, John Stratton, Edward Thornton. - p. 333

HICKMAN, WILLIAM - 25 Apr. 1683 - 3 July 1683 - To my 7 sons Richard, William, Joseph, Benjamin; Henry, Roger & John Hickman 1000 A. to be equally divided between them, eldest son Richard to have first choice & the rest as they come to age. 3 daus. (no names), To godson William Heubanck, Wife Exec. until my son John comes to age then he to join with her as my Ex'r. Roger Ternon & John Wheeler to see my will performed. Witt: Rodger Ternan, John Wheeler - p. 341

WILLSON, WILLIAM - 27 Dec. 1682 - Partly proved 21 Feb. 1682 - Prob. 3 July 1683 - To Naomy Anderson, dau. of William Anderson whole est. real & personal. William Anderson Ex'r. Witt: Sam: Taylor, George Hope, Thomas Briggs. - p. 342

SMITH, JOSHUA - 9 July 1683 - 14 Nov. 1683 - Wife Margaret Exec. To sons John & Joshua my planta. to be divided between them. To dau. Mary. Witt: John Drummond, Timothy Coe, Wonie Mackannie - Children under 18 - p. 361

PITMAN, JOSEPH - 14 Mar. 1678 - 16 Mar. 1679 - Rec. 12 Feb. 1683 - To son Obed. To dau. Mary. Wife Elizabeth Exec. Son Obedience to be at age at 18, dau. at 15. Witt: Obed: Johnson, Thomas Johnson - p. 363

LORING, WILLIAM - 5 Oct. 1683 - 5 Feb. 1683 - Wife Alice to sell my 300 A. at St. Marys in Somerset County, Md., proceeds to be divided between William Loring, Elizabeth Loring and wife Alice. To son William 200 A. Purchased of Benjamin Eyres. To dau. Elizabeth. Wife Alice & Nicholas Millechop & George West Ex'rs. Son to be at age at 18, dau. at 17 - Witt: John Stratton, Daniel Harwood, Sarah Harwood - p. 364

MAJOR, WILLIAM - Not dated - 3 June 1684 - To son John planta. at Occohannock. To son William planta. at Skippers Gut where I now live. To unborn child, to be named Rowles if a son, land adj. that given my son William, if a dau. then my bros. John Rowles & Obe: Johnson to divide said land between my sons William & Peter. To son Peter land called Osborne Neck. To son Thomas 200 A. at Mattepeny. To dau. Alice. To dau. Mary. Wife Mary. Sons to be at age at 18, daus. at 16. Wife & children Ex'rs. Brothers Obedience Johnson & John Rowles to divide property. Witt: George Hislop, Alecksander Richards, John Mussay. - p. 379

WATTS, JOHN - 29 Apr. 1680 - 4 June 1684 - To son John. Bal. personal est. 1/3 to wife Dorothy & the other 2/3 to my children Margery, Jannett & John (all under 16). Wife & friend John Drumaond to be guardians of my children. To son John 450 A. where I now dwell at Accocomson & 250 A. on Teasers Island in Somerset County, Md.

granted me by patent & 300 A. in Somersat County being the Souther-most part of 600 A. granted me by patent. To dau. Tabitha, now wife to John Tarr, the remaining part of my 600 A. in Somerset County for life then to her heirs with reversion to her heirs at common law. Wife Exec. Witt: John Wallop, Thomas Mitchell - p. 381

STURGIS, JOHN - 6 Mar. 1683 - 5 Aug. 1684 - Wife Elizabeth - To son John. To son Richard (under 21). To son Jonathan (under 20). To son Daniel (under 16). To dau. Dorothy Nevill, To dau. Ann Sturgis, Witt: Richard Bundick, David Jones. - p. 383

STEVENS, WILLIAM - 21 July 1683 - 2 Dec. 1684 - To bro. in law Robert Hutchinson 1/2 the sloop purchased of Issac Jacob. To Harry Read, Jr. 150 A. at Pungotege, being part of a patent for 700 A. pur-chased of John Cole. To Richard Read 200 A. being part of said tract. To the children of Henry Read, Sr., viz: John, Henry & Richard. To Charles Leatherbury's wife, Henry Read, Sr., resid. legatee & Ex'r. Witt: Robert Hutchinson, John Charles, Robert Maccoller.- p. 390

MICHAEL, JOHN - 12 Sept. 1684 - Partly proved 11 Feb. 1684 - Prob. 7 Apr. 1685. To wife Ann land where I live at Matompkin for life, except such part of the woodland as I have given unto some of our children to build & live on. To eldest son Joachim planta. at Nusswat-tox, being 400 A. formerly belonging to Richard Hinman, reversion to unborn child if a boy & if a girl to be divided between all my daus. To son John 1/2 of a neck of land & marsh between Cattail Creek & Messongo Creek, the whole being 2700 A., 1600 A. of which I bought of my father in law Lt. Col. John Tilney, reversion to my son Symon. To son John at his mother's death the plantation. where I now live at Matompkin, being 200 A., reversion to my son Symon. To my son Symon the other 1/2 of said neck, reversion to my son John, & 100 A. at Matompkin. To unborn child the bal. of my land at Masongo, sup-posed to be 1100 or 1200 A. To daus. Ann, Elizabeth, Adrians & Grati-ana 200 A. out of my dividend of 1100 A. at Matompkin, Ann's 200 A. at the head of James Walker's Branch, Elizabeth, Gratiana & Adri-ana's 200 A. at the head of the mill branch. Wife Ann Exec. & resid. legatee. Sons to be at age at 18, daus. at 16. Friend Mr. Thomas Teackle, my cousin Capt. John Custis, Mr. William Anderson, Mr. William Burton, Mr. John Bagwell & Mr. Thomas Bagwell assistants & overseers. Witt: Charles Scarburgh, Isaac Dix, Jane Marriner - p. 401

MACCOMB, JOHN - 8 May 1684 - 7 July 1685 - Son James - Wife Elizabeth. Daus. Esther & Elizabeth - Wife resid. legatee & Exec. Witt: Edward Ashbye, Thomas Dant, James Gray, Daniel Darby. - p. 405

MITCHELL, WILLIAM - 20 Aug. 1685 - 1 Sept. 1685 - Nunc. Robert Higgons Ex'r. of est. which concerns those persons that employed me as supercargo of all ye goods imbarked in ye good ship called the Katherine of London, to be sold for the payment of debts and the best advantage of the owners of said goods, an inventory whereof is now in the hands of the said Robert Higgons & John Rolls of Nandewy in the county of Accomack. Wife (no name) Exec. of whole est. in Scotland, real & personal - Proved by John Rowles & William Fletcher. - p. 406

JENKINS, JOHN - 9 Oct. 1685 - 17 Nov. 1685 - To eldest dau. Elenor Jenkins 200 A. being part of the divident where I now live. To second dau. Margaret Jenkins 200 A. of said tract where Steven Warrington now lives, reserving to the said Warrington 4 years possession thereof. To third dau. Ann Jenkins 200 A. of said tract. To grandson John Warrington, son of Steven Warrington, 200 A. where I now live. To son John planta. where I now live, being 400 A. Son John & daus. re siduary legatees - Son John Ex'r. Witt: Edward Revell, Charles Fleetwood, John Kellam - p. 409

SAVAGE, GRIFFITH - 6 July 1680 - 11 Mar. 1685 - To wife Bridget planta. where I now live for life then to my son Griffith Savage (under 19). Son Griffith to be in the care of his mother, and should she die to be in the care of his godfather Roger Mikell. Wife Exec. Witt: Edward Brotherton, Roger Mikell, William Prettiman. - p. 421

RATCLIF, ELIZABETH - 3 Oct. 1684 - 11 May 1686 - John Price, husband of my dau. Sarie, to have no part of my est., her share to be held in trust by my son in law Edward Whalle of Somerset County, Md. for the use of her and her children. To dau. Bridget Tailer. To son Nathaniel Ratclif. To son in law Nathaniel Enis. To dau. Elizabeth Whalee. Son Nathaniel Ratclif Ex'r. Witt: John Wallop, Woodman Stockley, Marie Paine - p. 423

ALEWORTH, WILLIAM - 14 Feb. 1685 - 6 July 1686 - To wife Dorcas & son Jonathan my planta. at Massongo: being 200 A., & at my wife's death the whole to my said son. Son in law John Sanders. Witt: John Morris, John Glading - p. 425

STOCKLEY, WILLIAM - 23 July 1686 - 7 Oct. 1686 - Wife Mary to have use of planta. where I now live during her life. Bal. of est. to wife in fee. Wife & brother Joseph Stockley Ex'rs. Witt: John Stratton, Elizabeth Stratton, Thomas Perry - p. 429

BAGWELL, JOHN - 18 Sept. 1685 - 30 Nov. 1686 - To son Henry (under 18) 1/2 of the planta. where I now live & his equal share of my 3rd part of an Island purchased by Thomas Bagwell, Isaac Medcalfe & myself. To son Alexander the other 1/2 of my plantation & his part of said Island. (Alexander under 18) Dau. Rebecca (under 17). The profits of my water mill to be used for the maintenance of my wife & children. Wife to enjoy whole est. until children come to age. Wife Ann Exec. Bro. Thomas Bagwell & William Burton Ex'rs. in trust. Witt: William Parker, Isaac Metcalf, Robert Watson - p. 433

PARKER, Peter - Declaration made Sept. 1686 - 30 Nov. 1686 - Nunc. Whole est. to wife & children (no names) Proved by William Parker, age about 34, & Mary Martiall, age about 55 - p. 434

SMITH, WILLIAM - Nunc. Declaration made Oct. 1686 - 2 Dec. 1686 - To cousin Roger Miles whole est. with the exception of my land which I give to his son Roger - Proved by Isaac Dix, age about 42 & Mary Dix, age about 31 - p. 436

PHILBY, STEPHEN - 11 Dec. 1686 - 30 Mar. 1687 - To son George (under age) planta. where I now live being 300 A. To Pheby Philby. To Catherine Philby - John Bayley Ex'r. Witt: Charles Fleetwood, Thomas Blake - p. 448

TAYLOR, WILLIAM - 21 Sept. 1686 - 21 June 1687 - To son Elias Taylor land on Assawoman Creek containing 850 A. , 600 A. being granted me by patent dated 1664, & the remaining 250 being part of 1050 A. purchased of Col. John Stringer, remainder to his heirs, with remainder to my son William Taylor, with remainder to my dau. Winefred, formerly wife of Peter Parker, dec. To son Elias 450 A., being the South end of said 1050 A. between Geangoteage & Assawoman Branches. To dau. Winefred, formerly wife to Peter Parker, dec. To son William land on the seaboard side between Geangoteage & Assawoman Branches, containing 800 acres, being the northermost part of said 1050 A., also 450 A. in the woods. To my 4 grandaus. Elizabeth, Mary, Rachell & Sarah Parker, daus. of Winefred Parker. To dau. Elizabeth Ratclif & her husband Charles Rattclife - To grandau. Elizabeth Rattclife. To grandson William Taylor, Jr. Son Elias resid. legatee & Ex'r. Witt: William Whittington, William Paine, John Elliot - p. 453

BULL, TOBIAS - 29 Apr. 1687 - 16 Nov. 1687 - To wife Rebeccah Whole est. Wife Exec. Witt: John Wallop, Nathaniel Tunnell, Thomas Conaway - p. 458

FITZGARRELL, JOHN - 13 Aug. 1687 - 16 Nov. 1687 - To eldest son John 100 A. situate in little Anamessick in Maryland. To son Thomas. Daus. Elizabeth & Katherine. Sons to be at my friend John Wise's until they are 21. Dau Elizabeth to Mrs Barbary Robins until of age & dau. Katherine to her mother, or if she see fit to the disposal of her godmother also. Wife (no name) Exec, John Wise & William Sill overseers. Witt: George Nicho: Hack, Thomas Busshell - p. 459

EYRE, BENJAMIN - Not dated - 15 Nov. 1687 - Wife Martha Exec. To wife 250 A. where I now live during her widowhood, then to my son Regnold Eyre. Wife resid. legatee - Witt: Richard Coopr, Elizabeth Morgane, Sarah Harrod - p. 459

MACKWILLIAN, FINLA - 25 Mar. 1687 - 10 Nov. 1687 - To sons Fenla & Overton planta. where I now live being 400 A. To dau. Sarah. To dau. Patience. Sons to be at age at 19. Wife Mary Exec. Daus. Sarah & Patience to remain with their mother till their marriage. To dau. Margaret Litchfield. To dau. Elizabeth Willett. To dau. Ann

Scott. To George Middleton 12 pence as a portion for his dec. wife. Wife to have planta, during her widowhood. Should my wife marry personal est. to be divided between my said wife & four children Finla, Overton, Patience & Sarah. Col. John West, Capt. Richard Hill & John Drummond to be overseers of my will. Witt: John Ayres, Thomas Rila, John Cary. - p. 459

REVELL, EDWARD - 6 Oct. 1686 - 17 Jan. 1681 - To Frances Custis, dau. of Henry Custis & Rachell, his wife, silver tankard stamped with H.Y. To dau. Rebeca Revell planta at Nickawamson containing 500 A., pewter marked R.R. To son John Revell land at Pungoteague. Should Rebeca & John die without issue the land at Nickawamson to Elizabeth Custis, dau. of Henry Custis, & est. at Pungoteague to Frances Custis, dau. of Henry Custis. To Dorothy Washbourne. Wife to have her maintenance on the plantation at Pungoteague during her widowhood. Son John Ex'r. (wife Frances - p. 484) Witt: John Washbourne, John Fenn, Daniel Ograhan, Jr. p. 461

PALMER, CAPT. THOMAS - 11 Mar. 1687 - 24 Mar. 1687 - Whole est. to Elizabeth, Sabra, Esther, Scarburgh, Barbara, Margaret & Sarah Robins, daus. of Arthur Robins, to be divided between them, only my goddau. Barbara to have 2 shares. Arthur Robins Ex'r. Witt: Daniel Jenifer, John Wise, Sr. Math: Scarburgh, William Wise, Elizabeth Wise - p. 468

PRETTIMAN, JOHN - 7 Mar. 1687 - 21 Mar. 1687 - To Mary Grice. Personal property at my landlord Thompson's to Robert Thompson. Witt: William Jones, Samuell Benton - p. 469

DIX, ISAAC - 28 Oct. 1687 - 2 Apr. 1688 - Wife Mary Exec. To sons John & Isaac land near Gargatha containing 1000 A., John to have the planta. where I live & Isaac to have his part in the little neck; wife to live upon the land of my son John during her life. Daus. Elizabeth, Lucretia, Annabella & Mary. Wife resid. legatee. Sons to be at age at 18 if my wife marry, if not at 21. Witt: Thomas Crippin, John Lewis, William Dennison. - p. 470

SHIPP, MATTHEW, wheelright - 1 Apr. 1688 - 18 Sept. 1688 - To bro. Francis Shipp of Lower Norfolk County whole est., real & personal, as also my several dividents of land & marsh in Accomack County. Friend George Johnson of Muddy Creek Ex'r. until my bro. shall come over into Accomack County, Witt: Thomas Welburne, Micajah Sadler, James Smith, Peter Walker, William Wyat, Diana Wyat - p. 479

WATKINSON, PETER - ____ 1687 - 10 Sept. 1688 - To son Cornelius planta. in the main woods containing 475 A. purchased of Col. John Stringer. To dau. Elizabeth. To son Peter. To wife Dorothy personal est. during her widowhood, then to be divided between my sons Peter & Cornelius & dau. Elizabeth - Wife Exec. James Gray, Joseph Ames & Richard Bally overseers of my will & children's estates. Witt: James Gray, Joseph Ames, Richard Bally. - p. 480

HILL, HENRY - 8 Oct. 1688 - 20 Nov. 1688 - Eldest son Richard. Son Henry. Wife Jane Exec. of the rest of my est., only giving to each one of the rest of my children one breeding hog as each comes to age. Witt: Daniel Darby, Richard Neblet, Will: Sill - p. 482

?SARKER, WILLIAM - 7 Nov. 1688 - 21 Nov. 1688 - Uncle Henry Custis Ex'r. To cousin Elizabeth Custis, dau. of my uncle Henry Custis of Metompkin, my planta. at Metompkin betwixt my grandfather Capt. William Custis & my uncle Thomas Bagwell, there being by estimation 300 A., also my moveable est., & should she die before coming to age reversion to her sister Frances Custis. Witt: William Dennison, Henry Allen, Jr., James Walker, Jr. - p. 484

WATSON, RICHARD - 2 Oct. 1688 - 20 Feb. 1688 - To goddau. Ann (under age) the dau. of Mary Scale, which is now wife to Thomas Iremonger, whole est. except the following legacies - Edmund Allen & Ann Allen, his wife, to be overseers of the child's estate. To Thomas Franklin. To Mary, the dau. of John Stockley of Northampton. Should Ann die before her marriage, reversion to Elizabeth & Edward, the two children of Thomas Iremonger. Witt: Rebeckah Bagwell, Joan Chance, William Dennison - - p. 493

COE: TIMOTHY - 7 Sept. 1688 - 18 June 1689 - To son Timothy all my land from the Bridge over the gutt along George Johnson & so downward. To son John the remainder of my land. Bal. of est. to be divided between my wife & the rest of my children - Sons to be at age at 21, daus. at 18 - George Johnson, Thomas Brown, William Knock, Thomas Fookes to be assistants to my wife (no name) Witt: George Johnson, Richard Moore, Mary Johnson - p. 496. Presented by Sarah Coe, wid. of Timothy.

SMALLEY, JOHN - 2 May, 1689 - 18 June 1689 - To dau. Sarah Tailor. To dau. Elizabeth Smalley. To dau. Rebecka Smalley. To dau. Bridgett Smalley planta. where I now live. William Fletcher Ex'r. Witt: Elizabeth Fletcher, Mattildah Harrison, William Fletcher - p. 497

METCALFE, ISAAC - 19 Mar. 1688 - 17 Sept. 1689 - To my 3 sons John, Isaac & Samuel (All under age) planta. where I now live being 530 A. To 2 daus. Ann & Ellzabeth (both under 16). Wife Ann Exec., she to have whole est. until children come to age. William Burton & Thomas Bagwell overseers of children's estates. Witt: Henry Allin, Lancelot Sawkild, William Dennison - p. 502

JORDAN, DOROTHY, of Ockahanock - 15 May 1683 - 18 Feb. 1689 - To grandau. Ann Shepheard 450 A. where I now live. To grandau. Elizabeth Shepheard the lower planta. where my son in law John Shepheard now lives. Should both Ann & Elizabeth die my grandson John Shepheard to have the said land. 2 grandaus. resid. legatees & Executrices. Henry Parke, son in law Mr. John Shepheard & Mr.

Robert Watson overseers - Witt: Thomas Teackle, Fra: Wainhouse, John James - p. 516

AREW, JOHN - 18 Jan. 1689 - 18 Mar. 1689 - To sons John, Thomas & Wony planta. where I now live. Daughters (no names) To son John 118 A. of my seat of land lying along the Creek & the branch. To son Thomas 116 A. next my son John. To son Wony 116 A. on the Southern side of my seat. James Truet Ex'r. with the advice of Col. John West & William Willett. Witt: Thomas Rily, Sr., Sarah Rily, Elizabeth Silverthorn - p. 521

BAGWELL, THOMAS - 15 Apr. 1690 - 16 Sept. 1690 - Wife Ann Exec. To sons William & Francis all my land at the Horekill in Sussix County in the teretory or Penselvaina, To son John planta. where I now live. To son Thomas all the rest of my divident of land here (John & Thomas under 18) My part of Cedar Island to be divided between my sons Thomas & John. Daus. Ann & Valeance 225 A. adj. John Abbott. To son Thomas 200 A. adj. William Burton's Branch. Dau. Elizabeth Tilney. Dau. Comfort Leatherbury. Grandchildren Comfort & Ann Tilney & Patience Leatherbury. Wife & children resid. legatees. Sons to be at age at 18, daus. at 16. Capt. William Burton & William Parker overseers of my children. Not witnessed - Proved by Jane Nicholson & William Dennison. - p. 525

Orders 1676-1678(vii)

HOGBEN, JOHN - Adm. his est. to Maj. Edmund Bowman - 18 Dec. 1676 - p. 19

FLACK, JOHN - Adm. his est. to John Cole - 18 Dec. 1676 - p. 19

ARMSTRONG, HENRY - Ordered that the Sheriff take into his custody the est. of the said Henry Armstrong, dec. where it may be found in this county, & sell same at outcry. 17 Apr. 1677 - p. 38

BOWMAN, ELLINOR - Adm. her est. to Maj. Edmund Bowman, husband of the said Ellinor - 17 Apr. 1677 - p. 39

HANSON, JOHN - Adm. his est. to Arthur Robins, he having died intest. & leaving no relations in these parts to care for & look after his est. 20 Nov. 1677 - p.74

D. & W. 1678-1682 (viii)

SMITH, JOHN - Adm. his est. to Maxamillian Gore as marrying the relict of the said John - 16 Dec. 1678 - P. 41

YEO, HUGH - Petition of William Yeo for adm. denied & est. committed to the hands of Edward Revell until next Court, or a will or

18

some person by law qualified shall appear – 17 Mar. 1678 – p. 62

JEKELL, JOSEPH, dec., late mate of the ship called George's Adventure, of Hull – Adm. his est. to William Marr, of the Town of Kingston upon Hull, mariner & master of the good ship Prosperous of Hull, now bound for Virginia, attorney for John Jekell, bro. of the said Joseph – Mr. Tankard attorney for William Marr. 18 Mar. 1678 – p. 72

SMALLY, EDWARD – Adm. his est. to Walter Harges as marrying the relict of said Edward – 16 July 1679 – p. 96

WELSH, RICHARD – Adm. his est. to Mary Welsh, wid. of sd. Richard – 7 Oct. 1679 p. 117

YEO, HUGH – Adm. his est. to William Cleverdon, bro. in law of sd. Hugh – 8 Nov. 1679 – p. 120

BROWNE, EDMUND – Adm. his est. to Martha Browne, wid. of sd. Edmund – 3 Aug. 1680 – p. 177

RATCLIFFE, GEORGE – Adm. his est. to Nathaniel Ratcliffe, bro. of sd. George – William Stockley & William Blake sec. – 17 Dec. 1680 – p. 192

WREATHWELL, WILLIAM – Adm. his est. to Mary Wreathwell, wid. of sd. William – 17 Mar. 1680 – p. 209

DAVIS, HOPKIN – Nunc. 22 July 1681 – 16 Aug. 1681 – Declaration made at the house of Henry Reade. Whole est. to Henry Reade – Proved by Thomas Bell & Morgan Thomas – p. 248

REVELL, JAMES, Indian – Adm. his est. to Edward Revell – 18 Nov, 1681 – p. 271

CLEVERDON, WILLIAM – Adm. his est, to Deborah Cleverdon, wid. of sd. William – 16 Feb. 1681 – p. 281

DUNBARR, ROBERT – Adm. his est. to Mary Dunbarr, wid. of sd. Robert – 17 Aug. 1682 – p. 314

Wills & c. 1682–1697(ix)

WHITE, WILLIAM * Adm. his est. to Elizabath White, wid. of sd. William – 21 Feb. 1682 – p. 3

GOODMAN, JOHN – Adm. his est. to William Stevens – 16 Mar. 1682 – p. 8

FRANKLIN, RICHARD – Adm. his est. to Joan Franklin, wid. of sd. Richard – 6 Aug. 1684 – p. 47

FOSTER, THOMAS – Adm. his est. to Elizabeth Foster, wid. of sd. Thomas – Thomas Blake & Nicholas Millechop sec. – 12 May 1685 – p. 65

BOTE, ANN – Adm. her est. to Geo: Nicholas Hack & Peter Hack, sons of sd, Ann – 8 July 1685 – p. 68

SMITH, WILLIAM – Adm. his est. to Leonard Goring – Richard Kellam, Sr. & Richard Kellam, Jr. sec. 17 Nov. 1685 – p. 73

QUINTON, PHILLIP – Adm. his est. to Ann Quinton, wid. of sd. Phillip – George Hope & James Bonewell sec. 7 Sept. 1686 – p. 93

PORTER, ABEL – Adm. his est. to William Anderson – 21 June 1687 – p. 118

SACKER, FRANCIS – Adm. his est. to John Parker, Jr. – Francis Sacker bro. of Bridget Parker, wife of John Parker, Jr. – 17 Jan. 1687 – p. 124

HOLLIDAY, ROBERT – Adm. his est. to Elizabeth Holliday, wid. of sd. Robert – 17 Jan. 1687 – p. 124

PRETTIMAN, JOHN – Adm. his est. to John Prettiman, son of sd. John – Henry Williams & Thomas Stockley sec. – 2 Apr. 1688 – p. 129

SMITH, ELIZABETH, orphan – Adm. her est. to James Glenn, father of Lazarus Glenn – 22 Nov. 1688 – p. 145

SMITH, ELIZABEIH – Nunc. Declaration made 8 July 1688 – 18 June 1689 – After father "Anderson" is satisfied what would be due him, whole est. to godson Lazarus Glenn, son of James Glenn – Proved by Comfort Anderson, Alice Timberlake & Elizabeth Lawrence – p. 159

NIXSON, THOMAS – Adm. his est. to Ann Nixson, wid. of sd. Thomas – 17 Dec. 1689 – p. 173

SUARBURGH, MARY, now resident at the house of Anthony West at Merry Branch – 14 June 1691 – 15 Dec. 1691 – To grandson Anthony West – To his dau. Matilda. To dau. Matilda West. Son Charles Scarburgh. Dau. Tabitha Custis. Son Edmund Scarburgh. To grandson Edmund Scarburgh (under 12), son of Edmund Scarburgh. Grandau. Mary West. Grandau Tabitha Custis. Dau. Matilda West & grandson Anthony West resid legatees & Ex'rs. Witt: James Alexander, Edward Marten, Tully Robinson, Richard Bally, Jr. – Codicil revoking legacy to son Charles Scarburgh on account of his neglect. – p. 228

BOWMAN, EDMUND – 26 Feb. 1691 – 15 Mar. 1691 – To wife & dau. Gertrude Cropper planta. where I now live from the Cowpen Branch to the seaboard side & all marsh belonging to it for life, then to grandson

Sebastian Cropper. To grandson Edmund Bowman Cropper land called Church Neck binding upon Folly Branch. To grandson Nathaniei Cropper land between small beare branch & Cowpen branch. To grandau. Elizabeth Atkins 200 A. Land on Messongo to be sold for the good of my est. To grandson Southy Littleton. To grandau. Gertrude Littleton – Wife (no name) & dau. Gertrude Cropper resid. legatees & Executrices. Witt: William Parker, William Bunting, William Martiall – p. 235

NEWTON, JOSEPH – 29 Feb. 1691 – 15 Mar. 1691 – My shallop to be sold & the proceeds & what other estate to be equally divided between my wife & children. Son Joseph to be now at age & son John to assist my wife in bringing up my 5 younger children – Dau. Ann. Samuel Sandford & William Anderson overseers. Witt: Joseph Robinson, William Milburn, Richard Digges. – p. 237

SILEVANT, DORMAN – 22 Mar. 1691 – 22 June 1692 – To sons Daniel & Dorman (both under 18) planta. where I now live. To dau. Mary Selevant. Wife (no name) Exec. Witt: Christopher Stokelee, Daniel Darby, William French. – p. 241

WILLIAMS, HENRY – 15 Nov. 1689 – 21 June 1692 – To son John Williams all my land. To Elizabeth Richard, Jr. To William & Thomas Marriner – Witt: Isaac Metcalf, Robert Adkins, Edmond Allen – p. 242 – Presented by Mary Marriner.

JOHNSON, GEORGE, the elder, written at my now dwelling house at Muddy Creek – 10 Dec. 1690 – 20 Sept. 1692 – To son George 200 A. near Blocksomes Bridge. To dau. Sara Stevens. To son John planta. where I now live. To son Samuel land & marsh. George Truet, William Nock, Thomas Browne, John Drummond & Daniel Ayres overseers – Wife Mary Exec. Witt: Thomas Evernden, John Drummond, William Nock. p. 245

Orders – 1690–1697 (x)

BRADFORD, NATHANIEL – Adm. on his est. to Joane Bradford, wid. of sd. Nathaniel & William Bradford, son & heir of sd. Nathaniel – 19 Nov. 1690 – p. 4

MORRIS, DENNIS – Adm. his est. to Elizabeth Morris, wid. of sd. Dennis – Edward Brotherton sec. 21 Feb. 1692 – p. 94

JENIFER, Col. DANIEL – Adm. his est. to Capt. Daniel of St. Thomas Jenifer, son of sd. Col. Daniel, to take effect when he becomes 21, which will be 3 day of May next – 21 Feb. 1692 – p. 97 – Adm. granted June 20, 1693 – Capt. William Custis, William Anderson, William Parker of Matompkin & Edward Brotherton sec. p. 104

NOBLE, JAMES – Adm. his est. to Maj. Isaac Foxcroft as greatest

21

creditor – Ester Noble, wid. of sd. James, relinquishing her right – 20 Feb. 1693 – p. 121

DENNIS, MORRIS – Adm. his est. to Martha Dennis, wid. of sd. Morris – Gervas Baggaly sec. 19 Nov. 1695 –.p. 168

EVANS, JOHN – Adm. his est. to Sarah Evans, wid. of sd. John – Gervas Baggaly sec. 17 Mar. 1695 – p. 185

NEWTON, JOHN – Adm. his est. to William Anderson as greatest creditor – Elizabeth Newton, wid. of sd. John, relinquishing her right. John Bradhurst sec. 17 June, 1696 – p. 192

TAYLOR, WILLIAM – Adm. his est. to Bridgst Taylor, wid. of sd. William – William Parker & Elias Taylor sec. 15 Sept. 1696 – p. 199

GLENN, JAMES – Adm. his est. to Catherine Glenn, wid. of sd. James – Henry Toles & John Morris sec. – 15 Sept. 1696 – p. 199

EYRE, MARTHA, dec., wid. of Benjamin Eyre – Ordered that the sheriff sell her est. at outcry – 21 Nov. 1696 – p. 208

ATKINSON, JAMES – Adm. his est. to Henry Allen as marrying Elizabeth Atkinson, wid. of sd. James – 7 Apr. 1697 – p. 237

HILL, NICHOLAS – Adm. his est. to Hester Hill, wid. of sd. Nicholas – Richard Cutler sec. 5 Oct. 1697 – p. 252.

Wills &c. 1692-1715 (xi)

CLOVELL, PETER – 6 Aug. 169_ – 21 Feb. 1692 – To wife Elizabeth planta. where I now live, being 200 A. for life then to 3 sons Peter, Selbe & Thomas Clovell – To dau. Comfort. To 3 sons marsh purchased of William Jarman, but the rest of my children to have provision for their stock. Wife Exec. Witt: John Drummond, John Abbot, John Parker, Henry Young. – p. 1

BLAKE, WILLIAM – Page mutilated, date gone – 21 Feb. 1692 – To son William 1 s. To son John 1 s. To daus. Mary Owen & Sarah Willis 1 s. To daus. Rebecka & Isbella 1 ewe lamb @. To sons Daniel, Joseph & Elias planta where I now live. Wife Jane resid. legatee & Exec. Should my wife marry personal est. to be divided between Elias, Rebecka, Isebella Blake & my son Elias to be at age at 18 – Witt: Thomas Perry, Jonathan Owen – p. 2

DANIEL, WILLIAM – 27 Feb. 1688 – 21 Feb. 1692 – To son Alexander Daniel. To grandson (no name) – Two sons, but only names Alexander – Wife Sarah Exec. Witt: John Williams, Sr. Henry Bech – p. 2

OSBORNE, Capt. JOHN, of Somerset County, Md. 23 Feb. 1686 – 21 Feb. 1692 – To wife Attalanta & dau. Martha whole personal est. to be divided between them, should unborn child live to be divided in three parts. Wife Exec. to have power to sell 1200 A. at Messongo Creek for payment of debts, and if this should not be sufficient to sell land called Watermellon Point; should there be no occasion to sell Watermellon point I give the same to my dau. Martha Osborne. In case of wife's death brother Thomas Welburne to be Ex'r. Witt: Mathew Scarburgh, Bryan Parfe, Hanah Hopkins, Alexander Williams, Dorrithy Cary, Jane Cort – Proved 1687 – Rec. in Accomack 1692 – p. 6

WALLOP, alias WADLOW, JOHN – 4 Apr. 1693 – 19 Sept. 1693 – To son Skinner Wallcp als Wadlow, 1985 A. on the East & South-east side of Gingoteage Creek on the main land of Accomack County, also house on Mr. Anderson's planta. at Crooked Creek & land belonging to it. To dau. Sarah Wallop, als Wadlow, 400 A. on Gingoteage Creek, being part of my dividert of 2385 A., & 2000 A. on my Island formerly called Keeckotanck Island on the seaboard side – To son Skinner 500 A. on Keeckotanck Island – Son Skinner & dau. Sarah resid. legatees & Ex'rs. Dau. Sarah to make division. Witt: Samuel Taylor, Nathaniel Tunnell, Will: Wright, James Glenn, Thomas Conway – p. 18

COLLONY, OWEN – 5 Dec. 1693 – 19 Sept. 1693 – To son Owen Collony planta, where I now live containing 380 A. To dau. Ester Sill. To grandson Brian Collony, son of Owen Collony a neck of land adj. 300 A. formerly given his father, Owen
Collony. Son in law William Sill. Son in law Stephen Warrington. Son in law Arnold Harrison. Son Owen resid. legatee & Ex'r. Thomas Teackle trustee & overseer of grandson Brian Collony – Witt: Thomas Teackle, Provost Nellson – p. 20

SPIERS, JOHN – Nunc. 29 Nov. 1693 – 18 Dec. 1693 – To wife Sarah whole est. during her life then to be divided between my children – Son John (other children not named) – Proved by Jane Bird & Bridget Bird – p. 36

HILL, Capt, RICHARD, of Hunting Creek – 26 Mar. 1688 – 21 Nov. 1694 – To grandson Francis Ayres 200 A. at the head of Hunting Creek known as Drakes Neck. To John Ayres, Jr. 200 A. adjoining his bro. Francis. To Richard Hill Ayres 300 A. at Chingoteage, to his two brothers, Edmond & Henry Ayres planta. where his father now lives after the death of their mother & father. To 2 grandsons Richard & John Drummond, which said John Drummond was born 21 Mar. 1687/8, sons of John Drummond, 1100 A. where I now live. To grandson Hill Drummond 300 A. at Chingotege, being 1/2 of my dividert & planta. & the other 300 A. to Richard Ayres aforesald. To grandson Steven Drummond 300 A. in Drakes Neck. To Drake Drummond 300 A. in Drakes Neck. Wife Mary Hill Exec. John Ayres & John Drummond Ex'rs. Wife to have personal est. for life then to my daus. Mary Ayres & Patience Drummond. Witt: Nicholas Hill, John Lewis, Richard Grinnold – p. 62

23

HODSON, JOHN - 7 Oct. 1694 - 20 Mar. 1694 - To eldest son John Hodson 100 A. where I now live. To youngest son Anthony Hodson the other 1/2 of my planta. containing 100 A., To second son James Gray Hodson. Wife Mary Hodson. Sons under 18. Three daus. (no names) under 16. Witt: Joseph she, James Duer, William Carte - p. 71

ABBOT, JOHN, Sr. 7 Nov. 1694 - 19 Mar. 1694 - Wife Ann Exec., she to have use of dwelling house & planta. during her life; personal est. to be divided between wife & two daus. Patience & Elizabeth. To son William 100 A. To son Roger (under age) 100 A. where I now dwell - To sons William & Roger my 250 A. of marsh, reversion to the eldest son of my son Robert. To Samuel Thomas cow. Dau. Mary Justis & Son John Abbott 12 pence @, they having received their estates. Witt: Roger Ternal, Thomas Rily, William Willet - p. 73

TERNALL, ROGER - 23 Dec. 1694 - 17 Sept. 1695 - To son Thomas Ternall 150 A. being the South-west part of the planta. where I now live. To son John 150 A. where I now live (both under 21) Dau. Ann Ternall. To dau. Margaret Hill. To Grandson Roger Hill. Children Thomas, Ann & John resid. legatees. Wife Ann Exec. William Willet, Richard Hill, John Lewis & Larance Rily to guard & protect my children in their minority. My 20 A. of marsh to be in equal privilege among all my children. Witt: Richard Grinnall, Edward Burman, William Chance, John Lilliston - p. 77

PARKER, JOHN, Sr., of Mattapany - 9 Jan. 1692 - 19 Sept. 1695 - To eldest son George Parker 20 s. To each of his children (no names) sheep &c. To second son John Parker planta. called Mattapany where I now live, containing 400 A. after the decease of my wife Amy. To son John 1/2 of my great sloop to hold in partnership with my wife. To son William Parker 300 A. in Pocomoke River in Somerset County, Md. called Winter Quarter, also my sloop called Arlington. To son Edward Parker 200 A., being part of 600 A. of Mattapany patent, as by deed of gift to him dated 21 Dec. 1692. To son Matthew Parker my planta. called Little Gargaphia containing 400 A., also 1/2 the hammocks & marshes at Marumscoe in Maryland to hold with his brother Thomas Parker. To son Anderson Parker 385 A. near Bloxoms Bridge. To son Thomas 200 A. at the head of Messongo Branch & planta. purchased of Maximilian Gore containing 295 A. & 1/2 the marshes at Marumscoe in Maryland. To grandson John Ayres. To William Williamson. Bal. of est. including the 1/2 of my great sloop to my wife Amy - Wife Exec. Witt: Charles Scarburgh, Bennett Scarburgh, John Watts. Codicil dated 12 Jan. 1692 - Whereas I have 200 A. of marsh, being the northermost of Pungoteague Island not expressed in the foregoing will, the said 200 A. to be appropriated to my 400 A. at Mattapany & I give the same to my son John Parker; likewise I have 200 A. of marsh by a later patent upon Pungoteague Island to the southward of the aforesaid 200 A. which is also omitted in the aforesaid will, but is given by deed of gift to my son Edward Parker, which said 200 A. I give and bequeath to the said Edward.

Witt: William Anderson, George Hope, George Parker, Sr. – p. 80

READE, HENRY – 2 Mar. 1694 – 18 Sept. 1695 – To son Henry Reade 150 A. at the head of a branch called Smith Shop Branch. To son Richard Reade 200 A. being part of said tract. To son James 200 A. To son William 150 A. adj. my son James. To son John Reade 1 s. To kinsman John Reade. To bro. John Reade. Wife (no name) resid. legatee & Exec. Witt: Thomas Bushell, John Read, Phillip Willson – p. 82

WALLIS, JOHN – 12 Apr. 1695 – 19 Nov. 1695 – To landlord Will: Taylor my chest & all that is in it. Bal. of est. to James Bonewell – James Bonewell Ex'r. Witt: William Yeo, Thomas Cannaday – p. 84

WISE, JOHN, Sr. – 21 Oct. 1693 – 19 Nov. 1695 – To eldest son John Wise planta. where I now live on Checconessex Creek adj. the land of Capt. George Parker. To son William Wise land on Onancock Creek. To John Wise, my second son of that name & usually called Johannes, land on the North side of Checconesssx Creek adj. his bro. John Wise. To dau. Barbara Robins. To dau. Hannah Scarburgh, To friend Mr. Thomas Teackle a small silver tankard as a token of my love. To James Lee. To Neome Mikemie & Comfort Taylor, my grandaus. 20 s. @ to buy them a ring. eldest son John Wise Ex'r. Witt: George Parker, John West, Jr. Nich: Hill, John West, minor. – p. 85

CONNOWAY, THOMAS – Nunc. 12 Dec. 1695 – 17 Dec. 1695 – To Will Paine. Will Paine's children Bridget, Martha & William, Jr. resid. legatees. Proved by Bridget Collins & William Paine. – p. 93

NEWTON, JOSEPH – 29 Nov. 1695 – 17 Dec. 1695 – To bro. Sterlin Newton planta. purchased of Robert Pitt. To bro. Jonathan. To sister Sarah Newton. To sister Rachell. Robert Pitt Ex'r. Witt: Edward Needom, Henry Dixy, Richard Small. – p. 93

TEACKLE, THOMAS – 20 Jan. 1695 – 19 Feb. 1695 – To dau. Margaret planta. which was once James Atkinson's on Cradock Creek, till my son John comes to the age of 18, but should she marry a man who has no land then I give her the said land for- ever. To dau. Elizabeth planta. at the head of Muddy Creek. To dau. Catherine planta. at Pungoteague. Son John Teackle to be my heir of all my lands, houses &c. in Virginia or elsewhere not above disposed of, also a silver tankard given me by John Wise, dec. Bal. of est. to be divided between all my children. Joseph Milby to be guardian to my son. William Willett to take my dau. Catherine, Nicholas Mellichop, Sr. to take my dau. Elizabeth. Jacob Johnson & John Revel to divide est. Four children & their guardians Ex'rs. The land I have given my dau. Margaret I mean is only for her natural life. Witt: Agnes Milby, Mary Mason, James Ferefax. – p. 98

BURTON, WILLIAM – 5 Jan. 1695 – 18 Feb. 1695 – To eldest son William land on the seaboard side, situate in Forked Neck near where

I now live. to 3rd son Thomas Burton the South side of the said Forked Neck. To 6th son Stratton Burton land purchased of Col. John West & adj. the land given Thomas. To 2nd son John Burton 500 A., being 1/2 of 1000 A. in Sussex County in the Territories of Pennsylvania granted me by patent called Long Neck. To 4th son Benjamin 600 A. near Assateag on the seaboard side in Somerset County, Md. The other 1/2 of the 1000 A. in Sussex County was conveyed by me to Thomas Bagwell, of Accomack, dec. To 5th son Joseph Burton 387 1/2 A. on the North side of Indian River in Sussex County, Pa. being 1/2 of 775 A. purchased of John Parker. To 7th son Woolsey Burton 387 A. being the other 1/2 of said tract. To sons William, Thomas & Stratton my interest in Cedar Island in Accomack County. To 8th son Jacob Burton 450 A, near Lewis Towne in Pennsylvania on Indian River, being part of 600 A. purchased of Thomas Jones & adj. the land given my son John – The other 150 A. was due William Bagwell of Accomack. To 9th son Samuel Burton 500 A. on the South side of Indian River. Wife Ann Burton. To dau. Agnes Revell – To grandchildren Frances, Elizabeth & Edward Revell. Wife Ann & son William Ex'rs. Capt. William Custis, William Nock & son in law John Revell overseers in Accomack & John Hill of Lewis Town, Pa. Witt: John Revell, Robert Scott, James Smith, Robert Edge – p. 100

CARY, JOHN – 6 Feb. 1695 – 17 Mar. 1695 – To son Jeremiah 100 A., being the same land I formerly gave to my son John Cary, dec. To son Solomon planta. where I now live. Son Solomon resid. legatee & Ex'r. Witt: William Willett, Edward Burman, John Gosle. – p. 104

TAYLOR, SAMUEL – 1 Feb. 1695 – 7 Apr. 1696 – To son Samuel Taylor planta. where I now live & 182 A., being 1/2 of 365 A. granted me by patent, & 300 A. of marsh, being 1/2 of an Island containing 600 A. granted me by patent. To son Charles 182 A. the remaining 1/2 of said 365 A. To dau. Mary 300 A. marsh, being the other 1/2 of said Island. To son Charles my Island of marsh on the seaboard side containing 300 A. called George's Island. Sons Samuel & Charles & dau. Mary Ex'rs. Witt: Thomas Perry, Nicholas Millechop, John Blake.

LITTLETON, BOWMAN – 2 May 1696 – 16 June 1696 – To cousin William Wittington all my lands in King's Neck containing 50 A. To cousin Edward Robins, son of Maj. John Robins, land on the East side of Popelar Branch. To bro. Nathaniel Littleton & bro. in law Ricbard Waters my neck of land called Farsalia during their lives & the lives of their wives, then to return to the male heir of my bro. Nathaniel, reversion to the male heir of my bro. Southy Littleton. To bro. Southy Littleton. To sistor Custis. To sister Harmanson. To cousin Southy Whittington. Nathaniel Littleton & Richard Waters Ex'rs. Witt: John Purnell, John Jones, John Roussalle – p. 110

BYLES, DANIELL – 21 Jan. 1695 – 16 June 1696 – To friend Patriack Morgan. To Will: Barnes "my most usefull instrument for distillation", worm, casks & what brandy shall be in his custody at my dec. Will: Barnes Ex'r. Witt: John Straford, Thomas Budd, Steven

TUNNILL, NATHANIEL - Not dated - 16 June 1696 - To son Washbourn Tunnill house where I live & 1/5 part of 400 A., To 4 youngest sons, Nathaniel, Edmond, Scarbrough & Elias the residue of my land. Wife Mary. Witt: Samuel Taylor, Jonathan Owen, James Glenn. - p. 112. Mary "now wife of Charles Stockley" qualified.

TAYLOR, THOMAS - 6 Mar. 1693 - 17 Mar. 1695 - Wife Elizabeth to have use of house & planta. where I now live, being 100 A., for life then to my son Edward Taylor, situate at Burtons Branch. To son Thomas Taylor 100 A. bounded Northerly on the North side of Dry Swamp. To son James 100 A. on the South side of Dry Branch. Daus. (no names) & wife resid. legatees. Daus. under 16, sons under 21 - Wife Elizabeth Exec. Witt: William Smith, John Marshall. - p. 113

MARTINO, JULIAN - 14 May 1696 - 16 June 1696 - To Lewis Knight, my Ex'r. To goddau. Magdalen Knight. To Lewis Knight, Jr. 100 A. purchased of Col. Jenifer. Witt: Joseph O'Kain, Edmond Tataham, John Scott. - p. 114

GORE: MAXIMILIAN - 31 Mar. 1696 - 17 June 1696 - To son in law Thomas Smith 225 A. bought of Jonathan Owen, except timber which I leave to my son Daniel Gore. To son in law James Smith 500 A. on Assateage Island, being part of 3005 A. purchased of Col. Jenifer. To son in law John Smith 500 A. on Assateage Island. To son in law Thomas Smith 300 A. on Assateage Island. To son in law Arthur Roberts. Son Daniel Gore resid. legatee, he to maintain his mother during her natural life. Sons in law James Smith & John Purnell overseers. Son Daniel Ex'r. Witt: John Deane, James Walker, John Duberley - p. 114

BLAKE, JANE - 5 Mar. 1695 - 16 June 1696 - To 3 youngest children (no names) all my est. left me by my dec. husband, William Blake. To dau. Mary Owen. To dau. Sarah Willis. Witt: Jonathan Owen, John Wheelton, Sarah Plumsted - p. 115

SNELLIT, WILLIAM - Nunc. Declaration 17 Jan. 1695 - Proved 20 Jan. 1695 - Rec. 16 June 1696 - To Ann Mary Ayres 2 yards of Blew cotton at Christopher Thomson's house. Christopher Thomson resid. legatee - Proved by Henry Ayres & ___ Ayres. - p. 116

NIXSON, THOMAS - Nunc.- Declaration 12 Feb. 1695 - Proved 11 June 1696 - Rec. 16 June 1696 - To mother Ann Nixson. Bros. Edward & Richard Nixson. Proved by Richard Bundick & Jonathan Sturgis - p. 116

STURGIS, RICHARD - 12 Feb. 1695 - 15 Sept. 1696 - To son John Sturgis (under 16) To son Richard Sturgis & dau. Elizabeth Sturgis (both under 16). Wife Sarah Exec. Witt: Thomas Crippen, George Parker, Sr. Thomas Jones. - p. 124

WALKER, PETER - 18 Mar. 1695 - Partly proved 17 June 1696 -
Prob. 15 Sept. 1696. To sons Henry & Peter Walker, Jr., 250 A. at the
head of Pitts Creek at the Virginia-Maryland line. To son James
Walker 1/2 of 400 A. where I now live. To son Daniel Walker (under
21) 200 A. where I now live, being the remainder of the said 400 A. To
son Peter Walker, Jr. 275 A. of marsh which Mr. Thomas Welbourne
& I took up, being 1/2 of an Island between Gengoteage Island &
Muskeedo Point. To dau. Mary Walker. Wife (no name) resid. legatee.
Sons Henry & Peter Walker Ex'rs. Witt: John Pitts, James Smith,
Richard Flowers. - p. 129

JOHNSON, ALEXANDER - Not dated - 15 Sept. 1696 - To daus.
Elizabeth & Sarah Johnson (both under 16). To bro. in law John Bowen.
To my cousin George Hall. To bro. Barnitt Ramsy. To bro. Alexander
Marsy. To eldest dau. Elizabeth planta. where I now live. Bro. Alex-
ander Marsy & Henry Toles Ex'rs. Witt: Joseph Stockley, Joseph
Staton. - p. 130

MASSEY, ALEXANDER - 25 Sept. 1696 - 19 Nov. 1696 - To Alexan-
der Massey planta. where I now live containing 100 A. To Sarah
Massey. To Joseph & Comfort Stockly, son & dau. of Joseph Stockley.
To William Massey. To Thomas Massey, son of John Massey. To
Mary Stockley, wife of Joseph Stockley. Alexander Massey Ex'r. To
son John Massey. Witt: John Massie, John Upshur, John Die - p. 135

LEWIS, JOHN, Sr., of Hunting Creek - 15 Aug. 1690 - No order of
Prob. (1697) - To son John Lewis planta. on Hunting Creek for life
then to his two sons, William & John Lewis. To son Robert Lewis
land on Hunting Creek. To son Richard Lewis land on Hunting Creek.
To 3 sons John, Robert & Richard marsh land. To wife Lucresia.
Richard Drummond Ex'r. Witt: Daniel of St. Thomas Jenifer, Nich:
Hill, Richard Hill, John Drummond - p. 154

STUART, ANDREW - 24 Feb. 1696 - 6 Apr. 1697 - To wife Judith
planta. where I now live containing 737 A. until my son Andrew comes
to age of 21 years, then to my said son Andrew, together with 500 A.
adjoining where I now live. To dau. Anna Stuart. To daus. Margaret &
Abigale Stuart. (daus. under 16) Wife resid. legatee & Exec. John
Washbourne, Robert Watson & William Nock overseers. Witt: Will:
Sill, Richard Kellam, Jr., Robert Scott. - p. 160

RILY, THOMAS, Sr. - 1 Aug. 1696 - 1 June 1697 - To son Thomas
Riley planta, containing 300 A. where I now live. To son Lawrence
Rily planta. at Back Creek containing 200 A. To dau. Mary Truit. To
grandson James Truit. Daus. Elizabeth, Sarah & Margaret. Grandson
Thomas Liliston. Sons Thomas & Lawrence Riley & John Lewis of
Hunting Creek Ex'rs. Witt: John Ayres, Finley Mackwilliam, Nich:
Hill - p. 161 - Sarah Riley, wid. of Thomas, Sr., qualified.

PARKER, WILLIAM, of Matompkin - 13 Aug. 1696 - 2 June 1696 -
To dau. Comfort 215 A. being one moiety of 430 A. belonging to me at
St. Martins in Somerset Co. Md. Bal. of land at St. Martins to son
William Parker (under 18). To wife Elizabeth the one moiety of my
land at Matompkin for life, & the other moiety to my son William
when he reaches the age of 18 years, and at the death of my wife to
enjoy the whole 373 A. Wife Exec. Bro. in law John Powell & friend
George Parker Overseers - Witt: Robert Scott, Richard Hill Ayres,
Charles Campleshon - p. 162

STRATTON, JOHN, of Accomack - 1 May 1696 - 2 June, 1697 - To
Joseph Stockly. To Thomas Stockley, To Francis Conner. To wife
Elizabeth. Joseph & Thomas Stockly feo fees in trust of will, & Ex'rs.
To Eliner Massie planta. containing 80 A. for term of lease after the
dec. of my wife. Witt: Thomas Perry, Nathaniel Price, Alexander
Massie. - p. 164

REVELL, Mrs Frances - Nunc. Died 23 June, 1697 at the house of Mr.
Robert Coleburne - Prob. 3 Aug. 1697 - To Frances Coleburn. To
Frances Custis. To Frances Revell. To my dau. Custis & my dau.
Rebecca Coleburne. Proved by Johannah Ogleby & Sara Beech - Rec.
at the request of Mr. Henry Custis & Mr. Robert Coleburn - p. 166

BIRD, EDWARD - 12 Apr. 1697 - 3 Aug. 1697 - To son in law William Rodgers, my Ex'r., whole est., he to maintain me and my now
wife Jane Bird during our natural lives. To son John Bird cattle. Witt:
Edmund Allen, William Dennison, Thomas Agen - p. 166

ROBERTS, FRANCIS - 22 Oct. 1697 - 8 Dec. 1697 - To wife Sarah for
life the brick house I now live in, mill planta. &c. To son Arthur
(Sarah his stepmother) planta. where I now live. To son Francis
Roberts the remaining part of my dividend of 550 A. of land at Mache-
pungo. Son in law John Downing. Daua. Frances & Bethulia. To
grandson Arthur Barker (under 21) son of Bethulia.
      Died before signing and recorded at the request of the heirs,
Sarah Roberts, Arthur Roberts, Francis Roberts, Frances Downing &
Bethulia Barker. Proved by Robert Scott. p. 184

WALTHAM, JOHN - 14 Jan. 1697/8 - 5 Apr. 1698 - To friend Christopher Stokely land adjoining Richard Kellam. To son Stephen Waltham land known as Little Neck. To son Charleton Waltham planta.
where I now live bet. Little Neck & Tobacco House Branch; wife to
have use of same during her life. To son John Waltham 200 A. bet.
Tobacco House Branch & the Pined Neck Branch. To son Teakle
Waltham 200 A. from the Pined Neck Branch to Schoolhouse Gut. To
son Peter Waltham 200 A. at the head of land devised Teakle. To
dau. Bridget Waltham. Wife Elizabeth Exec. Witt: Luke Layler,
Bethula Barker, William Barnes - p. 193

COULBURN, ROBERT - 6 Apr. 1698 - 7 June 1698 - To son Robert
Coulburn planta. where I now live. To dau. Frances 50 A. in Maryland

called Prayers Neck. To my unborn child, if a son, 200 A. in Maryland called Heart's Ease, if a girl the whole divident cont. 250 A. to be divided between my dau. Rebecca & that dau. which is yet unborn. Wife (no name) Exec. Witt: William Nock, James Lee, Johanna Ogleby – p. 196 – Rebecca Coulburn, wid. of Robert, qualified.

TAYLOR, JOHN, of Pungatege – 13 Apr. 1698 – 7 June 1698 – 210 A. to be divided as follows: To son Bartholomew 60 A., to unborn child, if a son, then to two sons John & Abraham & that son, if it live, 50 A. each, if a dau. then the said 210 A. to be divided between my three sons only, Bartholomew to have 10 A. more. Sons under 18 – Daus. Deborah & Mary, both under 16. Wife (no name) Exec. Witt: John Lecatt, Sr., Robert Hutchinson, Tomason Lecatt.– p. 196

MILLECHOPPE, NICHOLAS, Sr. 20 Dec. 1697 – 7 June 1698 – 650 A. in Pungoteague Neck on Assawoman Creek to 3 sons: eldest son Nicholas to have 218 A. at the head of said Neck where my son in law William Lucas now lives; to second son John 216 A. to youngest son Richard 216 A. at the botton of said Neck where I now dwell. Wife Mary. To dau. Mary Lucas 100 A. in Messongo Swamp late bought of Capt. Daniel of St. Thomas Jenifer, the other 200 A. in Messongo Swamp to be divided between my 3 sons. To the 3 children of my dau. Mary Lucas, viz: Thomas, William & Comfort Lucas. Wife & 3 sons Ex'rs. Witt: Samuel Jester, John Abbot, William Dennison – p. 197

STOCKLEY, FRANCIS – 23 May 1698 – 2 Aug. 1698 – 300 A. to be divided bet. 3 sons Joseph, Francis & John. To wife Sarah & unborn child the remaining part of my land where my dwelling planta. is situate adjoining Nicholas Millechops. Children under age. If any of them are not willing to stay with their mother then to be with their uncle Joseph Stockley until 18. Brother Joseph Stockley & bro. Richard Webb, Jr. Ex'rs. Witt: Roger Adams, Judith Taylor, Walter Lane – p. 206

ANDERSON, WILLIAM – 23 July 1698 – 4 Oct. 1698 – To Mr. Francis Makemie & Naomi his wife, my eldest dau. all my lands at Matchatanck, being 1000 A. & for want of heirs to my 3 grandaus. Elizabeth, Naomi & Comfort Taylor, daus. of Elias & Comfort Taylor – To Francis Makemie all the money lent him & that he may have his sloop at my death &c., he paying 6 L ster. to my sister Barns; 5 L to my sister Hope & 5 L to my sister Nock, and bestowing education to the value of 50 L on my 3 grandchildren. To Francis & Naomi Makemie planta. at Pocomoke cont. 950 A. for life & for want of issue to Taylor grandchildren. To wife Mary planta. at Accomson for life then to Taylor grandchildren. Land at Sikes Island not already given my dau. Comfort, being 350 A. to the next dau. my dau. Comfort shall have, if none then to the 3 daus. now living. To nephew & godson Anderson Parksr 400 A. at Pungoteague & for want of heirs to Thomas Parker, & for want of heirs to Matthew Parker. To sister Comfort Scott debts now due me in the county of Sussex. To nephew William Hope, son of George & Temperance Hope, 250 A. at Forked Neck at the head of

Pitts Creek in Somerset County, Maryland, being 1/2 of 500 A. called Fookes Choice. To nephew William Parker. Son in law & dau. Naomi Ex'rs. Edmund Custis, Edward Moore, Bro. George Hope & Thomas Perry to appraise est. Witt: William Bloxham, Abraham Bancks, Sara Pritchet, Edmund Custis, Gervis Baggale - p. 209.

OGROHONS, DANIEL - Nunc. 18 Feb. 1698/9 - 4 Apr. 1699 - To grandson John. To grandson William. To grandau. Jane. Son Daniel Ogrohons resid. legatee & Exr. Proved by Nathaniel & Elizabeth Walker. - p. 226

WHARTON, FRANCIS - 6 Oct. 1695 - 4 June 1700 - Wife Elizabeth Exec. Planta. where I now live to my son Francis Wharton, & for want of issue to my son Charles Wharton - Ditto to son John Wharton - Ditto to son Daniel Wharton - Ditto to son Thomas Wharton - Ditto to dau. Elizabeth Wharton. To dau. Sarah Sturgis, wife of Richard Sturgis 1 s. Witt: Robert Hawley, John Grey, John Arue - p. 251

NIBLIT, RICHARD - 16 Mar. 1699 - 6 Aug. 1700 - To wife Elizabeth 100 A. where I now live. To grandau. Margaret, dau. of Abraham Banks by Sarah, my dau. 100 A. out of my divident of 300 A. & for want of heirs to grandsons Richard & Burnell Niblet, sons of Burnell Niblet & Margaret his wife. To grandsons Richard & Burnell Niblet 100 A. being the remainder of my land. After my death my son in law & his wife to come down to my planta. where I now live at Marrumsco, there to dwell & be assistant to my wife. To friend John Washbourne. Wife Elizabeth Exec. John Washbourne to aid & assist her. Witt: Richard Jones, Joseph Clarke, Henry Clarke - p. 253

CUSTIS, EDMUND. of Deep Creek - 12 Aug. 1700 - 14 Feb. 1700 - To son Thomas (under 20) To dau. Tabitha Scarburgh Custis (under 17) 850 A. given me by my honoured Uncle Coll. John Custis of Arlington in Northampton County, dec., at or near Deep Creek. To Naomi Makemie, wife of Mr. Francis Makemie. To Robert Pitt. To Mary Anderson, my housekeeper. To Francis Makemie. To John Broadhurst. To son Thomas Custis & dau. Tabitha Scarburgh Custis bal. of est. in Virginia, Maryland, Europe & elsewhere. Two children Ex'rs. Francis Makemie & Naomi his wife to act as Ex'rs. with the advice of Madame Tabitha Hill, their great grandmother, during their minority. To my servant William Darter. Witt: Robert Logan, William Darter, Joane Thomson. Memo: 7th paragraph omitted by error & ordered to be inserted: To Margaret Robins, dau. of Arthur Robins, cattle. Codicil: To Francis Makemie my sloop called Tabitha. Witt: Thomas Thornbury, Mary Anderson. - p. 262

LITTLEHOUSE, WILLIAM - 24 Sept. 1700 - 1 Apr. 1701 - Whole est. to wife Dorithy & 3 children William, Simon (under 18) & Floriana (under 16) Friends James Gray, Thomas Dent & James Mecombe overseers. Witt: Joseph Ash, Mary Amos, Elizabeth Watkinson - p. 268

31

LECATT, PHILLIP ALEXANDER - 26 Nov. 1700 - 3 June 1701 - To sons Richard & John Lecatt planta. where I now live (both under 16) Dau. Elizabeth (under 14) Wife Mary resid. legatee & Exec. Witt: Richard Jones, Rowland Savage, John Lecatt - p. 270

FITTIMAN, SAMUEL - 2 Nov. 1701 - 2 Dec. 1701 - To Meshack Fittiman 200 A. where I now live. To son Shadrack Fittiman 200 A. To son Joseph Fittiman 200 A. being the remainder of 600 A. To dau. Elizabeth Fittiman. To dau. Mary Fittiman. To William Benston, son of Francis Benston, Sr. To William Williamson. Wife Elizabeth Exec. Witt: Robert Pitt, Elizabeth Brodhurst, William Pattison - p. 276

CUDDY, JAMES - 3 Feb. 1700 - 2 Dec. 1701 - Daus. Mary, Martha, Elizabeth & Jane. To wife Jane my mill during her life, then to one of my daus. to whom she shall think fit. Unborn child. Wife resid. legatee. Witt: Christopher Hays, William White, Thomas Jenkinson - p. 277

SCARBURGH, CHARLES - 6 Aug. 1701 - 6 Oct. 1702 - To eldest son Bennet Scarburgh 521 A. near Kikotanck formerly called Hogneck, now Antingham; land in Jollys Neck & his one share of Benefield in Pocomoke containing 3000 A., and his share of 2500 A. in Wickocomo in Maryland, to be equally divided between him & his sister Ann Parker. To son Charles Scarburgh planta. at Great Matomkin where he now lives cont. by patent. 2100 A. To son Henry Scarburgh planta. where I now live at Pungoteague after the death of my wife, & my Island called Scarburgh Winter Island in the mouth of Pungoteague. To dau. Ann, wife of George Parker of Onancock, Gent: her share of 3000 A. at Pocomoke called Benefield & of 2500 A. at Wickomoco, Maryland, called Bennet's Adventure, and 1/2 of 2000 A. at Poco-moke, in Virginia, to be divided bet. her & her bro. Bennet Scarburgh. To dau. Mary Scarburgh land at Pungoteague called Yeo's Neck, now Bradfield, purchased of Justinian Yeo. To dau. Sarah 2000 A. on the South side of White Marsh. To dau. Tabitha Scarburgh land near the Court House, land at Anancock, called the Town, land in Burton's Branch. To wife Elizabeth lot at Anancock Town, Tangier Island, at Bundicks & Muddy Creek & 3000 A. called Hogquarter in Maryland & all other land not already by me given, also my planta. & land & Winter Island for life. Wife resid. legatee & Exec. Witt: John West, minor, John Lilliston, Edmund Scarburgh. John Morragh. - p. 292

NIGHTINGALE, THOMAS - Nunc. 26 July 1702 - 2 Feb. 1702 - To Edmund Ayres' two daus. Tabitha & Ann Mary Ayres. To Ann Denni-son. Edmund Ayres resid. legatee - Proved by Christopher Thomson & William Dennison - p. 298

BENTS, KANUTUS - 3 Aug. 1702 - 3 Feb. 1702/3 - To dau. Margaret Howard. Grandson William Howard. Wife Elizabeth Exec. John Marshall overseer. Witt: Capt. Thomas Welburne, Daniel Welburne - p. 300

LECATT, JOHN - 1 Dec. 1702 - 2 Mar. 1702/3 - To dau. Tabitha & to her dau. Susanna & her son Nathaniel Bradford. To son John. To grandson Augustin Lecatt. Wife Tomasin. To dau. Elizabeth. To the children of my dau. Mary that she had by John Taylor. Wife Exec. Witt: Robert Hutchinson, Richard Rogers, Joseph Milby - p. 302

WALTHAM, ELIZABETH - late wife of John Waltham dec. - 28 Aug. 1699 - 3 Mar. 1702 "Being bound up to Wiccocomoco by Water" To 3 sons Teackle, John & Peter Waltham 600 A. left them by the will of my said dec. husband which was escheat land, and which after his death was patented in my name. Witt: Luke Layler, Christopher Stockley, Judith Brereton - p. 305

TULLY, KATHERINE - 8 Oct. 1702 - No ord. of prob. To eldest son Hemry Lamberson 1/2 of the worth of the land Richard Lamberson lives on in Somerset County, Maryland. To son Richard Lamberson the remainder of the plantation where he now lives. To Sarah Lamberson. To son Abraham Lamberson planta where I now live & all the rest of my personal est. To grandson Henry Lamberson. Should my son Abraham marry with Sarah Timmons all my personal est. to be divided bet. his 2 bros. Henry & Richard - Witt: James Taylor, William Taylor. - p. 306

WATSON, ROBERT, Sr. - 24 July 1702 - 1 June 1703 - To son Robert 1/2 of 400 A. where I now live. To son David the other 1/2. To son in law Samuel Berston & Joanna, his wife, 200 A. on Pratts Branch. To grandson John Benston 100 A. be- longing to the divident given his father & mother. To grandson Joseph Watson, son of Peter Watson. To grandson John Bonwell. Bro. Peter Watson. Day. Mary Hughbank. To dau. Susanna Stott. Dau. Sarah Kellam. Dau. Joanna Benston. Son in law Henry Stott. Wife (no name) Exec. Son Robert Overseer. Witt: John Watscn, Francis Darby, John Procter - p. 308 - Presented by David Watson, youngest son. Susan Watson, wid. of Robert.

BLAKE, JOSEPH - 24 Feb. 1702/3 - 3 Aug. 1703 - To son Dennis (under 18) land where I now live - Daus. Naomy & Rachell (both under 16) - Wife Ann Exec. Friends & Bros. Robert Pitt & Dennis Morris overseers. Witt: Comfort Morris: Elias Blake, John Read. - p. 310

WHITE, WILLIAM - Nunc. 29 June, 1703 - 3 Aug. 1703 - Whole est. to son William White - (other children but not named) Proved by Peter Rogers & Richard Rogers. p. 313

WEST, JOHN - 6 Feb. 1702/3 - 4 Aug. 1703 - To son Anthony land at Nandua - Elizabeth wife of Anthony. Grandson John, son of Anthony. To grandaus. Matilda, Mary Scarburgh & Jean West, daus. of my son Anthony, the Ridge land without the Neck where Anthony now lives. To son Alexander planta. at Mossongo formerly known by the name of old Brookes land, To 4 youngest daus. Catherine, Mary, Ann & Scarburgh West (all under 16) To eldest son John and son Benony land at

Deep Creek; should both die without issue Benony's part to go to Alexander's eldest son and John's part to my son Jonathan. To son Jonathan land at Chicconessick Creek. To son John land at Pungoteague. To 5 daus. Catherine, Mary, Ann, Scarburgh & Matilda land at Deep Creek. To dau. Matilda Wise & her dau. Mary Cade Wise 300 A. at Deep Creek. To dau. Sarah Robinson, wife of Capt. Tully Robinson, planta. at Onancock called ye Folly, cont. 600 A. for life, & then to her 5 children, West, Elizabeth, Scarburgh, Sarah & Susanna. To dau. Frances Kellam land given her by deed. To Sarum, son of my dau. Frances, cattle, personalty. To John, the son of Sarah Glanning, dec., 100 A. at Gingoteague. To youngest son John West. To sons John West the younger & John West the elder. Wife Matilda Exec. & after her dec. I appoint my son Jonathan Exr. Son in law Capt. Tully Robinson to assist my wife. To grandson Anthony, son of John West. To grandson John, the eldest son of my dau. Matilda Wise 100 A. Witt: William Wise, John Wise, Jr. Tabitha Hill, Geo: Nich: Hack, Patrick Morgan, Robert Hutchinson – p. 317

KELLAM, RICHARD – 1 June 1703 – 6 Oct. 1703 – To 2 sons Edward & William Kellam 5 s. each. To dau. Sarah Kellam, now Curle. Dau. Ann Kellam, now Wallis. Dau. Rachel Lingo 5 s. each. To dau. Rose Kellam, now Garretson, 60 A. on Burrells Branch. To godson William Onely, son of Clement Onely. To son William 50 A. adj. his own land on Beaver dam branch. To son Richard 5 s. Wife Sarah Exec. Witt: Stephen Waltham, William Sill – p. 321

THORNTON, EDWARD – 6 May 1703 – 6 Oct. 1703 – To son Edward Thornton 100 A. where I now live. Son Thomas. Son Jonathan. To son William 100 A. being the other 1/2 of my 200 A. Wife Patience resid. legatee & Exec. Sons under 18 – Daus. (no names) under 16 – Witt: Thomas Perry, Nathaniel Rackcliffe, Jr., Joseph Staton, Jr. – p. 322

STRIPE, WILLIAM – 25 June 1698 – Proved in Somerset Co. Md 30 Nov. 1703, Pro. in Accomack 7 Dec. 1703 – To sons William & John 1 s. To daus. Abigail, Ann & Mary 1 s. To son Robert whole est. after the dec. of my wife. Wife Elizabeth Exec. Witt: William Anderson, John Custis, Pock, Wealthyana Booth – p. 326

ANDERSON, MARY, wid. of William Anderson – Nunc. 12 Nov. 1703 – 7 Dec. 1703 – To Betty Makemie – To Betty Taylor. To Betty Shepheard's dau. Proved by William Shepheard, Elizabeth Shepheard & Sarah Ginn – Presented by Mr. Francis Makemie – p. 326

MORRIS, ELIZABETH, wid. of Dennis Morris – Nov. 1703 – 6 Feb. 1703/4 – To sons John, Dennis & Joseph Morris 1 s. each. To daus. Sarah Read & Elizabeth Pitt 1 s. each. Dau. Ann Blake. Dau. Mary Morris – Dau. Ann Blake's youngest son born this present year. Grandau Sarah Read. Son Jacob Morris & dau. Mary Morris resid. legatees – Robert Pitt & John Morris to make division. Son Jacob

Exr. Witt: John Blockson, Sr. John Dimzie. - p. 327

TAYLOR, JAMES - 12 Oct. 1703 - 1 Feb. 1703/4 - To son William Taylor planta. where I now live after his mother's death. Dau. Lyshia Sadberry. To dau. Sarah Green, wid. Wife Elizabeth Exec. Witt: John Marcy, James Soward. John Bowen - p. 328

BEECH, SAMUEL - 25 Nov. 1700 - 1 Feb. 1703 - To son Samuel planta. where I now live cont. 150 A. To son Ben: Beech planta. where my son Thomas lately lived cont. 150 A. To wife (no name) 100 A. at the head of the land given my son Ben: Wife Exec. p. 328

TOMSON, CHRISTOPHER - 9 Dec. 1703 - 7 June 1704 - After the death of my wife to my son in law Edmund Ayres planta. where I now live cont. 300 A., being part of 500 A. as by patent will appear. To Francis Ayres, son of my son in law Francis Ayres 100 A. of said land. To Richard Ayres, son of Richard Ayres, my son in law, 100 A. of said tract. To son in law Henry Ayres 100 A. of said tract. To Ann Mary Ayres my dau. in law 100 A. of said tract. To Edmund Ayres & Ann his wife planta. cont. 800 A. at Blackwater Creek in Maryland for life, then to their two daus. Tabitha & Ann Mary Ayres. Wife (no name) resid. legatee & Exec. Witt: John Drummond, Robert Davis, Regnald Eyre, Isaac Metcalfe, Simon Michael - p. 345

EWELL, JAMES - 7 Aug. 1703 - 13 July 1703 - To son Mark. To wife Anne all my land & planta. Dau. Patience Ewell. Dau. Ann Ewell. Son Solomon. Dau. Comfort Tatham. Grandau. Jane Tatham. Grandau Tabyther Tatham. Son Charles. Son Mark Exr. Son George. Witt: John Drummond, Robert Norton, William Willet, Sarah Ryley - p. 347

BENSTON, WILLIAM, Sr. 17 Oct. 1703 - 1 Aug. 1704 - To son Alexander Benston land at Beaver Dam. To son William land beginning at the valley & including the branch. To son Ambrose land at Beaver Dam. To son in law Edward James land at Beaver Dam for the term of 8 years. Wife Rebecca resid. legatee & Exec. Daus. Ester Rickets & Elizabeth Rickets 12 pence each. Witt: John Bowen, Henry Richy, John Gillet - p. 347

WALKER, PETER - 29 Oct. 1703 - 1 Aug. 1704 - To bro. Daniel Walker planta. left me by my father Peter Walker. Bros. Henry, James & Daniel Walker. Sister Mary Walker. Bro. Henry resid. legatee & Exr. Witt: Edward Robins, Robert Ardis, George Parker - p. 351

CUTTING, WILLIAM - 11 Aug. 1704 - 3 Oct. 1704 - To cousin William Bell, son of Robert Bell. To cousin Thomas Bell planta at Nasswadox cont. 250 A. To cousin Robert Bell. To cousin Nathaniel Bell. Bro. in law Robert Bell. To sister Dorothy Lursen. Sister Ann Layler. Bro. in law Robert Bell resid. legatee & Exr. Witt: William Taylor, William Nicholson, Robert Scott - p. 354

35

HACK, Lt. Col. GEORGE NICHOLAS – 20 Mar. 1704/5 – 4 Apr. 1705 –
To son George all my land at Pungoteagus, 1/2 my land at Sassafrax
River in Maryland, cont. 800 A. To son Peter all my land at Andue
purchased of Capt. Matthew Trim & Martha his wife & 1/2 my land at
Sassafrax River in Maryland. To dau. Frances. To dau Mary Margaretta, she to be in the care & tuition of Mr. Arthur Davis until 16. To
dau. Elizabeth, To dau. Anne, she to live with my Ex'rs. until 16,
land at Massongo cont. 700 A. to be div. between my sons George &
Peter. 5 children, George, Peter, Elizabeth, Anne, & Mary Margaretta
resid. legatees. Friends Col. John Custis of Northampton, Col. William Custis & Capt. John Washbourne to assist Exrs. Sons George &
Peter Ex'rs. Witt: William Custis, John Washbourne, Robert Scott –
p. 362 – Presented by Capt. George Hack to be recordcd.

MEERS, MARY – 28 July 1703 – 3 Apr. 1705 – To son William. To
son John. To children Richard, Robert, Elizabeth, Mary & Dorothy.
Son William Exr. Witt: Joseph Aymes, James Maccome, Robert
Scott. – p. 365

JOHNSON, HENDRICK, Cooper – 27 Feb. 1704/5 – 5 June 1705 – To
friend William Danniell, whom I app. my Exr. To Ann Danniell, wife
of William. To Comfort Danniell. Nicholas Millechops to be satisfied for any trouble of being at his house. Witt: Nathaniel William,
John Bradford, William Havett. – p. 366

CLARK, JOSEPH – 10 Sept. 1703 – 5 Dec. 1705 – To son in law
James Leary. To my dau. Mary, his wife. To 2 grandsons & 2 grandaus., children of James & Mary Leary. Wife Ann & son Henry resid.
legatees – Wife Exec. Witt: John Rowles, Richard Jones – p. 376

DAVIS, ROBERT – Not dated – 4 June 1706 – To son Samuel Davis
land on the South side of Gilford or Muddy Creek. To son Thomas
Davis land on the North side. To son James Davis 100 A., being part
of my dividend of 350 A. To son Robert Davis. Dau. Elizabeth Parks
1 s. To dau. Mary Read 1 s. Daus. Sarah, Gean, Comfort & Easter
Davis. Wife Elizabeth Exec. Witt: John Morris, Obedience Pitman,
Thomas Bell – p. 393

NELSON, David – 21 Apr. 1706 – 6 Aug. 1706 – To son William
Nelson. Son David Nelson. Dau. Naomi Nelson. Wife Jeane to have
custody of sons William & David & Dau. Margaret until they arrive to
age. Wife resid. legatee & Exec. Witt: Robert Logan, John Hutton,
Eliazbeth Hutton – p. 393

THORNE, ARTHUR – "Being only in company with the subscriber,
knocked overboard in Potomack River by boom on the sloop Diamond
of Accomack County, about 4 o'clock on Sunday morning last past &
drowned" Deposition of Charles Bayly – 6 Aug. 1706
p. 393

BOOTH, JOHN, of Pocomoke River – 6 Nov. 1706 – 4 Mar. 1706 – To sons George & John Booth (under age) my 300 A. of land. Wife Katherine. To daus. Ann Garret, Elizabeth Jenkinson, Weltheana Clark, Isabell Booth, Sarah Booth & Naomi Booth 1 s. each. Witt: Richard Sterling, William Flear, Sebastian Silverthorne – p. 407

STRATTON, ELIZABETH.– 17 June 1697 – 6 Aug. 1707 – To Joseph Atkins, son of my dau. Ann Atkins. To Matilda & John Atkins. Grandson Woodman Stockley. To Henry Toles Jr. To Stockly Toles. To Thomas Toles. To Job Toles. To John, Frances, Thomas. Joseph & Charles Stockly. Dau. Hannah Bally. Woodman & Thomas Stockly Ex'rs. Witt: John Bradford, Mary Sampell – p. 422

SCOTT, ROBERT – Nunc, 18 Aug. 1707 – 7 Oct. 1707 – 1/2 of est. to Barbery Nicholson & the other half to my Landlord. Proved by William Nicholson, Barbery Nicholson, Margaret Wainhouse, Ann Harman – p. 426

WILSON, THOMAS – 8 May 1707 – 4 Nov. 1707 – To Peter Turlington, Sr. To his son Peter Turlington. To Mary Turlington. To Thomas Turlington. To John Turlington. To Mamefield Turlington – Witt: John Spiers, John Simcock – p. 428

MARVILL, JOHN – 29 July 1707 – 3 Feb. 1707/8 – To son Thomas Marvill. To Jonathan West. To Mrs Catherine West. Friend Mrs Matilda West resid. legatee & Exec. Witt: Tully Robinson. John West, John Lewis. – p. 431

HARMAN, CORNELIUS – 22 Feb. 1706/7 – 2 Mar. 1707/8 – To eldest son William Harman planta. where I now live, being 325 A. wife to have use of same for life, William to pay my sons Cornelius & Symon when they come to age. Daus. Anne, Hannah & Sarah. Youngest dau. Mary. Wife Elizabeth Exec. Witt: Timothy Truelove, Francis Wainhouse, Jr. – p. 434

BROWNE, EDMUND, son of Devorax Browne & Tabitha (Scarburgh) Browne, his wife, born 1660 and died in Turkey in 1678, being taken in captivity, being 18 years old or thereabouts when he died. Capt. John Martin reporting that he died, and Timothy Low saying he carried the said Browne to his grave. Deposition of Tabitha Hill, formerly Tabitha Browne, & Matilda West. 2 June, 1708 – p. 440

BAYLY, RICHARD, Jr. – 15 Nov. 1707 – 1 June 1708 – To son Henry Bayly 200 A. in Somerset County, Maryland at the head of Pitts Creek. To dau. Lacey Bayly. To sons Richard, Edmund, Henry & Whittington Bayly. Daus. Ursilia Whittington & Joyce Bayly. Eldest son Richard. Wife Ursilia & son Richard Ex'rs. Children under 18. Father, Bro. Edmund Bayly & friend Joseph Milby overseers. Witt: Richard Bally, John Taylor, Thomas Bowles, Edmond Bayly. – p. 441

CHARLES JOHN - 1 July 1707 - 1 June 1708 - To wife Ann 120 A. purchased of Col. Edmund Scarburgh - Wife resid. legatee & Exec. Witt: Robert Hutchinson, Margaret Hutchinson, John Hutchinson - P. 441

MIDDLETON, THOMAS - 15 Apr. 1707 - 1 June 1708 - To eldest son Daniel Middleton 70 A., being part of land purchased of William Sill. To son in law Thomas Budd & Anna Danela, his now wife, part of the above land. To 3 youngest sons Thomas, John & Gabriell bal. of said land. To dau. Mary Middleton by my now wife Elenor. Wife Exec. Witt: Henry Read, William Mason, John Washbourne - p. 442

MAKEMIE, FRANCIS - 27 Apr. 1708 - 4 Aug. 1708 - To kinsman William Bagg of Accomack. To wife Naomi & 2 daus. Elizabeth & Ann Makemie. To Mr. Jedidah Andrew, Minister at Philadelphia, books & after his death or removal then to the minister or ministers succeeding him in that place, and to such only as shall be of the Presbyterian or Independent persuasion. To Andrew Hamilton my law books. To eld. dau. Elizabeth 850 A. patented by me on the South side of Sykes Island & 200 A. of swamp near Pokamok Bridge known as Dumfriece, lots at Scarburgh Town. To youngest dau. Ann 174 A. an Island on the South side of Watts Great Island, 350 A. on the South side of Matchetank Creek, 180 A. patented by me, lot at Scarburgh Town. To wife Water & Grist Mill at Assawoman Branch for life then to daus. Wife & 2 daus. resid. legatees of whole est. not already disposed of by the will of Mr. William Anderson or this will. Should daus, die without issue, then to my youngest sister Ann Makemie of the Kingdom of Ireland and the two eldest sons of by brothers John & Robert Makemie, both of the name of Francis Makemie. Daus. under 18. To 2 daus. my 1/3 part of 3804 A. patented on Smith's Island, cont. by estimation 1268 A. & should they die without issue to my sister Ann & the two eldest sons of my brothers John & Robert. Wife Naomi Exec. & should she die before my will is proved then Col. Francis Jenkins, of Somerset County, Maryland & Mary his wife to be my Ex'rs & guardians of my children. Mr. Andrew Hamilton Capt. John Wales, Robert Pitt, James Kemp in Accomack County, or any two of them, to assist my Ex'rs. Witt: John Parker of Mattaponi, Elizabeth Davis, Elizabeth Pichee, A: Hamilton, Tully Robinson, John Lewis - p. 443 -

WAITE, WILLIAM - 21 Mar. 1705/6 - 3 Aug. 1708 - To son Joseph Waite planta where I now live. To son Nathaniel Waite land in Maryland called Tanners Hall. To son William Waite 3000 lbs. tobacco. Wife (no named) Exec. Witt: John Martiall, Seb: Cropper, Daniel Walker, Annabella Walker - p. 444 - wife "Diana" - p. 448

GIBBINS: HENRY, Sr. - 17 Dec. 1707 - 5 Oct. 1708 - To son John Gibbins. To son Henry Gibbins. To son Thomas Gibbins (under 18) To son David Gibbins (under 18) To daus. Ellinor & Sarah (under 14) Wife Frances resid. legatee & Exec. Witt: Thomas Jenkinson, William Howard - p. 450

CAMPLESHON, CHARLES. Mariner – 18 May 1708 – 5 Oct. 1708 – To son Charles (under age) all my lands. Richard Kitson guardian of son. Wife Mary Exec. Witt: Thomas Crippen, Roger Miles, William Mills – p. 450

PERRY, JOHN – 5 Sept. 1708 – 5 Oct. 1708 – To son John (under 21) all my lands after his mother's death. Should he die without issue to my son in law Francis Hill – Wife Jane Exec. Witt: William Custis, William Spiers, Christopher Brooks. p. 451

WILLIAMS, JONES – 17 Aug. 1708 – 5 Oct. 1708 – To wife Margrett my sloop Indeavor & whole personal est. To son Jones Williams. Wife Exec. Witt: Morgan Bradshaw, Robert Norton, Thomas Sanders. – p. 452

SIMCOCK, JOHN – 26 Sept. ____ – 5 Oct. 1708 – To wife (no name) To her dau. Mary cattle. Witt: Thomas Nicholson, Peter Burnley, Peter Turlington – p. 452

TAYLOR, THOMAS – 8 Sept. 1702 – 2 Nov. 1708 – To son David planta. where I now live cont. 100 A. To dau. Mary Taylor. To son Thomas Taylor. Unborn child. To Peter Turlington the younger my shoemaker's tools. To Jonathan James Tanner's Tools. Wife (no name) Exec. John Washbourne & William Nock overseers. Witt: Peter Turlington, John Wylie. – p. 456

PIWELL, CHARLES – 7 Oct. 1708 – 2 Nov 1708 – Planta. where I now live to my mother & sister for life, reversion to Piwell Richardson. To Peter Turlington, Jr. To Sarah Richardson. To William, Charles, John, Jr., Thomas & George Richardson. Mother (no name) Exec. Witt: John Lurton, Henry Lurton, Peter Turlington – p. 458

DARBY, CHURCHILL – 23 Nov. 1708 – 7 Dec. 1708 – To Churchill Darby (under 21) son of my bro. Dormund Darby, planta. cont. 125 A. To William Darby (under 21), son of my bro. William Darby, 125 A. formerly the land of my bro. Francis Darby, dec. To John Dormund Darby. Should Churchill Darby die without issue his land to go to his bro. John Darby. To bro. Daniel Darby. To my father. To Ann, the wife of my bro. Daniel. To Pricila Darby, dau. of my bro. William Darby. To Dority, dau. of my bro. Daniel. To cousin Elizabeth Walter. To Dority Darby, dau. of my bro. Dormund Darby. Father Daniel Darby Exr. Witt: Arthur Layler, Robert Barly, James Oustes – p. 460

DELASTIUS, SEBASTIAN – 25 Jan. 1705/6 – 1 Feb. 1708 – To son Sebastian Delastius. Son in law George Philbe. Grandson Peter Delastions. Grandaus. Batillina & Frances Delastions. Dau. Roda (under 15) 300 A. purchased of George Layfield, being part of 700 A. Dau. in law Katherine Hall. To my now wife Katherine 200 A. where I now live purchased of John Baily. Wife & dau. Roda resid legatees.

39

Wife Exec. Witt: Robert Pitt, Robert Smith, George Philbe – p. 461

WATTSON, ROBERT – 22 Nov. 1708 – 1 Feb. 1708 – To son John Wattson planta. where I now live with 130 A. after the death of my wife Elizabeth. To son David 135 A. where my son John now lives. To sons Robert & Peter land on the North side of Occohannock Creek. To sons Benjamin & Moses (under 18) my part of the Shallop &c. Dau. Susanna. Dau. Mary Bell. Dau. Elizabeth. Wife & 6 sons resid. legatees. Wife Exec. Witt: Fra: Wainhouse, Thomas Stringer, Luke Layler. – p. 462

ALEXANDER, JAMES – 14 Jan. 1708 – 1 Feb. 1708 – To son in law William Burton after the dec. of his mother, my wife. To John, Thomas, Benjamin, Joseph, Stratton, Woolsey, Jacob & Samuel Burton 100 A. at Jengoteague. To wife Ann 1/2 of my new sloop now in Pungoteague & the other 1/2 of my kinsman Benjamin Clugston, but if he come not within 12 months to claim this gift I give the same to Stratton Burton. Wife Ann resid. legatee & Exec. Witt: William Custis, Francis Wharton, Delight Sheald – p. 463

UPSHUR, ARTHUR – 12 Feb. 1707 – 1 Feb. 1708/9 – To son Arthur Upshur, Jr. planta. where I now dwell cont. 2000 A., 1000 A. being formerly given by me to my son John Upshur. To dau. Ann, now the wife of Benjamin Dolby 300 A. where she now dwells at Naswadox for life, then to her husband for life & then to my grandson Abel Upshur – Grandau. Susanna Upshur. To grandson Abel Upshur (under 19) 250 A. adj. the aforesaid 300 A. To son Arthur Upshur, Jr. the remainder of my land. To 5 grandchildren Amy Stott, Lydia Stott, Margaret Stott, Bridget Stott & Jonathan Stott. To dau. in law Sarah Upshur. Grandson Arthur Upshur. Grandaus. Sarah & Abigail Upshur. Son Arthur resid. legatee & Exr. Witt: William Bradford, John Layler, John Willis, John Washbourne. – p. 463

WARRINGTON, STEPHEN – 23 Dec. 1708 – 1 Feb. 1708/9 – To son Walter Warrington 100 A. To son Alexander 100 A. To sons William & Thomas, as my Ex'rs., & to my daus. Susanna, Rachell & Elizabeth Warrington all my moveable goods in Virginia. To sons John & Stephen Warrington & dau. Mary Hutchinson. – Witt: Thomas Roby, John Stanton, John Lasster – p. 464

CUSTIS, HENRY – 28 May 1698 – 1 Feb. 1708 – To son Reavell Custis. Son Henry Custis. Son Joseph Custis. Daus. (no names) Wife Rachel Exec. Sons under 21, daus. under 16 – Witt: Thomas Ironmonger, Mary Ironmonger, Francis Croston – p. 466

QUINTON, PHILLIP – 17 Dec. 1708 – 1 Feb. 1708 – To Rachel Warrington. Father in law Alexander Harrison – Mother Ann Harrison Exec. To mother planta. cont. 200 A. at the head of Onancock Branch – Witt: Thomas Roby, Steven Warrington, John Stanton – p. 467

40

HITCHINS, JARRETT - 30 Nov. 1708 - 1 Feb. 1708 - To son Major Hitchins 170 A. where I now live. Daus. Abigail & Rosanna Hitchins. Son Edward Hitchins (under 21). Wife Mary resid. legatee & Exec. Witt: John Taylor, William Twiford, William Savage - p. 467

LAYLOR, JOHN - Not dated - 1 Feb 1708 - To dau. Leah Laylor my planta. at her mother's death or marriage, should she die without issue then to my sons in law Cornelius & Bayley Johnson, sons of my wife. Dau. in law Rebecca Johnson - Wife (no name) Exec. Witt: Henry Lurton, Francis Wharton, David Allford, Charles Marshall - p. 467

DARBY, DANIEL - 20 Dec. 1708 - 1 Feb. 1708/9 - To son Daniel Darby planta. where I now live. To grandson George Darby, son of my dec. son Dormond Darby 100 A. where my dau. in law, his mother, now lives. To grandson Daniel, son of my son William 50 A. adj. the land given George Darby. To son William Darby. Dau. Sarah Walter. Son Daniel & neighbor Arthur Laylor Ex'rs. Witt: Robert Bally, James Ouster, Arthur Laylor - p. 467

JESTER, FRANCES - 14 Dec. 1708 - 1 Feb. 1708/9 - To Margaret Jester. To Richard & Samuel Jester. To Margaret, dau. of Samuel Jester. To son Thomas Jester & to his dau. Mary. To Susanna Sprune & her husband William Sprune. To son Francis Jester personal property left me by Thomas Church. Dau. Ann Jester. Son Thomas Jester Exr. Witt: Thomas Jenkinson, Thomas Towles, John Glading - p. 468

SAVAGE JOHN - 10 Feb. 1701/2 - 1 Feb. 1708/9 - To son John Savage 1/4 of my land where I now live cont. 350 A. To son Thomas 1/4 of my land. To son William 1/4 of my land. To son Robert 1/4 of my land. To dau. Elizabeth, wife of Robert Wattson, Jr. Daus. Mary Ann & Sarah Savage. Wife Dorothy Exec. Friends William Nicholson & Richard Garrison overseers. Witt: John Luke, John Bagwell, William Nicholson - p. 469

GARRISON, WILLIAM - 13 Oct. 1708 - 1 Feb. 1708/9 - To mother Rose Garritson. Wife Elizabeth resid. legatee & Exec. Witt: Edward Kellam, Francis Roberts, John Milby, Jr. - p. 469

WEST, BENNONY - 17 Jan. 1708/9 - 1 Feb. 1708/9 - To wife whole est. Goddau. Ann Snead. To wife Sarah negro Robin now in the possession of my mother. Wife Exec. Bro. & friend Capt. Snead to assist her. Witt: Charles Snead, Evan Edwards - p. 470

HAZLOP, GEORGE - 3 Nov. 1708 - 1 Feb. 1708/9 - To sons William & George Hazlop planta. cont. 300 A. on Hunting Creek. Son Charles. Wife Ann resid. legatee & Exec. Witt: Stephen Walthan, Francis Wainhouse. Jr. - p. 470

DARBY, DORMAND - 14 Dec. 1708 - 1 Feb. 1708/9 - To son John 100 A. bought by my father of Arnold Harrison. To son Smith Darby.

To unborn child 125 A. bought of Nathaniel Littleton if a boy, & if a girl to my son Smith. Dau. Dorithy. Son George. Son Churchill. Sons under 18 - Wife Ann resid. legatee & Exec. Witt: John Foscue, Hewett Smith, Arthur Laylor - p. 470

WEST, JOHN, the elder, son of Col. John West - 9 Nov. 1708 - 2 Feb. 1708 - To John Sparrow, son of Thomas Sparrow by Ann, his now wife, land at Court House provided my mother & his grandmother, Mrs Matilda West, have use of same until he is 18. To Thomas Preson 200 A. at Gingoteag provided he pay 2000 lbs. of tobacco to my Exr. To sister Sarah Robinson. To cousin Susanna Robinson, dau. of Tully Robinson & my goddau. To mother, Mrs Matilda West. To cousin Anthony West, son of my brother John West the younger. To cousin Elizabeth Robinson. To cousin John West, son of my bro. Alexander West. To bro. John West. Bro. in law Tully Robinson & bro. John West the younger Ex'rs. Witt: Timothy Coe, John Lewis, Mathew Oneale - p. 471

MILBY, WILLIAM - Nunc. Declaration 31 Dec. 1708 - Proved 3 Jan. 1708/9 - Prob. 1 Feb. 1708/9 - Whole est. to bros. John & Joseph Milby. Proved by Christopher Stockly & Dorothy Osbourne - p. 471

PARKER, CHARLES - 16 Jan. 1708/9 - 2 Feb. 1708/9 - To wife Elizabeth all my real est. for life then to my children, should they die to my cousin John Parker, son of my bro. George Parker, land in the Indian Town upon Pokamoke River near my bro. John Parker's land, being 200 A., & land on Seaside called Rumly in Somerset County, Maryland & for want of heirs to Bennit Parker, son of my bro. George Parker. Should my wife die without heirs by me then to my cousin John Parker, son of my bro. John Parker land in the Indian Town near the Great Bridge on Pokemoke River, cont. by patent 400 A. & for want of heirs to Charles Parker, son of my bro. John. To cousin Bayly Parker all my interest in my lands in Accomack. Wife Exec. Witt: George Parker, George Parker, Jr., John Istall - p. 472

MILLS, THOMAS - 17 Feb. 1708/9 - 5 Apr. 1709 - To son Edmond Mills. To son Thomas Mills planta. at head of Back Creek. To son Alexander Mills land on the seaside on the North side of Gargapha Neck & 100 A. To Elizabeth Mills. Dau. Ann Mills. To son William Mills. Wife Rebecka Exec. Bro. Alexander Bagwell & friend Richard Kitson overseers - Witt: John Nock, Edward Mills, Mary Nock - p. 479

WATSON, JOHN - 3 Dec. 1708 - 5 Apr. 1709 - To son Peter Watson house & 1/2 the land given me by the last will of my father Robert Watson. To son John Watson (under 18) the other half of said land. To dau. Margaret (under 16) Wife Elizabeth Exec. Witt: Arthur Layler, Cornelius Wadkinson, Floryana Littlehouse - p.480

EYRE, REGNOLD - 17 Jan. 1708/9 - 5 Apr. 1709 - To sister Elizabeth 1/2 my land with the planta. & 150 A. & the other 1/2 to my sister Martha. Sisters Elizabeth & Martha Executrices. Witt: Henry Scarburgh, James Drummond, Delight Shield - p. 480

DIX, ISACK - 25 Jan. 1708 - 5 Apr. 1709 - To son Richard (under 18) 250 A. To son Isack (under 18) 250 A. beginning at the fork called Winneyfritt Woodund's Branch. Dau. Margaret (under 16) Wife Margaret Exec. & in case of her dec. friends George Parker, John Barnes, Jr., Bro. John Dix & Richard Kitson to see my will carried out. Witt: John Barnes, Jr., John Mellson, John Crippen, John Oneony - p. 480

COBB, INGOLD - 10 Dec. 1708 - 6 Apr. 1709 - To bros. & sisters children (no names) 1 s. To bro. Sammwell Cob 1 s. Wife Sarah Exec. & to have the disposal of my est. Witt: Thomas Jenkinson, William Flear, Simon Smith - p. 480

BAGWELL, EDWARD, Indian - 30 Jan. 1708 - 5 Apr. 1709 - Wife Mary sole legatee & Exec. Witt: Thomas Iremonger, Thomas Bagwell, Elizabeth Fosque - p. 481

LEATHERBURY, PERRY - 19 Feb. 1708/9 - 5 Apr. 1709 - To son Perry planta. where I now live cont. 300 A. To sons Edmund & Charles 600 A. being part of 1000 A. & adj. the land given Perry, & should both die under age to be divided between all my daus. To Thomas Bagwell 150 A. to pay my debts & educate my sons Charles & Thomas. To son Thomas the remaining part of the above tract & 600 A. formerly rented to Daniel Boyd. Daus. Comfort, Patience & Ann. Sons under 18 - Daus. under 16 - Wife Comfort Exec. Bros. Thomas & John Bagwell trustees. Witt: John Stanton, John Martin, Thomas Ward. - P. 481

SHEPHARD, JOHN - 10 Feb. 1708/9 - 5 Apr. 1709 - To son Morris Shepheard - To grandson John Shepheard (under 21) Dau. Ann. To grandson Jacob Johnson planta. known as Forked Neck cont. 200 A. in Northampton County & for want of issue to grandau. Abigail Wattson. To grandau. Elizabeth Wattson land at the head of Anduey. Dau. Elizabeth Shepheard, alias Andrews. Dau. Jane Smith. Grandson Robert Andrews. Dau. Ann Simkins resid. legatee & Exec. Witt: Francis Wainhouse, Richard Kellam, William Nicholson, Luke Layler - p. 482

SAVAGE, THOMAS - Nunc. - 14 Jan. 1708/9 - 5 Apr. 1709 - Dau. Susanna. Son John Savage (under 21). Dau. Sarah (under 16) Bro. Robert Savage & bro. in law John Henderson. Youngest son Abell Savage. Son Jacob Savage (under 21) Proved by William Nicholson, Thomas Clark, Richard Savage. - p. 482

BRITTINGHAM, WILLIAM, Sr. - 18 Mar. 1708/9 - 5 Apr. 1709 - To son Samuel planta. where he now lives being on the gut leading out of Pitts Creek. To son Nathaniel planta. where I now live & for want of heirs to my son Samuel. To son John. To dau. Rebecca Brittingham 150 A. where William Brittingham, Jr. lately lived. To son William 400 A. in Somerset County, Maryland, being part of a divident cont. 700 A. called Winter Quarter. To son Joseph 200 A. in Somerset County being part of the above tract. To son Samuel 100 A. of said tract. To dau. Sarah Horsey. To son Isaac 5 s. as a bar to cut him off. Son in law Mr. Francis Thorrowgood 1/2 of the marsh land adj. planta where I now live in Somerset County, Maryland, & the other 1/2 to my son Nathaniel. Dau. Ann Thorowgood. Wife Mary & son in law Francis Thorowgood Exrs. Witt: Robert Pitt, Ralph Milbourne, Elizabeth Pitt, Thomas Baker - p. 487 - Codicil: Land in Maryland to son Samuel.

HUDSON, WILLIAM - 23 Jan. 1705/6 - 3 May 1709 - To dau. Margaret Darter my planta. cont. 150 A., also 20 A. Salt Marsh purchased of William Jarman. Wife Mary & son in law William Darter Exrs. Witt: John Barnes, John Barnes, Jr., Charles Campleshon - p. 488

PRICE, ELIAS - Not dated - 1 May 1709 - Sister Bridget Blake. Eld. bro. Nathaniel Price. To the children of Elias Blake, dec., viz: Jane, Elias, William & Charles - Witt: John Whelton, Francis Johnson - p. 488

BOWLS, THOMAS - 1 Jan. 1708 - 1 May 1709 - To wife Ann whole est. for life then to be equally div. between my 4 children, Zacharias, Thomas, Henry & Jeane. Wife Exec. Witt: Prisilla Bayly, Joseph Milby, Henry Mason - p. 488

BLAKE, ELIAS - 20 Jan. 1707/8 - 3 May 1709 - To son Elias 130 A. & 50 A. & for want of heirs to my son William, & for want of heirs to my son Charles. Personal est. to be divided between wife & 4 children. Wife Bridget Exec. Witt: Thomas Allen, Jonathan Owen, Samuel Taylor - p. 489

WATSON, DAVID - 15 Nov. 1708 - 7 June 1709 - To dau. Sarah Watson. 100 A. to be sold by her for debts, & she to have the bal. if any. To wife Elizabeth 170 A. where I live for life. To sons Daniel & David planta. where I live after the dec. of my wife. Should wife marry est. to be div. between children Daniel, David, Sarah, Martha, Elizabeth, Mary, Susanna & Hannah Watson. Wife Elizabeth Exec. Cousin John Watson to have inv'y. of est. taken. Witt: John Watson, Peter Watson, Joseph Dent - p. 491

FISHER, PHILIP - 17 Feb. 1708/9 - 7 June 1709 - To son John Fisher. To my wife's dau. Ann James. Dau. Mary Fisher. Dau. Elizabeth Fisher. Son Phillip. Son Bally Fisher. Wife Elizabeth resid. legatee & Exec. Children under age. Robert Brimer, William Lucas, Sr., John Morris & John Johnson trustees. Witt: John Morris, William Lucas. - p. 492

SMITH, JAMES - 26 Mar. 1708 - 7 June 1709 - To son Thomas Smith planta. where I now live being about 90 A. To son John 200 A. called Addition, being in Maryland at the head of Swansagutt Creek. To son James 300 A. called Lakefield adj. land given John on the same Creek. To 3 sons Thomas, John & James 644 A. on Assateag Island. To dau. Director Smith. To dau. Joyce Smith, Dau. Comfort Smith - Sons under 18 - Daus. under 14 - Wife Ellinor Exec. Bro. Thomas Smith & Bro. Daniel Gore overseers. Witt: John Parridice, Mary Harris, Daniel Gore. - p. 492

HOUTTEN, JOHN - 1 Apr. 1709 - 7 June 1709 - To son William 1/3 of my land. Dau. Eve - (other children but not named) Wife Elizabeth & bro. John Fitzgarell Exrs. Witt: John Duggan, John Fisher, Oin Scanlon - p. 493

TAYLOR, THOMAS - 25 Oct. 1707 - 2 Aug. 1709 - To 3 sons William, John & Thomas Taylor (under age) 200 A. purchased of Samuel Taylor. Wife Elizabeth Exec. Witt: John Watt, John Bradford, Bartholomew Taylor, Andrew Crawford - p. 499

CLUGSTON, CAPT. BENJAMIN - Nunc. 1 Oct. 1709 - 6 Oct. 1709 - To Stratton Burton Sloop which my kinsman James Alexander left me. Proved by Robert Hollingsworth (his cabin boy) & William Burton. - p. 501. Memo: Robert "Hutchinson" in order of probate.

ROWLES, JOHN - 9 Aug. 1709 - 1 Nov. 1709 - To son John Rowles 1/2 my land at Nandua being the part where I now live. To son Daniel the other 1/2 my land. To son Jonathan 1/2 my land at Pungoteague. To son Major the other 1/2 at Pungoteague. Dau. Elizabeth West. Dau. Ellinor Rowles. 6 childred Ex'rs. Witt: Richard Jones, John Lecatt, George Farmer - p. 506

TAYLOR, JOHN - 13 Jan. 1708/9 - 1 Nov. 1709 - To William Phillips, Sr. To Patience Leatherbury. William Phillips, Sr. Exr. Witt: James Leary, Henry Speakman, John Wylie - p. 508

BENSTON, FRANCIS - 7 Dec. 1708 - 7 Feb. 1709/10 - To son Francis Benston 100 A. adj. where I now dwell at the Virginia-Maryland line, & land in Maryland called Benston's Lott adj. where he now lives. To son William Benston bal. of land cont. 300 A. adj. my son Francis. Son William Exr. Witt: Starlin Newton, Alexander Benston, Joseph Fittiman - p. 515

TOWNSON, JOHN - 11 Feb. 1709/10 - 7 Mar. 1709/10 - To son Richard Townson planta. on Kickotanke Branch where I now live cont. 100 A. To wife Faith Townson. Dau. Mary Townson. Son Henry Townson. Sons John & James Townson. Dau. Easter Flenne. Dau. Ann Norwood. Wife Faith Exec. John Morris & Walter Warrington to divide Est. Witt: Walter Warrington, John Morris - p. 517

BRINMER, ROBERT - 23 Dec. 1709 - 2 May 1710 - Planta. & dwelling house known as Dunkirk & tract of land cont. 385 A. on North side of Muddy Creek I leave in the care & under the management of my Exec. Mary Brinmer, als Brimer, until my sons arrive to 21, then to my son John Brinmer, als Brimer, 129 A. when 21; to son Samuel 128 A. when 21; to youngest son Robert 128 A. of the aforesaid tract of land at the dec. of his mother. Should they all die without issue then to my dau. Mary Brinmer als Brimer. Wife Mary Exec. Friends James Kemp, Price Bray & John White (son in law to the said Bray) to be assistants. Witt: Thomas Wharton, John Jenkins - p. 518

FLETCHER, WILLIAM - 2 Nov. 1710 - 5 Dec. 1710 - To wife Elizabeth. To son William Fletcher planta. where I now live. To son Mathew. To son Thomas. Two sons Batterton & Brandon. Dau. Elizabeth Hill. Dau. Dorithy Parker. Dau. Mary Croucher. Dau. Rosanah Fletcher. Dau. Frances Fletcher. Wife Elizabeth & son William Ex'rs. Witt: Thomas Hall, George Farmer p. 537

DRUMMOND, STEPHEN, being now intending to go to sea - 26 Aug. 1707 - 5 Dec. 1710. To Stephen Allen 300 A. on Hunting Creek bequeathed to me by my grandfather Capt. Richard Hill. To my mother. To bro. Richard Drummond money due me by him. To Edmund Allen. Father resid. legatee & Exr. Witt: William Chance, Robert Drummond - p. 538

COLLINS, JOHN - 3 Jan. 1710/11 - 5 June 1711 - Son Thomas Collins - 5 grandchildren (no names) Wife Bridget Exec. Witt: Charles Taylor, Andrew Crawfford, John Hollock, Thomas Hogshur - p. 548

SANDFORD, SAMUEL, Sometime of Accomack County, Virginia, but now living in the City of London. - 27 Mar. 1710/11 - 1 Jan. 1711/12 - To be buried in the Parish burial place at____ in the County of Gloucester. To sister Mary Freeman, wid., 25 shillings to be paid her each month for life out of the interest or yearly income for what money I have in the Bank of England. To Mary Freeman, dau. of my sister Mary Freeman, & to her bro. & sister Jane & Thomas Freeman. To Sandford Green, son of Mordicay & Thomazine 50 L sterling. To Susanna Sandford, dau. of my bro. John Sandford, sometime of Princess Ann County, Virginia. To Mary Sandford, dau. of my bro. John. To John Parry, son of Thomas Parry, my kinsman in Maryland. To Thomas Sandford, my kinsman living in Fenchurch Street in London. To Kathrine Sandford, my sole Exec., dau. of my bro. Gyles Sandford, bal. of est. not otherwise beq. in Virginia, Maryland or elsewhere in America, Great Britain or any other Kingdom &c. & should she die without issue then to Susanna & Mary Sandford, daus. of my bro. John. Friend Thomas Sheppard, late of Avening, Gloucester County, now of London, & John Parr? overseers. Witt: Lewis Smith, Thomas? Sheppard, Thomas? Witherby - p. 556 - Will badly mutilated.

SCARBURGH, COL. EDMUND - 21 May 1711 - 5 Feb. 1711/12 - To dau. Ursley 1 s. she having had her part of my est. To dau. Hannah ditto. To dau. Elizabeth ditto. To dau. Mary ditto. To dau. Tabitha ditto. To dau. Matilda ditto. To dau. Edmund Memoria ditto. To dau. Sarah (under 14) Eldest son Edmund Scarburgh 832 A. out of my Neck of 2000 A. surveyed for him by me. To second son Edmund Scarburgh 604 A. out of my 2000 A. surveyed for him by me. To son Michell 500 A. out of my 2000 A. surveyed for him by me. To wife Elizabeth 1/2 my planta. & Neck of land for life & then to my three sons. Wife Exec. Witt: James Drummond, Charlton Walthan, Morris Shepheard, Edmund Bayly, John Hall, Jacob Duey - p. 559

MAJOR, PETER - 5 Aug. 1704 - 5 Feb. 1711/12 - To Nephew Littleton Scarburgh Major all my land in Accomack. To sister in law Mary Major, wife of my bro. William Major. Bro. William resid. legatee & Exr. Witt: Edmund Scarburgh, Elizabeth Scarburgh, Edmund Scarburgh, Sr., Elizabeth Parker. - p. 559

TWARTON, MARGARET - 18 Dec. 1711 - 5 Feb. 1711/12 - To Ann Bundick. To Elinor Millechop. To Sarah Williams. To Elizabeth Bundick - To Nicholas Millechop. Bal. of est. to Nicholas Millechop & he to be my Exr. Witt: John Millechop, James Grey Hudson - p. 560

ALEXANDER, ANN - 6 Sept. 1711 - 4 Mar. 1711/12 - To son Stratton Burton. To son William Burton. To my son William's son William. To son Thomas Burton. To son Thomas Burton's wife & to his 2 children Thomas & Patience. To Ann Burton, dau. of my son Thomas. To son Benjamin Burton & to his son William, dau. Ann & son John. To my son Joseph & to his son. To son Stratton's dau. Leeze. To son Benjamin's wife Elizabeth. To son Woolsey Burton. Sons Jacob & Samuel Burton. Grandau. Agnes Burton. Grandaus. Elizabeth & Ann Revell. Son in law John Revell. Grandaus. Rachell & Sarah Revell. Grandson Edward Revell. Son William Exr. Witt: William Custis, Christopher Brooks, John Daggen - p. 560

HUGHES, JOHN - 23 Aug. 1710 - 3 June 1712 - To son William Hughes planta. with 100 A. Son Joseph Hughes. Wife Elizabeth. Sons Woodman, Edmund, Thomas & Joseph (all under 21) resid. legatees. Wife Exec. Witt: John Morris, Walter Warrington, Richard Tounsin - p. 580

HUTCHINSON, ROBERT - 18 Mar. 1711/12 - 5 Aug. 1712 - To son Stephen (under 21) planta. where I now live cont. 650 A. To son John 50 A. bought of George Parker. To daus. Mary, Elizabeth & Ann 5 s. each. Wife Margaret Exec. Witt: Hancock Custis, John _____. Peter Roggers. - p. 585

HACK, GEORGE - 18 Feb. 1711 - 2 Sept. 1712 - To wife Sarah planta. where I now live during her widowhood, then to my 2 daus. Francina & Betty. Land at Massongo to my 2 sisters Ann & Mary Margaretta. To bro. in law Zerobabell Preeson. To Capt. Henry Scarburgh my sword, boat, wearing apparel &c. To bro. Peter Hack my Hatt & wigg. Wife Exec. Friends Capt. Richard Drummond, Mr. John Revell, Capt.

Henry Scarburgh to assist her. Witt: Robert Makey, Henry Scarburgh, John Rowles, Peter Hack – p. 588

SILVERTHORNE, SEBASTIAN – 1 Jan. 1712/13 – 6 Jan. 1712/13 – To wife Tabitha, dau. of Mary Hubank. To son John land & planta. where I now live. To son Sebastian. Dau. Mary. Friends James Kempe & Naomi his wife & Robert Mills to be tutors to my 2 children Sebastian & Sarah. William Williamson tutor to my son John. Son John Exr. when he is 21 – James Kempe & William Williamson to act until then. Witt: Simon Smith, William Boggs – p. 591

BAGWELL, THOMAS – 15 Aug. 1712 – 6 Jan. 1712/13 – To son Thomas planta. where I now live cont. 165 A. To son John my part of Cedar Island. Wife & 5 daus. Elizabeth, Susanna, Ann, Comfort & Sara resid. legatees. Sons under 18 – Daus. under 16 – Wife (no name) Exec. Bro. John Bagwell & cousin Henry Bagwell trustees. Witt: Sarah Metcalf, John Metcalf, James Davis. – p. 592

HEALY, JOHN – 30 Jan. 1710/11 – 3 Mar. 1712/13 – Dau. Rachell Healy – To John Martin. John Martin & son William Healy Ex'rs. Witt: William Phillips, James Leary – p. 594

EVINS, SARAH – 12 Sept. 1711 – 3 Mar. 1712/13 – To dau. Grace Smith. Dau. Sarah Attle. Bal. of est. to son John Evins & his eld. son John Evins & his eld. dau. Sarah Evins. Son John Exr. Witt: George Boothe, John Boothe – p. 594

SNEAD, CAPT. ROBERT – 27 Aug. 1711 – 4 Mar. 1712/13 – To son Robert 90 A. near Bagwills Island & to each of his children a ewe lamb. To son Charles all my est. real & personal in the Island of Jameco. To dau. Frances Snead who is now in England, who I understand is married to one Mr. _____ Ossester, who has sometime merchant to Virginia, but now keeps a great still house near Hatton Gardens in Holbourne, 10 L to buy her a silver tankard, and I desire that my coat of arms be put upon it. Son John. Wife Mary. Daus. Mary, Ann & Catherine Snead (John, Mary, Ann & Catherine children of Mary – all under age) To son John land at Indian River in Maryland called Snead's Purchase. Wife Exec. In case of her death or marriage William Burton & my son Charles Snead to act. Witt: Robert Hutchinson, John Lurton, Thomas Lurton – p. 595

DAVIS, JAMES – 9 Apr. 1712 – 2 June 1713 – To 2 sons James & Henry Davis 200 A. near the head of Mussongo Creek. To sons Thomas & Charles Davis 170 A. where I now live. Daus. Sarah & Ann Davis. Grandson James Benston. Son James Exr. Friends Capt. Richard Drummond & James Kempe to see my will performed. Witt: John Metcalfe, Christopher Brooke, Delight Shield. – p. 599

HUTCHINSON, JAMES – 30 Dec. 1712 – 2 June 1713 – To son Thomas Hutchinson (under 18) plantation where I now live cont. 366 A. & should he offer to sell the same I give it to my son James (under age)

Dau. Elizabeth. To Howell Butey. To Howell Glading. To Martha Pitt. To William Howard. To Patience Simson. Unborn child. Wife Elizabeth & friend John Gladden Ex'rs. Witt: James Wessells, Kendall Towles, Thomas Towles. - p. 602

PARKER, GEORGE, Sr. - __1708 - 7 July 1713 - To son George Parker 1/2 the land on the West side of the branch where I live & the other 1/2 at his mother's death, cont. 400 A., also my 1/2 of Ship Rack Island, should he die without issue to my daus. Abygall Parker alias Lafbury & Elizabeth Parker. Grandaus. Ruth Lafbury, alias Parker & Mary Lafbury. Dau. Abygall Laufbary 400 A. called Mr. Hope near the head of St. Martin's Branch, also 30 A. of Marsh in Romly Marsh, being 1/3 of 90 A. called Wocitt, the other 60 A. to my dau. Amy Hutson & my dau. Mary Warrington. Cousin Scarburgh Parker (under 18), dau. of my bro. William Parker, the land our father William Parker gave to me at the head of the Sound in Maryland. To dau. Elizabeth 375 A. called Kickotanck. To Hennere Sachell 150 A. which I sold him on the South side of Indian Town Branch, & to Thomas Copes 100 A. on the North side. Son in law John Laufbury. Godson John Danell. Goddau. Jane Shipard. To John Calvirt. Wife & 5 children resid. legatees. Wife Exec. Kinsman Maj. George Parker, Capt. Richard Drummond & Henere Bagwell & Godson George Hope to assist my Exec. Witt: William Willett, John Read, Henry Read - p. 602 - Presented by John Parker.

FOGG, ANN - 8 Apr. 1712 - 5 Aug. 1713 - To dau. Ann. To first born son Aaron Fogg whole est. both at home & abroad, He paying John Watts Fogg, John Fogg, Daniel Fogg, Moses Fogg & Ann Fogg each of them as they come to age a feather bed, &c. John Watts Fogg to have liberty to choose with whom he shall live. My bro. John Watts to have the care of my two sons John & Daniel. Son in law Steven Costen to have Moses & Ann, provided he bring up the boy to read & write & the girl to read & sew. Son Aaron Exr. - Witt: John Watts, Denis Connar, Mary Watts - p.604

FISHER, JOHN - 17 Sept. 1713 - 3 Nov. 1713 - Wife Grace. To sons Jonn & Phillip 200 A. where I live. Grandson William Martin. Dau. Bridget Martin. Dau. Ester Fisher. Son William Fisher. Wife & 5 children resid. legatees. Wife & 2 sons Ex'rs. Witt: John Parker of Mattopani, Sarah Pollson, Thomas Bolls - p. 610

DRUMMOND, JOHN - 10 Oct. 1713 - 6 Jan. 1713/14 - To 2 sons James & Robert 550 A. on the seaside, James to have that part lying on Arcadia Branch. Son Hill Drummond. Son Richard Drummond. Grandau. Patience Allen. Dau. Margaret Bagwell. Dau. Mary Chance. Grandson John Drummond, son of Hill. Son John Drummond. 5 sons Richard, Hill, James, Drake & Robert Ex'rs. Grandson James Allen. Grandsons Scarburgh & Richard, his brother. Grandson Richard Drummond. Witt: Robert Jones, William Northam, Ann Drummond, Patience Miles - p. 615

BELL, TABITHA - 30 Nov. 1713 - 6 Jan. 1713/14 - To my mother. Bro. Edmund Scarburgh, Jr. Bro. Michaell Scarburgh. Sister Elizabeth Duey. Sister Sarah Scarburgh. Cousin Beautyfiler Duey. Sister Mary, now the wife of William Major & sister Matilda, wife of Jacob Duey 250 A. in Northampton on the North side of the head of Nuswadox Creek. Sister Edmund Memore, now wife of Morris Shepheard. Sister Matilda Duey Exec. Witt: John Metcalfe, Edmund Bayly, John Hall - p. 615

BAKER, JOHN - 15 Nov. 1712 - 2 Mar. 1713/14 - To wife Elizabeth 100 A. on Gargaphy Branch for life then to my son John Baker. To son William Baker. Daus. Lishea, Mary, Elizabeth, Ann, Comfort, Sebrou,_____? Wife Exec. Thomas Crippen, John Barnes & Richard Kitson overseers. Witt: Richard Kitson, Thomas Crippen, Margritt Crippen - p. 618

PITT, ROBERT - 20 July 1711 - 4 May 1714 - To son John Pitt land & Marsh where Dennis Morris now lives, except a piece of marsh called Impossible Marsh. If he should die without issue to my son Robert Pitt. To son John all my land or est. in England by right belonging to me by virtue of the last will & test. of Mary Pitt, of Bristoll, dec. To dau. Martha Pitt planta. cont. 300 A. To son Robert (under 21) all my remaining land, including Impossible Marsh. Capt. John Brodhurst & James Kemp trustees & to divide personal est. between wife Elizabeth & children. Wife & son John Ex'rs. Witt: John Morris, Dennis Morris, John Bradhurst - p. 622

SCARBURGH, EDMUND - Nunc. Oct. 1713 - 6 July 1714 - "The words of the verbal will of Edmund Scarburgh late dec., late of this County Accomack, spoken in the hearing of the evidenced hereunder named. I do desire that what I have received of my father's estate given to me by my father's last Will may be Equally divided between my two Brothers Scarburgh & Mittchell" Luke Johnson, John Teackle - Sworn to before Henry Scarburgh 1 Oct. 1713 - p. 630

LURTON, HENRY - 6 Feb. 1713 - 7 July 1714 - To son William Lurton 100 A. where I now live. To son Thomas 100 A. on the North side of my land. To son Lazarus 50 A. adj. the above. To son Jacob 50 A. of the same dividet. 63 A. of White Marsh to be divided between 4 youngest sons. Son John. Dau. Dorothy Lurton. Wife Dorothy. Dau. Hannah Lurton. Sons William & Thomas Ex'rs. Witt: Nathaniel Badger, Henry Stakes - p. 634

KELLAM, WILLIAM - 21 Aug. 1714 - 5 Oct. 1714 - To 4 sons Nathaniel, William, John & Thomas Kellam planta. where 1 now live cont. 450 A. Dau Sarah Kellam. Wife Ann. Dau. Tabitha Kellam. Son Nash Kellam. Son in law Charles Hazlop. Dau. in law Elizabeth Hazlup. Wife Exec. Witt: Francis Roberts, John Meers, Arthur Laylor. - p. 636

50

WALE, WILLIAM – 17 Jan. 1713/14 – 7 Dec. 1714 – To eldest son William Wale planta. where I now live cont. 110 A. Wife Margaret to have use of same until William arrives to age of 26, which will be in the year 1723. Dau. Elizabeth Wale. Son John. Son Robert. Wife & children Robert, John, Margaret, Mary Ester & Sarah resid. legatees. Richard Rogers, Jonathan Rowles, Henry Read & Luke Johnson to divide personal est. Sons under 18 – Daus. under 16 – Wife Exec. Witt: Phillip Parker, Henry Read. – p. 640

REW, JOHN – 28 Feb. 1710/11 – 4 Jan. 1714/15 – Wife Leshe. Son Thomas. Dau. Catherine Rew. Bro. Wony Rew. Major Frame, John Evens & Peter Cleavel to div. est. Witt: William Darter, Mark Ewell, Thomas Prescoe – p. 642

BLOXAM, JOHN , Carpenter – 22 July 1713 – 5 Apr. 1715 – To wife Mary. To son Woodman Bloxam 200 A. where I now live & 200 A. of Marsh on France Creek. To son William Bloxam 200 A. where he now lives, 100 A. adj. his bro. Woodman & 100 A. adj. his bro. Johnson . To son Johnson Bloxam 80 A. adj. his brothers Woodman & William for life then to my grandchild Nicholas. To son John Bloxam. To son Richard Bloxam 1 s. to cut him off from receiving any benefit from my est. Wife Exec. John Johnson & John Morris to advise my wife & children. Witt: Samuel Justis, Anthony Hudson, Thomas Ward. – p. 645

BARNES, JOHN – 27 Apr. 1714 – 5 Apr. 1715 – To Henry Truite, als Barns 1 s. Dau Ann Mills 1 s. To dau. Mary Nock 1 s. Son John Barnes resid. legatee & Exr. Witt: Richard Kitson, Thomas Evans, William Hastins.

ORDERS – 1697 – 1703

TAYLOR, WILLIAM & BRIDGET, his wife – Adm. on their estates to Elias Taylor, bro. of the said William, for the use of their 6 children – Timothy Coe & Samuel Taylor sec. 8 Dec. 1697 – p. 2

ROBERTS, FRANCIS – Adm. his est. to Sarah & Arthur Roberts, wid. & son of sd. Francis – 8 Dec. 1697 – p. 4

YOUNG, Henry – Adm. his est. to his bro. William Young. William Hudson sec. 7 June 1698 – p. 29

SMITH, GEORGE – Adm. his est. to his wid., Mary Smith – Richard Baley & Dormant Darby sec. – 2 Mar. 1702/3 – p. 40

EDGE, ROBERT – Adm. his est. to his wid. Joan Edge – 7 Dec. 1698 – p. 48

BUSHELL, THOMAS – Adm. his est. to Charles Scarburgh as greatest creditor, he having neither wife, child nor kindred – 8 Nov. 1699 – p.

51

FULLING, HUGH - Adm. his est. to his wid.. Sarah Fulling - John Barnes, Sr. & George Parker, Sr. sec. - 7 Oct. 1701/ - p. 119. Before giving bond Sarah Fulling married John Newby, therefore Adm. is granted him in right of his sd. wife on the est. of the said Hugh Fulling. Charles Stockly & William Jerman sec. 4 Dec. 1701 - p. 123

LEWIS, JOHN - Adm. his est. to his wid., Elizabeth Lewis - Ralph Justice & William Chance sec. 2 Dec. 1701 - p. 121

DOE, SAMUELL - Adm. his est. to his wid., Mary Doe - Thomas Simpson & Jonathan Chambers sec. - 3 Feb. 1701/2 - p. 125

ROBERTS, ARTHUR - Adm. his est. to his wid., Joyce Roberts - Edward Kellam & William Kellam sec. 1 Dec. 1702 - p. 132

WELBURNE, CAPT. THOMAS - Adm. his est. to his wid., Arcadia Welburne - John Watts & Daniel Welburne sec. 3 Feb. 1702/3 - p. 136

JONES, DAVID - Adm. his est. to John Gerrat as marrying Ann, the wid. of sd. David _____ Cobb & Sebastian Silverthorne sec. 2 Mar. 1702/3 - p. 141

ORDERS - 1703 - 1709

SIMKINS, WILLIAM - Adm. his est. to his wid., Ann Simkins - Francis Wainhouse & Thomas Hall sec. 3 Oct. 1704 - p. 33

WATSON, PETER - Adm. his est. to his wid., Ann Simkins, relict of William Simkins. Francis Wainhouse & Thomas Hall sec. 3 Oct. 1704 - p. 33

AMES, JOSEPH - Adm. his est. to his wid., Ester Ames - Edward Kellam & Thomas Ames sec. - 5 Apr. 1709 - p. 134

ORDERS - 1710 - 1714

MASON, WILLIAM & SARAH - Adm. on their estates to their son, William Mason - 1 Aug. 1710 - p. 7

SMITH, THOMAS - Adm. his est. to Francis Benston as marrying Ann, wid. of sd. Thomas Smith - Daniel Welbourn sec. - 2 Aug. 1710 - p. 8

STERLING, RICHARD - Adm. his est. to Col. Tully Robinson as Greatest creditor. Robert Snead sec. - 4 Aug. 1710 - p. 10

STATON, JOSEPH – Adm. his est. to his son, Joseph Staton – Charles & Thomas Stockly sec. – 6 Mar. 1710 – p. 16

Orders 1710–1714

ALLEN, EDMUND – Adm. his est. to his wid., Margaret Allen – James Drummond & John Drummond sec. – 2 Oct. 1711 – p. 27

DARBY, WILLIAM – Adm. his est. to his son Daniel Darby & John Walter – Arthur Laylor & Daniel Darby, Sr. sec. – 1 Jan. 1711/12 – p. 30

CHAMERS, JOHN & PHILOCLEARE – Philocleare being dead & John being gone in some remote parts 15 years since & not being heard of, Adm. on their estates to Robert Norton as marrying Frances Chambers, mother of John & Philocleare – 1 Jan. 1711/12 p. 31

DAVIS, WILLIAM – Adm. his est. to his wid., Margaret Davis – Marcus Andrews & Walter Warrington sec. – 1 Jan. 1711/12 – p. 32

MILLS, EDWARD – Adm. his est. to his wid., Ann Mills – John Barnes, Sr. & Walter Warrington sec. – 1 Jan. 1711/12 – p. 32

WELCH, MARGARET – Adm. her est. to Maj. George Parker, she having no known relatives in this country – 2 June 1713 – p. 59

MILES, STEPHEN – Adm. his est. to his wid., Patience Miles – Thomas Simson, Sr. & Thomas Simson, Jr., sec. – 3 Nov. 1713 – p. 67

MOORE, RICHARD – Adm. his est. to his bro. Edward Moore – James Kempe & Simon Smith sec. – 2 Feb. 1713/14 – p. 69

HALL, THOMAS – Adm. his est. to his wid., Jane Hall – 2 Feb. 1713/14 – p. 69

HOPE, GEORGE, Jr. – Adm. his est. to his wid., Catherine Hope – Capt. John Watts & William Taylor sec. – 7 Apr. 1714 – p. 73

ORDERS – 1714 – 1717

CAMPBELL, WILLIAM, of North Britain, Merchant – Adm. his est. to John Henry of Somerset County, Maryland – Capt. John Watts sec. – 5 Feb. 1716 – p. 27

WILLS, DEEDS &c. 1715 – 1729 v.i

BELL, THOMAS – 31 June 1715 – 1 Nov. 1715 – To son Elias Bell planta. where I now live cont. 150 A. To son Joseph Bell the remain-

der of my land cont. 150 A. Wife "Cohole" resid. legatee & Exec. To
the rest of my children, Thomas Bell, Jr., Sarah Kelle, Oliver Bell,
Edward Bell, Mary Hard 12 pence each. Witt: Witherinton Fitchett,
Samuel Davis, Benjamin Coe – p. 6

ONEONS, JOHN – 20 Apr. 1714 – 5 June 1716 – To son Thomas
Oneons 100 A. where I now dwell. To son Selby Oneons 100 A., being
1/2 the divident where I live. To son John Oneons. Dau. Ann. Dau.
Grace. To son Samuel Oneona. Dau. Elizabeth. Wife Elizabeth
resid. legatee & Exec. Witt: Richard Kitson, John Nock, Mary Kitson
– p. 24

BAYLEY, CHARLES – 27 Feb. 1715/16 – 3 July 1716 – To son John
Bayley 1/2 my sloop Diamond. To son Charles Bayley 959 1/2 A. on
Pungoteage Creek known as Yeo's Neck which Hon. Charles Scarburgh
bought of Justinian Yeo. Daus. Elizabeth & Edith Bayly. My 1/2 the
Court House land containing 225 A. to be sold for education of children. Wife Mary resid. legatee & Exec. Capt. John Bradhurst, Richard Kitson, Arthur Upshur, John Purnall or any three of them trustees.
Witt: William Finne, John Stott. All children under age – p. 30
　　　Mary Bayley, wife of Charles, objects to the clause devising
959 1/2 A., stating that she was possessed of same before her marriage with the said Charles, and was and still is possessed of an
estate of inheritance in fee simple, and which the said Charles without
her consent devised to her son Charles – For further dispositior of lend
see will of John Bayley.

COLLONY, OWEN – 10 Apr. 1711 – 2 Oct. 1716 – Land to be equally
divided between sons Owen & Benjamin Collony. To son Brian Collony. Dau. Isabel Repentans Collony. Dau. Hester. Wife Winifret
resid. legatee & Exec. Witt: Christopher Stockely, John Osborn,
Arthur Layler – p. 35

WATT, JAMES – 12 July 1716 – 2 Oct. 1716 – To Nehemiah Watt, my
son, the planta where I now live on the heybridge Branch. To son
Adam Watt balance of land on heybridge Branch. To son William
Watt. To son James Watt. Wife Mason Watt resid. legatee & Exec.
Children under 18. Bro. in law John Kendall, Hancock Custis &
Thomas Custis overseers. Witt: Hill Drumaond, Richard Hill Ayres,
John Thomson. – p. 36

MORRIS, DENNIS – To wife Easter. Son Joseph Morris. Sister Elizabeth Anders to have dau. Tabitha until she arrives at age. Daus.
Elizabeth & Mary (under age) Wife Exec. Witt: Sebastian Delastatius, John Morris, James Wessells – p. 42

BLOCKSOM, MARY, wid. of John Blocksom – 19 Nov. 1716 – 6 Mar.
1716/17 – To son Richard Blocksom. Son William Blocksom. To son
William's wife. To Ann Jones. All my sons except Richard resid.
legatees. John Johnson & Edward Bell to divide est. To grandau. Ann
Blocksom. Son William Exr. Witt: Edward Bell, Mary Bell, John

BAILY, JOHN - 3 Jan. 1716/17 - 7 May 1717 - To grandson John Baily, son of Charles & Mary Baily, planta. where I now dwell, as also the planta. where my son Charles Baily lived in his lifetime after my wife's dec. Dau. in law: Mary Baily, mother of my grandson John Baily, to enjoy the planta. where she now lives & the planta. where my son Charles lived for life, provided she make over by deed to her second son, Charles Baily, that tract of land given her by her dec. father, Charles Scarburgh at the head of Pungoteague Creek, commonly called Yeo's Neck, cont. 959 1/2 A., reserving to herself the profits therefrom for life. After my wife's dec. Madam Tabitha Hill shall, if she so desire, dwell on the planta. whwre I now live and enjoy the profits from same. To grandson John Scarburgh, son of Charles & Edith Scarburgh, planta. near Assawoman Church, cont. 250 A. and also my part of Foxes Island. To grandson Parker Selby, son of Parker Selby, & Tabitha, now wife to John Purnell of Somerset County, Maryland, land in Jolleys Neck cont. 500 A. To dau. Tabitha Purnell. Grandchildren Parker & Edith Selby. Grandau. Elizabeth Scarburgh. Grandsons John & Charles Baily my sloop. Son in law Charles Scarburgh, Dau. Edith Scarburgh. To 4 grandchildren John, Charles, Elizabeth & Edith Baily. Wife (no name) Exec. & should she die before this will is proved I app. my son in law John Purnell Exr. Witt: John Wise, Matilda Wise, Thomas Wilkinson, Daniel Selby, John Whelton - p. 51

BAYLY, EDWARD - 2 Dec. 1716 - 7 May 1717 - To wife planta. where I live during her widowhood reversion to my son Edward Bayly. To 3 sons Edmund, John & Robert the land I now hold at the head of Masongo Creek. To dau. Hannah Conty. To dau. Elizabeth Glading. To dau. Comfort Ginkinson. Wife, daus. Ann Catherine & Rachel Bayly & sons Edmund, John & Robert resid. legatees. Wife Exec. Friends Thomas Stockly, Jr. & Joseph Stockly, Jr. to divide the land at Masongo & to assist my wife in her business. Witt: Thomas Stockly, Joseph Stockly, Thomas Stockly, Jr. p. 54

WHELTON, JOHN - 18 Aug. 1716 - 7 May. 1717 - To wife Catherine whole est. during her widowhood. To son John Whelton at the death of his mother. To son William Whelton land cont. 90 A. at the dec. of his mother. Son William Exr. Witt: Jonathan Owen, Elias Taylor, Jr., Francis Johnson. Codicil: Son William to have whole est. at the dec. of his mother & also the care of his two sisters, Ann & Comfort, and to deliver to each sister out of the est. the value of 12 pence, viz: to Bridgett & Mary & Catherine & Ann & Comfort - p. 55

WISE, JOHN - 27 Mar. 1717 - 7 May 1717 - To son John planta. where I now live with 500 A., being part of 800 A. , wife Matilda to have 1/3 for life. To son Thomas 300 A. adj. his brother John, being the remaining part of the said 800 A. Wife Matilda to sell my part of Foxes Island & my part of Smith's Island in Somerset County, Maryland, proceeds to my son Samuel Wise. 6 children John, Thomas,

Samuel, Mary Cade Scarburgh, Elizabeth & Hannah Scarburgh Wise.
Wife Exec. Witt: Tully Robinson, Jonathan West, Elizabeth Bradhurst, Sarah Robinson - p. 55

TAYLOR, ELIAS - 19 Apr. 1717 - 4 June 1717 - To son Joshua (under
18) all my land at Assawoman devised me by my father William
Taylor, also 450 A. called Queenhive at Assawoman. To daus.
Hannah & Esther Taylor 500 A. purchased of Col. John Custis of
Northampton. To dau. Mary Taylor. To dau. Elizabeth Whittington.
To dau. Naomi Davis. To dau. Comfort Ewell. Wife Comfort Exec.
Should she die before my son becomes 21 then my son in law William
Whittington to be Exr. Witt: Thomas Perry, William Taylor, Mary
Taylor - p. 58

GARRISON, RICHARD - 23 Feb. 1708/0 - 6 Aug. 1717 - To wife 1/2
of planta. where I now live for life. To son Jonathan the other 1/2 of
my planta. & to have the whole at my wife's dec., & should my son
die without heirs 1/2 to Thomas Mears & the other 1/2 to John Roberts, son of Francis Roberts. To Richard Armitrader. To dau. Rose
Roberts. Dau. Tabitha Milby. Dau. Ann Read. Dau. Margaret Mears.
Wife (no name) Exec. Witt: Edward Kellam, John Mears, Peter
Wilkinson - p. 61

WEST, ANTHONY - 26 Oct. 1716 - 6 Aug. 1717 - To son John 1/2 of
my land on the South side of Nandua Creek where I now live, also 1/2
of my part of Tangear Island. To son Anthony West 1/2 of my Nandua
land & 1/2 of my part of Tangear Island. Dau. Jane West. Wife
Elizabeth Exec. Witt: Daniel Rowles, Major Rowles, Rowles Major -
p. 62

HACK, PETER - 4 May 1717 - 6 Aug. 1717 - To son George Nich:
Hack all my land at Sasifricks in Siscell (Cecil?) County. To son
Peter, which is my will to be baptised Peter, all my lands at Andua.
Dau Ann. Wife (no name) Exec. Hancock Custis to assist her. Witt:
Anthony West, Major Rowles, Ana Allen, Daniel Rowles - p. 64

ADKINS ROBERT - 17 Feb. 1715 - 3 Sept. 1717 - To dau. Sibella
Tomson & John Tomson 200 A. where I now live at the head of Gingo-
teague Neck. Son Robert Adkins. Dau. Catherine Whealton. Dau. Mary
Mason. Dau. Ann Ternall. Dau. Elizabeth Walker. Son & dau. John &
Sibella, his wife, Exrs. Witt: Daniel Welburne, Samuel Welburne,
Francis Welburne - p. 70

OWEN, JONATHAN - 12 May 1717 - 6 Nov. 1717 - To dau. Indie
Morris. Dau. Elizabeth Collins. Dau. Ann Millman. To eldest son
Timothy Owen 120 A. To son Jonathan Owen 120 A., being the re-
maining part of my land. Son Samuel. Son Peter - Wife Mary. Son
Timothy Exr. Witt: Samuel Taylor, Elias Taylor, Francis Johnson -
p. 82

SAVAGE, ROWLAND - 23 Aug. 1709 - 5 Nov. 1717 - To wife Mary whole est. during her widowhood. To son Rowland Savage planta. where I now live at Pungoteague cont. 200 A. To son William Savage 125 A. adj. the above. To son Charles 125 A. adj. his bro. William. To son Richard 1/3 of planta. at Mattchipungo. To son Robert 1/3 of Mattchipungo Planta. To son John the remaining 1/3. Dau. Mary Roads, wife of John Roads. Dau. Patience Lecatt, wife of John Lecatt. Wife Exec. Witt: Henry Stakes, Jr., William Ward, John Washbourne - p. 83

LEWIS, SAMUELL - 2 June 1717 - 3 Dec. 1717 - Wife Mary - Children (no names) Wife Exec. Witt: James Kempe, Naomi Kempe, Thomas Ginkinson - p. 88

KELLE, JAMES - Nunc. 10 May 1717 - 7 Jan. 1717/18 - Son Nathaniel Kelle to be bound as an apprentice to a shoemaker & tanner when he is 15 years of age until he is 21. Dau. Cattarn Kelle (under 18) Wife Susanna resid. legatee & Exec. Proved by Daniel Stuart, William Ellis - p. 94

MOORE, EDWARD - 18 Jan. 1713/14 - 7 Jan. 1717/18 - To wife Katherine land & planta. where I now live on the North side of Mossongo Creek cont. 500 A. To Elizabeth Flear, dau. of William & Heaster Flear. To Samuel Cowly, son of Mary Cowly that was, but now Mary Shahe. Wife Exec. Witt: James Kempe, John Sandford, Simon Smith - p. 94

FOSCUE, SIMON - 10 Aug. 1717 - 7 Jan. 1717/18 - To wife Ann 1/3 of planta. where I now live known as Neville Neck during her wid. & all the corn & wheat to bring up my children. To eldest son Simon, now at the Southerd. To son John the North part of the land where I live. To youngest son Simon Fosque (under 18) the Southern part of my plantation. To son Luke Fosque 500 A. in Somerset County, Maryland patented to me by the name of Land Down. To son John & youngest son Simon 400 A. in Somerset County as by patent will appear. To dau. Elizabeth Hill 2 s. 6d. Arthur Upshur, Francis Wainhouse, John Savage & Arthur Laylor to div. est. Wife & son John Exrs. Witt: John Lawrence, Arthur Laylor, Robert Miliken. p. 95

HILL, TABITHA - 23 Aug. 1717 - 7 Jan. 1717/18 - To great grandson Thomas Custis 700 A. near the place called White Marsh. To Ann Custis, wife of said Thomas my wearing stays embroidered with gold, my black suit & silk clothes & black stays set with bugles with one cloath of silver pettycoat. Great grandson Thomas Custis resid. legatee of all my est. in Virginia, England or elsewhere. Thomas Custis Exr. Witt: John Morrogh, Elizabeth Tilney - p. 97

BAYLY, EDMUND - 6 Feb. 1717/18 - 2 Apr. 1718 - To dau. Elizabeth Crippen. To dau. Tabitha. To son Edmund all my land on the seaside cont. 800 A. & for want of heirs to unborn child, if a boy, but if a girl I give 1/2 the personal est. given by this will to my son Edmund to the said child. Should my wife not be with child & my son dies without issue, I give 350 A. to my dau. Elizabeth & the remaining part of my land to my dau. Tabitha. To wife Mary all her est. that belonged to her dec. husband Charles Bayly & all legacies left her by her dec. husband. To Nephew Whittington Bayly. 3 children Elizabeth, Tabitha & Edmund resid. legatees. Edmund Scarburgh, Morris Shepheard & Henry Scarburgh to inventory est. Son Edmund to be under the guide & direction of his uncle Morris Shepheard. Wife & son Edmund Exrs. Witt: Henry Scarburgh, Morris Shepheard, Seb: Cropper – p. 113

BLARE, JOHN, Tanner – 8 Feb. 1717/18 – 2 Apr. 1718 – (of Somerset County, Md.) Eldest son Robert. Youngest son Fenton Blare. Eld. dau. Elizabeth. 2nd dau. Margrett. 3rd dau. Hanna. Youngest dau. Agnes. Father in law Capt. Moses Fenton & mother in law Margaret Fenton to care for children. Friend Robert Mills Exr. Witt: Lazrius Maddox, Frances Newbole, Thomas Layfield, Edward Johnson – p. 119

AYRES, RICHARD HILL – 21 Dec. 1717 – 3 June 1718 – Wife Esther Exec. To son Richard Ayres (under age) planta. where I now live cont. 150 A. being 1/2 the tract of land left me by my grandfather, Richard Hill. To son John Ayres (under age) the other 1/2 cont. 300 A. Daus. Mary, Esther & Frances Ayres. Witt: Hill Drummond, Francis Welburne, Mary Chance, Samuel Welburne – p. 122

BENSTON, WILLIAM – 24 Nov. 1717 – 5 Aug. 1718 – To son Robert Benston 370 A. where I now live adj. my bro. Francis Benston. To son John Benston part of said land. To son William Benston the remainder of said land. To son Holston. Son James. Son Benjamin. Dau. Ellener. Wife Grace Exec. Witt: William Benston, Michael Nedum, Joseph Benston, John Morris. – p. 136

DOWNING, JOHN – 6 June 1718 – 5 Aug. 1718 – To son John Downing planta. cont. 70 A. in Northampton, being part of the land that was Samuel Cobb's. Dau. Maru Walter. Wife Frances. Son John Exr. (other children not named) Witt: William Bell, William Harman, Simon Harman – p. 137

WEBB, SCARBURGH – 16 May 1718 – 2 Sept. 1718 – To son Thomas Webb (under 21) planta. where I now live cont. 100 A. To son John Webb (under 21) 100 A. being the remainder of 200 A. where I now live. Bal. of est. to be divided between all my children after they arrive to age. Friends John Dicks & Thomas Blake to care for stock at my planta. until children come to age. Daus. Elizabeth & Patience (under 16) – Bro. in law Thomas Dicks. To Sarah Harrison. Son Scarburgh Webb (under age) John Dicks & Thomas Blake Exrs. Witt: John Morrogh, Mason Abbott, John Lewis – p. 142

SHEPHARD, WILLIAM – 19 May 1718 – 7 Oct. 1718 – To grandson William Shephard Foster, son of John & Elizabeth Foster planta. in Accomack, said John & Elizabeth to have life int. in said land provided they care for my wife Mary Shephard. Friends James Kempe & Naomi his wife to see that my wife is well taken care of during her life. Elizabeth & John Foster Exrs. Witt: Simon Smith, James Wishart, Naomi Kempe, James Kempe - p. 144

STANTON, JOHN - "Should I not live to return to Virginia again" - 14 Feb. 1717/18 - 4 Nov. 1718 - To 3 youngest sons Robert, Stephen & Jonathan (other children not named) Capt. John Bradhurst Exr. Witt: Thomas Stockly, Samuel Prier - p. 159

LITCHFIELD, WILLIAM - 2 May 1718 - 5 Nov. 1718 - To son Francis. son William. Son Joseph. To son Joseph planta. where I now live cont. 138 A. Dau. Tabytha. Dau. Margaret. Wife Margaret Exec. Witt: William Willet, Sarah Hurst, Sarah Rily. - p. 161

COPES, MATHIAS - 25 Dec. 1718 - 3 Feb 1718/19 - To Giles Copes, youngest son of my bro. Giles Copes. To bro. Giles Copes. To the son of Hugh Roberts. Wife Margaret resid. legatee & Exec. Witt: William Foster, Hugh Roberts - p. 165

YEO, WILLIAM - 30 Dec. 1717 - 3 Feb. 1718/19 - To dau. Sary Yeo (under 16) whole est. & should she die without issue to Sabrah Drummond, dau. of my friend Hill Drummond. Hill Drummond Exr. Witt: Hill Drummond, William Chance, Joseph Allen, William Chance, Jr. - p. 165

HOPE, WILLIAM - 5 Dec. 1718 - 4 Mar. 1718/19 - Whole est. to dau. Joanna Custis Hope. To be buried near my dear wife late dec. Father Capt. George Hope Exr. & in case of his death my friend Mr. Richard Kitson to take charge of all my est. & said dau. until 18 or marriage. Witt: Robert Fleek, John Bradhurst, Samuel Turner - p. 177

ROGERS, PETER - 20 Oct. 1717 - 7 Apr. 1719 - To son John Rogers planta. where I now live, being the 100 A. which was my father's. To son Peter land purchased of Richard Hufington. Dau. Cazia Rogers. Son Jacob. Son Solomon. Dau. Tabitha. Sons Lazarus, Isaac & Gilbert. Sons under 18 - daus. under 16 - Wife Sisela Rogers & son John Exrs. Friends Philip Parker, John Lecatt, Morris Shepherd & Arthur Laylor to divide est. Witt: Philip Parker, John Lecatt, Richard Rogers, Jr., David Wattson - p. 178

WALKER, NATHANIEL - 2 Feb. 1718/19 - 7 Apr. 1719 - To father in law John Clift planta. where I now live cont. 100 A., also planta bought of Charles Trueford cont. 100 A. To bro. John Walker. Bro. Joseph Walker. Bro. Nehemiah Walker. Sister Mary. Sister Elizabeth Walker. Father in law resid. legatee & Exr. Witt: John Millechop, Anthony Hudson, John Tank--d. - p. 182

DIX, JOHN - 11 Mar. 1718/19 - 8 Apr. 1719 - To son Isaac (under 18) 200 A. being part of 500 A. where I now dwell. To son John (under 18) 150 A. where I now live. to son Jacob the remaining part of said 500

A. Wife Patience. Dau. Mary Dix. Dau. Elizabeth Dix. Son William & 2 daus. resid. legatees. Dau. Mary to be & remain with my bro. William & Mary Nicklson until 18 - Elizabeth to live with her bro. Iassc until 18 - Wife Exec. Friends Thomas Evans & John Barns overseers. Witt: Richard Kittson, Samuel Thomas, Richard Sturges - p. 186

STOCKLY, CHARLES, Yeoman - 6 May 1718 - 5 May 1719 - To sons Joseph & Charles all my lands & planta. where I now live. To son Jacob land adj. where I now live. Dau. Elizabeth. Wife Rebecca. Son in law William Mills personal property which was his mothers. Friend Sebastian Delastatius Ex'r. Richard Kittson & my Exr. to divide planta. Witt: Richard Kitson, Nathaniel Williams, Samuel Turner - p. 188

MIDDLETON, GEORGE, Sr. - 22 Feb. 1715/16 - 7 Apr. 1719 - To Bridget Middleton 100 A. being the Eastern part of the Planta. where I live. To younger son George Middleton, minor, the remaining part of my planta. To eldest son George Middleton Jr. 1 s. Youngest son, George, minor, Exr. Witt: Elizabeth Bradhurst. Catherine Willett - p. 191 -

FOSTER, JOHN - 28 Jan. 1718/19 - 5 May 1719 - Whole est. to be div. bet. wife Elizabeth & sons William & John. Friend Ralph Corbin trustee to see that my son William has 3 years schooling. Wife Exec. Witt: Simon Smith, Robert Corbin, Ralph Corbin - p. 192

KILLAHAWN, WILLIAM - 10 Apr. 1719 - 6 May 1719 - Dau. Mary. Sons John, William & Solomon - Wife dead - Son John to live with Robert Watson; William with Richard Rogers, Jr.; Mary with Ester Sill & Solomon with Luke Foscue. If they will not take the children Court to app. guardian. Court to app. Exr. Witt: Thomas Stringer, William Mears, Arthur Layler - p. 197

ANTHONY, GEORGE - 12 Sept. 1717 - 2 June 1719 - To son in law Arthur Laylor planta. where I now live cont. 100 A. on the North side of Occahannock Creek. Wife to have use of same for life. Grandau. Tabitha Laylor. Godson William Sill. Son in law Arthur Laylor resid. legatee & Exr, Witt: Andrew Stewart, Robert Watson, Elizabeth Stewart - p. 197

SCARBURGH, ELIZABETH - 2 June 1719 - 4 Aug. 1719 - To son Bennett. Son Charles. Son Henry. Dau. Mary Leatherbury. Dau. Sarah Black. Dau. Tabitha Bagwell. To 3 daus. my int. in Tangier Island, to each 1/3 & not to sell except to each other. To grandson Scarburgh Drummond. To grandson Henry, son of my said son Henry Scarburgh. To grandson Charles, son of my said son Charles Scarburgh. Grandau. Ann Parker. Grandau. Elizabeth Bagwell. Grandau. Edith Baily. Daus. Mary, Sarah & Tabitha resid. legatees & Executrices. Witt: Sacker Parker, Samuel Turner, Leah Parker, William Finney, Jr. - p. 211

60

AYRES, EDMUND - 10 Dec. 1718 - 4 Aug. 1719 - Planta. where I now live cont. 300 A. to 5 daus. Comfort, Tabitha, Patience, Huldah & Elizabeth Ayres. Dau. Tabitha Onions. Dau. Ann Mary. Wife Ann. To bro. Francis Ayres & Capt. Richard Drummond 250 A. at Hunting Creek, being 1/2 of 500 A. given by Capt. Richard Hill to me & my bro. Henry Ayres, which for a valuable consideration received by me I give to them & their heirs. Wife Ann Exec. Bro. Francis & Richard Drummond overseers. Witt: Charles Snead, Thomas Copes, Edmund Bowman Cropper. - p. 214

TRUITT, HENRY - 26 Mar. 1718 - 1 Sept. 1719 - To son Elias Truitt (under 18) planta. where I now live. Daus. Elizabeth, Tabitha, Hannah & Sarah. Wife Elishe Exec. Witt: William Nock, Jr. George Bonwell, Samuel Turner - p. 217

GRAY, JAMES - 21 Aug. 1719 - 3 Nov. 1719 - To dau. Ester Gray, alias Aymes, planta. where I now live for life, cont. 200 A. then 100 A. to my grandson James Aymes & 100 A. to William Aymes. To dau. Elizabeth Gray, alias Hinman, 200 A. adj. the above for life, then to grandau. Ester Macome, alias Hornsby, & for want of heirs to the heirs of my dau. Elizabeth by her present husband Richard Hinman. To dau. Dorothy Gray, alias Littlehouse, 200 A. adj. the above for life, then to grandson Peter Wadkinson, & for want of heirs to the next heir of my dau. Dorothy. Grandsons William & Simon Littlehouse. Grandson James Gray Hudson. Daus. Elizabeth, Dorothy, Mary & Ester resid. legatees & executrices. Witt: Arthur Layler, Robert Watson, William Mears - p. 229

WILLETT, WILLIAM - 17 Mar. 1718/19 - 4 Nov. 1719 - To wife use of 1/2 planta. & personal property for life, then to be div. between my children. To son Ambrose planta where I live & 110 A. To dau. Elizabeth 145 A. adj. same. To dau. Catherine 143 A. adj. Elizabeth. To dau. Ann 120 A. purchased of Francis Ayres. To son John the other part of land purchased of Francis Ayres, supposed to be 60 A. To grandson William Willett, son of Ambrose, mill & 2 A. given me by Richard Hill dec., also 12 A. purchased of John Cary. Son Ambrose & grandson William Exrs. Francis Young, Thomas Rily, Francis Ayres & Thomas Simson, Jr. overseers. - Witt: - Jacob D. Litchfield, John Rily. Robert Ternall. - p. 231.

FLETCHER, MATTHEW - 13 Dec. 1719 - 5 Jan. 1719/20 - To Brand Fletcher planta. where I now live cont. 150 A. & for want of heirs to William Fletcher. To Batterton Fletcher 50 A.. To sisters Elizabeth Tench, Mary Croucher & Frances Haket. To Phillip Parker, Jr. To Winnfret Parker. To Thomas Fletcher. To Dorothy Parker. To John Shipard. Bros. William, Batterton & Brandon Fletcher resid. legatees. Bro. William Exr. Witt: Morris Shepheard, Philip Parker, John West - p. 237

LITTLEHOUSE, WILLLIAM - 8 Jan. 1719/20 - 2 Feb. 1719/20 - To bro. Peter Wadkinson. To Abigal Wadkinson. Bro. in law John Oakly. Sister Floriana. Bro. Cornelius. Sister Elizabeth Twyford & her son William Twyford. My 2 bros. & 2 sisters resid. legatees. Bro. Peter Wadkinson Exr. Witt: Arthur Layler, Philip Parker - p. 240

CARY, TIMOTHY - 24 Jan. 1719/20 - 1 Mar. 1719/20 - To wife Margaret planta. where I live for life then to son Edward. Son James. Son Edw. to live with my friend Richard Kitson until he is 21 - Dau. Mary Cary. Son James to live with my friend Solomon Ewell until 21. Dau. Mary with friend Elis Abbott until 16 - Wife Margaret resid. legatee & Exec. Witt: Thomas Hope, Richard Kitson, Elizabeth Abutt. p. 243

STOCKLY, THOMAS - 1 May 1719 - 1 Mar. 1719/20 - To wife Hannah whole est. during her wid. for the maintenance of herself & children. To son Charles my planta where I now live at the head of Assawoman Creek. To son John land at Assawoman Creek. Grandson Thomas Stockly Merrill. Daus. Neomi & Jemina Stockly. Dau. Hannah Merrill. Grandau. Hannah Merrill. Bro. Joseph Stockly & friend John Staton Exrs. Witt: Samuel Paine, Alexander Stockly, Samuel Turner, Thomas Wormsly. p. 244

GORE, DANIEL - 3 Jan. 1719/20 - 5 Apr. 1720 - To son William land where I now live & my Neck of land called Great Neck. To son Selby planta where John Duberly now lives with the neck of land called Little Neck. To dau. Joyce 300 A. being part of the above tract. To dau. Mary 300 A. in Maryland where Robert Ardis lives. To son William two necks of land & marsh on Assateague called Raged Point & Little Neck, also 1/3 part of 500 A. on said Island bought of my bro. John Smith. To son Selby land on Assateague called Great Neck. Bal. of beach & land on said island to be div. bet. 2 sons. Sons under 18 - Daus. under 16. Wife (no name) & 4 children resid. legatees. Wife Exec. Friends Edward Robins, William Selby & John Purnell overseers or trustees. Witt: John Jenifer Osburn, John Smith, John Duberly, Ann Benston - p. 252

DRUMMOND, CAPT. RICHARD, of Hunting Creek - 24 Feb. 1719/20 - 3 May 1720 - To son Scarburgh Drummond. To son Richard Drummond planta. where I now live including 1/2 of Half Moon Island. Grandson Richard Drummond. Grandau. Elizabeth Drummond. Grandson Spencer Drummond. Bro. Hill Drummond & son Richard Exrs. Witt: Hancock Nickless, Joseph Litchfield, Jacob Litchfield, Joaokim Michael. - p. 253

HARRISON, FLOWERDEW - Nunc. 21 Feb. 1719/20 - 5 Apr. 1720 - To Matilda clothing. To Sisceley clothing - "And Mr. Rickets having the said Flowerdew by the hand asked her to whom she left the child, she answered to you, and all the rest I have in the world I leave to my child" Proved by Sarah Poulson & Sisceley Rogers. p. 254

CUSTIS, RACHELL - 8 Dec. 1718 - 3 May 1720 - To son Edward. Son Henry. Son Joseph. Son Revell. Dau. Rachell Custis. Dau. Jane Custis. Dau. Ann Custis. Dau. Frances Stringer. Dau. Elizabeth Shield. Dau. Sarah Watson. Grandson John Stringer. Grandson William Sacker Shield. Grandson William Custis. Grandau. Ann Watson. Son Edward Custis & Thomas Stringer Exrs. Witt: John Metcalfe, Charles Scarburgh, Charles Scarburgh, Jr. - p. 255.

WAINHOUSE, Francis - 7 Mar. 1719/20 - 3 May 1720 - (of Occahannock Creek) To wife Margaret land & planta for life then to grandson Francis Wainhouse (under age) & for want of heirs to grandson Michel Scarburgh & grandau. Margaret Wainhouse. To Thomas Godding 10 L- if he comes to claim it within 3 years after my death, if not to my grandchildren Francis & Margaret Wainhouse. To dau. Dorothy Scarburgh. Wife Margaret & son in law Michel Scarburgh Exrs. Witt: James Hilton, Arthur Lsyler, Jonas Beloat, Richard Kitson - p. 256

MARAIN, JOHN - -- --- 1720 - To son Mager Marain 250 A. To dau. Mary her mother's clothing. 2 youngest sons Jonathan & Joseph. Friend Joseph Staton Exr. Son Joseph to Joseph Staton; Jonathan to Jonathan Laws, dau. to Mr. John Kendal, & Mager to Samuel Pain. Witt: Joseph Goutey, Mary Luecraft, Samuell Paine - p. 261

SAVAGE, ROBERT - 7 May 1720 - 2 Aug. 1720 - To cousin Jacob Savage 262 A. "formerly left to me & my two brothers as Thomas & John & William Savage by their father left to me by his last will & testament" & for want of heirs to Abel Savage, bro. of Jacob, & for want of heirs to Parker Savage, son of my bro. William Savage. To cousin Abell Savage 87 A. which I formerly bought of his bro. John Savage & for want of heirs to his bro. Jacob. & for want of heirs to Parker Savage. Cousin Sarah Nelson. Goddau. Susanna Kellam. To Richard Savage, Jr., (under age) son of Sarah Warrenton. Bro. William Savage. To friend John Henderson Cousins Jacob, Abell & John Savage, Sarah Nelson & Susanna Joynes resid. legatees. Cousin Jacob Savage & John Henderson Exrs. Witt: John Bryant, Robert Henderson. p. 265

COLLEE, SYLVANUS - 15 June, 1720 - 2 Aug. 1720 - To son Job (under age) planta. cont. 250 A. & for want of issue to dau. Abigail Eliot. Wife Diana. Daus. Elizabeth & Diana Collee - Wife Exec. Witt: Thomas Perry, Joseph Stockly, Jr. John Mathews - p. 267

MINNION, OWING - 12 Sept. 1719 - 6 Sept. 1720 - To Rowland Hogson. To godson Joshua Lary. Grandau. Sarah Hodgson. Dau. Ann - Wife Margaret Exec. Witt: Bishop Henderson, Thomas Hogshare - p. 271

OWEN, TIMOTHY - 24 Apr. 1720 - 6 Sept. 1720 - To wife Patience & my child Mary all my moveable est. & should she die without issue

my planta. to my youngest bro. Peter Owen - Wife Exec. Witt: Elias
Taylor, Thomas Collins, James Taylor. p. 271

GUNTER, EDWARD - 9 Oct. 1716 - 6 Sept. 1720 - To son William
Gunter. Son Joseph. Dau. Sarah Gunter. Dau. Mary Collins. Grandson Thomas Collins. Dau. Susanna "if she ever come in these parts
again" Dau. Ously. Bal. of est. to wife Mary during her wid. then to
be div. bet. son Edward & dau. Ously - Sons under 18 - Daus. under
14 - Wife Exec. Witt: Thomas Jones Mary Jones, John Johnson - p.
272

JONES, RICHARD - 16 Aug. 1720 - 4 Oct. 1720 - To dau. Elizabeth
Jones 300 A. where I now live & for want of heirs to dau. Lisia Jones
& for want of heirs to my cousin William Savage & for want of heirs to
my cousin Charles Savage. To dau. Lisia Jones 200 A. being the
other part of my planta. & for want of heirs to dau. Elizabeth & for
want of heirs to my cousin George Smith, & for want of heirs to my
cousin John Smith. Daus. Abigall, Elizabeth & Lisia resid. legatees
& Executrices. Witt: Henry Read, Mary Savage, Arthur Laylor - p.
277

TOWNSEND, THOMAS, Jr. - 26 Apr. 1720 - 4 Oct. 1720 - To bro. in
law John Townsend 200 A. where I now live which my fatner gave me
by deed of gift. To Benens Morris, son of Hester Morris. To mother
in law Sarah Townsend. Sister Jaen Marsy. Sister Sarah Townsend.
Father Thomas Townsend resid. legatee & Exr. The residuary est.
left my father to be used to bring up Benens Morris, he to remain with
my faherr until he is 18. Witt: Sebastian Delastatius, Sr., Sebastian
Delastatius, Jr. - p. 278

CHAPMAN, WILLIAM - 6 Oct. 1720 - 7 Dec. 1720 - To bro. Silas
Chapman 164 A. & should he die without heirs to the next heir at
common law. Sister Mary. Bro. Silas Exr. Witt: John Robins,
Christopher Paradis, Barbary Robins - p. 289

FOSQUE, ANN - 27 July 1719 - 6 Dec. 1720 - Dau. in law Elizabeth
Hill. Dau. Barbary Blear. Dau. Ann Fosque. Grandson Clark Blear.
Dau. Sarah Fosque. Son in law Henry Blear. Son in law John Fosque.
Son in law Luke Fosque. 3 daus. & grandson Clark Blear resid.
legatees. Friends William & Nathaniel Bell to div. est. Son in law
Henry Blear Exr. Witt: William Bell, William Harman - p. 290

WATSON, ELIZABETH - 5 Sept. 1713 - 7 Feb. 1720/21 - Son Robert.
Son Peter, Son David. Son Benjamin. Son Moses. Dau. Elizabeth
Riggs. Dau. Mary Bell. Dau. Susanna Watson. Son Benjamin Exr.
Witt: Arthur Layler, Robert Savage - p. 295

PARKER, JOHN - 26 Jan. 1720/21 - 7 Feb. 1720/21 - To son John
land where he lives on in my Neck & 100 A. of land & marsh on the
Island near Pungoteague. To two youngest daus. Bridget & Betty. To
son Sacker land adj. that given John & also 100 A. on the said Islands.

To sons William & George all my lands at Indian River known as Piny or Ferry Neck; cont. 500 A. by a Maryland Patent & 900 A. by a Pennsylvania Patent. Daus. Abigail & Ann Parker. To dau. Frances Wise & her children George & Tabitha Wise. To dau. Amy Drummond & her children John, Drake & Patience. To John, Frances, Robert & William Parker, children of my son John Parker. To Susanna, dau. of my son Sacker. Sons John & Sacker & my wife (no name) Exrs. Witt: W. Bagge, Hillary Griffin, Thomas Leatherbury, John Stockley. p. 296

CROPPER, SEBASTIAN - 14 Dec. 1720 - - Mar. 1720 - To son Bowman Cropper land adj. the land of Edmund Bayly dec. To son Sebastian land ad . his bro. Bowman. Wife Rachell. Dau. Ester (under 16) - Sons under 21 - Should wife marry friend Henry Satchell & bro. in law Samuel Simson to take my two sons under their care. Wife Exec. Witt: John Metcalf, Samuel Simson, Edmund Bowman Cropper, Michael Ward - p. 307

LAYLOR, ARTHUR - 30 Jan. 1720/21 - 7 Mar. 1720/21 - To wife Ann whole est. for life to bring up my children & at her death or marriage I give my land & planta. where I now live cont. 200 A. to my sons Arthur & John Laylor. Daus. Mary & Derecture - Wife Exec. Witt: Robert Watson, Arthur Roberts, David Watson, John Savage - p. 308

HUTCHINSON, STEPHEN - 13 Dec. 1720 - 7 Mar. 1720/21 - Wife Elizabeth - Daus. Mary & Susanna Hutchinson. 1/2 my land to dau. Mary & the other 1/2 to dau. Susanna at the death of my wife. To Richard Williams & Daniel Patterson, my servants. Friends Arthur Laylor, Daniel Rolls & Thomas Evans to div. bal. of est. bet. wife & 2 daus. Wife Exec. Witt: Thomas Evans, Sisley Rodgers, Hilliard Fadre - p. 309

HAYES, ALICE - Nunc - Declaration made 12 Aug. 1720 - Pro. 7 Mar. 1720/21 - To dau. Elizabeth Hayes. To dau. in law Joan Bucklin. To Samuel Collins, son of John Collins. Proved by John & Mary Collins & Joan Bucklin - p. 310

PARKER, PHILLIP - 21 Oct. 1719 - 4 Apr. 1721 - To son Phillip land & planta at Nanduey where I now live cont. 220 A. also my land & marsh in Maryland at a place called Runbelde Marsh, wife to have use of same until Phillip is 18. To dau. Mary Parker, alias West, land in Maryland at Pocomoke near the head of Pitses Creek cont. 200 A. To dau. Elizabeth Parker 100 A. near Wallops Road. Wife, son Phillip & dau. Winefreet Parker resid. legatees. Bro. George Parker, Mr. Teackle, Richard Rodgers & Arthur Layler to div. est. Wife (no name) Exec. Witt: George Parker, Arthur Layler, John Rogers. - p. 319

BONEWELL, JAMES - 14 Jan. 1721 - 4 Apr. 1721 - To mother Mary Huebank land at Ekekses Creek cont. 100 A. To cousins Mary Silverthorne & Susana Wise. Sister Elizabeth Bonewell. Bro. James Bonewell. Sister Mary Wise. Sister Susana Mychell. Sister Sarah Wise - Mother Exec. Witt: William Wise, John Wise, Sr., John

Wise, Jr. - p. 320

PARKER, WILLIAM - 20 Feb. 1720/21 - 4 Apr. 1721 - To grandson in law William James planta. where I now live cont. 200 A. To Rachel James. To David James. To dau. in law Sarah Booles. To William Spiers. To Jackcoby Spiers. To Luke Spiers. To Sarah Spiers. Dau. in law Sarah Boles resid. legatee & Exec. Witt: Jacob Sare, Richard Sheald, William Burton - p. 321

HUGHS, WILLIAM - 27 Aug. 1720 - 4 Apr. 1721 - To the children of Peter Milby the debt which he owes me. To Sabrah Milby. Son in law Dormund Sullvant Exr. To Susanna Sulevant. Witt: Ester Sill, Arthur Layler - p. 321

TAYLER, JOHN - 3 Feb. 1720/21 - 4 Apr. 1721 - To son Robert 100 A. To son Joseph my manor planta. where I live with 100 A. To son William 100 A. on the West side of Love long Branch. Wife to have use of land until Joseph is 18. Dau. Mary Tayler. Sons Robert & William Exrs. Witt: Thomas Simson, Jr. Thomas Simson, Sr. William Willson, Samuel Onions. - p. 322

NELSON, PROVIS - 5 Mar. 1721 - 2 May 1721 - To sons John (eldest) & Provis land where I now live being 100 A. Dau. Comfort Foster. Dau. Betty Nelson. Wife Elizabeth & son John Exrs. Witt: William Finney, Jr., A. Finney, William Foster, p. 323

ROGERS, JOHN - 27 Sept. 1720 - 4 Apr. 1721 - To son John 75 A. where I now live. To son William. Dau. Newbery Sheild. To my said dau's. son Jonathan. Son John (under 18) Son William Exr. Witt: William Burton, Jr. William Burton. Edward Taler - p. 323

LEATHERBURY, CHARLES - To son Thomas planta. where I now live. To son John Planta. where Rose Macabe now lives, planta. where William West lives & planta. where Robert Tisekar lives. To son Perry planta. where Peter Turlington lives, also the land between the line by Tisekar's fence to Pungoteague Road. To dau. Elizabeth Leatherbury land on the East side of Pungoteague Road. To dau. Ann Leatherbury land which was in dispute between me & Edmund Leatherbury. Wife (no name) & daus. Elizabeth & Ann resid. legatees. - Wife Exec. Witt: W. Bagge, Elizabeth Ward, William West, Thomas Davis. - p. 324

COPES, THOMAS - 16 Dec. 1720 - 4 Apr. 1721 - To son Thomas (under 18) all the land I am now possessed with except from the old road to the new road & the branch left clear which I give to Elijah Simpson. Should my son die without issue 200 A. to Samuel Simpson provided my bro. Giles will make an exchange, then to my said bro. & his heirs. Should my son die without heirs I give to my son in law Abraham Hooton the land Patrick Clark lives on cont. about 140 A. To dau. in law Ester Hooton. Should my son in law Abraham Hooton decline the aforesaid land, then his brother Samuell to have it, Samuel to pay his bro. Abraham 6 cows & calves or 3000 lbs. of tobacco which Abraham shall think fir in case he refuse the land & my will is that Samuel Hooten shall have the land left by his father John Hooten at Bogetenorton which doth belong to Abraham, & if Giles Copes refuse to make the exchange before mentioned, then Samuel Simson & his now wife Sarah & heirs to have 100 A. at the head of the Neck. To Ester Hooten 1 suit of clothes which belonged to my dau. Mary. The remainder of her clothes to Sarah Simpson & Esther Cropper. Son Thomas to have 7 years schooling in Virginia. Wife, Henry Custis & Samuel Simson Exrs. Mr. William Tazewell to be my attorney both in Virginia & Maryland. Witt: John Metcalf, Henry Custis, Edmund Bowman Cropper, Giles Copes, Pattrick Clark. - p. 325

CUSTIS, THOMAS - 3 Oct. 1719 - 4 Apr. 1721 - To wife Ann all the land I had with her near Oak Hall. To son John Custis planta. where I now live cont. 1750 A. on Deep Creek. To son Edmond 1000 A. adj. the above & all my interest in the lands on Jingoteague & Morrys Island beq. by Hon. John Custis of Hungars, dec. to me & my wife Elizabeth. To son Thomas Whittington Custis 300 A. on Old Plantation Creek in Northampton County. Daus. Tabitha, Sarah & Elizabeth. To friends Capt. John Broadhurst, Charles Snead & Henry Custis each a gold ring. Sister Tabitha Scarburgh Custis. Wife, Capt. John Broadhurst, Mr. Charles Snead & Mr. Henry Custis Exrs. Children under 18. To unborn child 700 A. near Burton's Branch which descended to me from my Hon. Grandmother Mrs Tabitha Hill - Witt: John Lewis, Mary Collier, John Chambers, John Mead - p. 327

ANDREWS, NATHANIEL - 16 Feb. 1720/21 - 2 May 1721 - Wife Elizabeth. To dau. Elizabeth (under 16) 200 A. near Pocomoke Road & should she die without issue to my bro. Isaac Andrews. To son in law Jabez Pitt. Sister Dorothy Hastings. Wife Exec. Friends Capt. John Bradhurst & Hancock Custis to assist her. Witt: Robert Dalrymple, Martha Pitt, Elizabeth Morris, James Houlston, Thomas Merrill - p. 333

AYRES, RICHARD - 14 Feb. 1720 - 2 May 1721 - The 150 A. which my father Richard Hill Ayres beq. to my bro. John Ayres, & he dying the same did revert to me by my father's will, I give to my sister Ann Francis Ayres & for want of heirs to my sister Easter Ayres, & for want of heirs to my sister Mary Ayres, & for want of heirs to my cousin Nathaniel Wilkins, son of William Wilkins. Mother Easter Ayres resid. legatee & Exec. The 100 A. which my grandfather Christopher Tomson beq. to me I give to my sister Mary Ayres. Cousin Thomas Wilkins, son of Thomas Wilkins. Witt: John Watts, Daniel Welburne, John Tomson - p. 335

GLADDIN, JOHN - 16 Jan. 1720/21 - 2 May 1721 - To grandson Thomas Gladdin all my land in Forked Neck cont. 207 A. & for want of heirs to the next male heir of my son Howell Gladdin & if there be no male heir to the eld. of my grandaus. & heirs. To wife land she is now possessed of during her wid. To son Howell planta. he now lives on for life. Should my wife die before my grandson Thomas comes to age my son Howell to be possessed with the whole tract until said Thomas marries or comes to age of 21. Wife & son Howell resid. legatees & Exrs. Witt: Thomas Jenkinson, William Broadwater, Job Towles, Howell Bootin - p. 335

DYER, JOHN - 8 Feb. 1721 - 6 June 1721 - To wife & John Fish whole est. Should either die survivor to have all; that there be no division between them & that they live together. Wife & John Fish Exrs. Francis Croston & Ralph Lisney overseers. Witt: Francis Croston, Elizabeth Walker, William Beavans - p. 344

SNEAD, ROBERT - 7 Apr. 1721 - 6 June 1721 - To 3 sons Robert (under 16) Thomas & Charles Snead 150 A. where I now live. To wife Margaret dwelling house & land for life. To son John gun, sword &c. Bal. of est. to be div. bet. the rest of my children. Wife Exec. Bro. Charles & John Fitzgarrell Exrs. Witt: Catherine Snead, Mary Snead, John Morrogh - p. 345

TOWLES, HENRY - 17 Jan. 1720/21 - 6 June 1721 - To son Kendall my planta. where I live - Wife to have use of same for life. Sons Job & Thomas the rest of my land adjacent to the above. To son Henry Towles 1 s. To son Stockle Towles 1 s. Friends Thomas Jenkinson & Thomas Jenkinson, Jr. Exrs. Witt: John Glading, Howell Bootin, William Broadwater - p. 346

BONWELL, GEORGE - 12 Feb. 1720 - 6 June 1721 - Bro. Thomas Bonwell. Grandmother Mrs Frances Norton. Sister Mary. Sister Arabella Bonwell. To friend Solomon Ewell. To friend Mason Abbot. To John Tankard. Solomon Ewell Exr. "I request of the said Solomon his Christian care of my Brethren". Witt: Samuel Turner, John Wilkins - p. 346

WASHBURNE, CAPT. JOHN - 28 Mar. 1721 - 6 June 1721 - To wife Susanna 400 A. where I now live for life then to grandson Washburne Johnson, son of my dau. Dorithy Johnson. Grandchildren Richard, Temperance & Bridgitt Johnson, children of my sau. Dorithy Johnson. Wife Exec. Friend Richard Rodgers to assist her. Witt: John Metcalfe, Daniel Willis, Dorrythea Parker, Henry Willis. - p. 347

AYRES, FRANCIS - 19 Jan. 1720/21 - 6 June 1721 - To son Francis Ayres 289 1/2 A. where I now live. To son Richard Ayres 200 A. at the head of a branch of Hunting Creek, being the planta. where my father lived, & for want of heirs to my 3 daus. Sarah, Elizabeth & Ann Ayres. 5 children resid. legatees. Thomas Riley & Charles White overseers of my children & their estates. Son Francis Exr. Witt: Middleton Melson, William Haizlup.- p. 348

GRIFFIS, DANIEL - 27 Aug. 1719 - 1 Aug. 1721 - Wife Mary sole devisee & Exec. Witt: Edmund Scarburgh, William Only - p. 362

HINMAN, RICHARD, of Guilford Creek – 24 July 1721 – 1 Aug. 1721 – To son John 800 A. land & marsh at Gilford Creek. To sons Argill & Baly 1000 A. to be div. bet. them, that is 400 A. where I now live & 600 A. below the land of Weatherington Fitchett. Wife & children resid. legatees. Wife Elizabeth Exec. Witt: Edmond Tatham, Benjamin Royall, John Johnson, Weatherington Fitchett – p. 363

BUDD, THOMAS – 5 May 1721 . 1 Aug. 1721 – To sons Thomas & John my mill. Wife to have use of same to bring up children until they come to age. Friends William Fletcher & Thomas Gascoyne to div. est. bet. wife & children. Wife Annadaneelah Exec. Witt: William Fletcher, Thomas Gascoyne, Jann Randall – p. 363

MILBY, JOHN, Jr. – 6 Feb. 1720 – 1 Aug. 1721 – To son Salathiel water mill at head of Occahannock Creek & 100 A. adj. Should my son John die without heirs then the planta. where my father now lives to go to my son Salathiel, and the water mill & land to my son Garrison. Unborn child. Wife Tabitha. Daus. Tabitha & Patience. sons under 18 – Daus. under 16 – If wife should die before children come to age Jonathan Garrison to take care of their estates. Wife Exec. Witt: Henry Read, John Milby, Sr., Francis Downing, John Teackle – p. 364

LITTLETON, JOHN, of Back Creek – 15 Sept. 1718 – 1 Aug. 1721 – To son William Littleton 200 A. where I now live. To dau. Tabitha Warde. Son Thomas Littleton. Son John Littleton. Dau. Comfort Crowson. Dau. Ann Mary Littleton. Son Charles Littleton. Sons Mark & Edmund & Thomas resid. legatees. Son William Exr. Witt: Richard Drummond, Edmund Tatham, Richard Drummond, Jr. – p. 365

BROTHERTON, EDWARD – 3 Sept. 1721 – 3 Oct. 1721 – To Solomon Sanders, son of Richard & Rachell Sanders, his wife, 1/2 my land where I now live, that is the part where Richard Sanders now lives. To dau. Mary Brotherton the remainder of my land. To wife Mary. To Mary Sanders, dau. of Richard & Rachell Sanders. Wife & dau. Mary resid. legatees & Executrices. Witt: Edmund Tatham. James Tatham, John Johnson – p. 368

SMITH, SIMON – 6 Sept. 1721 – 3 Oct. 1721 – To son Simon. To dau. Elizabeth & for want of heirs to her two youngest bros. Dau. Johana Littleton. Bal. of est. to be div. bet. all the rest of my children not herein mentioned except Johana. Son Simon Exr. Witt: John Sandford, Robert Corbin – p. 363

ROBERTS, HUGH – 3 Nov. 1720 – 3 Oct. 1721 – Wife Mary Exec. To son Hugh planta. where I now live. Daus. Elizabeth & Katherine. Wife & children resid. legatees. William Black & George Kutler trustees for my children. Witt: William Gilchrist, Richard Cutler, Jr., John Cutler – p. 369

SMITH, HENRY – 12 Feb. 1720/21 – 7 Nov. 1721 – To 2 sons William & Henry Smith & John Arrington land where I live to be div. bet. them. Should John Arrinton die without issue his part to my sons William & Henry. Wife (no name) & John Arrington Exrs. Witt: Sacker Parker, John Powell, Andrew Martan – p. 381

EVANS, JOHN – 6 Jan. 1720 – 8 Nov. 1721 – To son John 200 A. on Smith's Island where John Park now lives in Maryland. To son Mark 200 A. on Smith's Island. To son Richard the old planta. where Arthur Park now lives on Smith's Island. To dau. Mary Evans all my Island called Point Comfort & 50 A. on Silverthorn's Ridge. To son Mark 50 A. adj. where I now live. To son John planta. where I now live & 148 A., also 100 A. marsh after the death of my wife. Wife Elizabeth & son John Exrs. Witt: Darby Linton, Elizabeth Johnson, John Johnson – p. 381

KEMPE, JAMES – 23 Oct. 1721 – 6 Mar. 1721/2 – To bro. George Kempe the gun my father gave me. To kinsman James Wishart, at the day of his marriage. To sister Mary, wife of Thomas Wishart of Princess Anne County, Virginia, 200 A. in said county at Back Bay. Wife Naomi resid. legatee & Exec. & should she die my bro. George Kempe & kinsman James Wishart Exrs. Witt: Hancock Custis, Comfort Finney, Ann Makemie – p. 399

DONOS, ARTHUR, Carpenter – 18 Oct. 1721 – 6 Mar. 1721/2 – To wife (no name) To Even Edwards. To Jacob Lear. To Rannals Badger. To Frances Alaston – John Warrinton, Sr. Exec. To Mary Chace. Witt: Thomas Lurton, Jacob Lurton, Stephen Warrinton – p. 400

CONNOR, PATRICK – 21 Feb. 1720/21 – 6 Mar. 1721/2 – To wife Anna Margareta. Dau. Anne Mary Connor. Father in law William Kane. Wife Exec. Friends Thomas Morrel, Nicholas Millman & Thomas Taylor joint Exrs. Witt: Robert Dalrymple, Sebastian Delastatius, William Howard – p. 401

BRYANT, WILLIAM, Yeoman – 2 Mar. 1720 – 3 July 1722 – Wife (no name) Dau. Tabitha Bryant. Son Benet. Wife resed. legatee. Friend Thomas Gin Exr. Witt: John Tankred, Jacob Stokly, Francis Brooks – p. 417

HOPE, CAPT. GEORGE – 20 Jan. 1721/2 – 7 Aug. 1722 – To son Thomas 700 A. where I now live & 100 A. of swamp. To son & dau. Mark & Comfort Ewell 30 A. where I now dwell. Grandson George Hope Ewell. Grandau. Johannah Custis Hope (under 18) dau. of William Hope, dec. Son George Hope dec. To Mary & Patience Savage, daus. of Griffeth Savage. To servant Elizabeth Dutton 100 A. where my son Thomas now lives for life, reversion to her dau. Margaret, also her freedom as soon as I am dead. To dau. Temperance Scarburgh all the money I have in England. Son Thomas Hope & friend Richard Kitson Exrs. Son Thomas & 3 daus. Comfort. Temperance & Patience resid. legatees. Witt: William Nock, Jr., John Tankred, Elizabeth

LEATHERBURY, EDMUND – Not dated.– 3 Oct. 1721 – To son Perry Leatherbury land where I now live. The remaining 1/2 of 1000 A. in Accomack County opposite to Onancock Creek to be sold for the benefit of my son Perry for his education, & should he die before coming to age to receive the benefit then to the next heir of me the testator. Wife Mary Exec. Witt: Charles Leatherbury, William Parker, John Stockly, Thomas Fitzgrall, Henry Scarburgh – p. 425

ROSE, THOMAS, age 33 – 2 Nov. 1722 – 4 Dec. 1722 – To friends George, Thomas & William Hook my sloop called the Rosanna, about 18 tons. To godson George Cutler Jr. To Mary Roberts & Nathaniel Riggin. To friends Richard Cutler, Sr., Elizabeth Cutler, John Cutler, William Cutler, Richard Cutler, Jr., Elizabeth Bagwell, George Cutler, Sr. George Cutler, Jr., Comfort Lurton, Arcadia Cutler, Maj. George Parker, Ann Parker, Mr. William Black each a gold ring. To William Pritchett & John Warrington, Sr. each a ring. George Cutler, Sr. Exr. Witt: William Whitford, Henry Parker – p. 441

FOOKES, THOMAS – 25 Oct. 1720 – 5 Feb. 1722 – To son Daniel 300 A., being all that I hold. Son William Fookes. Son James Fookes. Son Benjamin Fookes. Dau. Neomy Edmonds. Dau. Mary Warrinton. Dau. Rachell Prichard. Dau. Elizabeth Cripin. Dau. Sarah Idlet. Sons Benjamin & Daniel Exrs. Witt: Thomas Brown, Hugh Roberts Mary Roberts, William Cup – p. 456

HINMAN, ELIZABETH, wid. of Richard Hinman – 22 Sept. 1722 – 5 Feb. 1722 – To dau. Esther Hornby. Dau. Comfort Mary Hinman. Grandchildren William Hinman, Naomi Maccome, Thomas Hinman, Baly Hinman, Argill Hinman. To Rachell Fitchett. To Neall Mackenny's dau. Katherine. Grandson Richard Hinman. Son Argill Hinman, Son Baly Hinman. Grandson John Maccome. To Richard Sanders. Dau. Neome Maccome. Grandau. Sarah Hinman. Son in law John Hornby. Dau. Comfort Mary Hinman resid. legatee & Exec. Witt: John Johnson, Weatherington Fitchett – p. 459

BENSTON, FRANCIS – 17 Oct. 1722 – 5 Mar. 1722 – To son Joseph land in Virginia at the head of my planta. & land on the West side of my planta. in Somerset County, Maryland. To son Jonathan my planta. in Virginia & land in Maryland adj. that given Joseph. To son Joshua bal. of my land in Virginia & Maryland. Wife Edith & son Joseph Exrs. Witt: Daniel Welburne, William Benston, Dennis Blake – p. 463

MOORE, EPHRAM – 12 Nov. 1713 – 5 Mar. 1722/3 – "Now bound out of the County" To bro. in law John Rowles. Mother Catherine Moore. Bro. in law John Rowles Exr. Witt: Daniel Rowles, Major Rowles. – p. 465

WISE, MATILDA, Widow - 6 Sept. 1721 - 6 Mar. 1722 - Son John.
Son Thomas. Dau. Elizabeth. Dau. Mary Cade Scarburgh. Dau.
Hannah Scarburgh. Son Samuel. Son Thomas to take his bro.
Samuel & sister Hannah into his care and give them their maintenance &
education. Son Thomas Exr. Witt: Charles Snead, Jonathan West,
James Davis, Henry Davis - p. 465

BRADHURST, CAPT. JOHN - 2 May 1720 - 6 Aug. 1723 - To wife
Elizabeth planta. where I now live cont. 400 A. for life & then to
Tabitha Custis, dau. of Thomas Custis & Elizabeth, his wife & for
want of heirs I give 200 A. to Margaret Custis, dau. of Henry & Tabitha Custis, & the other 200 A. to Sarah Custis, dau. of Thomas &
Elizabeth Custis. To godson Jabez Pitt 100 A., being part of 500 A.
given me by my dec. uncle Col. John Custis in Jollys Neck. To my
little nephew Edmund Custis, son of Thomas & Elizabeth Custis a gun
which was given him by the last will of his grandfather, Mr. Edmund
Custis, dec. To wife bal, of est. except my wearing apparel, which I
give to the sons of my sister's dau. whose sir names I do not know,
but if living she dwells on the North side of Nuswadox Creek in Northampton County. Wife Elizabeth Exec. Witt: Issac Pypar, John
Morris, Edward Robins, Thomas Wilkinson, John Brittingham, Sebastian Delastatius, Thomas Taylor. Codicil dated 31 Aug. 1722 - To
wife negro girl Jenny & increase - Witt: George Douglas, Jacob Merrill, Pheobe Delastatius - p. 490

JAMES, JONATHAN - 14 Feb. 1721 - 6 Aug. 1723 - To two sons
Joshua & William James 150 A. in Somerset County at a place called
Back Creek. To five sons John, Joseph, Uzeziah, Joshua & William
70 A. in Somerset County at a place called Rumblete Marac Beech.
To eldest son John James 100 A. in Somerset County on the North
side of St. Martins River. To son Uzeziah 100 A. adj. John. To son
Joseph 100 A. of same tract. To youngest son William. All my hogs
to be div. bet. wife & children when they come to age of 18. Wife
Mary & son John Exrs. Witt: Thomas Marshall, Kelley Johnson, John
White - p. 491

TOWLES, JOB - 23 July 1723 - 3 Sept. 1723 - To Mary & Susana
Huchason, daus. of Steven Huchason, dec. 10 L each when they come
to age of 18. In case their mother marries to be paid out of the est., if
not to keep it in her possession during her life. To bros. Thomas &
Kendall Towles. Wife Elizabeth resid. legatee & Exec. Witt: William Groton, John Window, Elizabeth Gareitt - p. 495

TATHAM, EDMUND - 1 Feb. 1720 - 3 Dec. 1723 - To wife whole est.
during her wid. To son James planta. where I now live cont. 200 A. at
his mother's death or marriage. Dau. Tabitha Tatham. Daus. Comfort
& Sarah Tatham. Ann, Comfort & Sarah resid. legatees. Son James
Tatham Exr. Witt: Robert Snead, John Drummond, Richard Drummond
- p. 510

TURNALL, THOMAS - 25 Aug. 1723 - 4 Mar. 1723/4 - Wife to have use of house & planta. during her wid. & if she marry to be divided bet. my children. I acquit my eldest dau. Anow Bellow Evens with paying 1 s. "so takeing Leave of all the world I bid adew" - Witt: John Young, Thomas Riley - p. 527

KELLY, JOHN - 6 Apr. 1724 - 2 June 1724 - To 2 sons Edmund & Joseph Kelly all my land on the South side of the Sedgey Branch. To 2 sons Daniel & David Kelly planta. where I now live on this side the said branch. To two sons George & Dennis Kelly all my land from Edward Bell's line to the slash by Timothy Coe's old saw pit. To son John Kelly my old planta. with all the remainder of my land. To dau. Sarah Kelly. To son Thomas Kelly. Sons Daniel & David resid. legatees. Son John Exr. with the assistance of John Johnson. Witt: John Johnson, Elias Bell, Charles Pringle. - p. 535

JENKINSON, THOMAS - 17 Jan. 1720/21 - 2 June 1724 - To son Thomas Jenkinson for life one point of marsh called the Little Island, reversion to my son Moses Jenkinson. To son Thomas land where he now lives called Plators point provided he give so much of the land he bought of Sacker Parker to join the land I shall give my son Moses, & if he refuse Moses to have Plators poynt to make up his full quantity. Wife Elizabeth residue of est. for life, but if she marry my son John to take possession of my now dwelling house with 187 A., it being 1/2 of my 374 A. in Joyys (Jollys) Neck, & I give to my son Moses the remaining 187 A. Should John die without issue Moses to have his part, and Moses' part to go to my son Jesse Jenkinson, & should all three die without issue the whole 374 A. to go to my dau. Frances Jenkinson. & for want of heirs to my dau. Mare Jenkinson, & for want of heirs to my dau. Neome & for want of heirs to my dau. Catherine & should there be no living heir then to the Church of this Parish, but if any of my daus. inherit the said plantation it shall be called Thomas Jenkinson's Plantation forever & if they alter the name they shall be disinherited & the land to fall to the next to bear up the name forever. After the death of my wife bal. of est. to be divided bet. my children John, Catherine, Naome, Frances, Mare, Moses, Jesse & Elizabeth Jenkinson & if my wife marry I set my children free at 18. Bro. in law Ralph Corbin Exr. & wife Exec. Witt: Thomas Towles, Job. Towles, Howell Bootin. p. 536

STICIKAR, JAMES - 28 Mar. 1724 - 7 July 1724 - To son & dau. John & Sarah Sticikar Exrs. Personal property to be div. bet. them. Son Robert. Dau. Alice. Dau. Mary Fitzgarold. Grandson Solomon West. Grandson James Fitzgarold. Grandau. Sarah West. Wife Jane. Witt: John McClester, John Bonwell, Francis White - p. 557

ROBINSON, COL. TULLY - 1 Nov. 1723 - 5 Aug. 1724 - To Jacoba Spires for life 35 A. near Burton's Branch, reversion to the eld. son of John Spires, dec. then living. To John Williams of Northampton 100 A. near Old Plantation Creek, formerly the land of Mr. Benjamin Robinson of Northampton, dec., provided he pay his bond due me by

73

the last of April 1724. To youngest dau. Ann Robinson (under 18) To dau. Mary Robinson. To son William Robinson. Dau. West Smith. Dau. Scarburgh Wise. Dau. Sarah Smith, Dau. Sarah McClenahan. To dau. Elizabeth Smith & John Smith, her husband. Grandson William Robinson Smith, son of Elizabeth & John Smith. Wife (no name) Exec. Witt: William Black, Daniel Fookes, Sarah Fookes - p 558

PARKER, GEORGE, of Accomack - Not dated - 7 July 1724 - To son George Parker 1/2 my land on the North side of Anancock Creek, being 825 A. To sons George, Henry & Philip my large copper still. To son Charles all my land on Pungoteague Creek cont. 950 A. which I purchased of Justinian Yeo. To son Henry land on Back Creek adj. his bro. George. To son Bennet Parker 1/2 my land in Indian Town in Somerset County. Maryland, called Wickenoughs Neck cont. 300 A. To son Richard the remainder of my land in Wickenoughs Neck, the whole cont. 600 A. To son Philip all my land in my Neck on Onancock Creek not already given to my sons George & Henry. To dau. Ann. Son George to pay her 6 L Children to receive their legacies as soon as my will is proved. Sons George, Charles & Henry Exrs. Witt: Henry Scarburgh, Winnefred Scarburgh, John Bonwell - p. 561

MORRIS, ANN - 4 Feb. 1723/4 - 7 July 1724 - To dau. Naomie Tull 1 s. To son Dennis Blake 1 s. Son Joseph Blake to have whole personal est. to bring up the children. Son Gilburd & son John Morris to be with Joseph Blake until they are 18. To Elizabeth Morris. Joseph Blake Exr. Witt: Charles Ramsey, William Baker, Jacob Morris. - p. 563

RILEY, THOMAS - 17 Feb. 1721/2 - 5 Aug. 1724 - To eld. son John Riley planta. where I now live cont. 300 A., also 1/2 of marsh purchased of Col. Solomon Ewell, being in all 250 A. To son Thomas Riley the other 1/2 of the said marsh. To 2 sons William & Lawrence all my marshes & Hammocks at Guilford. To son Benjamin. To dau. Mary Riley. To dau. Sarah Riley. To wife Planta. &c. for life. To cousin Ryley Slocomb a years schooling to be allowed him when he arrives to the age of 15 years. Wife & 7 children, John, Thomas, William, Lawrence, Benjamin, Mary & Sarah Riley resid. legatees. Wife (no name) & son John Exrs. Witt: Richard Drummond, Alexander Edwards, John Evans - p. 567

WAGGAMAN, JONATHAN - 23 July 1723 - 17 Oct. 1724 - "I Jonathan Waggaman of Accomack, being about to take a voyage" &c. To son William Elliot Waggaman 500 A. near the seaside, 400 A. of which I bought of my mother Mrs Frances Waggaman & the other of Thomas & John Gascoins, & for want of heirs to my son Ephraim Waggaman. To son Henry Waggaman 200 A. on Pitts Creek in Accomack County & for want of issue to son Ephraim. Should my son William rather have the planta on Pitts Creek he shall enjoy the same provided he makes over to my son Henry the 500 A. above given him, and that between the 21st and 22nd years of the said William's age. 3 sons William Elliot, Henry & Ephraim Waggaman resid. legatees. Bro. Mr. Jacob

Waggaman & Mr. Richard Kitson Exrs. Witt: John Walker, Thomas Merrill, Comfort Merrill - p. 575

BELL, ROBERT - 4 Oct. 1724 - 5 Jan. 1724/5 - To wife Mary planta. where I now live & 250 A. for life & then to my son Thomas Bell. To son William Bell 250 A. adj. where I now live provided he do not molest my son Nathaniel Bell or his heirs of a parcel of land I shall give him at Naswadox which was left me by my father's last will. To son Nathaniel 150 A. being part of the land where I now dwell, also my planta at Naswadox, also a small parcel of land which I leased of Thomas Maddux during the term of the lease. To grandau. Tabitha Bell, dau. of Nathaniel & Mary Bell. Bal. of est. to wife Mary for life then to my three sons. 3 sons, William, Thomas & Nathaniel Exrs. Witt: Hancock Nickless, John Foscue, John West. - p. 585

ROSS, ANDREW, 6 Dec. 1724 - 5 Jan. 1724/5 - To Mrs Francinia Hack 10 L- for a suit of mourning &c. To friend Capt. Richard Drummond all my interest of whatsoever kind in this American parts, he to pay funeral charges, legacies & other debts in American parts. Capt. Richard Drummord Exr. Witt: Alexander Wordie, Thomas Wise, Thomas Wise, Benjamin Drewitt - p. 588

SCARBURGH, CHARLES - Nunc. Declaration 22 Dec. 1724, proved 23 Dec., prob. 8 Jan. 1724/5 - "On the 22 day of this Instant December being at the house of Capt. Charles Scarburgh, dec., did here his son Charles Scarburgh, being to the best of our knowledge in his perfect scences, by word of mouth give to his brother John Scarburgh all his estate that was known & called his, he declaring he most deserving it for his kindness to which wee have sett our hands and are ready to declare on our Oaths. Attested this 23 day of December, 1724" Proved by Catherine Fouler, Roger Fouler - p. 590

GRINALD, RICHARD - Nunc. Proved 3 Feb. 1724 - 3 Feb. 1724 - To 2 sons Richard & Henry 100 A. of land and marsh on Jobe Island. Whole personal est. to wife Mary to bring up 2 sons, & if there be any left at her death she to dispose of it as she shall think fit. Proved by Jacob Litchfield, Joseph Thorn, William Sherwood. p. 592

Wills, Deeds &c. 1715-1729 - v. ii

ROBBINS, WILLIAM - 27 Nov. 1718 - 3 Aug. 1725 - To son Joseph Robbins planta. where my father John Robbins lived which fell to me by inheritance, cont. 200 A. To 3 daus. Diana Robbins, Sarah Robbins & Ann Starling Robbins. Dau. Elizabeth. Daus. under 18 - Sons John & Joseph to be at liberty at 18 - Friends Williamson & Thomas Townsend, Jr. trustees of my son Joseph & to look after his planta. Wife Sarah resid. legatee & Exec. Witt: Sebastian Delastatius, James Taler, Sr. Sebastian Delastatius, Jr. - p. 34

BALEY, EDMUND - 20 Feb. 1724 - 5 Oct. 1725 - To wife Rosana planta. on Cradock Creek for the term of 20 years if she marry & if not for her natural life. At the expiration of 20 years or if she should die then to my unborn child, male or female. Bal. of est. to wife & unborn child to be divided when said child shall arrive at 18 or marry. Land in Somerset County to my said child. Wife to have possession until child is 18 or marries, & if said child should die before coming to age, then to my wife for life & then to Ursilla Whittington Hermon & her heirs. Wife Exec. Witt: Mittchell Scarburgh, Richard Bayly, Henry Bayly - p. 36

HALL, JOHN - 23 June, 1725 - 5 Oct. 1725 - To the poor of Accomack County 25 L to be disposed of at the discretion of the Churchwardens. To bro. Maurice Sheppard clothing & to his son John my part of the schooner which I have with Maurice Shephard & Robert Anderson. To Abbigale Bailey, wife of Richard Bailey, 15 L To Sarah Laler, dau. of Luke Laler, dec. 15 L To Naomy Rodgers 10 L & to Thomas Hall & Mickal Hall 10 L each. To Hancock Nickless my "Scrutore" I give my planta. to the first son born of Mathew Vandegrught, called & known by the name of Obiddiah Vandegrught, & for want of heirs to my heirs at common law, not excluding John Shephard. Bal. of est. to be div. bet. the first born son of Rebecca Pratt, she is now wife of Wilcock Johnson, called & known by the name of John, and Obiddiah Vandegrught, son of Mathew Vandegrught when they arrive at 18 years of age. Hancock Nickless Exr. Witt: Daniel Rowles, Major Rowles, Thomas Sadler - p. 37

BUGERSBEE, WILLIAM - 23 Apr. 1723 - Proved 3 Nov. & Prob. 7 Dec. 1725 - To wife planta which is within fence for life provided she care for my children, otherwise to have as the law directs. At my wife's death of marriage planta. to be divided between my two children, Jean & George Bugersbe - Bal. of est. to wife to bring up my children. To son William Bugersbe 1 s. & to be at age at my dec. Wife Exec. Witt: John Fittchgrall, Thomas Hickman - p. 45 - Wife Elizabeth.

SIMSON, THOMAS - 6 Jan. 1725/6 - 2 Feb. 1725/6 - To son Thomas Simson 225 A. purchased of Thomas Parker, also 50 A. purchased of Peter Claywell. To son William Simson 200 A. purchased of William Darter, also 50 A. where I now live, also 112 1/2 A. of marsh. To son John Simson 200 A. where I now live, also 112 1/2 A. of marsh. Dau. Sarah Simson. To the poor of the Parish 1000 lbs. of tobacco or 5 L money, 9 children Thomas, Elizabeth, Mary, Margaret, Rachel, William, Patience, John & Sarah resid. legatees. Sons Thomas, William & John Exrs. Witt: John Tankred, John Oakley, Mark Littleton - p. 51

EVANS, JOHN - 29 Oct. 1725 - 1 Mar. 1725/6 - Planta. in Maryland adj. the planta. of Peter Wattson cont. 150 A. to my wife Mary for life & then to my sons John, Arthur, Levin & Jobe Evans when they arrive at 18 to choose 2 honest men to sell the said land & div. the proceeds between them. Personal est. to wife during her wid. & at her marriage to be div. bet. my children, John, Arthur, Leaven, Job, Elizabeth & Mary Evans & William Shipman. Wife Mary Exec. Witt: James Wishart, Comfort Ewell, Hannah Wishart – p. 56

WATTS, CAPT. JOHN – 2 Jan. 1724/5 – 5 Apr. 1726 – To son John Watts. To son William Watts my island called Wolfes Denn Island at Mattoponey in Somerset County, cont. 90 A., also my Island called Temp Island at Mattopony in Somerset County, Maryland, cont. 725 A. To dau. Easter Watts my two tracts of land called Smithfield & Farloworth cont. 367 A. in the County of Somerset. To dau. Sarah Finney. To dau. Mary Selby. To dau. Jannat Narn. To son John Kendall negroes for life reversion to Lemuel Kendall, heir of Tabitha Kendall as is recited on the back of a bill of sale endorsed by me to the said Kendall being in his possession. To grandson Lamuel Kendall negro to be delivered to him at 18. To son William negro & liberty to get timber on my land at Mattapony called Wattses Conveniency for the building of houses on Temp Island. To dau. Elizabeth Colliar. Beds & furniture to be div. bet. wife & 6 children, Sarah Finne, John Watts, William Watts, Mary Selby, Jannet Nairn, Ester Watts. To wife Priscilla 1/3 of all my lands & 1/3 of personal est. not disposed of & the other 2/3 to be div. bet. my above named children. Wife Exec. Richard Kitson & Mr. William Tazewell overseers. Witt: Solomon Ewell, Comfort Ewell, Sarah Wallop, Charles Littleton, John Wallop. Codicl dated 9 Dec. 1725 – I app. my friend Richard Kitson & my son in law John Kendall assistant Exrs. until my son John arrive at 20 years. – p. 58

BROADWATER, WILLIAM – 9 Mar. 1725 – 3 May 1726 – To eldest son William Broadwater 125 A. at the head of my whole divident of 500 A. at the head of Ewamus branch. To son Jacob Broadwater 125 A. of said tract. To son Elias Broadwater 125 A. on Crooked Creek Branch. To son Joshua Broadwater 125 A. at the head of my 500 A. in Jollys Neck on Crooked Branch. To son Caleb Broadwater 200 A. "being near ye farerest of Nanticooke River in Maryland" near the head of said River, same land purchased of Thomas Gordon & is called Gordon's Lot in Deep Creek. This being all my land & my youngest son James Broadwater is left without any land, if any of his bros. should die without issue their land to descend to the said James. To dau. Leshia 1 ewe, & what things I lent her husband Turlo Hobryant I give to her children. Wife's clothing to be div. bet. 3 daus. Elizabeth Ellis, Lishia Hobryant & Mary Ellis. Son in law Thomas Ellis. Children resid. legatees. Friends William Beavans & Hancock Custis to make division. Six sons William, Caleb, Elias, Joshua, Jacob & James Exrs. Witt: Joseph Feddaman, John Aleworth, Charles Taylor, John Jenkinson – p. 66

WILLIT, ANN – Nunc. – 28 Nov. 1725 – 4 May 1726 – To grandson William Willett. Grandau. Comfort Conner. Bal. of est. to be div. bet. 3 daus. (no names) Proved by Jacob Litchfield & John Melson – p. 69

COPES, MARY – 10 Feb. 1723/4 – 4 Oct. 1726 – To son Abraham Outten all the money I am now possessed with & all the money due me abroad. Children Abraham & Hester Outten resid. legatees & Exrs. Grandau. Mary Truitt. Grandson John Outten, son of my son Thomas Outten. Witt: Andrew Allen, Matilda West, Elizabeth Smallsbe, William Selby, Sabrow Outten – p. 97

CLARK, JAMES – 24 Jan. 1722/3 – 4 Oct. 1726 – To wife Bridget personalty for life & then to son David Clark. Son James. Dau. Isabel. Son George. Dau. Sarah. To my wife's children Lewezer, Philip & Ann Mew. To sons John & Major 1 s. each. Wife & 5 children James, Isabel. George, David & Sarah resid. legatees. Friends Hancock Custis & Robert Corbin Exrs. Witt: William Burton, Thomas Jenkinson, Daniel Rowles – p. 97

CUSTIS, COL. WILLIAM – 27 Nov. 1725 – 1 Nov. 1726 – To wife Bridget 200 A. where Churchill Darby now lives & whole personal est. except what I have already given my dau. Bridget Custis; also 1/3 of all my lands & Islands besides the above 200 A., for her life. To dau. Bridget Custis & heirs, except what is above named, all my lands, Islands, marshes &c. but should she die without heirs then to my grandau. Joanna Custis Hope, & for want of heirs to my wife Bridget Custis & heirs. To grandau. Joanna Custis Hope when she arrives to 18 years or marriage, provided my wife Bridget should die without disposing of them, 2 of the slaves given my wife, viz: Joe & Daniel, also the 200 A. devised my wife, provided she die without disposing of it, but should the said Joanna Custis Hope die without heirs, then I give the two slaves & the 200 A. to my dau. Bridget. To grandau. Joanna Custis Hope slaves' increase that I lent to my dau. Joanna Mary Hope, & should she die without heirs to my dau. Bridget. Wife & dau. Bridget Exrs. Witt: Robert Coleburn, William Burton, Charles McClester, William Wood. – p. 107

SELMAN, HENRY – 6 Dec. 1725 – 7 Dec. 1726 – To dau. Mary 1 s. To Harburt Rapwell & heirs the use of my whole estate, real & personal, forever, provided he or they send a letter on board some ship bound for London directed to Francis Selman or his heirs at Old Ford 2 miles from Long Acre in London, giving the said Selman an account of this my will, and if the said Francis Selman or any of his children, or their heirs, shall come & defend the est. above mentioned, that then the said Selman or his heirs, or any claiming under them, shall possess & enjoy the est. real & personal – If they do not come & defend the est. Harburt Rapwell & his heirs to possess & enjoy the same forever, provided the said Harburt Rapwell find me a sufficient maintenance during my natural life – John Watts, Ship Carpenter & Hancock Nicless Trustees. Witt: Daniel Rowles, Edward Martin, Nickles Done, Hanneane Seasbrigs – p. 114

BLAKE, JOHN – 8 Aug. 1721 – 7 Dec. 1726 – To adopted grandson John Blake, son of Charles Blake, alias Price, dec., 200 A. adj. a tract of land formerly belonging to Capt. John Wallop, now in the possession of Mr. John Kendall, with all the appurtenances belonging & appertaining "to the said 200 acres I to ye sd. John Blake, son of Mary ye daughter of Charles Ratcklif of Somerset County in Maryland, to him the said John & the heirs of his body lawfully begotten forever" & for want of heirs to my grandau. Sarah Willson. To my adopted grandson 100 A. on Gingoteage Island. Should the said John Blake attempt to sell or mortgage any of the said 300 A., then it shall revert to my grandson John Turvil of Somerset County. To dau. Rebecca Willson 150 A. adj. Capt. Watts. To dau. Arcadia Turvil. To grandau Rachel Scott. Adopted grandson resid. legatee, he to be at age at 18. Thomas Robins & John Turvill of Somerset County Exrs. Witt: Thomas Perry, Samuel Taylor, Charles Taylor, John Taylor. - p. 115

NOCK, WILLIAM - 4 Sept. 1724 - 8 Feb. 1726 - To son William 400 A. where he now lives on the seaside, also 200 A. of land & marsh on the Bayside between Gilford & Messongo Creeks provided he neither sell nor rent same without the consent of his bro. Benjamin Nock that is to have the other 200 A. of land & marsh belonging to that tract. To son John Nock 250 A. where he now lives. To son Benjamin Nock planta cont. 400 A. where I now live & 150 A. adjoining, also the other 200 A. of land & marsh between Gilford & Messongo Creeks. To dau. Ann Nock. To son Thomas Nock. To grandson William Nock, son of William Nock. to 4 daus. Patience, Ami, Temperance & Ann 20 L to be div. bet. them. Grandson John Nock, son of John Nock. Sons William & Benjamin Exrs. Est. not to be appraised - Witt: W. Bagg, Jacob Chance, Jacob Lurton - p. 119

RIGGS, ABRAHAM - 5 Oct. 1726 - 7 Mar. 1726/7 - To son Joseph Riggs planta. where I now live with all the land from the hogg penns against Baly Hinman's to the end of the burnt Ridge "where William Gott a Keele for a Sloop" To son Joshua Riggs all the rest of my high land next to the schoolhouse branch. The rest of my land being swamp I give to my two sons to get timber. To wife personal est. during her wid. then to be div. bet. my children. Son Moses. Wife Rosanna Exec. Witt: John Johnson, Eborn Bird, Thomas Dove - p. 127

MILBY, PETER - 5 July 1726 - 7 Mar. 1726/7 - Wife Mary Exec. to have use of planta. until my son Nathaniel comes to age of 21 & then to have her thirds. Son Nathaniel to receive that part of the est. that his grandfather left him in his will when he receives the est. I give him. To son Peter Milby 1 A. & for want of heirs to his two youngest sisters then alive. Should wife marry son Peter to be at age at 18 & to receive the est. left him by me, his father, & by his grandfather. Bal of est. to be div. bet. wife & daus. & youngest son; daus. Rosanna, Elizabeth, Sabra, Lukecreshe & son Peter & dau. Agnes not to receive their estates until they are 18. Should wife die before children come to age, Francis Roberts to take my son Nathaniel & youngest dau. Agnes until they come to 18. John Fosque to take my son Peter & dau. Lukcresha & their estates until they come to 18. Witt: John

Robertson: John Smith, Arthur Downing. - p. 128

SNEAD, CHARLES - 13 Apr, 1727 - 6 June 1727 - To son John Planta. on Checonessex bought of Maj. John Custis. To son Smith Snead planta. at Merry Branch. Wife Catherine & 2 sons above named resid, legatees. Should my sons die without issue I give to my bro, John Snead planta. where I now live. Wife Exec., and in case of her death I app. Capt. Richard Drummond & William Wood to demand & receive what debts are due me in favor of my children. Witt: Jonathan West, George Parker, Mary Snead - p. 133

EWELL MARK - Not dated - 6 June 1727 - To son James planta. where I now live & marsh thereto belonging cont. 400 A. To son Mark 400 A. adj. the land beq. James. To son George Hope Ewell the remainder of the land where I now live. To sons Mark & George Hope Ewell my Island known by the name of "Shoaris" Island, cont. 200 A. Daus. Ann, Elizabeth & Sarah. Bal. of est. to my wife during her wid. and at her marriage to be div. bet. wife & children. Wife (no name) Exec. Witt: R: Drummond, Solomon Ewell, Elizabeth Lewis. - p. 134

SAVAGE, WILLIAM - 4 Jan. 1725/6 - 6 June 1727 - To son Parker Savage my house & planta. & 100 A. belonging with it. To dau. Abigail Savage. To son William Savage. Dau. Mary Savage. Wife Feby Savage resid. legatee & Exec. Witt: Benjamin Watson, West Kellam, John Warrington - p. 135

STAKES, HENRY - 11 Mar. 1726/7 - 6 June 1727 - To son Jacob planta. where I now live with 158 A. & in case of death without issue to the heirs of my son William Stakes. To dau. Mary Stakes. To son Samuel Stakes. Son Simon Stakes. To Sarah Layler. To 3 grandchildren of my son Henry Stakes. To grandson William Stakes. To grandson Major Davis. To all the rest of my grandchildren not named herein. Five children William Stakes, Sarah Layler, Margaret Heath, Simon Stakes & Ann Davis resid. legatees. Son William Stakes Exr. Witt: W. Lurton, Thomas Lurton, Jacob Lurton - p. 136

LISNEY, RALPH - 4 Feb. 1725/6 - 4 July 1727 - To dau. Jane Fogg. To grandau Cannedy Fogg. To dau. Mary Lisney planta. where I now live after her mother's dec. & for want of heirs to my dau. Jane Fogg. To John Tempellen. Wife (no name) resid. legatee & Exec. Witt: Anderson Patterson, Atkins Massey, William Beavans. p. 138

BEECH, BENJAMIN - 20 Feb. 1726/7 - 4 July 1727 - To son Benjamin planta. where I now live cont. 150 A. Son Thomas. Son Luke. Wife Hannah resid. legatee, she to have use of my planta. during her wid. Wife Exec. Witt: Jacob Chance, Revell Wharton, Robert Coleburne. p. 139

CUSTIS, BRIDGET, Jr. - 26 Apr. 1727 - 4 July 1727 - To mother Bridget Custis, Sr. all my personal est. & app. her my Exec. Witt: George Drewe, Ralph Rutherford, Mary Drummond, Criffith Bowen - p.

WEST, JONATHAN - 3 May 1727 - 4 Oct. 1727 - To wife Rachel West land & marsh called Pumeno Island cont. 500 A. taken up by Col. Tully Robinson & myself in 1705, also a small parcel of land cont. 50 A. called the prizeing House on Chiconesick Creek. Wife resid. legatee & Exec. - Witt: John Watts, John West, Job Kincaid, John Hanniford - p. 158

BRITTINGHAM, SAMUEL - ___ Mar. 1727 - 4 Oct. 1727 - To be buried in my own orchard near my late wife Elizabeth. To eld. son John planta. in Somerset County, Maryland where he now lives called Capt. Thomas, cont. 200 A. for life, reversion to my grandson Jedediah Brittingham, son of the said John. To 2nd son Samuel Planta. near Robert Mills, being part of a tract called Cowley at Winter Quarter Branch. To 4th son Micajah Brittingham the remaining part of my land called Cowley with 50 A. adj. to it called Paggetts Old fields. To 3rd son Elijah Brittingham planta. where I now live in Virginia adj. my bro. Nathaniel Brittingham & a parcel of land adj. to it called Line Lott in Somerset County. My dwelling planta. as given above to be for the use of Sarah Brittingham during her wid. & if she marry, provided she & her husband bring up my 4 youngest children, Elijah, Micajah, Sarah & Earlie, they to enjoy the said planta. until my son Elijah comes to age. To dau. Margaret. To dau. Sarah. To youngest dau. called Early. To dau. Betty, now wife of John Powell. Son John Exr. Bro. Nathaniel overseer. Witt: Nathaniel Brittingham, Peter Dickeson, Jr., Thomas Layfield - p. 160

WEST, ALEXANDER - 30 Nov. 1727 - 3 Jan. 1727/8 - To wife Mary negro Jack for life reversion to her dau. Anne Hurtley & for want of heirs to my son Scarburgh West. To dau. Mary West. To son John West. To grandson Alexander West. To grandson John West. Wife to have the orphan boy Thomas Harris that lives with me till he is at age. To wife Mary 100 A. at Mattompkin for life, reversion to her dau. Anne Hurtley, & for want of heirs to my grandson Alexander West. Wife & son John Exrs. Witt: John Custis, Mary Snead, William Tilney - p. 184

TALER, EDWARD, Cordwinder - 30 May 1727 - 5 Mar. 1727/8 - To wife Sarah 1/2 the planta where I now dwell & 1/2 the 100 A. left me by my father Thomas Taler during her wid. & then to return to my youngest dau. Sarah. To dau. Mary Taler 100 A. on the North-east side of Dry Branch left by my father to my bro. Thomas. To dau. Sarah the other 1/2 of my planta. where I now live, also the 100 A. where I live at the marriage of my wife. Should my dau. Mary die without issue her land to fall to my dau. Sarah, & if Sarah die without issue the land to fall to my eld. dau. Elizabeth Hedge. Wife & daus. Elizabeth & Roseana resid. legatees. Dau. Roseana to live with Alexander Harrison & Susanna, his wife, they to have charge of her est. To godson John Harrison. To son in law John Harrison. Wife Exer. Witt: Delight Shield, Stratton Burton, John Wharton - p. 187

BIRD, JOHN - 26 Jan. 1727/8 - 5 Mar. 1727/8 - To son Nathaniel Bird land where he now lives. To son Solomon Bird all the remainder of my land & marsh, & for want of issue to my son Major Bird. 4 sons Eborn, Daniel, Major & Solomon Bird resid. legatees. Son Nathaniel Exr. (Major under 18) Witt: John Johnson, John Wimberry, Samuel Johnson - p. 188

PARKER, HENRY - 15 Feb. 1727/8 - 5 Mar. 1727/8 - To bro. George Parker. To bro. Charles Parker. Bro. Charles resid. legatee & Exr. Witt: John McClester, Isaack Rodgers, Elizabeth Rodgers. - p. 188

STEWARD, DANIEL - 4 Jan. 1727/8 - 5 Mar. 1727/8 - To son Daniel all my land & for want of heirs 125 A. to my youngest dau. Martha Steward and the other 125 A. to my dau. Tabitha Steward. Dau. Elizabeth Steward. To godson John Edome. To Joseph Stoakly, son of Joseph Stoakly. Bal. of est. to daus. Martha & Tabitha when they come to 18 years. Son Daniel to be at age at 18. I leave my two daus. to Alexander Daniell & if he will not take them to John Edome & if neither will take them Joseph Stoakly to do what he will with them. Bro. in law Joseph Stoakly Exr. Witt: Samuel Owen, William Taylor, John Edome - p. 189

SALTER, SILVESTER - 20 Feb. 1727/8 - 5 Mar. 1727/8 - To Wife Ann whole est. during her wid. & then to be div. bet. my wife & 2 children Nannie & Mary. Wife Exec. - Witt: Ralph Gorbin, Elizabeth Boggs. - p. 193

TAYLOR, Samuel - 30 Mar. 1727 - 6 Mar. 1727/8 - To son Samuel my land & water mill. Bal. of est. to be div. bet. wife Sarah, son Samuel & dau. Mary, the wife of Samuel Owen. Son Samuel & Bro. Charles Taylor, Mr. John Kendall & Col. Solomon Ewell Exrs. Witt: George Douglas, Samuel Welburne, Prisila Watts, John Watts, Scarburgh Tunnel - p. 195

CRIPPEN, THOMAS - 27 Dec. 1727 - 5 Mar. 1727/8 - (Son of Thomas Crippen the elder) To wife Elizabeth. Son William Crippen. Son Robert Crippen. Dau. Catharine Crippen. Dau. Elizabeth. Son George. Sons John & Thomas. To father Thomas Crippen. Wife Exec. John Kitson & Uncle Henry Bagwell overseers. Witt: Richard Kitson, Isaac Dix. - p. 197

WATTSON, DANIEL - 23 Apr. 1728 - 7 May 1728 - To son Daniel planta. where I now live. I give my son Daniel to Joseph Custis until he comes to 20 years to learn him a trade. To Amey Kellam. To dau. Ann Wattson. To dau. Susanna Wattson. Friend Joseph Custis Exr. Witt: Thomas Stringer, David Watson - p. 205

NICHOLSON, WILLIAM - 10 Feb. 1725/6 - 7 May 1728 - To wife Mary whole personal est. during her wid. & then to be div. bet. my

wife & 2 sons in law Robert & Isaac Baly. Wife Exec. Witt: Richard
Kittson, John Kittson - p. 208

EWELL, GEORGE - 24 Apr. 1728 - 7 May 1728 - To sister Ann
Glading 1/2 my planta. on Hunting Creek where I now live for life &
the use of the other 1/2 to my cousin Tabitha Gray for life & then I
beq. the whole to Thomas Tatham whom I now keep at school to
William Willson. To sister Comfort Tatham, To cousin Comfort
Young, she to pay my cousin Sarah Tatham 10 L- To sister in law
Comfort Ewell (meaning the widow Ewell). To bro. Solomon Ewell.
To cousin Jane Barincastle. To kinsman Thomas A'Rew. To Matilda
Lewis. To Ann Lewis, the first born of Matilda Lewis. To the wife of
my bro. Solomon. To cousin Naomi Ewell. To Margaret Peal. To
cousin George Glading. Bro. Solomon Ewell, sister Ann Glading &
cousin Tabitha Gray Exrs. Witt: Southey Rew, Baly Hinman, Sarah
Gibbens. - p. 210

BLAKE, DIANER - 5 Nov. 1727 - 7 May 1728 - To dau. Abigail
Taylor. To daus. Elizabeth & Dianer Coley bal. of est. Should both
die without issue to dau. Rosaner Baly. William Mathews & William
Welten Exrs. Witt: John Mathew, Thomas Bonewell, Solomon Cary. -
p. 211

SANDERS, MARY - 25 Apr. 1728 - 8 May 1728 - To bro. William
Sanders. To bro. John Sanders. To Clery Skersburgh. To Hanna Dun.
To Margaret Daves. To Mary Williams. To Elizabeth Polson. To
Franciner Hack. To Sarah Gibson. To sister Olinda Sanders. To
sister Sarah Scot. To Tabitha Maiden. To Elizabeth Chisly. To
Walter Annyhom. To Ann Allen. Walter Anningham Exr. Witt:
Charles Campbell, William Dunlop - p. 212

WELBURNE, Samuel - 12 Dec. 1727 - 8 May 1728.- James Watts
children Nehemyah, Adam & William to be paid their estates due
them by their father's will. To son Daniel Welburne. Hill Drummond
to be paid 4000 lbs. of tobacco for 200 A. of Assateag Island Beach in
Somerset County, Maryland, provided the said Drummond makes over
the said 200 A. to my son Daniel. To dau. Mason Welburne. To wife
Sarah Welburne. To Nehemyah & Adam Watts. To 2 daus. Ann &
Mason clothing that was my former wife Mason's. Wife & 4 children
Daniel, Ann, Mason & Elizabeth resid. legatees. Wife Exec. Bro.
Daniel Welburne Exr. Witt: Solomon Ewell, Nehemiah Watt, Charles
Taylor, Elizabeth Taylor. - p. 213

BAYLY, RICHARD - 19 Apr. 1726 - 4 June 1728 - To grandson Henry
Bayly, son of Richard & Rosana Bayly, dec., 250 A. on the North side
of Craduck Creek & for want of heirs to grandson Southy Bayly. To
grandson Richard Bayly the rest of my land on Craduck Creek. To
grandson Whittington Bayly. To grandson Edmund Bayly a silver
dram cup marked R:B. To grandson William Bayly 100 A. near
Matomkin. To Scarburgh West 3 A. on small bear branch adj. the land
of the said West. To wife Elizabeth 1/3 of my planta. during her wid.

Bal. of est. to be div. in 6 parts between wife Elizabeth, Richard
Bayly, Henry Bayly, Whittington Bayly, Lacy Harman, Henry Bayly,
the son of Richard & Rosanna. Grandson Richard Bayly, Henry Bayly
& William Harman Exrs. Witt: Mitcheall Scarburgh, William Smith,
Rosanna Bayly - p. 217

FITCHETT, WEATHERINGTON - 4 Nov. 1727 - 4 June 1728 - To son
John Fitchett all my land after the death of my wife & privilege for my
3 daus. to live & use the same until marriage. Dau. Rachel. Bal. of
est. to wife during her wid. then to be div. bet. my children & wife.
Wife Exec. Witt: John Johnson, Baly Hinman, Dennis Kelly - p. 218

MICHAELL, SIMON, 12 Jan. 1727/8 - 4 June 1728 - To son John
Michaell planta. where I now live with 350 A., also 148 A. purchased
of Capt. Richard Drummond. To son Joachim Michaell planta. on the
seaside with 300 A. when he is 18 years of age. To wife Susanne land
where I live for life. To dau. Sarah Milbourn. To dau. Ann Michaell.
To dau. Mary Michaell. Wife & children resid. legatees. Wife Exec.
Witt: John Johnson, John Aleworth, Samuel Cowly - p. 219

DRUMMOND, HILL - 22 Mar. 1723/4 - 4 June 1728 - To wife Sabra
planta. where I now live, being 300 A. & my water mill for life & then
to my youngest dau. Sabra, & for want of heirs to my dau. Tabitha
Drummond. To dau. Patience Drummond 200 A. purchased of John
Jenifer Osburne, & for want of heirs to my dau. Elizabeth. All my
other lands in Virginia & Maryland to my 3 daus. Barbara, Elizabeth &
Tabitha. Wife & 5 daus. resid. legatees. Thomas Preson's heirs to
make over & convey the land according to bond to those to whom I
have given it. Wife & Daniel Welburne Exrs. Witt: Charles Taylor,
William Chance, Jr., Cuthbert Russell. Codicil - Dated 28 Oct. 1726
- Bro. in law Henry Bagwell & Capt. Charles Snead to be Exrs. with
Daniel Welburne. Witt: George Douglas. William Chance, Esther
Chance - p. 222

ONIONS, SELBY - 26 Mar. 1728 - 2 July 1728 - To son John Onions
250 A. in Somerset County, Maryland on Indian River between Vinesis
Branch & Blackwater Branch. To son Ears (Eyres) Onions 100 A. in
Accomack County where I now live & bounded according to my father's
will. Eyres under age - To dau. Elizabeth Onions. To wife Ann Mary
Onions, bal. of est. for the support of my children. Wife Exec. Witt:
Thomas Evans, Samuell Onions, Thomas Onions - p. 226

STOKLY, CHRISTOPHER - 12 May, 1728 - 2 July 1728 - To wife
Mary planta. where I now live & personal est. for life, then personal
est. to be div. bet. my 3 children Christopher, Christian & Isabel
Stokly. To son Christopher all my land & for want of heirs to my 2
daus. Christian & Isabel & for want of heirs to Allison Rose. Wife
Mary Exec. Witt: Andrew Allen, Bridgett Allen, John Rose. - p. 227

MILBY, JOHN, Sr. - 20 June 1727 - 3 July 1728 - To wife Mary
planta. where I now live & whole est. for life. To grandson Nathaniel

& his mother Mary Milby. To grandson John Milby. To grandau Tabitha Milby. To grandson Salathiel Milby. To grandson Peter Milby. To son Nathaniel Milby. Wife Mary Exec. John Meers, Sr., William Meers, Sr. & Richard Savatch (Savage), Sr. to divide est. not before devised between my grandchildren Salathiel Milby, Garrison Milby, Patience, Sabra, Tabitha, Mary, Peter, Rosanna, Elizabeth, Lewcreatia & Agness Milby after the death or marriage of my wife. Witt: Andrew Allen, Stephen Waltham, Bridgett Allen. - p. 228

WALTHAM, STEPHEN - 2 May 1728 - 2 July 1728 - To John Heath, als Waltham, son of my wife Elizabeth Waltham, Planta. where I now dwell, cont. 250 A. & for want of heirs to 2 daus. Elizabeth & Bridget Waltham, Elizabeth to have her part the full breadth on Occahannock Creek & Bridgst the planta. where her grandfather now lives, & for want of heirs to my daus. Grace & Hester Waltham, & for want of heirs to Marget Allen, dau. of Andrew & Bridget Allen. To son John Heath, als Waltham "the planta. where his grandfather Heath dwells". Personal est. to 4 daus. Elizabeth, Bridget, Grace & Hester Waltham and their mother Elizabeth Waltham. Wife Elizabeth Exec. Witt: Andrew Allen, Nathaniel Pratt, Christopher Stokely - p. 232

WARRINGTON, JOHN - 18 June 1728 - 6 Aug. 1728 - To sons Stephen & John Warrington planta. where my father Stephen Warrington lived, being 200 A. at the head of Anancock Creek, adj. where I now live, that I bought of Charles Leatherbury. To son Jonathan planta. where I now live, cont. 100 A. & for want of heirs to son James Warrington. To son Thomas Warrington. To dau. Ann Warrington. To wife whole est. during her wid. Personal est. to my 7 children by my wife Sarah, James, Margaret, Rachel, Sarah, William, Benjamin & Jacob Warrington. Wife Sarah & son Jonathan Exrs. Witt: John Lurton, Sacker Parker, John Nelson - p. 238

ROBINS, EDWARD - 13 Feb. 1720/21 - 6 Aug. 1728 - Wife Elizabeth 1/2 the benefit of a parcel of land & marsh adj. my dwelling planta called Little Pasture, also 1/2 my dwelling planta. for life. To dau. Barbara cattle her grandfather John Robins gave her. To son John all my land in Virginia or Maryland that was given me by my father John Robins & Mr. Bowman Littleton, part being my dwelling planta. & for want of heirs to my 3 daus. Barbara, Easter Littleton Robins & Elizabeth Robins. Should all my daus. die without issue I give 1/2 the land to my nephew Bodon Robins, son of Thomas Robins & the other 1/2 to my nephew Edward Robins, son of John Robins. To 3 daus. Barbara, Easter Littleton & Elizabeth all my land & marsh on Gingoteague Island & all creatures according to my father's will. Wife & 4 children resid. legatees - Wife Elizabeth & son John Exrs. Witt: Dan: Welburne, William Cord, William Porter, Giles Jones - p. 239

BRITTINGHAM, JOHN, Sr. - 22 June 1728 - 6 Aug. 1728 - To eldest son William Brittingham that part of my dwelling planta. lying in Virginia, also 100 A. in Maryland adj. the Virginia-Maryland line after my wife's dec. To second son John Brittingham 250 A. in Maryland, being the remaining part of my land in Md. after my wife's dec. To youngest son Samuel Brittingham after the dec. of his mother, Christian Brittingham. Son Thomas Brittingham. Dau. Christian Brittingham. To son Nathaniel Brittingham. Dau. Elizabeth Brittingham. Bal. of est. to wife for life then to be div. bet. my children. Wife Christian & son William Exrs. Witt: Philip Quinton, James Houston. Thomas Layfield. - p. 250

CHANDLER, JOHN - 1 June 1728 - 3 Sept. 1728 - To wife whole est. until this present crop is finished, then 1/3 to my wife & the bal. to be div. bet. my children (no names) Wife Exec. Witt: John Metcalfe, Jacob Leare - p. 254 Presented by Joanna Chandler, Exec., who qualified.

NIBLET, BURNAL - Not dated - 3 Sept. 1728 - To 2 sons Richard & Burnal Niblet land adj. the Beaver dam Branch, being 200 A. To son William Niblet my other land. To my now wife Margaret. To dau. Rosana Niblet. To dau. Barbara Niblet. Son Richard Exr. Witt: Philip Parker, Henry Clarke. William Jacob. - p. 255

TOWNSEND, THOMAS - 4 July 1728 - 3 Sept. 1728 - To son John planta. where I now live cont. 200 A. He to make over to his bro. Stephen 200 A. beq. his, the said John, by his bro. Thomas sometime before the said John arrives to the age of 23 years., should he refuse Stephen to have my Manner planta. Should Stephen die before John makes over the said planta., then John to make it over to my son William and if he fails to do so my Manner planta. to be William's. Dau. Jane Mercy. Dau. Sarah Townsend. Dau. Catherine Marcy. Dau. Elizabeth Townsend. Bal of est. to 3 sons for their maintenance & when they arrive to lawful age to be div. bet. them. Dau. Sarah & sons John & Stephen Exrs. Witt: Anderson Patterson, William Patterson, Nicholas Milman - p. 255

BURTON, SAMUEL - 29 Mar. 1728 - 3 Dec. 1728 - To wife Procilla. To son John Planta. at Magette Bay in Northampton called Golden Quarter, cont. 534 A. To son Samuel planta. where I now live cont. 216 A. To son Eligals Burton 100 A. in the woods near Gingoteague. Dau. Ann Burton. Dau. Mary Burton. Wife & 4 of my children, Samuel, Eligals, Ann & Mary resid. legatees. Bro. Stratton Burton to have the care of my son John & his est. until he is 21. Wife Exec. Witt: Bennet Scarburgh, John Tankerd, Elizabeth Abbott, Temperance Scarburgh - p 272

GOUTY, JOSEPH - 2 June 1728 - 6 Feb. 1728/9 - To wife Elizabeth. To bro. John Gouty. To dau. Mary (under 16) Bro. John & friend John Tankard Exrs. Witt: Pricilla Burton, Robert Leonard, Elizabeth Tankard - p. 287

SHEPHERD, MORRIS - 6 July 1727 - 4 Feb. 1728 - To wife Edmond Memora 1/2 my land during her wid. then to revert to my son John Shepherd. To son John planta. where I now live on the South side of

Nandua Creek, also 1/2 the mill belonging to me & Robert Andrews, also my part of the sloop. Wife & son John Exrs. Witt: William Fletcher, Brenden Fletcher, Daniell Rogers. - p. 287

PERRY, THOMAS - 26 Jan. 1725/6 - 4 Mar. 1728/9 - To Jeptha Samson alias Perry my adopted son, all my personal est. except my cane which I leave to Samuel Jestor, the father in law of my adopted son Jeptha Perry. Jeptha Perry Exr. Witt: Joseph Stockly, Jr., Edward Bayley, Gabriel Waters - p. 295

CHANDLER, JOHN - 23 Jan. 1728/9 - 4 Mar. 1728/9 - To son Hathen fettaplace Chandler. To son Solomon Chandler. Dau. Bridgett Powell. Dau. Abigail Phillips. Dau. To dau. Charity Arlington. To son in law William Phillips. Son in law John Arlenton Exr. Witt: Isa: Smith, Sarah Smith - p. 296

BONWELL, JOHN - 19 Jan. 1728/9 - 1 Apr. 1729 - To sons John & James Bonwell planta. where I now live cont. 400 A., beginning at the head of a gut called Stevens gut. To son Joachim Mikeall Bonewell 200 A. at the seaside which I had by my wife, it being the land former- ly of John Mekeall. Sons Thomas & Richard Bonewell. Personal est. to wife for life then to my 4 children Thomas, Richard, Ann & Sarah. Wife (no name) & son James Exrs. Witt: John Smith, Daniel Fookes, William Wise, Jr. - p. 318

Orders - 1717-1719

WELBURNE, BENJAMIN - Adm. his est. to his bro. Daniel Welburne - Samuel Welburne sec. 3 Sept. 1717 - p. 1

LEATHERBURY, PERRY - Adm. on his est. to Robert Burton, his father in law, of Sussix County upon Delaware, as greatest creditor, with the consent of Edmund Leatherbury, brother of sd. Perry. Wil- liam Burton & Samuel Welburne sec. - 3 Sept. 1717 - p. 1

ELLIS, HENRY - Adm. his est. to Thomas Custis, Sheriff, he having no kindred known here - 7 Jan. 1717 - p. 8

WALLOP, SKINNER - Adm. his est. to Elizabeth Wallop, wid. of Skinner - Samuel & William Taylor sec. - 2 Apr. 1718 - p. 10

BONIWELL, THOMAS - Adm. his est. to his son George Boniwell - William Taylor & Sebastian Cropper sec. - 2 Apr. 1718 - p. 10

BLAIR, JOHN, Tanner - Adm. his est. with will annexed to Capt. Moses Fenton, he being grandfather of the orphans of said Blair. Thomas Custis sec. - 2 Apr. 1718 - p. 11

WARD, THOMAS - Adm. his est. to William Andrews as marrying Ann, the wid. of said Ward - John Justice & John Rodgers sec. 3 Apr.

BOGGS, WILLIAM – Adm. his est. to his wid., Alice Boggs – Charles Leatherbury & Sacker Parker sec. 11 July 1718 – p. 14

BENSTON, WILLIAM – Adm. his est., with will annexed, to Grace Benston, wid. of sd. William – Marcus Andrews & Robert Benston sec. – 5 Aug. 1718 – p. 16

COE, SARAH – Adm. her est. to her son Berry Coe – Charles Stockly & John Metcalfe sec. – 5 Aug. 1718 – p. 16

NEDAM, MICHAEL – Adm. his est. to Francis Benston, he being the grandfather of the orphans of said Nedam – 7 Oct. 1718 – p. 20

STANTON, JOHN – Adm. with will annexed. to his son Robert Stanton & his son in law (stepson) Charles Leatherbury – John Parker & John Parker sec. – 4 Nov. 1718 – p. 25

STOCKLY, THOMAS, Jr. – Adm. his est. to his father, Thomas Stockly – Francis Benston & John Foster sec. – 5 Nov. 1718 – p. 24

MACKCOME, JAMES – Adm. his est. to his mother, Elizabeth Hinman – 5 Nov. 1718 – p. __

COLE, JOHN, a free Christian Negro man – Adm. his est. to Anthony West as greatest creditor – 3 Feb. 1718/19 – p. 26

DRUMMOND, JAMES – Who 4 years since took a voyage to Jamaica & yt none of his relations can tell what became of him, save one person who went with the said James, and he told the sd. James' friends that he, James Drummond was dead – Adm. on his est. to his bro. Hill Drummond – Capt. Richard Drummond eldest bro. of James, Hill Drummond next eldest. – Charles Leatherbury & Samuel Welburne sec. – 3 Mar. 1718/19 – p. 27

MACCOMES, JAMES – Adm. his est. to Samuel Justis – Marcus Andrews, Mason Abbott sec. 6 May. 1719 – p. 36

KELLAHAWN, WILLIAM – Adm. with will annexed to William Meers, he having no relations in this county. – Edm: Scarburgh & Thomas Stringer sec. – 6 May 1719 – p. 36

WILLIS, JOHN – Adm. his est. to his son, John Willis, eldest son & heir – Sebastian Cropper & Henry Armitrading sec. – 2 June 1719 – p. 37

Orders 1719 – 1724

FLACK, ROBERT – Adm. his est. to his wid., Comfort Flack – 2 Aug.

READ, JOHN - Adm. his est. to John Rodgers as marrying Sarah, the dau. of John Read, & Jonathan Rowles, guardian of Richard Read, son of John Read - Henry Read & Richard Rodgers sec. 4 Oct. 1720 - p. 25

CONER, JAMES - Adm. his est. to his bro. in law Ambrose Willett - Thomas Simson sec. - 7 Feb. 1720 - p. 27

WHITE, SIMCOCK * Adm. his est. to his wid. Mary White - John Justice; Jonas Davis sec. - p. 28

WARRINGTON, ALEXANDER - Adm. his est. to his wid., Anne Warrington - John Nock & Jacob Bishop sec. - 2 May 1721 - p. 29

LEATHERBURY, CHARLES - Adm. his est. with will annexed to his bro., John Leatherbury - John Bagwell & John Metcalfe sec. - 2 May 1721 - p. 30

WHITE, CHARLES - Adm. his est. to his wid. Tabitha White - Richard Grinall & Jos: Hickman sec. - 6 June 1721 - p. 31

COE, BENJAMIN - Adm, his est. to his wid. Mary Coe - Ralph Justis & John Justis sec. - 3 Oct. 1721 - p. 35

MORRIS, ESTHER - Adm. her est. to Elizabeth Morris, oldest child of Esther Morris. William Bevans & John Jenifer Osbourne sec. - 5 Jan. 1721/2 - p. 39

WALTHAM, CHARLTON - Adm. his est. to Stephen Waltham, eld. bro. of the said Charlton. Mitchell Scarburgh & Andrew Steward sec. - p. 41

ONLY, JOHN - Adm. his est. to Jacob Rogers & Micall, his wife, wid. of John Only. William Rogers & William Rogers, Jr. sec. - 3 Apr. 1722 - p. 41

COLE, ROBERT - Adm. his est. to Phillis Cole, wid. of sd. Robert - Henry Satchell & Jonathan Bunting sec. - 3 Apr. 1722 - p. 41

LITCHFIELD, WILLIAM - Adm. his est. to his bro. Joseph Litch-field, he being the next eldest bro., the eldest bro. being summoned & not appearing - Jacob Litchfield & Francis Young sec. - 4 Apr. 1722 - p. 41

TEACKLE, JOHN - Adm. his est. to his wid. Susanna Teackle - Arthur Upshur & Rich: Rogers sec. - 3 July 1722 - p. 44

SLOCOMB, ROBERT - Adm. his est. to his son & heir Thomas Slocomb - Mason Abbott & John Wilkins sec. - 7 Apr. 1724 - p. 77

JUSTICE, ABBOTT - Adm. his est. to his wid. Mary Justice - Bayly Hinman & Mason Abbott sec. - 7 Apr. 1724 - p. 77

Orders - 1724 - 1731

LINGO, NATHANIEL - Adm. his est. to his father, William Lingo - Richard Rogers & John Fitchgarell sec. 1 Sept. 1724 - p. 4

SPIERS, JOHN - Adm. his est. to William Rogers as marrying the wid. of John Spiers. Jacob Rogers & Walter Warrington sec. - 7 Oct. 1724 - p. 4

SCARBURGH, CAPT. CHARLES - Adm. his est. to his son John Scarburgh - Col. Henry Scarburgh & Maj. Edmund Scarburgh sec. - 5 Jan. 1724/5 - p. 10

SCARBURGH, CHARLES, Jr. - Adm. his est. to his next eldest bro., John Scarburgh, with nunc, will annexed - Col. Henry Scarburgh & Maj. Edmund Scarburgh sec. - 8 Jan. 1724/5 - p. 12

GRINALL, RICHARD - Adm. his est. with will annexed to his wid., Mary Grinall - Jacob Litchfield & William Sherwood sec. 3 Feb. 1724/5 - p. 18

NOTTINGHAM, SARAH - Adm. her est. to her bro. Bartholomew Nottingham, being the nearest kin - Henry Read Sec. - 4 May, 1725 - p. 26

KNIGHT, GEORGE . Adm. his est. to his wid., Elizabeth Knight - Richard Kitson sec. 3 Aug. 1725 - p. 34

CHANCE, WILLIAM - Adm. his est. to his son William Chance - Henry Bagwell & Thomas Wise sec. - 5 Feb. 1725/6 - p. 46.

TILLOTT, JAMES - Adm. his est. to John Wise as greatest creditor - George Parker sec. - 5 Apr. 1726 - p. 51

WILLETT, ANN - Adm. her est. to her son Ambrose Willett - John Riley sec. - 4 May 1726 - p. 54

STURGIS, DANIEL - Adm. his est. to his wid. Elizabeth Sturgis - John Barnes & Thomas Simson sec. - 7 June 1726 - p. 56

SELLMAN, HENRY - Adm. his est. with wiil annexed to his son in law Hobert Raphell. resid. legatee - 7 Dec. 1726 - p. 69

HURTLY, WILLIAM - Adm. his est. to his wid. Mary Hurtly - Alexander West & Scarburgh West sec. - 8 Feb. 1726/7 - p. 71

MILLICHOP, JOHN - Adm. his est. to Nicholas Millichop - Solomon Ewell & John Tankred sec. - 6 June 1727 - p. 75

OAKLEY, JOHN - Adm. his est. to John Scarburgh - 6 Oct. 1727 - p. 88

DAVIS, HENRY - Adm. his est. to James Davis - 2 Jan. 1727/8 - p. 92

BROWN, JAMES - Adm. his est. to Joseph Gouty - 5 Mar. 1727/8 - p. 95

SHERWOOD, WILLIAM - Adm. his est. to his wid. Lucretia Sherwood - 5 Mar. 1727/8 p. 95

DAVIS, JAMES - Adm. his est. to Charles Springle - 5 Mar. 1727 - p. 96

MORROUGH, DANIEL - Adm. his est with will annexed to Nicholas Fountain - 5 Mar. 1727 - p. 96

VIRGIN, ANN - Sheriff ordered to sell her est. at outcry for the use of her children - 5 Mar. 1727 - p. 97

SIMPSON, THOMAS - Adm his est. to Rhody Simpson - 6 Mar. 1727 - p. 98

SILL, WILLIAM - Adm. his est. to his wid. Esther Sill - 6 Aug. 1728 - p. 116

GRAY, THOMAS - Adm. his est. to his wid. Tabitha Gray - 7 Aug. 1728 - p. 116

TAYLOR, JAMES - Adm. his est. to William Rogers - 7 Aug. 1728 - p. 117

DANIEL, ALEXANDER - Adm. his est. to Jane Daniel - 1 Apr. 1729 - p. 149

DRUMMOND, DRAKE - Adm. his est. to Pricilla Watts - 2 Sept. 1729 - p. 167

WAIR, JOHN - Adm. his est. to Thomas Blair - 3 Dec. 1729 - p. 173

OWEN, MARY - Adm. her est. to Nicholas Milman - 6 Jan. 1729 - p. 177

BAGWELL, JOHN - Adm. his est. to his wid. Keziah Bagwell - 7 Jan. 1729 - p. 177

LURTON, WILLIAM - Adm. his est. to Tabitha Lurton - 3 Mar. 1729 - p. 178

RICHARDSON, CHARLES - Adm. his est. to his wid. Elizabeth Richardson - 3 Nov. 1730 p. 214

BAKER, JOHN - Adm. his est. to William Baker - 2 Dec. 1730 - p. 218

WATTS, JOHN - Adm. his est. to Parker Selby - 6 Apr. 1731 - p. 233

Deeds & Wills - 1729 - 1737

CUSTIS, HANCOCK - 30 Aug. 1725 - 7 May 1728 - To son John Custis planta. at Hungars in Northampton cont. 1840 A., and all the other lands my father John Custis beq. me. To son Southy Custis all that part of my now dwelling planta. in Jolleys Neck on this side of Crooked Creek, together with an Island called Cobham Island, cont. 100 A. Bro. Henry Custis. To son Levin Custis the remainder of my land in Jollys Neck beq. me by my father, the whole cont. 1200 A. To son Theophilus Custis all my land at Kings Creek in Northampton County which my uncle Adam Michael beq. to me. To sons Southy & Levin 300 A. at or near Oak Hall which my father gave me. To son Theophilus all land & swamp at or near Mosohgo Creek in Accomack County which I bought of Darby McCarty cont. 133 1/3 A. To son Levin silver tankard marked "M.L.", silver spoons marked "M.L." To son Theophilus small silver tankard marked "S.B." Sons John, Southy, Levin & Theophilus resid. legatees. To son & dau. in law Levin & Leah Gale each a ring with this inscription "In remembrance of Hancock Custis and Mary his wife" To Madam Broadhurst a ring with the same inscription. Four sons Exrs., they to consult with my son in law Levin Gale until they arrive to the age of 21 years: Witt: Anne Blair, Thomas Towles, Howell Bootin, Ralph Rutherford.
Codicil: 30 Aug. 1725 - Should my son John die without issue the land beq. him to go to my son Southy; Southy's land to my son Levin; Levin's land to my son Theophilus, and should they all die without issue I give all the negroes I had by my late wife Mary Custis and 1/2 their increase to my dau. in law Leah Gale, and the other 1/2 to be div. bet. my brother's & sister's childred, and the negroes I had by my father & their increase, to my bro. Henry Custis. Should Southy die without issue his land to go to my son Levin & Levin's land to my son Theophilus. Same witnesses.
Another Codicil: 10 Sept. 1725 - Son in law Levin Gale to take under his care Southy, Levin & Theophilus Custis until they arrive to 18 years of age, and to then deliver them their estates. Witt: Susanna Preeson, Ralph Rutherford. Another Codicil: 3 Apr. 1727 - To sons Southy, Levin & Theophilus negroes. To son John negroes. Should

my sons die without issue 1/2 the negroes to my dau. in law Leah Gale & the other 1/2 to the children of my brothers & sisters. The other 1/2 of my negroes left after my dau. in law Leah has her choice to be div. bet. my cousins Susanna Preeson & Hannah Preeson, her sister & Elizabeth Upshire, the dau. of Arthur Upshur & Sarah, his wife. Should my sons die without issue 1/2 my household goods, plate &c. to the children of my son in law Levin Gale & Leah his wife, and the other 1/2 to be divided between Robinson Custis, son of my bro. Henry Custis & Ann, his wife, Littleton Kendall, son of my sister Sorrowful Margaret, and James Hamilton, son to Andrew Hamilton & Ann, his wife. None of my negroes who are husband and wife to be parted. Witt: Howell Bootin, Thomas Cane.
Another Codicil: 17 Aug. 1727 - Should my son John to be advanced in estate by his uncle John at any time to be more worth in land than Hungars Neck, then I give 1/2 my Hungars lands to my son Theophilus & for want of heirs to my son Levin & for want of heirs to my son Southy to div. it bet. any 2 of his children. Should my son John marry near kin, as a first cousin, then I will he shall have no part of my est., only the point of land where the dwelling house is down to the mill - Sons Southy, Levin & Theophilus joint Exrs. Witt: Thomas Blair, Howell Booting, John Jenkins. - p. 5

DARBY, DANIEL - 20 Apr. 1729 - 3 June 1729 - To son Daniel Darby 165 A. where I now live, he paying his bro. Churchell Darby 1500 lbs. of tob. for 1/2 the planta. To son John Darby 125 A., he to pay his bro. Francis 800 lbs. of tobacco for 1/2 the land. To son Francis Darby. To dau. Ann Darby. To dau. Tabitha Darby. To son Churchell Darby. Sons to be at age at 21, or if their mother marry at 18. Bal. of est. to wife Ann for life then to my children. Wife Exec. Witt: Thomas Stringer, John Darby, John Hornby - p. 16

BENSTON, WILLIAM - 22 Mar. 1728/9 - 5 Aug. 1729 - To wife Anabell all my land for life then to my son Nathaniel Benston. Son Jacob. Son Daniel. Dau. Ann. To wife whole est. for life then to be div. bet. my children as she sees fit. Wife Exec. Witt: John Jenifer Osburn, Samuel Gillitt, John Benston - p. 24

FLETCHER, WILLIAM - 19 May 1729 - 5 Aug. 1729 - To wife Sarah Planta. where I now live at the head of Andua Creek for life then to my son Mathew Fletcher. To unborn child. To John Evans. Wife & child or children resid. legatees. Wife Exec. - Witt: John Shepherd, Brandon Fletcher, Dorothy Parker - p. 25

JUSTICE, RALPH - 17 Sept. 1729 - 2 Dec. 1729 - To son Richard my dwelling planta. & 600 A. thereto belonging after the death of his mother, also 200 A. of land & marsh leased of Thomas Hope for the term of the lease. To son Robert 300 A. land & marsh where he now lives during his life reversion to his son Richard. To dau. Elizabeth Johnson. Dau. Sarah Kitson. Grandau. Mary Parramore. Dau Mary Baker. To grandson Richard Bundick. To grandson Abbot Bundick. To grandau. Sarah Justice, dau. of Abbot Justice 280 A. which I bought of Mr. Jenifer. To sons Richard & John 100 A. of swamp. Wife Mary to have use of my planta. during her life. Bal. of est. to be divided in 6 parts & to my children John, Robert, Richard, Elizabeth, Sarah and the children of my dau. Susanna Bundick when they come to age or marry. Wife & son Richard Exrs. Witt: Richard Kitson, Elias Bell, William Dalton - p. 47

LUCAS, WILLIAM - 29 May 1719 - 2 Dec. 1729 - To wife Mary whole est. during her wid. & if she marry personal est. to be div. bet. my 3 daus. Comfort Northam, Rachel Wimbury & Elizabeth Lucas. To son William Lucas 100 A. being 1/2 the planta. where I now live beginning at Mosongo. To son Thomas Lucas the remaining 1/2 of my planta where he now lives cont. 100 A. Witt: William Nock, Jr., Nicholas Millichops, Henry Gibbs. - p. 48

PARKER, DORITHY - 25 Jan. 1729/3O - 4 Mar. 1729/30 - To son in law Sollomon Rogers and his wife 217 A. on Indian River at Rumbly Marsh for life & then to my grandson Mathew Rogers (under 18) To son Phillip Parker. To dau. Winney Rogers. To Mary Budd. Son in law Sollomon Rogers Exr. Witt: Thomas Johnson, George Dewey - p. 58

SAVAGE, ROWLAND - 7 Oct. 1729 - 3 Mar. 1729/30 - To wife Frances Savage land & planta. where I now live cont. 450 A. & all my other est. Wife Exec. Witt: Whitentun Bayly, Joseph Lary, Daniell Rogers. - p. 60

PHILLIPS, WILLIAM, Sr. - 21 Dec. 1729 - 7 Apr. 1730 - To eldest son William Phillips planta. where he now lives cont. 140 A. To my second son John Phillips planta. where I now live with all the lands purchased of Thomas Nickison, also the remainder of the tract I bought of Richard Baily adj. the land of his bro. William cont. 140 A. To grandson Jacob Philllps, son of William Phillips & for want of heirs to Mattathias Phillips. To dau. Mary Turlington 100 A. purchased of Thomas Bagwell. To wife Margaret & son John personal est. Wife & son John Exrs. Witt: Benjamin Nock, Richard Rogers, Jacob Lurton, John Lewis. - p. 67

MAJOR, WILLIAM - 11 Dec. 1729 - 7 Apr. 1730 - To wife Mary Major 1/2 the land & planta. where I now live during her wid. To son Littleton Scarburgh Major all my land. Wife & son Littleton Scarburgh Major resid. legetees & Exrs. Witt: Walter Cunningham, Sabra Milby, Mitchell Scarburgh - p. 68

WEST, JOHN - 28 Jan. 1729/30 - 5 May 1730 - To son Jonathan all my land in Chiconessick & for want of heirs to my wife Ann for life reversion to my bro. Argoll Yardley West, provided he make over his planta. at Pungoteague to Charles West, & if he refuse the whole divident to be div: bet. Charles West & my sister Sarah Smith. Son Jonathan to be put at school at 10 years of age & kept there until he is 15. Wife & son resid. legatees. Should wife die before my son is at lawful age, my bro. Isaac Smith to take care of him & his est. To

Isaac Smith. Wife & bro. Isaac Smith Exrs. Witt: Samuel Spooner, Rachel Spooner, Richard Hope. - p. 78

LONGO, JAMES - 13 Aug. 1729 - 1 Sept. 1730 - To son James Longo planta. where I now live cent. 70 A. To dau. Mary Huton land & planta. where Pratt formerly lived cont. 70 A. To dau. Elizabeth Longo 70 A. known as Fox Ridge. Bal. of est. to wife during her wid. & then to my 3 children James, Mary & Elizabeth - Wife Isabel & daus. Mary & Elizabeth Executrices. Witt: Woodman Hughs, Daniel Rogers, Joseph Hughes - p. 101

SAVAGE, JOHN - 29 Dec. 1728 - 1 Sept. 1730 - To son Charles (under 18) planta. where I now live. To dau. Patience Savage. To dau. Mary Savage. Bal. of est. to wife during her wid. Overseers Francis Savage & John Savage. Should all my children die whole est. to Francis & John Savage & should either of them die without heirs their est. equally to be given to Rowland Savage, son of Robert Savage, & Richard Savage, son of Richard Savage, but if the said Francis Savage should die without heirs then his part to fall to his bro. Richard, and if John should die without heirs his part to be his brother Rowland's. Wife (no name) Exec. Witt: John Foscue, Richard Savage, William Harmon - p. 102

WATTS, PRISCILLA - 7 Nov. 1730 - 5 Jan. 1730/31 - To son William Watts. To dau. Elizabeth, wife of Peter Collier. To grandau. Elizabeth Collier. To dau. Esther Watts. To grandau Mary Collier. To cousin Mary Riley. Son William, dau. Esther and all my grandchildren by my 3 daus. Elizabeth, Mary & Jannet resid. legatees. Son William & son in law Peter Collier Exrs. Witt: George Douglas, Charles Taylor, Thomas Taylor - p. 113

BURTON, WILLIAM - 18 Nov. 1730 - 2 Feb. 1730/31 - To wife Mary. To daus. in law Ann Snead & Catherine Snead. To dau. Agnes & for want of heirs to her children. To son William 250 A. of land & marsh bought of William Clark on Pothook Creek near Lewis Town. To nephew Thomas Burton. To nephews Joshua, Samuel & Joseph. To nephews Caleb & Abner Burton. To grandson John West. To the children of my dau. Agnes already born or to be born. Wife & 2 children resid. legatees. Wife Exec. Witt: Stratton Burton, William Arbuckle - p. 122

KELLAM, RICHARD - 8 Feb. 1730/31 - 6 Apr. 1731 - To dau. Catherine 200 A. adj. my son William's land & for want of heirs to my son William. To dau. Sarah Sill 100 A. at the head of Sarah's Neck adj. John Sill's land. To son Jonathan Kellam. To son Richard. Bal. of est. to wife Frances during her wid., then to be div. bet. 4 of my children, Sarah Sill, William, Jonathan & Catherine. Wife Exec. Witt: Littleton Scarburgh Major, Edward Kellam, Bryant Coneley - p. 133

MATHEWS, WILLIAM - 9 May 1730 - 6 Apr. 1731 - To son John Mathews a parcel of land adj. the nearest branch to Pocomoke Road with 250 A. purchased of Samuel Taylor adj. to it. To son Joseph Mathews 270 A. running from Stockley's head line to the great swamp. To son William Mathews planta. & all the rest of my land I purchased of Richard Lee. To son Thomas Mathews 250 A. purchased of Charles Taylor. To dau. Sarah Mathews. To dau. Jane Stockley. To dau. Elizabeth Tunnell. Wife Rebecca planta. where I live during her wid. Wife Exec. Witt: Caleb Broadwater, Gabriel Waters, Robert Lumbers - p. 134

JACKSON, ELIZABETH - 10 Feb. 1730/31 - 6 Apr. 1731 - To goddau. Hannan Truett. To friend John Tankred. To goddau. Elizabeth Savage, dau. of Griffeth Savage & Patience, his wife. To Tabitha Vos. John Tankred resid. legatee & Exr. Witt: William Wilson, John Tankerd - p. 135

BUNDOCK, RICHARD - 23 May 1731 - 6 July 1731 - To son George Bundock planta. where I now live cont. 200 A. To son Abbot Bundock (under 21) 100 A. in the woods near Gargathy adj. my son Richard's land. To grandson William Bundock Pearson 73 A., being the remainder of the tract of land given my son Abbot on Gargatha Branch. To son Justis Bundook (under 21) 100 A. near Guilford between the land I gave John Onions & Richard Jones' land. Grandson John Onions. To son George Bundock the remainder of my land at tbe head of Guilford. 3 daus. Mary Evans, Tabitha Bundock & Keziah Bundock. Son in law John Onions. To daus. Ann Abbot, Susanna Onions & Mary Evans. Son George resid. legatee & Exr. Witt: Thomas Evans, William Wilson, William Hastings. - p. 153

ROGERS, WILLIAM - 8 Feb. 1723/4 - 3 Aug. 1731 - To 2 youngest sons Samuel & Henry planta. where I now live. To son Edmund Rogers. To son Richard Rogers 100 A. adj. the Dry Swamp. To dau. Bridget. To son William Rogers. To son Isaac Rogers. Children resid. legatees. Dau. Bridget Exec. Bro. Richard Rogers, Capt. John Bagwell & Delight Shield to div. est. Witt: James Reyliee, John Bagwell, Tabitha Bagwell, Richard Rogers - p. 154

WINDOM, GEORGE - 11 Nov. 1730 - 7 Dec. 1731 - To wife Sissoly the use of my whole est. during her life & then to my two children in law, Lawrence Rogers & Tabitha Reide. To son in law Peter Rogers. Wife Exec. Witt: John Rogers, Susana Moor, John Evans, Edmund Scarburgh - p. 183

BLAKE, JOSEPH - 13 Mar. 1730 - 4 Jan. 1731/2 - To son Charles Blake 165 A. where I now live & for want of issue to unborn child & for want of heirs to Rachel Wilson. Jonathan Thornton to have free possession of a parcel of land on Jengoteague Branch where he now lives for 14 years, being 150 A. provided he pay the Quit Rents & plant 150 apple trees, and after the expiration of the sd. 14 years I give the said land to my unborn child & for want of heirs to my bro. in law John

Morris. To bro. Gilbert Morris. Wife Rebecca & bro. Dennis Blake Exrs. Witt: Uriah Collins, William Watts, John Melten - p. 184

ROWLES, MAJOR - 1 Jan. 1731/2 - 7 Mar. 1731/2 - To bro. Jonathan Rowles all the land which my father, John Rowles, gave me at Pungoteague. To bro. Daniel Rowles personal est. Bros. Daniel & Jonathan Exrs. Witt: Jacob Rogers, John West, Hancock Nickless - p. 193

DRUMMOND, RICHARD - 9 June 1730 - 4 Apr. 1732 - To wife Ann Drummond. To son Richard (under 21) planta. where I now live being 600 A., including 1/2 of Half Moon Island. To son Spencer Drummond planta. purchased of Col. Solomon Ewell, being 300 A. To son William Drummond planta. purchased of James Tatham lying on Guilford, being 200 A. To son Georgs Drummond planta. purchased of William Littleton lying on Hunting Creek being 200 A., also my planta. which I bought of my bro. Thomas Wise, lying near the Court House, being 450 A. To dau. Elizabeth Drummond. To dau. Ann Drummond. My Exrs. to have power to sell 1500 A. of the land at Mossongo which I bought of Richard Lee, being in all 2500 A., not to sell the part lying on the Creek, but to dispose of the back part, & the remaining 1000 A. I give to my 2 sons Spencer & William. Wife & 6 children resid. legatees. Mother Ann Drummond to have her choice of a room in my house, a negro woman to wait on her & maintenance suitable for her during her natural life. Wife, Capt. Hancock Nickless & son Richard Drummond Exrs. (sons under 21) Witt: Samuel Spooner, John Justice, John Snead - p. 197

HEATH, WILLIAM - 19 Feb. 1731/2 - 6 June 1732 - To wife Mary planta. where I now live for life then to my bro. Jacob Heath. To wife whole personal est., reversion to my brothers & sisters, Joseph, Robert & James Heath, Elizabeth Walthum & Mary Budd. Wife Exec. Witt: Andrew Allen, Christopher Stockley, Christian Stockley - p. 201

LEWIS, ELIZABETH - 30 Sept. 1731 - 4 Jan. 1731/2 - To son William Lewis. To daus. Elizabeth & Comfort. To son John Lewis my full right of 70 A. in Somerset County, Maryland, he to dispose of the same, and I give the proceeds to my grandson Josiah Lewis, & for want of heirs to my grandson Rodulphus Scott. To 3 children John Lewis, Elizabeth Scott & Comfort Rew. Son John Exr. Witt: Richard Drummond, Jacob Litchfield, Anne Drummond - p. 209

JENKINSON, THOMAS - 3 Dec. 1731 - 4 Jan. 1731/2 - To son Robert Jenkinson 200 A. where I now live & for want of heirs to my son Custis Jenkinson (under 21) To my 2 youngest daus. To sister Mary Jenkinson. To wife Comfort. Dau. Naomie Jenkinson. To dau. Leah Jenkinson. To sister Frances Jenkinson. Dau. Comfort Jenkinson. Dau. Welthy Jenkinson. Wife Comfort resid. legatee. Wife & Ralph Corbin Exrs. Witt: Uriah Collins, Thomas Lord, Turlough Bryan - p. 210

SALSBERY, JOHN - 5 Feb. 1722 - 1 Aug. 1732 - To wife Sarah whole est. for life & then to be div. bet. my 2 children William & Mary Salsbery - Wife Exec. Witt: John Watts - Daniel Fogg - p. 217

ROBINS, JOHN - 10 June 1732 - 1 Aug. 1732 - To cousin George Harmanson, son of Argill Harmanson, all the land from Oyster Shell Gut to the Maryland line, including that that was Bowman Littleton's in it, also my 1/2 of the Maryland land adj. the planta. of the said George Harmanson. To sister Esther Littleton Robins all my land in Virginia & Maryland not already given. To sister Barbara Harmanson. To Argill Harmanson & his wife Barbara. Bro. Argill Harmanson & sister Esther Littleton Robins resid. legatees & Exrs. Witt: Thomas Robins, William Cord, Bowdoin Robins, Giles Jones - p. 219

JOHNSON, GEORGE - 15 Jan. 1731/2 - 3 Oct. 1732 - To son George land where he now lives. To son Affradosie Johnson planta. where I now live with the remaining part of my land. To sons George & Affradosie my marsh cont. 50 A., the rest of my children to have free privilege in the same until they marry. To daus. Rachel, Susanna & Elliner Johnson. To wife Liddya bal. of est. for life & then to my 6 children, Rachel, Susanna, Samuell, Elliner, William & Shadrack. To grandson Johnson - Wife Exec. - Witt: John Johnson, John Brymer, Elizabeth Johnson - p. 232

ABBOTT, JOHN - Nunc - Declaration made 30 Dec. 1718 - proved Jan. 1718/19 - Prob. & Rec. 3 Oct. 1732 - To goddau. Elizabeth Bundick all that is in the hands of George Bundick. To bro. Mason Abbott. To bro. William. To my mother in law's dau. Mary. To John Tankred. To Elizabeth Jackson. George Bundick & Mason Abbott to bury me. Proved by Rodger Abbott & Thomas Lewis. - p. 240

CUSTIS, JOHN - 7 Jan. 1732/3 - 7 Feb. 1732/3 - Wife Ann. To son Thomas planta. where I now dwell on Deep Creek cont. 1500 A. To son Hancock Custis 700 A. near Burton's Branch near the White Marsh which was given my father by my grandmother Tabitha Hill, also my planta. where Walter Stot lives cont. 250 A. To dau. Betty all her mother's wearing clothes. To dau. Susanna. Plate to be div. bet. my 4 children, Thomas, Betty, Hancock & Susanna. Wife & 4 children resid. legatees. Wife to maintain & educate my children until they are 18, & if she refuse my Exrs. to take them & their estates out of her custody. John Smith, John Jackson, George Douglas & Abel Upshur Exrs. Witt: John Wise, William Clark, James Davis. - p. 260

CUSTIS, HENRY - 11 Oct. 1729 - 6 Mar. 1732 - Wife Ann. Wife to have use of my dwelling planta. during her wid. Eldest son to have liberty to seat himself on that part I bought of William Selby when he comes to age or marries. To sons Henry & Robinson Custis land where I now live cont. 1333 A. To sons Henry, Robinson & Thomas all my land & marshes on Jengoteague Island. To son Thomas 600 A. at Massongoe, also 600 A. near Deep Creek. To daus. Ann, Tabitha & Frances. Children to be at age at 18. Should my wife be with child, said child to have an equal share of my est. with my other children. Wife Ann & son Henry Exrs. To dau. Leah Custis. Dau. Margaret Scarburgh, wife of Henry Scarburgh, Jr. Wife & children resid. legatees. Witt: John Scarburgh, Richard Cooper, Sarah Custis. Codicil: 10 Dec. 1732 - To wife Ann my schooner called Ann for her better support to maintain & educate my children. To dau. Margaret, wife of Henry Scarburgh, Jr. a child's share of my cattle & horses. Witt: William Wood, Samuel Simson, Thomas Simson - p. 262

PARK, MARY, wid. of John Park, dec. - 22 Jan. 1732/3 - 3 Apr. 1733 - Whole est. which did properly belong to my husband to be div. bet. all my children. Bal. of est. which I have got by my care since the death of my husband I give to my 3 children Mary, Sarah & William Park. Mary, Sarah & William Park Exrs. Witt: Joseph Walker, John Johnson - p. 271

DIX, WILLIAM - Nunc - Declaration 4 Feb. 1732/3 - Proved 10 Feb. 1732/3 - Pro. 3 Apr. 1733 - To Mackwilliams Rite 500 lbs. tobacco for the schooling of my godson William Rite, son of Mackwilliams Rite. Sister Mary Rite resid. legatee & Exec. Proved by William White & Ann Mills - p. 272

EDWARDS, EVAN - 23 Jan. 1732/3 - 5 June 1733 - To wife Elizabeth Edwards use of whole est. during her wid., after her marriage to have 1/3. To son John Edwards planta. where I now live with 120 A. of land. Son David Edwards. To dau. Betty Edwards. Son David & dau. Betty resid. legatees. Sons John & David to be at age at 18. Wife Exec. Witt: George Cutler, Jacob Badger, John Badger - p. 278

WELBURNE, DANIEL - 18 May 1733 - 7 Aug. 1733 - To wife Barbara the use of 1/3 of all my lands during her life, then to my eldest son Daniel Welburne the planta. where I now live which was conveyed to me by my mother Arcadia Welburne. To younest son Thomas Welburne. To son Francis Welburne land on Cattail Branch adj. the land devised my son Daniel & the land of the heirs of my dec. bro. Samuel Welburne. To son Thomas Welburne all the residue of my land in Jengoteague Neck. To 3 sons Daniel, Francis & Thomas all my swamp land at the head of Jengoteague Neck. To wife negroes for life & then to my dau. Arcadia, if alive, & if not to her children. To sons Daniel, Francis & Thomas my interest in Hopes Island & my will is that Thomas Stayton & his wife Elizabeth convey the moiety of their interest on Assateague to my said sons pursuant to bond given by the said Stayton for that purpose. Wife to have the custody of my 4 children & their estates. Wife Exec. Friends Col. Solomon Ewell, Capt. James Wishart to assist my wife & children. Witt: George Douglas, Arcadia Cutler, Grace Ramsey, Mary Marshall, Sarah Marshall - p. 299

CUTLER, RICHARD - 17 May 1730 - 6 Nov. 1733 - To sons George & William Cutler planta. where I now live being 300 A. To son Richard Cutler 150 A. in the Forked Neck. To son John Cutler 100 A. pur-

chased of William Lewis, with my lot of land & house in Onancock.
To dau. Mary Roberts. To grandson Snead. To 5 children Mary.
George, Richard, John & William. Sons Richard & John Exrs. Witt:
William Tilney, Daniel Fookes, John Banfield - p. 318

BENSTEN, AMBROSE - 14 May 1733 - 6 Nov. 1733 - To son James
Bensten planta. where I now live with all my land in Virginia or
Maryland thereto adjoining except 1/2 of 130 A. which I give to Jonathan Bensten, and except all such land as is contained in the following
bounds: beginning at a marked white oak standing near the head of the
Branch at the upper end of my planta., thence South to the Swamp by a
line of trees also marked, thence along the swamp to my bro. Alexander's line, thence along my said bro's. line to the Branch, thence down
the said branch to the first mentioned white oak, all of which I give to
my son Ambrose. Wife Rebeccah & daus. Mary, Elizabeth, Sarah &
Tabitha resid. legatees. Son James & bro. in law John Bensten
Exrs. Witt: John Pitts, Nathaniel Bensten, John Pitts, Jr. - p. 319

YOUNG, FRANCIS - 29 Sept. 1733 - 6 Nov. 1733 - Wife to have use
of my dwelling planta. during her wid. To son John Young 50 A.
purchased of Francis Wharton & the orchard that my bro. Samuel
formerly lived on. To wife "and the rest of my children" To sons
Thomas & Ezekiel. Bal. of est. to wife & the rest of my children.
Children under age. Wife Exec. Witt: Henry Hickman, Joseph
Hickman, William Simpson - p. 320

CROSTON, FRANCIS - 6 Sept. 1733 - 5 Mar. 1733 - To William
Warrington & Rachel his wife, whole personal est. To Jane Warrington, dau. of William & Rachel. To the second child of Rachel Warrington the land where I live, being 272 A. if it be a boy, & if not then
to be div. bet. the first two girls after the dec. of the said Warrington
& his wife, & for want of such heirs I give the said land to Steven
Fitzgarell. To Frances, the wife of John Fitzgarell. William Warrington Exr. Witt: Andn? Patterson, William Beavans - p. 336

MARTIAL, JOHN - 9 May 1733 - 5 Mar. 1733/4 - To sons William &
Daniel the land I formerly conveyed them. To son Charles Martial
planta. where I now live adj. the land of his bro. Daniel, cont. 300 A.
To son Peter Martial all the rest of my land to the West of the King's
Road cont. 200 A. To sons Daniel, Peter & Charles my swamp land
cont. 330 A. adj. the head of the land given Peter. To wife Mary
during her wid. 130 A. known as Shingle House adj. Impossible Branch
& then to my son John Martial by my said wife Mary. To William
Martial Richardson son of my wife Mary, 140 A. which I lately took up
in the fork of the Impossible branch. To dau. Elizabeth Dickeson. To
grandson Martiall Townsend, son of my dec. dau. Ann Mary. To daus.
Annabella, Mary & Comfort by my wife Mary. My said 3 daus. & son
John by my wife Mary to be under the tuition of their mother until they
come to lawful age. Wife Mary Exec. Son Peter & kinsman William
Gore Exrs. Witt: George Douglas, William Mersey, Sebastian Delastatius, Jr. Codicil: 17 Dec. 1733 - To wife Mary during her wid.

negroes, then to my son John Martial.   Witt: George Douglas, James Walker, William Chance - p. 337

PARKER, GEORGE - 26 Sept. 1733 - 6 Mar. 1733/4 - To wife 1/2 the planta. where I now live, 1/2 the marsh & all my negroes during her wid. to bring up the children, but should she marry to have 1/3 & the bal. to be div. bet. my children Ann, Sarah, Prissilla, Betty, Levin, John, Charles & Clement.   To son George, after his mother dec. all my lands & marshes where I now live except 400 A. where Mr. Watts now lives at the head of Back Creek, which I give to my son John.   To son Thomas 300 A. on Pocomoke.   To son Levin 140 A.   on Pocomoke.   Wife, son George & Mr. George Dashawle Exrs.   Witt: W: Bagge, John Bayley, William Wise.   - p. 339 Wife "Elizabeth" in ord. of prob.

SCARBURGH, BENNET - 24 Feb. 1733 - 7 May 1734 - To wife Temperance 1/3 the planta. where I now live for life.   All my lands in Somerset County, Maryland, to be held by her & her heirs forever.   To wife all my land at or near White Marsh.   To kinsman Henry Scarburgh, Jr., son of my bro. Col. Henry Scarburgh, all my interest on Tangier Island.   Godson William Gore.   To kinsman Charles Parker. To bro. Col. Henry Scarburgh my lot & interest in Port Scarburghtown in Accomack County.   To my aforesaid kinsman Capt. Henry Scarburgh, son of my bro. Col. Henry Scarburgh.   To kinsman John Bayley. Wife resid. legatee & Exec.   Witt: William Andrews, William Lewis, George Douglas - p. 349

HARMANSON, ARGAIL - 2 June 1732 - 7 May 1734 - To second son Benjamin Harmanson (under 18) all my right of the land on which my father George Harmanson now lives, being 600 A.   To eldest son George Harmanson the fee simple of that 100 A. of land that belonged formerly to Henry Pike and now belongs to Gertrude Harmanson.   To wife Barbara.   Bal. of est. to be div. as my wife pleases for the better bringing up & taking care of my children above mentioned - Wife Exec.   Witt: Alexander Melvin, Sabrath Drummond, Mary Jones, Will: Cord, John Murray. William Chance - p. 350

LAUGHLAN, CORNELIUS - 21 Mar. 1733/4 - 7 May 1734 - To wife Mary planta. where I now live cont. 115 A. for life, she to permit her dau. Rhoda to live in one of the houses on said planta. After the death of my wife, I give the said planta. to the eldest dau. of the said Rhoda, the wife of William Chance, & for want of heirs to Mary Daniel, dau. of William Daniel & Mary his wife.   "the eldest dau. of the said Rhoda who is now unbaptised, and whom I desire may be named Margaret" Wife to have liberty to dispose of any part of my personal est. among her grandchildren by William Daniel's wife or William Chance's wife.   Wife Exec.   Witt: George Douglas, Thomas Collins, William Daniel - p. 350

HOPE, THOMAS - 12 May 1734 - 4 June 1734 - To wife Lydia & my 3 children George, William & Temperance all my personal est.   John

Jackson, Clerk of the Court for this county to have the tuition of my eldest son George & the management of his est. until he arrives at lawful age. Wife Exec. Witt: Benjamin Bull, John Sanders - p. 352

LINSEY, ELIZABETH, Wid. of Hampton Linsey - 7 Apr. 1734 - 4 June 1734 - To son John Linsey planta. where I now live & all my land on the North side of the road that leads from where my barrs now stand unto John Stanton's planta., being part of the land given me by my father John Jenkins, dec., also the piney old field that lies just without my barrs except 50 A. on the North branch which I give to my dau. Elizabeth Guy for life, reversion to my son John Linsey, his sisters Catherine & Margaret to have their living with him until they marry. Son James Linsey to be in the care of his bro. John. To son James all the rest of my land on the South side of the aforesaid road. To daus. Elizabeth Guy, Catherine & Margaret Linsey. William Guy & his wife Elizabeth to live on my son James' plantation until he comes to the age of 21. Son John Exr. Witt: Richard Cutler, John Cutler, Provis Nelson - p. 353

BENSTEN, JAMES - 25 Mar. 1734 - 6 Aug. 1734 - To wife Elizabeth all my lands for life & then to such child or children that she may have by me, & for want of such issue to my bro. in law Ambrose Benstene. Wife resid. legatee & Exec. Witt: George Douglas, Robert Pitts, John Pitts, Jr. - p. 370

MERCY, JOHN - 5 June 1734 - 3 Sept. 1734 - To son William Mercy & to his eldest surviving son the manor planta. where I now live, being 100 A. devised to me by my father, & 10 A. adj. the said land, being part of the land purchased of Joseph Gouty. Wife to have her thirds in the manor planta. or that at the Indian River as she chooses. To son Thomas Mercy the remaining part of the land purchased of Joseph Gouty, being 90 A., reversion to his eldest surviving son. To sons William & Thomas 100 A. lying in the swamp which I purchased of Thomas Layfield, & then to their eldest sons. To sons John & Adkins Mercy planta. on the seaside in Somerset County at the head of the Sound, and at their deaths to their eldest surviving sons. Wife (no name) & 7 children Thomas, John, William, Adkins, Sarah, Mary & Neomy resid. legatees - Son William Exr. Witt: Isaac Wheler, Flowerdue Russel, Thomas Mercy - p. 371

READ, HENRY - 9 Mar. 1724/5 - 3 Sept. 1734 - To dau. Rose Read. To son Richard 74 A. where I now live after the death or marriage of his mother. To sons Richard & Henry my mill, each of them to give my son John 500 pence when he comes to the age of 18 or at their mother's death or marriage. To cousin Richard Read, son of John Read. To son Henry 74 A. beginning in the Mill Branch. Bal. of est. to wife Ann Read & my son John & Susanna & Tabitha & Smithee & Sarah. Wife Exec. provided she be ruled by my friend Jonathan Rowles & her bro. Jonathan Garason in the management of it. Witt: Jonathan Rowles, Henry Perry. Sons to be at age at 18 & the girls at 14 - p. 372

GRIFFIN, ELIZABETH – 5 June 1734 – 3 Sept. 1734 – To my children, viz: Emanuel, Benjamin, Susanna & Elizabeth all the est. that belonged to my husband Luke Griffin, dec., to be div. bet. them according to his will. Dau. Elizabeth to have one years schooling. To dau. Ann Hook 1 s. To grandau Betty Hook. Bros. John & Hilliard Fatherly Exrs. Witt: W: Bagge, Henry Satchel, George Hutten – p. 381

BAGWELL, HENRY – 12 Aug. 1734 – 1 Oct. 1734 – To son Thomas planta. in Northampton in Old Plantation Neck cont. 160 A. To wife Margaret planta. where I now live & my water mill for life. To son Henry all the land in my neck below the land devised my wife, cont. 50 A., and after the death of my wife I give my son Henry my water mill & 150 A. of the land where I now live, also my marsh & Hammocks on the South side of a gut coming out of tbe Bay into France Creek, cont. 100 A. The rest of my marsh, being 125 A. I give to my wife for life, reversion to my grandson Charles Bagwell, son of my son John Bagwell. To grandson Charles the rest of my land at the head of Matompkin not already devised, being 100 A. To dau. Tabitha. To dau. Ann chest that was her grandmother's. To dau. Elizabeth, wife of Isaac Rogers, bed & bolster that was her mother's. Wife, son Thomas & 2 daus. Ann & Tabitha resid. legatees. Witt: James Poolman, John Cole, John Medcalfe – p. 384

EWELL, SOLOMON – 30 Aug. 1734 – 1 Oct. 1734 – To son William Ewell land purchased of Samuel Davis & Naomi, his wife, being 450 A. To son Edward land purchased of Elias Taylor and devised to me in his will, also the water mill purchased of Thomas Blair & Ann his wife. To William Mason 461 A. out of a tract of land purchased of Henry Custis & Ann his wife, Samuel Welburne & Mason his wife, & of John Kendall, according to deed which I have already assigned to him. To wife Comfort use of all the rest of my negroes during her wid. then to be div. bet. my children Naomi, Jedodiah, William, Ann, Mary Ann & Edward. To son Jedodiah my silver hilted sword. My sloop the Comfort & Mary now at sea to be sold for the payment of my debts. Bal. of est. to my wife to whom I devise the tuition of all my daus. Wife, Capt. Hancock Nickless, Mr. George Douglas, Scarburgh Tunnell & James Wishart Exrs., they to have the tuition of my sons to educate them out of the profits of my est. Witt: Samuel Davis, Ralph Corbin, Richard Townsend – p. 386

JOHNSON, JOHN, of Muddy Creek – 14 July 1734 – 1 Oct. 1734 – To son Isaiah Johnson all my land & negroes after the dec. of my wife Elizabeth, & for want of heirs to my dau. Dinah Johnson. To son Samuel Johnson. Dau. Mary Lingo. Dau. Sarah Meers. Wife & 4 children Susanna, Elizabeth, Dinah & Isaiah resid. legatees. Wife Exec. Witt: William Andrews, Ralph Corbin, Nathaniel Bird – p. 386

CRIPPEN, THOMAS – 17 Dec. 1730 – 5 Feb. 1734/5 – To son Paul Crippen 350 A. where I now live beginning at the old house branch &

for want of heirs to my son William Crippen. To grandsons John & Thomas Crippen, sons of Thomas & Elizabeth Crippen, 200 A. on the seaboard side on Ambrocomoco at the mouth of said Creek & so up to the old house branch, John to have the 1/2 where his father Thomas lived, & for want of heirs to my son William. To grandsons Robert, son of Thomas & Elizabeth Crippin, & grandson Bennet, son of Thomas & Elizabeth Bennet the bal. of my land lying on the head line, being 298 A. Robert to have the part adj. my son Paul & Thomas Bennet to have the part lying on the head line. Son Paul to give my grandson Thomas Bennet 2 years schooling. To Margaret Crippen. Son Paul resid. legatee & Exr. Witt: Richard Drummond, William White, John Cooke - p. 411

ARMITRADER, HENRY - 13 Jan. 1734/5 - 6 Mar. 1734/5 - To 2 sons Liddleton & William Armitrader 300 A. purchased of John Morris. To son Henry Armitrader land & planta. purchased of Robert Taylor, also my right & title to the mill dam adj. the land of Jacob Chance. To son Richard Armitrader land & planta. where I now live, also a piece of land adj. Jonathan Garrison cont. 60 A. To son Richard all my land in Northampton. Son John Armitrader. Dau. Roxe Willis. Son Arthur Armitrader. Son Richard resid. legatee & Exr. Witt: Robert Coleburn, William Spiers, Jacob Chance - p. 432

BRITTINGHAM, NATHANIEL, Jr. 13 Jan. 1734/5 - 1 Apr. 1735 - To mother & sister Elizabeth. To bro. Samuel Brittingham. To bro. John Brittingham. To bro. Thomas Brittingham. To bro. William Brittingham. To sister Criston. Mother Exec. Witt: Peter Dickeson, Abigall Quinton, Dixon Quinton - p. 436

THOMSON, JOHN - 9 Dec. 1734 - 6 May 1735 - To dau. Mary. To son John. To son William. Son Robert to pay each of my aforesaid sons 4 L in country pay when they come to lawful age. Bal. of est. to son Robert whom I app. my Exr. Thomas Stayton & Robert Ardies to have the care of my son Robert until he is 21. Witt: George Douglas. John Wallop, Charles Taylor - p. 439

BAGWELL, HENRY - 1 Mar. 1734/5 - 3 June 1735 - To son Heli Bagwell planta. where I now live cont. 50 A. devised me by my father Henry Bagwell, also that part of Marsh & Hammock lying on the South side of a gut running out of the Bay into France Creek, being 100 A. devised me by my said father. To son Spencer Bagwell after the dec. of my mother in law Margaret Bagwell, 150 A. devised my said mother in law for life, the reversion to me, also the water mill beq. me at the death of my mother in law. Wife Sabra resid. legatee, she to have the tuition of my 2 sons until they arrive at lawful age. Wife Exec. Witt: John Allen, Thomas Bagwell, John Snead - p. 442

CUSTIS, LEVIN, of Somerset County, Maryland - 7 Mar. 1733/4 - 3 June 1735 - Whole est. to my sister Leah Gale and her 3 children, Betty, Sarah & Leah Gale. Bro. in law Levin Gale and sister Leah Gale Exrs. Witt: Katherine Ryland, Patrick Stewart, John Williams -

BURTON, THOMAS – 4 May 1735 – 1 July 1735 – To son Joshua land & planta. where I now live being 500 A. & for want of heirs to my son Samuel & for want of heirs to my son Joseph. To son Joshua my part of Cedar Island & for want of male heirs to my son Samuel & for want of male heirs to son Joseph, & for want of male heirs to dau. Patience Armitrader. Bal. of est. to all my children except my dau. Patience, only my wife to have 2 parts with my children. Son Joshua Exr. Witt: Samuel Beech, John Wharton, Robert Coleburn – p. 459

SCARBURGH, HENRY – 31 Aug. 1735 – 4 Nov. 1735 – Dau. Comfort. Dau. Ann. To son Henry the land where I now live. To dau. Sarah land on Pocomoke River in Maryland cont. 300 A. upon condition that Richard Bennet, Esq., according to his promise give my son William the planta. on Nancemond, and should he not do this before he arrive to the age of 21 years I give the said 300 A. to my son William. To dau. Henrietta a little Island called Winter Quarter Island lying at the mouth of Pungoteague Creek. Wife (no name) & children resid. legatees. Wife & son Henry Exrs. Witt: W: Bagge, John Egles – p. 468

ROWLES, DANIEL, Sr. – 10 Dec. 1733 – 3 Feb. 1735 – To sister Eleanor Nickless all my lands during her life & then to my bro. Jonathan Rowles. To kinsman John Rowles, son of my bro. Jonathan Rowles my tools, provided he permit Capt. Hancock Nickless, Jacob Rogers, John West & Anthony West to use same during their natural lives. To Eastland Rogers, dau. of Jacob Rogers. Bal. of est. to sister Eleanor Nickless & bro. Jonathan Rowles. Bro. in law Capt. Hancock Nickless & bro. Jonathan Rowles Exrs. Witt: George Douglas, George Hack, Peter Hack, Codicil: 27 Apr. 1734 – Revokes bequest of land to sister Eleanor unless she be in necessity or want. To grand nepnew Major Rowles my biggest silver cup & my gun that is now in possession of his father, John Rowles. To grand nephew Daniel Nickless Rowles my small gun. Witt: Michael Rickards, Mary Nablet, James Holmes. p. 475

BRADFORD, WILLIAM – 4 July 1735 – 1 June 1736 – To sons Nathaniel, William, Thomas & Bayly Bradford 1 s. To son John Bradford. To son in law Jeodiah Bell & Sarah his wife land & marsh adj. the land of West Kellam cont. 10 A. To son John Fisher Bradford planta. where I now live with 600 A. belonging to it & for want of heirs to son John Bradford. To grandson William Bradford Gascoyne. Wife Bridget. To son Fisher Bradford all my lands not before given, negroes &c. wife to have use of negroes during her life. Son John Fisher Bradford to pay in lieu of said negroes as follows: In lieu of the negro Jack 10 L to Bridget Addison or else deliver her the negro; in lieu of the negro Appy 10 L to the dau. of Henry Armitrader called Comfort when she is 16 years of age or else deliver her the said negro; In lieu of the negro Hannah 18 L to my dau. Anne Bonawell or else deliver her the said negro. In lieu of the negro Levin 20 L to my son John Bradford or else deliver him the said negro. Wife Bridget resid. legatee &

Exec. Witt: Samuel Benston, John Kellam, Thomas Bryan, Robert Coleburn – p. 494

Deeds & Wills 1729 – 1737 – v. ii

WEST, ARGOL YARDLY – 4 Apr. 1736 – 6 July 1736 – To son John West planta. where I now live, wife to have use of same during her wid. Bal. of est. to wife during her wid. then to be div. bet. my 2 daus. Sarah Yardly & Anne West – Wife Comfort Exec. – Witt: Henry White, John Fisher, John Arenton, Isaac Smith – p. 4

DRUMMOND, ANNE – 1 Apr. 1733 – 6 July 1736 – To dau. Ann Drummond, wid. of my son Richard Drummond, whole est. real & personal. Ann Drummond Exec. Witt: William Arbuckle. Jonathan Baker. Richard Drummond – p. 4

HUTCHINSON, JOHN – 10 Nov. 1735 – 6 July 1736 – To son John Hutchinson. To wife Elizabeth use of all my est. during her life then to be div. bet. my children John, Barsheba, Anne, Rachel, Betty & Tabey. Wife & son John Exrs. Witt: Littleton Scarburgh Major, Halbert Raphael – p. 4

ARDIES, EDWARD – Nunc. – Declaration 8 Jan. 1735/6 – Proved 5 Apr. 1736 – Pro. 6 July 1736 – To bro. Hazard Ardies. Bro. Robert Ardies. Wife Comfort Ardies. To Robert Ardies, eld. son of James Ardies – Proved by John Tapman & Andn? Patterson – p. 7

PATRICK, JOHN – 5 Aug. 1736 – 7 Sept. 1736 – To mother Elizabeth Patrick. To my landlady Elizabeth Abbott. To Mason Abbott. William Crippen, son of my landlady Elizabeth Abbott. Mason Abbott Exr. Witt: Stephen Fitzgerrald, Thomas Crippen, Joshua Sprewance – p. 20

MURRAY, JOHN – of Somerset County, Maryland – 19 Sept. 1736 – 2 Nov. 1736 – To friend Hannah Henderson of the City of Philadelphia 50 Ł Philadelphia currency. Whole est., real & personal, to the care of my friends Capt. John Walker of Somerset County, Maryland, & Mr. George Douglas of Accomack County, Virginia, for the use of my father George Murray, they paying all debts due as shown by books & othwr writings in the hands of Mr. George Parker of Accomack. Goods & merchandise in the hands of Mrs. Barbara Harman to be inventoried & sold. Witt: Michael Higgins, Richard Martin – p. 49

WATSON, BENJAMIN – 9 Oct. 1736 – 2 Nov 1736 – To son Edmund Watson all my land between Occahannock Creek & the main road. To second son Benjamin Watson land where Timothy Kelly now lives, being the remaining part of the first patent. To 3rd son Peter Watson all the land lying between my son Benjamin & Arthur Robins & Wainhouses. To youngest son Francis Watson my water mill. To eldest dau. Amy Watson. To dau. Margaret chest that was her mother's. To dau. Priscilla Watson. All my children, except Edmund, resid. legatees. Bro. William Simkins & sister Elisha Hilton Exrs. Witt: Francis Roberts, David Watson, Benjamin Watson – Children under age – p. 55

ASHBY. CHARLES – 11 Oct. 1724 – 4 Jan. 1736/7 – To youngest son Charles Ashby my now dwelling planta. cont. 100 A. To dau. Eleanor Ashby. Wife Sarah & son Charles Exrs. – Witt: – Alexander Stockly, John Stockly, John Morrogh – p. 67

TAYLOR, CHARLES – 28 Dec. 1736 – 4 Jan. 1736/7 – To son in law John Walker & dau. Sarah, his wife, planta. where I now live for life, reversion to my grandson John Walker. To my said son in law & dau. my planta. in Maryland purchased of Richard Waters & wife for life, reversion to their next male issue except their son John, & if such issue die without heirs then to my said grandson John. Grandau. Ann Walker. To friend Capt. John Kendall. Bal. of personal est. to son in law John Walker & Sarah his wife. John Walker Exr. Witt: George Douglas, Daniel Marshall, John Wallop – p. 73

FLETCHER, THOMAS – 1 Nov. 1736 – 1 Feb. 1736/7 – To the first male heir of my son Henry Fletcher the planta. where I now live, cont. 300 A. & for want of such heirs to the first female heir. Henry to enjoy same during his life, & should he die without heirs I give the said land & planta. to William Fletcher, son of William Fletcher, wife to have 1/3 of same during her wid. Bal. of est. to be div. in 3 parts by my friends Ralph & Robert Corbin, wife to have 1/3 & son Henry 2/3 – Son Henry Exr. Witt: Timothy Donnohos, John Snead, Robert Lockard – p. 77

OSBURNE, JOHN JENIFER – 26 Jan. 1736/7 – 1 Mar. 1736/7 – To son Obadiah Osburne land adj. my son John Osburne, & for want of heirs to my 2 youngest daus. Olive Osburne & Attalanta Osburne. To son in law Lazarus Davis & his wife Patience land lying between John Fish & Robert Ardies during their lives, reversion to the heirs of my said dau. Patience, & for want of heirs to my dau. Martha. To son John Osburne Exr. Witt: John Walker, Daniel Martiall, Peter Ensworth – p. 82

PRITCHET, WILLIAM – 21 Oct. 1723 – 2 Mar. 1736/7 – To son Joshua Pritchet all my land between the branch above Tom Sawers so called & the mill road. To son William Pritchet all my land between the mill road & Mr. John Smith's land. To dau. Mary Pritchet land between the aforesaid branch & Alexander Harrison's land. Dau. Ann Pritchet. To dau. Betty Pritchet. Bal. of est. after wife's dower is taken out to be div. bet. all my children. William Bagge Exr. Witt: Joseph Cox, William Pritchet, Snead Cutler, Joachim Michael Bonnewell – p. 82

O'GRAHAN, DANIEL – 20 Nov. 1736 – 1 Mar. 1736/7 – To friend Johh Sheppard. To Arnol Adderson O'Grahan (under 21). To Matthew

Parish. Bal. of est. to be sold & proceeds to my mother Margaret
Ozburn & should she die to my friend John Shephard - John Shephard
Exr. Witt: John Jenkens, John Prat, Matthew Parish - p. 83

STOCKLEY, JOSEPH, Yeoman - 27 Dec. 1731 - 3 May 1737 - To son
Joseph Stockley land where he now lives being 364 A. Planta. where I
now live to my 2 sons Alexander & Elias Stockley, beginning in the
Creek called Asawaman. I give all my swamp land to my 3 sons
above named. To grandson Joseph Stockley. Grandau. Comfort Stockley. Sons Joseph, Alexander & Elias Exrs. Witt: Bennet Scarburgh,
Samuel Raine, John Stockley - p. 87

MILBY, GARRISON - 26 Feb. 1737 - 3 May 1737 - To bro. John
Milby. Bal. of est. to be div. bet. my bro. John Milby & my 3 sisters
& my bro. Salathiel Milby's son John, but should the sd. John inherit
the land where his mother now lives then his two sisters Ann & Mary
Milby to inherit the part left him. Bro. John Milby Exr. Witt: Nathaniel Milby, Edmund Johnson - p. 90

KELLAM, EDWARD - 18 Oct. 1736 - 2 Aug. 1737 - To son John
Kellam 130 A. where he now lives as it is patented in my own name,
also the planta. where I now live with all the land between a branch
called Bussells Branch & the line of Arthur Roberts land, cont. 150 A.
To son Arthur Kellam all my land on the other side of Bussells
Branch, cont. 150 A. To son Richard Kellam 1 s. To dau. Mary
Groton 1 s. To Grandson Benjamin Stewart 1 s. To son Edward
Kellam. To wife Sarah bal. of est. during her wid. then to my 4 chil-
dren John Kellam, Arthur Kellam, Scarbrough Addison & Rachel
Meers. Wife Sarah & son John Exrs. Witt: Littleton Wyatt. William
Wyatt, Robert Coleburn - p. 111

MELSON, JOHN - 30 Dec. 1736 - 3 Aug. 1737 - To son John Melson
land where he now lives known by the name of Hunting Creek cont. 50
A. To dau. Elizabeth Lewis 1 s. To dau. Mary Elliot 1 s. To son
Daniel Melson. To dau. Adra Gunter 1 s. To son Joshua Melson 1 s.
To dau. Tabitha Gary 1 s. To son Smith Melson. To dau Abigail
Melson. To wife Mary bal. of est. during her wid. then to my children
that are not named. Wife Exec. At the death or marriage of my wife
Tobias Bull, Roger Abbott, John Simpson & Thomas Riley to div. est.
Witt: Robert Caldwell, Henry White, Sarah White - p. 115

AYMES, JAMES - 18 July 1737 - No order of probate (1737) - To dau.
Esther. To Bro. William Aymes. Wife Mary & dau. Esther resid.
legatees - Bro. William Aymes Exr. Witt: Abigail Watkins, Thomas
Stringer, Bartholomew Meers - p. 116

CLARK, BLAKE - Nunc. 29 Nov. 1737 - 7 Dec. 1737 - Whole est. to
wife (no name) Proved by William Ames & Bartholomew Mears. - p.
128 Tabitha Clark, widow, qualified.-

JACKSON, JOHN - 19 Feb. 1735/6 - 7 Dec. 1737 - To wife whole est. during her wid. for her own & children's maintenance, 3 children William, Elizabeth & Ann. To dau. Jane Snead, wife of John Snead 1 s. Wife Mary Exec. Witt: James Davis - p. 129

JONES, RICHARD - 14 Nov. 1737 - 3 Jan. 1737/8 - To John Sparrow, son of David & Mary Sparrow, whole est. real & personal, for life, but should the said John mortgage or attempt to cut the entail of the said land I give the same to David Sparrow, son of David & Mary, & for want of heirs to the dau. of the said David & Mary. David Sparrow, John Onions & Southey Rew Exrs. Witt: Griffith Savage, David James, Timothy Silaven, Tabitha Onions - p. 129

Orders - 1731-1736

DUNTON, WATERFIELD.- Adm. his est. to Mary Dunton - 7 Sept. 1731 - p. 2

BYZWICK, JAMES - Adm. his est. to William Andrews, Gent. - 8 Sept. 1731 - p. 3

SMITH, VALENTINE - Adm. his est. to Roger Miles - 5 Oct. 1731 - p. 4

BLAKE, JOSEPH - Adm. his est. to William Andrews, Gent: - 4 Nov. 1731 - p. 9

TISDALE, JAMES - Adm. his est. to Darby Macarty - 7 June 1732 - p. 31

HUGHBANK, MARY - Adm. her est. to John Wise - 5 July 1732 - p. 34

ASH, BRIDGET - Adm. her est. to James Richards & Isaac Chace - 5 Sept. 1732 - p. 45

SAVAGE, MARY - Adm. her est. to Richard Savage - 5 Sept. 1732 - p. 45

COLLINS, JOHN - Adm. his est. to James Thornton - 4 Oct. 1732 - p. 49

TILLOTT, JAMES - Adm. his est. to Arnold Addison - 8 Nov. 1732 - p. 53

COE, SARAH - Adm. her est. to Jonathan Baker - 6 Dec. 1732 - p. 57

HUGHS, JOSEPH - Adm. his est. to Nicholas Guy - 4 Jan. 1732/3 - p. 63

BIDLE, THOMAS – Adm. his est. to William Andrews, Gent: 6 Feb. 1732/3 – p. 64

JACKSON, HENRY – Adm. his est. to Agnes Jackson – 7 Feb. 1732/3 – p. 66

WEST, EDWARD – Adm. his est. to his wid., Martha West, 7 Feb. 1732/3 – p. 66

RICE, WILLIAM – Adm. his est. to Mary Rice – 6 Mar. 1732/3 – p. 70

RAIN, SAMUEL – Adm. his est. to Solomon Ewell – 5 June 1733 – p. 79

HINMAN, BAILY – Adm. his est. to Mary Hinman – 5 June 1733 – p. 80

HARISTON, JOHN – Adm. his est. to Esther Hariston – 5 June 1733 – p. 80

CUSTIS, SOUTHEY – Adm. his est. to John Custis, Gent: – 7 Aug. 1733 – p. 87

BRYMER, SAMUEL – Adm. his est. to his wid. Ann Brymer – 4 Sept. 1733 – p. 93

CROPPER, EDMUND BOWMAN – Adm. his est. to his wid. Elizabeth Cropper – 5 Dec. 1733 – p. 106

DUBBERLY, JOHN – Adm. his est. to his wid. Grace Dubberly – 5 Mar. 1733/4 – p. 114

PREESON, BROWN – Adm. his est. to James Gibson – 3 Apr. 1734 – p. 119

SMITH, WILLIAM – Adm. his est. to Thomas Gardner – 2 July 1734 – p. 127

READ, HENRY – Adm. his est. to Richard Read – 6 Aug. 1734 – p. 131

WEST, WILLIAM – Adm. his est. to John Guy – 1 Oct. 1734 – p. 135

DAVIS, SAMUEL – Adm. his est. to his wid. Naomi Davis – 4 Mar. 1734/5 – p. 147

MOORE, EPHRAIM – "On the motion of John Rowles setting forth that the will of Ephraim Moor was proved in this Court believing the said Moore to be dead, after which the aforesaid Ephraim Moore returned and lived some years in Northampton County, and being now supposed to be dead, it is ordered that the Clerk of this Court deliver the afore-said will to the said John Rowles" - 3 June 1735 - p. 160

WATT, NEHEMIAH - Adm. his est. to his wid. Barbara Watt - 7 Oct. 1735 - p. 171

WHALE, WILLIAM - Est. comitted to the hands of the Sheriff - Rachel Whale wid. of William - 4 Nov. 1735 - p. 172

SCOT, THOMAS - Adm. his est. to his wid. Elizabeth Scot - 3 Feb. 1735/6 - p. 177

RODGERS, JOHN - Adm. his est. to his wid. Naomi Rodgers - 3 Dec 1735 - p. 176

GREEN, JOHN - Adm. his est. to George Green - 1 June 1736 - p. 184

ISDALE, GEORGE - Adm. his est. to John Scarburgh - 2 June 1736 - p. 187

PREWETT, CATHERINE - Adm. her est. to John Willett - 7 Sept. 1736 - p. 195

MILBY, SALATHIEL - Adm. his est. to his wid. Frances Milby - 5 Oct. 1736 - p. 196

BAILY, RICHARD - Adm. his est. to his son Richard Baily - 4 Jan. 1736/7 p. 200

MCGAHAN, CHARLES - Adm. his est. to James Wishart - 1 Feb. 1736/7 - p. 203

BURTON, STRATTON - Adm. his est. to Caleb Burton - 2 Feb. 1736/7 - p. 203

SLAUGHTER, WILLIAM - Adm. his est. to his wid. Abigal Slaughter - 2 Feb. 1736/7 - p. 203

Orders - 1737-1744

WYATT, JOHN - Adm. his est. to Nathan Addison - William Parker sec. - 1 Nov. 1737 - p. 1

DALTON, SARAH - Adm. her est. to John Brymer - William Andrews, Gent: sec. - 6 Dec. 1737 - p. 3

HASTINGS, WILLIAM - Adm. his est. to John Onions - William Andrews sec. - 6 Dec. 1737 - p. 4

CHASE, WILLIAM - Adm. his est. to Richard Dickinson - Nehemiah

Walker sec. – 7 Dec. 1737 – p. 8

THOMAS, SAMUEL – Adm. his est. to George Bundic – John Young & George Bundic, Jr. sec. – 3 Jan. 1737 – p. 18

THOMAS, MARGARET – Adm. her est to Isaac Dix, Jr. – William Andrews, Gent: sec. 7 Feb. 1737 – p. 29

CRIPPEN, GEORGE – Adm, his est. to Thomas Crippen – Griffith Savage, Gent: sec. 9 Feb. 1737 – p. 35

DAVIS, JAMES – Adm. his est. to his bro. Charles Davis – George Douglas, Gent: sec. – 7 Mar. 1737 – p. 37

ADDISON, Nathan – Adm. his est. to his wid. Bridget Addison – Isaac Riggs & John Hutchinson sec. – 2 May 1738 – p. 48

MARSHALL, ANNABELLA – Adm. her est. to her mother Mary Marshall, wid. – George Douglas & William Arbuckle, Gent: sec. – 2 May 1738 – p. 49

FEDDEMAN, SHADRACK – Adm. his est. to his bro. Joseph Feddeman – Jonathan Chambers & John Blake sec. – 3 May 1738 – p. 51

ADAMS, ANNE – Ordered that the Sheriff take her est. into his possession & sell same at public auction – 3 May 1738 – p. 54

GASCOIGNE, THOMAS – Adm. his est. to his wid. Sarah Gascoigne – William Andrews & John Justice sec. – 7 June 1738 – p. 62

ROGERS, WILLIAM – Adm. his est. to his wid. Anne Rodgers – John Fitzgerrold & John Cole sec. – 7 June 1738 – p. 63

ONELY, WILLIAM – Adm. his est. to his wid. Anne Onely – William Tilney & Caleb Burton sec. – 7 June 1738 – p. 65

RYLEY, JOHN – Adm. his est. to his bro. & heir at law, Thomas Ryley – John Smith & Southey Rew sec. 7 June 1738 – p. 66

BULL, DEWY – Adm. his est. to Rebccca Bunting, wid. of the said Dewy Bull & George Douglas, Gent: sec. – 7 June 1738 – p. 66

SAVAGE, ABEL * – Adm. his est. to his wid. Elizabeth Savage – William Harman sec. 4 July 1738 – p. 74

MARTIN, EDWARD – Adm. his est. to his son William Martin – John Arlington & Edw. Martin sec. – 5 July 1738 – p. 81

BENSTON, JAMES – Adm. his est. to John Goutee – John Tankred & Scarburgh Tunnell sec. – 2 Jan. 1738 – p. 114

ANDERSON, ROGER – Ordered that the Sheriff take his est. into his custody & sell same at public auction – 13 Oct. 1738 – p. 115

STOCKLEY, JOHN – Adm. his est. to Mason Abbot – John Tankred & Jonathan Warrington sec. – 6 Feb. 1738 – p. 122

WATSON, THOMAS – Adm. his est. to his wid. Sarah Watson – William Andrews & John Fitzgerrald & John Parker sec. – 25 June 1739 – p. 154

HASTINGS, JOHN – Adm. his est. to John Brown, wid. Dorothy Hastings relinquishing her right to qualify – William Andrews sec. – 25 Sept. 1739 – p. 192

BEECH, SAMUEL – Adm. his est. to his son Samuel Beech – Jonathan Burton sec. – 29 Jan. 1739/40 – p. 219

MILICHOP, JOHN – Adm. his est. to Nicholas Milechop – William Andrews sec. – 29 Jan. 1739/40 – p. 223

PEARCE, JOHN – Adm. his est. to his ward, Bridget Pearce – Fisher Bradford & Bartholomew Twiford sec. – 29 Jan. 1739/40 – p. 223

BAGWELL, THOMAS – Adm. his est. to his wid. Elizabeth Bagwell – Edward Revell & Robert Coleburn sec. – 26 Feb. 1739/40 – p. 232

WATSON, THOMAS – Adm. his est. unadministered by Sarah Watson, his wid. & late Adm'x. dec., to William Arbuckle – George Holden sec. – 26 Feb. 1739/40 – p. 234

PARKER, CHARLES – Adm. his est. to Henry Custis – Henry Scarburgh, Gent: sec. – 27 Feb. 1739/40 – p. 235

WHITTINGTON, WILLIAM – Adm. his est. to his wid. Betty Whittington – James Wishart & William Beavans sec. – 25 Mar. 1740 – p. 240

SHEPHARD, JOHN – Adm. his est. to his wid. Catherine Shepherd – Edmund Baily & Edmund Allen sec. – 25 Mar. 1740 – p. 240.

WATSON, SARAH – Adm. her est. to John Scarburgh – George Douglas sec. – 27 May 1740 – p. 263

MARSHALL, CHARLES – Adm. his est. to his wid. Betty Marshall – John Wallop & John Blake sec. – 29 July 1740 – p. 275

POWELL, JAMES * – Adm. his est. to Winifred Scarburgh & Henry Scarburgh, Gent: sec. 28 Oct. 1740 – p. 290

DAVIS, THOMAS – Adm. his est. to Anne Davis – Charles White & Henry White sec. – 28 Oct. 1740 – p. 290

STOCKLEY, EYRE – Adm. his est. to his wid. Mary Stockley – Henry Custis & John Bagwell, Jr. sec. – 25 Nov. 1740 – p. 298

TAYLOR. WILLIAM – Adm. his est. to his wid. Mary Taylor – John Simpson & Mason Abbot sec. – 27 Jan. 1740/41 – p. 304

PARKER, PHILIP – Adm. his est. to his wid. Tabitha Parker – John Rogers & Robert Coleburn sec. – 27 Jan. 1740/41 – p. 304

LEWIS, JOHN – Adm. his est. to Fenn Lewis – John Rogers sec. – 24 Feb. 1740/41 – p. 308

TILNEY, WILLIAM – Adm. his est. to his wid. Elizabeth Tilney & William Bagge – John Smith sec. – 24 Feb. 1740/41 – p. 309

FITZGERALD, THOMAS – Adm. his est. to Mary Fitzgerald – John Fitzgerald & James Fitzgerald sec. – 25 Feb. 1740/41 – p. 312

SCARBURGH, BENNET, JR – Adm. his est. to John Scarburgh –Southey Rew, Gent: sec. – 31 Mar. 1741 – p. 320

WHARTON, REVEL – Adm. his est. to his wid. Bridget Wharton – William Custis & . John Parker sec. – 28 Apr. 1741 – p. 321

WATTS, JOHN – Adm. his est. to John Goutee – Robert Slocomb & Elias Taylor sec. 30 June 1741 – p. 340

BAILY, HENRY – Adm. his est. to his wid. Rose Baily – Richard Read sec. – 30 Sept. 1741 – p. 366

ROSS, RICHARD – Adm. his est. to John Gilchrist – George Douglas sec. 29 June 1742 – p. 408

WHITE, BENJAMIN – Adm. his est. to William Wyatt – Thomas Parramore, Gent. sec. 26 Oct. 1742 – p. 428

ARMITRADER, ARTHUR – Ordered that the Sheriff take charge of his est. and sell same at public auction – 26 Jan. 1742/3 – p. 459

TAYLOR, MARY – Adm. her est. to Jonathan Warrington – Johh Nock & Robert Nock sec. – 22 Feb. 1742/3 – p. 464

TOWNSEND, HENRY – Adm. his est. to his wid. Rhody Townsend – George Philbey & John Townsend sec. – 30 Aug. 1743 – p. 496

TOWNSEND, THOMAS – Adm. his est. to his wid. Elizabeth Townsend – John Wallop sec. 30 Aug. 1743 – p. 495

ROBINS, SARAH – Adm. her est. to Susannah Kendall, wife of Lemuel Kendall George Douglas & Henry Scarburgh sec. – 27 Dec. 1743 – p.

535

LUCAS, PASAVELL – Adm. his est. to George Douglas – George Holden & William Arbuckle sec. – 27 Dec. 1743 – p. 536

BRADFORD, NATHANIEL – Adm. his est. To his wid. Elizabeth Bradford – George Parker & Robert Carruthers sec. – 28 Feb. 1743/4 – p. 550

FISHER, JOHN – Adm. his est. to his wid. Elizabeth Fisher – Thomas Bonnwell & Thomas Parramore sec. – 28 Feb. 1743 – p. 551

CHANCE, JACOB – Adm. his est. to his wid. Rose Chance – Richard Armitrader sec. 27 Mar. 1744 – p. 562

TOWLES, THOMAS – Adm. his est. to Mary Towles, wid. – Daniel Shae sec. – 27 Mar. 1744 – p. 564

GLADING, JOSEPH – Adm. his est. to George Glading – George Scott & John Willet sec. 25 Apr. 1744 – p. 572

CUSTIS, REVEL – Adm. his est. to Edward Revell – Hancock Nickless sec. 29 May 1744 – p. 576

MORRIS, GILBURT – Adm. his est. to Mary Morris – John Walker & John Smith of Swansigut sec. – 29 May 1744 – p. 580

KELLAM, SARUM – Adm. his est. to Richard Kellam – Isaac Smith sec. – 30 May 1744 – p. 583

WHITE, CHARLES – Adm. his est. to Elizabeth White – Edmund Ironmonger & Jacob White sec. – 1 Aug. 1744 – p. 603

NOCK, GEORGE – Adm. his est. to Anne Hack. wid. – Joseph Bell & John Nock sec. 28 Aug. 1744 – p. 641

VANDEGRAUGH, OBEDIAH – Adm. his est. to Elizabeth Vandegraugh, wid. – George Holden sec. – 28 Aug. 1744 – p. 642

Wills – 1737 – 1743

BLACK, WILLIAM – 10 June 1728 – 7 Mar. 1737/8 – Whole est. to wife Margaret – Wife Exec. Witt: Henry Bagwell, Delight Shield, William Nowell, William Haizlup, John Allen, John Bagwell, William Tazewell, Thomas Parramore – p. 7

WATSON, BENJAMIN – 31 Aug. 1732 – 7 Mar. 1737/8 – To son Arthur 1/2 the land which was my father's. Bro. Robert Watson & cousin Benjamin Watson to divide my land. To son Benjamin Watson. To son Mitchel Watson. Son Robert Watson. Son Moses Watson. Dau.

Directer Watson. Dau. Elizabeth Watson. Wife Joice Watson. Wife & children resid. legatees - Wife Exec. - Witt: Benjamin Watson, Robert Watson, William Simkins - p. 12

WALKER, MARY - Nunc - Declaration 7 Nov. 1737 - Proved 24 Dec. 1737 - Pro. 7 Mar. 1737/8 - To Mrs Gibson a ring. To Mr. George Douglas a stone ring. To Patrick Stewart a plain ring. To Anne Douglas, dau. of George Douglas, a pair of ear rings, all in the custody of George Douglas. To Elizabeth Stewart. To Mrs. Douglas, wife of George Douglas. George Douglas resid. legatee & Exr. To Ann Stewart, dau. of Patrick Stewart a guinea to buy her ear rings. proved by Patrick Stewart, Chirurgeon - p. 15

OSBORN, JOHN - 10 Mar. 1737/8 - 2 May 1738 - To wife Ratchel all my lands during her wid. To eld. son Ezkell Osborn all my lands at the death of my wife. Son John Osborn. Wife & 3 children (only 2 named) resid. legatees - Wife & George Douglas Exrs. Witt: Daniel Cutler, Jesse Jenkinson, Lazarus Davis - p. 18

NOCK, WILLIAM - 26 Feb. 1737/8 - 2 May 1738 - To son Elijah Nock 250 A. with my planta., but should my son William be destitute for a home then he to have his life on my planta. To son John Nock 150 A. above the main county road for life, reversion to his son Joseph Nock, his now wife having her widowhood in same. To wife Elizabeth my dwelling planta. cont. 250 A. with the use of 200 A. of marsh on the Bayside during her life. To sons John & Elijah 200 A. marsh on the Bayside. To my 6 sons William, John, Nehemiah, Solomon, George & Elijah. To dau. Sarah Nock. To grandson Joseph Nock, son of John Nock & Margaret, his wife. To grandson William Ratlif, son of Charles Ratlif & Waddelo his wife. Son Elijah & dau. Sarah to be with their mother until capable of taking care of themselves. Sons William & John Exrs. Witt: John Nock, John Tankard, Steaven Warington. - p. 25 In ord. of prob: William Nock eld, son & heir at law.

BARNS, JOHN - 16 Dec. 1737 - 2 May 1738 - To son John Barns 70 A. at the head of Hogshead Branch. To son Arthur land beginning at a cedar post between the upper landing point & the little Island. To son Robins Barns 100 A. on the Bayside. To dau. Easter Barns. To dau. Frances Barns. To son William land between the upper landing point & the little Island. To son William my water mill. To Ezekiel Barns. To wife Esther - Son William resid. legatee. Should anything accrue on a bond given Henry Satchell on account of Waterfield Dunton's est., that there is one shilling paid out of my est. on the account of Waterfield Dunton's est., then I cut my son John Barns entirely off with an English shilling, and what I have given him to go to my son Arthur - Son William Exr. Witt: William Parker, John Drummond, Job Faddersick - p. 28
In ord. of prob: John Barns heir at law.

ONIONS, THOMAS - 18 May 1737 - 2 May 1738 - To daus. Ann & Grace Onions a tract of land I had by my wife Tabitha Onions cont. 250 A., being part of a tract of land that fell to her by the death of Christophor Thompson, situate between Blackwater Creek & Venesses Creek in the Province of Maryland. To 2 youngest daus. Elizabeth & Comfort Onions land where I now live, wife to have use of same until my youngest child is 21. Wife Exec. - Bro. John Exr. Witt: Peter Harlee, William Sturgis, Andrew Finney - p. 31

KENDALL, JOHN - 12 Mar. 1738 - 6 June 1738 - To son Lemuel Kendall the land & planta. where he now lives, cont. 200 A. being the same I purchased of him. To son John Kendall one moiety of all my lands on Jengoteague Island & the other moiety of said lands to my son William Kendall. To son William Kendall all my lands at or near Oak Hall being 370 A. To son Joshua planta. where I now live Purchased of John Wallop. Wife Mary & children John, William, Joshua, Theophilus, Ann, Elizabeth & Molly resid. legatees. Wife to have use of whole est. heretofore beq. by me to any of my children by her begotten until they arrive at age or marry, Wife & friends Capt. James Wishart & Capt. John Walker Exrs. Witt: George Douglas, John Wallop, William Rowley, Robert Slocomb. - p. 33
In ord. of prob: Lemuel Kendall eld. son & heir at law.

ONLEY, FAIRFAX - 6 Mar. 1737/8 - 6 June 1738 - To bro. William Onley's son William 1/2 the land which was my father's. To bro. Smith Onley the other 1/2 of the land. To cousin Tabitha Custis. To Hewett Onley. To sister in law Ann Onley. To sister Mary Custis. To Margaret Satchel. To uncle William Onley. Bros. & sisters Smith Onley, Hewet Onley, Mary Custis & Ann Onley resid. legatees. Bro. Smith Onley Exr. Witt: Jacob Lurton, Mansfield Turlington, Daniel Rodgers - p. 59

UPSHUR, ARTHUR - 26 May 1738 - 4 July 1738 - To wife Sarah Upshur - Dau. Rachel. To son Thomas Upshur. To dau. Abigall Waters. To dau. Elizabeth Finney. To grandson Arthur Upshur. To grandson Hancock (under 21). To grandson William Kendall. To grandau. Susanna Custis. To grandson Thomas Teackle. To grandau. Margaret Teackle. To grandau. Prosillah Scarburgh. To grandson John Teackle. To grandson Caleb Teackle. To grandson Levin Teackle. To grandson Upshur Teackle. To son Abel Upshur all the remainder of my est. in Virginia & elsewhere. Son Abel Exr. - Witt: Edward Revell, John Foscue, Nathaniel Foscue - p. 69

PAYNE, SAMUEL - 20 ___ ___ 1723 - 6 June 1738 - To bro. in law Daniel Mitchel 275 A. purchased of John & Thomas Gaskins & for want of heirs to my sister Esther's eld. son. To sister Esther. To sister Susannah. To friend William Miles. To Ann Miles. Mother Ann Mitchell resid. legatee. Friend Sebastian Delastatius, Sr. Exr. Witt: Sebastian Delastatius, Jr., John Clement - p. 75
In ord. of prob: Sebastian Delastatius, Sr. refused to act & George Douglas qualified as adm'r C.T.A.

GRAY, JAMES – Nunc – Declaration 25 Oct. 1737 at 8 o'clock at night – Proved 26 Oct. 1737 – Pro. 4 July 1738.– Whole est. to Solomon Gray & Betty Thomas – Proved by John Dix & Southy Littleton – p. 77 Southy Littleton qualified.

HOGSHEAR, THOMAS – 9 June 1738 – 3 Oct. 1738 – To 2 sons Robert & Kendall Hogshear my tract of land called "parkall"; to my 2 sons my right of the Beach called Winter Quarter pasture for the time I have leased it. To grandson Alexander Taylor. Pewter & plate to be div. bet. wife, 2 sons & 2 daus. To Sarah Taylor. Wife Anne & son Robert Exrs. Witt: John Hall, William Shield, Robert Hogshear – p. 94

FINNEY, WILLIAM – 16 Feb. 1737/8 – 3 Oct. 1738 – To son William land & planta. on Onancock Creek. To son Andrew land where he now lives. To dau. Athalia Bell. Son William resid. legatee. Sons William & Andrew Exrs. Witt: John Wise, John Bayly, Alexander Sloughter – p. 104

KITCHEN, TEMPERANCE – 17 Aug. 1737 – Proved 4 Oct. 1738 – Prob. 15 Oct. 1738 – To Col. Henry Scarburgh my planta. in Somerset County on Pocomoke River & 1/2 the land thereto, Mr. William Kitchen to have the use of same during his life. To William Tankred, son of John Tankred & Elizabeth, his wife, planta. in Somerset County where Hancock White now lives & 1/2 the land thereto belonging, Hanna White to have use of same during her life. To George Hope, son of Thomas Hope, 700 A. at the White Marsh. To Joanna Parramore. To friend Mary Broadwater. To Caleb Broadwater. To friend John Tankred. To niece Sarah Ewell. To Sophia Abbott, dau. of Major Abbott & Elizabeth, his wife. To friends Mason Abbott & William Dryas. To sister Patience Savage. To sister Comfort Justice riding horse for life then to return to her dau. Sarah Ewell. To Richard Parker. Robert Justice to give bond to Mr. William Kitchen for my est. in Somerset County not already disposed of. To Temperance Scarburgh Savage. To George Savage. To Temperance. Hope, dau. Thomas Hope. To my Exrs. "all the remainder of my est. not already given for the bricking in Major Scarburgh's Grave with my own". Friends Henry Scarburgh & John Tankred Exrs. Witt: Richard Kitson, William Welford – p. 105

PARKER, SACKER – 3 July 1738 – 2 Jan. 1738/9 – To son John planta. where I now live & all my right to Islands lying between Pungoteague & Onancock Creeks. To dau. Jemimah Parker (under 21). To dau. Keziah Parker (under 21) To son Thomas (under 21) to son Cornelius Parker (under 21) To son Hancock (under 21) To dau. Sinah (under 21) To son Sacker (under 21) To unborn child. To dau. Susannah, now the wife of William Barns. Unborn child & wife Leah resid. legatees. Wife & son John Exrs. Witt: John Parker, Henry Scarburgh, Baly Johnson – p. 107

TISEKER, JOHN – 13 Jan. 1738/9 – 6 Feb. 1738/9 – To bro. Robert Tiseker. To Sarah Turlington. To sister Alice West. To niece Susanna Turlington. To my bro. Robert's dau. Mary. To Sarah Rogers. To James Turlington. To Mary Fitzgerrald. To bro. Robert's son Robert. To Edmund Turlington. To Solomon West. Bro. Robert & Thomas Turlington Exrs. Witt: William Bagge, John Connyer, John Guy – p. 109

WILSON, WILLIAM – 7 Sept. 1738 – 6 Feb. 1738/9 – "I give & bequeath for the good of the Middle Church my great Common Prayer Book with Singing Psalms in it" To godson William Abbott. To William White "that lives on the seaside" to him & his wife & his sister Elizabeth Claywell. To George Trewit living in Maryland called "Accomack George" & to his dau. Comfort & to his cousin Sarah Trewit, dau. of Henry Trewit. To godson Isaac Dix. To goddau. Mary Evans, wife of Jestinian Evans. To Mary Nickleson. To Leah White. To Patience Tankred. Goddau. Mary Evans, dau. of Capt. Thomas Evans. To Esther Barns & Mrs. Sacker Parker, wid. To Mason Abbott. To Francis Young's children. To John Young's wife. To Elizabeth Riley, wife of Thomas Riley. To Wise Middleton, wife of William Middleton. To my landlord John Young. To Tabitha Stockly. Francis Young's children resid. legatees. Friends John Young, Thomas Riley & William White Exrs. Witt: George Bundick, William Hickman, Joseph Hickman – p. 113

PARKER MAJ. GEORGE, of Onancock, Gent: Not dated – 7 Mar. 1738/9 – To son George Parker 1/2 my land on the North side of Onancock Creek, being 825 A. To son Charles Parker all my land on Pungoteague Creek which I purchased of Mr. Justinian Yeo, being 959 A. To son Henry Parker all my land on Back Creek adj. his bro. George. To son Bennet Parker 1/2 my land in the Indian Town in Somerset County, Maryland, called Wickenoughs Neck, being 300 A. To son Richard Parker the remaining 1/2 my land called Wickenoughs Neck, the whole being 600 A. To son Phillip all my land in my neck on Anancock Creek not already given my sons George & Henry. To dau. Anne. Children resid. legatees – Sons George, Charles & Henry Exrs. Witt: Henry Scarburgh, Winnefred Scarburgh, John Bonwell – p. 133

MCCOMB, JOHN – 26 Mar. 1738 – Partly proved 6 Mar. 1739/9 – Pro. 27 Mar. 1739 – To Abraham, the son of Joseph Rigs planta. where I now live. To sister Naomi Rigs. To Mary Hinman "meaning the widow" To Sarah Hinman. To Mary Hinman. To Bayly Hinman, son of Bal: Hinman, dec. Bal. of est. to my sister, the wife of Joseph Rigs. Joseph Rigs Exr. Witt: James Tolman, John Gilchrist, Southy Rew – p. 139

DRYAS, WILLIAM – 24 Mar. 1738/9 – 29 May 1739 – To wife Lydia all my goods, chattels &c. belonging to the planta. where I now live until my children Edward Dryas, William Dryas & Betty Dryas & George Hope, William Hope & Temperance Hope come to age, then to be div. bet. my wife & said children. To William Conner. Wife Exec. - Witt: Thomas Webb, William Conner, Thomas Ginn - p. 140

SAVAGE, RICHARD - 2 May 1739 - 29 May 1739 - To son Francis Savage planta. where I now live, also 50 A. adj. Hewit Smith. To son Richard Savage 150 A. purchased of James Smith. To son Rowland Savage land purchased of Parker Savage. To son John Savage the remainder of the land. To dau. Mary Dix. To dau. Tabitha Fletcher - To dau. Elizabeth Roberts. To dau. Michal Burton. To dau. Redegel Savage. Robert Andrews, Littleton Major & Robert Coleburn to div. est. Sons Rowland & Francis Savage Exrs. Witt: Robert Coleburn, Littleton Wyatt, William Wyatt - p. 140

SAVAGE, GRIFFITH - 5 Feb. 1738/9 - 7 June 1739 - To son Griffith Savage planta. where I now live cont. 300 A. To son George Savage 200 A. adj. the above. To son William 212 A. purchased of Charles Leatherbury &. Isaac Dix. To son in law William White. To dau. Elizabeth Riley. To dau. Patience. To dau. Sarah Savage. To son in law Isaac Dix. To dau. Scarburgh Savage. To son in law Ralph Justice. To dau. Bridget Dix. Roger Abbott, George Bundick, Sr. & Southy Rew to div. est. bet. wife & 6 children, George, Elizabeth, Patience, William, Scarburgh & Sarah. Wife (no name) & sons Griffith & George Savage Exrs. Witt: Southy Rew, David Sparrow, John Bell - p. 157
In order of prob: Presented by Patience Savage, wid., & Griffith Savage, son of Griffith Savage, dec. Griffith Savage heir at law.

TUNNELL, NATHANIEL - 5 Apr. 1739 - 31 July 1739 - To son William 170 A. where I now live. Wife Sarah to have use of same for life. Wife & 3 children Comfort, William & Mary Tunnell resid. legatees. Children under age. Wife Exec. Witt: Nathaniel Morgan, Catherine McKenny, William Beavans, Jr. - p. 159

CUTLER, GEORGE - 17 Mar. 1738 - 1 Aug. 1739 - To wife Arcadia land where I now live purchased of Phillip Quinton for life, then to my son George Cutler. To wife use of planta. given to me by my father Richard Cutler during her wid. then to my son Daniel Cutler. To son Daniel Cutler a pair of silver shoe buckles & my Wigg that was made of his own hair. To son Thomas Cutler 50 A. between the Court House road & Daniel Foxes, said land adj. his bro. George. To son George one gold ring, the posey on it is "strike while the iron is hot" & G.C. in the ring. Son Richard Cutler. Son Samel Cutler. Dau. Arcadia Cutler a gold ring with the posey "love near dies where virtue lives". To son Richard a gold ring with T:Rose in it. 4 children Betty, Richard, Samuel & Arcadia resid. legatees. Wife & son Thomas Exrs. Witt: Michael Hall, John Smith - p. 174
In order of Prob. Daniel Cutler heir at law.

CUSTIS, EDWARD - 3 June 1739 - 1 Aug. 1739 - To son William Custis. To son Thomas Custis (under age) Dau. Bridget Wharton. Dau. Susanna Custis. Grandson Spencer Bagwell. To daus. Ann &

Susanna all their mother's wearing apparel (both under 18) Wife to have use of land given Thomas until he comes to age. Son Thomas & daus. Ann & Susanna resid. legatees. Thomas & Susanna to live with my wife until they come to age & dau. Ann to live with Revel Wharton until she comes to age. Wife (no name) & Revel Wharton Exrs. Witt: W: Bagge, Stephen Allen, Thomas Bagwell - p. 175

STOCKLY, HANNAH - 30 Nov. 1739 - 30 Jan. 1749/40 - To grandson Thomas Stockly. Dau. Jemimah Stockley. Grandson William Stockly. Grandson John Stockly. Grandau. Temperance Stockly. To Emanuel Harman. To Mary Townsend. To grandau. Martha Merril. To Argillus Merril. Grandson William Merril. Grandson Stockly Cain. Grandau. Naomi Cain. Grandau. Sophia Cain. Dau. Jemimah Stokly & grandson Thomas Stockly resid. legatees. Grandson Thomas Stockly Exr. Witt: Joseph Stockly Sr., Edward Bayly, Emanuel Harman - p. 202

ROWLES, DANIEL - 6 Mar. 1736/7 - 6 Feb. 1739/40 - To father John Rowles, Sr. To Margaret Scarburgh. Bro. John Rowles, Sr. resid. legatee & Exr. Witt: Litt: Scarburgh Major, Rowles Major - p. 204

TYRE, THOMAS - 13 Oct. 1739 - 26 Feb. 1739/40 - To wife Johanna whole est. for life then to be div. bet. son William Tyre & dau. Anne Tyre. Wife & son William Exrs. Witt: Lemuel Kendall, Robert Slocomb, Esther Miles - p. 204

BLAIR, THOMAS, Merchant - 17 Feb. 1739 - 25 Mar. 1740. - To Edward Dickeson land purchased of Col. Solomon Ewell cont. 250 A. (being the land formerly sold the said Dickeson but never deeded to him) To wife Anne Blair all my lands in Virginia and all negroes & personal est. in Virginia or Maryland, except my ready cash, my goods of merchandise in any or all of my storegouses, my outstanding debts & my sea vessels, she to pay my debts. To my mother in glasgow & my bro. Walter Blair all those things excepted out of the above devise to my wife, & all my other est. not already beq., but if neither of them outlive me I will the same to their legal representatives. Wife Exec. as so far as relates to the legacies beq. her, and Mr. Alexander Buncle, merchant, & George Douglas Exrs. in trust for my mother & brother or their representatives - Witt: John Kincaid, Naomi Ewell - p. 214

ROGERS, RICHARD, Sr. - 6 Jan. 1737/8 - 25 Mar. 1740 - To son Richard Rogers 265 A. where he now lives. To son Nathaniel 150 A. where he now lives. To wife Mary 200 A. adj. the land hereafter beq. my son Daniel during her life then to my son Daniel. To my grandchildren by my daus. Mary Johnson & Comfort West. To son Daniel 240 A. where he now lives. To son John 200 A. where I now live. To grandau. Sophia Rogers, dau. of my son Nathaniel Rogers. Wife & 6 children resid. legatees. Maj. Hancock Nickless, Capt. John Shepherd, Mr. Robert Andrews & Adam Muir to div. est. Wife Mary, John Rogers & Daniel Rogers Exrs. Witt: Adam Muir, John Kincaid, Philip Parker - p. 215

In order. of Prob: Richard Rogers eldest son & heir at law.

NOCK, JOHN – 24 Dec. 1739 – 29 Apr. 1740 – To sons George & William Nock the younger, land left me by my father William Nock, to be div. bet. them as my bro. Benjamin Nock & Nicholas Guy see fit. To son John Nock, Patience Bishop, Elizabeth Jarmine, Amy Bishop, dau. Comfort Mannering & the children of Mary Justice, my dau., & Ann Bundick bal. of est. not before given. Grandson John Baker, son of Comfort Mannering – Wife (no name) son George Nock & Richard Bundick Exrs. Witt: Ralph Justice, Joseph Bell, Jacob Shephard – p. 222
In order of prob: John Nock eld. son & heir at law. Wife "Rose" – see div. of est. p. 248

FOOKS, DANIEL – Not dated – 24 June 1740 – To dau. Elizabeth planta. where I now live. To dau. Sarah 100 A. in the woods. To dau. Leah. To dau. Rachel. 4 daus. resid, legatees. Nathaniel Milby Exr. Witt: John Smith, John Cutler, Thomas Cutler – p. 237

KITSON, RICHARD – 23 Feb. 1739/40 – 24 June 1740 – To Thomas Parramore my gold watch. To goddau. Johanna Parramore gold ring. To goddau. Ann Kitson. To kinswoman Johanna Kitson. To godson & kinman John Kitson "when he comes to 21 or sooner if his father sees fit, silver Tankard marked "A.K. 1714" To godson Ralph Justice. To nephew John Kitson 400 A. where I now live for life, reversion to his son John Kitson, the use of the same to continue to his heirs. To nephew John Kitson 300 A. adj. the said 400 A. Nephew John Kitson resid. legatee & Exr. Witt: Arthur Emmerson, William White, Mary Parramore – p. 238

WATKINSON, PETER – 2 June 1740 – 29 July 1740 – To wife Abigail whole est. real & personal – Wife Exec. Witt: Francis Savage, Benjamin Darby, William Darby. p. 240

ROGERS, RICHARD – 3 July 1740 – 30 July 1740 – To bro. Edmund Rogers. To bro. Henry Rogers. Bro. Samuel Rogers. To Mary Young. To Francis Stockly. To John Rogers & John Spiers. To Caleb Burton. Friend Francis Stockly Exr. Witt: Tabitha Young, Robert Carruthers – p. 256

LEWIS, WILLIAM, of Hunting Creek – 14 Feb. 1739 – 30 July 1740 – To son William 100 A. called Hills land or planta. lying on back creek branch. To sons William & Thomas & Isaac & to my bro. John Lewis all my salt marshes. To son John Lewis 1 s. To daus. Comfort & Lueser 1 s. Bal. of est. to wife during her wid. then to be div. bet. my wife Anne Tabitha's children then alive. Wife & bro. John Lewis Exrs. All my children by my last wife to live with their mother until they are of age. Witt: Thomas Riley, Jacob Litchfield, Robert Turnall – p. 257
In order of prob: The citation issued for John Lewis, son & heir at law of the within William Lewis, dec., being returned by the sheriff of this

county that the said John Lewis was not found within his Bailiwick &c., will admitted to record.

PATTERSON, WILLIAM - 20 Nov. 1732 - 26 Aug. 1740 - To son Anderson Patterson whole est. and for want of heirs to be equally div. bet. all my grandaughters by my 3 daughters, Mary, Elizabeth & Eupheme. Son Anderson Exr. Witt: George Douglas, Charles Stockly, William Peavans.
Codicil: 12 Oct. 1734 - To dau. Eupheme, the wife of Samecl Gillet, chest that was my late wife's, her mother. To grandau. Margaret Gillet. Witt: George Douglas. Codicil: 1 May 1736 - To grandaughters Isabel & Mary Ramsey. To grandsons William & Samuel Gillet. Witt: George Douglas, Coventon Corbin. - p. 258
In order of prob: William Ainsworth & Jenne, his wife, and Tabitha Patterson, heirs at law to the above testator, appeared and offered no objection to the probate of said will.

ROBERTS, ARTHUR - 26 Sept. 1740 - 28 Oct. 1740 - To bro. John Roberts. To bro. in law William Simpkins my shallop. To bro. Abel Roberts. To father Francis Roberts. Father Exr. Witt: Francis Savage, William Wyat, Jonathen Garrison - p. 274

TEACKLE, CALEB - 31 Jan. 1735/6 - 28 Oct. 1740 - Whole est. to be div. bet. my brothers & sister Margaret. Bro. John Teackle Exr. - Witt: Abel Upshur, Edward Palmer - p. 281

DIX, ISAAC - 30 Dec. 1740 - 27 Jan. 1740/41 - To son John Dix planta. where I now live & all my other lands. Solomon White to have the tuition of my son John until he arrive at the age of 21 years. Dau. Mary Dix (under 18) Thomas Evans to have the care & tuition of my dau. Mary. Should either of my children die before coming to the age of 21, the survivor to enjoy the whole est. without accounting to any of the half blood. Mr. Edmund Bayly, Mr. John Simpson & Southy Rew to appraise & div. my est bet. my wife & children. Wife (no name) & bro. John Dix & Solomon White Exrs. Witt: Southy Rew, Peter Copes, Leah White. In order of Prob: Presented by Mary Dix, widow of Isaac.

STOCKLY, FRANCIS - 18 Nov. 1740 - 28 Apr. 1741 - To the child my dau. in law goes with, if a son, the planta. his father lived upon, the planta. where I now live & my part of Pamco Island, known as Tobacco Island. To grandau. Elizabeth Stockly planta. I purchased of Samuel & Henry Rogers. To grandau Ann Stockly planta. at the head of a gut upon Assawoman. To son in law Ezekiel Young (under age) 80 A. that I had of my uncle Joseph Stockly, & for want of heirs to Mary Young. Should the child my dau. in law goes with be a girl then I give the planta at Town where her father lived to my grandau. Elizabeth Stockly, and the planta. where I now live to my grandau Ann Stockly "and the child my daughter in law goeth with Mary Stockly if a Girl the plantation that I bought of Samuel and Henry Rogers and that plantation at Assawoman" and my part of Pamco Island to my grandau

123

Elizabeth Stockly. Wife to have use of the planta. where I now live & the planta. where John Rogers lives, & the profits of 1/2 my part of Pamco Island for life. To Mary Stockly, wid. of Eyre Stockly, the use of my planta at Town during her wid. & the use of 1/2 my part of Pamco Island. To George Green, son of John Green, dec. land lying over the Slash that Phillip Hargas lives on and where his father lived, provided Capt. John Bagwell makes over to me or the grandchild to whom the planta. where I live will belong, 25 A. adj. the land I bought of Robert Carruthers. Should all my grandchildren die before age or marriage, Mary Stockly to have the planta. at Town & Pamco Island; the planta. I bought of Samuel & Henry Rogers to Sarah Bagwell Carruthers; the planta. at Assawoman to John Carruthers & the planta. where I now live to Ezekiel Young. Witt: Robert Carruthers, Mary Adams, Smith Only.
In order of prob: Tabitha Stockly qualified – Elizabeth & Ann Stockly, infants, heirs at law.

BRITTINGHAM, NATHANIEL – 13 Mar. 1740 – 26 May, 1741 – To son Jesse Brittingham planta. where I now live and all the land on the West of the land I have hereafter given to my son Beaverly Brittingham. To son Beaverly land & marsh beginning at the mouth of a gut issuing out of Pitts Creek. To dau. Rachel Pitts. To dau. Betty Waugh. To dau. Sarah Brittingham. To dau. Mary Brittingham. Wife Sarah, son Beaverly & daus. Sarah & Mary Brittingham resid. legatees. Sons under 18 – Wife Sarah Exec. & in failure of my wife my son in law Mr. Robert Pitt. Witt: Elijah Brittingham, John Brittingham, John Benson. – p. 315
In order of prob: Robert Pitt, Gent: app. guardian to Jesse Brittingham, heir at law.

GUY, NICHOLAS – 20 Mar. 1740 – 30 June 1741 – To wife Ann. To son Major Guy. To son William Guy. To dau. Catherine Guy. Wife & children resid. legatees. Wife & Caleb Burton Exrs. Witt: Robert Coleburn, John Guy – p. 322

LUCAS, THOMAS – 1 Sept. 1735 – 25 Aug. 1741 – To son Thomas Lucas planta. where I Now live, cont. 100 A. To son Levin Lucas 80 A. adj. said planta. Bro. William Lucas Exr. Witt: William Lewis, Nehemiah Walker, Solomon Lucas. – p. 335
In order of prob: William Lucas refused to qualify, and Adm. granted Persevella Lucas, wid. of Thomas.

WISE, JOHN, Sr. – 20 Sept. 1741 – 29 Dec. 1741 – To son Thomas Wise 1s. To son Matthew Wise 1s. To son Ezekiel Wise 1s. To dau. Tabitha Stockly 1s. To dau. Drummond Simpson 1s. To wife Abigail 1/3 of personal est. Bal. of est. to my aforesaid children & wife & to my two sons Johannis Wise & Joseph Wise. Wife Exec. Witt: John Smith, George Parker – p. 341

SMITH, JOHN – 2 Dec. 1741 – 26 Jan. 1741/2 – The 100 A. I sold Jacob Fox to be deeded to him. Bal. of est. to wife (no name) provided

she bring up my children. Wife Exec. Witt: Littleton Lecatt, Daniel
Rogers - p. 347
In order of Prob: Presented by Keziah Smith, wid. & exec. of John
Smith, who qualified.

THORNTON, JAMES - 20 Nov. 1741 - 26 Jan. 1741/2 - To son John
Thornton. To son James Thornton. To son Southy Thornton. To son
William Thornton. To son Thomas Thornton. To dau. Sarah Thorn-
ton. 3 youngest children Southy, William & Thomas. Wife Bridget.
Wife & 6 children resid. legatees - Wife Exec. Witt: John Wallop,
Thomas Townsend, Henry Townsend - p. 348

RATCHFIELD, THOMAS - 27 Jan. 1741/2 - 28 Jan. 1741/2 - Nunc. -
Died at the house of Richard Brooks. To Richard Brooks servant man
Thomas, stating that he had no relations to whom he would give any-
thing - Proved by John Watts Fogg & Hugh Brooks - Richard Brooks
qualified - p. 351.
In order of prob: "Ratchford".

SLOCOMB, ROBERT - 6 Mar. 1718/19 - 24 Feb. 1741 - Bro. Thomas
Ryley Exr. Eld. son Thomas Slocomb. Youngest son Ryley Slocomb
my land. After payment of debts bal. of est. to be div. bet. all my
children. Richard Grinalds to keep my dau. Sarah untll she is 16.
Francis Young to have the care of my son Bennitt until he is 21.
Witt: Thomas Ryley, Richard Sanders, Edward Brotherton - p. 361

BURLEY, PETER - 9 Mar. 1741/2 - 22 Apr. 1742 - To wife Director
Burley - Dau. Mary Burley. Dau. Elizabeth Burley. Dau. Ann Burley.
Dau. Unice Burley. Wife Exec. Witt: Darmon Darby, George D.
Darby, George Hazleup, Richard Meers - p. 362

PARKS, EDMUND BALEY - 19 Feb. 1741 - 25 May 1742 - To dau.
Rhoda Ewell 1s. & to her dau. Levinah Ewell. To dau. Tabitha Ewell
& Mark Ewell, her husband. To Mark Ewell the piece of marsh I
bought of him. To son Benjamin Parks 100 A. where I now dwell. To
dau. Keziah Parks. To dau. Sinah Parks. Dau. Ann Parks. Bal of est.
to wife during her wid. & if she marry to be div. bet. my wife, Keziah,
Sinah, Ann & Levinah Ewell. Wife Ann & son Benjamin Exrs. Witt:
Cesar Evans - Joshua Chapman - p. 364

PARKS, WILLIAM - 9 June 1741 - 29 June 1742 - All my right & title
to the 100 A. where I now dwell to my 2 sisters Mary & Sarah Parks.
Sisters Mary & Sarah resid. legatees & Executrices. Witt: Cesar
Evans, Joshua Chapman - p. 371
In order of prob: Arthur Parks, eldest bro. & heir at law to William
Parks being returned by the sheriff not to be found in his Bailiwick,
the above will was duly probated - Mary Parks qualified.

SHARPLEY, WILLIAM - 5 Nov. 1741 - 30 Mar. 1742 - To son William Sharpley all my land - Wife to have use of same during her wid.
Dau. Tabitha Sharpley - Dau. Elizabeth Sharpley. Youngest dau.

Sinah Sharpley. Wife (no name), son Thomas, dau. Comfort, son Joseph, dau. Elizabeth & dau. Sinah resid. legatees. Friends James Wishart & William Beavans Exrs. Witt: Joseph Stockly, Sr., Samuel Hosier, Cuzilina Vanelson - p. 382
In order of prob: Tabitha Sharpley, wid. of William qualified.

BENSTEN, ALEXANDER - 13 Mar. 1741 - 29 June 1742 - To son Edward Bensten all my lands reversion to his son Alexander Bensten. To my several daus. & their husbands & their children what I have given them now in their possession. Children of my son in law Charles Davis resid. legatees. Son Edward Exr. To William Merrils 2 youngest children by my dau. Witt: George Douglas, William Chance. p. 393
In order of prob: Levin Bensten heir at law to Alexander Bensten.

FINNEY, ANDREW - 24 Sept. 1741 - 28 July 1742 - To son Abel. To son Andrew. To dau. Sarah Finney. To son Arthur Finney. To dau. Betty Finney. To son William. To Benjamin Littleton. To wife Elizabeth 300 A. where I now live & all my other est. during her wid. then my son Abel Finney to have my manor planta. & 200 A. To son Andrew Finney the remaining 100 A. children Abel, Andrew, Sarah, Arthur, Betty & William Finney resid. legatees. Bro. William Finney & friend Abel Upshur Exrs. Not witnessed. - p. 394

RIGGS, ISSAC - 11 Sept. 1742 - 26 Oct. 1742 - To dau. Margaret Riggs planta. where I now live & for want of heirs to my bros. Watson & Benjamin Riggs. Witt: Ardrew Allen, Elizabeth Hutchinson, Mary Rodgers -
Codicil: To mother her choice of 6 hogs, cattle &c. To kinswoman Elizabeth Smith. p. 402
In order of prob: Presented by Naomi Riggs, wid. of the testator, who qualified.

SIMPSON, JOHN - 23 Dec. 1741 - 26 Oct. 1742 - To wife Mary. To son Thomas Simpson planta. & marsh where I now live being 442 A. reserving his mother's thirds. To dau. Sinah Simpson. Dau. Mary Simpson. Dau. Ann Simpson (wife Mary mother of all the children) Wife & children resid. legatees. Wife Exec. Witt: Southy Rew, Job Haddersick, William Riley - p. 403

HICKMAN, HENRY - 20 Aug. 1738 - No order of probate (1742) - To 3 sons Henry, George & Edward my right & title to land & marsh on South side of Guilford Creek known as Cedar Island. To wife whole personal est. to bring up my grandson Richard Hickman, and at her death to be div. bet. my 4 sons & 3 daus. Wife (no name) & son Henry Exrs. Witt: Southy Rew, George Bundick, Elizabeth Scott - p.404

ROOSE, JOHN - 12 Aug. 1742 - 30 Nov. 1742 - To son John Roose. To wife Ellison use of whole est. during her wid. then to be div. bet. wife & all my children. Wife Exec. Witt: Edmund Scarburgh, James

Roose, William Scarburgh, Christian Stockley – p. 405

MILLICHOPS, NICHOLAS – 8 Aug. 1742 – 30 Nov. 1742 – To son Nicholas 108 A. purchased of John Riggs adj. my dwelling planta. To son Nicholas my dwelling planta. & 218 A. & water grist mill adj. the same. To grandau. Elizabeth Millichops, dau. to John Millichops, dec. 164 A. where Robert Jarvis formerly lived & 200 A. on Mosongo Swamp. To Nicholas Abbott, son of William Abbott. To dau. Naomi Millichops. Daus. Tabitha, Naomi & Mary resid. legatees. Son Nicholas Exr. Witt: John Tankred, Charles Ashby, Stephen Warrington – p. 406
In order of prob: John Tankard app. guardian to Elizabeth Millichops, heir at law to the testator.

COPES, THOMAS – 4 Dec. 1741 – 1 Dec. 1742 – To son Southy Copes 200 A. where John Sterling now lives. To dau. Mary. Wife (no name) & Peter Parker Copes Exrs. Witt: Zophar Simpson, Giles Copes. – p. 420
In Order of prob: Thomas Copes heir at law to the above testator cited to appear by Southy Rew, his guardian, & no objection being made said will was admitted to probate. Comfort Copes, wid. of the testator qualified.

VANELSON, GUZALINE, the younger – Nunc – 15 Dec. 1742 – 28 Dec. 1742 – To bro. Elias' son Elias. To Comfort Tunnel. Bal. of est. to Sarah Tunnel. To bro. Joseph. Proved by Elias Vanelson & Sarah Roberts – p. 420
In order of prob: Sarah Tunnell, widow, devisee of the testator qualified.

NOCK, ELIZABETH – 4 Feb. 1742/3 – 22 Feb. 1742/3 – To grandson Joseph Nock. To son Robert Abbott, son Richard Abbott, dau. Peggy Nock. Son in law Elijah Nock, he to pay his bro. John Nock 4 bbls. of corn &c. Dau. Mary Chambers. To son Richard Abbot's wife. To John Nock, Jr. Bal. of est. to be div. bet. son Robert Abbot, Richard Abbot, John Nock, Stephen Warrington & John Chambers. "children" Robert Abbot & John Exrs. Witt: John Wilkins, Thomas Webb, George Nock. In order of prob: "John", one of the executors referred to as John Nock.

DELASTATIUS, SEBASTIAN – 30 Sept. 1738 – 29 Mar. 1743 – To son Sebastian planta. where I now live cont. 400 A., being the land deeded to me by my dec. father, also all my right & interest in the 300 A. purchased of Thomas Stockly & Rhoda, his wife. To son Peter all my land purchased of Mr. Richard Lee not already sold by me, the same being 450 A., also my water mill. Son Sebastian resid. legatee. Sons Peter & Sebastian Exrs. Witt: Charles Stockly, Joseph Stockly, Jr., Joseph Robins. – p. 449
In order of prob: Ezekiel Delastatius, heir at law to the within Sebastian, appeared by Samuel Feddiman, his guardian, and there being no

objection the said will was admitted to probate.

DELASTATIUS, PETER – 5 Feb. 1742 – 29 Mar. 1743 – Wife to have 1/2 of est. and son the other 1/2. Wife to bring up my son and learn him to work and not bring him up as a vagabond. Proved by Joseph & Meshack Feddeman. – p. 452
In order of prob: Esther Delastatius, wid. of the dec., qualified.

TAYLOR, JOHN – 5 Mar. 1742 – 29 Mar. 1743 – To son John 100 A. purchased of Thomas Layfield where I now live. To son Levin. To son Jeremiah. To son Samuel. To dau. Patience Johnson. To dau. Mary Wilkinson. Son John to bring up my two youngest children Jacob & Jeremiah. Children Levin, Jacob, Jeremiah & Edith Taylor resid. legatees. Son John Exr. Witt: Samuel Feddeman, Joseph Robins, Thomas Mersey. – p. 452
In order of prob: Samuel Taylor heir at law.

BRITTINGHAM, CHRISTIAN – 4 Feb. 1742/3 – 31 May 1743 – To eld. son William Brittingham. To son John Brittingham. To son Thomas Brittingham. To son Samuel Brittingham. To dau. Christian. To Zorobable Gill. To dau. Elizabeth Hall. To grandau. Ann Hall. Grandau. Betty Hall. Grandau. Mary Hall. Son in law John Hall & his wife Elizabeth. To grandau. Christian Hill. Son in law John Hall resid. legatee & Exr. Witt: Richard Ayres, Stephen Hall, William Hopkins – p. 465

FINNEY, COMFORT – 21 Jan. 1742 – 31 May 1743 – To dau. Elizabeth Whittingham (Whittington) To grandaus. Naomy, Ann & Mary Ann Ewell. To dau. Naomy Stockly for life, reversion to grandau. Comfort Davis. To dau. Mary Kendall. Grandchildren Joshua, Jabez & Mary Kendall. Grandson William Kendall. Grandau. Elizabeth Beavans till her son Samuel Beavans comes to the age of 21. Grandson Elias White. Grandau. Comfort Wishart. Grandsons John Kendall & Thomas Wishart. To son in law James Wishart. Dau. Hannah Wishart. Grandau. Betty Williams. Dau. Ester Williams. Grandau. Naomi Davis. Son in law John Williams. To 5 daus. Elizabeth Whittingham, Naomy Stockley, Mary Kendall, Hannah Wishart & Ester Williams 200 A. of land & marsh called Sister Island. 5 daus. resid. legatees & Executrices. Witt: Thomas Teackle Taylor, Stephen Shay. – p. 467
In order of prob: Jedidiah Ewell, one of the heirs at law appeared by William Arbuckle, his attorney, and the rest of the heirs at law appeared by George Douglas, their attorney, and having nothing to object the said will was admitted to probate.

MIFFLIN, EDWARD – 7 Sept. 1740 – 31 May 1743 – To son Daniel the tract of land where I now live lying in the mouth of Swans Gut Creek, with my water mill & planta. in Maryland. To son Samuel planta. situate in the Northern Liberties of Philadelphia near Schoolcill whereon my father John Mifflin lived, cont. 270 A. To son Southy my house & lot in High Street in Philadelphia in Pennsylvania, near the great meeting house. "whereas there is a dispute with my brothers & sisters children about part of my above given planta. near Philadelphia, which if they recover their claim I desire that my son Samuel Mifflin may have 200L in lieu of what they recover" To grandau. Ann Eyre. Bal. of est. to wife & 3 sons. Wife Mary to have her natural life in the planta. where I live, also my water mill & planta. in Maryland, the profits of my house in Philadelphia & all my planta. on Schoolkill until my sons Samuel & Southy come to the age of 21. Est. not to be divided until son Daniel is 21. Son Daniel, Joseph Maxfield & wife Mary Exrs. Witt: Joseph Maxfield, John Watson. Jacob Hill, William Gore - p. 470

In order of prob: Joseph Maxfield a Quaker. Daniel Mifflin heir at law.

MARCHANT, BENJAMIN - 4 Feb. 1742 - 31 May 1743 - To son Zorobabell Marchant (under 21) at his mother's dec. To dau. Catharine Marchant, at her mother's dec. To son Shadrack Marchant. To daus. Margaret & Esther. To sons William & John land & planta. where I now live at their mother's dec. Wife to have use of whole est. To bring up my children. Wife Elizabeth Exec. Witt: Samuel Feddeman, Howel Bootin, Jacob Broadwater, Joshua Milbourne - p. 472

In order of prob: Zorobabell Marchant heir at law.

HADDERSICK, JOB - 30 Sept. 1742 - 31 May 1743 - To Elizabeth Ayrs whole est. real & personal. Elizabeth Ayrs Exec. Witt: Thomas Riley, George Drummond, John Willet - p. 473

SHIELD, WILLIAM - Not dated - 31 May 1743 - To Roger Taloar. To Kendall Hogsheare. To John Reed. Wife (no name) resid. legatee. Witt: Abraham Shavers, Mary Shavers - p. 474

In order of prob: Presented by Ann Shield, wid. of the testator, who qualified.

HOGGHERE, KENDALL - Not dated - No order of probate (1743) - To bro. Kindel Hoggher my sorrel horse &c. To William Shield personalty & my right of Marsh upon pop's Island. To Sarah Grimes. To cousin Alexander Taylor. "I give unto Sarah Grimes my large Chest & my bible & Common Prayer book Robert Hoggshear Leaves William Sheild Executor of his Last Will & testament" Signed Kendall Hogghere. Witt: Sarah Grimes, William Sheild - p. 475

FILBY, GEORGE - Not dated - 28 June, 1743 - My father to hold the land & planta. where he now lives for life reversion to my wife Mary & to her first heir if she have any by me, & if not to whom she please. Witt: Edward Hitchlns, Febe Filby, Howell Bootin. Wife & William Bootin Exrs. - p. 477

In order of prob: Stephen Filby heir at law to the testator - Sheriff's return not found in his Bailiwick.

SHEPHERD, JACOB - 15 Mar. 1742 - 30 Aug. 1743 - To son John 3 pewter plates marked "J.S." To dau. Elizabeth Shepherd. To dau. Esther Shepherd. Wife Esther resid. legatee. Wife & friend John Kitson Exrs. Witt: Thomas Crippen, John Nock, Thomas Webb - p. 478

COLLINS, JOHN - 6 Mar. 1742/3 - 30 Aug. 1743 - To dau. Bridget Thornton. To grandchildren Sarah & Rachel Townsend. To son John Collins "if he does come back". To son John Collins' children. Bal. of est. to wife & the rest of my children. Sons to be at age at 18, daus. at 16. Son Thomas Exr. Witt: Thomas Townsend, William Collins, Joseph Taylor - p. 479

PARKS, JOHN - 20 Apr. 1743 - 30 Aug. 1743 - To wife Liddia Parks. To son Mark Parks. To dau. Jemina Taylor. To son John Parks. To dau. Rachel Parks. Dau. Elizabeth Parks. Dau. Sabra Parks. Son Sacker Parks. Dau. Jemima "Tiler". Bal. of est. to wife Liddia. Son Mark, dau. Jemima Tiler, sons John, Rachel, Elizabeth, Sabra & son Sacker Parks. Wife & son Mark Exrs. Witt: Cesar Evans, Mary Parks - p. 487

CORBIN, ROBERT - 8 Sept. 1743 - 25 Oct. 1743 - To Wife Ann whole est. for life then to my son Ralph Corbin planta. where I now live. To son David land on Massongo which I bought of George Philby. Daus. Leah, Scarburgh, Wealthy, Susannah & Mary Ann. Wife Ann Exec. Witt: John Snead, Jane Snead, Daniel Hall. p. 499
In order of prob: David Corbin heir at law.

CUTLER, THOMAS - 24 Apr. 1743 - 25 Oct. 1743 - To bro. Richard Cutler my land which was given me by my father George Cutler for 50 A. & negro London given me by my father at my mother's death, & for want of issue to my bro. Samuel Cutler. To bro. George Cutler. To Caleb Burton. To sister Betty Hall. To sister Arcadia Cutler. Betty Hall, Richard Cutler, Samuel Cutler & Arcadia Cutler resid. legatees. Caleb Burton Exr. Witt: Hugh Roberts, Isaiah Evans, Arcadia Cutler. "my will is that my brother Daniel Cutler nor his heirs Should never Inherit any Part or Parcel of what I ever Owned" "Interlined before Signed" - p. 503
In order of prob: Daniel Cutler heir at law.

TAYLOR, ELIAS - Nunc. 6 Sept. 1743 - 15 Oct. 1743 - Wife Judith & unborn child to have that estate I have & my bro. John must take back the Miln he sold me as he has promised to do. Proved by Anne Milman - p. 504
In order of prob: Judith Taylor, wid. of the testator, qualified.

FENN, PHILIP - 14 Aug. 1743 - 25 Oct. 1743 - "I appoint my wife Mary Finn my Executrix first and William Underhill my second I make my daughter Mary my heir to my plantation where I live containing 120 A. during her life & then to her son Elijah" Wife to have use of Planta. during her wid. 3 grandchildren Catherine Ansello, William

Ansello & Charles Finn resid. legatees after my wife's dec. Witt: George Cutler, James Poolman, John Warrington. - p. 505

In order of prob: "Jacob Badger, guardian to the son of Joseph Powell & Susanna his wife and to William Angelo, son of James Angelo & Sarah his wife, (for this purpose appointed) two of the daughters & co heirs of the within Philip Fenn, dec., & William Underhill who inter-married with Mary, the other daughter & co heir of the said Philip, appeared and having nothing to object against the proving of the within will the same was proved and admitted to probate"

WATTS, WILLIAM - 2 Oct. 1743 - 29 Nov. 1743 - To son John Watts land where I now live, also Mills Island & Wolfs Denn. To son Charles Watts planta. in Maryland called Mattapany & likewise Accomsick Island. To son William Watts land in Maryland called New Port pannel. To wife Comfort 1/3 of all my personal est. & 1/3 of my land during her life. Wife & son John Exrs. Witt: Robert Nairn, John Smith, Lemuel Kendall - p. 506

In order of prob: Henry Scarburgh app. guardian of John Watts, heir at law to the testator. - Henry Scarburgh qualified on estate.

BELL, EDWARD - 24 July 1742 - 29 Nov. 1743 - To wife Mary 1/2 my land & planta. during her wid. & then to my son William Bell. To son William Bell planta. where I now live cont. 101 A. on Muddy Creek Branch. To grandau. Susanna Bell. To son John Bell. Son Elias Bell. Dau. Tabitha Tathan. Daus. Elizabeth & Rachel Bell, they to be at age at 18. Daus. Mary, Elizabeth & Rachel resid. legatees. Son William & wife Mary Exrs. Witt: Major Bird, John Bloxsom, Tabitha Bloxsom. p. 511 In order of prob: John Bell heir at law to the testator.

SCARBURGH, JOHN - 12 July 1743 - 29 Nov. 1743 - To son Charles (under age) land & planta. where I now live cont. 975 A. also my planta. called Hog Neck cont. 500 A. To dau. Bradhurst Scarburgh land at Pocomoke cont. 400 A. To dau. Elizabeth Scarburgh planta. at Assawoman cont. 200 A. To dau. Tabitha Scarburgh. To dau. Sarah Scarburgh. Wife Tabitha. Col. Henry Scarburgh, Edmund Bayly & John Selby in Maryland Exrs. Witt: William Bagg, Richard Bonny-well, Robert Cole - p. 513

In order of prob: Charles Scarburgh infant heir at law to the testator.

BONNYWELL, THOMAS - 1 Dec. 1743 - 27 Dec. 1743 - To two sons George & Thomas land I bought of Anthony Hudson lying on the head of Mosongo on the North side of Guilford Road cont. 100 A. To Hannah Bonnywell. wife of James Bonnywell. To Sarah Savage. To Elizabeth Ewell. To bro. James Bonnywell. Bal. of est. to be re-served for my two sons George & Thomas. Bros. James & Joachim Bonnywell Exrs. Witt: Griffith Savage, Elizabeth Ewell, John Bonny-well - p. 520

NOCK, GEORGE - 8 Jan. 1743/4 - 1 Feb. 1743/4- To bro. Elijah Nock. Bro. William Nock. Bro. Solomon Nock. Bro. John Nock. To cousin Joseph Nock. To sister Sarah Chambers. To bro. Nehemiah Nock. Bal. of est. to be div. bet. all my bros. & 2 sisters. Bros. John & William Exrs. Witt: Richard Justice, Thomas Webb, Elias Truit - p. 525

SHIELD, DELIGHT - 16 Nov. 1742 - 1 Feb. 1743/4 - To son William Sacker Shield. To son John Shield. To Abel Badger. To Rachel Badger "the chest that was her mothers with all that is in it" 7 children Sacker, Reuben, John, Rachel, Elizabeth, Sarah & Anne Shield resid. legatees. Sons William Sacker Shield & Reuben Shield Exrs. Witt: Thomas Parramore, Robert Coleburn, John Bagwell - p. 533

Orders 1744-1753

STOCKLEY, CHRISTOPHER - Adm. his est. to Sabra Stockley - Andrew Stewart & George Smith sec. - 30 Oct. 1744 - p. 2

FITZGERALD, PETER - Adm. his est. to his wid. Anne Fitzgerald - Rodolphus Scott & Jacob Badger sec. - 29 Jan. 1744/5 - p. 25

JENKINSON, JOHN - Adm. his est. to Jesse Jenkinson - Andrew English & Thomas Parramore sec. 29 Jan. 1744/5 - p. 25

COLONEY, O'BRYAN - Adm. his est. to Floriana Coloney - Daniel Shae & John Fitzgerald sec. - 30 Jan. 1744/5 - p. 28

NEEDOM, JOHN - Adm. his est. to his wid. Elizabeth Needom - Joseph & Alexander Stockly sec. - 26 Feb. 1744/5 - p. 31

BEAVANS, WILLIAM - Adm. his est. to his wid. Tabitha Beavans - Teackle Taylor & Mason Abbot sec. - 26 Mar. 1745 - p. 36

SMITH, DANIEL - Adm. his est. to his wid. Mary Smith - William Marshall sec. 28 May 1745 - p. 44

THOMSON, ROBERT - Adm. his est. to his wid. Jemima Thomson - 28 May 1745 - P.44

WALKER, NEHEMIAH - Adm. his est. to his wid. Mary Walker - Joseph Walker sec. 28 May 1745 - p. 44

CUTLER, JOHN - Adm. his est. to William Cutler & Mary Roberts - William Bagge & George Wise sec. 28 May 1745 - p. 45

EWELL, ELIZABETH - Ordered that the sheriff take her est. into his hands & make sale thereof - 28 May 1745 - p. 53

LARY, MARY - Ordered that the sheriff take her est. into his possession & make sale of the same - 25 June 1745 - p. 59

132

TAYLOR, JOSEPH – Adm. his est. with will annexed to John Taylor – George Douglas sec. – 30 July 1745 – p. 65

STOCKLEY, JOSEPH – Adm. his est. with will annexed to John Michael – George Douglas sec. – 31 July 1745 – p. 68

SMITH, JOHN – Adm. his est. to Elizabeth SMITH – William Arbuckle sec. – 27 Aug. 1745 – p. 73

ANDREWS, ANDREW – Adm. his est. to his wid. Sarah Andrews – William Rowley sec. 24 Sept. 1745 – p. 81

WISE, WILLIAM – Adm. his est. to his father, John Wise – Isaac Smith sec. – 26 Nov. 1745 – p. 92

LINTON, SARAH – Adm. her est. to Thomas Bloxom – Robert Abbott sec. – 26 Nov. 1745 p. 92

DOWNING, ROBERT – Adm. his est. to his wife Mary Downing – 28 Jan. 1745/6 – p. 106

FITZGERALD, MARY – Adm. her est. to her son John Fitzgerald – John Drummond sec. 28 Jan. 1745/6 – p. 108

SIMPSON, MARY – Adm. her est. to Charles Rew – Thomas Crippen sec. – 25 Mar. 1746 p. 123

HOOTEN, DAVID – Adm. his est. to his wid. Esther Hooten – Thomas Northam & Thomas Lucas sec. – 29 Apr. 1746 – p. 124

SNEAD, MARY – Adm. her est. to her husband Smith Snead – William Arbuckle sec. – 24 June 1746 – p. 147

OBRYAN, Furlough – Adm. his est. to William Conner – George Douglas & William Arbuckle sec. – 29 July 1746 – p. 154

ABBOT, JOHN – Adm. his est. to Mary Abbot – William Hickman & George Bundick sec. 29 July 1746 – p. 155

WILKINSON, THOMAS – Adm. his est. to Jacob Wilkinson – George Douglas sec. – 26 Aug. 1746 – p. 160

WILKINSON, ELIZABETH – Adm. her est. to Jacob Wilkinson – George Douglas sec. – 26 Aug. 1746 – p. 160

GRIFFIN, EMANUEL – Adm. his est. to his wid. Margaret Griffin – William Bagge sec. – 30 Dec. 1746 – p. 177

CUSTIS, JOSEPH – Adm. his est. to Mary Custis – Richard Rogers sec. – 27 Jan. 1746/7 – p. 179

ASHBY, CHARLES - Adm. his est. to William Beavans - George Douglas sec. - 27 Jan. 1746/7 - p. 179

HARRISON, JOHN - Ordered that the sheriff take into his possession the est. of the said Harrison & make sale of same - 26 May 1747 - p. 198

SMITH, SIMON - Adm. his est. to Henry Fletcher - Isaac Smith sec. - 30 June 1747 - p. 205

SCOTT, RODOLPHUS - Adm. his est. to his wid. Patience Scott - West Kellam & John Kellam sec. - 28 July 1747 - p. 214

ROBERTS, SAMUEL - Adm. his est. to Thomas Roberts - Jacob Stakes & George Cutler sec. - 27 Oct. 1747 - p. 231

ABBOT, RICHARD - Adm. his est. to his wid. Anne Abbot - Ebon Bird & Henry White sec. - 24 Nov. 1747 - p. 233

WALKER, JOHN - Adm. his est. to his wid. Esther Walker - George Douglas & Robert Ardis sec. - 31 May 1748 - p. 266

JOHNSON, EDMUND - Adm. his est. to his wid. Patience Johnson - George Douglas & Levin Taylor sec. - 31 May 1748 - p. 266

KERSON, ALEXANDER - Adm. his est. to William Bagge - George Holden sec. - 31 May 1748 - p. 267

GOWTEE, JOHN - Adm. his est. to his wid. Mary Gowtee - Mason Abbot & Thomas Parramore sec. - 31 May 1748 - p. 268

BANKS, CHRISTOPHER - Adm. his est. to his wid. Naomi Banks - Elias Stockley & Daniel Cutler sec. - 31 May 1748 - p. 269

READ, RICHARD - Adm. his est. to his wid. Tabitha Read - Robert Pitt & John Rowles sec. - 29 Nov. 1748 - p. 296

BYLES, JAMES - Adm. his est. to Hancock Nickless - George Holden sec. - 30 Nov. 1748 - p. 299

BRADFORD, NOAH - Adm. his est. to Elizabeth Bradford - James Richards & William Niblet sec. - 30 Nov. 1748 - p. 299

GRIFFITH, JAMES - Ordered that the sheriff take possession of his est. & make sale of same - 27 Dec. 1748 - p. 305

JEPSON, HENRY - Ordered that the sheriff take possession of his est. & make sale of same - 31 Jan. 1748/9 - p. 313

MACMATH, JANE - Adm. her est. to Thomas Wise - William Arbuckle sec. - 28 Feb. 1748/9 - p. 320

HUTCHINSON, ELIZABETH, Ordered that the sheriff take possession of her est. & make sale of same - 28 Feb. 1748 - p. 320

TAYLOR, NEHEMIAH - Adm. his est. to Thomas Parramore - George Douglas sec. - 1 Mar. 1748/9 - p. 321

WATKINSON, ABIGAL - Adm. her est. to Whittington Bayly - John Rowles sec. 28 Mar. 1749 - p. 325

NICKLESS, HANCOCK - Adm. his est. to his wid. Eleanor Nickless, Thomas Teackle & James Rule sec. - 30 May 1749 - p. 333

POOLMAN, JAMES - Adm. his est. to George Holden - "Douglas" sec. - 26 July 1749 - p. 352

MARSHAL, JOHN - Adm. his est. to Mary Marshal - George Douglas & William Arbuckle sec. - 29 Nov. 1749 - p. 370

NEWBERRY, JOHN - Adm. his est. to James Pettigrew - George Douglas sec. - 26 Dec. 1749 - p. 374

ABBOTT, MASON - Adm. his est. to George Abbott - Ralph Justice & Samuel Burton sec. 26 Dec. 1749 - p. 375

ADAMS, THOMAS - Adm. his est. to Alexander Adams & Ralph Justice - George Abbott sec. - 26 Dec. 1749 - p. 275

ARMITRADER, HENRY - Adm. his est. to Abigail Armitrader - John Bradford & Samuel Beech sec. - 30 Jan. 1749 - p. 381

HALL, JOSHUA - Adm. his est. to Martha Hall - Daniel Hall & Wrixom White sec. - 30 Jan. 1749 - p. 381

ANDERSON, RALPH - Adm. his est. to Mary Gowtee - George Douglas sec. - 30 Jan. 1749 - p. 382

NICHOLS, GEORGE - Adm. his est. to Ann Nichols - James Gibson & Thomas Bonnewell sec. - 30 Jan. 1749 - p. 382

VANNELSON, THOMAS - Adm. his est. to Jane Vannelson - Charles Vannelson sec. - 30 Jan. 1749 - P. 382

HARRIS, JOHN - Adm. his est. to James Richards - Jacob Stakes & Joshua Burton sec. 30 Jan. 1749 - P. 382

ROWLES, JONATHAN - Adm. his est. to John Rowles - Charles West sec. - 31 Jan. 1749 p. 385

RODGERS, JACOB – Adm. his est. to Richard Kelly – Edmund & Thomas Kelly sec. – 27 Feb. 1749 – p. 388

SCOTT, ROBERT – Adm. his est. to Robert Pitt – George Douglas sec. 27 Feb. 1749 – p. 389

BROADWATER, JOSHUA – Adm. his est. to Jacob Broadwater – Robert Pitt sec. 27 Feb. 1749 – P. 389

HARGRESS, GEORGE – Adm. his est. to Rachel Hargress – Charles West & Caleb Burton sec. – 27 Feb. 1749 – p. 389

McBRIGHT, HUGH – Adm. his est. To Sabra McBright – John Walker sec. – 28 Feb. 1749 – p. 393

HORNSBY, JOHN – Adm. his est. to Esther Hornsby – Bartholomew Twiford, Jr. & Eborn Bird sec. – 28 Feb. 1749 – p. 393

HARRISON, STEPHEN – Adm. his est. to Henry Pike – Daniel Cutler sec. – 28 Feb. 1749 – p. 394

GLADING, JOHN – Adm. his est. to Leah Glading – Robert Jenkinson sec. – 27 Mar. 1750 – p. 399

SMITH, JOHN – Adm. his est. to George Douglas – George Holden sec. – 27 Mar. 1750 – p. 399

WHALEY, THOMAS – Adm. his est. to Barbara Whaley – Jacob Badger & Thomas Savage sec. – 27 Mar. 1750 – p. 399

SHARPLEY, FRANSCINA – Adm. her est. to William Sharpley – Jessey Jenkinson sec. 27 Mar. 1750 – p. 399

ANDREWS, ROBERT – Adm. his est. to Elizabeth Andrews – Charles West & John Rowles sec. – 27 Mar. 1750 – p. 400

RIGGS, WATSON – Adm. his est. to Mary Custis, wid., Thomas Custis & Edmund Allen sec. – 27 Mar. 1750 – p. 401

WIMBROUGH, THOMAS – Adm. his est. to Salathiel Simpson – Edmund Bayly ssc. – 31 July 1750 – p. 428

SMITH, JOHN – Adm. his est. to John Wallop – George Douglas sec. – 29 Jan. 1750 – p. 458

ONLEY, WILLIAM – Adm. his est. to Solomon Powell – John Smith sec. – 29 Jan. 1750 – p. 458

FADREE, HILLYARD – Adm. his est. to Elizabeth Fadree – Charles West & Southy Satchell sec. – 29 Jan. 1750 – p. 459

CUTLER, SNEAD - Adm. his est. to William Arbuckle - George Douglas & George Holden sec. - 31 Jan. 1750 - p. 464

JUSTICE, ANNE - Adm. her est. to Ralph Justice - William Arbuckle & George Douglas sec. - 31 Jan. 1750 - p. 465

DULANY, WILLIAM - Adm. his est. to Joseph Kellam - Joseph Lecatt sec. 26 Feb. 1750 - p. 468

DAVIS, THOMAS - Adm. his est. to Major Davis - Jacob Stakes sec. - 26 Feb. 1750 - p. 468

DAVIS, WILLIAM - Adm. his est. to Major Davis - Jacob Stakes sec. - 26 Feb. 1750 - p. 468

DOWNING, Francis - Adm. his est. to John Robins Downing - William Kellam, Bayside, sec. - 26 Feb. 1750 - p. 468

ABBOT, GEORGE - Adm. his est. to Mary Abbot - Thomas Parramore sec. - 27 Feb. 1750 - p. 471

WOOLD, THOMAS - Adm. his est. to Ralph Justice - William Arbuckle sec. - 27 Feb. 1750 - p. 471

DRUMMOND, RICHARD - Adm. his est. to Katherine Drummond - Thomas Parramore, George Douglas & George Holden sec. - 26 Mar. 1751 - p. 474

STEWART, DANIEL - Adm. his est. to Michael Needham - Elias Stockley sec. - 26 Mar. 1751 - p. 475

DRUMMOND, JOHN, Jr. - Adm. his est. to Elizabeth Drummond - William White & John Kitson sec. - 26 Mar. 1751 - p. 475

CORD, ARTHUR - Adm. his est. to Joseph Cord - George Douglas sec. - 26 Mar. 1751 - p. 476

ASHBY, RACHEL - Adm. her est. to Thomas Parramore - Thomas Teackle sec. - 26 Mar. 1751 - p. 476

CUTLER, SNEAD - Adm. his est. unadministered by William Arbuckle, to George Holden - George Douglas sec. - 26 Mar. 1751 - p. 477

STOTT, DANIEL - Adm. his est. to Christopher Piper - John Dix & John Dix, Jr. sec. 26 Mar. 1751 - p. 477

SHERWOOD, WILLIAM - Adm. his est. to Rachel Sherwood - Henry White & Henry Grinnalds sec. - 26 Mar. 1751 - p. 478

BLOXOM, RICHARD - Adm. his est. to Nicholas Bloxom - William Bloxom sec. - 26 Mar. 1751 - p. 478

ANDREWS, ROBERT - Adm. his est. unadministered by Elizabeth Andrews, to his son William Andrews - Thomas Hall & Jacob Andrews sec. - 30 Apr. 1751 - p. 479

ANDREWS, ELIZABETH - Adm. her est. to her son William Andrews - Thomas Hall & Jacob Andrews sec. - 30 Apr. 1751 - p. 479

BAYLY, BAGWELL - Adm. his est. to William Jackson - William Sharpley & William Conquest sec. - 30 Apr. 1751 - p. 480

BAYLY, EDWARD - Adm. his est. to William Jackson - William Sharpley & William Conquest sec. - 30 Apr. 1751 - p. 480

STRINGER, DANIEL - Adm. his est. to Susannah Stringer - John Bell, William Abbot & John Kitson sec. - 30 Apr. 1751 - p. 480

GIBSON, JAMES - Adm. his est. to Andrew Gilchrist - Tully Robinson Wise & Abel Finney sec. - 30 Apr. 1751 - p. 482

LECATT, JOHN - Adm. his est. to William Aimes - West Kellam sec. - 30 Apr. 1751 - p. 483

TANKRED, ELIZABETH - Adm. her est. to William Tankred - David James & Robert Crippen sec. - 30 Apr. 1751 - p. 484

TANKRED, JOHN - Adm. his est. unadministered by Elizabeth Tankred, his exec., to William Tankred - David James & Robert Crippen sec. - 30 Apr. 1751 - p. 484

SAVAGE, JOHN - Adm. his est. to his wid. Rachel Savage - Simon Harmon sec. - 28 May 1751 - p. 493

ENGLISH, ANDREW - Adm. his est. to Daniel Cutler - Jacob Badger sec. - 29 May, 1751 - p. 503

EWELL, JEDIDIAH - Adm. his est. to his wid. Arcadia Ewell - George Douglas sec. 26 June, 1751 - p. 506

TAYLOR, ROBERT - Adm. his est. to John Taylor - Henry Wright & William Miles sec. 26 June 1751 - p. 506

DAVIS, JOHN - Adm. his est. to Robert Davis - Samuel Davis sec. - 26 June, 1751 - p. 507

BIRD, DANIEL - Adm. his est. to his wid. Margaret Bird, who made oath that the will of the said Daniel was destroyed as she believes - Middleton Mason & Benjamin Parks sec. - 26 June 1751 - p. 507

BELL, ELIAS - Adm. his est. to Elizabeth Bell - Thomas Tatham & William Bell sec. 30 July 1751 - p. 515

BRIMER, JOHN – Adm. his est. to Samuel Lewis, Mary Brimer, wid. of John, relinquishing her right to qualify – George Corbin sec. 30 July 1751 – p. 515

BIRD, MAJOR – Adm. his est. to Sarah Bird – William Bell & Thomas Bloxom sec. 30 July 1751 – p. 516

CHAPMAN, HUMPHREY – Adm. his est. to Mary Chapman – John Blake & William Kendall sec. – 27 Aug. 1751 – p. 518

MORGAN, JACOB – Adm. his est. to Arnold Morgan – William Andrews sec. – 27 Aug. 1751 – p. 518

RATCLIFFE, JEMIMA – Ordered that the sheriff take her est. in his possession & make sale of same – 27 Aug, 1751 – p. 520

SANDERS, JOHN – Adm. his est. to James Sanders – Arthur Robins sec. – 27 Aug. 1751 – p. 520

SCOTT, WALTER – Adm. his est. to his wid. Rebecca Scott – Benjamin Bull & Drake Drummond sec. – 30 Oct. 1751 – p. 538

COPES, JONATHAN – Adm. his est. to George Douglas – George Holden sec. – 30 Oct. 1751 – p. 539

CUSTIS, HENRY – Adm. his est. to his wid. Scarburgh Custis – Charles West & George Holden sec. – 26 Nov. 1751 – p. 546

BAGWELL, WILLIAM – Adm. his est. to Smith Snead – George Parker sec. – 27 Nov. 1751 – p. 552

JENKINS, WILLIAM – Adm. his est. to Gawin Sill – John Jenkins the heir at law relinquishing his right to qualify. John Sill sec. – 27 Nov. 1751 – p. 552

ARMITRADER, ABIGAL – Adm. her est. to Littleton Armitrader – Joshua Burton & Bartholomew Taylor sec. – 28 Jan. 1752 – p. 566

GRIFFITH, OLIVER – Adm. his est. to Edmund Kelly – William Andrews ssc. – 28 Jan. 1751 – p. 568

RAPHIEL, HALBERT – Adm. his est. to John Rodgers, Jr. – Richard Cutler & John Willet sec. – 28 Jan. 1751 – p. 568

ABBOTT, MASON – Adm. his est. unadministered by George Abbot, to Mary Abbot – Thomas Parramore sec. – 29 Jan. 1751 – p. 569

ROWLEY, JOHN – Adm. his est. to Arthur Rowley – William Ewell sec. – 25 Feb. 1751 – p. 575

HARRIS, THOMAS - Adm. his est. to Tabitha Harris - Nathaniel Stockley sec. - 25 Feb. 1751 - p. 575

SHIELD, SACKER - Adm. his est. to Sarah Shield - Reuben Shield & Argol Kellam sec. 31 Mar. 1752 - p. 580

PARKER, SACKER - Adm. his est. to Mark Parks - Drake Drummond sec. - 31 Mar. 1752 - p. 581

PRITCHET, JOSHUA - Adm. his est. to William Pritchet - Isaac Rodgers sec. - 31 Mar. 1752 - p. 582

ANDERSON, JOHN - Adm. his est. to Thomas Parramore & James Rule, Catherine Anderson, wid. of John, relinquishing her right to qualify - George Douglas sec. - 26 May, 1752 - p. 589

CRIPPEN, WILLIAM - Adm. his est. to Thomas Crippen - Paul Crippen sec. - 27 May 1752 - p. 594

PHILBAY, WILLLAM - Adm. his est. to James Stevens - Henry White sec. - 27 May, 1752 - p. 594

PRITCHET, WILLIAM - Adm. his est. to Keziah Pritchet - Nathaniel Lecatt & Charles Bagwell sec. - 1 July 1752 - p. 605

ARBUCKLE, WILLIAM - Adm. his est. unadministered by Katherine, his late wid. dec., to Mary Burton - George Douglas & George Holden sec. - 26 Aug. 1752 - p. 616

ROBERTS, THOMAS - Adm. his est, to Jacob Stakes - Henry White sec. - 27 Aug. 1752. - p. 625

WOOD, DAVID - Adm. his est. to Major Guy - Littleton Armitrader sec. - 28 Nov. 1752 - p. 631

ABBOT, MARY - Adm. her est. to Thomas Parramore - Robert Pitt sec. 31 Jan. 1752 - p. 650

SAVAGE, PARKER - Adm. his est. to Sarah Savage - John Bandfield & Littleton Lurton sec. - 31 Jan. 1752 - p. 651

SHAE, NATHANIEL - Adm. his est. to Amey Shae - Nicholas Milichop & Jabez Lucas sec. - 27 Feb. 1753 - p. 653

GORE, WILLIAM - Adm. his est. to his son Daniel Gore - Thomas Teackle & Thomas Parramore sec. - 27 Mar. 1752 - p. 655

GIBBINGS, THOMAS - Adm. his est. to Ralph Justice - Tabitha, wid. of the said Thomas refusing to give security, George Douglas sec. - 28 Mar. 1753 - p. 675

BARNS, JOHN - Adm. his est. to his wid. Mary Barns - John Drummond sec. - 29 May 1753 - p. 677

Wills &c. 1743-1749

MERCY, MARY - 20 Dec. 1742 - 28 Feb. 1743/4 - Grandson Thomas, son of Thomas Mercy. To son William. To son John Mercy's son Atkins Mercy. Grandson William, son of Atkins Mercy. Grandau Leach, dau. of Atkins Mercy. "To my said son Atkins' children a cow & heifer in the possession of William Evans, their father in law. To dau. Mary, the wife of Edward Benstene. To Leah, the dau. of Mary Benstene. To Leah the dau. of Atkins Mercy. Dau. Mary resid. legatee - Son William Exr. Witt: George Douglas, Tabitha Douglas - p. 1

MELSON, MARY, wid. - 1 Feb. 1739/40 - 28 Feb. 1743/4 - To son Smith Melson planta. where I now live & for want of heirs to my grandson Daniel Melson. To son John Melson forever the land I have given him to use in my life time. My 3 daus. that is now single to have use of the planta. where I now live until they are married. Witt: Charles White, Edward Edwards, Jacob White. - p. 4
In order of prob: John Melson heir at law.

ELLIOTT, ROBERT - 20 Jan. 1733/4 - 28 Mar. 1744 - Wife Mary Elliott sole legatee & Exec. Witt: George Cutler, Joseph Gunter. - p. 19

LITCHFIELD, JACOB - 5 Feb. 1743/4 - 28 Mar. 1744 - To son William Litchfield - To son Joseph Litchfield (under 21). To son Jacob. To dau. Margaret Litchfield. To dau. Tabitha Litchfield. To son Ezekiel Litchfield. To dau. Mary Litchfield. Bal. of est. to wife Mary during her wid. then to be div. bet. my children except my son William. Wife Mary & cousin Ezekiel Litchfield Exrs. Witt: Thomas Riley, John Melson, Middleton Melson - p. 20

MILES, ROGER - 25 Jan. 1743/4 - 24 Apr. 1744 To son William Miles planta. where my father now lives cont. 180 A. Son in law Baley Smith. Wife (no name) & children resid. legatees. Friend Henry Fletcher Exr. Witt: John Hall, Timothy Donoho, Elizabeth Brymer - p. 21

JUSTICE, MARY - 1 Apr. 1744 - 24 Apr. 1744 - To grandson William Justice a gold ring now in the hands of my son Richard Justice. To grandson Ralph Justice, Jr. a gold ring in the hands of my son Richard Justice. To grandson Richard Justice a gold ring now in the hands of my son Richard. To grandau. Ann Kitson, a gold ring in the hands of my son in law John Kitson. To grandson John Kitson. To grandau. Joanna Kitson. To grandau. Ann Justice. To Mary Justice, dau. of Robert Justice. To dau. Elizabeth Nock. Son in law John Kitson Exr. Witt: Thomas Webb, John Wilkins. - p. 23
In order of prob: John Kitson relinquished his right, & Richard, Robert

& Ralph Justice qualified as Exrs. –

WHALEY, SOLOMON – Ordered that the Sheriff take his est. into his hands & make sale of same – 1 Mar. 1743/4 – p. 33

BELL, WILLIAM – 17 Dec. 1742 – 29 May 1744 – To son Robert Bell 250 A. in Accomack & 150 A. in Northampton. Grandsons Nicholas Powell & Robert Clark Jacob. Grandaus. Betty & Mary Jacob. To dau. Elizabeth Jacob. To grandson Nicholas Powell negroes, his grandmother Elizabeth Bell to have his est. until he is 21. Son in law Hancock Jacob. Son in law Abell Powell. Wife to have use of whole est. during her wid. Son Robert Bell, dau. Elizabeth Jacob & grandson Nicholas Powell resid. legatees. Wife Elizabeth & son Robert Exrs. Witt: William Harmanson, Baley Harmon, John Harmon – p. 38

CUTLER RICHARD – 5 Apr. 1744 – 29 May 1744 – To wife planta. in the Forked Neck where I now live cont. 150 A. which was devised to me by my father, during her natural life, reversion to George Holden. To wife negroes for life, reversion to William Herring. Wife (no name) resid. legatee. Wife & George Holden Exrs. Witt: John Cutler, John Nelson, William Cutler. – p. 41
In order of prob: Mary Culter, wid. of the testator, & George Holden qualified.

STURGIS, RICHARD, Sr. Nunc. – 30 Apr. 1744 – 30 May 1744 – Son Absalom Sturgis. Dau. Sarah Sturgis. Son Richard Sturgis. Grandau. Betty Sturgis, dau. of John Sturgis, dec. Proved by William Hickman & John Abbott. – p. 50
In order of prob: Absalom Sturgis qualified.

WARRINGTON, JONATHAN – 23 July 1743 – 28 Aug. 1744 – To bro. Stephen Warrington. To bro. John Warrington. To bro. Thomas Warrington. To sister Ann Aonins (Onions). Wife Sarah resid. legatee & Exec. Witt: William Beavans, Jr., Churchill Darby, George Abbott – p. 98

TAYLOR, JOHN – 7 May 1744 – 30 Oct. 1744 – To son Bartholomew Taylor 100 A. where I now live adj. William Wail, down the creek to a Valley called the Sunken Marsh. To wife Tabitha Taylor for life the use of the remaining part of the land where I live, being 110 A., also the use of 1/2 the land I bought of Arthur Armitrader. To son John Taylor 170 A. purchased of Arthur Armitrader. To son Abraham Taylor. To son William Taylor. To dau. Agness. Bal. of est. to be div. bet. wife & "son William & Agnes & Gilbert & Leah & Levin". To son Levin 110 A. where I now live – Wife Exec. Witt: Edward Edwards, Nathaniel Lecatt, Hanah Grimes – p. 120

CUSTIS, PATIENCE – 2 Oct. 1744 – 30 Oct. 1744 – To Edmund Allen. To Stephen Allen. To James Allen. To James Rule. To sister Margaret Rule. To Ann Bagwell. To sister Tabitha Custis & to her dau. Scarburgh Custis. To bro. Thomas Bagwell. To Abigail Drum-

mond. To Bridget Chandler. To Ann Chandler. To Susannah Chandler.
To dau. in law Susannah Custis. Bro. John Allen resid. legatee & Exr.
Witt: Thomas Parramore, Thomas Custis, William Bagwell. Bro.
John Allen to.pay Susannah Custis her estate. - p. 121

WHARTON, JOHN - 5 Sept. 1742 - 30 Oct. 1744 - To son John
Wharton. To son James Wharton. To dau. Anne Wharton all her
mother's wearing clothes &c. Father in law Capt. John Bagwell resid.
legatee & Exr. Witt: Thomas Parramore, John Allen, John
Bagwell - p. 123

MERCY, WILLIAM - 12 Nov. 1744 - 29 Jan. 1744/5 - 350 A. & stock
on Assateague Island to be sold & proceeds div. bet. wife Patience,
dau. Nanny Mercy, son William Mercy & son John Mercy - Children to
receive their estates at 21 or marriage. To son Joshua Mercy. Wife &
4 children resid. legatees. Wife Patience & Capt. George Douglas &
John Walker Exrs. Witt: Robert Ardes, John Walker, Jr., Robert
Thompson - p. 132

MEERS, WILLIAM - 16 June 1744 - 29 Jan. 1744/5 - To son Bartholomew planta. where he now lives cont. 150 A. reversion to his son
Elijah Meers, & for want of heirs to my son Elisha Meers. To son
William Meers planta. where I now live cont. 150 A. To son Richard
150 A. purchased of Thomas Window. To son Elisha 130 A. adj. his
bro. Richard. To dau. Mary Bird. To dau. Elizabeth Stringer. Bal. of
est. to wife Mary during her life. Wife & son William Exrs. Witt:
Francis Savage, John Foskue, John Kennahorn - p. 133
In ord. of prob: Bartholomew Meers heir at law.

ROWLEY, RICHARD - 12 Oct. 1743 - 29 Jan. 1744 - To son Arthur
Rowley. To wife Grace & her 3 children by me what pewter I had with
her at our marriage. Bal. of est. to be div. bet. wife, sons William,
John & Arthur, dau. Sarah, the wife of Andrew Andrews & my 3 children by my wife Grace. Son Arthur Exr. Witt: George Douglas, William Davis - p. 135

ONIONS, ELIZABETH - 22 Dec. 1744 - 30 Jan. 1744 - To John
Bennet (under 21), son of John Bennet & Elizabeth, his wife. To
Elizabeth Onions. Eyres Onions resid. legatee. Friend Eyres Onions
Exr. Witt: John Drummond, Elizabeth Drummond - p. 151

GALE, LEVIN - Of Somerset County, Maryland - 16 Feb. 1742/3 -
Proved in Somerset County 24 Apr. 1744. Prob. in Accomack 26 Feb.
1744/5 - To bro. Matt: Gale land I bought near White Haven Town
from Thomas Walker, and the place called Priviledge adjoining to it,
he allowing my dau. Leah what the said land cost me. To Day Scot
that part of a tract of land which he has purchased called Akam, being
part of a tract called Sunken Ground adj. the land devised by Col.
Evans to Rachel, now the wife of Daniel Cordry, & being the land
formerly sold Edward Day. To bros. George, John & Matt: Gale &
their wives. Dau. Leah resid. legatee. my aforesaid 3 bros. & dau.

143

Leah Exrs. Bros. guardians of my dau. until she is 21 or marries.
Witt: Hester Ann Hodson, Patrick Stewart, Henry Wanchope. - p. 157
In order of Prob: Presented in Accoomack by Matthias Gale.

SCARBURGH, HENRY - 4 Oct. 1744 - 26 Mar. 1745 - To son Charles
Scarburgh all my lands on Tangier Island. To son Bennet Scarburgh
all my lands in Worcester County formerly Somerset County, Mary-
land. Wife Margaret. Eldest son Henry Scarburgh. Wife & 5 children
resid. legatees. Daus. Margaret & Ann. Unborn child. Bro. in law
Henry Custis & friends William Bagge & Thomas Teackle to div. est.
Wife to have the tuition of all my children until they arrive at 21 or
marry. Wife, Henry Custis, William Bagge & Thomas Teackle Exrs.
Witt: George Douglas, George Holden, James Mitchel, Richard
Drummond - p. 165
In order of prob: William Bagge app. guardian to Henry Scarburgh,
eld. son & infant heir at law to the testator.

CORBIN, DAVID - 2 Mar. 1744 - 28 May 1745 - To bro. Ralph Corbin
planta. on Mossongo after the dec. of my mother. To sisters Leah,
Scarburgh, Wealthy, Susannah & Mary Ann. Witt: Henry Fletcher,
Henry Hill, Elizabeth White - p. 180
In order of prob: Ralph Corbin app. guardian to Ralph Corbin, Jr.,
Inf't. to contest the said will, and having nothing to object the same is
admitted to probate.

LINSEY, JOHN - 8 Sept. 1744 - 25 June 1745 - To John Warrington 50
A. at the head of my land adj. land of the said Warrington. To cousin
Benjamin Griffin all my land & planta. lying to the South & West of
the Schoolhouse adj. the land given John Warrington. To Benjamin
Griffin all my personal est. To cousin Caleb Guy all my land lying to
the North of the Schoolhouse path aforesaid. John Warrington &
Emanuel Griffin Exrs. Witt: John Smith, James Warrington, Stephen
Warrington - p. 183
In order of prob: Huit Onley & Elizabeth, his wife, Emanuel Griffin &
Margaret, his wife, & Richard Jones & Catherine, his wife, sisters &
heirs at law to the testator, appeared in Court and having nothing to
object the said will was admitted to record.

BENSON, SAMUEL - 29 Dec. 1742 - 30 July 1745 - To son Jonah
Benson planta. where I now live with 200 A. adj. thereto. To son
Samuel Benson 100 A. at Watchapreague, also 100 A. being part of a
tract my father in law gave me & my wife on the Southwest side of
Pratts Branch. To dau. Sarah Kellum. To dau. Martha Bradford. To
dau. Mary, she to live on my land until she marries. To wife Johan-
nah use of whole est. during her wid, then my moveable est. to son
Jonah & dau. Mary. Son Jonah Exr. Witt: David Watson, Sarah
Watson, Francis Savage - p. 187
In order of prob: Samuel Benson heir at law to the testator.

TAYLOR, JOSEPH, of Somerset County - Dated "Worcester County"
15 Dec. 1744 - Pro. in Maryland 1 June 1745. Pro. in Accomack 6

June 1745 - To bro. James Taylor 200 A. in Accomack known as West Ridge. To bro. Samuel Taylor 100 A. out of the tract called West Ridge, also 100 A. in Somerset County on Barren Creek known as Guacason Ridge. To bro. John Taylor. To bro. Mathast. To Henry Graham for taking care of me in my sickness & burying of me. To Joseph Melson. Witt: Andrew Sanders, Lance James, Henry Graham. - p. 189

DELASTATIUS, SEBASTIAN - 20 Jan. 1743/4 - 30 July 1745 - To son Lemuel Delastatius (under age) planta. where I now live with 200 A. adj. & one water mill belonging to the same, being part of a tract of land given by my grandfater to my father by deed of gift. To eld. son Sebastian Delastatius 200 A., being part of the tract where I now live, and 300 A. more lying in the swamp that my father bought of Thomas Stockly & Rhoda, his wife. To wid. dau. Phebe Delastatius. To 2nd dau. Mary Delastatius. To 3rd dau. Leah Delastatius. Wife Mary & "her children" resid. legatees. Wife & eld. son Sebastian & Anderson Patterson Exrs. Witt: William Beavans, Anderson Patterson, John Robertson, Ralph Corbin - p. 191 In order of prob: Anderson Patterson, Gent: app. guardian to Sebastian Delastatius, Inf't. helr at law to the testator.

DELASTATIUS, SEBASTIAN - Nunc. - 15 June 1745 - Proved 19 July 1745 - Prob. 30 July 1745 - "you know I have left the child last born nothing in my will let it have part among you" Proved by Mary Delastatiua, wid. of Sebastian Delastatius, age 40 years & upwards, & Phebe Dias - p. 193

MELICHOPS, NAOMI - 6 Jan. 1744/5 - 27 Aug. 1745 - To sister Mary Bradford, wife of Fisher Bradford. To cousin Elizabeth Abbott, dau. of William Abbott. To sister Tabitha Abbott. To William Abbott. To bro. Nicholas Milichops. To cousin Elizabeth Melichops. Bro. Nicholas Milichops resid. legatee & Exr. Witt: William Beavans, Jr., Mary Mason, Temperance Abbott - p. 219

WARRINGTON, STEPHEN - 14 Aug. 1745 - 24 Sept. 1745 - To son Abbott Warrington 140 A. purchased of Churchill Darby. To second son Stephen Warrington 1 silver spoon marked IFA&c. To 3rd son Southy Warrington. To 4th son Jonathan Warrington. To dau. Betty Warrington. To 5th & last son George Warrington. Wife Tabitha & children Stephen, Southy, Jonathan, Betty & George Warrington resid. legatees. Wife & Friend Robert Abbott Exrs. Witt: William Beavans, George Johnson, Comfort Watson, Mary Justice. - p. 239
In order of prob: Robert Abbott guardian to the heir at law.

PITTS, JOHN - 3 Mar. 1744/5 - 24 Sept. 1745 - To wife Hannah, whom I app. my Exec. To son John Pitts, after the dec. of his mother, land on the North side of the Mill Branch. To son Isaac Pitts land on the South side of the Main Mill Branch after the dec. of his mother. To son Samuel Pitts the remainder of my tract of land after my said wife's dec. To son William Pitts. To dau. Jemina Pitts. To

son Robert Pitts all my lands in Maryland. To dau. Mary Blades. To dau. Elizabeth Merril. To dau. Hannah Benston. To grandau. Ann Blades. To grandau. Hannah Blades. To grandau. Levinah Benston. Sons William & Samuel & dau. Jemima resid. legatees. Witt: George Douglas, Robert Pitt, Joseph Feddeman, Arthur Emmerson - p. 245
In order of prob: John Pitts heir at law to the testator.

HINMAN, ARGOL - 22 Aug. 1745 - 26 Nov. 1745 - To 2 sons Thomas & Bayly Hinman 400 A. where I now dwell. To son Argol Hinman. To dau. Mary White. To son Benjamin Hinman. Wife Anne Hinman Exec. Witt: Richard Justice, Samuel Cowley, Caesar Evans. - p. 248
In order of prob: Thomas Hinman heir at law to the testator.

TRUIT, ELIAS - 16 July 1745 - 26 Nov. 1745 - To unborn child planta. where I now dwell cont. 240 A. & for want of heirs to my wife Anne Truit for life then to my godson George Truit Taylor. Father in law Joseph Bell Exr. Witt: Thomas Webb, Truit Wilkins, Kendal Towles - p. 249

STEWART, ANDREWS - 26 Oct. 1745 - 31 Dec. 1745 - To Wife Sarah Stewart 1/3 of my land in Virginia & Maryland during her life. To son Andrew Stewart land & planta. at Watchapreag & land & marsh on Cedar Island. To son George Stewart 300 A. in Worcester County, Maryland, near Swansegut. To dau. Sabra Smith. To dau. Lishey Stewart. To dau. Elizabeth Stewart. To dau. Ziller. To dau. Agnes. To son John Stewart. To son Levin Stewart. To dau. Sarah James. To son Benjamin Stewart. Robert Andrews, John Rowles & Littleton Scarburgh Major to appraise & divide est. Wife Sarah & son Andrew Exrs. Witt: Littleton Scarburgh Major, Robert Watson, Arthur Laylor - p. 250
In order of prob: Benjamin Stewart eldest son & heir at law to the testator.

BELL, NATHANIEL - 9 Dec. 1745 - 28 Jan. 1745/6 - To wife Mary planta. where I now live during her wid., then to my son Nathaniel Bell. Wife to have use of slaves for life then to be div. bet. my 4 children, Nathaniel Bell, Betty Bell, Rachel Bell & Mary Stockly. To son Nathaniel all the rest of my land. To dau. Tabitha Lecatt. Children Mary Stockly, Nathaniel, Betty & Rachel Bell resid. legatees. Friends Abel Upshur, Joachim Michael & Nathaniel Fosque to div. est. Wife Mary, John West & son Nathaniel Bell Exrs. Witt: Joachim Michael, John Joynes, Harmanson Joynes.
In order of prob: Nathaniel Bell heir at law to the testator.

ROBERTS, FRANCIS - 24 Mar. 1744/5 - 25 Feb. 1745/6 - To wife Rose 170 A. where I now live during her wid. & then to my son Abel Roberts planta. where he now lives that was left me by the will of Japhat Davis, also 30 A. of the tract where I now live adj. the land before given him. To son John Roberts planta, where I now live cont. 170 A. To grandson Edmund Watson. To grandson Benjamin Watson.

To grandaus. Amy, Margaret & Priscilla & grandsons Peter & Francis Watson. To dau. Sabra Simpkins. To grandau. Rose Green. Bal. of est. to be div. in 3 parts, wife Rose to have 1 part, dau. Sabra Simpkins 1 part & the other part to sons John & Abel Roberts. Wife Rose & son John Exrs. Witt: Francis Savage, John Hutchinson, Jonathan Garrison. - p. 258
In order of prob: John Roberts heir at law to the testator.

EWELL, ELIZABETH - Ordered that the sheriff take her est. into his possession & make sale of same - 29 May 1745 - p. 270

MIDDLETON, GEORGE - 27 Feb. 1745/6 - 29 Apr. 1746 - To son George Middleton. To son William Middleton. Bal. of est. to wife for life & then to be div. bet. my children - Sons William & George Exrs. Witt: Thomas Riley, George Melson - p. 271

WALKER, JOHN - 13 Apr. 1746 - 27 May, 1746 - To dau. Anne land at Assateague Island in Maryland purchased of Charles Ramsay, also lands in Accomack purchased of Francis Brooks, being 200 A. "Whereas my father in law Mr. Charles Taylor devised to my said daughter Ann the planta. in Maryland where I formerly lived" provided that if my wife Sarah should after that bequest have male issue the said land should go to such issue; should my dau. loose the said land by means of such male issue of my wife Sarah, then, and not otherwise, she to enjoy the land formerly conveyed to me in Accomack County by Charles Stockly. To wife Sarah slaves for life then to be div. bet. my son John & dau. Ann. Wife, son & dau. (both under age) resid. legatees. Slaves to be div. by John Wallop, Daniel Mifflin, George Douglas. Wife, son & dau. Exrs. Witt: John Baldwin, George Douglas, Robert Ardies, Daniel Martiall - p. 273

SNEAD, ANNE - 27 Feb. 1745/6 - 24 June 1746 - To mother, slaves. To cousin Euphamia Arbuckle. Cousin Ann Arbuckle. Cousin Mary Snead. Cousin Anne Gaskins. Cousin John Gaskins. I give my share of my father's negroes due me at my mother's death to be div. bet. Katharine Arbuckle, dau. of William & John Snead, son of John, my bro. To Mary Snead, dau. of John. Mother resid. legatee & Exec. Witt: Ann Guy, John Chandler, William Arbuckle - p. 284
In order of prob: Mary Burton qualified as executrix.

FOSQUE, JOHN - 14 Apr. 1746 - 29 July 1746 - To son John. To wife Mary. To son Nathaniel. To son George. To son Luke. To dau. Rachel Fosque. To dau. Barbara Harmon. To dau. Mary Meers. Wife to have use of planta. & bal. of est. during her wid. then to be div. bet. all my children aforesaid. Abel Upshur, John Darby & Francis Savage to appraise & div. est. Wife Mary & son Nathaniel Exrs, Witt: Francis Savage, William Hamron, Richard Savage - p. 287

BURTON, AMEY - 24 Nov. 1745 - 30 July 1746 - To son Joseph Burton. To dau. Patience Armitrader. To dau. Agnes Garrison. 3 daus. Susannah, Amey & Anne Burton resid. legatees. Son Joseph &

dau. Susannah Burton Exrs. Proved by William Spiers & John Shield –
p. 296

CORBIN, RAPLH – Nunc. – Proved 30 Sept. 1746 – Prob. 30 Sept.
1746 – "What is in the closet wherein I keep my books & medicines I
give to my son Covington – Proved by Mary Evans. Covington Corbin
qualified – p. 305

JESTER, SAMUEL – 17 Nov. 1731 – 25 Nov. 1746 – To wife Mary use
of my planta. & 50 A. of swamp land during her life, then to my son in
law Jeptha Perry & Margaret, his wife for life, reversion to Amey &
Elizabeth Perry, daus. of Jeptha & Margaret Perry. Bal. of est. to
wife for life then to be div. in 4 parts, 1 part to my son Jeptha &
Margaret, his wife, the bal. to be div. bet. the children of Jeptha Perry
& Bridget Dalton. Son in law Jeptha Perry Exr. Witt: John Tankred,
Robert Abbott, Anthony Hudson – p. 307

BONNEWELL, RICHARD – 5 Jan. 1746/7 – 27 Jan. 1746/7 – To
cousin John Bonnewell. To sister Anne Lee. To bro. Joachim Michael Bonnewell. To bro. John Bonnewell. To bro. James Bonnewell.
To cousin Rachel Bonnewell. Bro. Joachim Michael Bonnewell Exr.
Witt: Philip Parker, Susanna Wise, Mary Wise – p. 314

ROWLEY, WILLIAM – 29 Mar. 1747 – 26 May 1747 – To dau. Rachel
Rowley 200 A. where I now live which I bought of William Daniel,
also 50 A. purchased of Charles Dickason adj. the said 200 A. To bro.
Arthur Rowley. To bro. Richard Rowley 150 A. purchased of Charles
Dickason, provided he will make over in the room or stead of his part
of his father's estate to my wife Margaret Rowley, the planta. where I
now live during her wid. To dau. Rachel whole personal est. not
before given. Wife Margaret & bro. Arthur Exrs. Witt: Joseph Robins, John Field, John Townsend – p. 342
In order of prob: Anderson Patterson guardian to Rachel Rowley, Inf't.
heir at law to the testator.

ROBINS, JOSEPH – 29 Sept. 1746 – 25 Aug. 1747 – To son Levi
Robins 125 A. where I now live purchased of Stephen Townsend. To
son Josias Robins all the rest of my land, being the land bought of
John Townsend. To wife whole est. not already given during her wid.
& at her marriage to have 1/2 and the other 1/2 to be div. bet. my 3
youngest children, Levinah Robins, Sarah Robins & William Robins.
To wife Catherine planta. where I now live during her wid. Wife Exec.
Witt: John Townsend, Joseph Feddeman – p. 373

PITTS, ISAAC – 29 June 1747 – 25 Aug. 1747 – To bro. William Pitts
land beq. me by my father John Pitts. To mother Hannah Pitts. To
bro. Robert Pitts. To bro. Samuel Pitts. To bro. John Pitts. To
sister Jemima Pitts. To cousin Anne Blades. Bro. William Exr.
Witt: Robert Pitts, Samuel Feddeman, Joseph Feddeman, Christopher
Banks – p. 374
In order of prob: John Pitts heir at law to the testator.

WALKER, JOSEPH - 22 Apr. 1747 - 25 Aug. 1747 - To son Littleton Walker 100 A. purchased of William Northam. To son Southy Walker. To wife Mary use of whole est. during her life & then to my 2 sons Joseph (under 21) & Littleton Walker. To Joyce Walker, dau. of Nehemiah Walker. Son Littleton Exr. Witt: Major Bird, Sarah Hudson - p. 382
In order of prob: Southy Walker heir at law to the testator.

STRINGER, THOMAS - 6 Sept. 1744 - 29 Sept. 1747 - To son Fereby Stringer 110 A. where Timothy Kelly formerly lived. To son Thomas Stringer. To dau. Ann. To son Jacob Stringer 50 A. at the head of my land, also my water mill & 2 A. adj. Son Jacob resid. legatee & Exr. Witt: Thomas Goffigon, Thomas Hunt, John Goffigon, Jr. - p. 386

MEERS, JOHN - 14 Aug. 1745 - 29 Sept. 1747 - To son Thomas planta. where I now live cont. 150 A., reversion to my grandson John Meers, son of John. To son John Meers planta. where he now lives cont. 150 A. that my father Bartholomew Meers gave me. To son Mark Meers planta. purchased of Major Hitchens with 50 A. of land adj., also 50 A. adj. it off the tract where I now live. Son Bartholomew Meers. To sons John & Thomas 70 A. to be sold for the payment of my debts. Sons John, Thomas & Mark Meers & daus. Elizabeth Major & Mary Ames resid. legatees. Sons John & Thomas Exrs. Witt: Francis Savage, William Garrison - p. 388
In order of prob: Bartholomew Meers heir at law to the testator.

BENSTON, JONATHAN - 15 Aug. 1747 - 24 Nov. 1747 - To wife Hannah use of all my lands during her wid. then to my son Rosewell Benston. To son Jonathan Benston. To dau. Catharine. Bal. of est. to be div. bet. wife & all my children. Bro. Joseph Exr. - Children under age. Witt: George Douglas, John Gowtee, Joseph Gowtee, Ambrose Benston, John Merril - p. 394
In order of prob: John Gowtee app. guardian to Rosewell Benston, heir at law to the testator.

SATCHELL, HENRY - 21 Mar. 1746/7 - 29 Dec. 1747 - To wife Elizabeth planta. where I now live, being 100 A., during her wid. & then to my son Southy Satchell. To son Henry Satchell planta. where he now lives including 75 A. To dau. Sarah White & her husband Henry White, negroes for life, then to their children. To dau. Elizabeth Bundick & her husband John Bundick, negroes for life, then to their children. To dau. Ann Abbott & her husband Richard Abbott, negro for life then to any child of the said Ann to when she may see fit to give it. Grandson William Satchell, son of my son Southy Satchell. Grandau Ann, dau. of Southy Satchell. Wife, son Henry, dau. Elizabeth Bundick, dau. Ann Abbott resid. legatees. Wife Elizabeth & sons Southy & Henry Exrs. Witt: Stephen Fitzgerald, John Blaxton, Anne Blaxton - p. 404
In order of prob: Southy eldest son & heir at law to the testator.

149

ROSE, JACOB - 3 Feb. 1747/8 - 23 Feb. 1747/8 - To William Bigeroa. Wife Tabitha Rose. James Rose resid. legatee. Witt: Mitchel
Scarburgh, Jr., John Rose, Griffith Pritchet - p. 411

GASCOIGNE, WILLIAM BRADFORD- 14 Jan. 1747/8 - 24 Feb.
1747/8 - To son Harmon Gascoigne. To son William Gascoigne. Bal.
of est. to wife Sarah to bring up my children. Robert Coleburn to be
guardian to my eldest son. To Robert Coleburn 60 A. at the head of
Mattchapungo if the said land can be recovered by law or any other
means. Wife Sarah Exec. Witt: John Case, John Bradford, William
James - P. 414
In order of prob: William Bagge app. guardian to Harmon Gascoigne,
heir at law to the testator.

LEATHERBURY, THOMAS - 27 Dec. 1747 - 29 Mar. 1748 - To son
Charles Leatherbury all the land from where Findlay's mill stands
toward the branch where John Leatherbury now lives, all to the North
side of the horse road. To sons Thomas & John & dau. Elizabeth the
profits of all the remainder of my land to bring them up. To son
Thomas negro, wife to have use of him during her wid. or as long as
she shall keep my children. What cash I have to be reserved for the
law suit concerning the land that is in dispute between Mr. George
Holden & I. Wife & 3 children, John, Thomas & Elizabeth resid.
legatees. Wife Rachel, Mr. Thomas Parramore, & Mr. James Rule
Exrs. Witt: Edward Revell, John Leatherbury, William Phinney, Jr.
p. 416
In order of prob: Edward Revell guardian to Charles Leatherbury, Inf't.
heir at law to the testator.

YOUNGE, WILLIAM - 22 Feb. 1745 - 28 June 1748 - To Wife Patience use of slaves, 1/2 of planta. where I now live & 1/2 my person-
al est. during her wid. & then to be equally div. bet. my 2 sons John &
William. To dau. Anne Collins negro, reversion to my grandson
Thomas Jenkins. To son John negroes, house & orchard where I now
live & 1/2 the remaining part of my land & marsh. To son William
negroes & 1/2 my land & marsh. Sons John & William resid. legatees
& Exrs. Witt: John Wise, Jr., Richard Sanders, Anne Hindmane,
Southey Rew, Southey Rew, Jr. - p. 431
In order of prob; John Younge heir at law to the testator.

FOGG, JOHN WATTS - 18 Feb. 1745/6 - 26 July 1748 - To wife
Elizabeth negro York during her wid. & if she marry negro to be sold &
the money paid my unborn child. Dau. Grace Fogg. Son John Watts
Fogg & dau. Grace Fogg resid. legatees. Bro. John Fogg Exr. Witt:
Robert Pitt, Henry Jones - p. 458

VENELSON, CHARLES - 23 May 1748 - 30 Aug. 1748 - To son
Charles Venelson planta. where I now live, cont. 200 A. To wife
Tabitha Venelson. Dau. Anne Venelson. Son Elias Venelson. Son
Lisha Venelson. Wife & 3 children, Elias, Lisha & Anne Venelson
resid. legatees unless my wife be with child, & if so that child to have

1/5 part of what is not before given. Wife & son Charles Exrs. Witt: Caleb Broadwater, Jacob Broadwater, Mary Broadwater, James Wishart. p. 460
In order of prob: Thomas Venelson heir at law to the testator.

PARKER, GEORGE. Seaside - 18 July 1748 - 29 Nov. 1748 - To wife Amey Parker. To son John Parker. To son George Parker. To son Sacker Parker (under 19) To son William Parker. To dau. Anne Parker. To dau. Rachel Parker. 3 youngest children Amy, Rachel & William Parker. To John Blackstone. Wife Amey & son John Exrs. Witt: Nathaniel Sheaff, Elizabeth Bradford, Elizabeth Sheaff - p. 467

MASON, EDE - 17 May 1748 - 29 Nov. 1748 - To Middleton Mason. Father & mother resid. legatees. Mother Exec. Witt: Middleton Mason, Bennet Mason, Zorobable Mason - p. 469
In order of prob: Middleton Mason relinquishes his legacy.

LECATT, JOHN - 1 Mar. 1747/8 - 29 Nov. 1748 - To son John Lecatt 100 A. where he now lives, reversion to grandson Leven Lecatt. To son Littleton Lecatt 208 A. where he now lives. To son Joseph Lecatt 200 A. in Sommerset County, Maryland, adj. the lands given my son Littleton. To son Nathaniel Lecatt all the land I hold lying on Pocomoke Branch where I now live cont. 300 A. Gun marked "B.L." "whereas my son Charles Lecatt sometime ago went to Sea, and not having any certain account whether he be living or dead", in case the said Charles should return within 10 years from this date, my son Nathaniel to give him a good and sufficient maintenance out of the est. above given him, the said Nathaniel. To son in law John Rowles. To dau. Tabitha Rowles. Grandau. Patience Rowles. Grandaus. Rachel & Jane Rowles. Grandau. Anne Parker. 3 children Nathaniel, Joseph & Tabitha Rowles resid. legatees. Son Nathaniel Exr. Witt: Thomas Teackle, Richard Read, Sr., John Lecatt, Jr. - p. 469
In order of prob: John Lecatt eldest son & heir at law to the testator.

BLOXOM, WILLIAM - 16 July 1744 - 29 Nov. 1748 - To wife Elizabeth 72 A. during her natural life & then to my son Moses Bloxom, being the land I purchased of Jeptha Perry. To wife 1/3 of all my lands during her life. To son William Bloxom planta. where I now live cont. 100 A. To 2 sons William & Moses all my right in the marsh lying below William Young's. Son Richard Bloxom. Grandson Richard, son of Richard. Son Nicholas Bloxom. Dau. Mary Baker. Grandson William Baker. Dau. Fortain Bloxom. Grandau. Siner Bloxom. To William Bloxom, son of Nicholas Bloxom. Bro. Woodman Bloxom. Wife Elizabeth & son Richard Exrs. Witt: Woodman Bloxom, John Bloxom, Major Bird. - p. 473
In order of prob: Richard Bloxom heir at law to the testator.

STOCKLEY, JOSEPH - 15 Oct. 1748 - 27 Dec. 1748 - To wife Rebecca Stockley 1/2 my personal est. during her life & then to her dau. Sarah Stockley. Wife to have use of my dwelling planta. during her life, & then to return to my bro. Charles Stockley's first male heir, &

151

for want of such heir to his dau. Ann Stockley. To grandau. in law
Leah Stockley. Cousin Sarah Stockley. Bal. personal est. to bro.
Charles Stockley. To Major Davis the planta. where he now lives.
Bro. Charles Stockley & Joseph Stockley, Clerk, Exrs. Witt: Samuel
Burton, Joseph Stockley, Anne Mackemy - p. 482
In order of prob: John Stockley heir at law to the testator cited to
appear - Sheriff's return "not found within my Bailiwick"

BADGER, REGINALD - 27 Sept. 1748 - 27 Dec. 1748 - To son Jacob
Badger planta. where I now live. To son John Badger land bought of
Morris Shepherd. To Frances Badger. To Leanna, the dau. of
Frances. Dau. Anne Moore. To dau. Rachel Lurton's 2 children,
Henry & Hannah. Dau. Sabra. To Joseph Gunter. To grandson David,
son of Nathaniel Badger. Wife Bridget. Sons John & Jacob resid.
legatees & Exrs. Witt: William Spiers, John Phillips, Robert Barry -
p. 483
In order of prob: Stephen Harrison app. guardian to the heir at law.

TOWNSEND, JAMES - Nunc. - Proved 23 Jan. 1738/9 - Prob. 31 Jan.
1748/9 - "Made in the Christmas Holy Days last past" To bro. Caleb.
To John Paradice. John Paradice resid. legatee. Proved by John
Thornton, age 26, William Davis, age 21, & John White, age 18.
In order of prob: Presented by John Paradice who qualified.

LURTON, JOHN - 30 July 1748 - 31 Jan. 1748/9 - To son Jacob
planta. where I now live. Wife Rachel to have use of planta. during
her wid., cont. 150 A. Son in law John Edwards. Dau. Hannah. Dau.
Rachel. Dau. Elizabeth. Dau. Susanna. Dau. Mary. Bal. personal
est. to wife Rachel. Wife & son Jacob Exrs. Witt: William Wise,
Robert Barry, Joshua Nelson - p. 489

WISE, WILLIAM - Not dated - 1 Feb. 1748/9 - To wife Sarah land
called Wises Addition during her natural life & at her death to Jesse
Brittingham. To wife all my negroes & at her death I give to Mary
Brittingham, her dau. negro Hagar.
To wife 1/3 part of the Shallop called Sally & Polly. To Sarah Brit-
tingham, her child, 1/3 part of the Shallop. To Mary Brittingham, her
child, my dau. in law. To Beverly Brittingham horse called Prince &
1/3 my Shallop. To bro. John Christian Wise. Wife & Robert Pitt,
Major I mean, Exrs. Witt: Robert Nairne, William Holland, John
Holt. - p. 495

JEPSON, HENRY - Ordered that the Sheriff take his est. into his
possession & make sale of same - 31 Jan. 1748/9 - p. 500

ROGERS, REUBEN - 22 Oct. 1748 - 28 Mar. 1749 - To unborn child
planta. where I now live if a boy & if not then to go to my eldest dau.
Sarah Rogers & for want of issue to Leah Rogers, reversion to my
youngest child - Wife Leah Rogers & father Jacob Bishop Exrs. Witt:
Thomas Webb, Elizabeth James, Jacob Bishop, Sr. -p. 501

WARRINGTON, WALTER – 25 Oct. 1746 – 25 Apr. 1749 – To wife Arnashai Warrington whole est. during her life. To grandson Edmond Warrington. Grandau. Levina Park. 5 children, William, Alexander & Walter Warrington, Jemima Park & Rachel Thornton resid. legatees. Wife Exec. – Witt: James Wichart, Thomas Wishart. – p. 503

SATCHELL, ELIZABETH – 12 May 1748 – 25 Apr. 1749 – To dau. Sarah White. Dau. Elizabeth. Dau. Anne Abbott. Son Southy, provided he pay to my mother Elizabeth Ansil 20 s. country produce during her nat life. To son Henry Satchell, he to pay my mother 10 s. Bal. of est. except my clothing to be div. bet. my 5 children, Southy Satchell, Henry Satchell, Sarah White, Elizabeth Bundick & Ann Abbott. To dau. in law Susan Satchell, wife of Southy. To Rachel, wife of Henry Satchell. To Tabitha White, dau. Henry White. Sons Southy & Henry Exrs. Witt: Stephen Fitzgerald, Jacob Dunton, Benjamin Dunton – p. 504

WILLIS, DANIEL – 5 Nov. 1744 – 27 June 1749 – To son Peter Willis. Dau. Bridget Richards. To wife Isabella Willis all my personal est. Wife Exec. Witt: George Hewitt, John Richardson, Ann Frances Lewis – p. 521

WATKINSON, CORNELIUS – 2 June 1749 – 26 July 1749 – Son Thomas Watkinson. Son Cornelius Watkinson. Dau. Tabitha Philips. Son Peter Watkinson. Son Levin Watkinson. Wife Susanna Watkinson resid. legatee – Son Thomas Exr. Witt: Robert Coleburn, John Taylor. – p. 533

Wills 1749–1752

CHAPMAN, SILAS – Nunc – Declaration 17 Aug. 1749 – Proved 16 Sept. 1749 – Prob. 28 Nov. 1749 – Dau. Elizabeth. Dau. Mary. Son Silas. Wife Elizabeth. To my wife's son Ambrose Willis. Proved by Luke Watson & Elias Price – Wid. Elizabeth qualified. – p. 10

STOCKLEY, REBECCA, wid. of Joseph Stockley, dec. 29 Oct. 1749 – 28 Nov. 1749 – Grandau. Leah Stockley. Grandau. Rebecca Mathews. Dau. Sarah Stockley & grandau. Leah Stockley resid. legatees. Son in law Joseph Stockley Exr. Witt: Alexander Stockley, Jane Stockley, Anne McKenney – p. 11

NOCK, JOHN – 11 Oct. 1749 – 28 Nov. 1749 – Son Joseph Nock. Bal. of est. to wife Margeret Nock during her life or wid. then to be div. bet. all my children. Wife Exec. Witt: Comfort Watson, John Evans, William Smith – p. 11

TANKRED, JOHN – 4 Sept. 1749 – 26 Dec. 1749 – Wife Elizabeth to have use of planta. where I now live during her wid. also my personal est. To son Stephen Tankred planta. where I now live cont. 160 A.

Son William Tankred. Son Robert Tankred. Wife Elizabeth Exec. -
Witt: William Beavans, Mary Beavans. - p. 22
In order of prob: William Tankred heir at law to the testator.

ROWLES, JOHN - 29 Dec. 1746 - 30 Jan. 1749 - To wife Phebee
whole est. real & personal. Wife Exec. - Witt: Thomas Hall, Richard
Cutler, Ann Mary Niblet - p. 24

TURLINGTON, PETER - 19 Jan. 1749 - 27 Feb. 1749 - Son Thomas
Turlington. Wife Sarah Turlington. Son Peter Turlington. Grandson
Benjamin Turlington. Wife Sarah resid. legatee. Wife & son Thomas
Exrs. Witt: Daniel Cutler, William Wise, William Tiseker - p. 32

LEWIS, FENN - 10 Dec. 1749 - 27 Feb. 1749/50 - Whole est. to
friends William Nock & Benjamin Nock. William Nock Exr. Witt:
Reuben Shield, Benjamin Nock - p. 42

BAGWELL, ELIZABETH - 20 Oct. 1748 - 27 Feb. 1749/50 - To son
Isaiah Bagwell 200 A. at the head of Guilford Creek, being the same
land I bought of my father Francis Wharton & John Young. To son
John Bagwell. Dau. Elizabeth Bagwell. Dau. Adah Bagwell. Dau.
Ann Bagwell. Bal. of est. to be div. bet. my daus. then living. Son
William Bagwell & Smith Snead Exrs. Witt: Robert Coleburn, Wil-
liam Sacker Shield, Adoniah White - p. 50

BAGWELL, JOHN, Sr. - 1 Nov. 1748 - 28 Feb. 1749/50 - To grandson
Thomas Bagwell, son of my son John Bagwell, planta. where I now
live & all my land on Cedar Island. To grandson John Wharton 250 A.
"being part of the tract of land I hold by the Curtesy of England in
right of my wife Tabitha, deceased", said land to be laid off at Muns
Branch or Walkers Branch. To son John Wharton my land on Chi-
conessex Island. To William Bagwell, son of my nephew Thomas
Bagwell, all the land his father held adj. the planta. I now live on. To
Betty or Elizabeth Stockley meaning Ayres Stockley's eldest dau. 25
A. which he purchased & paid me for adj. my planta. where William
Underhill lives. Grandson James Wharton. Grandau. Ann Wharton.
Bal. of est. to my 4 grandchildren before mentioned. Son in law John
Colcburn. Friends Capt. Edward Revell, Capt. Coleburn & my cousin
Stockley & grandson John Wharton Exrs. Witt: Robert Barry, Adaniah
White, William Kellam, William Sacker Shield. - p. 52
In order of prob: Charles Stockley guardian of Thomas Bagwell, heir
at law to the testator.

DANIEL, William - 10 Jan. 1749 - 27 Mar. 1750 - To dau. Mary
Daniel all my lands, reversion to my sister Elizabeth, the wife of
Elias Bell. Dau. resid. legatee. Mother Jean Collins to have the
tuition of my dau. until she arrive at full age. Should my mother die
before that time, then her grandmother Joyce, the wife of William
Whealton to take her. Mother Exec. Witt: George Douglas, William
Chance, Daniel Collins - p. 54

JAMES, JOSHUA - 23 Jan. 1749 - Proved 27 Feb. 1749/50 - Prob. 27 Mar. 1750 - 200 A. bought of Edmund Custis lying on the North side of Deep Creek to be sold, & after payment of debts I give the remainder to my wife Rachel James. My 56 A. in Worcester County, Maryland, on Fenix Island, I give in the manner aforesaid. To wife negroes for life should she be with child, & then to the said child, but if not then I give Walthy to my wife, Tony to Rachel West, dau. of John West, Nandewy, & Taby to Abel West, son of the said John West. Godson Henry Custis (under 21). Son in law Charles Leatherbury. Wife resid. legatee. Capt. Edward Revil, William Bagge & wife Rachel Exrs. Witt: Edward Revil, John Poalas, William Wise. - p. 55
In order of prob: John Taylor, Cooper, heir at law, cited to appear, & failing to appear said will is ordered to be probated.

LINGO, WILLIAM - 28 Jan. 1749/50 - 27 Mar. 1750 - Wife Hannah to have use of all my land & moveable est. during her wid. & then to son William Lingo planta. where he lives with 65 A. adj. To son John Lingo planta. where he now lives with 60 A. adj. To son Littleton Lingo planta. where I now live. Personal est. to be div. bet. all my children. Wife Hannah Exec. Witt: Francis Savage, Thomas Custis, Thomas Elliott - p. 56
In order of prob: Robinson Lingo heir at law to the testator appeared, & having nothing to object said will was admitted to probate.

JARVIS, ROBERT - 22 Jan. 1749 - Proved 27 Feb. 1749 - Pro. 27 Mar. 1750 - Son William Jarvis. To dau. Prudence McDaniel all my land & personal est. Dau. Prudence Exec. Witt: Major Bird, Arnold Morgan, Thomas Webb - p. 59
In order of prob: William Jarvis heir at law.

HORNSBY, ESTHER - 15 May 1750 - 29 May 1750 - Daus. Esther Kellam, Comfort Stakes, Ann Bradford. Sons James, John & Argol resid. legatees. To Jacob White 1 s. & he to have no further part of my est. Son John Hornsby Exr. Witt: John Darby, Jr., Churchill Darby, Jr., John Dayson - p. 63
In order or prob: James Hornsby heir at law to the testator.

TOWNSEND, RICHARD - 28 Nov. 1743 - 29 May 1750 - Son John Townsend. Son Richard Townsend. Son Samuel Townsend. Daus. Leah, Ann & Rachel. Dau. Sarah. Bal. of est. to wife Susannah during her wid. then to be div. bet. my wife & 6 children, Leah, Ann, John, Richard, Samuel & Rachel. Wife & son John Exrs. Witt: James Wishart. Charles Stockly - p. 64

YOUNG, JOHN - 13 Mar. 1749 - 29 May 1750 - All my lands to be divided between my sons Thomas & John. Wife Keziah to have use of whole est. during her wid. To dau. Elizabeth Young my personal est. Wife Exec. Witt: George Bundick. John Abbott Bundick, William Middleton, Thomas Riley - p. 65
In order of prob: Thomas Young heir at law to the testator.

CARY, SOLOMON - 25 Feb. 1749/50 - 29 May 1750 - To grandau. Esther Taylor land where I now live cont. 150 A., Betty Morrice to live & have a right in the said land during her maiden life. Grandson John Buckly. Grandson Bartholomew Taylor. Grandson Jermiah Taylor. Dau. Betty Buckly. Dau. Mary Melson. Grandau. Esther Taylor Exec. Witt: Joseph Taylor, Charles Vannelson, James Taylor, Baly Smith - p. 76
In order of prob: Elizabeth Buckly heir at law to the testator.

PHILBEE, GEORGE - 25 Apr. 1749 - 29 May 1750 - Dau. Esther Fogg. Grandson Stephen Philbee, son of Stephen Philbee. Grandson George Philbee, son of George Philbee. Grandaus. Leah & Arcadia Townsend. Dau. Catherine Warrrington. Dau. Phebee Collins resid. legatee - Son Thomas Collins Exr. Witt: Walter Warrington, Joseph Collins - p. 78
In order of prob: Stephen Philbee heir at law to the testator.

ROACH, MICHAEL - of Accomack, formerly of Sommerset County, Maryland. 23 Jan. 1749/50 - 26 June 1750 - To bro. William Wheatly all my land in Maryland. Bro. Sampson Wheatly. Cousin William Wheatly, son of my bro. Sampson Wheatly. Cousin Mary Wheatly, dau. of my bro. Sampson Wheatly. Bro. William Wheatly Exr. Witt: Edward Jones, William Wise, Nathan White - p. 91

JOHNSON, WASHBOURNE - 23 Apr. 1750 - 31 July 1750 - To cousin Joshua Johnson all my lands in Accomack & for want of heirs to my bro. Richard Johnson, father of the said Joshua. Cousin Sarah Wainhouse. To Obedience Johnson, son of John Johnson. Sister Temperance Hews. Cousin Joshua Johnson, Elizabeth Johnson & Sarah Johnson resid. legatees. Bro. Richard Exr. Witt: William Simkins, Edmund Watson, John Eshon - p. 98
In order of prob: John Johnson heir at law to the testator.

WILLIS, HENRY - 18 Dec. 1742 - 31 July 1750 - Goddau. Rachel Willis. To Elizabeth Melson. To George Richardson. Cousin John Richardson that lives with me at the present time redid. legatee & Exr. Witt: Rowland Savage, Ezekiel Ashby. Joseph Huff - p. 101

BELL, JEODIAH - 20 Feb. 1749/50 - 28 Aug. 1750 - To son George Bell planta. where I now live & all my land on the Eastern side of the creek. To son William Bell land & planta. on the Western Side of Matchapungo Creek. Wife Sarah to have use of whole est. during her life, but if she marry to have 1/4 my personal est. 5 daus. Rachel. Sarah, Hannah, Ann & Betty Bell resid. legatees. Wife Sarah Exec. Witt: Francis Savage, Samuel Benson, Whittington Addison. - p. 109
In order or prob: Francis Savage app. guardian to George Bell, infant heir at law to the testator.

TUNNEL, EDMUND - 9 Aug. 1750 - 28 Aug. 1750 - To son Joseph land where I now live cont. 150 A. Dau. Naomi Tunnel. Dau. Scarburgh Hastings. Son Joseph & Dau. Naomi resid. legatees. Son

Joseph Exr. Witt: Charles Stockly, Philip Fisher, Mary Fisher - p. 110

DUNNAHOE, TIMOTHY - 8 Aug. 1750 - 28 Aug. 1750 - Wife Mary Dunnahoe sole legatee. Wife & John Dix Exrs. Witt: Daniel Hall, William Bootin - p. 112

TYNDLE, WILLIAM, Nunc. Late of Kent County, Delaware. Died at his father in law Luke Manlove's house 31 Aug. 1750, about the rising of the sun. Proved 31 Aug. 1750 - Proved in Accomack 25 Sept. 1750 - Whole est. to Luke Manlove. Proved in Kent County by Paree Trippett, age 19 or thereabouts, & Luke Manlove, Quaker age 61 or thereabouts. Luke Manlove qualified on est. in Virginia - p. 113

PARKER, THOMAS, of Kent County in the Province of Pennsylvania - 24 Mar. 1750 - 25 Sept. 1750 - Personal est. to be div. bet. all my children, Susannah, Betty, Matthew, Thomas, Sarah, John & William Parker & Naomi Hill. To son Thomas Parker all the land I owned & lived on in the County of Kent on Delaware in Pennsylvania, and any other lands I may have a title to. Bro. Anderson & son Thomas Exrs. Witt: John Parker, Sr., Leah Parker, Betty Nelson - p. 120

MERRILL, ESAU - 17 Dec. 1749 - 26 Sept. 1750 - To wife Hannah planta. where I live during her wid. Dau. Elizabeth Merrill. Dau. Hannah Merrill. Dau. Peggy Merrill. Dau. Sarah Stockley. Dau. Mary Milburne. Son in law Joshua Milbourne. To son Issac Merrill land called Merrills Adventure and planta. where I now live. Bro. Joshua Merril Exr. Wife Hannah & 3 youngest daus. Elizabeth, Hannah & Peggy Merrill resid. legatees. Witt: Thomas Merrill, Scarburgh Merrill, Simpson Merrill, William Merrill - p. 123
In order of prob: Isaac Merrill heir at law to the testator.

MERRILL, WILLIAM - 25 June 1749 - 27 Nov. 1750 - To grandson William Merrill 100 A. adj. my son Scarburgh Merrill; gun now in the possession of Nathaniel Stockley. To son Thomas Merrill 100 A. adj. my grandson William Merrill. To son Scarburgh Merrill 2 tracts of land one called Hoop Ridge & the other called Security & that part of Oracoco within the divisional line of marked trees beginning at a marked hicory standing near Phillip Quinton's road, & also 22 A. called Floyd's Grove which I bought of Smith Mills. To son Simpson Merrill 2 tracts of land one called Merrills Priviledge & the other Merrills Delight, also 8 A. part of Corton Lott bought of Samuel Lamberson. To wife Rachel Merrill all my planta. in Virginia where I now live during her life & then to my son Thomas. Daus. Leah & Rebecca Merrill resid. legatees. Witt: Isaac Merrill, Levinah Merrill, Jacob Merrill. p. 139
In order of prob: Nathaniel Stockley app. guardian to William Merrill, Inf't. grandson & heir at law to the testator.

CUTLER, ARCADIA - 2 Jan. 1749/50 - 27 Nov. 1750 - Son Richard Cutler. Son Samuel Cutler. To dau. Betty Hall, wife of Michael Hall negro, reversion to my grandau. Betty Hall. Grandau. Comfort Hall. Dau. Arcadia Cutler. To son Richard Cutler silver spoon marked "R E C" To dau. Arcadia Cutler silver spoon marked "A R W" Son Daniel Cutler. Son George Cutler. Son Richard & daus. Betty Hall & Arcadia Cutler resid. legatees. Son Richard Exr. Witt: William Beavans, Solomon Powell, Isaiah Evans. - p. 141

LURTON, THOMAS - 25 Sept. 1750 - 27 Nov. 1750 - To cousin Littleton Lurton 150 A. at White Marsh. To cousin Jacob Lurton 100 A. at Deep Branch. To bro. Jacob Lurton 150 A. & 15 A. of the White Marsh land. To my wife Mary all that was hers before I married her. Cousin Henry Lurton. To Rachel Willis. To son in law Charles Richardson. Cousin Hannah Lurton. To Benjamin Richardson. Wife Mary resid. legatee. Bro. Jacob Lurton & Cousin Jacob Lurton Exrs. Witt: Caleb Burton, Thomas Roberts. - p. 144
In order of prob: Jacob Lurton cousin & heir at law.

WATSON, ROBERT - 3 Feb. 1749/50 - 29 Jan. 1750 - To son Littleton Watson 1/2 my land adj. Benjamin Stewart, cont. 125 A. To son Robert the other 1/2 of my land adj. Churchill Darby, beginning at the Creek on the South side of Island Branch, cont. 125 A. To son Abel Watson. Dau. Tabitha Watson. Dau. Elizabeth Smith. Dau. Mary Bayley. To son Robert chest marked "R W S" To Lisha Mears. Children Littleton, Robert, Abel, Elizabeth, Mary & Tabitha resid. legatees. Son Robert Exr. Witt: Churchill Darby, Arthur Laylor, Owen Darby, John Dawson. - p. 152
In order of prob: Littleton Watson heir at law.

WATSON, DAVID - 15 Dec. 1750 - 29 Jan. 1750/51 - To son Moses Watson 130 A. with my Water Mill, also 25 A. bought of Arthur Robins. To son Solomon the remainder of my land cont. 125 A. To wife negro Vinor during her wid. & should she marry to fall to Mary & Joyce. To son David Watson (under age) To son John Watson (under age) To dau. Patience Anderson. Daus. Mary & Joyce Watson. To dau. Lisha Meers. Wife & children Moses, Solomon, David & John Watson, Comfort Anderson, Mary Watson, Joyce Watson, Sarah Watson, Lisha Meers resid. legatees. Wife Sarah. Son Moses Exr. Witt: John Dayson, Benjamin Watson. - p. 154
In order of prob: Moses Watson, Jr., heir at law to the testator.

BURTON, SAMUEL - 7 Jan. 1750/51 - 29 Jan. 1750/51 - Exrs. to sell so many of my slaves as they shall think fit to make a purchase of all the land & planta. where I now live for my son John. Wife & 3 children Ann, John & Priscilla resid. legatees. Friend Edmund Bayley Exr. Witt: William Gray, George Abbott, John Sturgis. - p. 157
In order of prob: Tabitha Burton, widow of the testator, qualified.

STURGIS, WILLIAM - 7 Jan. 1745/6 - 29 Jan. 1750/51 - To wife Martha whole est. during her wid. & then to my son William Sturgis planta. where I now dwell, he to allow my son Joshua Sturgis a sufficient maintenance during his natural life out of the profits of the

same. Son Isaiah Sturgis. Soh Jacob Sturgis. Dau. Martha Sturgus. Dau. Elizabeth Sturgis. Dau. Bathsheba Sturgis. Dau. Mary Coverly. Bal. of est. to be div. bet. the rest of my children. Wife Martha & son William Exrs. Witt: Abel Finney, John Barnes, William Arbuckle, Wonne Rew - p. 158
In order of prob: Joshua Sturgis heir at law to the testator.

KIRKMAN, ROGER - 9 Dec. 1750 - 29 Jan. 1750/51 - Son George Kirkman. To dau. Comfort Kirkman all her mother's wearing apparel. Dau. Elizabeth Kirkman. Son George resid. legatee & Exr. Joshua Riggs, Richard Onions, Joseph Riggs & Thomas Webb to appraise & divide est. Witt: Thomas Webb, Patience Hinman. - p. 160

THOMSON, WILLIAM - Nunc - 12 Jan. 1750/51 - 29 Jan. 1750/51 - Whole est. to sister Mary Thomson. Proved by Robert Ardis, age 47 & upwards, & John Taylor, age 39 & upwards - p. 162

JONES, GILES - 9 Feb. 1744 - 26 Feb. 1750/51 - To dau. Mary, wife of James Cary. Dau. Esther, wife of Thomas Dubberly. To son John Jones all my lands in Maryland. To wife Ann Jones "all the right I have to that personal estate in the possession of the said wife's son Daniel Smith in his lifetime & now in the possession of the said Daniel's widow; Mary Smith" 1/2 the balance of my est., real & personal, to my wife during her life or wid. & then to my son John Jones. The other 1/2 to my son John Jones. Son John Exr. Witt: George Douglas, John Cord, Nathaniel Sheaff, Ambrose Willet - p. 163

WALKER, ELIZABETH - 15 Sept. 1750 - 26 Feb. 1750/51 - Daus. Sebella Davis, Jemima Cathell & Arcadia Paradice. Grandson Daniel Walker (under 18) Grandau Mary Walker. Grandau. Elizabeth Paradice. Grandchildren Daniel & Mary Walker resid. legatees. 3 sons in law, Samuel Davis, John Paradice & Jonathan Cathell Exrs. Witt: Nathaniel Bensten, William Gillet, William Marshall - p. 164
In order of prob: The executors named in the above will refusing to act Jacob Benstine qualified.

GILCHRIST, JOHN - 17 Jan. 1750/51 - 26 Feb. 1750/51 - Wife Mary. Bro. Andrew Gilchrist. Uncle James Gibson. To mother in law Hannah Wishart. To Thomas Wishart. Should my wife be with child I give it the whole of my est., real & personal in the Town of Glasgow, in North Britain, given to me by my mother Agness Gibson, alias Gilchrist, but if she should not be with child I give the said est. to my bro. Andrew Gilchrist. To wife Mary 1/2 my est. in this country & the other 1/2 to my brother Andrew. Wife Mary Gilchrist, Bro. Andrew Gilchrist & James Wishart Exrs. Witt: William Gray, Anne Wishart, Elizabeth Wishart - p. 167

ROWLES, JOHN - 16 Jan. 1750/51 - 27 Feb. 1750/51 - To wife Tabitha whole est. during her wid. To son Major Rowles this plantation with the mill Whittington Bayley has the care of. Daus. to live with their mother until marriage or death. To son Hancock Rowles all

159

the reversion of the lands on Nanduey which I should have. To son
John Rowles (under age) 1/2 of my largsst Water Mill. To bro. in law
Nathaniel Lecatt the other 1/2 of my great mill. To son Hancock
Rowles the Water Mill that formerly belonged to Edmund Polson.
Dau. Anne Parker. Dau. Patience Rowles. Dau. Eleanor. Dau.
Rachel Rowles. Dau. Jane Rowles. Unmarried children resid. lega-
tees. Wife & son Major Exrs. Witt: John Rodgers, Daniel Rodgers,
John Dayson. - p. 169
In order of prob: Major Rowles heir at law to the testator.

WISHART, JAMES - 19 Nov. 1749 - 27 Feb. 1750/51 - To son William the lands called Queen Hithe which I bought of Capt. John Williams & Esther, his wife, & the same estate in all the lands I purchased on Sexes Island. Wife Hannah Wishart. Son Thomas. Wife &
children Thomas, William, James, Joshua, Mary, Ann, Elizabeth &
Jacomin resid. legatees. Wife, son Thomas & George Douglas Exrs.
Witt: Patrick Stewart, Southy Whittington - p. 170
In order of prob: Thomas Wishart heir at law to the testator.

BROADWATER, ELIAS - 28 Jan. 1750/51 - 27 Feb. 1750/51 - Son
Caleb Broadwater. Son Elias Broadwater. Son Ezekiel Broadwater.
Sons Charles & Scarburgh Broadwater. Son George Broadwater. Wife
Phebe Broadwater, Caleb, Elias, Ezekiel, Charles, Scarburgh & George
Broadwater resid. legatees. Son Caleb Exr. Witt: Jacob Broadwater,
William Sterling, Charles Parks, William Broadwater. - p. 171

ALLEN, STEPHEN - 23 Sept. 1738 - 27 Feb. 1750/51 - Mother
Margaret Bagwell. To bros. John & James Allen 300 A. Bro. Edmund
Allen. Bro. Thomas Bagwell. Sister Margaret Rule. Sister Patience
Custis. Sister Ann Bagwell. Sister Tabitha Bagwell. Bros. John &
James Allen resid. legatees. Bro. John Exr. Witt: Stephen Fitzger-
ald, Sarah Fitzgerald, John Metcalf, William Custis - p. 172
In order of probate: Edmund Allen, eldest bro. & heir at law to the
testator. William Custis, who married one of the legatees, relin-
quished his right to said legacy.

TOWNSEND, MARY - Nunc. Proved 9 Mar. 1750/51 - Pro. 26 Mar.
1751 - To James Fleson. James Townsend resid. legatee., reversion
to "Gemima Children to Jonathan Caree to keep" Proved by John
Taylor & Mary Townsend. - p. 173
In order of prob: Jonathan Catheel qualified.

BAYLEY, EDMUND - 13 Jan. 1750/51 - 26 Mar. 1751 - Son Edmund
Bayley (under age). To dau. Tabitha Burton, slaves & all the rest of
my est. that my dau. hath received since marryed to Samuel Burton.
Son John Bayley. Dau. Rose. Wife Tabitha. Rest of my slaves to be
div. bet. my wife & the following children, John Bayley, Rose Bayley,
Thomas Bayley, Ismy Bayley, Levin Bayley, Hancock Bayley &
Tabitha Burton. Wife & children resid. legatees. Wife Tabitha, my
loving friend Joachim Michael, living in Northampton & my son John
Bayley Exrs. Witt: Thomas Crippen, William Drummond, Bridget

160

Dorton.
Codicil: To George Polson the planta. where he now lives cont. 100 A. beginning at the Black Slash running along the road South toward the Court House. Witt: Thomas Crippen, William Drummond, Bridget Dorton. - p. 186
In order of prob: Littleton Scarburgh Major app. guardian to Edmund Bayley, heir at law to the testator.

FOX, GOLDEN - 2 Feb. 1750/51 - 26 Mar. 1751 - To wife Sarah Fox, use of whole est. during her wid. then the land where I now live, being 150 A., to my son Jacob Fox. Personal est. to be div. bet. my 6 children Jacob, Ann, Thomas, Levin, Amy & Golden Fox. Wife Exec. Witt: Ezekiel Ashby, William Harrison, Elizabeth James.
In order of prob: Thomas Fox, heir at law to the testator, under age, Thomas Parramore app. his guardian. 29 Nov. 1752, Jacob Fox granted letters of adm. on the est. of the within Golden Fox unadministered by Sarah, his wid. & Exec. therein named, the said Sarah being now dec. - p. 187

FLETCHER, MATTHEW - 22 Jan. 1750/51 - 26 Mar. 1751 - To Bezaleel Watson 125 A. adj. Harrison's land. To bro. in law Daniel Watson 125 A. adj. Robert Heath. Bro. in law Bezaleel Watson & Littleton Scarburgh Major Exrs. Witt: William Meers, John Wells, Perces Watson - p. 191
In order of Prob: West Kellam qualified.

JOHNSON, AFRADOZY - 31 Dec. 1750 - 26 Mar. 1751 - To bro. Samuel Johnson planta. where I now live & for want of heirs to bro. William Johnson. Brothers & sisters resid. legatees. Bro. William Exr. Witt: Thomas Webb, William Bloxom, Ezekiel Bloxom - p. 192

HICKMAN, ROGER - 12 June 1750 - 26 Mar. 1751 - To sons Solomon & Benjamin 50 A. of land & marsh that I hold on Jobs Island. To wife all remaining part of my moveable est. during her lifetime then to be div. bet. my 5 children. Son Solomon Exr. Witt: Richard Hickman, Richard Grinnalds, Salathiel Russel. - p. 192
In order of prob: Solomon Hickman heir at law to the testator.

ONIONS, JOHN - 27 Aug. 1743 - 26 Mar. 1751 - To Wife Susannah whole est. for life to bring up my children & then to be equally div. bet. my children. Son William Selby Onions, wife Susannah Onions & son Richard Onions Exrs. Witt: Southy Rew, Justicc Bundick - p. 193
In order of prob: Richard Onions heir at law to the testator.

ARBUCKLE, WILLIAM - 18 Oct. 1746 - 30 Apr. 1751 - Wife to have use of whole est. during her wid. To son James planta. where I now live. "I give to my poor little fellow and Dear Child William my plantation I bought from Timothy Coe" Bal. of est. to be div. bet. all my children, first making allowance for what my sister Ann Snead has bequeathed to my daus. Euphama & Ann, so that all my children be made equal. Wife Exec. Witt: Comfort Rew, James Strann, Wonny

Rew.

Codicil dated 21 June 1747: To unborn child an equal share of my est. with the other children. – p. 197

In order of prob: Thomas Parramore app. guardian to James Arbuckle, heir at law to the testator. Katherine Arbuckle, wid. of the testator qualified.

MORGAN, JOHN, Sr. – 15 Apr. 1751 – 30 Apr. 1751 – To son Arnold Morgan 1/2 my land including the planta. where my said son now lives. The remainder of the land, being the planta. where I now dwell, I lend to my wife Mary Morgan during her wid. & then to my son William Morgan, & for want of heirs to my son James Morgan, & for want of heirs to my son Jacob Morgan. Bal. of est. to wife during her wid. then to be div. bet. my 4 children, Jemima, Jacob, James & William Morgan. Wife & son Arnold Exrs. Witt: William Abbott, Mary Morgan, Jr., John Evans. – p. 202

In order of prob: Arnold Morgan heir at law to the testator.

LUCAS, WILLIAM – 20 Mar. 1751 – 30 Apr. 1751 – To son Solomon Lucas planta. where he now lives. To son Jabez Lucas planta. where I now live cont. 125 A., also the land I bought of Daniel Shae. To son Solomon all the land I bought of Mason Abbott. Sons Solomon & Jabez resid. legatees & Exrs. Witt: Joseph Stockley, Robert Hutson, Daniel Shae.

In order of prob: Solomon Lucas heir at law to the testator.

CARY, JAMES – 17 Jan. 1750/51 – 30 Apr. 1751 – To son Jessey Cary the planta. that was my father's, wife to have use of same until my son comes to age. Dau. Tabitha Cary. Son James Cary (under age). Bal. of est. to wife Mary during her wid. then 2/3 to be div. bet. my last wife's children. Wife Exec. Witt: Joshua Chapman. Peter Watson, Samuel Gillet – p. 203

CLEMENS, ANN – Son Stephen Clemens. To dau. Jane Brooks Clemens planta. where I now live cont. 100 A., reversion to son Stephen Clemens, reversion to my grandau. Sorrowfull Booth Underhill & for want of heirs to the heirs of my son Stephen Clemens. Dau. Jane Brooks Clemens resid. legatee & Exec. Witt: Thomas Crippen, John Kitson, William Baker. – p. 204

In order of prob: Stephen Clemens qualified.

HOWARD, NATHANIEL – 5 Oct. 1750 – 30 Apr. 1751 – To son Nathaniel 75 A. where I now live. To son Solomon Howard 50 A. adj. William Mason & John Custis. To son Daniel Howard 50 A. adj. John Custis & Mathias Gale. Son in law John Ross. To wife Mary the use of personal est. during her wid. then to be div. bet. my 3 children Patience, Elias & Ambross Howard – Wife & son Nathaniel Exrs. Witt: John Watson, Moses Hinman, Ezekiel Ross – p. 205

In order of prob: Daniel Howard son & heir at law to the testator.

DRUMMOND, JOHN – 19 Dec. 1750 – 30 Apr. 1751 – To son John Drummond 100 A. of land & marsh. To son Drake 100 A. of land & marsh adj. his bro. John. To son Stephen Drummond 100 A. land & marsh adj. his bro. Drake. To son Robert Drummond 100 A. land & marsh adj. his bro. Stephen. To son William Drummond 100 A. land & marsh adj. his bro. Robert. Wife to have the use of my planta. during her life. Dau. Abigail Drummond. Dau. Amy Drummond. To son Drake Drummond's 2 children. All my sons, John, Drake, Stephen, Robert & William to have an equal privilege of all my lands and marshes on half Moon Island. Bal. of est. to wife for life & then to be div. bet. all my children. Wife (no name) & sons John & Drake Exrs. Witt: Thomas Ryley, Betty Crowson, William Parker. – p. 207
In order of prob: Amy Drummond, wid. of the testator, & Drake Drummond qualified.

CUSTIS, THOMAS – 24 Jan. 1749/50 – 1 May 1751 – Cousin Tabitha Scarburgh Custis. To Cousin Margaret Custis negroes & all the bal. of my est., real & personal. Henry Custis & Scarburgh Custis Exrs. Witt: Edmund Poulson, George Poulson, Archibald Milby – p. 213

MAJOR, ROWLES – 22 Jan. 1750 – 1 May 1751 – To son John Major land where I now live. Dau. Mary Major. Children resid. legatees. Son John to be guardian to my 3 young sons, Caleb, Levin & Kendall till they come to the age of 21 years. Son John Exr. Witt: Thomas Teackle, Darmon Darby, Mary Ames. – p. 214
In order of prob: Phillip Major, heir at law to the testator, qualified.

WATT, ADAM – 13 Jan. 1749/50 – 28 May 1751 – To eldest son James Watt planta. where I now live. Son Nehemiah Watt. Dau. Ann Watt. I desire the est. I had of Ralph Corbin to be equally div. bet. my sons James & Nahemiah. Bro. William Watt. All the est. I had by my wife Scarburgh to be div. bet. my wife & her 2 children. Wife Exec. Bro. in law Ralph Corbin & James Wallop overseers. Witt: Jacob White, William Collins, Jane Nedham – p. 218

METCALF, JOHN – 19 July 1749 – 28 May 1751 – To wife Elizabeth my planta. during her wid. & then to my son Thomas Metcalf the planta. he now lives on cont. the 1/6 part of the tract of land where I now live. To son Samuel the planta. I now live on, being 1/6 of my tract of land. To son Mark Metcalf 1/6 of my land adj. my son Thomas. To son William Metcalf 1/6 of my land on the South-west corner. To son Isaac Metcalf 1/6 of my land between my sons William & Mark Metcalf. To son William 1/6 of my land where Rachel Ashby now lives. Daus. Sarah & Tabitha Metcalf. Wife Elizabeth resid. legatee & Exec. Witt: Thomas Parramore, John Bagwell, Rachel Ashby – p. 219
In order of prob: George Holden app. guardian to John Metcalf, Inf't. heir at law to the testator.

WALLOP, JOHN – 11 Apr. 1751 – 28 May 1751 – 1/2 the Sloop Success, negro Will, book accounts, notes, bonds &c. to be sold for the payment of my debts. To wife Ann Wallop all my living during her wid. to bring up my children, then to be equally div. bet. all my children, Sarah Leatherman, Rebeceah Kendall, Ann Wallop, Sophia Wallop, Skinner Wallop, John Wallop, Parker Wallop & William Wallop. Wife Ann Exec. Witt: John Kendall, Betty Smith, Annabella Marshall - p. 220

SNEAD, KATHERINE - 5 May 1748 - 28 May 1751 - To son Smith Snead land & planta. on Mary Branch left me by my father Col. John West, reversion to my grandson John Snead, son of my son John Snead. Grandson Charles Snead, son of John Snead. To grandson John Snead, son of John Snead, a pewter dish marked "K W" To Ann Snead, dau. of John Snead. To the children of my son Smith Snead. Sons John & Smith Snead Exrs. Witt: Katherine Arbuckle, Jemima Booth, William Arbuckle. Codicil: 23 Nov. 1750 - To dau. in law Scarburgh Snead. To Mary Snead, dau. of my son John Snead. Witt: Euphamia Arbuckle, James Arbuckle, William Arbuckle - p. 222
In order of prob: John Snead heir at law to the testatrix.

CHANCE, WILLIAM - 30 Apr. 1751 - 25 June 1751 - To grandson John Cord planta. where I now live cont. 364 A. To grandson William Cord 250 A. at the head of Hunting Creek, & for want of heirs to my Grandau. Esther Cord. To grandau. Esther Cord negro & all the personal est. of Arthur Cord & all the personal est. of which I am possessed. Maj. George Douglas Exr. Witt: Anderson Patterson, Edward Joynes, William Watt - p. 225

SIMPSON, WILLIAM - 7 Mar. 1751 - 26 June 1751 - To eldest son Thomas Simpson 100 A. adj. the tract where I now live. To son Solomon Simpson 50 A. land & marsh on the Bayside. To wife Drummond Simpson. Dau. Rachel Simpson. Dau. Tabitha Simpson. Son William Simpson. Son Drummond Simpson. Son John Simpson. Bal of personal est. to wife Drummond Simpson for life then to be div. bet. all my children. Wife & son Thomas Exrs. To son William, upon condition that he never marry Comfort Taylor, 50 A. of land adj. the branch over my father's land, also 50 A. adj. the land of Richard Grinalds. Witt: Richard Grinalds, Thomas Simpson, Jacob White - p. 243
In order of prob: Thomas Simpson heir at law to the testator.

BUNDICK, GEORGE, Jr. - 14 Apr. 1751 - 30 July 1751 - Son Richard Bundick. Dau. Ann Bundick. Dau. Elizabeth Bundick. Wife to have use of personal est. during her wid. then to be div. between my children. Wife & son Richard Exrs. Witt: Henry Satchell, Richard Onions, John Abbott Bundick. - p. 259

KENDALL, LEMUEL - 20 Apr. 1751 - 30 July 1751 - To wife Susanna Kendall planta. where I now dwell during her wid. then to my son John Kendall, provided he make over to my son William Kendall 1/2 my land on Wallops Island. Dau. Ann Kendall. Dau. Peggy Kendall. Wife & children resid. legatees. Son John & cousin William Phinney, Jr.

Exrs. Witt: William Phinney, Jr., John White, Mary Kendall, William Kendall. – p. 261
In order of prob: Anderson Patterson app. guardian to John Kendall, Inf't. heir at law to the testator.

TAYLOR, JOHN – 23 Apr. 1751 – 27 Aug. 1751 – Son William Taylor. To wife Patience negro Pleasant, "and if she goes to keep any of the increase of the aforesaid woman from her three children John Taylor, Mary Tayler or Stephen Taylor, then for the woman & her increase to go to my four children Teackle Taylor, William Taylor, Amy Taylor & Betty Taylor. Wife & children resid. legatees. Teackle, William, Amy & Betty to receive their estates when they come to the age of 16 years. Bros. Matthews Taylor & Samuel Taylor Exrs. Witt: Robert Ardies, Robert Copes, Nathaniel Bensten – p. 289
In order of prob: Samuel Taylor, surviving Exr., relinquished his right, & Patience Taylor, wid. of the testator, qualified.

BENSTON, JOSEPH – 23 Apr. 1751 – 27 Aug. 1751 – To wife Elizabeth whole est. during her wid. Son Joseph Benston. Son Hill Benston all the land that lies to the West side of the gulley that runs through my land. Son Francis Benston. To son Jesse Benston all my land on the East side of the gully that runs through my land. Wife to div. the rest of my est. bet. my children as she sees fit. Wife & son Hill Exrs. Witt: Nathaniel Benston, Massey Benson, Samuel Pitts – p. 292
In order of prob: Francis Benston heir at law.

DIX, ISAAC – 8 Feb. 1750/51 – 27 Aug. 1751 – To son Richard Dix planta. where I now live with 200 A. to begin at the first fork that makes out of Rooty Branch. adj. the land of John Dix. To son George Dix 150 A. where my son Isaac is now settled, provided my son Isaac refuse to make over all his right & title of his mother's maiden land to my son George, which is 100 A. adj. William Savage, but if he does make the said property over to my son George, then I give the said 150 A. to my son Isaac. To son Solomon Dix 150 A. at the head of my land where Thomas Clark now dwells. Dau. Elizabeth Dix. 4 children Richard, Solomon, George, & Elizabeth resid legatees. Son Richard Exr. – Witt: Richard Hickman, John Dix, Heli Bagwell – p. 293
In order of prob: Isaac Dix heir at law to the testator.

WATSON, MOSES – 14 Mar. 1751 – 27 Aug. 1751 – Dau. Rachel Watson. Son Robert Watson. Son Barthemy Watson. Son Ezekiel Watson. Dau. Comfort Watson. Dau. Betty Watson. Son Benjamin Watson. Son Esau Watson. Son Jacob Watson. To unborn child. To wife Direcktor Watson, whom I app. my Exec., all the rest of my personal est. during her wid. then to be div. bet. my wife & children. Witt: Arthur Robins, John Henderson, Benjamin Watson. – p. 294

BOOTIN, WILLIAM – 9 Apr. 1751 – 27 Aug. 1751 – To wife Agnes Bootin the land & planta. where I now live until my son John arrives to the age of 21 years, then the said John to possess the said land, also

the swamp land adjacent to my planta. & for want of heirs to my dau. Nanny Bootin, except my unborn child should be a boy "and if he is I leave the aforesaid land to him". Dau. Elizabeth Bootin. Wife resid. legatee. Wife Agnes Bootin & James Hutchinson Exrs. Witt: Anderson Patterson, Andrew Samplar, Jabis Blake – p. 295
In order of prob: Robert Pitt app. guardian to John Bootin, heir at law to the testator.

HARRISON, JOSEPH – 16 Aug. 1749 – 29 Oct. 1751 – Wife Elizabeth Harrison. Son William Harrison. Son Stephen Harrison. Grandson William Harrison. Son Josias Harrison. Dau. Sarah Watkinson. Dau. Susanna Harrison. Dau. Tabitha Tignal. Bal. of est. to wife Elizabeth for life then to be div. bet. all my children. Wife & son Josias Harrison Exrs. – Witt: Bartholomew Meers, Stephen Harrison. – p. 310

EVANS, THOMAS – 18 May 1751 – 29 Oct. 1751 – To son Thomas Evans 150 L which I have already lent him to buy his land which he bought of Mr. Thomas Custis, lying at Mossongoes. Grandson John Evans, son of Thomas. To son John Evans planta. where I now live cont. 150 A. Dau. Mary Evans. To son Isaiah Evans 191 A. which I bought of Thomas Bennett & Robert Crippen, reversion to grandson Zerrobabel, son of Isaiah Evans. To dau. Mary all her mother's wearing clothes. 4 children, Thomas, John, Isaiah & Mary resid. legatees. Sons John & Isaiah Exrs. Friends Caesar Evans, Paul Crippen & John Dix to div. est. Witt: Caesar Evans, John Dix, William White – p. 311
In order of prob: Thomas Evans heir at law to the testator.

CHRISTALL, WILLIAM, Merchant – 20 Aug. 1751 – 30 Oct. 1751 – Friend John McMillion to have the care & management of disposing of my est. to the best advantage with the concuring advice of Mr. Andrew Sproul, Merchant in Norfolk, & Adam Muir of this County. To friend John McMillion, after payment of debts. Bal. of est., real & personal in Virginia or elsewhere, to my nephew William Chrystall, son of my bro. James Chrystall, in Kippen, in North Britain. Andrew Sproul, Merchant in Norfolk Adam Muir of this County, & John McMillion Exrs. Witt: John Rodgers, Abel Rodgers – p. 313

TAYLOR, JOSEPH – 8 Mar. 1750/51 – 26 Mar. 1751 – To wife Bridget Taylor whole est during her wid. & then to my son John Taylor my manor planta. cont. 100 A. Son Joseph Taylor. Son William Taylor. Son Jacob Taylor. Son Severn Taylor. Son Shadrack Taylor. Dau. Bridget Taylor. Children to be of ago at 18 years. Son John Exr. & wife Exec. Witt: Abel Finny, Samuel Stakes, Mary Stakes. – p. 324

EDWARDS, EDWARD – 20 June 1751 – 26 Nov. 1751 – To Samuel Simpson. To Laban Simpson. To William Spiers. To Jacob Stakes. Samuel Simpson Exr. Witt: Sacker Parker, Comfort Simpson – p. 325

PITTS, WILLIAM – 5 Apr. 1751 – 26 Nov. 1751 – To bro. Samuel Pitts the land that was my brother Isaac's given to him by his father,

John Pitts & also one man called Jack & negroes Pleasant & Peter to Samuel Pitts to school Hannah Pitts, the dau. of Robert Pitts, & also my part of the negro Little Harry left me by my mother to the said Samuel Pitts. To Hannah Benston negro, reversion to her dau. Hannah Benston. To Sophia Blades negro Rachel, & the first child of the said Rachel to be delivered to John Benstone, the son of Ezekiel Benstone. To John Merril's son William Merril. To Samuel Pitts all my part of the cattle belonging to me by my mother's death. To John Blades, Jr. To Levin Merril, son of John Merril. To Zepheniah Benston, son of Jonn Benston. To John Pitts, son of Robert Pitts. To bro. Robert Pitts. To sister Jemimah Moss. Brothers & sisters resid. legatees. Samuel Pitts Exr. Witt: Anderson Patterson, Samuel Feddiman. Massey Benson – p. 326

STEPHENS, CHRISTOPHER – 24 Apr. 1751 – 26 Nov. 1751 – Son John Stephens (under 21) Wife to have the use of my planta. during her wid. & then all my lands & planta. to descend to my son John Stephens. Son George Stephens. Son William Stephens. Dau. Elizabeth Stephens. Bal. of est. to wife during her life or wid. then to be div. bet. my 3 children George, William & Elizabeth Stevens. Wife Exec. Witt: Thomas Ryley, Richard Grinalds, Martha Sturgis, John Abbott Bundick. – p. 327
In order of prob: John Abbott Bundick app. guardian to John Stephens, heir at law to the testator – Elizabeth Stevens, wid. of the testator qualified.

Orders – 1753–1763

CHANCE, WILLIAM – Adm. his est. to Sophia Wise Chance – Richard Armitrader sec. 31 July 1753 – p. 6

VANDEGRAH, OBEDIAH – Adm. his est. to Henry Martin – West Kellam & Americus Scarburgh sec. – 25 Sept. 1753 – p. 19

MILLICHOP, NICHOLAS – Adm. his est. to Hannah Millichop – Joseph Tunnel & William Jackson sec. – 27 Nov. 1753 – p. 22

CUMMINS, THOMAS – Adm. his est. to Francis Welburne – Southy Simpson sec. – 27 Nov. 1753 – p. 23

EDWARDS, FRANCIS – Adm. his est. to Sarah Edwards – Thomas Parramore sec. 29 Jan. 1754 – p. 30

SHAE, AMEY – Adm. her est. to William Drummond – George Drummond sec. – 30 Jan. 1754 – p. 34

JONES, HENRY – Adm. his est. to Sarah Jones – Covington Corbin & William Selby sec. 26 Mar. 1754 – p. 42

LINTON, WILLIAM – Adm. his est. to Isaiah Johnson – Solomon Bird & Joseph Bell sec. – 26 Mar. 1754 – p. 43

BADGER, JACOB - Adm. his est. to Ann Badger - John Badger & John Dawson sec. 28 May 1754 - p. 44

WIESE, Sarah - Adm. her est. to William Selby - Robert Pitt & Joseph Feddiman sec. 30 July 1754 - p. 57

PROBATE, WILLIAM - Adm. his est. with will annexed to George Holden - George Douglas sec. - 28 Aug. 1754 - p. 60

JENKINSON, CUSTIS - Adm. his est. to Alexander Stockley, Jr. - William Matthews sec. - 29 Oct. 1754 - p. 66

GRIFFIN, MARGARET - Adm. her est. to Charles West - Luke Lucar sec. - 27 Nov. 1754 - p. 71

STURGES, WILLIAM - Adm. his est. to Elizabeth Sturges - William Johnson sec. 28 Jan. 1755 - p. 76

SAUNDERS, JAMES - Adm. his est. to John Saunders - William Savage sec. 29 Jan. 1755 - p. 77

GALE, MATTHIAS - Adm. his est. to Levin Gale - James Rule & Robert Pitt sec. - 27 May 1755 - p. 86

LUCAR, GEORGE - Adm. his est. to Luke Lucar - Southy Simpson sec. - 27 May 1755 - p. 87

WALKER, SARAH - Adm. her est. to Ann Walker - Covington Corbin & William Cord sec. 27 May 1755 - p. 87

SAVAGE, PARKER - Adm. his est. to Southy Simpson - Henry Greenalds sec. - 24 June 1755 p. 92

WINDOW, JOHN - Adm. his est. to Elizabeth Window - John Window & James Rodgers sec. - 29 July 1755 - p. 98

ARBUCKLE, KATHERINE - Adm. her est. to Mary Burton - James Rule sec. 25 Nov. 1755 - p. 114

PARKER, GEORGE - Adm. his est. to Susannah Parker - Smith Snead, George Drummond, Thomas Custis & George Holden sec. - 30 Dec. 1755.- p. 120

WHITTINGTON, WILLIAM - Adm. his est. to Southy Simpson - George Holden sec. - 26 May 1756 - p. 143

STOCKLFY, EYRE, an infant, Adm. his est. to William Beavans - Elijah Nock sec. 29 June 1756 - p. 146

ARNOLD, LAWRENCE - Adm. his est. to William Marshall Richardson - John Finney & Arthur Rowley sec. - 28 Dec. 1756 - p. 163

ELLIS, THOMAS - Adm. his est. to John Taylor - Nathaniel Stockley & Joseph Gowtee sec. - 28 Dec. 1756 - p. 163

BENSTON, REBECCA - Adm. her est. to William Melvin - Southy Simpson & Littleton Dennis sec. - 28 Dec. 1756 - p. 164

BALDWIN, JOHN - Adm. his est. to William Jackson - Thomas Bonnewell & William Andrews, Jr. sec. - 29 Dec. 1756 - p. 168

PARRADICE, JOHN - Adm. his est. to Skinner Wallop - William Nicholson sec. - 25 Jan. 1757 - p. 169

ARDIES, JAMES - Adm. his est. to Southy Whittington - Elizabeth Ardies, wid. of James relinquishing her right to qualify - George Holden sec. - 26 Jan. 1757 - p. 171

FITZGERALD, SHADRACK - Adm. his est. to Arnold Morgan - Simpson Bloxom sec. - 26 Jan. 1757 - p. 171

BALEY, ELIZABETH - Adm. her est. to Margaret Baley - Alexander Stockley, Jr. sec. 22 Feb. 1757 - p. 174

SCARBURGH, CHARLES - Adm. his est. to John Coleburn - Thomas Parramore sec. - 27 Apr. 1757 - p. 185

WHEELTON, JOHN - Adm. his est. to Mary Wheelton - Skinner Wallop sec. - 31 May 1757 - p. 187

BLAKE, William - Adm. his est. to Sarah Blake - Skinner Wallop & William Robins sec. - p. 187

PARKER, JOHN - Adm. his est. to Sarah Parker - Thomas Riley & Henry Greenalds sec. - 28 June 1757 - p. 192

SCARBURGH, JOHN - Adm. his est. unadministered by Tabitha Scarburgh, dec., his admx., to James Henry - John Coleburn sec. - 29 Nov. 1757 - p. 210

BUCKLEY, ROBERT - Adm. his est. to Bartholomew Taylor - Warrington Staton & William Nicholson sec. - 29 Nov. 1757 - p. 211

STOCKLEY, ELIAS - Adm. his est. to Sacker Parker - William Barns & Robert Parker sec. - 29 Nov. 1757 - p. 211

MILBURN, JOSHUA - Adm. his est. to Mary Milburn - James Broadwater & George Broadwater sec. - 30 Nov. 1757 - p. 212

169

CROPPER, BOWMAN - Adm. his est. to Sebastian Cropper, Jr. - William Nicholson & John Baley sec. - 30 Nov. 1757 - p. 212

BISHOP, JACOB - Adm. his est. to Elizabeth Bishop - Robert Abbott & Solomon Lucas Wimbrough sec. - 30 Nov. 1757 - p. 212

FISHER, ELIZABETH - Adm. her est. to Thomas Fisher - Thomas Parramore sec. - 28 Dec. 1757 - p. 217

TAYLOR, SARAH - Adm. her est. to Daniel Kelly - Andrew Simpler sec. - 1 Feb. 1758 - p. 223

MIDDLETON, WILLIAM - Adm. his est. to Thomas Wise - John Wise, Jr. sec. - 28 Mar. 1758 - p. 231

GREENALDS, HENRY - Adm. his est. to Catherine Greenalds - Isaiah Johnson & Elijah Lilliston sec. - 28 Mar. 1758 - p. 234

CRIPPEN, THOMAS - Adm. his est. to Thomas Crippen - Southy Simpson sec. - 27 June 1758 - p. 247

CONQUEST, NATHANIEL - Adm. his est. to Elizabeth Conquest - William Drummond & Joseph Stockley sec. - 27 June 1758 - p. 247

NOCK, JOHN - Adm. his est. to Rachel Nock - John Kitson sec. - 15 July 1758 - p. 251

DICKERSON, SARAH - Adm. her est. to Mary Dickerson - William Andrews, Jr. & Joseph Matthews sec. - 31 Oct. 1758 - p. 264

WISHART, WILLIAM - Adm. his est. to Jannah Wishart - George Holden sec. - 28 Nov. 1758 - p. 266

MELSON, JOHN - Adm. his est. to Robert Turnal - William Young sec. - 28 Nov. 1758 - p. 268

BRITT, BILLINGS - Adm. his est. to Abraham Riggs - John Fitchet sec. - 26 Dec. 1758 - p. 273

THORNTON, WILLIAM - Adm. his est. to Anne Thornton - Joseph Feddiman & Warrington Staton sec. - p. 288

WIMBROUGH, JOHN - Adm. his est. to Rachel Wimbrough - Solomon Lucas Wimbrough & Thomas Fisher sec. - 29 May 1759 - p. 288

MEERS, WILLIAM - Adm. his est. to Mary Darby - Charles Bagwell & William Groten, Jr. sec. - 29 May 1759 - p. 289

DARBY, CHURCHILL - Adm. his est. to Custis Darby - Benjamin Darby sec. - 29 May 1739 - p. 289

LEATHERMAN, JOHN – Adm. his est. to Sarah Leatherman – Skinner Wallop & William Wheelton sec. – 26 June 1759 – p. 294

PARKER, AGNES – Adm. her est. to Robert Russell – George Hope & Thomas Evans sec. 29 Jan. 1760 – p. 319

VANNELSON, JANE – Adm. her est. to Charles Vannelson – Ezekiel Delastatius & Meshack Feddiman sec. – 29 Jan. 1760 – p. 320

LILLISTON, JOHN – Adm. his est. to Mary Lilliston – Elijah Lilliston & Jacob Dunton sec. – 26 Feb. 1760 – p. 325

GASCOIGNE, THOMAS – Adm. his est. to Henry Gascoigne & John Darby sec. – 26 Feb. 1760 – p. 326

COOK, THOMAS – Adm. his est. to William Cook – Richard Hinman sec. – 25 Mar. 1769 – p. 332

OWEN, PETER – Adm. his est. to Elizabeth Owen – William Finney, Jr. & William Wheelton sec. – 25 Mar. 1760 – p. 332

FITZGERRALD, STEPHEN – Adm. his est. to Edward Gunter, Susanna Fitzgerrald, eld. child & only heir of age, relinquishing her rignt to qualify – George Drummond & Robert Drummond sec. – 26 Mar. 1760 – p. 334

COPES, PARKER – Adm. his est. to Parker Copes – Charles Bagwell & Sebastian Cropper, Jr. sec. – 26 Mar. 1760 – p. 335

MASON, ELEANOR – Adm. her est. to Middleton Mason – Littleton Armitrader sec. – 29 Apr. 1760 – p. 339

MILLS, MOSES – Adm. his est. to Samuel Mills – Adam Hall sec. – 27 May 1760 – p. 344

WEST, SCARBURGH – Adm. his est. to Alexander West – Littleton Scarburgh Major sec. – 30 July 1760 – p. 357

WIMBPOUGH, PAUL – Adm. his est. to Covington Corbin – Tully Robinson Wise sec. – 30 July 1760 – p. 357

DOUGLAS, ANNE – Adm. her est. to Walter Douglas – John Wise sec. – 26 Aug. 1760 – p. 357

NICHOLSON, WILLIAM – Adm. his est. to Arcadia Nicholson – Covington Corbin sec. – 7 Oct. 1760 – p. 369

HERBERT, JOHN – Adm. his est. to Jonathan Bunting, a creditor, Tabitha Herbert, wid. of John, relinquishing her right to qualify. John Drummond sec. – 7 Oct. 1760 – p. 369

EVANS, JOHN - Adm. his est. to Anne Evans - John Kitson & Thomas Cropper sec. - 30 Dec. 1760 - p. 372

DIX ISAAC - Adm. his est. to Southy Simpson - Littleton Dennis sec. - 30 Dec. 1760 - p. 373

HASLES, MOSES - Adm. his est. to John Willet - Southy Simpson sec. - 30 Dec. 1760 - p. 374

SIMPSON, Mary - Adm. her est. to Ralph Justice - Arnold Morgan & Thomas Bloxom sec. - 30 Dec. 1760 - p. 374

MORGAN, JAMES - Adm. his est. to Mary Morgan - Arnold Morgan sec. - 30 Dec. 1760 p. 374

SPIERS, JOHN - Adm. his est. to Anne Spiers - Richard Rodgers, Jr. & William Spiers sec. - 30 Dec. 1760 - p. 374

ARMITRADER, HENRY - Adm. his est. to Littleton Armitrader - William Andrews sec. - 31 Dec. 1760 - p. 377

SHAE, DANIEL - Adm. his est. to John Shae - William Matthews sec. - 27 Jan. 1761 - p. 378

TOWNSEND, RICHARD - Adm. his est. to Sarah Townsend, widow - Skinner Wallop & Adam Hall sec. - 27 Jan. 1761 - p. 379

HOWELL, JOHN - Adm. his est. to Sarah Howell - Edmund Scarburgh & Francis Wainhouse sec. - 27 Jan. 1761 - p. 380

WAINHOUSE, BRIDGET - Adm. her est. to Francis Wainhouse - Edmund Scarburgh sec. - 27 Jan. 1761 - p. 380

LITTLETON, SARAH - Adm. her est. to Mark Littleton - Ambrose Willet & Richard Hickman sec. - 27 Jan. 1761 - p. 380

ALLEN, JAMES - Adm. his est. to William Custis - Thomas Bagwell sec. - 25 Feb. 1761 - p. 385

BLAKE, JOHN - Adm. his est. to Sarah Blake - William Lane & Arthur Rowley sec. 31 Mar. 1761 - p. 389

TWIFORD, HILLARY - Adm. his est. to Rosannah Twiford - Major Rowles & Litt: Read sec. - 31 Mar. 1761 - p. 389

DOUGLAS, TABITHA - Adm. her est. to James Rule - John Coleburn sec. - 1 Apr. 1761 p. 392

DOUGLAS, ANN - Adm. her est. unadministered by Walter Douglas, dec., to James Rule. - John Coleburn sec. - 1 Apr. 1761 - p. 392

DAVIS, SAMUEL – Adm. his est. to Justice Bundick – John Taylor & Sebastian Cropper sec. – 1 Apr. 1761 – p. 394

SHIELD, JONATHAN – Adm. his est. to Sacker Shield – Ezekiel Young sec. – 26 May 1761 – p. 400

NOBLE, EDWARD – Adm. his est. to William Finney, Jr. – John Smith sec. – 29 Sept. 1761 – p. 420

BURTON, CALEB – Adm. his est. to Michael Burton – Major Rowles & John Taylor sec. 24 Nov. 1761 – p. 430

ROSE, JAMES – Adm. his est. to Edmund Heath – Noah Belote sec. – 24 Nov. 1761 – p. 430

CASE, EZEKIEL . Adm. his est. to Ezekiel Case – John Giddens sec. – 24 Nov. 1761 – p. 430

CUSTIS, HENRY – Adm. his est. unadministered by Scarburgh, his wife, now dec., to James Arbuckle – George Stuart sec. – 30 Dec. 1761 – p. 437

SHIELD, SACKER – Adm. his est. to Richard Shield – George Bonnewell sec. – 26 Jan. 1762 – p. 441

WALKER, JOHN – Adm. his est. to Nathaniel Walker – Adam Hall & Thomas Fisher sec. – 26 Jan. 1762 – p. 441

SCANDLIN, JAMES – Adm. his est. to Margaret Scandlin – William Patterson & Ayres Gillet sec. – 23 Feb. 1762 – p. 442

PARPADICE, WILLIAM – Adm. his est. to Daniel Gore – Covington Corbin sec. – 30 Mar. 1762 – p. 445

MEERS, JOHN – Adm. his est. to Sabra Meers – John Meers & Littleton Armitrader sec. – 30 Mar. 1762 – p. 445

ROWLES, MAJOR – Adm. his est. to Elizabeth Rowles & James Rodgers – Hancock Nickless Rowles & Zorobable Rodgers sec. – 30 Mar. 1762 – p. 446

WATKINSON, THOMAS – Adm. his est. to James Rickards – Samuel Beech & John Willis sec. – 27 Apr. 1762 – p. 448

LAWRENCE, BARTHOLOMEW – Adm. his est. to Jacob Stakes – Zorobabel Rogers sec. – 27 Apr. 1762 – p. 449

BARKER, MARY – Adm. her est. to John Downing – Ambrose Howard & Major Davis sec. – 25 May 1762 – p. 451

PARKER, ANDERSON - Adm. his est. to Betty Parker - William Tisaker sec. - 25 May 1762 - P. 451

ONIONS, WILLIAM - Adm. his est. to James Pettigrew, the wid. relinquishing her right to qualify - Southy Simpson sec. - 28 July 1762 - p. 469

RODGERS, EDMUND - Adm. his est. to Edmund Rodgers - Zerrobabel Rodgers & Stratton Burton sec. - 2 Dec. 1762 - p. 496

HALL, MICHAEL - Adm. his est. to Betty Hall - Thomas Hall & Richard Cutler sec. - 28 Dec. 1762 - p. 499

GARRISON, PHILLIS - Adm. her est. to William Garrison - John Taylor & Littleton Armitrader sec. - 28 Dec. 1762 - p. 499

WEBB, THOMAS - Adm. his est. to Charles Snead - Severn Guthrey & Smith Bunting sec - 29 Dec. 1762 - p. 503

BAKER, JOHN - Adm. his est. to Ezekiel Dalastatius - William Patterson sec - 26 Jan. 1763 - p. 511

SIMPSON, JOHN - Adm. his est. to Southy Simpson - Littleton Dennis sec. - 27 Jan. 1765 - p. 517

HARTFEILD, ELIAS - Adm. his est. to Edward Parrish (Quaker) - Ezekiel Young & John Smith, Jr. sec. - 23 Feb. 1763 - p. 521

BAYLY, EDMUND - Adm. his est. with will annexed, unadministered by Dorothy Wainhouse, his wid. & Exec., to John Custis - Sebastian Cropper, Jr. sec. - 30 Mar. 1763 - p. 531

KELLAM, PETER - Adm. his est. to Solomon Kellam - Jonathan Kellam & John Kellam sec. - 30 Mar. 1763 - p. 531

GOODAY, WILLIAM - Adm. his est. to David James - Abbott Bundick sec. - 30 Mar. 1763 - p. 534

LEIGH, JOHN - Adm. his est. to William Black Bunting - Sebastian Cropper, Jr. sec. - 31 May 1763 - p. 548

TOWLES, Daniel - Adm. his est. to Patience Towles - George Hope & John Smith sec. - 31 May 1763 - p. 548

MAJOR, JOHN - Adm. his est. to John Gowtee - Ralph Justice sec. - 1 June 1763 - p. 552

RULE, JAMES - Adm. his est. to Agnes Rule - Thomas Parramore & Skinner Wallop sec. - 26 July 1763 - p. 586

SCANDLIN, EDWARD - Adm. his est. to Edward Parrish (Quaker) - Southy Simpson sec. - 31 Aug. 1763 - p. 607

BUNTING, JOHN - Adm. his est. to William Black Bunting - Smith Bunting sec. - 31 Aug. 1763 - p. 607

READ, SOUTHY - Adm. his est. to Richard Read - Henry Read sec. - 25 Oct. 1763 - p. 629

WISE, GEORGE - Adm. his est. to Edmund Wise - Perry Leatherbury & Samuel Cutler sec. - 7 Nov. 1763 - p. 635

BRADFORD, CHARLES - Adm. his est. to Naomi Bradford - John Parker & William Bradford sec. - 27 Dec. 1763 - p. 643

WATSON, THOMAS - Adm. his est. to Tabitha Watson - Thomas Tatham sec. - 27 Dec. 1763 - p. 643

FURNACE, SAMUEL - Adm. his est. to Simpson Bloxom - William Andrews sec. - 27 Dec. 1763 - p. 643

Wills 1752-1757

AUSTIN, MOSES - Nunc - Declaration 29 Dec. 1751 - Proved 10 Jan. 1752 - Prob. 28 Jan. 1752 - Whole est. to Mary Chapman - Proved by Isaac McKenny & Betty Rain - p. 10
In order of prob: Mary Chapman qualified.

FEDDIMAN, JOSEPH - 3 Jan. 1752 - 29 Jan. 1752 - To son Samuel land & planta. where I now live. To dau. Elizabeth Mercy. To son Meshack Feddiman. To son Joseph Feddiman. To dau. Esther Mathews. Sons Meshack & Joseph resid. legatess. Sons Samuel, Meshack & Joseph Exrs. - Witt: Edward Dickeson, Joseph Mathews, Ezekiel Delastatius - p. 15

ROBINS, JOHN - 2 Dec. 1751 - 25 Feb. 1752 - To wife Mary whole est. for life. Will not to be proved until death or marriage of my wife. To bro. William Robins. Bro. William Exr. & to have my son when he will take him. Witt: John Spalding, Dennis Blake, William Robins, William Holston - p. 22
In ordder of prob: Nathaniel Stockly app. guardian to Michael Robins, heir at law to the testator.

LITCHFIELD, FRANCIS - 10 Feb. 1752 - 31 Mar. 1752 - To wife Sarah 1/3 of personal est. To dau. Comfort Ailworth bal. of personal est. Thomas Evans Exr. Witt: William Chase, Susanna Evans - p. 55
In order of prob: Thomas Evans relinquished his right, & Ezekiel Litchfield qualified.

RODGERS, DANIEL – 12 Oct. 1751 – 31 Mar. 1752 – To wife Hannah whole est. during her wid. Dau. Elizabeth Rodgers. To son James land where I now live on this side of a little branch after his mother's death or marriage, also 12 1/2 A. on Cedar Island, & for want of issue to my son John Rodgers. To son Zerobabel Rodgers land on the West side of the branch at his mother's death or marriage, also 12 1/2 A. on Cedar Island, & for want of heirs to my son Thomas Rodgers. To son John. To son Thomas. Bal. of est. to be div. bet. my 5 children (sons under age) Wife & sons James & Zerobabel Exrs. Witt: Robert Wale, Luke Lucar, Mary Rodgers – p. 40

PARKS, SARAH – 24 Nov. 1751 – 31 Mar. 1752 – To sister Mary Parks use of land & moveable est. for life, then the land to Daniel Lewis. To Thomas Bloxom. Bal. of est. to Benjamin Parks, Daniel Lewis & Thomas Bloxom, they to be my Exrs. Witt: William Young, George Hope Ewell, Elizabeth Parks – p. 44

DICKESON, ABRAHAM – 5 Feb. 1752 – 26 May 1752 – Wife Rachel whole est. during her wid. to bring up my children. To son Michael Dickeson all my land. To son Georgs Dickeson. Son Boyer. Dau. Sarah Broadwater. Dau. Ann Mary Beavans. Dau Martha Dickeson. Dau. Rachel Dickeson. Children resid. legatees. Son Michael Exr. Witt: Edward Dickeson, Nicholas Milman, Peter Milman – p. 53

COLEBURN ROBERT – 25 Mar. 1752 – 26 May 1752 – To Comfort Spiers, wife of William Spiers, planta. where the said Spiers now lives. To Robert Spiers, son of William Spiers, land I bought of William Lingo, Leah Lingo to have use of the house & kitchen during her wid. To the said Robert Spiers all the marsh I own on Matchapungo Creek. To son John Coleburn planta. where I now live & all the land not already given during his natural life, & then to my grandson Robert Coleburn. Wife (no name) John Coleburn & Comfort Spiers, my son & dau., resid. legatees. Son John Exr. Witt: Thomas Parramore, Joshua Burton, James Wharton – p. 54
In order of prob: John Coleburn heir at law to the testator.

DELASTATIUS, MARY – 21 Dec. 1749 – 26 May 1752 – To son Lemuel Delastatius. To dau. Phebe Delastatius. Dau. Mary Delastatius. 2 youngest daus. Leah & Rhoda. Bal. of est. to be div. bet. my 4 daus., Son Lemuel & bro. in law Anderson Patterson Exrs. – Witt: Samuel Feddiman – p. 54

PITTS, HANNAH – 29 Mar. 1751 – 30 June 1752 – Grandsons John & William Pitts (under 21) To sons Samuel & William Pitts. To dau. Elizabeth Merril. Dau. Hannah Benston, Grandau. Sophia Blades. Grandau. Levinah Pitts. Grandau. Hannah Pitts, dau. of John Pitts, dec. Daus. Elizabeth Merril & Hannah Benston resid. legatees – Witt: Robert Pitt, Robert Pitts.
Codicil: To son William Pitts. To dau. Jemimah Morse. – p. 58
In order of prob: Proved by Robert Pitts – Samuel Pitts qualified.

COLEBURN, WILLIAM – 13 Jan. 1751 – 30 June 1752 – To son Spencer Coleburn my land & housings, provided he pay his bro. William when he comes of age 20 L & his bro. John 20 L, & should he refuse I give my land to my son William, he to pay the same sum to Spencer & then to my youngest son. Dau. Ann. Dau. Susannah. Bal. of est. to be div. bet. all my children. Wife (no name) Exec. Witt: Richard Justice, Levin Teackle, John Coleburn – p. 59
In order of prob: Spencer Coleburn heir at law to the testator. Temperance Coleburn, wid. of the testator qualified.

LUCAS, SOLOMON – 30 Dec. 1751 – 25 Aug. 1752 – To son Southy Lucas 100 A. where I now live. To son Elijah Lucas 100 A. which my father bought of Mason Abbott. To son Solomon Lucas 50 A. which fell to me by the death of my bro. Robinson Lucas. Friends Middleton Mason & William Mason Exrs. Bal. of est. to be div. bet. all my children. Witt: Middleton Mason & William Mason – p. 90
In order of Prob: Robert Pitt app. guardian to Southy Lucas, heir at law to the testator – The executors named in said will relinquished their right and Eleanor Lucas, wid. of the testator qualified.

DONOHOE, MARY – 27 Apr. 1752 – 28 Nov. 1752 – Grandson Nathaniel Milby, son of Nathaniel Milby. Son Nathaniel Milby. Grandau. Anjeletter Evans. Son Peter Milby. Dau. Agnes Buty. Son in law George Polson. Bal. of est. to my sons & sons in law as follows: Nathaniel Milby, Peter Milby, John Dix, George Polson & my dau. Agnes Buty. Grandson John Evans. Son Peter Milby & John Dix Exrs. Witt: Leah Fletcher, Abigail Hall, Thomas Evans, Henry Fletcher.
Codicil: 9 Oct. 1752 – Should both my gandau. Anneletter Evans & my grandson John Evans die without heirs negro Candace & her increase to son Nathaniel Milby, Peter Milby, Sarah Dix, Elizabeth Polson & Agnes Simple, to be equally div. bet. my 5 children. Witt: Henry Fletcher, Leah Fletcher, Abigail Hall – p. 123

LECATT, JOSEPH – 17 Nov. 1752 – 25 Dec. 1752 – Friends John Huffington the elder & his son Gilbert Huffington of Somerset County, Maryland. or either of them, to sell 209 A. in Somerset County devised me by my father John Lecatt, dec., for payment of debts, & the residue to be applied toward bringing up my son. To wife Anne negro for life, then to my son Augustine Lecatt, & if he die before his mother without issue to my goddau. Comfort Taylor. To son Augustine Lecatt negroes, & for want of issue to my goddau. Tabitha Parker. To bro. John Lecatt. Wife & son resid. legatees. Bro. Nathaniel Lecatt Exr. Witt: Thomas Teackle, John Milby, Littleton Darby – p. 146
In order of Prob: Thomas Teackle app. guardian to Augustine Lecatt, heir at law to the testator.

CRIPPEN, PAUL - 2 Dec. 1752 - 27 Feb. 1753 - Wife Margaret to have Planta. where I now dwell with my son Thomas Crippen, negroes, cattle &c., they to school my 3 small children, Mary, John & James Crippen. Son Thomas to have the whole of the above effects at the death of my wife. To son George land in Worcester County, Maryland called Obeds Willingness to Try - Bal. of est. to 4 children George, Mary, John & James. Wife & son Thomas to have care of children until they come to age or marry. Friends Daniel Mifflin, John Kitson, William White & John Evans to div. est. Daniel Mifflin & son Thomas Crippen Exrs. Witt: Wrixom White, John Evans, William White, Robert Crippen - p. 160
In order of Prob: Thomas Crippen heir at law to the testator. Probate granted "on the motion of Thomas Crippen & Daniel Mifflin, the Exrs., and they affirming thereto, being the People called Quakers".

INGERSON, TABITHA - 15 Oct. 1752 - 27 Mar. 1753 - To son Solomon Gray. Dau. Mary Ann Gray. Dau. Tabitha Kelly. Son Samuel Ingerson. Bal. est. to dau. Mary Ann Gray & son Samuel Ingerson if they will pay Sarah Drummond 1 lb. of wool & Creshey Smith 3 s. in Linnen. Son Thomas Tatham. Thomas Ryley Exr. Witt: John Lewis, Elizabeth Lewis, Solomon Gladding - p. 163

PARKS, MARY - 7 Aug. 1752 - 27 Mar. 1753 To Daniel Lewis all my land. To Benjamin Parks. Benjamin Parks, Daniel Lewis & Thomas Bloxom resid. legatees & Exrs. Witt: William Young, Thomas Ryley, Ann Parks, Sinah Parks - p. 165

ABBOTT, ROGER - 13 July 1751 - 27 Mar. 1753 - To grandson Roger Abbott all my lands on the North side of the Branch where I now live cont. 175 A. To grandau. Betty Abbott, dau. of Richard Abbott 125 A. on the South side of the branch where my son Richard did live, & for want of heirs to my grandson John Abbott. To 3 grandchildren Roger, John & Betty Abbott 255 A. land & marsh. Bal. of est. to wife (no name) during her wid. & then to be div. bet. Susanna Belote, Elizabeth Bloxom, Patience Hindman & my grandson John Abbott. Wife & Caesar Evans Exrs. Witt: Thomas Ryley, Robert Turnal, Thomas Turnal, Robert Turnal, Jr. - p. 167
In order of Prob: Southy Simpson app. guardian to Rodger Abbot, grandson of the testator.

MILMAN, NICHOLAS - 23 Mar 1753 - 28 Aug. 1753 - To eldest son Thomas Milman all my land & planta. where I now live on the South side of Wamoes Branch, but should he offer to sell the same then to fall to my second son Jonathan. To 3rd son Peter Milman my field over the said branch with 1/2 my land over the aforesaid branch. To youngest son Ephram Milman my small Planta. where my son Thomas now lives with 1/2 my land over the aforesaid branch. To dau. Sarah Milman Daus Mary & Elizabeth Milman. To wife Ann personal est. during her life then to be div. bet. my children which have no land given them. Sons Thomas & Jonathan Exrs. Witt: William Mathews, Michael Dickson, David Thornton - p. 195

178

BLAXTON, JOHN – 22 July 1753 – 28 Aug. 1753 – To wife Ann Mary Blaxton. Son William Blaxton. Dau. Mary Blaxton. Wife & 2 children William & Mary Blaxton resid. legatees. Wife Exec. Witt: Stephen Fitzgerald, Thomas Cropper, Susanna Trader – p. 197

WEST, ELIZABETH – 21 Apr. 1749 – 25 Sept. 1753 – To son Anthony West. Dau. Mary Bell. Dau. Jean Rogers. To my four grandchildren my dau. Matilda had by Jacob Rogers. To grandson Anthony, son of my son John. Son John resid. legatee & Exr. Witt: Littleton Scarburgh Major, West Kellam – p. 199

REVELL, EDWARD – 22 Mar. 1753 – 25 Sept. 1753 – Wife Rebecca to have 1/2 my personal est & 1/2 my land, Island, water mill &c. during her natural life, then to my son John all my land Island &c. & for want of heirs to my 2 daus. Agnes Horsey & Catharine Revell. To son John large silver Tankard marked IRA. To grandson William Custis. Dau. Rachel Tilnay. Grandau. Elizabeth Leatherbury. Wife & 2 children John & Catherine resid. legatees. Est. to be div. by friends Abel Upshur, William Bagg, Robert Parker & William Spiers. Wife & son John Exrs. Witt: James Falconer, James Rodgers, Anthony West, John Custis. – p. 200

SILVERTHORN, SEBASTIAN – 7 Oct. 1751 – 29 Jan. 1754 – To eld. son John Silverthorn. To wife Elizabeth, Bal. of est. for life & then to be div. among my children Southey, Thomas, Levin, Anne, Arthur & Sebastian Silverthorn. Wife to have care of my children until my sons come to age of 21 & daus. to 16. Wife Exec. Witt: Thomas Northam, Edward Dickeson, William Melson – p. 207

UPSHUR, ABEL – 2 Sept. 1753 – 29 Jan. 1754 – To son Arthur 1300 A. in Accomack on Matchapungo River where I now live provided he permit my son John Upshur to hold & enjoy 550 A. in Northampton County on Nassawadox Creek and which I hereby give to my son John, and should he refuse my son John to possess the said 1300 A. & if my son John should die before he comes to lawful age without issue, then I give the Northampton land to my son Caleb, and my son Arthur to be subject to the same conditions as above. To son Caleb 800 A. in Accomack County near the head of Watchaprig Creek lately Purchased of William Burton of Northampton County, & for want of issue to my son John, & should John die to my 2 daus. Susanna & Elizabeth. Son Arthur to be guardian to my 2 sons John & Caleb & dau. Elizabeth until they come of age. Son Arthur resid. legatee. Son Arthur, William Bagge & Thomas Teackle Exrs. Witt: W: Bagge, Henry Lurton, Abel Bradford, Ezekiel Badger, Nicholas Dolby – p. 209

CARRUTHERS, ROBERT – 24 Feb. 1750 – 29 Jan. 1754 – To son John Carruthers planta. in Sussex County which I bought of John Reed, lying upon Pemberton's Branch, cont. 150 A. To dau. Leah Bagwell Carruthers. To son Robert Carruthers planta. where I now live which I bought of Thomas Adams, cont. 125 A. Wife (no name) & 2 sons

resid. legatees. Wife & son Robert Exrs. Witt: Thomas Ryley, John Young, Nicholas Powell, Ann Turnall - p. 212
In order of Probate: Tabitha Carruthers, wid. of the testator qualified.

BENSTEN, JOHN - Not dated - 26 Feb. 1754 - To wife Hannah Bensten the manor planta. for 5 years, then to my son Micajah Bensten & for want of heirs to my son Zepheniah Bensten. To son Ezekiel Bensten the remaining part of my land. Sons Isaish & Zepheniah Bensten. Grandchildren John & Elizabeth Gray. Grandson John Bensten. Bal. of est. to be div. bet. 5 of my children, Micajah, Zefeniah, Levineah, Leah & Hannah Bensten. Sons Ezekiel & Micajah Bensten Exrs. Witt: Hill Bensten, Joseph Gouty - p. 218

MELSON, JOSEPH - 10 Apr. 1747 - Partly Proved 28 May 1751; Further proved 28 Feb. 1754 - Prob. 6 Mar. 1754 - To son George Melson 1/2 my Manner planta. Whole est. real & personal to wife Ann Melson during her wid. & then to be div. bet. my sons Edmund, Isaac, Middleton, Joseph, William, George & John Melson & Elizabeth Barns & Arcadia Bull, my sons & daus. Wife Ann & son Isaac Exrs. Witt: Stephen Fitzgerrald, William Reid - p. 222

EVANS, ISAIAH - 7 Dec. 1753 - 26 Mar. 1754 - To eld. son William Evans planta. where I now live cont. 200 A. to 2nd son Zerubbabell Evans 191 A. near Gargathy devised me by my dec. father Thomas Evans. To dau. Sarah Evans. To wife Elizabeth. Bal. of est. to be div. bet. all my children including unborn child. Wife & bros. Thomas & John Evans Exrs. Witt: Denwood Turpin, Edward Jones, George Cutler - p. 223
In order of Prob: Willlam Beavans app. Guardian of William Evans, eld. son & heir at law to the testator.

TIZZAKER, ROBERT - 10 Dec. 1753 - 28 May 1754 - To wife Fetaplace Tizzaker planta. where I live for life then to my son William. To son Joseph Tizzaker the remaining part of my land. Dau. Betty. Dau. Nanny. Dau. Marry. Dau. Sarah. Dau. Ann. 6 children Sarah. William, Mary, Betty, Joseph & Nanny resid. legatees. Wife & son William Exrs. Witt: George Cutler, Perry Leatherbury, Daniel Cutler. - p. 229

PROBART, WILLIAM Mariner, being bound on a voyage to Great Britain - 6 Aug. 1752 Proved 28 May 1754 - Prob. 28 Aug. 1754 - Immediately upon my death my Exr. to app. someone to receive of & from the Exr. of my cousin Elizabeth Gronans dec. such sum or sums of money which shall be due & owing me by virtue of the last will & test. of the said Elizabeth, same to be divided in 6 parts, one part to my wife & the remainder to be div. in 2 parts, one to my sons Yelverton & William & the other between my 3 daus. Eleanor, Elizabeth & Leah. Property to remain in my wife's hands until the respective legatees arrive at age of 21 or marry with the consent of their mother. Whole est. to wife for life, then to be div. bet. my children. Friends Patrick McDowall & George Holden trustees. Wife (no name) Exec.

Witt: John Dayson, Stephen Fitzgerrald, William Lee –
Codicil: 17 July 1753 – Since writing the above will my son William is dead, & I have had a child born whose name is Mary – After my wife s 6th part is set aside est. to be div. in 4 parts, & 1/4 to be allotted to my son Yelverton & the other 3 parts to my 4 daus aforesaid. Witt: William Hubbard, Robert Roberts – p. 236
In order of Prob: Elizabeth Probart, wid. of the testator, relinquished her right & George Holden qualified.

EDMUNDS, JONATHAN – 4 Mar. 1754 – 28 May 1754 – To son Southey Edmunds 150 A. 50 A. adj. Edmund Alen's line to be sold to pay my debts. To wife Elisha Edmunds. To dau. Leah Edmunds. Wife & children resid. legatees – Wife & son Southey Exrs. Witt: John Wharton, Isaiah Bagwell, Peine Chapman – p. 238
In order of Prob: James Rodgers app. guardian to Southey Edmunds, heir at law to the testator.

AMES, THOMAS, Sr. – 16 Mar. 1754 – 25 June 1754 – To wife Mary Ames whole personal est. during her life, then to be div. bet. my 3 children Joseph Ames, Esther Harrison & Thomas Ames, Jr. Son Joseph Exr. Witt: Thomas Johnson, Hillery Bellot Bartholomew Meers – p. 240

VESSELS, JAMES, Sr. living on Fisher's Island – 7 Apr. 1751 – 25 June 1754 – To son Ephraim Vessels 1 s. To son Shadrack 1 s. To son Elijah 1 s. To son James planta. & land where he now lives being 50 A. Bal. of est. to wife Elizabeth during her wid. & then to my 3 daus. as my wife sees fit, viz: Keturah, Betty & Rebecca Vessels – To dau. Hannah 1 s. Wife & son James Exrs. Not witnessed – Proved by James Vessels – p. 243

ALWORTH, JONATHAN – 6 June 1752 – 24 Sept. 1754 – Grandson Jonathan Alworth land & planta. where I now live being 200 A. To son John Alworth 140 A. where he now lives. To grandson John Taylor, Dau. Elizabeth Taylor, dec. To Jonathan Alworth the son of my grandson Jonathan Alworth. Bal. of est. to be div. bet. son John & grandson Jonathan by the discretion of Daniel Hall & Henry Fletcher. Grandson Jonathan Exr. Witt: Henry Fletcher, Joachim Michael, Susanna Michael. – p. 247
In order of Prob: Jonathan Alworth grandson & heir at law to the testator.

DICKESON, EDWARD – 3 Oct. 1754 – 29 Oct. 1754 – To son Jessie Dickeson (under age) all my lands, & for want of issue to my 4 daus. Mary, Martha, Sarah & Leah Dickeson. Wife Sarah & 4 daus. resid. legatees. Wife Exec. Witt: William Mathews, Sophia Peal, Sarah Brimer – p. 257
In order of Prob: Littleton Dennis app. guardian to Jessie Dickeson, heir at law to the testator.

PARKER, JOHN, Sr. - 25 Aug. 1754 - 1 Jan. 1755 To son John Parker. Sons William & Robert Parker. Sons Anderson & Edward Parker. Dau. Frances White. Dau. Susannah Wise. 4 daus. Ann Lacey, Rachel Boggs, Betty Guy & Bridget Parker. Children not to have any part of their est. without the consent of their mother. Wife Frances Parker to have use of whole est. during her wid. Wife & son Robert Parker Exrs. Witt: David Neilson, Francis Boggs, Sacker Parker, Southey White. p. 261
In order of Prob: John Parker heir at law to the testator - Frances Parker qualified.

WISHARD, THOMAS - 21 Oct. 1752 - 1 Jan. 1755 - To mother Hannah Wishard during her life then to my bro. Joshua Wishard. To bro. William Wishard. 3 sisters & bro. James, to-wit: Ann, Elizabeth & "Gaeamen" Wishard. Cousin Southey Whittington & William Wishard Exrs. Witt: Joseph Blades, Thomas Bennet, Charles Parker, Southey Whittington - p. 263
In order of prob: Hannah Wishart qualified.

TOWNSEND, ELIZABETH - 29 Jan. 1754 - 28 Jan. 1755 - To Skinner Wallop. To dau. Elizabeth Davis during her life, reversion to her 2 daus. Betty Smith & Mary Smith. Sarah Martial & Sophia Wallop resid. legatees. Skinner Wallop Exr. Witt: John Thornton, Charles Thornton - p. 266

WEST, JOHN - 13 Sept. 1754 - 28 Jan. 1755 - To wife 1/3 of est. during her life. To son John West. To son Major West (under 21) To dau. Agnes Snead. To dau. Cathrine Chambers. To dau. Ann Bunting. To dau. Betty Goffigon. To daus. Susannah & Comfort West. To dau. Scarburgh Topping. Sons John & Major West resid. legatees. Son John Exr. Witt: Smith Snead, Thomas Webb, Noah Belote - p. 268

MEERS, WILLIAM - 10 Jan. 1755 - 25 Feb. 1755 - To son John Planta. where I now live. To son William land at the head of Nandua Creek being 100 A. To dau. Mary Meers. To son Richard Meers. To son Elisha Meers. To wife Mary Meers bal. of est. for life, & then to be div. bet. all my children, John, William, Mary, Richard & Elisha Meers. Wife Mary, Son John & friend & bro. in law Thomas Stringer Exrs. Witt: John Kennahorn, Jacob Bird, William Tray - p. 269
In order of Prob: Anthony West app. guardian to John Meers, Inf't. heir at law to the testator.

ARMITRADER, RICHARD - 24 Feb. 1755 - 25 Mar. 1755 - To wife Elizabeth whole est. during her wid., then to dau. Sabrah Meers Planta. where I live. Grandsons William & Benjamin Knock. Grandau. Patience Knock. Grandson Levin Knock. Dau. Sabra Meers resid. legatee. Son in law John Meers Exr. Witt: Francis Savage, Rowland Savage, William Red. - p. 271
In order of Prob: John Meers, husband of Sabra, one of the daus. & co heirs of the testator, & William Knock, son & heir at law of Rose

Knock, dec., the other dau. & co heir of the said testator, being present & having nothing to object, the said will was admitted to Probate.

SPIERS, WILLIAM - 14 Nov. 1754 - 27 May 1755 - To wife whole est. during her wid. & should she marry to have an equal share with the children. Bal. of est. to be div. bet. my children - Wife (no name) Exec. - Witt: John Spiers, Henry Heath. In order of Prob. John Coleburn guardian to John Spiers, heir at law of the testator. Comfort Spiers, wid. of the testator qualified.

WARRINGTON, JOHN - 28 Dec. 1753 - 24 June 1755 - To son John Warrington "land over the bridge where he now lives" Bal. of land & planta. where I now live to wife during her life, then to my son John. Daus. Elizabeth, Anne, Mary, Comfort & Rachel. Bal. of est. to wife for life then to be div. bet. my 5 daus. Wife (no name) Exec. - Witt: William Bagge, Samuel Bagge, Jeremiah Bagge - p. 285
In order of Prob: John Warrington heir at law to the testator. Mary Warrington, wid. of the testator qualified.

NEADOM, ELIZABETH - 24 May 1755 - 24 June 1755 - Daus. Mary & Betty Neadom sole devisees & Executrices. Witt: Sarah Thornton, Joseph Stockly - p. 286

HOWARD, SOLOMON - Nunc. - 7 June 1755 - 24 June 1755 - Bro. Daniel Howard. Wife Ann Howard resid. legatee. Proved by Elijah Nock, Elias Vernelson, Joseph Kelly. p. 286
In order of Prob: Ann Howard, wid. of the testator qualified.

CART, MONSER, of the Island of St. Domingo, but now in Worcester County in Maryland - 8 Mar. 1748/9 - Prob. in Maryland 10 Mar. 1748/9 - Rec. in Accomack 24 June, 1755 - To my attorney Monsieur Lanse Geseran in the Island of St. Domingo all my land in said Island, City of New York, in the Province of Maryland or elsewhere. All my effects in the City of New York which are in the hands of Capt. Peter Brown to be put in the hands of Monsieur Pentare in New York, & by him remitted to Monsieur Legarde in Cape Fransway & by him delivered to my Attorney Monsieur Lange Geseron. Capt. Moses Chaille, Jr. Exr. in Worcester County, Province of Maryland & Accomack County, Colony of Virginia, & Monsieur Pentare Exr. in the City of New York & my Attorney Mons: Lange Geseran Exr. in the Island of St. Domingo. Witt: Moses Chaille, Peter Chaille, William Allen - p. 287

KING, ROBERT, of Somerset County, Maryland - 30 May, 1750 - Prob. in Maryland 26 June 1755 - Rec. in Accomack 26 Aug. 1755 - To Richard Waters, son of William Waters late of Somerset County, dec., by his wife Abigail, that tract of marsh land called Londons Advisement near the head of Teagues Creek in Somerset County Maryland, being the parcell I promised the said William Waters in his life time. To William & Thomas Walston the remainder of Londons

Advisement adj. the land formerly belonging to Benjamin King. To Edward Waters of Somerset land on Stevens Branch in Somerset County purchased of me & which has never been conveyed to him. To son Nehemiah King my dwelling planta. in Manokin in Somerset County where my dec. father Maj. Robert King lived, cont. about 300 A. to him & his male heirs, & for want of heirs to my grandson Thomas King & his male heirs. Whereas my son Robert King hath departed this life intestate leaving 2 sons Thomas & Robert Jenkins King, & as Thomas will inherit as eldest son & heir at law all the lands possessed by his said father & his younger bro. be deprived of inheriting any part of his dec. father's est., that all the land in Worcester County whereof my said son was seized in fee simple, being about 200 A. where my said son last settled be sold by my son Nehemiah King & the purchase money to be put at interest for the benefit of my grandson Robert Jenkins King &c. To my grandson Thomas King all my land on the South side of Great Annamessex River where his dec. father first settled and Murrumsco Branch in Somerset County, cont. by est. 1566 A. To grandson Robert Jenkins King land on Stevin's Branch called Timber Track in Somerset County. I desire all that moiety or 75 A, of Cypress swamp, part of a tract called Conveniency, lying on Pokomoke River in Worcester County, conveyed by Peter Collier & others to my sister Mary Hampton & myself, that having been her part thereof, to my sister's eldest son Robert Jenkins Henry. To grandau. Mary Barns, dau. of Maj. Abraham Barns. Grandau. Mary King, dau. of my son Nehemiah. To 3 grandsons Thomas King, Robert King & Robert Jenkins King. Wife Anne bal. of moveable est. on the Eastern Shore of Virginia. To nephew Maj. Henry Ballard. Nephew Col. John Henry. To niece Sarah Leatherbury, wife of John Leatherbury. Niece Elizabeth Dashield, wife of Charles Dashield. To Rev. Mr. John Hamilton. Bal. of personal est. to be div. bet. son Nehemiah King, Thomas King & Robert Jenkins King. Nephews Robert Jenkins Henry & his bro. John Henry. Wife Anne & son Nehemiah Exrs. Witt: Jarvis Ballard, Revell Horsey, John Givan, John Leatherbury.
Codicil: 12 July 1754 - To grandson Robert Jenkins King land called Wharton's Folly, purchased of my son Nehemiah & by him this day conveyed to me. Witt: Levin Wilson, Joshua Riggin, Rachel Stockam.
Codicil: 27 Feb. 1755 - To the children of my dec. son Robert King. To wife land purchased of John Sanford adj. her dwelling planta, negroes at the home Planta. in Accomack & Matchetank planta. in the same county. Cattle at the Virginia Plantations & at the Tangier Islands. - p. 292

BOOTH, GEORGE - 10 Nov. 1753 - 26 Aug. 1755 - To 3 daus. Sophia, Jemima & Martha all my personal est. To son John Booth. Stephen Fitzgerald Exr. Witt: Susanna Fitzgerald, Rachel Fitzgerald, Stephen Fitzgerald - p. 305

FITZGERALD, JOHN - 12 Mar. 1749 - 30 Sept. 1755 - To youngest son Charles Fitzgerald all my est. I give nothing of my est. to any other person. Son Charles Exr. Witt: Stephen Fitzgerald, William Clarke, Sarah Fitzgerald – p. 306

ROWLES, PHEBE – 11 June 1754 – 28 Oct. 1755 – To Ephraim More, son of Ephraim More. To cousin John Hall. Cousin Santeke Hallet negro for life, reversion to the 3 children she had by her first husband, William, Francis & Santeke Hallet. To Daniel Rowles Hall. Cousin Isaac More, Sr. Cousin John Hall resid. legatee & Exr. Witt: Michael Hall, Peter Watson, Robert Wale – p. 314

SNEAD, THOMAS – 7 Aug. 1755 – 28 Oct. 1755 – To wife Agnes one gold ring marked T.S. To son William Snead. Son William resid. legatee. Bros. Robert & Charles Snead Exrs. Witt: Stephen Fitzgerrald, Vallance Doe, Edward Gunter. – p. 315

KENDALL, JOSHUA – 13 Jan. 1755 – 28 Oct. 1755 To bro. Jabez Kendall my dwelling Planta. To bro. John Kendall. To bro. William Kendall. Bros. & sisters resid. legatees. Bros. John & William Exrs. Witt: Charles Ballard, Joseph Mathews, Mary Gray. – p. 316
In order of Prob: John Kendall heir at law to the testator.

WATSON, SOLOMON – 18 Feb. 1755 – 28 Oct. 1755 – Land & moveable est., except pewter, to be sold & proceeds to my son Shadrack Watson (under age) & for want of heirs to my wife Mary Watson. Edmund Watson Exr. Witt: John Henderson, Peter Watson, Edmund Watson – p. 317
In order of Prob: Southy Simpson app. guardian to Shadrack Watson, heir at law to the testator.

DICKERSON, SARAH – Nunc. – Declaration 17 Oct. 1755 – Pro. 25 Nov. 1755 To dau. Leah Dickerson. Proved by William Northam & Sarah Brimer – p. 322
In order of Prob: Mary Dickerson qualified.

HALL, THOMAS – 17 Apr. 1755 – 27 Jan. 1756 – To son James Hall. Son Thomas Hall. Grandau. Mary Filbey. Son Thomas Exr. Witt: Skinner Wallop, Sarah Hall – p. 325

BROADWATER, CALEB – 11 Mar. 1756 – 29 Apr. 1756 – To wife Mary Broadwater my dwelling planta. for life & then to my dau. Massey & for want of heirs to my 3 youngest daus. Mary, Scarburgh & Sinah Broadwater. Wife resid. legatee & Exec. Witt: Jacob Broadwater, Charles Vanelson, Anne Vanelson – p. 342
In order of Prob: William Tunnel & Mary his wife, Stephen Massey & Ann. his wife, & Scarburgh & Sinah Broadwater, daus. & co heirs of the testator, appeared by William Tunnel, their guardian & having nothing to object said will was admitted to Probate.

SCARBURGH, WILLIAM – 17 Aug. 1756 – 28 Sept. 1756 – To son William Scarburgh land which my grandfather gave to my father lying on Cradock Creek. To wife Alice all the surplus land to be found in

all the lands I Possess for life, & then to my son William. Wife Alice Exec. Witt: Mitchel Scarburgh, Norwich Rodgers, Daniel Fisher. - p. 351
In order of Prob: Mitchel Scarburgh, guardian of Edmund Scarburgh, infant heir at law of William Scarburgh.

SMITH, ROBERT - 11 Sept. 1755 - 28 Sept. 1756 - To wife Neaomy Smith whole est. during her wid. & then to be equally div. bet. my 2 children, John Smith & Jane Smith. Wife & son John Exrs. Witt: Thomas Hall, Littleton Wyatt, John Rodgers, William Wyatt - p. 351

PARKER, SACKER - 23 Aug. 1756 - 28 Sept. 1756 - 100 A. at Deep Creek including the house & cleared ground called Ohio to be sold for Payment of debts. To my father all my clothes. To unborn child 100 a. at Deep Creek adj. that called Ohio & 30 A. on Half Moon Island, also 50 A. given to me by my father. Should my child die before coming to age est. to be div. bet. my father, wife, bro. & sister. Bro. John Parker, father & wife (no name) Exrs. Witt: Thomas Wise, John Drummond, Drake Drummond - p. 352
In order of Prob: William Parker & Mary Parker, wid. & Exec. of the testator qualified.

PITT, ROBERT - 16 Oct. 1755 - 30 Nov. 1756 - To wife Ann Pitt. To son John Pitt land where I now live cont. 2180 A. To dau. Anne Pitt. To son Robert Pitt 165 A. purchased of Dennis Blake & Joseph Gootee, lying on the head of Pitts Creek & mill dam branch & for want of heirs to dau. Anne Pitt, & for want of heirs to my brother's son Jabis Pitt, & for want of heirs to Robert Pitt, son of Jabis Pitt & for want of heirs to Slocomb Blake, & for want of heirs to Matilda Hack & for want of heirs to John Blake. Bro. Jabis Pitts 2 daus. Elizabeth & Susanne Pitt. Son Robert & dau. Anne Pitt resid. legatees. To Thomas Wilkerson. Cousin Dennis Blake & Frances, his wife. Wife & friend George Douglas Exrs. Witt: John Cam, Dennis Blake, Tobis Blake - p. 353
Codicil: To sister in law Elizabeth Rodgers.

STEWART, SARAH - 4 Oct. 1756 - 30 Nov. 1756 - To son Levin Stewart (under age) land & planta. where I now live & for want of heirs to my son John Stewart. To son George Stewart. To dau. Agnes Roberts. Grandson John Easham. Grandau Sarah Easham. Son George Stewart Exr. Witt: Thomas Parramore, George Easham - p. 356
In order of Prob: George Stewart heir at law to the testatrix.

REVELL, ANNE - Nunc. - Prob. 30 Nov. 1756 - "The Substance of the will of Anne Revell deced. the sixth of November 1756 (viz) I Give all my Estate to my two sisters Sarah & Mary" - p. 357

KELLAM, THOMAS - 26 July 1756 - 30 Nov. 1756 - To wife Abegal whole est. for life. To son Stephen. Son Elijah. Dau. Anne. Dau. Sarah. Son Peter. Son Jonathan. Sons Stephen & Elijah & daus.

Anne & Sarah resid. legatees. Wife & son Jonathan Exrs. Witt: Littleton Scarburgh Major – John Kellam, Susannah Kellam – p. 357

SCARBURGH, WINEFRIED – 8 Sept. 1756 – 30 Nov. 1756 – To grandson John Watts. Grandau. Anne Scarburgh. Dau. Henrietta Deshel. Dau. (Grandau?) Elizabeth Watts & her sister Sarah Watts. Grandau. Sarah Watts. Grandson Henry Scarburgh & his bro. Bennet & their sister Tabitha. To William Teackle, son of Upshur Teackle. To Edmund Scarburgh, son of William Scarburgh. To Charles Watts. To grandson Henry Wright. To Nanny Wright. To my sister Elizabeth Coleburn. To William Scarburgh, son of William Scarburgh. Dau. Henrietta Dashiel resid. legatee. Grandson John Watts & Mr. William Bagge Exrs. Witt: Adam Muir, Sarah Smith – p. 358

BENSTON, EDWARD – 9 Oct. 1756 – 30 Nov. 1756 – To wife Mary 1/3 of my est. during her life. To son Edward Benston Planta. where I now live. To son Joseph Benston land known as Chestnut Ridge, cont. 100 A. To son Massey Benston. To dau. Leah Benston my water mill & 1 A. adj. & 1/2 the pewter which was her brother John's. To dau. Mary Benston the hogs that was her bro. Alexander's &c. Children Massey, Edward, Joseph, Leah & Mary resid. legatees – Wife & son Edward Exrs. Witt: Epharim Waggoman, Nathaniel Benston – p. 360

MILLS, ROBERT – 25 Sept. 1751 – 28 Dec. 1756 – To cousin Robert Mills, son of Smith Mills, 100 A. in Accomack County and 25 A. in Worcester County adj. the said 100 A., called Chapman's Adventure. To bro. Nathan Mills. "To my well beloved Elizabeth Shanklin" Unto my well beloved William Mills & Smith Mills" Bro. William Mills Witt: Hugh Mills, John Mills, Barnet Ramsey – p. 363
In order of Prob: "On the motion of Robert Mills, Guardian to the Heir at Law, citation being issued for his appearing & returned not to be found"

CHANDLER, SOLOMON – 30 Sept. 1756 – 29 Dec. 1756 – To Bridget Fitzgerrald, my dau. now the wife of David Fitzgerrald. To dau. Anne Chandler "the sum of Twenty Shillings which I justly owe her, it being a Legacy left her by my son Jacob Chandler" To son George. Dau. Comfort. Bal. of est. to my present wife Anne Chandler & my daus. Susannah, Anne, Comfort, Betty & Mary & sons William & George, to share equally. Son William & Present wife Anne Exrs. Witt: Samuel Midcalf, Jacob Phillips, Benjamin Phillips – p. 365

RODGERS, JOHN – 31 Oct. 1756 – 25 Jan. 1757 – To wife Elizabeth whole est. for life or wid. To son Abel Rodgers Planta. where I now live. To son Robert Rodgers. To son Richard Rodgers. Dau. Anne Rodgers. To Margaret Cloud. To grandson Robert Rodgers, son of Abel Rodgers & grandson Robert Rodgers, son of Robert Rodgers. Children Robert, Richard & Anne Rodgers resid. legatees. Wife Elizabeth & sons Abel & Robert Rodgers Exrs. Witt: John Rodgers, Peter Rodgers, John Smith – P. 366

BAYLEY, EDMUND - 18 Dec. 1756 - 26 Jan. 1757 - To dau. Rosey Bayley. Son Thomas Bayley. Wife Dorothy Bayley. To bro. John Bayley 100 A. which my father Edmund Bayley, dec. bought of William Bayley near Small Beer Branch. Wife, dau. Rosey, & son Thomas Bayley resid. legatees. Wife & bro. John Bayley Exrs. Witt: Tabitha Gilchrist, Salathiel Simpson, Rebecka Bull - p. 384 In order of Prob: Americus Scarburgh app. guardian to Thomas Bayley, Inf't. heir at law to the testator. Dorothy Wainhouse Bayley, wid. of the testator qualified.

BEAVANS, TABITHA - 31 Oct. 1756 - 22 Feb. 1757 - To dau. Sophia Beavans. Clothing to be div. between my 4 daus. Son Joshua Beavans resid. legatee & Exr. Dau. Sophia Exec. Witt: William Beavans, Mary Beavans, Hannah Wishart - p. 387

REVELL, REBECCA - 7 Nov. 1756 - 22 Feb. 1757 - To son John Revell. To grandson Edward Revell. To grandson Isaac Horsey. Grandau. Elizabeth Revell Horsey, "A large diaper table cloth marked R.R." To cousin Robert Parker. To Edward Custis. To Nicholas Dun. Dau. Katherine Revell resid. legatee. Son John & dau. Katherine Exrs. Witt: James Rule, James Scott, Thomas Bagwell - p. 388

BARNS, ARTHUR - 6 Sept. 1756 - 23 Feb. 1757 - To wife Elizabeth whole est. during her wid. To son John Barns planta. where I now live. Bro. William Barns Exr. Witt: Thomas Riley, Southy Simpson, Richard Bundick. - p. 390 In order of Prob: James Henry app. guardian of John Barns, Inf't. heir at law to the testator. William Barns refusing to qualify est. committed to the hands of the Sheriff to make sale of same and make return at the next Court.

WEBB, THOMAS - 22 Feb. 1754 - 29 Mar. 1757 - To wife Rachel whole est. for life, she to school my son William Webb & my godson Custis McCloud. Bal. of est. to be div. bet. my son William & godson Custis McCloud & should they both die without heirs est. to be div. bet. my wife's 3 daus., Keziah Townsend, Elizabeth McCloud, & Peggy McCloud. To Reuben Rogers' 3 children Sarah, Leah & Rachel - Wife Exec. Not witnessed. Proved by Elijah Nock, George Hope & Southy Simpson - p. 399

WEST, CHARLES - 10 July 1756 - 30 Mar. 1757 - To Isaac Smith, son of my sister Sarah Smith, planta. I bought of William Pritchet & all my lots & houses on the North side of Onancock Town & the land I bought of Hugh Roberts. To Thorowgood Smith, son of my said sister, 400 A. on the South side of Nantecoke which I bought of Smith Snead, & for want of heirs to Isaac Smith. To Charles West, son of Jonathan, my lot & houses on the South side of Onancock & the land I bought of Daniel Cutler. To my sister Anne Chambers & to her 2 daus. by Thomas Clapton. To Jamimy Booth the land I bought of Chambers. To Elizabeth White, dau. of Solomon White.

To Col. Thomas Parramore. To John Smith, son of my sister Sarah. To Jonathan West. To John Hall, son in law to John Nelson. Bal. of est. to be div. bet. my sister Sarah Smith's children, except Isaac & Thorowgood, & Ann Chambers children that she had by Thomas Clapton. Isaac Smith, son of my sister Sarah Exr. Col. Parramore & Col. Eyre overseers. Codicil: 16 Aug. 1756 – Before there is any division of my est., my Exrs. to buy in London such a tombstone as is at Mr. John Smith's & put it over my grave. Witt: Littleton Eyre, George Holden, Luke Lucar. – p. 400

In order of Prob: "Americus Scarburgh in right of Sarah, his wife, & Charles Parker, legatees in an old will dated 24 day of Oct. 1747, and Elizabeth West, wid. & Exec. of Charles West, dec., therein named, having first come into Court & said that they claim no benefit thereby, & consented that the said will shall be of no effect, and that the will now Produced by Isaac Smith should be admitted to record"

JINKENSON, COMFORT – 7 Oct. 1751 – Partly proved 7 Feb. 1757 – Prob. 26 Apr. 1757 – To son Custis Jinkenson. Dau. Neoma Marcey. Son Robert Jinkenson. Dau. Weltha Parks. Grandson Thomas Glading. 5 children Neoma, Leah, Comfort, Robert, Weltha & Custis resid. legatees, to be div. by my 2 neighbors Jonathan Bunting & Nathaniel Stockly. Son Robert Exr. Witt: Nathaniel Stockly, Jonathan Bunting, Sarah Stockly – p. 409

DARBY, WILLIAM – 19 Sept. 1754 – 27 Apr. 1757 – To bro. Benjamin Darby use of my Planta. cont. 200 A. for life, reversion to my cousin Littleton Darby, son of Benjamin. Cousins Elishe & Sarah Darby. Cousin Leah Darby, sister of Elishe & Sarah. Elishe, Sarah & Leah Darby resid. legatees. Bro. Benjamin Exr. Witt: John Milby, Nathaniel Lecatt, Francis Darby. – p. 417.

In order of Prob: Sheriff's return – "Unlce Darby, heir at law to the testator, not found within my Bailiwick"

PRATT, BALY – 17 Nov. 1756 – 23 June 1757 – To son Aron Pratt. Dau. Elizabeth Pratt. Bal. of est. to wife Ann Pratt during her wid. & then to be div. bet. my 5 children, Moses Pratt, Baly Pratt, Susanna Pratt, alias Melscn, Elizabeth Pratt & Aaron Pratt. Wife Exec. – Witt: Thomas Ames, Rowland Savage – p. 423

BISHOP, JACOB – 7 Feb. 1756 – 28 June 1757 – To son John land where he now dwells during his life, cont. 50 A. reversion to my son Muns Bishop & for want of heirs to my dau. Margaret Bishop. To wife Patience planta. where I now live during her wid. Daus. Temperance & Margaret to have a home on said planta. until they marry, & at the death of my wife I give the said planta. to my son Jacob Bishop. To dau. Leah Cowley. To dau. Patience Taylor. To grandau. Sarah Rogers. Daus. Temperance & Margaret Bishop resid. legatees. John Kitson, Sr., John Nock & Thomas Webb to div. est. Wife Patience & sons Muns & Jacob Exrs. Witt: Richard Justice, James Fitzgearld, Thomas Webb – p. 424

In order of Prob: John Bishop heir at law to the testator.

DARBY, ANN - Not dated - 26 July 1757 - Son John Darby.   Son Churchel Darby. 3 children John, Churchel & Tabitha resid. legatees. Sons John & Churchel Exrs. Witt: Littleton Scarburgh Major, Bartholomew Meers, Nathaniel Lecat - p. 430

TUNNELL, SCARBURGH - 1 Mar. 1757 - 30 Aug. 1757 - To wife Elizabeth whole est. during her wid. To son Washpan (Washbourne) Tunnell land where I now live cont. 150 A. To son Jediah Tunnell. Son Scarburgh Tunnell. Son William Tunnell. Son Elias Tunnell. Son Ezekiel. Son Charles.   Dau. Comfort. All my children resid. legatees. Wife & son Washpan Exrs. Witt: Charles Stockley, Joseph Stockley, Sarah Ewell - p. 434
In order of Prob: Washborn Tunnell heir at law to the testator.

RICKARDS, MICHAEL - 11 Feb. 1749 - 30 Nov. 1757 - To grandson Michael Hall Part of the planta. where I now live cont. 200 A. on Nandue, to be taken off the West side of the tract.   To grandson Michael Rickets Tatum the remainder of the land where I now live, being 100 A., his mother Ann Tatum to have use of same for life.   To Betty Hall, dau. of Michael Hall. To Comfort, dau. of Michael Hall. To dau. Jean Jackson. Wife Mary. To grandau Lydda Rogers. Grandau. Comfort Brazier. Household goods to my wife for life then to my daus. Jean Jackson, Ann Tatum, Michael Hall, Michael Rickards Tatum & James Tatum. Michael Hall & Michael Rickards Tatum Exrs. Witt: Adam Muir, John Rodgers, John Rodgers. - p. 443

Wills &c. 1757-1761

MARSHALL, MARY - 30 Sept. 1757 - 27 Dec. 1757 - To dau. Mary Jackson, reversion to her children. To dau. Comfort Merill, reversion to her children. To Euphamy Cutler. Daus. Mary Jackson & Comfort Merill & their husbands Exrs. Witt: Anderson Patterson, Robert Ardis. - p. 11
In order of Prob: William Jackson & William Merrill qualified.

DOUGLAS, GEORGE - 9 Nov. 1757 - 31 Jan. 1758 - To Mr. Isaac Morris of Worcester County, Maryland my silver watch.   "To friend George Holden my best Night Gown" To friend Ephraim Waggaman. To Peter Martial. To dau. Ann. To Rev. Arthur Emmerson 5 L to Preach my funeral sermon. To Mr. Littleton Dennis 5 L for advice in directing my Exrs. Wife to have the tuition of my dau. Ann. To dau. Agnes. "to my 2 married daus. or their husbands, whatever things I have given them & they are in possession of" To Tully Robinson Wise my silver shoe & knee buckles. To dau. Peggy. To son Walter (under 21) Wife to have planta. where I live for life. To dau. Tabitha. To dau. Elizabeth. To George Holden in trust for my son, all my lands of inheritance to be delivered to him at the end of 7 years. Wife & daus. Tabitha, Agnes, Peggy & Anne resid. legatees. Wife (no name), dau. Agnes, Mr. Holden & Mr. Waggaman Exrs. Witt:

John Martil, Mason Martial, Caleb Townsend. p. 18
In order of prob: Tabitha Douglas, wid. of the testator, & George Holden qualified.

PARKER, WILLIAM - 20 Dec. 1757 - 31 Jan. 1758 - To grandson Sacker Parker the remainder of the land where I now live. To son John Parker - To dau. Sophah Scott. To grandson William Scott. Son John & dau. Sophiah resid. legatees. Son John Exr. Witt: Thomas Custis, Spencer Drummond, John Lewis - p. 33

CARROTHERS, TABITHA - 11 Apr. 1749 - 28 Feb. 1758 - Son Ezekiel Young to have all the est. paid him which belonged to him out of the est. of his father, Francis Young without account or discount. Dau. Mary Young what is due her from her father's est., & 34 yards of check linnen that was left her by one Rodgers. Bal. of est. to be div. bet. all my children. Son John Young & William Middleton Exrs. Witt: John Doe, Mary Cortney, Thomas Slatter - p. 39

BIRD, DANIEL - Nunc. ----1751 - 29 Mar. 1758 To dau. Susannah Bird my land where I now live cont. 125 A. My now wife to have use of same during her wid. To my 2 daus. Mary & Scarburgh. To Solomon Bird. 4 daus. Rachel Mason, Elizabeth Parks, Mary Bird & Scarburgh Bird. Wife Margaret. Proved by Henry Fletcher & William Melson.
The depositions of Henry Fletcher & William Melson were filed in the suit of Susannah Bird, complainant, vs. Margaret Bird, Middleton Mason & Rachel, his wife, Benjamin Parks & Elizabeth, his wife, Mary Bird & Scarburgh Bird, defendants. Ordered that the said depositions be recorded and that the substance thereof be established as the last will & testament of Daniel Bird, dec., and that the former administration granted on his est. be revoked, and that the defendant, widow of the said testator, be summoned to take upon her the administration on the said estate. - p. 39

WATSON, PETER - 22 Oct. 1753 - 28 Nov. 1758 - To dau. Esther Ayelott land called Black Ridge in Worcester County, Maryland, cont. 300 A. reversion to Peter Watson, son of my bro. Euriah Watson. To son in law Benjamin Ayelott 50 A. being part of a tract called Peterson lying in the aforesaid County. To bro. John Watson. Wife Mary Watson. To dau. Esther bal. of my est. in Maryland "provided she gives my mother a decent maintenance out of it" Wife to pay my dau. in law Atalanta Smith all her est. due her by the death of her father. Wife & Benjamin Aydlott resid. legatees. Friends Daniel Gore, John Smith & Samuel Gillet to inventory est. Son in law Benjamin Aydlott & wife Mary Exrs. Witt: William Andrews, Samuel Gillet, Daniel Gore - p. 41

NORTHAM, WILLIAM - Nunc - Died 1 Feb. 1758 - Prob. 28 Mar. 1758 - To son William land purchased of Southy Northam. To dau. Nanny Northam. The things conveyed me by Thomas Northam to remain in his possession during his life. Proved by John Northam &

Rachel Northam – p. 42
In order of Prob: John Northam qualified.

PARKER, JOHN – 21 Feb. 1758 – 30 May 1758 – To son John (under 21) all the lands I have any right or title to. Wife Sarah & 2 daus. Neomy & Esther Parker resid. legatees. Wife Exec. Witt: Southy Simpson, Solomon Dix, Sacker Parker – p. 58

MARTING, ANDREW – 17 Apr. 1757 – 30 May 1758 – To wife Briget whole est. for life Then to be div. bet. whom she please. Wife & son Henry Exrs. Witt: Americus Scarburgh, Sarah Raffeld – p. 58

BONNEWELL, THOMAS – 25 Nov. 1753 – 25 July 1758 – To wife Ann Bonnewell whole est. real & Personal. Wife Exec. – Witt: David James, Elizabeth James, Thomas Webb – p. 63
In order of Probate – Sheriff's return that George Matthews, one of the heirs at law of Thomas Bonnewell, dec., was summoned to appear & that George Stockley, the other heir at law of the said Thomas Bonnewell was not found within his Bailiwick.

DARBY, CHURCHEL – 17 Mar. 1755 – 25 July 1758 – To wife Mary use of whole est. during her wid. To son Eliah Darby land & planta. where I now live. Dau. Agnes. Son John. Dau. Elizabeth. Son Churchel. Wife & son Eliah Exrs. Witt: Littleton Scarburgh Major, Arthur Laylor, Robert Watson – p. 64
In order of Prob: Eliah Darby heir at law to the testator.

KENDALL, WILLIAM – 17 Apr. 1758 – 27 June 1758 – To wife Mary Ann Kendall whole est. during her wid. To son John Kendall planta. called Oak Hall. To dau. Margaret Kendall. Bro. Jabez Kendall. Wife & 2 children resid. legatees. Wife & friend John Watts Exrs. Witt: Jonathan Groten, Peggy Groten, Hancock Tayler. Signed "Thomas Kendall" "William Kendall" in order of Prob. p. 65
In order of Prob: William Nicholson app. guardian to John Kendall, Inf't. heir at law to the testator.

NEWTON, ABRILIHO – 15 June 1758 – 29 Aug. 1758 – To 3 daus. Sophia Walton, Levinah Newton & Sarah Newton. To son William Newton. Bal. of est. that is coming to me in Newcastle County in Pennsylvania to my son Abraham Newton & dau. Sarah Newton. Son in law Job Walton Exr. Witt: Bowdoin Robins, Robert Bell, Major Guy – p. 76

WAGGAMAN, EPHRAIM – 2 June 1758 – 26 Sept. 1758 – To wife Mary planta. where I now live & 250 A. known as Layfields Swamp for life then land where I live to son Ephraim Waggaman & the 250 A. to my son Joseph Waggaman. To wife silver Tea Tongs marked EMW &c. To son William Elliott Waggaman (under 21) land in Worcester County, Maryland known as Kings Neck together with 50 A. in the same Neck but in the bounds of Accomack County, Virginia, also the lands & marshes I purchased of Hezekiah Purnell, being part of two

tracts of land, one called Bantray & the other called Piney Island, wife
to have use of same for life. To dau. Sarah Waggaman tea spoons
marked S.W. in a cypher. To dau. Mary Waggaman silver spoons
marked EMW & one small one marked W.W. Son William to be in
the tuition of William Hayward, said son to be educated in Latin & in
the study of Law. Bal. of personal est. to be div. bet. wife & 4
children, Joseph, Ephraim, Sarah & Mary (all under age) Wife Mary &
friend William Hayward to have the tuition of my sons Joseph &
Ephraim until they arrive at the age of 16. Daus. Sarah & Mary to be
under the tuition of Wife Mary until 16 or marriage. Should all my
children die before coming to age or marriage, I give to William
& Elizabeth Scott, children of John Scott, dec., who was brother to
my wife, the 1/2 of my slaves & personal property. To niece Sarah
Waggaman, dau. of my bro. Henry, the remaining 1/2. To nephew
George Waggaman, one of the sons of my bro. Henry, all my lands
in Viriginia. Wife Mary & friend William Hayward, of Somerset
County, Maryland, Exrs. Witt: Priscilla Gray, Stephen Warrington,
Joseph Ankers. - p. 76
In order of Prob: William Elliot Waggaman heir at law to the testa-
tor. William Hayward, one of the surviving Exrs. named in said
will relinquished his right, & Henry Waggaman qualified.

OWEN, JONATHAN - 18 Oct. 1758 - 28 Nov. 1758 - Wife Rachel
100 A. on Jengoteague Island & 100 A. where I now live during her
wid. & then to my son Peter Owen. Grandson Isaac Hill. Grandson
Major Owen. Bal. of est. to wife during wid. then to Esther Owen,
Mary Owen & Sally Owen. Wife Exec. Witt: John Blake, Littleton
Taylor, Abel Taylor - p. 84
In order of Prob: Peter Owen heir at law to the testator.

THORNTON, WILLIAM - 14 Nov. 1758 - 28 Nov. 1758 - To son
William. To son David Thornton. Son Thomas Thornton. Grandau.
Jacaman Thornton. Wife Sarah. Dau. Mary Thorp. Two eld. sons
Exrs. Witt: Bartholomew Taylor, Mary Broadwater, Mary Tunnel,
Thomas Matthews. - p. 85
In order of prob: William Thornton, heir at law to the testator, &
David Thornton qualified.

GUNTER, JOSEPH - 6 Oct. 1758 - 26 Dec. 1758 - To son Edward
Gunter 1 s. Dau. Sheba Savage, wife of Abel Savage. To son Joseph
Gunter 60 A., not entitling his wife Sarah any thirds, & at Joseph's
death my son to turn her cut of doors & rent the said land for the
benefit of my son Joseph's heirs. To son Mesheck the othor 60 A.
where I live. To son Abednego Gunter. Bal. of moveable est. to be
div. bet. my 2 youngest daus. & 2 youngest sons. Daus. Abigal &
Adria. Witt: John Cade, Joseph Jefferys, Joseph Custis, Nash
Kellam. - p. 86
In order of Prob: Edward Gunter, heir at law to the testator, cited to
appear, and failing to do so Adiax Gunter qualified.

BALEY, JOHN - 23 Feb. 1759 - 27 Feb. 1759 - To bro. Thomas Baley all my land. Bro. in law Andrew Gilchrist. Bro. Levin Baley. To Ann Burton. Bro. Thomas resid. legatee. Bro. Thomas Baley & Andrew Gilchrist Exrs. Witt: John Milligan, Sebastian Cropper, Joseph Nock - p. 116
In order of Prob: Thomas Bayley the younger, heir at law to the testator, cited to appear; sheriff's return that he had left a copy of said citation at the place of his abode, and he failing to appear the said will was proved and Thomas Bayley, one of the Exrs. qualified.

TWIFOOT, BARTHOLOMEW - 4 Jan. 1759 - 27 Feb. 1759 - To wife Sarah house & planta. during her wid. then to be sold & money div. bet. my 3 sons, Daniel, John & Bartholomew Twifoot. To Sarah Lingo. To Rachel Lingo. Sons James, Levin & William Twifoot resid. legatees. Wife & Thomas Custis Exrs. Witt: Elishe Custis, Southe Savage, Brigit Chance - p. 125
In order of Prob: Bartholomew Twifoot, Jr., heir at law to the testator - Sheriff returned said citation "Bartholomew Twifoot not found within my Bailiwick".

SANDERS, RICHARD - 29 Mar. 1759 - 24 Apr. 1759 - Dau. Keesier Sparrow. Dau. Catherine Ingerson. Wife Rachel. Grandau. Rachel Bundick. Wife & 2 daus. resid. legatees. Wife Rachel, John Sparrow & Samuel Ingerson Exrs. Witt: William Young, Rachel Bundick, Robert Jones - p. 126

DRUMMOND, SPENCER - 13 Mar. 1759 - 29 May 1759 - To son William Drummond planta. where I live on Hunting Creek Wife Ann to have use of same till my son comes to age of 21. To son Spencer two tenements & plantations on Messongo Creek upon Pessimon Gut, to include 250 A., & for want of heirs to my son Richard. To son Charles planta. where Walter Warrington lives, adj. William Drummond & George Holden, to include 250 A., which land was devised to my by my father Richard Drummond for 500 A., & for want of heirs to my son Richard Drummond. Daus. Elizabeth, Anne & Sarah. Wife & children, except William, resid. legatees. Wife & friends James Stran & James Henry Exrs. Witt: John Selby, John Purnell, Ann Selby p. 130.
In order of Prob: James Henry app. guardian to William Drummond, heir at law to the testator.

DARBY, ELIJAH - 10 Mar. 1759 - 30 May 1759 - To dau. Sarah Darby planta. where I live. Wife Mary. Dau. Elizabeth. My mother to have free privilege of my dwelling house during her life. Wife & dau. Elizabeth resid. legatees. Wife & Benjamin Darby Exrs. Witt: Churchlll Darby, Robert Watson, John Meers - p. 140
In order of Prob: Littleton Scarburgh Major app. guardian to Sarah & Elizabeth, heirs at law to the testator.

PARKER, HANCOCK - 10 Mar. 1756 - 30 July 1759 - To Eleanor Nicholass whole est. Witt: Sacker Parker, William Boggs - p. 146

194

In order of Prob: Sacker Parker qualified.

DOWNING, HANNAH SCARBURGH – 14 Sept. 1759 – 25 Sept. 1759 – To son Thomas Wise Rodgers. Dau. Elizabeth Wise Rodgers. Son Thomas & dau. Elizabeth resid. legatee Son James Rodgers Exr. Witt: Luke Lucar, William Harrison, Jane Rowles p. 154

BELL, JOSEPH – 21 Sept. 1759 – 27 Nov. 1759 – To Woodman Bloxom 53 A. Wife Comfort to have use of the remainder of my land during her wid. Son Oliver Bell. Dau. Comfort Bell. Dau. Mary Bell. 5 children Susannah, Grace. Oliver, Comfort & Mary Bell resid. legatees. Wife Exec. Not witnessed – Proved by Thomas Bloxom, John Ross – p. 101
Deposition of Thomas Bloxom: That the foregoing will was written by him at the direction of the testator, and that the devise to Woodman Bloxom was not by his direction, but was desired so to do by Woodman who had the consent of the said Joseph for that purpose, as he told him, and that after he had wrote it he read it to the said Joseph who made no objection, but before he signed it the said Joseph was taken out of his senses and so remained while this deponent stayed. John Ross also deposed that he heard the said will read to the said testator. It is the opinion of the Court that the same is sufficiently proved, and ordered to be admitted to record.

THORNTON, EDWARD Sr. – 8 Nov. 1759 – 27 Nov. 1759 – To dau. in law Rachel Thornton planta. where she lives during her wid. Dau. Susannah Taylor. Son John Thornton Dau. Rhody Wheelton. Dau. Scarburgh Broadwater. Dau. Esther Broadwater. Children Edward Thornton, Rachel Thornton. Comfort Warrington & Ann Mary Taylor resid. legatees. Son Edward Thornton & dau. in law Rachel Thornton Exrs. Witt: Joshua Beavans, Edmund Warrington, William Dunston. – p. 162
In order of Prob: William Beavans guardian to Edward Thornton, Inf't heir at law to the testator.

LUMBERS, ROBERT – 12 Dec. 1757 – 27 Nov. 1759 – To wife Easther 1/3 of my est. To Crosby Lewis 1/4 of my est. Wife Exec. Witt: William Matthews, Joseph Matthews – p. 163

MASON, WILLIAM Sr. – 12 Feb. 1758 – 28 Nov. 1759 – To son Middleton Mason 200 A. where he now lives on the South side of Masongo. To son William Mason 100 A. purchased of Ann Drummond. To son John Mason 450 A. purchased of Solomon Ewell. Dau. Ann Pickeran, wife of Francis Pickeran. Dau. Hannah Major. Dau. Susannah Andrews, To Ismael Mason. Dau. Elinor Howard. Grandson Daniel Mason. Wife Eleanor Mason. To son Bennet Mason 200 A. where I now live. Wife & son Bennet resid. legatees & Exrs. William Beavans, Ephram Waggaman & Henry Fletcher to appraise est. Witt: John Milligan, Daniel Howard, Lewis Biswick – p. 164
In order of Prob: Middleton Mason heir at law to the testator.

BURTON, AMEY - 13 Nov. 1759 - 29 Jan. 1760 To Joshua Burton enough to pay him for burying me. Son John resid. legatee. Joshua Burton Exr. Witt: John Spiers, Robert Peel, Thomas Burton - p. 166

PHILLIPS, JOHN - 18 Nov. 1756 - 29 Jan. 1760 - To son William Phillips, after his mother's death, planta. where I live & 50 A. purchased of David Taylor. Dau. Mary Bennet. Wife Tabitha & children William, Nanny, Abigal, Tabby & Sarah Phillips resid. legatees. Wife & son William Exrs. Witt: William Hough, Joseph Heath, John Macnamarra - p. 167

MAGRATH, EDWARD - Nunc - 6 Jan. 1760 - 29 Jan. 1760 - Bro. in law Phillip Whitchard to be his Exr. & receive all that is due his est., to pay debts & make return to Mr. Mitchell and the other merchants in Philadelphia so far as his est. will pay off. That he left in Mr. Zadock Purnel's care $150. and one watch & left in the care of Mr. Parrish & Mr. Purnal one green silk purse having in it four Doubloons & some Pistols; there was likewise one stone ring & one small trunk that Mr. Parish had in his chest, & that he had on board the Schooner 100L or more of Europing goods belonging to Magrath & Justice between them in partnership, & that he, Magrath, had 70 or 80 lbs. of cheese on board and one cask of dye holding 5 1/2 galls., & that he left in the care of Robins Collins one suit of cloaths of Superfine broadcloth, & that he left on board several shirts. Proved by Eli Campbell & Patrick McCormick - p. 168
In order of Prob: Phillip Whishart qualified.

JUSTICE, RALPH - 12 May 1757 - 29 Jan. 1760 - To son William Justice planta. known as Kickatank, conveyed to me by Mrs Margaret Gale, also my Island between the Inlet called Assowoman & Gargaphy Inlet. To son James all my other lands with my planta. called Gargaphy & my land at Parkers & Island & swamp land in Maryland. Dau. Joyce Teackle. To Sarah Justice, dau. of Susannah. To Levin Teackle. Wife & 3 children resid. legatees. Arthur Emmerson, John Kitson, Levin Teackle & James Justice overseers Witt: William Bains (Barns in Probate) John Kitson. Jr., John Nock.
Codicil: 27 Jan. 1758 - Son William Justice to make over that moiety of land that I & my wife conveyed to him as a deed of trust in Northampton, to Mr. John Harmanson - p. 169
In order of prob: William Justice heir at law to the testator. Catherine Justice, wid. of the testator, relinquished her claim to any bequest in said will. Exrs. refused to act and Levin Teackle qualified.

TANKRED, WILLIAM - 16 Dec. 1759 - 29 Jan. 1760 - To bro. Robert Tankred 20L current money due me by him, he to convey to my bro. Azariah Tankred all the houses I am now possessed of, together with 1 A. of land, for the term of 10 years, & should he refuse the accounts against him to be paid which I give to my bro. Azariah. To William Drummond, son of Elizabeth Parker. To Elizabeth Parker, wife of George Parker. To Peggy, dau. of Robert Tankred. To Sarah, dau. of William Jackson. To Nanny Drummond, dau. of Elizabeth Parker.

Bro. Stephen Tankred. Bro. Robert & bro. Azariah resid. legatees & Exrs. Witt: Southy Simpson, Henry White, Hely Bagwell, William Melson – p. 171

SMITH, ELIZABETH – 6 Jan. 1755 – 30 Jan. 1760 – Son John Smith. Son William Robinson Smith. Dau. Elizabeth Phiney. Grandaus. Anne & Ellzabeth Phiney. Son William Robinson Smith Exr. Witt: Jane Bonnewell, John Bonnewell – p. 177

SMITH, WILLIAM ROBINSON – 14 Dec. 1759 – 30 Jan. 1760 – My present wife Mary Robinson Smith to have use of my planta., being 350 A. & personal est. to bring up my child or children. Should she marry I give my Planta. where I live to my unborn child, if a boy, & if a girl I give my said planta. to my present dau. Elizabeth Smith. To unborn child, if a girl, my house & lot in Onancock Town, if a boy my said house & lot to my dau. Elizabeth. So much money to be saved will pay for a gravestone for myself & my mother. Bro. John Smith & wife Mary Exrs. Witt: John Spendelow, Susanna Wise, Sophia Bagwell – p. 177
In order of Prob: John Wise app, guardian to Elizabeth Smith, Inf't. heir at law to the testator.

LILLISTON, JACOB – Not dated – 31 Jan. 1760 – Nunc. Bro. Elijah Lilliston. Bro. Thomas Lilliston. To my mother. Proved by John Willet & Ann Lilliston – p. 181
In order of prob: Ann Lilliston relinquished her right & Elijah Lilliston qualified.

WAINHOUSE, FRANCIS – 28 Jan. 1760 – 26 Feb. 1760 – Wife Bridget. To son Francis Wainhouse planta. where I now live. Son William to have the use of the planta where John Howell now lives when he comes to age or marries. To son Francis all my land between the Creek & the main county road after his mother's death or marriage. To son William all the remaining part of my land on the E. side of County Road after his mother's death. Children Margaret, Sarah, Patience, William & Rose Wainhouse resid. legatees. Wife & son Francis Exrs. Witt: Francis Savage, Edmund Watson, Benjamin Watson – p. 182

CUTLER, DANIEL – 11 Mar. 1757 – 26 Feb. 1760 – To wife Ann Cutler 1/2 my land & personal est. during her wid. then to my dau. Betty Ironmonger. Bal. of est. to dau. Betty Ironmonger, & for want of heirs to my bro. George Cutler. Bro. George & son in law Major Ironmonger Exrs. Witt: Daniel Maxwell, Henry Scarburgh, Fairfax Smith, Clement Parker, John West, William Wishart. – p. 183
In order of Prob: George Holden guardian to John Marshall Cutler, Inf't. heir law to the testator.

MERCY, THOMAS – 27 Oct. 1759 – 26 Feb. 1760 – "I give to my son in law one shilling sterling of my estate & no more". To Naomi Mercy 1 s. To son John Mercy the things I lent him at his marriage.

To son Stephen Mercy the things I lent him at his marriage. To son Littleton Mercy 25 A. of land. Daus. Jane & Agnes Mercy. Grandau. Mary Mercy. Wife Jane Mercy. Wife & son Littleton, daus. Jane & Agnes resid. legatees. Wife & son Littleton Exrs. Witt: Slocomb Blake, Stephen Townsend, David Baker - p. 184
In order of Prob: Joseph Walker app. guardian to Mary Mercy, heir at law to testator.

COPES, PETER PARKER - 11 Feb. 1760 - 26 Feb. 1760 - To wife Rhody planta. where I live with my water mill during her wid., then to my two sons Charles & Parker Copes to be div. bet. them. Two youngest sons Thomas & Solomon Copes resid. legatees. Wife Exec. Witt: Southy Simpson, Laban Simpson, Richard Dix p. 187
In order of Prob: Peter Parker Copes heir at law to the testator.

BLAKE, DENNIS - 13 Dec. 1759 - 27 Feb. 1760 - Son Jabez Blake. Son Joseph Blake. Son John Blake. Dau. Sarah. Dau. Ann Blake. To son Slocomb Blake my land. Sons Joseph & John resid. legatees. Slocomb to bring up my son John & to school him. Son Slocomb Exr. Witt: John Taylor. - p. 190

DELASTATIUS, SEBASTIAN - 3 Feb. 1760 - 25 Mar. 1760 - To son William planta. where I now live. Wife to have use of same to school & bring up my children until William arrives to the age of 21. Dau. Ann Delastatius. Bal. of est. to wife & all my children not before mentioned. Wife Mary & her father John Matthews Exrs. Witt: Samuel Feddiman, Robert Jenkinson, Samuel Delastatius, Levi Robins. - p. 194
In order of prob: William Delastatius heir at law to the testator.

MILBY, PETER - 12 Mar. 1760 - 25 Mar. 1760 - Whole est. to two daus. Nanny & Tabitha Milby. Friends John Dix & George Poulson Exrs. Witt: Southy Simpson, Nanny Dix, Elizabeth Dix - p. 196

BELL, JOHN - 8 Feb. 1753 - 25 Mar. 1760 - Wife Elizabeth. Son William Bell 100 A. where I live. Bal. of est. to all my children except William. Wife Exec. Witt: Stephen Fitzgerald, Tabitha Foster, John Foster - p. 196

PATTERSON, ANDERSON - 24 July 1758 - 25 Mar. 1760 - To eldest son William Patterson planta. where I live. To son James Patterson planta. in Worcester County, Maryland cont. 300 A. purchased of Samuel & William Ramsey. Sons William & James resid. legatees & Exrs. Witt: Sebastian Delastatius, Alexander Warrington, Thomas Beavans, Samuel Beavans - p. 202

WEST, SCARBURGH - 14 Mar. 1760 - 29 Apr. 1760 - Dau. Elizabeth Miles, Mary Bunting & Edmund West each 2 s. & no more of my est. To 3 grandchildren Leah Dunton, Dealy Dunton & Edmund Dunton. To son Alexander West 1/2 my land. To son Philip Parker West the other 1/2 my land, being the manor planta. where I now live.

Daus. Parker & Adah West resid. legatees. Sons Alexander & Philip Parker West Exrs. Witt: Laban Simpson, Thomas Cropper, William Evans. - p. 211
In order of Prob: Alexander West heir at law.

TEACKLE, JOHN - 2 May 1755 - 27 May 1760 - To bro. Thomas Teackle my divident of land. Bro. Levin Leackle. Bro. Upshur Teackle & sister Margaret Robins resid. legatees. Bro. Upshur Exr. Witt: Abraham Turner, Thomas Jacob.
Codicil: 20 Feb. 1760 - Bequest to nephew Thomas Teackle, Jr. - p. 214

GRAY, BENJAMIN - 24 Mar. 1760 - 27 May 1760 - Wife Rachel to have use of land where I now live during her wid. & then to my 2 sons Thomas & Levin Gray & for want of heirs to Jacob Sherwood, said tract cont. 25 A. Wife resid. legatee. Witt: Thomas Batson, Thomas Sherwood. - p. 220
In order of Prob: Rachel Gray, wid. of Benjamin, qualified.

EVANS, CAESAR - 12 July 1759 - 27 May 1760 - Whole est. to wife during her wid. then personal est. to be div. bet. all my children. To sons Thomas & Hillary the use of my land during their lives. I debar Kezia, the wife of my son Thomas from any dower in my land. After the death of my 2 sons I give my land to my grandson George Collony, son of Herman Collony. Son Hillary & Herman Collony Exrs. Witt: William Savage, John West - p. 220 In order of Prob: Thomas Evans heir at law of the testator.

TAYLOR GEORGE - 24 Mar. 1760 - 27 May 1760 - To bro. Shadrack Taylor my land cont. 80 A. that my mother gave me, & for want of heirs to my 3 bros. Joseph, William & Jacob Taylor. Bal. of est. to my mother after payment of debts. Mother (no name) Exec. - Witt: Thomas Batson, Thomas Clark p. 221
In order of Prob: Bridget Taylor qualified.

HARRISON, ALEXANDER - 13 May 1760 - 28 May 1760 - Dau. Ann Phillips. Dau. Welthyanna Dix. Grandson Alexander Harrison. Dau. Sarah Harrison. Son Alexander Harrison. Son John Harrison. Son Phillip Harrison. Grandau. Euphamy Harrison. Alexander, John & Phillip Harrison resid. legatees. Son Alexander Exr. Witt: Clement Parker, George Cutler - p. 222
In order of prob: John Harrison heir at law to the testator.

GARRISON, JONATHAN - 6 Mar. 1760 - 24 June 1760 - To wife Fillis Garrison use of all my land during her wid. then to my son Jonathan Garrison 200 A. where he now lives. To son William, at his mother's marriage, the remainder of my land being 240 A. Dau. Margaret. Son Richard Garrison. Son George Garrison. Bal. of est. to be div. bet. sons Richard & George & all my daus. Wife & son Jonathan Exrs. Witt: Littleton Scarburgh Major, William Wyatt, John Darby - p. 223
In order of Prob: William Garrison heir at law.

STOCKLEY, JOSEPH, Sr. – 17 May 1758 – 24 June 1760 – To son Nehemiah Stockley land where I live cont. 380 A. Wife Naomi. Dau. Mary Riche. Son Joseph Stockley. Son Nathaniel Stockley. Dau. Comfort. Son Nehemiah resid. legatee. Sons Joseph, Nathaniel & Nehemiah Exrs. Witt: William Thornton, Jr., Thomas Stockley, William Tunnell – p. 223
In order of Prob: Joseph Stockley heir at law to the testator.

WHITE, HENRY – 7 Apr. 1760 – 24 June 1760 – Wife to have use of whole est. during her wid. To dau. Tabitha what she hath had of me. Bal. of est. to children that now live with me. Wife (no name) Exec. Witt: Thomas Batson, Southy Satchell, Jacob White – p. 224
In order of Prob: Sarah White qualified.

SMITH, ISAAC – 6 May 1760 – 29 July 1760 – Son John Smith. To son Thorowgood Smith (under age) Dau. Sarah West. Dau. Ann West. Grandson Isaac West. Dau. Briget Smith. Son Isaac Smith. Grandau. Sarah West, dau. of Ann West. Grandau. Betty Smith. Wife Sarah. Children not to disturb my son Isaac concerning what he has already advanced my dec. dau. Betty of the estate of Charles West dec. – Wife Exec. Witt: John Spendelow, Edmund Custis – p. 234

PARKS, JOHN – 13 Oct. 1759 – 30 Sept. 1760 – To wife Jemimah whole est. during her wid. then to my 6 children Levinor, Astor, Susannah, Mary, Ann & John. Wife Exec. Witt: Henry Fletcher, Leah Fletcher – p. 249

GILCHRIST, ANDREW – 21 Aug. 1760 – 30 Sept. 1760 – To wife 1/3 of Personal est. Son George Gilchrist. Dau. Agnes. Son in law John Burton. Wife (no name) Exec. Witt: Arthur Emmerson, Major Davis, Anne Emmerson, John Leigh – p. 251
In order of Prob: Tabitha Gilchrist, wid. of the testator qualified.

BELL, MARY – 19 June 1759 – 30 Sept. 1760 – Dau. Mary Bell. Dau. Tabitha Thatam. Grandau Luse Northam. Son William Bell. To John Northam. Son William Bell resid. legatee & Exr. Witt: Arnold Morgan, George Johnson, Solomon Johnson. – p. 253

NICKLESS, ELENOR – 19 Sept. 1760 – 25 Nov. 1760 – To Hancock Rowles. To friend John Walker. To Nanny Muir, dau. of Adam Muir. To George Gale, son of Levin Gale of Somerset County, Maryland. Slaves to be div. bet. Mr. Adam Muir & Mr. Levin Gale. To Elizabeth Hall, wife of John Hall in Northampton. Friends Adam Muir & Levin Gale resid. legatees & Exrs. Witt: James Henry, Peter Hack, George Hack – p. 263
In order of Prob: Major Rowles heir at law to the testatrix.

WEST, PARKER – 15 Nov. 1760 – 26 Nov. 1760 – To sister Adah. Alexander West, Phillip Parker West & Adah West resid. legatees –

Witt: Mary West Elijah Cropper, Thomas Cropper – p. 273

GASCOYNS, ELIZABETH – 11 Apr. 1759 – 30 Dec. 1760 – Sister Sarah
Joynes. Bro. Thomas Gascoyns. Bro. William Gascoyns. William
Joynes Exr. Witt: John Waltham, Adah Waltham, Susanna Gascoyns
– p. 274

WILKINSON, JACOB * 14 Nov. 1760 – 30 Dec. 1760 – To wife whole
sst. to bring up my children. Wife (no name) Exec. – Witt: Samuel
Feddeman, William Drummond, Moses Verdain – p. 274
In order of Prob: Mary Wilkinson, wid. of the testator qualified.

BULL, TOBIAS – 4 May, 1751 – Partly proved 25 Nov. 1760 – Prob.
30 Dec. 1760 – Wife Frances Bull. To sons Tobias & Daniel Bull 350
A. on the head of the South Branch of Hunting Creek. Grandson Daniel
Bull, son of Tobias Bull. To son Benjamin Bull 200 A. on a branch
formerly called James Walker's Branch where he now lives. Grandson
Tobias Bull, son of Benjamin. Dau. Ann Bird, wife of Solomon Bird.
Grandau. Frances Bird dau. Peggy Bonnewell, wife of Joachim Michael Bonnewell. Grandau. Sarah Bonnewell. Dau. Esther Lilliston,
wife of Willet Lilliston land purchased of Major Dunton, being 90 A.
& for want of heirs to grandson Tobias Bull, son of Benjamin. 1/3 of
the remainder of my est. to my wife Frances & the other 2/3 to my
son Daniel Bull. Wife & son Daniel Exrs. Witt: Major Ironmonger,
John Ironmonger, Cornelius Ironmonger – p. 275
In order of Prob: Tobias Bull heir at law to the testator.

WATSON, MOSES – 24 Nov. 1756 – 30 Dec. 1760 – To son Sacker
Watson 100 A. where I now live & for want of heirs to my 3 bros.
Benjamin Watson, Mitchell Watson & Robert Watson. Wife Rachel
Exec. Witt: Mitchell Watson, Ezekiel Watson, Robert Watson – p.
276

SIMPSON, SAMUEL – 16 Aug. 1756 – 30 Dec. 1760 – Dau. Sarah
Cropper. Grandsons Sacker Barnes, Elijah Simpson & Zopher (Chris-
topher?) Simpson. Son Laban Simpson resid. legatee & Exr. Witt: John
Dix, William Dix, Nanny Dix – p. 277

HARRISON, STEPHEN – 29 Oct. 1760 – 30 Dec. 1760 – To son James
Harrison Planta. where I live & 100 A. To wife Mary my mill that is
now building during her wid. to bring up her children & then to my son
Robert Hutchuson. Bal. of est. to all my children. Bro. in law Dennis
Tigner & Wife Exrs. Witt: Littleton Lurton, Richard Rodgers, Jr.,
Elizabeth Roberts. – p. 278

In order of Prob: Dennis Tigner guardian to James Harrison, inf't. heir
at law to the testator.

DOUGLAS, WALTER – 19 Mar. 1760 – 30 Dec. 1760 – To my Honored
mother all my est. during her life & then to my 4 sisters & my
nephew James Douglas. Deceased sister Ann Douglas. Nephew

George Douglas. Skinner Wallop Exr. Witt: Thomas Collins, John Townsend, Phebe Collins. - p. 279

SIMPSON, THOMAS - 10 Dec. 1759 - 30 Dec. 1760 - To 3 sisters Siner, Mary & Ann Simpson all my lands & marshes. Mother to have use of same during her life. Mother Mary Simpson Exec. Witt: Thomas Riley, Major Pettit, Bridget Taylor - p. 279
In order of Prob: Mary Simpson, the executrix named in the foregoing will being dead, Ann Simpson qualified.

DIX, RICHARD - 8 Nov. 1760 - 30 Dec. 1760 - Wife Molly - To son Griffin Dix land & planta. Personal est. to be div. bet. all my children Griffin, Nanny & unborn child. Friend Southy Simpson Exr. Witt: Arthur Emmerson, Parker Copes, George Dix p. 280
In order of Prob: Southy Simpson app. guardian to Griffin Dix, heir at law to the testator.

PARKER, SACKER - 2 Nov. 1760 - 30 Dec. 1760 - Sister Rachel Parker. Bro. George Parker. Mother Naomi Parker. Bro. William Parker. Bro. in law Richard Justice. Cousins Esther Parker, dau. of John; Ann Justice, dau. of Richard & Susey Parker, dau. of George. Mother Exec. Witt: Southy Simpson, Abel Finney, Mary East. p. 281

CLARK, THOMAS - 11 Oct. 1758 - 30 Dec. 1760 -To sister Rhody Clark my land & planta. & all the rest of my est. & for want of heirs to John Bull, son of Benjamin Bull. Sister Rhody Exec. - Witt: Southy Simpson, Comfort Simpson, Elizabeth Dix p. 282

WARRINGTON, ABBOTT - 17 Nov. 1760 - 30 Dec. 1760 - To son Stephen Warrington my land that my father gave me. To my second son John Warrington. Dau. Betty Warrington. Unborn child. Wife Elizabeth & Stephen Warrington Exrs: Witt: Stephen Warrington, Betty Warrington, Sarah Melichops - p. 282
In order of Prob: Stephen Warrington app. guardian to Stephen Warrington, Inf't. heir at law to the testator.

KELLY, JOSEPH - 7 Sept. 1760 - 30 Dec. 1760 - To wife Esther Kelly planta. where I formerly lived at the Bayside during her wid. & then to my son Joseph Kelly. To son John Kelly planta. where I now live. To wife Esther Kelly what property that came by her. Dau. Sarah Kelly. Dau. Warrington Kelly. Wife & children resid. legatees. Thomas Bloxom Exr. Witt: Thomas Bloxom, George Hope, William Sacker James - p. 283
In order of Prob: Thomas Bloxom app. guardian to John Kelly, heir at law to the testator.

EWELL, MARK - 10 Oct. 1760 - 30 Dec. 1760 - To son George Ewell planta. where I now live & that part of land I hold by my father's will. To son William Ewell 50 A. Dau. Sarah Ewell. To dau. Ann Ewell. Dau. Famey Ewell. Wife Tabitha & Ephraim Vessells Exrs. Witt: George Hope Ewell, Thomas Lewis, William Young - p. 284

In order of Prob: Tabitha Ewell app. guardian to George Ewell, heir at law to the testator.

WEST, AGNESS – Nunc. 29 Oct. 1760 – 31 Dec. 1760 – Son Major West. Dau. Comfort West. Dau. Scarburgh Topping. Dau. Agnes Willett. Dau. Susannah Scott. Grandau. Agness Chambers – Proved by Anthony West & Scarburgh West. – p. 295

MARSHALL, WILLIAM – 26 Sept. 1760 – 27 Jan. 1761 – Eldest son William Marshall. Son John Marshall. To son Daniel Marshall planta. purchased of Charles Dickerson, being 300 A. To son Solomon Marshall planta. where John Whaly lives, also 50 A. adj. which I bought of Kendall Toles. Dau. Mary Welburn, wife of Francis Welburn. Son Charles Marshall. Dau. Elizabeth Marshall. Dau. Leah Marshall. Son George Marshall. Son Levin Marshall. Son Solomon to have the planta. where I live 15 years from this time, he to keep my 2 youngest sons George & Levin until they are of age. To son William planta. where I live at the end of 15 years. Wife Elizabeth. Sons Daniel & Solomon Exrs. Witt: Daniel Marshall, Peter Marshall, Sr., Nehemiah Holland – p. 298

EVANS, JOHN – 30 Jan. 1760 – 27 Jan. 1761 – To son Thomas Evans 210 A. where I now live. Dau. Mary Evans. Dau. Grace Evans. –––––––– Will not completed – Not signed – Not witnessed. Proved by Thomas Crippen, Thomas Evans, bro. of John, & John Kitson. – p. 300
In order of Prob: The above writing produced as the last will of John Evans, found since the last Court. Ann Evans, wid. of the testator qualified.

HICKMAN, WILLIAM – 14 Nov. 1760 – 25 Feb. 1761 – To bro. George Hickman 100 A. adj. the land of Solomon Hickman & for want of heirs to my bro. Richard. Bro. Jesse Hickman. Bro. Selby Hickman. Sister Bridget. Bro. "Rayth". Witt: William Barns, William White, Sarah White. – p. 302
In order of Probate – Richard Hickman qualified. Selby Hickman, heir at law to the testator, cited to appear – Sheriff's return "not found within my Bailiwick".

GROTEN, JONATHAN – 10 Feb. 1761 – 24 Feb. 1761 – Whole est. to my wife to bring up my children. Witt: Lazarus Townsend, John Kendall, James Taylor – p. 307
In order of Prob: Peggy Groten qualified.

BULL, TOBIAS – 17 Jan. 1760 – 24 Feb. 1761 – Wife to have use of whole est. during her wid. & then personal est. to be div. between all my children. To son John Bull 100 A. on that part of my land adj. Daniel Bull. To son Daniel all the remainder of my land. Wife Arcadia Exr. Witt: Thomas Ryley, Daniel Bull, Catherine Bull – p. 308
In order of Prob: John Bull heir at law to the testator.

BELL, JOSEPH - 5 Feb. 25 Feb. 1761 - To Mary Nock 2/3 of my whole est. To Rachel Warner 1/3 of my est. To Mary Baker 1 s. To Ann Ramsey 1 s. William Warner & Mary Nook Exrs. Witt: John Bishop, Bridget Gooday, William Gooday - p. 313

BAGWELL, HELY - 21 Mar. 1761 - 31 Mar. 1761 - Mother Sabra Dix planta. on Folly Creek with 100 A. of marsh on the Bayside for life & then to my brother Spencer Bagwell. Cousin John Milby. To Henry Bagwell, son of my bro. Spencer. To father in law John Dix & mother Sabra Dix bal. of est. for life & then to be div. bet. my brothers & sisters, Ann Dix, Elizabeth Dix, John Dix the younger, Mary Dix & Levin Dix. Mother & father in law Exrs. Witt: Laban Simpson, Southy Simpson p. 314
In order of Prob: Charles Bagwell heir at law to the testator.

STRINGER, JACOB - 22 Jan. 1761 - 31 Mar. 1761 - To son Benjamin Stringer 150 A. to wife Elizabeth. Dau. Custis Stringer. Dau. Joynes Stringer. Dau. Elizabeth Stringer. Son Thomas Stringer. Son Jacob Stringer. Elizabeth Stringer Exec. Witt: Littleton Ames, John Ames, Mitchell Watson - p. 315

MOONEY, NICHOLAS - 5 Feb. 1761 - 31 Mar. 1761 - Corn to be sold to discharge my Virginia debts. To friend Daniel O'Gallachor. Est. to be sold & the money transmitted to my friend James White of Philadelphia, near the Draw Bridge, in trust that he will pay the same to my mother Rose Malone, my bro. John Mooney, my sister Jane & Alice Moonah, children of Daniel Moonah near to Minimore in the County of Tyrone, and Kingdom of Ireland to be div. bet. my said mother, bro. & sisters equally. Friends William Bagge & Capt. John Coleburn & Daniel O'Gallachar Exrs. Witt: John Thompson, James Henry - p. 315

STATON, WARRINGTON - 5 Dec. 1760 - 31 Mar. 1761 - Son Thomas Staton. To son Joseph Staton planta. where I now live cont. 200 A. & for want of heirs to my youngest son Warrington Staton. To son George Staton. Youngest dau. Sophia Staton. Dau. Keziah Taylor. Dau. Elizabeth Mathews. Dau. Ann Conquest. Son James Staton. Bal. of est. to wife Catherine during her wid. then to be div. bet. my children Jacob, Comfort, Sophia & Warrington Staton. Wife & son Joseph Exrs. Witt: Nehemiah Stockly, William Tunnel, William Matthews. p. 316
In order of Prob: Thomas Staton heir at law to the testator.

WEST, ALEXANDER - 19 Nov. 1760 - 26 May 1761 - To wife Judah whole est. during her wid. & then to my 3 daus. Nanny, Rachel & Abigal West, & should they all die without issue to my bro. Phillip Parker West all my land. Wife Exec. Witt: Laban Sympson, Rachel Gray, Rachel Thorgood. - p. 351
In order of Prob: John West, of Deep Creek, app. guardian to Nanny, Rachel & Abigal West, Inf't. heirs at law to the testator.

ROBERTS, ABEL - 22 Dec. 1760 - 28 July 1761 - Dau. Peggy Savage, wife of Major Savage, land where I now live cont. 200 A. & for want of heirs to my 2 daus. Rachel Garrison & Sinah Roberts. Daus. Rachel Garrison & Sinah Roberts resid. legatees. Son in law George Garrison & dau. Sinah Roberts Exrs. Witt: Thomas Savage, Jonathan Garrison, "Arcabl" Harrison - p. 354

BEAVENS, WILLIAM - 13 June 1761 - 28 July 1761 - To son Samuel Beavens planta. where father lived & 200 A. To son Will: Beavens 200 A. being part of said tract. To son John Beavens 200 A. of the same tract on the Seaside. To son Nathaniel planta. where I now dwell cont. 164 A. & 100 A. purchased of George Booth, 50 A. of swamp at Masongo, 65 A. purchased of Thomas Upshur, also the right of dower purchased of Felia Hall & Hannah, his wife. To sons Samuel & William Beavens 120 A. on Wallops Island purchased of Skinner Wallop. To sons Nathaniel & John Beavens 167 1/3 A. of Marsh at Muddy Creek. To son Samuel Beavens negro Jacob formerly given him by his grandmother, silver spoons marked ETC & 2 more marked TEC. Dau. Mary Beavens 3 silver spoons marked ETC, 2 marked SDN & small silver spoon which was her mother's marked EXD, a gold ring marked C.J. To son William Beavens silver spoon marked WMB. To son Nathaniel spoon marked WMB. To son John silver spoon marked WMB. To dau. Rachel Beavens silver spoon marked WMB. To wife Mary a gold ring that her father left her &c. To George Milachops a silver stock buckle which I bought of his father's est. Wife & son William Exrs. Witt: Southy Simpson, Solomon Dix, Billy Young, Anne Emmerson, William Drummond. Ezekiel Young - p. 355
In order of Prob: Samuel Beavens heir at law.

ROGERS, RICHARD - 17 Sept. 1756 - 28 July 1761 - To wife that Part of my land I now live on. To son Richard Rogers land he now lives on. To son Laban Rogers land he now lives on adj. that given his bro. Richard, as also the land I lent my wife. Son John Rogers, Ann Speers, Mary Wise & Robert Rogers resid. legatees. Wife & Son John Rogers Exrs. Witt: James Rodgers, Luke Luker, Zerobabel Rogers. p. 357
In order of Prob: Richard Rogers heir at law to the testator.

JUSTICE, WILLIAM - 18 June 1761 - 28 July 1761 - To wife Eleanor Justice whole est. Thomas Bloxom Exr. Witt: Bally Hindman, Ruben Shield - p. 358

GITTINS, WILLIAM - 11 Jan. 1761 - 26 Aug. 1761 - To grandson William Watson Gittins. Bal. est. to wife Jean for life & then to my 4 children, Elisha, Jain, Susey & Margaret Gittins. Wife Exec. Witt: Joshua Burton, Abner Burton, William Banfield Walker - p. 392

MARTIN, PETER - 10 May 1761 - 29 Sept. 1761 - To son Smith Martin planta. where I live with 100 A. To son Peter Martin the other 50 A. adj. Stakes Cave & Abel Savage. Wife Margaret. Daus.

Ritter & Charity Martin. Bal. of est. to wife for life & then to 3 above named daus. Wife & John Earlington Exrs. Witt: John Cave, Edmund Mason, Henry Willis – p. 409

STOCKLEY, ISABEL – 27 Oct. 1761 – 24 Nov. 1761 – To John Rose & his 2 daus. Rachel & Eberson. To Griffin Pritchet. To Ann Henderson. To Christian Sill. To Mary Satchell. John Rose Exr. Witt: John Waltham, Ann Waltham – p. 447

JOHNSON, BAYLY – 26 Mar. 1761 – 26 Nov. 1761 – To kinsman Abner Burton. To Caleb Burton, son of Abner. To Sinah Parker, dau. of my sister Leah Boggs. To sister Rebecca Burton – Abner Burton resid. legatee & Exr. Witt: Leah Boggs. James Henry – p. 451

Orders – 1764–1765

GRAHAM, GEORGE – Adm. his est. to Isaac Smith, Bridget Graham, widow of George, relinquishing her right to qualify – James Henry sec. – 3 Feb. 1764 – p. 18

BELOTTE, NOAH – Adm. his est. to Sarah Belotte – Solomon Bunting, Daniel Twiford & Michael Bonnewell sec. – 28 Feb. 1764 – p. 28

RODGERS, NORWICH – Adm. his est. to Mary Rodgers – Arthur Robins sec. – 28 Feb. 1764 – p. 30

SMITH, THOMAS – Adm. his est. to John Smith Joseph Walker & Richard Hinman sec. 29 Feb. 1764 – p. 37

JACKSON, WILLIAM – Adm. his est. to Mary Jackson – Solomon Martial & Skinner Wallop sec. – 27 Mar. 1764 – p. 53

BELL, WILLIAM – Adm. his est. to Bridget Bell John Northam & William Warner sec. 27 Mar. 1764 – p. 56

MASSEY, JOHN – Adm. his est. to Skinner Wallop Tully Robinson Wise & Solomon Martial sec. 28 Mar. 1764 – p. 62

MILES, WILLIAM – Adm. his est. to Jacob Stakes. Henry Heath sec. – 29 Mar. 1764 – p. 87

EMMERSON, ARTHUR – Adm. his est. to Anne Emmerson – John Kitson & George Holden sec. – 24 Apr. 1764 – p. 90

REVEL, JOHN – Adm. his est. to Leah Revel – James Scott & Luke Luker sec. – 26 June 1764 – p. 146

THOMAS, AGNES – Adm. her est. to her husband, George Thomas, Jr. – Jonathan Powell sec. 29 Aug. 1764 – p. 214

FINNEY, WILLIAM, Jr. – Adm. his est. to Elizabeth Finney – John Smith sec. – 30 Oct. 1764 – p. 237

JOHNSON, WILLIAM – Adm. his est. to Mary Johnson – Samuel Johnson sec. – 30 Oct. 1764 – p. 238

BLAKE, JABEZ – Adm. his est. to Littleton Dennis – Skinner WalloP sec. – 29 Jan. 1765 – p. 290

HARRISON, ALEXANDER – Adm. his est. to Elizabeth Harrison – John Parker, Jr. sec. 31 Jan. 1765 p. 302

THOMSON, JOHN – Adm. his est. to William Bagge James Kemp sec. 26 Feb. 1765 – p. 326

WATTS, WILLIAM – Adm. his est. to Esther Watts James Watts & Joshua Collings sec. 26 Feb. 1765 – p. 328

WHITE, WRIXOM – Adm. his est. unadministered by his wid. Grace White, dec., to Robert Russell Solomon White sec. – 26 Feb. 1765 – p. 329

WHITE, GRACE – Adm. her est. to Robert Russell Solomon White sec. – 26 Feb. 1765 – p. 329

CRIDLEY, MARY – Adm. her est. to Bowdoin Robins George Stewart sec. – 26 Feb. 1765 – p. 330

WHARTON, WILLIAM – Adm. his est. to Thomas Custis – Fairfax Smith & Richard Rodgers sec. – 30 Apr. 1765 – p. 403

CHAMBERS, KATHERINE – Adm. her est. to her husband, Edmund Chambers – Sebastian Cropper, Jr. & Severn Guthrey sec. – 1 May 1765 – p. 408

HUDSON, ROBERT Adm. his est. to George Millichops – Levin Stewart sec. – 26 June 1765 – p. 450

WEST, JUDITH – Adm. her est. to John West – Thomas Cropper sec. – 29 Aug. 1765 – p. 499

DRUMMOND, RICHARD Adm. his est. with will annexed to Thomas Bayly who intermarried with Ann, dau. of the testator. Littleton Dennis & Thomas Riley sec. – 31 Oct. 1765 – p. 588

Orders – 1765–1767

BUNDICK, RICHARD – Adm. his est. to John Bundick – Richard Bundick sec. – 27 May 1766 – p. 33

HICKMAN, ANNE - Adm. her est. to Samuel Cowley - John Shae sec. - 25 June 1766 - p. 67

HOLT, JOHN - Adm. his est. to John Holt - Edward Parish sec. - 29 July 1766 - p. 129

EMMERSON, REV. ARTHUR - Adm. his est. unadministered by Anne Emmerson, his late wid. & admx., to John Kitson & George Holden - Littleton Dennis & James Henry sec. 30 Sept. 1766 - p. 234

CORBIN, ROBERT - Adm. his est. with will annexed, unadministered by Anne, his late wid. & Exec., dec., to Ralph Corbin - Covington Corbin & Southy Simpson sec. - 30 Sept. 1766 - p. 236

MARTIAL, JOHN - Adm. his est. to Mason Martial - Francis Welburne, Timothy Collings & Covington Corbin sec. 27 Oct. 1766 - p. 289

POPE, THOMAS Adm. his est. to Polly Pope - Lisney Gootee & John Gootee sec. 26 Nov. 1766 p. 307

HICKMAN, KNEVIT - Adm. his est. to George Hickman - Thomas Wise Rodgers sec. - 30 Dec. 1766 - p. 365

NORTHAM, WILLIAM - Adm. his est. to Thomas Northam - Thomas Bloxom sec. - 30 Dec. 1766 - p. 365

THORNTON, THOMAS Adm. his est. to Martha Thornton & Michael Dickenson - Samuel Beavans & William Patterson sec. - 27 Jan. 1767 - p. 375

Orders - 1767-1768

OUTTEN, JOHN - Adm. his est. to Jesse Outten - John Gootee sec. - 24 Feb. 1767 - p. 1

STRANN, James - Adm. his est. to Thomas Parramore - John Coleburn sec. - 25 Feb. 1767 - p. 4

BROADWATER, JACOB - Adm. his est. to Jacob Broadwater - Sebastian Cropper & John Townsend, Jr. sec. - 25 Feb. 1767 - p. 8

BENSTON, MICAJAH - Adm. his est. to Elisha Hill - John Taylor sec. - 25 Feb. 1767 - p. 8

GOOTEE, JOSEPH - Adm. his est. to Rachel Gootee - George Stewart sec. 31 Mar. 1768 - p. 18

MASSEY, THOMAS – Adm. his est. to Naomi Walker – Robert Jenkinson & William Stockly sec. – 31 Mar. 1767 – p. 18

STEWART, JAMES – Adm. his est. to John Potter – Jammes Henry sec. – 31 Mar. 1767 – p. 21

BEAVANS, WILLIAM – Adm. his est. to Anne Beavans & Samuel Beavans – Joseph Matthews & Southy Matthews sec. – 26 May 1767 – p. 90

STURGIS, ISAIAH – Adm. his est. to Adah Sturgis – William Sturgis & Parker Copes sec. – 26 May 1767 – p. 93

PITTS, SAMUEL – Adm. his est. to Andrew Gootee – Littleton Dennis sec. – 1 July 1767 – p. 159

COLEBURN, TEMPERANCE – Adm. her est. to William Coleburn – John Coleburn sec. – 1 July 1767 – p. 162

LEATHERMAN, WALLOP Adm. his est. to Thomas Broadwater – Jonathan Bunting & Jacob Broadwater sec. – 30 SePt. 1767 – p. 262

LOMBARD, SAMUEL – Adm. his est. to Mary Anne Lombard – Scarburgh Tunnel & Joseph Matthews sec. – 27 Oct. 1767 – p. 311

LUCAS, THOMAS – Adm. his est. to Fortune Lucas Littleton Armitrader sec. – 29 Dec. 1767 – p. 370

PEAL, ROBERT – Adm. his est. to Comfort Peal Robert Spires sec. – 30 Dec. 1767 – p. 373

STAKES, WILLIAM – Adm. his est. to Rebecca Stakes John Sacker Barnes & Thomas Hickman sec. – 26 Jan. 1768 – p. 391

WIMBROUGH, SOLOMON Adm. his est. to Thomas Bloxom William Andrews & Ezekiel Delastatius sec. – 23 Feb. 1768 – p. 434

PARKER, AMEY – Adm. her est. to George Parker Richard Justice sec. 23 Feb. 1768 – p. 434

TAYLOR, WILLIAM – Adm. his est. to John Taylor (cordwainer) – James Rodgers & Robert Spires sec. – 24 Feb. 1768 – p. 438

BURTON, REBECCA – Adm. her est. to Abner Burton – John Coleburn & Henry Heath sec. 29 Mar. 1768 – p. 460

MASON, BENNET – Adm. his est. to Anne Mason Littleton Armitrader, John Bunting & Thomas Bloxom sec. – 30 Mar. 1768 – p. 478

SMITH, GEORGE - Nunc - 24 Nov. 1761 - 29 Dec. 1761 - Wife Sabra. Sons John, Simon & Machel. Dau. Margaret Smith. To son George Smith 50 A. purchased of Richard Baley. Wife & children resid. legatees. Son John Exr. Proved by John Major & Jonathan Kellam - p. 8
In order of Proh: Sabra Smith, wid. of the testator qualified.

IRONMONGER, EDWARD - 26 Jan. 1760 - 29 Dec. 1761 - Wife to have use of 1/ my land & whole personal est. during her wid. To son John Ironmonger 100 A. called the Mill Branch. To son Jacob Ironmonger. Sons Jacob & Cornelius resid. legatees. Wife (no name) & son Cornelius Exrs. Witt: Thomas Ryley, Thomas Wise, Samuel Wise - p. 9
In order of Prob: John Ironmonger heir at law to the testator.

COOK, WILLIAM - 31 Jan. 1761 - 30 Dec. 1761 -To wife whole est. during her wid. then 1/2 to Tompson, son of my sister Margaret Tompson, & if he be dead then to the next eldest son or dau. To Benjamin Royal the debt due me. To John & Sarah Russell, son & dau. of Salathiel Russell. Godson William Cook. Friends Thomas Parramore & Benjamin Royal Exrs. Witt: Smith Bunting, Sebastian Cropper, Jr., William Evans. - p. 10

ARRINGTON, JOHN - 24 Jan. 1760 - 25 Jan. 1762 - To son John Arrington whole est. To son in law George Rew 1 s. Son John Exr. Witt: John Smith, Henry Scarburgh. p. 11

SCARBURGH, CHARLES - 3 Dec. 1761 - 25 Jan. 1762 - To son Henry Scarburgh (under age) To Col. Thomas Hall confirmation of sale of land willed me by my father, known as Tangier Island, & should the said Hall refuse to pay the balance due, then I give the said land to my son Henry & for want of heirs to my bro. Bennet Scarburgh. Wife Mary Ann. Should my son Henry die without issue ext. to be div. bet. my sister Margaret Watts, Ann Scarburgh, Bro. Bennet Scarburgh & sister Tabitha Scarburgh, except the silver plate which is to return to my wife Mary Ann. Wife Exec. Witt: Skinner Wallop, James Hall, Thomas Welburn - p. 11

LURTON, RACHEL - 8 Jan. 1762 - 25 Jan. 1762 - To son Jacob Lurton 1 s. Dau. Hannah Bonnewell 1 s. Dau. Rachel Bonnewell 1 s. Dau. Elizabeth West 1 s. Grandson John Evans 1 s. Dau. Mary Edwards 1 s. Grandau. Comfort Edwards resid. legatee. Witt: William PhilliPs, Thomas Lewis. - p. 12
In order of Prob: Isaac Lewis qualified.

McWILLIAMS, FINLEY - 29 Jan. 1762 - 23 Feb. 1762 - To Susanna Harrison. To Tabitha Rolley. To Ann Guy. To Jacob Ayres. Godson George Scott resid. legatee. Thomas Riley & Jacob Ayres Exrs. Witt: Wonne Rew, John Lewis, Jonathan Willet - p. 38

RUSSELL, SAMUEL - 10 July 1757 - 23 Feb. 1762 - Son Solomon. Son Salathiel. Son Andrew. Daus. Mary Mason & Rachel Prewit 1 s. each. Grandson William Prewit. Son Milby Russell resid. legatee after wife's death. Son Milby Exr. Witt: John Lewis, Wonne Rew - p. 39

LEWIS, JOHN - 1 Dec. 1762 - 30 Mar. 1762 - To wife whole est. during her wid. Son James Lewis. Daus. Sarah & Betty Lewis. To 3 youngest children. Son Leven Lewis & wife Johannah Lewis Exrs. Witt: Garret Toppin, Babel Rodgers - p. 67

DIX, JOHN - 1 Feb. 1762 - 30 Mar. 1762 - To wife Sabra whole est. during her wid. to bring up & educate my children. To son John my land & planta. To son Levin Milby Dix. Daus. Nanny, Elizabeth & Mary Dix & son Levin Milby Dix resid. legatees. Wife Sabra & dau. Nanny Exrs. Witt: Southy Simpson, John Dix, Jr., Laban SimPson - p. 85
In order of Prob: Charles Stockly app. guardian to John Dix, heir at law to the testator.

BENSTON, EDY - 9 May 1761 - 27 Apr. 1762 - Friend Joseph Feddiman Exr., he to Fay Elizabeth Conquest for her trouble during my sickness. Witt: John Spalding, Moses Winder - p. 87

WATSON, BENJAMIN - 24 Jan. 1762 - 29 Apr. 1762 - To son Levi (under age) 13 A. adj. Francis Wainhouse. To son William Watson all the remainder of my land. Land & planta. called Belhaven to be rented till my son William comes to age. To son William 20 A. adj. my son Levi when he is 21. Wife Peggy to have use of planta. where John Harmon lived & all the rest of my est. during her wid, to bring up my children. Daus. (no names) Bro. in law Thomas Adderson & wife Peggy Exrs. Witt: Francis Savage, Edmund Watson, Henry Harman - p. 93
In order of Prob: Edmund Watson guardian to William Watson, Inf't. heir at law to the testator.

BENSTON, EZEKIEL - 24 Feb. 1762 - 27 Apr. 1762 - To eld. son John Benston (under 21) all my land that I now hold. Bro. Micajah Benston. Son William Benston. Son James Benston. Daus. Mary & Grace Benston. Wife (no name) & Bro. Exrs. Witt: Lisney Goottee, Joseph Goote, Hannah Benston - p. 94
In order of Probate: Samuel Pitts app. guardian to John Benston, Inf't heir at law to the testator. Micajah Benston & Ann Benston qualified.

STOCKLY, NAOMI - Nunc. - --------- 27 Apr. 1762 - To Betty, the wife of Nehemiah Stockley. To Mary Filby. To Sarah, a slave belonging to Mrs Wishart. Hannah Mathews, Naomy Matthews resid. legatees. Proved by Catharine Staton & Naomi Ewell - p. 95
In order of Prob: Nehemiah Stockly qualified.

GUY, ANNE – 3 Apr. 1762 – 27 Apr. 1762 – To Elizabeth Guy. To Nancy Guy. To William Guy. To Nancy Cole & Jane Spiers. To Patience Spires, wife of John Spires negro for life, reversion to James Spires. John Spires Exr. Witt: William Nock, Thomas Burton - p. 96

WILLET, JOHN – 15 Apr. 1762 – 29 June 1762 – To wife all my land purchased of William Willet during her wid., also my water mill, then to my son Jonathan, he to Pay my son William 20L or get him 100 A. somewhere in Worcester County, & in case he refuse my son William to have the said land & mill. Dau. Anne Willet. Son Ambros 1 s. Dau. Betty 1 s. Dau. Mary 1 s. Dau. Sinah 1 s. Dau. Catharine. Tabitha Moor to have all the est. I had with her. To Bridget Ashby all that I have of her est. James Stran & son William Exrs. Witt: Thomas Riley, GeorSe Melson, John Onley. p. 102
In order of Prob: Jonathan Willet heir at law to the testator.

SAVAGE, ROBERT – 27 July 1761 – 31 Aug. 1762 – Wife Dorothy to have use of whole est. for life or wid. To 2 sons William & Charles all my marsh. To son William 1/2 my land & to my son Charles the other 1/2 my land, each to have the part they now live on. To dau. Elizabeth Savage. Grandson Rowland Savage. Daus. Mary Carpenter & Elizabeth Savage resid. legatees. Sons William & Charles Exrs. Witt: Francis Savage, John Kellam, Joseph Kellam – p. 134
In order of prob: – Rowland Savage heir at law to the testator.

JUSTICE, WILLIAM, Jr. – 10 Aug. 1759 – Partly proved 29 June 1762. Fully proved 1 Sept. 1762 Prob. 28 Sept. 1762 – Whole est. to wife, but if she should be with child the child to have all my lands & an equal part of my negroes & other est. Witt: John Harmanson, Sarah Mackmath – p. 137
In order of Prob: Edward Ker qualified.

HARRISON, ELIZABETH Sr. – 8 Apr. 1762 – 28 Sept. 1762 – To dau. Tabitha Tigner. To dau. Elizabeth Richardson. To dau. Susannah Pratt. Grandson Kendall Pratt. Bayly Pratt Exr. Witt: Bezaleel Watson – p. 139

KELLY, EDMOND – 25 Sept. 1762 – 30 Nov. 1762 – To son William Kelly the lower part of my land adj. Nathaniel Bird, John Kelly & Levin Gale. To wife Catherine Kelly. To eld. son Griffin Kelly the remainder of my land except 4 A. adj. William Bell which I give to my son Daniel Kelly. To dau. Catharine Howard. To dau. Atharliah Kelly. Dau. Mary Howard. Grandson Milven Rodgers. Dau. Sarah Rodgers, dec., her part to be div. bet. her 2 children. Wife Exec. Witt: Arnold Morgin, William Bell, Bridget Bell – p. 143

WHITTINGTON, ELIZABETH – 25 Apr. 1756 – 30 Nov. 1762 – To grandson William Whittington, son of William Whittington 1/2 of my 3rd part of my dec. husband's est. To the children of my son Joshua

Whittington, viz: William, Esther & Elizabeth Whittington all the remainder of my est. Son Joshua Exr. Witt: Elizabeth Wishart, Jacamen Wishart - p. 144
In order of Prob: Jacamen Wishart, now Jacamen Milligan Joshua Whittington relinquished his right & William Whittington qualified.

ARMITRADER, RICHARD - 13 Mar. 1762 - 30 Nov. 1762 - Wife Patience to have use of whole est. for life, reversion to 8 children Elizabeth Harrison, Robert Armitrader, Anne Armitrader, James Armitrader, Stephen Armitrader, Susanna Burton, Richard Armitrader & Mathew Armitrader. Wife Patience & son Stephen Exrs. Witt: Stratton Burton, Stephen Armitrader - p. 148

CHANDLER, ANNE - 15 Aug. 1757 - 2 Dec. 1762 - To Bridget Fitzgarald. To Susannah Fitsgarald. To Mary Kellam. To William Chandler. To Elizabeth Haly. To dau. Anne Chandler, Jr. To dau. Comfort Chandler. George. Anne & Comfort Chandler resid. legatees. Son William Chandler Exr. Witt: Samuel Metcalf, Thomas Metcalf, Jacob Phillips - p. 149

FLETCHER, BRANDON - 28 SePt. 1762 - 28 Dec. 1762 - Wife Jean to have use of land & Planta. during her wid. Dau. Rose Cutler. Grandson Thomas Cutler to have my land & planta. after the death or marriage of my wife. Dau. Comfort Heath. To William Randel 1 s. Bal. of est. to wife during her wid. then to my dau. Comfort Heath. Wife Exec. Witt: Littleton Scarburgh Major, Bezaleel Watson - p. 154

BOOTH, GEORGE - 21 June 1762 - 30 Dec. 1762 - To sister Jemima Booth 97 A. adj. land where she now lives; 16 A. on Gargatha Road to make up the 97 A. To sister Martha Booth 3 A. & the houses & orchard where I now live for life, reversion to my godson William Sterling, son of John Sterling. Bros. & sisters resid. legatees. Sister Jemina Booth Exec. - Witt: Isaac Rodgers, Thomas Martin, Babel Rodgers - p. 156

REW, WONNEY - 7 Jan. 1760 - 26 Jan. 1763 - To wife Comfort whole est. during her wid. Dau. Elizabeth Rew. To sons Wonny & Absalom Rew all my lands. Wonny to have planta. where I now live & he lives on. Son Ruben Rew. Bal. of est. to wife during her wid., & then to one or all of my children as she shall think Proper. Wife Exec. Witt: William Young, George Hope Ewell, George Middleton, John Lewis. p. 160
In order of Prob: The citation against Beverley Rew, heir at law to the testator, returned not to be found.

RODGERS, MAJOR - 9 Dec. 1762 - 25 Jan. 1763 - Wife Margaret whole est. during her wid., reversion to my 3 children now alive. Wife Exec. Witt: John Revell, Luke Luker, Leah Revell - p. 161

DUNTON, JACOB - 14 Sept. 1762 - 26 Jan. 1763 - To wife Elizabeth

1/2 my land during her wid. To dau. Elizabeth all my land on the North-east side of a branch or Gully running close along the side & through my Planta., my meaning is all the land on the North-east side of the Westermost fork of the Indian Town Branch & for want of heirs to my dau. Esther Ironmonger & for want of heirs to my 3 youngest daus. To son Benjamin Dunton all my land not already given. To my 4 youngest daus., Esther, Rachel, Bridget & Susey. To Elizabeth Jacob & Annaritta, the child of John Lilliston & to Sarah Dunton Guy, dau. of Robert Guy, dec. Wife & children resid. legatees. Wife & son Benjamin Exrs. Witt: Henry Satchell, John Leigh, Southy Simpson. p. 162
In order of Prob: Benjamin Dunton heir at law to the testator.

JOHNSON, RACHEL – 15 Apr. 1758 – 29 Mar. 1763 – Bro. Samuel Johnson sole legatee & Exr. Witt: Arnold Morgan, John Bloxom, Thomas Fisher – p. 175

KELLY, JOHN – 12 May 1758 – 29 Mar. 1763 – To son Richard Kelly planta. where I now live adj. Nathaniel Bird. Wife Ellis. To dau. Susannah Fitzgerrald. Dau. Esther Kelly. To 2 youngest daus., Mary Anne & Cadey Kelly the bal. of my est. at the death of my wife. Wife Exec. Witt: Nathaniel Bird, Sarah Bird, Richard Onions – p. 175
In order of Prob: "Alice" Kelly, wid. of the testator qualified.

CHANDLER, HATHAN FETTAPACE – 8 Nov. 1762 – 26 Apr. 1763 – To wife whole est. for life. Dau. Peggy Pilcher 1 s. To Elizabeth Chandler, wid. of John Chandler 1 s. To 2 sons Caleb & Hathan Chandler all my land. To younger son William Sacker Chandler (under age) To grandson Zorobabel Chandler. Bal. of est. to be div. bet. all my children except Peggy Pilcher, but her children to have equal part with all my children – Wife (no name) & son Caleb Exrs. Witt: John Philips, Laban Rodgers, John Rodgers. – p. 180
In order of prob: Zerrobabel Chandler heir at law to the testator. Rachel Chandler & Caleb Chandler qualified.

BRADFORD, ELIZABETH – 2 May 1763 – 31 May 1763 – To Violetta Addison all my est. which is in her father's & mother's custody. To son Nathaniel Bradford's 3 children 10L each. To his dau. Sarah. To dau. Naomi. Clothing to be div. bet. my 3 daus. Household goods to be div. bet. dau. Jemima & 2 grandchildren Jemima & Violetta. To William Bagge 40L cash. Daus. Jemima & Naomi resid. legatees. William Bagge Exr. Dau. Keziah. Witt: John Thomson, Elizabeth Jones – p. 190

HEATH, JOSEPH – 2 Feb. 1761 – 31 May 1763 To wife Margaret whole est. during her wid. To son Joseph planta. purchased of Maj. Bennet Scarburgh after his mother's death. To son Henry Heath planta. where I now live. To dau. Margaret Wise. To dau. Sophia. Children resid. legatees. Sons Joseph & Henry Exrs. Witt: John Spendelow, John Wise, Parker Vannelson.

In order of Prob: Joseph Heath heir at law to the testator.

TURNALL, ROBERT – 13 Apr. 1762 – 28 June 1763 – Cattle & sheep to be div. bet. my wife & all my daus. & my grandau. Amy Turnal. Sons George & William Turnal. Son John Turnal. Dau. Betty Turnal. Bal. of est. to wife & all my children except son Robert. To sons Robert & John. Son Robert & Thomas Riley Exrs. Witt: William Young, Richard Bundick – p. 196

PRITCHETT, GRIFFIN – 23 May 1763 – 26 July 1763 – To bro. in law John Rose. To Rachel. dau. of John Rose. John Rose, Mary Jacob, Lucresey Rafel, Eleson Wilson & Anne Hinderson resid. legatees John Rose Exr. Witt: Isaac Dunton, Abel Watson p. 202

MACKEE, WILLIAM – 8 Mar. 1763 – 30 Aug. 1763 – To wife Mary whole est. Bernard Grate of Philadelphia & William Bagge of Virginia Exrs. Witt: John Thomson, Littleton Townsend – p. 203

STOCKLY, ALEXANDER – 23 July 1763 – 27 Sept. 1763 – To dau. Rachel Donelson, wife of John Donelson. To grandau. Comfort Stockly Nock 70L to be in the hands of my son Alexander till she come to age or marry. To grandson William Nock. Son Alexander Stockly resid. legatee & for want of heirs to grandson Alexander Donelson. Son Alexander Exr. Witt: Charles Stockly, Mary Walker, Joseph Stockly –p. 206

CAIN, JOHN – 11 Feb. 1763 – 27 Sept. 1763 – To son William Cain my planta. & all lands belonging at his mother's death. Son John Cain. Dau. Elizabeth Cain. Dau. Anne Cain. Children resid. legatees. Wife Martha Exec. Witt: Jacob Broadwater, Stephen Lewis, Jacob Broadwater, Jr. – p. 207

WHEALTON, WILLIAM – 26 Aug. 1763 – 27 Sept. 1763 – To son Elisha Whealton 190 A. where I now live, also 75 A. of land & for want of heirs to my youngest son Smith Whealton. To all my children that is married, viz: William, James, Thomas & Joyce. To dau. Esther. Bal. of est. to my surviving children, William, James, Thomas, Elisha, Smith, Joyce & Esther. Son William Exr. Witt: Joseph Mathews, Jr., George Mathews, Henry Crossly – p. 208
In order of Prob: Thomas Teackle app. guardian to Nehemiah Whealton, heir at law to the testator.

SCARBURGH, MITCHEL – 27 Sept. 1762 – 28 June 1763 – To son Edmund all my lands & planta. & marsh & for want of heirs to my son Mitchel Scarburgh, & for want of heirs to my dau. Margaret Thorowgood. To wife Dorothy. To 2 grandsons Thomas Scarburgh Thorowgood & Mitchel Thorowgood. To grandau. Pennebruck Thorowgood. To dau. Sarah Scarburgh. To grandson Henry Custis. To daus. Matilda, Dorothy Wainhouse Custis & Sarah "deducting out of my dau. Dorothy's Part the bill I have of her last husband Edmund Bayley" To my neighbor John Finney. Son Edmund, son in law Benjamin Stuart &

215

son in law John Custis Exrs. Witt: Thomas Teackle, Benjamin Watson.
Codicil: 22 Mar. 1763 - To wife Dorothy all the legacy I gave in my will to my dau. Dorothy Wainhouse Custis, she having died since the writing of the within will. I app. my wife Dorothy my Exec. & my son Edmund my Exr. - p. 215

ANDREWS, WILLIAM - 24 Sept. 1763 - 29 Nov. 1763 - To wife Mary 1/2 my est. provided she consent that her son William Andrews divide same as he thinks fit, if not to have the 1/3 allowed by law. Bal. of est. to Ishmael Mason, als Ishmael Andrews, the child that was charged to my son by the oath of his now wife before he was married to her. Son William Exr. Witt: George Scott, Ann Scott, Rachel Bundick -
Codicil: Should Ishmael Mason, als Ishmael Andrews, die without issue my son William to have the est. Siven the said Ishmael. Same witnesses. p. 225

ROWLES, HAHCOCK NICHOLAS - 5 June 1763 - 29 Nov. 1763 - To bro. John Rowles whole est., to-wit: my land at Andue &c. James Rodgers Exr. Witt: Nathaniel Lecatt, Robert Spiers, Levin Taylor - p. 226

CUSTIS, JOHN - 16 Sept. 1763 - 29 Nov. 1763 - To wife Sarah whole est. during her wid. To son Robinson Custis & unborn child whole est. real & personal to be div. bet. them when my son Robinson comes to age. Should both my children die without issue I give my negroes to Mary Parker & Esther Parker, my daus. in law, & the rest of my est. to my 3 bros., William, Henry & Revel Custis. Wife & bro. William Exrs. - Witt: William East, Southey Simpson, Anne Cropper - p. 227

POULSON, GEORGE - Nunc - Declaration 11 Dec. 1763 - Pro. 28 Dec. 1763 - Whole est. to wife for life then to be div. bet. all my children. Proved by Robert Russell & George Polson - p. 237
In order of prob: Elizabeth Poulson, wid. of the testator qualified.

WISE, WILLIAM,, Jr. - Nunc - Declaration 26 Jan. 1764 - Prob. 1 Feb. 1764 - Whole est. to my father. Proved by Benjamin Pruit & Sarah Guy - p. 237
In order of prob: Thomas Wise qualified.

LURTON, LAZARUS - 12 Feb. 1764 - 28 Feb. 1764 - To cousin Littleton 15 A. in the White Marsh. Witt: Edmund Mason, Thomas Mason, Luke Fosque - p. 240 In order of prob: Littleton Lurton qualified.

WATSON, MOSES - __ __1764 - 28 Feb. 1764 - To youngest son Ephraim Watson (under age) 60 A. being part of the land that was formerly my father & adj. the land purchased by my father of Arthur

Robins. To son Meshack Watson (under age) the remaining part of my land with the water mill – Wife Lender, Daus. Elesha & Tabitha Watson. Mother Sarah Watson. 4 children, Meshack, Ephraim, Eleshe & Tabitha resid. legatees. – Bro. John Watson & wife Lender Exrs. Witt: Edmund Watson, George Harman, John Gores, Elijah Watson. – p. 240
In order of prob: Littleton Dennis app. guardian to Meshack Watson heir at law to the testator.

DIX, SABRA – 5 Jan. 1764 – 28 Feb. 1764 – To dau. Mary Dix. Bal. of est. to daus. Nanny, Elizabeth, & Mary & son Levin Milby. (under age) Son in law James Twiford Exr. Dau. Nanny Twiford Exec. Witt: Southey Simpson, Leah Simpson – p. 241

CUSTIS, THOMAS – 9 May 1763 – 28 Feb. 1764 – To wife whole est. during her wid. or until my son Robinson comes to age. To son Robinson Custis. Son Thomas Custis (under age) To son John Custis (under age) horses given him by his grandfather, Maj. John Wise. To dau. Anne Custis 1/2 doz. silver spoons marked IWS. Should my wife die before my children come to age my friend John Wise, Jr. to have the care & tuition of all my children until they come to age, and in case of my friends death Maj. John Wise, Sr., & my friend Tully R. Wise to have the care & tuition of my said children until they come to age. Wife (no name) & John Wise, Jr. Exrs. Witt: Joseph Cox, Edmund Chambers – p. 242
In order of prob: John Wise, Jr. & Casey Custis qualified.

BUNDICK, GEORGE – 28 June 1763 – 23 Feb. 1764 – To son John Abbott Bundick land on the seaside where I now live, cont. 200 A. To grandson Richard Bundick 200 A. where he now lives provided he let his mother Tabitha Bundick have a quiet & peaceable living during her wid. To Leah Townsend, dau. of Henry Townsend. Bal. of est. to 2 daus. Susanna Sturgis & Rachel Satchell & grandaus. Elizabeth Stephens & Betty Turrell. Son John Abbott Bundick Exr. Witt: William East, Archibald Barns, Charles Gill – p. 244

ABBOT, ROBERT – 26 Dec. 1763 – 28 Feb. 1764 – To son John Abbot 100 A. adj. Hacks Swamp with the place called Fortins Place during his life, reversion to his son. Thomas Abbot. To wife Elizabeth the remainder of my land during her wid. & then to my youngest son Robert Abbot. To 2 youngest sons George & Robert my marsh land cont. 150 A. To wife Elizabeth & her 4 children, Susanna Abbot, Ann Abbot, George Abbot & Robert Abbot 2/3 of the remainder of my est. To son John the other part of my est., he to pay 10 L to my eldest dau. Elizabeth Warrington & 5 L to my dau. Mary Nock, also to take care of & maintain his bro. Mason Abbot. Wife & son John Exrs. Witt: Arnald Morgan, Thomas Perry, Joseph More – p. 250 In order of prob: Mason Abbot heir at law.

BUNTING, JONATHAN – 26 Feb. 1763 – 29 Feb. 1764 – To wife Mary. To 3 youngest daus. Adah, Rebekah & Polly Bunting. To son William

217

Black Bunting all my lands being 150 A. which I bought of William Cole. Children Smith Bunting, William Black Bunting, Amy Milner, Betty Cropper, Adah, Rebekah & Polly Bunting resid. legatees. To sons Smith & William Black Bunting my mill. Wife "Polly" & sons Smith & William Black Bunting Exrs. Witt: Thomas Batson, John Bundick, Beershiba Bundick - p. 251
In order of prob: Smith Bunting heir at law to the testator.

SCARBURGH, MITCHELL - 19 Feb. 1764 - 27 Mar. 1764 - To sister Sarah Scarburgh. To cousin Mitchell Thorowgood. To cousin Scarburgh Stewart. To Edmund Reed. To cousin Sarah Scarburgh. Bro. Americus Scarburgh Exr. & resid. legatee. Witt: Henry Scarburgh, Elizabeth Scarburgh, Susanna Parker - p. 260

COKE, RICHARD - 11 Mar. 1764 - 28 Mar. 1764 - To father & mother negroes for life then to my elder bro. To bro. Samuel Coke. Thomas Bayly, my landlord, to deliver to Sarah Parker one plain gold ring which I had of her. My Exr. to carry my body over the Bay to my father's that I may be buried among my relations. To George Holden 20 s. for recording my will. Father & bro. Samuel Coke Exrs. Witt: William Williams, Littleton Townsend - p. 262
In order of prob: Samuel Coke qualified.

MATTHEWS, JOSEPH - 3 Nov. 1762 - 28 Mar. 1764 - Son George Matthews 180 A. Grandau. Hannah Matthews. To son Joseph Matthews planta. where I now live with 170 A. adj. & 130 A. of swamp adj. the same. To son Southey Matthews mill & 150 A. adj. & 1/2 my swamp land not already given. To son Robins Kendall Matthews 100 A. adj. Gum Branch & swamp land not already given. To son in law William Kendall. Dau. in law Peggy Kendall. Grandau. Esther Delastatius. Grandau. Mary Feddaman. Daus. Jean & Anne Matthews. Son in law Ezekiel Delastatius. Grandsons Peter, Joseph & William Delastatius. To dau. Elizabeth Feddeman all the negroes I lent to Meshack Feddeman. Son Joseph Exr. Witt: Thomas Matthews, John Brooks, Elizabeth Matthews. p. 264
In order of prob: George Matthews heir at law to the testator. Proved by Thomas Matthews & Elizabeth Matthews, now Tunnell.

SCARBURGH, EDMUND - 4 Feb. 1764 - 24 Apr. 1764 - Land purchased of William Read to be sold & 1/3 of proceeds to my wife. Wife to have land at Pungoteague till John Scarburgh comes to lawful age. Bal. of money from sale of land to be div. bet. my sister Sarah Scarburgh, Rosanna Bayly & Sister Mary Stewart's children. My Pungoteague land to John Scarburgh, son of Americus Scarburgh. Cousin Susanna Stuart. Wife Mary Exec. Witt: Henry Gascoyne, William Gascoyne, Teackle Waltham.
p. 266
In order of prob: Mary Scarburgh, wid. of the testator, refusing to qualify, Americus Scarburgh qualified.

ANDREWS, MARY – 13 Mar. 1764 – 24 Apr. 1764 – Dau. Joyce Robins. Dau. Leah Pettigrew. Grandau. Mary Andrews. Grandsons John, William & Gavin Pettigrew. Grandau. Leah Andrews. Son in law Bowdoin Robins & dau. Leah Pettigrew Exrs. Witt: John Bennitt, Ann Bennitt, William Young, Sr. – p. 268

ASHBY, EZEKIEL – 16 Mar. 1764 – 24 Apr. 1764 – Wife Sarah. To son William Ashby planta. where I live. To son John Ashby my small planta. called Fox Ridge. Son George Ashby. Son James Ashby. Son David Ashby. Son Ezekiel Ashby. Dau. Mary Beech. Dau. Thamar Ashby. Dau. Sarah Ashby. Dau. Susanna Ashby. Sons William & John Exrs. Witt: James Rodgers, Peter Watson, Zerobabel Rodgers, John Beach – p. 271
In order of prob: William Ashby, heir at law to the testator.

BAGWELL, ISAIAH – Nunc – 10 Mar. 1764 – 24 Apr. 1764 – I give my 1/2 part of the sloop between Archibald Milby & myself to be sold, also my negro James. Proved by Adah Parker & Archibald Milby – p. 273
In order of prob: Sarah Bagwell, wid. of the testator qualified.

BRADFORD, FISHER – 2 July 1763 – 29 May 1764 – To son Nathaniel Bradford all my land in Matchepungo Neck being 508 A., wife to have use of same during her life. To dau. Anne, wife of Samuel Bagge, 1 s. Dau. Susannah Bradford. Dau. Betty Bradford. Dau. Mary Bradford. Dau. Rachel Bradford. Dau. Esther Bradford. Wife Mary Bradford Exec. Witt: William Stockly, George Bell, John Bradford, James Bradford – p. 278
In order of prob: James Henry app. guardian to Nathaniel Bradford, heir at law to the testator.

BANFIELD, JOHN – 24 Sept. 1763 – 29 May 1764 – Grandson John Walker. Grandson Joseph Walker. Grandson Levin Walker. Grandson Robert Walker. Grandson Henry Walker. Grandson William Walker planta. where I live – Grandson William Walker resid. legatee & Exr. Witt: John Walker, Luke Luker – p. 285
In order of prob: Elizabeth Walker, dau. & heir at law to the testator.

RODGERS, LABAN – 8 Feb. 1764 – 29 May 1764 – Wife Margaret 50 A. where I live except my mother should die before my wife marries, then the first gift to be void & wife to have her thirds. Dau. Elizabeth Rodgers. Son Custis Rodgers land where my father lived & all other lands, he paying the rest of the children 5 L current money at the age of Levin Rogers, his son. To wife 1/2 my moveable est. & the other 1/2 to be sold. Wife & Zerrobabel Rodgers Exrs. Witt: Richard Rodgers, Robert Rodgers. – p. 286
In order of prob: Littleton Dennis app. guardian to Custis Rodgers, heir at law to the testator.
The wording of the foregoing will is vary confusing – Levin was evidently son of Laban & not Custis – S.N.

CUSTIS, JOHN, of Northampton – Not dated – 26 June 1764 – Whole est. to bro. Henry & sisters Anne & Sarah. Uncle Peter Hack Exr. Witt: William Pettit, Jonathan Savage, John Milby – p. 299

BAGWELL, THOMAS – Not dated – 28 June 1764 – Eldest son Stephen Bagwell planta. where I live. To 2 youngest children John & Rose my silver & gold. Wife Patience. Friend Isaiah Bagwell Exr. Witt: John Wharton, Sarah Bagwell, Mark Metcalf – p. 320

SMITH, RICHARD – 5 May 1764 – 30 Oct. 1764 – Wife Aradia. To Elijah Townsend. Wife & Elijah Townsend resid. legatees. Skinner Wallop Exr. Witt: John Smith, Jr., (unclear) Slocomb Blake – p. 342

STOCKLY, CHARLES – 14 Sept. 1764 – 30 Oct. 1764 – To wife Ann Stockly 1 silver spoon marked SDA &c. Dau. Betty Stockly. Grandau. Comfort Stockly. Grandson William Stockly. Grandson Charles Stockly. To dau. Ann Stockly planta. where I live & 100 A. purchased of Nathaniel Shay & William Barker, & for want of heir to Charles Stockly. Grandson Eyrs Stockly. Son in law Nehemiah Stockly. To Joseph Tunnell. Son in law Alexander Stockly, Grandson Joseph Stockly. To Elizabeth Lombard, dau. of Samuel Lombard. Daus. Ann & Betty Stockly resid. legatees. Wife Ann, Nehemiah Stockly, Alexander Stockly, Littleton Dennis & Southy Simpson Exrs. Witt: Joseph Stockley, William Hutson, Hannah Benston – p. 343

WISE, THOMAS – 7 Sept. 1764 – 30 Oct. 1764 – Son Samuel Wise 300 A. where I live, also part of land purchased of Ambros Willet, provided he pay my son Spencer Wise 50L To son Samuel my water mill. To grandau. Anne Wise, dau. of my son Thomas, 200 A., being the remainder of the land purchased of Ambrose Willet, her father. Thomas to have the privilege of living thereon during his life. To wife 1/3 of my land during her wid. Bal. of est. to be div. bet. all my children. Wife & son Samuel Exrs. Witt: Thomas Riley, Nathaniel Coverly, William Dunton, George Melson. – p. 345
In order of prob: Spencer Wise heir at law to the testator. Esther Wise & Samuel Wise qualified.

ARMITRADER, LITTLETON – 11 Oct. 1764 – 30 Oct. 1764 – To son "Arter" Son Henry. Son Samuel. To son Arthur Armitrader all my lands & my water mill. To daus. "Abgil" & Rose. Unborn child. John Tayler & Abraham Tayler Exrs. Witt: John Coleburn, John Spiers – p. 348

JAMES, DAVID – 2 Sept. 1764 – 31 Oct. 1764 – To wife Elizabeth planta. where I now live for life or wid. & whole personal est. To son William Sacker James planta. where I live & for want of heirs to my youngest son David James. Son Thomas. Children Laban, Thomas, Robert, Sarah & David resid. legatees. Wife & son William Sacker James Exrs. Witt: Arnold Morgin, John Cowley, Edward Gunter, Jr, – p. 348
In order of prob: William Sacker James heir at law to the testator.

WATSON, SARAH – 6 Nov. 1764 – 27 Nov. 1764 – Daus. Comfort Henderson, Patience Henderson, Mary Watson, Joyce Benson & Sarah Watson. To Philender Watson. Son John & David Watson. Son in law Edmund Watson & son John Watson Exrs. Witt: Elijah Watson, Benson Bradford, Elizabeth Stringer – p. 349

COURTNEY, CHARLES – 31 Oct. 1764 – 27 Nov. 1764 – To William Rolley 50 A. at the head of my land adj. Thomas Baleys land. Tabitha Rolley to have use of same during her life. To Garthery Taylor, dau. of Jacob Taylor the remaining 50 A. of my land. James Rolley's 5 children & Jacob Taylor's children resid. legatees. Thomas Riley Exr. Witt: Jacob Ayers, James Rolley, Marey Turner – p. 350
In order of prob: Abraham Turner, who intermarried with Mary, heir at law to the testator, being present & having nothing to object, said will admitted to probate.

STRINGER, THOMAS – 12 Apr. 1764 – 27 Nov. 1764 – Mill & 1 A. to be sold, also the 7 A. adj. the said mill formerly bought of Mr. Abel Upshur, & after payment of debts residue to be div. bet. my wife Elizabeth & daus. Elizabeth Ames, Mary Read & Elishe Stringer. To son John Stringer planta. where I live being 167 A. Wife & bro. in law William Savage Exrs. Witt: John Ambler, William Shea, Obedience Johnson – p. 351
In order of prob: John Stringer heir at law to the testator.

GARRITSON, RICHARD – 19 Nov. 1764 – 27 Nov. 1764 – To wife Esther whole est. during her wid. Son Jonathan. 3 daus. & unborn child resid. legatees. Wife & bro Jonathan Garritson Exrs. Witt: Richard Meers, Churchill Darby – p. 352
In order of prob: "Richard Garrison"

LAYLOR, ARTHUR – 22 July 1764 – 27 Nov. 1764 – Wife Sophia. Dau. Mary Laylor. Son Babel Laylor. Wife & friend William Joyne Exrs. Witt: Robert Watson, Bartholomew Meers. – p. 354
In order of prob: Babel Laylor heir at law to the testator appeared by James Rodgers, his guardian.

WAINHOUSE, FRANCIS – 8 Feb. 1764 – 22 Nov. 1764 – Mr. Thomas Rispass of Carolina, in "Bleadford" (Beaufort) County to make sale of my land in said County. Land on the South side of the road running from John Ambler's to a mill to be leased for 16 years, then to my youngest dau. Sarah Wainhouse. All my land on the North side of the road to my dau. Elizabeth Wainhouse. Wife Anne. My Belhaven place to be rented. Wife & 2 daus. resid. legatees. Bro. William Wainhouse & wife Exrs. Witt: Ismay Johnson, Thomas Howell – p. 357
In order of prob: Littleton Dennis app. guardian to Elizabeth & Sarah, daus. & co heirs of the testator.

GOWTEE, MARY - 20 Aug. 1764 - 27 Nov. 1764 - To son Joseph Gowtee planta. where I live. Son John Gowtee. Son Andrew. Son Lisney Gowtee. Dau Trephina. Dau. Mary. Sons Lisney & John Exrs. Witt: John Mercer, Leaven Taylor, William Shipham - p. 360 In order of prob: Joseph Gowtee heir at law to the testatrix.

KNIGHT, THOMAS - 2 Dec. 1760 - 29 Jan. 1765 - Son George Knight to be in the tuition of James Henry, Griffin Stith & Thomas Dolby until he is 21. James Henry, Griffin Stith & Thomas Dolby Exrs. Witt: Thomas Parramore, Andrew Newton, George Drummond. - p. 361 In order of prob: The Exrs. named in the foregoing will refusing to act Thomas Fisher qualified.

JOHNSON, GEORGE - 25 Feb. 1764 - 29 Jan. 1765 - To son John Johnson 70 A. purchased of Thomas Fisher. Dau. Sarah Bloxom. Son George Johnson 1 s. Dau. Mary Ann Johnson. To son Solomon Johnson planta. cont. 101 A. & the water mill & 30 A. purchased of Thomas Fisher & 20 A. of Marsh of Muddy Creek. To son John 30 A. Marsh on Muddy Creek. Son Solomon resid. legatee, "and for him to keep his mother". Son Solomon & bro. William Exrs. Witt: Arnold Morgin, William Bennet, Mary Morgin - p. 365 In order of prob: John Johnson heir at law to the testator. William Bloxom opposed the said will being admitted. Court ord. that the same be admitted to probate.

JOHNSON, SAMUEL - 12 Jan. 1765 - 20 Jan. 1765 - To cousin Joshua Johnson 100 A. where I live. Cousin Rachel Johnson. Sister in law Mary Johnson. John Johnson the elder, Solomon Johnson, Joshua Johnson & Rachel Johnson resid. legatees. Solomon Johnson Exr. Witt: Nathaniel Bird, Thomas Bloxom, Susanna Hinman - p. 369 In order of prob: John Johnson heir at law to the testator.

LITCHFIELD, WILLIAM - 24 Sept. 1764 - 29 Jan. 1765 - Wife to have use of my land during her wid. Son Francis Litchfield my land & planta. Son Jacob Litchfield. Bal. of est. to be div. bet. my children except Jacob. Wife (no name) Exec. Witt: Thomas Riley, Thomas Riley, Jr., James Rolley. - p. 370 In order of prob: George Holden guardian of Jacob Litchfield, heir at law to the testator. Tabitha Litchfield qualified.

BRADFORD, WILLIAM - 8 Oct. 1761 - 26 Feb. 1765 - Son Jacob. Son John, Wife Frances. Children Mary, Rachel, Margaret & William Bradford resid. legatees. Wife & son Jacob Exrs. Witt: Arthur Upshur, John Boggs, Henry Custis. - p. 376

COLLINGS, THOMAS - 24 Jan. 1761 - 26 Feb. 1765 - Son William Collings. Son Thomas Collings. Son James Collings. To son Timothy Collings planta. cont. 140 A. where I live. Son Timothy resid. legatee & Exr. Anne Hatfeld Exec. Witt: William Marshall, Thomas Beavans, Samuel Henderson.
Codicil: To grandau. Peggy, dau. of Timothy Collings & Anne his

wife, To grandson John Collings, son of Timothy & Anne, his wife. –
p. 377

JAMES, WILLIAM – 18 May 1764 – 26 Feb. 1765 – Wife Amey. To
son Thomas James planta. where I live being 109 A. & for want of
heirs to my dau. Fanny James. To dau. Johannah Bradford for life,
reversion to her 4 daus. Retter, Leagh, Fanny & Mettelder. To dau.
Margaret Lurton for life, reversion to her 2 daus. Tabitha & Semer
Lurton. To dau. Sarah Foskey for life, reversion to her 3 sons Luke,
George & John Foskey. Daus. Susannah & Rachel James. Wife Exec.
Witt: Mark Metcalf, Leah Badgers, William Savage. – p. 379

TIZEKER, JOSEPH – 30 Mar. 1764 – 26 Mar. 1765 – Bro. William
Tizeker. Bro. William Tizeker. Sister Betty Parker. Sister Sarah
Boggs. To my mother. Cousin Robert Boggs. Cousin Nanny Parker.
Cousin Betty Wise. Bro. William resid. legatee & Exr. – Witt:
Upshur Teackle – p. 389

FOGG, JOHN – 2⁷ Dec. 1763 – 30 Apr. 1765 – Grandau. Rosannah
Small. Cousin Grace Houseton Fogg. Son Elijah & dau. Canady Small
resid. legatees. Son Elijah Exr. Witt: Jacob Broadwater, William
Broadwater, Jr. – p. 418
In order of prob: 25 June 1765 – Robert Small qualified, the exr.
named in the foregoing will refusing to act.

TAYLOR, ABRAHAM – 30 Mar. 1765 – 25 June 1765 – Son Joshua
Taylor. Daus. Rachel, Comfort & Elizabeth Taylor. Son Teackle
Taylor. Unborn child. Wife Sarah & son Teackle resid. legatees &
Exrs. Witt: Bartholomew Taylor, Richard Read. – p. 433
In order of prob: Littleton Scarburgh Major app. guardian to Teackle
Taylor, heir at law to the testator.

CUSTIS, WILLIAM – Not dated – 25 June 1765 – Wife Anne. Son
John. Dau. Sarah. Dau. Elizabeth. Dau. Leah. Unborn child. Bro.
Henry Custis & John Boggs Exrs. Witt: Upshur Teackle, William
Bogs – p. 436

BELL, MARY – 19 Apr. 1759 – 25 June 1765 – Son Nathaniel Bell.
Grandson Mary Darby, dau. of Benjamin Darby. Grandau. Anne Stock-
ly. Dau. Rachel & to her son Nathaniel Darby. Grandson Nathaniel
Bevins. Grandson John Darby. Grandson Robert Bell. Grandson
Nathaniel Bell resid. legatee. Son Nathaniel Bell Exr. Witt: John
West, Agnes West, Abel West – p. 437

COOK, RACHEL – 23 Mar. 1765 – 25 June 1765 – To dau. Esther
Russel 40 A. where she lives for life, reversion to my son Benjamin
Ryall. Dau. Sarah Russell 40 A. where she lives for life then to my
son Benjamin Ryall. Son Benjamin Ryall Exr. Witt: William Young,
Sr., Leah Kelly, Esther Kelly – p. 442
In order of probate: "Benjamin Royal"

SMITH, JOHN – 23 Jan. 1765 – 30 July 1765 – To dau. Esther Savage. To son John Smith land where I live in Accomack & 2 tracts in Worcester County, Maryland, one called Waterfield & the other called Addition, also 300 A. on Assateague Island. To grandau. Leah Welburn 100 A. land & marsh on Assateague Island. To grandau. Esther Savage 100 A. on Assateague Island. To son in law Eyres Gillett, "for my dau. Mary, his wife' 100 A. on Assateague Island for life, reversion to my grandson John Gillett. To son in law Griffin Savage & my dau. Esther, his wife. To grandau. Ann Savage 100 A. on Assateague Island. Grandson Eyres Gillett. Grandau. Ann Gillett. Dau. Sarah Shankland. Grandson Daniel Welburn "all my right & title I have of a negro girl called Jenny that Mr. William Coard gave to my son Arthur Smith to my dau. Sarah Shankland". Son John Smith & son in law Eyres Gillett Exrs. Friends Bowdoin Robins, Griffin Savage & Daniel Gore overseers. Witt: Bowdoin Robins, Skinner Marshall, Daniel Walker, Love Ellis – p. 453

SMITH, HENRY – 26 May 1765 – 30 July 1765 – Son George Smith. Wife Exec. Witt: William Smith, John Arrington – p. 457
In order of prob: Susanna Smith, wid. of the testator qualified.

BELOTE, HANCOCK – 17 Mar. 1765 – 30 July 1765 – To wife Abigil all my land during her wid, then to be sold & the money div. bet. my 8 children, Mary, Hancock, Elisha, Sarah, Betty, John, William & Abbigil. To dau. Siner Ames. Dau. Elizabeth Belote. Sons John & William to live with their mother until 18 years of age. Bezaleel Watson & wife Exrs. Witt: Margaret Martin, Littleton Darby – p. 478

HEATH, JOSEPH – 22 June 1765 – 29 Oct. 1765 – To wife Comfort whole est. during her wid. To son Fletcher Heath 80 A. adjoining John Walker & James Rodgers. To son Joseph the remainder of my land. Daus. Leah & Margaret Heath resid. legatees. Wife Exec. - Witt: Henry Heath, Margaret Heath, Major Charnock, – p. 578
In order of prob: Joseph Heath heir at law to the testator.

DRUMMOND, RICHARD – __ Apr. 1744 – 31 Oct. 1765 – To wife Katherine Drummond land left me by my father Richard Drummond, being 600 A. of Hunting Creek, including the 1/2 of Half Moon Island during her wid., also the use of my water mill on Hunting Creek, & then to my dau. Elisha Drummond the above planta. at her mother's death. To dau. Ann Drummond water mill, & planta. my father bought of Jacob Litchfield; should both my children die without heirs I give the planta. on Hunting Creek to my bro. Spencer Drummond. Wife & John Kendall of Northampton Exrs. Not witnessed & not signed – p. 595
In order of prob: Presented by Thomas Bayly who intermarried with Ann Drummond, dau. of the testator, proved by Thomas Riley, George Drummond & George Holden, Gent: Thomas Bayly qualified.

MEARS, BARTHOLOMEW – 4 July 1761 – 29 Apr. 1766 – To son Meshack planta. where I now live with the land I bought of John Nock

& should he offer to sell same the said land to go to my son Robert Mears. Wife Rachel Mears. Son Shadrick Mears. Wife Rachel & children Jonathan, Robert, Susana, Rachel, Sarah, Elizabeth, Shadrack & Leah resid. legatees. Wife to bring up my son Meshack. Robert Abbott, Ralph Justice, Solomon Burd & John Watts to div. est. Wife Exec. Witt: John Watts, Isaac Williams, John Evans - p. 600
In order of prob: Jonathan Mears heir at law to the testator.

WATSON, ABEL - 31 Oct. 1765 - 29 Apr. 1766 - Bro. Littleton Watson. Bro. Robert Watson. Cousins Sarah Bayley & Susannah Bayley, & should either of them die without heirs their part to descend to Elizabeth Bayley. To the children of Mary Bayley, dec., Edmund, Welthy, John, Isme & Elizabeth. Cousin Richard Bayley. Sister Tabitha Rogers children, viz: John, Robert, Elizabeth & Jeaney resid. legatees. Bro. Robert Exr. Witt: William Puezey, Edmund Heath, Edmund Heath, Jr. p. 602

HINMAN, BAYLY - 18 Dec. 1765 - 20 Apr. 1766 - To wife Ann my land during her wid. & then to my dau "Jaca" Hinman & for want of issue to my 2 cousins Levin Hinman & John Hinman. To Solomon Gray. Wife Ann & dau. Jaca resid. legatees - John Young, Sr. & Wife Ann Exrs. Witt: William Young, Sr., Elizabeth Fitchet, Ann Hinman - p. 603
In order of prob: Littleton Dennis guardian to the heir at law.

LUKER, JOHN - 14 Nov. 1765 - 29 Apr. 1766 - Wife Mary. Grandson Charles Parker - To grandau. Mary Parker. Grandau. Peggy Parker. Dau. Peggy Parker. Wife Mary, son John Luker, grandson Charles Parker, grandaus. Mary & Peggy Parker resid. legatees. Luke Luker & Robert Parker Exrs. Witt: Luke Luker - p. 604

KELLUM, ELIJAH - Nunc. - Proved 23 Nov. 1765 - Prob. 29 Apr. 1766 - Mother Abigale Kellam whole est. Proved by John Walthom, William Joynce. - p. 605
In order of prob: Stephen Kellam qualified.

FISH, JOHN - 4 Apr. 1765 - 30 Apr. 1766 - "I bequeath all South pint the whole patten belonging to me unto Joseph Crockett". To Spencer Tyler all my part of hog neck. To Lazarus Bacor. To Jacob Tylor. To David Tylor. Joseph Crockett Exr. Witt: Butler Tylor, Arthur Parkes, Sarah Tylor - p. 608.

HICKMAN, WILLIAM, Sr. - 13 Sept. 1765 - 30 Apr. 1766 - To son Richard Hickman all the land I now own. Son William Hickman. Dau. Mary Stakes. Dau. Annabeller Willit. Wife Christian Hickman. Son Joshua Hickman. Dau. Keziah Hickman. Dau. Sarah Northam. Wife & son Joshua, dau. Kesiah & dau. Sarah Northam resid. legatees. Wife Exec. & son in law Thomas Northam Exr. Witt: Laban Simpson, George Hickman, Sarah Hickman - p. 609

BELOTTE, JOHN – 22 Feb. 1765 – 27 May 1766 – To bro. Noah Belotte land where my mother in law Sarh Belotte now lives, it being the land which descended to me by the death of my father Noah Belotte, & for want of heirs to my bro. Jonas Belotte. To bro. Noah my right & title to a tract of land near Deep Creek purchased by my father Noah Belotte of a certain Jonathan Chambers. To sister Leah Belotte. Uncle Solomon Bunting Exr. Witt: Peter Fitzgarrald, George Bonewell, Betty Waterfield – p. 611
In order of prob: Laban Belotte heir at law to the testator.

STUART, BENJAMIN – 18 Nov. 1765 – 27 May 1766 – To son Andrew. Wife Matilda. Dau. Margaret Stuart. Dau. Lizebethy Stuart. Dau. Sarah. Son Scarburgh Stuart. Dau. Nancy. Unborn child. Wife & children Margaret, Elizabeth, Sarah, Scarburgh, Nancy & unborn child resid. legatees. Thomas Hall & William Joyne Exrs. Witt: Thomas Delanaway, Elizabeth Larance – p. 613

LECATT, NATHANIEL – 6 Mar. 1766 – 24 June 1766 – To cousin Shadrack Lecatt. To friend John Read. Friend Luke Luker to have 1/2 the great mill which my bro. in law John Rowles gave me by his last well & testament. Bal. of est. to be sold & after payment of debts residue to be div. between Littleton Lecatt, Rachel, the wife of Robert Spiers & John Rowles. Luke Luker & Shadrack Lecatt Exrs. Witt: John Milby, Richard Walter, Labon Belote – p. 615

WELBURN, DANIEL – 7 May 1766 – 24 June 1766 – Wife Rebecca. To eld. son Daniel Welburn land where I live & for want of heirs to my 2nd son James Welburn. To son James Welburn all my swamp land given to me by my father Daniel Welburn's will. My Island land on Assateague to be div. bet. sons Daniel, James & Riley Welburn & my dau. Elizabeth Welburn. Sons Daniel, James & Riley Welburn & daus. Leah & Elizabeth Welburn resid. legatees. Bro. Francis Welburn & Ayres Gillett Exrs. Witt: Joseph Christopher, Leady Christopher, Tabithey Stevenson, William Gilett. – p. 620
In order of prob: Littleton Dennis guardian to Daniel Welburn, Inf't. heir at law to the testator.

EWELL, NAOMY – 8 Jan. 1757 – 24 June 1766 – To son William Whittington Ewell whole est. Friend John Watts Exr. Witt: Thomas Bayly, Tabitha Gilchrist, Andrew Gilchrist – p. 624
In order of prob: John Watts, the Exr. names in the foregoing will refusing to act, William Ewell qualified.

BLAKE, ELIAS – 9 Apr. 1766 – 24 June 1766 – Wife Bridget Blake sole legatee & Exec. Witt: Thomas Beavans, John Johnson, Samuel Taylor – p. 625
In order of prob: William Blake heir at law to the testator.

WHARTON, ANN – 26 Oct. 1765 – 24 June 1766 – Bro. James Wharton. To Tabitha Wharton (under 12) dau. of my bro. John. To John Wharton (under 12) son of my bro. John. To Nanny, dau. of Edmond

Poleson. To Nanny, dau. of my bro. John. To John Revel & Sally Revel, children of John Revel, dec. Bro. John Exr. Witt: James Scott, Pat: Colquhoun – p. 630

PARKER, JOHN, Ship Carpenter – 24 June 1766 – 30 July 1766 – To nephew Sacker Parker, son of my bro. Sacker Parker, dec., 1/2 of 100 A. purchased of my said bro. near Hunting Creek, adj. the land now in the possession of my said nephew, & the other 1/2 of said land to be sold for the payment of my debts. Wife Elizabeth "who now lays very sick". Dau. in law Sarah Evans. Son in law Zerrobable Evans. Bal. of est. to be div. bet the children of Isaiah Evans, dec., nephew Sacker Parker, the children of John Scott by my sister Sophia & my wife Elizabeth. Wife & Edmond Poulson Exrs. Witt: Isaac Smith, Anne Bushford – p. 632 In order of prob: Littleton Dennis guardian to Sacker Parker, Inf't. heir at law to the testator.

EVANS, ZERROBABLE – 29 June 1766 – 30 July 1766 – To Bro. Isaiah Evans 150 A. devised me by my dec. father Isaiah Evans. Mother Elizabeth Parker negro devised me by my father in law John Parker, dec., for life, reversion to my sister Sarah Evans. Bro. William Evans resid. legatee. Mother Elizabeth Parker & Isaac Smith Exrs. Witt: Sarah Belote, Rachael Hargrass – p. 633
In order of prob: William Evans heir at law to the testator.

FITCHETT, WITHERTUN – 18 Apr. 1764 – 26 Aug. 1766 – To Tabitha Fitchett whole est. & for want of heirs to Mary Fitchett & for want of heirs to her bro. John Fitchett. Bro. Jacob Fitchett Exr. Witt: Bayly Hinman, Jr. Stephen Walker – p. 643

FINNY, WILLIAM – 7 Nov. 1764 – 28 Aug. 1766 – Wife Joanna. To the children of my son William Finny, dec., 1 s. each. To each of the two youngest children of my dau. Sarah Bell, dec., 10 L viz: Levin & Leah. Daus. Attalanta & Tabitha. Wife & 6 children, John, Rachel, Attalanta, Agnes, Betty, or Elizabeth, & Tabitha resid. legatees. Son John & daus. Attalanta & Tabitha Exrs. Witt: John Bayly, Charles Bayly, Mary Bayly – p. 643

SIMPKINS, WILLIAM – 3 Feb. 1765 – 30 Sept. 1766 – Wife Sabra. To sons William & Arthur Simpkins all my lands in Accomack & Northampton to be equally divided bet. them at my wife's death or marriage. Rose Roberts, mother of my wife (now living). To son William all my Pott Mettle at my Macuty Bay Plantation. Dau Sabra. Dau. Mary Stott. Dau. Patience Roberts. Wife Sabra & Sons William & Arthur Exrs. Witt: Edmund Watson, Ferreby Stringer, James Henry – p. 647
In order of prob: William Simpkins heir at law to the testator.

TAYLOR, BARTHOLOMEW – 4 Feb. 1766 – 30 Sept. 1766 – To son John my land, houses & orchards – Wife Mary to have use of 1/2 my land for life. To sons Bartholomew & Major & dau. Margaret. Wife Exec. (had other children but names not given) Witt: Littleton Scar-

burgh Major, Leaven Taylor. p. 649
In order of prob: John Taylor heir at law to the testator.

SMITH, Huet – 5 May 1766 – 30 Sept. 1766 – Wife Isabella whole est. during her wid. To one of the children of my dau. Mary Savage. To one of the children of my dau. Ann. To grandson John Smith planta. at the seaside. To dau. Elizabeth Smith the use of my land at Cradock, if she be single at my wife's death, till my grandson George Smith comes to the age of 21, then 1/3 as long as she remains single. To grandson George Smith my planta. at Cradock at the expiration of the gifts to my wife & dau., & for want of heirs to be div. bet. my 3 daus. Elizabeth Smith, Mary Savage, Ann Kellam. Grandau. Margaret Smith. Wife Elizabeth Exec. 3 daus. resid. legatees, Witt: Littleton Scarburgh Major, Thomas Teackle, Jr. – p. 650
In order of prob: John Smith heir at law to the testator.

OWEN, RACHEL – 26 July 1766 – 30 Sept. 1766 – Dau. Sally Owen. Dau. Mary Morris. John Morris – Sally Owen Exrs. Witt: John Watts, Joseph Campbell – p. 651

REGGS, JOSEPH – 8 June 1766 – 1 Oct. 1766 – To son John Reggs my planta. cont. 100 A. To son Joseph Reggs. Dau. Rachel Regs. Bal. of est. to be div. bet. all my children. Son John Reggs Exr. Witt: William Young, Sr., Joshua Reggs, Richard Onions – p. 653
In order of prob: Abraham Reggs heir at law to the testator.

MARSHALL, PETER – 18 Oct. 1766 – 25 Nov. 1766 – To son Jenepher Marshall. To Thomas Marshall. Bal. personal est. to be div. bet. 2 sons Jenepher & Thomas. To dau. Scarburgh Hollen 1 s. Sons Jenepher & Thomas Exrs. Witt: Ayres Gillett, Peter Marshall, Jr., Patience Marshall – p. 663

DRUMMOND, GEORGE – 9 May 1765 – 25 Nov. 1766 – To son Richard Drummond all my land & planta. at Accomack Court House where I now live and my land at Back Creek on the Bayside. To dau. Anne Drummond all my land & my interest in any land at Messongo Creek. Should my said 2 children die under age & without issue the land at Accomack Court House to go to George Drummond, the son of my bro. William, & my land at Back Creek & Messongo to Richard Drummond, son of my dec. bro. Spencer Drummond. To mother Anne Buncle. Son Richard & dau. Anne Drummond resid. legatees. Bro. William Drummond & friend James Henry Exrs. Witt: J. Manby, David Bowman, John Powell – p. 664

COPES, ROBERT – 2 Aug. 1763 – 25 Nov. 1766 – To son Daniel Copes planta. where I now live which I purchased of Richard Smith, as far as a ditch between my son Giles Copes & the said planta., it being 1/2. Wife Elizabeth. To son Giles Copes. To son Daniel Copes. To son Peter Copes. Son Jesse (under 18) Sons Daniel & Jesse resid. legatees. Grandson Southy Marriner. Son Daniel Exr. with the advice of my friend Covington Corbin. Witt: Covington Corbin, John Holt, Jr.

Elizabeth Adams – p. 666
In order of prob: Giles Copes heir at law to the testator.

MARSHALL, SOLOMON – 9 Nov. 1766 – 25 Nov. 1766 – To bro. Charles Marshall planta. where I now live. Bro. William Marshall. To bro. George Marshall planta. where Stephen Townsend lives. To bro. Daniel. Sister Leah Marshall. Bro. Levin Marshall. Bros. George & Levin resid. legatees. Bro. Charles Exr. Witt: Thomas Marshall, Marshall Townsend, William Marshall – p. 668
In order of prob: William Marshall heir at law to the testator.

CUSTIS, WILLIAM – 10 Nov. 1766 – 25 Nov. 1766 – To son John. To son Bagwell Custis. To son William Custis. To dau. Betty all her mother's wearing clothes. To grandau. Leah Custis. Bal. est. to be div. bet. my children & their heirs. Sons John & Bagwell Exrs. Witt: James Arbuckle, Southy Bull – p. 670

MASON, BENNET – 17 Apr. 1762 – 30 Dec. 1766 – To son Edmund Mason planta. where I live for life, reversion to his heirs. To son Thomas planta. where he lives adj. the White Marsh. To son Jeremiah Mason. To son Jacob Mason. To dau. Bridget. To dau. Susannah Clemmoms. To dau. Nanny. Bal. of est. to 5 children, Nanny Mason, Bridget Mason, Jeremiah Mason & Jacob Mason & Susannah Clemmons. John Kitson, Thomas Crippen & Richard Justice to div. est. Sons Thomas & Jeremiah Exrs. Witt: John Cowley, Solomon Wimbrough, William Goodday – p. 675
In order of prob: Edmund Mason heir at law.

NOCK, BENJAMIN – 7 July 1765 – 31 Dec. 1766 – To son William 300 A. on the East side of the land where I now live. To son Benjamin 250 A. being the remaining part of the land where I live. To son Levi Nock 200 A. land & marsh on Muddy Creek that formerly belonged to George Johnson dec. To dau. Patience Accor. To grandchildren which my dau. Sarah bore to Henry Reed. Sons William & Benjamin Exrs. Witt: James Rodgers, Elijah Chance, Rachel Beach – p. 685
William Nock heir at law

BEAVANS, THOMAS – 5 Oct. 1766 – 31 Dec. 1766 – Wife Mary. To son William Beavans planta. where I now live cont. 125 A. To dau. Elizabeth Beavans. Bal. of est. to wife during her wid. to bring up my children, namely William Beavans, Thomas Beavans, Tabitha Beavans, George Beavans, Joshua Beavans & Mary Beavans. Wife & bro. Joshua Exrs. Witt: Joshua Collens, William Beavans – p. 688
In order of prob: George Holden guardian to William Beavans, Inf't. heir at law to the testator.

BURTON, MARY – 14 Apr. 1765 – 27 Jan. 1767 – Grandau. Anne Arbuckle, now Anne Teackle, wife of Levin Teackle. To great-grandau. Anne Purnall, dau. to my grandau. Euphime Purnell. To grandau Mary Stewart. To great-grandau. Anne Snead Stewart. To grandau.

Catherine Arbuckle. To grandson Archibald Campbell. To each of my grandchildren in North Carolina, viz: Leah & Eupheme Snead. To greatgrandson John Eustace. To grandau. Anne Snead, dau. of my son John Snead in North Carolina. To Anne Snead, dau. of John Snead in Accomack County. To my 4 grandchildren in North Carolina, viz: Jane, Catherine, Leah & Eupheme Snead. Jane & William Wilson Snead, children of my son John in North Carolina. Greatgrandau. Catherine Arbuckle, dau. of James Arbuckle. Great-grandau. Catharine Murray in Worcester County. Grandchildren Eupheme Purnall, Mary Stewart, & Catharine Arbuckle resid. legatees. Friends Col. Thomas Parramore, John Snead & grandson James Arbuckle Exrs. Witt: Levin Stewart, George Millechops, William Arbuckle – p. 707

EVANS, MARK – 4 Jan. 1767 – 28 Jan. 1767 – To son John Evans 75 A. where he now lives. To son Mark Evans 60 A. where he now lives. The remaining part ot my planta. I give to my dau. Rachel Evans and dau. Mary Evans. To children John, Mark, Rachel & Mary all my marsh, being 60 A. Children resid. legatee. Son John Evans Exr. Witt: William Young, Sr., Comfort West, Elizabeth West – p. 709. In order of prob: John Evans heir at law to the testator.

COULBURN, TEMPERANCE – 25 Jan. 1767 – 25 Feb. 1767 – To dau. Susannah Huffington. To grandson George Coleburn. To son William Coleburn. To son John Coleburn. Children William, John & Susannah Huffington resid. legatees. Witt: John Coleburn, John Wharton. – p. 717

JAMES, AMEY – Not dated – 24 Feb. 1767 – To son Thomas James 1 s. To dau. Sarah Fosque 5 s. To dau. Margaret, or Peggy, Lurton. To dau. Jonna Bradford. Dau. Famy James. Daus. Susannah, Rachel & Famy James resid. legatees. Dau. Susannah Exec. Witt: Thomas Mitcalf, Mary Dix, Levin Bunting. – p. 719

TOWNSEND, STEPHEN – 4 Feb. 1767 – 25 Feb. 1767 – To son Stephen Townsend. To dau. Jean Cambell. To son Littleton Townsend. Dau. Mary Townsend. To son James Townsend. 5 children before named resid. legatees. Sons Stephen & Littleton & dau. Mary Townsend Exrs. Witt: John Townsend. Jr., William Hutson, William Delastatius – p. 720

WHITE, WILLIAM – 5 Feb 1767 – 26 Feb. 1767 – To son William White 400 A. on the South side of my planta. To son George White 200 A. on the North side of planta. where my son William now lives. Wife Mary. To dau. Elizabeth Finney. To dau. Sarah Drummond. To dau. Annobellow White. Wife & son William Exrs. Witt: Charles Bagwell, Anne Bagwell. p. 721
In order of prob: William White heir at law to the testator.

WALKER, JOSEPH – 1 Feb. 1767 – 31 Mar. 1767 – Son Joseph Walker. Daus. Ann & Betty Walker. Daus. in law Sarah & Leah Massey. Bro. in law Nathaniel Stockly & wife Neoma Exrs. Witt:

Mary Ann Jenkinson, Leah Stockly - p. 730

HUTCHINSON, JAMES - 10 Dec. 1766 - 31 Mar. 1767 - To wife Sarah planta. where I now live cont. 138 A. during her life & then to my son James Hutchinson. To son John Hutchinson. Son Stephen. Daus. Martha & Nancy Hutchinson. Son Thomas (all under 21) Wife & friend Jonathan Bunting Exrs. Witt: Robert Jenkinson, George Holden - p. 731
In order of prob: James Hutchinson heir at law to the testator.

Orders - 1768-1769

BRITTINGHAM, JEDIDAH - Adm. his est. to Rachel Brittingham - Andrew Gootee sec. 26 Apr. 1768 - p. 5

FINNEY, WILLIAM - Adm. his est. to Mary Finney - Thomas Crippen & Charles Bagwell sec. - 26 Apr. 1768 - p. 8

MASON, EDMUND - Adm. his est. to Thomas Mason - Stephen Coleman & Stephen Bloxom sec. - 26 Apr. 1768 - p. 8

ARMITRADER, ISRAEL - Adm. his est. to Comfort Armitrader - Littleton Armitrader & William Morgan sec. - 31 May 1768 - p. 47

STRINGER, JOHN - Adm. his est. to Elizabeth Stringer - William Doote & William Joines sec. - 28 June 1768

PARKER, George Matompkin - Adm. his est. to Elizabeth Parker - William Drummond & John Dix. Jr. sec. - 26 July 1768 - p. 111

RULE, PEGGY - Adm. her est. to Edward Parrish, one of the people called Quakers. Tully Robinson Wise & James Arbuckle sec. - 30 Nov. 1768 - p. 225

FEDDIMAN, SAMUEL - Adm. his est. to George Stewart - Littleton Dennis sec. - 1 Dec. 1768 - p. 233

RODGERS, JOHN - Adm. his est. to Mary Rodgers - John Reid & William Groten sec. 31 Jan. 1769 - p. 250

Orders - 1769-1770

MARTIN, HENRY - Adm. his est. to Elizabeth Martin - John Hannaford, Jr. & Andrew Martin sec. - 28 Feb. 1769 - p. 5

ABBOTT, RICHARD - Adm. his est. to John Abbott - Thomas Parramore sec. - 3 Mar. 1769 - p. 49

SMITHERS, MOSES - Adm. his est. to Judith Smithers - Jonathan

Mears & Ralph Corbin Jr., sec. – 28 Mar. 1769 – p. 52

BEACH, BENJAMIN – Adm. his est. to Tabitha Beach – John Custis & Levi Nock sec. 28 Mar. 1769 – p. 54

NORTHAM, THOMAS – Adm. his est. to Sarah Northam – Richard Hickman, Jr. sec. – 29 Mar. 1769 – p. 60

ASHBY, WILLIAM – Adm. his est. to John Ashby – Zorobabel Rodgers sec. – 29 Mar. 1769 – p. 61

JOLLOFF, JOHN – Adm. his est. to Mary Jolloff – 29 Mar. 1769 – p. 61

BOGGS, WILLIAM, Jr. – Adm. his est. to Robert Boggs – 29 Mar. 1769 – P. 61

MASSEY, JOHN – Adm. his est. unadministered by his late wid. & Exec., Elizabeth Massey, to Meshack Feddiman, with will annexed – Jabez Pitt & James Selby sec. 30 May 1770 – p. 185

HOWARD, DANIEL – Adm. his est. to John Shae – Jonathan Meers sec. – 29 Aug. 1769 – p. 218

BRADFORD, ABEL – Adm. his est. to Jacob Bradford – James Rodgers & William Nock sec. – 29 Aug. 1769 – p. 220

WATT, THOMAS – Adm. his est. to Charles Bayly, Sr. – Luke Luker sec. – 28 Nov. 1769 – p. 267

DARBY, BENJAMIN – Adm. his est. to Edward Ker – Littleton Dennis sec. – 28 Nov. 1769 – p. 268

WHITE, LABAN – Adm. his est. to William Williams – George Holden, Jr. sec. – 26 Dec. 1769 – p. 298

LECATT, CHARLES – Adm. his est. to Esther Lecatt – John Downing & William Haislop sec. – 26 Dec. 1769 – p. 299

BELL, ANSELETA – Adm. her est. to Elijah Bird – 26 Dec. 1769 – Selv: Bird sec. – 26 Dec. 1769 – p. 301

ONIONS, RICHARD – Adm. his est. to Henry Fletcher – James Henry sec. – 27 Dec. 1769 – p. 303

STARLING, JOHN – Adm. his est. to Rachel Starling – Benjamin Royal & Woodman Bloxom sec. – 30 Jan. 1770 – p. 339

PARKER, GEORGE – Adm. his est. to William Drummond. William Drummond, son of Spencer, & Fairfax Smith sec. – 30 Jan. 1770 – p. 338

PARKER, ELIZABETH - Adm. her est. to William Drummond - William Drummond, son of Spencer & Fairfax Smith sec. - 30 Jan. 1770 - p. 339

FISHER, JOHN, Jr. - Adm. his est. to Benjamin Philips - Isaac Philips & William Smith sec. - 27 Feb. 1770 - p. 363

FISHER, JOHN, the younger - Adm. his est. to Lawrence White as marrying Ann, wid. of the said John Fisher, in place of Benjamin Philips. - Jonathan West sec. - 27 Mar. 1770 - p. 397

LEWIS, Stephen - Adm. his est. to Agnes Lewis - Joseph Feddiman & John Dixon sec. 28 Mar. 1770 - p. 406

REW, REUBEN - Adm. his est. to Sinah Rew - Ambrose Willet & Thomas Copes sec. - 29 May 1770 - p. 481

Orders - 1770 - 1773

WALKER, NAOMI - Adm. her est. to Robert Bayly - Jabez Pitt sec. - 28 Aug. 1770 - p. 56

RUSSEL, ROBERT - Adm. his est. to Lavina Russell - Zerrobable Rodgers & William Joyne sec. - 30 Oct. 1770 - p. 109

GARRIS, THOMAS - Ordered that the sheriff take into his hands the est. of Thomas Garris, dec., & make sale thereof, there having been no adm. on said est. - 29 Jan. 1770 - p. 143

KELLAM, ARTHUR - Adm. his est. to Abraham Kellam - Luke Luker & Robert Coleburn sec. - 31 Jan. 1770 - p. 159

WHEELTON, WILLIAM - Adm. his est. with will annexed, unadministered by Margaret Wheelton, his late wid. & Exec., to William Tunnel - Littleton Dennis sec. - 31 Jan. 1770 - p. 161

DUNTON, RACHEL - Adm. her est. to Elizabeth Dunton - John & Thomas Copes sec. - 26 June 1771 - p. 187

BEAVANS, JOSHUA - Adm. his est. to Elizabeth Stockly - Alexander Stockly sec. 30 July 1771 - p. 210

WATERFIELD, JACOB - Adm. his est. to John Watts - William Drummond sec. - 28 Aug. 1771 - p. 232

MORRIS, JOHN - Adm. his est. to Mary Morris - John Smith & Timothy Owen sec. - 28 Aug. 1771 - p. 232

NOCK, WILLIAM – Adm. his est. to Peggy Nock – John Spiers, Robert Coleburn & William Guy sec. – 28 Aug. 1771 – p. 234

GIBBENS, MAJOR – Adm. his est. to Babel Rodgers – Thomas Hickman sec. – 24 Sept. 1771 – p. 246

COOK, EDWARD – Adm. his est. to Thorowgood Smith – Isaac Smith sec. – 24 Sept. 1771 – p. 246

PREWET, BENJAMIN – Adm. his est. to George Middleton – Isaac Smith sec. – 25 Sept. 1771 – p. 249

WALKER, ROBERT – Adm. his est. to James Berry – George Hope sec. – 25 Sept. 1771 – p. 251

JUSTICE, THOMAS – Adm. his est. to William Young – James Berry sec. – 25 Sept. 1771 – p. 251

SAYRES, BENJAMIN – Adm. his est. to Sebastian Cropper, Jr. – George Holden sec. 26 Sept. 1771 – p. 252

GUY, JOHN – Adm. his est. to Betty Guy – Edward Parker & William Crowson sec. – 30 Oct. 1771 – p. 261

WIMBROUGH, ZOROBABEL – Ordered that the sheriff take into his possession the est. of Zorobabel Wimbrough & make sale thereof, no one having qualified on said est. 2 Jan. 1772 – p. 282

BRYMER, ROBERT – Adm. his est. to John Northam – Thomas Bloxom, John Bundick & John Shae sec. – 31 Mar. 1772 – p. 329

MAJOR, CALEB – Adm. his est. to Edward Ker – George Holden & S: Simpson, Gent: sec. 29 Apr. 1772 – p. 347

FLETCHER, READ – Adm. his est. to John Fletcher – Edward Ker & Thomas Jacob sec. – 29 Apr. 1772 – p. 349

STAKES, SAMUEL – Adm. his est. to Scarburgh Stakes – Nicholas Powell, Joshua Copes & Thomas Hickman sec. – 29 Apr. 1772 – p. 349

KELLY, JOSHUA – Adm. his est. to Sebastian Cropper – Ezekiel Delastatius sec. – 30 Apr. 1772 – p. 350

POULSON, EDMUND – Adm. his est. with will annexed, unadministered by Ann Poulson, wid. & Exec. of said Edmund, to George Parker & John Poulson – Littleton Dennis sec. – 30 Apr. 1772 – p. 350

MILLIGAN, JOHN – Adm. his est. to George Holden – Littleton Dennis sec. – 27 May 1772 – p. 374

DICKERSON, MICHAEL – Adm. his est. to Mary Dickerson – William Selby & William Patterson sec. – 30 June 1772 – p. 389

TAYLOR, WILLIAM – Adm. his est. to William Williams, Benjamin Peck & Clement Parker – Littleton Dennis & Nehemiah Stockly sec. – 30 June 1772 – p. 391

BARLOW, JOHN – Adm. his est. to William Williams – Littleton Dennis sec. – 1 July 1772 – p. 393

READ, HENRY – Adm. his est. to Southy Read. William Banfield Walker & John Ashby sec. – 28 July 1772 – p. 408

MOREY, LINSFORD – Adm. his est. to James Arbuckle – George Holden sec. – 29 July 1772 – p. 421

SMITH, MARGARET – Adm. her est. to John Smith – Zerobabel Rodgers & Thomas Custis sec. – 29 Sept. 1772 – p. 443

MAJOR, KENDALL – Adm. his est. to Able James – Luke Luker sec. – 27 Oct. 1772 – p. 466

PITT, MAJOR – Adm. his est. to George Stewart – John Coleburn sec. – 19 Nov. 1772 – p. 473

Orders &c. – 1773

WALLIS, WILLIAM – Adm. his est. to Arthur Rowley. – Sebastian Cropper, Jr. & John Riley Parker sec. – 23 Feb. 1773 – p. 9

MEERS, MARK – Adm. his est. to George Meers – Jonathan Meers & Andrew Meers sec. – 24 Feb. 1773 – p. 14

CRIPPEN, JAMES – Adm. his est. to Thomas Crippen – Charles Bagwell sec. – 30 Mar. 1773 – p. 37

JOHNSON, JOHN – Adm. his est. to Sarah Johnson – Woodman Bloxom & Stephen Bloxom sec. – 25 May 1773 – p. 79

HINMAN, JOHN – Adm. his est. to William Joyne – James Taylor sec. – 29 June 1773 – p. 107

WISHART, JAMES – Adm. his est. to Hannah Wishart – George Holden sec. – 27 July 1773 – p. 130

FOSTER, JAMES – Adm. his est. to John & Sarah Foster – Jacob Bird & William Bell sec. – 27 July 1773 – p. 138

FOX, THOMAS – Adm. his est. to Sarah Fox – William Seymour & John Ashby sec. – 26 Oct. 1773 – p. 274

KELLAM, BENJAMIN - Adm. his est. to Edward Ker - William Riley sec. - 26 Oct. 1773 - p. 276

BELL, ROBERT - Adm. his est. to William Bell - George Stewart & Ayres Gillet sec. 30 Nov. 1773 - p. 286

Wills &c. - 1767-1772

RODGERS, THOMAS WISE - 16 Feb. 1767 - 28 Apr. 1767 - Wife Anne Exec. & to have use of whole est. during her wid. then to have what est. she would have been entitled to had I died intestate. Witt: Laban Simpson, Adah Cole, Sarah Melson, John Bishop - p. 3
In order of prob: Southy Simpson app. guardian to Hannah Scarburgh Rodgers & Polly Rodgers, heirs at law to the testator.

SIMPSON, LABAN - Not dated - 28 Apr. 1767 - Father in law William Barns & wife Esther Exrs. Land bought of Capt Edmund Allen to be sold if personal est. is not sufficient to pay my debts - Wife to have use of whole est. during her wid. Not witnessed - Not signed - Proved by James Henry & Southy Simpson - p. 3
In order of prob: Littleton Dennis app. guardian to Hancock Simpson, heir at law to the testator.

ALLEN, JOHN - 6 Nov. 1764 - 28 Apr. 1767 - To sons Stephen, Edmund & John Allen 300 A. to be div. bet. them. Wife Esther to have use of land during her wid. to bring up her children. Wife Exec. Witt: Sebastian Cropper, Jr. Joseph Dunton.
p. 4
In order of prob: Sebastian Cropper app. guardian to Stephen Allen, heir at law to the testator.

SHIELD, RUBEN - 13 Apr. 1767 - 29 Apr. 1767 - To son Nioholas Shield land & planta. where I live & for want of heirs to my dau. Sarah Shield. Dau. Sarah resid. legatee. Son Nicholas Exr. Friend Littleton Wyatt, Jr. overseer. Witt: Littleton Wyatt, John Shield, Sarah Wyatt, Rachel Beach - p. 5
In order of prob: "Tabitha Shield, widow of the decedent, refused to abide by the said will".

BONNEWELL, JAMES - ___ ___ 1765 - 26 May 1767 - To son John Bonnewell planta. where I now live. To son Michael 200 A. which was my mother's maiden land lying on the seaboard side. To 3 sons John, Michael & James Bonnewell all my right & title of & in an Island called Tobacco Island which I purchased of Denwood Turpin, John Wharton & Thomas Upshur. To dau. Hannah. To dau. Leah. Dau. Rachel. Grandaus. Peggy & Nanny Budd. 3 daus. resid. legatees. Wife (no name) & sons John & Michael Exrs. Witt: Mickeel Bonnewell, Richard Bonnewell: Peter Fitzgerrald, Betty Bonnewell, Sarah Bonnewell - p. 19
In order of prob: John Bonnewell heir at law to the testator.

WARRINGTON, EDMOND - 23 Mar 1767 - 26 May 1767 - To dau. Mary. Dau. Rebecker. Son Stephen. Son Jacob. Wife Ann & 4 children resid. legatees. Witt: Jacob Broadwater, Stephen Taylor, Levinah Parks - p. 23
In order of prob: Mary Warrington, wid. of the testator, qualified.

SCARBURGH, BENNET - 2 Oct. 1764 - 26 May 1767 - To sister Tabitha Scarburgh & cousin Henry Watts, son of John Watts, whole est., real & personal. Bro. John Watts Exr. Witt: Edward Parrish, William Watts - p. 24
In order of prob: Edward Parrish, Quaker - Henry Scarburgh heir at law to the testator.

ARDIS, ROBERT - 18 Apr. 1767 - 30 June 1767 - Wife Anne. Son William Chance Ardis planta. where I now live on the East side of my land, cont. 100 A. To son Edward Ardis the Westward part of my land cont. 100 A. Son Robert Ardis. Children Patience, Joshua, John, Edward, Robert & William Chance Ardis resid. legatees - Sons Edward & William Chance Ardis Exrs. Witt: James Wheelton, Meshack Feddeman, John Taylor - p. 25

COPES, GILES - 7 Mar. 1767 - 30 June 1767 - To son Joshua Copes my land & planta. To each of my daus., Ann, Elizabeth & Leah Copes. 4 daus. Ann Copes, Elizabeth Copes, Esther Baker & Leah Copes resid. legatees. Son Joshua Exr. Witt: Charles Bagwell, William Warner - p. 27

STRINGER, ELISHA - 29 May 1767 - 33 June 1767 - Bro. John Stringer. Cousin Peggy Stringer, dau. of John. To cousin Peggy Ames. To cousin Rachel Aimes. To cousin Robert Read, & for want of heirs to cousin Nathaniel Ames. Sister Elizabeth Ames. Bro. John Stringer & Caleb Aimes Exrs. Witt: Joseph Ames, Jr., Robert Hutchinson, Joseph Ames, Sr. - p. 28

BIGGERBY, WILLIAM - 23 Apr. 1767 - 25 Aug. 1767 - To wife (no name) whole est. real & personal. Grandson William Rayfield. To Levin Joyne. Isaac Dunton & William Joyne Exrs. Witt: John Jacobs, Richard Bayly - p. 46

WISE, JOHN - 5 Aug. 1767 - 26 Aug. 1767 - Wife Scarburgh Wise. To son John Wise. To son Tully Robinson Wise. To dau. Casey Custis. "Slaves to be by my said daughter Casey disposed of to such of Major Thomas Custis's children as she shall think proper" To grandau. Elizabeth Custis. Grandaus. Elizabeth & Anne Smith. Bal. of est. to be div. bet. children & grandchildren, viz: John Wise, Tully Robinson Wise, Elizabeth Custis & Elizabeth & Anne Smith. Dau. Mary Smith. Sons John & Tully Robinson Wise Exrs. Witt: John Hanniford, Sr., Walter Scott, Jonathan Scott - p. 49

MASSEY, JOHN - 14 Mar. 1764 - 27 Oct. 1764 - To son John planta. where I live to be delivered at the death of his mother. To son William Massey. To dau. Esther Massey. Dau. Elizabeth Massey. Wife Elizabeth. (children under 21) Clildren William, Esther & Elizabeth resid. legatees. Wife Exec. - Witt S: Feddeman, William Lewis. - p. 68
In order of prob: Joseph Feddeman app. guardian to John Massey, heir at law to the testator.

WHITE, JACOB - 13 ___ 1767 - 24 Nov. 1767 - To wife Weltheaner personal property that came from her mother for the better support of herself & the children I had by her. To all the children that I had by my first wife all that part of my est. that came by their mother. To dau. Susanna one small mare in consideration of the one given her by her grandmother. Dau. Welthia, son Robert. Dau. Peggy. (all children by 2nd mar.) Wife & 6 children rcsid. legatees. Wife Exec. Witt: John Watts, William Sturgis, Robert Guy. - p. 82

BUDD, ZOROBABEL - 7 Sept. 1762 - 24 Nov. 1767 - To children Michael, Peggy, Major, Thomas & Nanney Budd 20 s. each. Wife (no name) resid. legatee. Wife & James Bonewell & Michal Bonewell Exrs. Witt: James Bonewell, Littleton Wyatt, Rebecca Belote - p. 84

GASCOYNE, WILLIAM - 24 Aug. 1767 - 26 Nov. 1767 - Wife Sarah. Dau. Elizabeth. Bro. Henry Gascoyne, he to have the tuition of my child. Bro. Henry Exr. Witt: Isaac Dunton, John Rose - p. 87

BEECH, SAMUEL - 4 Dec. 1767 - 29 Dec. 1767 - Wife Sarah. Won William. Son Rubin. Son William Exr. Wife Sarah, Ann Bennet, Elizabeth Young, Rachel Ashby, Rubin Beech, Samuel Beech, Leaven Beech & Sacker Beech resid. legatees. Witt: John Spires, John Coleburn - p. 87

STURGIS, ADAH - 17 Dec. 1767 - 29 Dec. 1767 - Son William Sturgis. Dau. Martha Sturgis. To son Jacob Sturgis. Dau. Adah Sturgis. 5 youngest children, Elizabeth, Adah, Abigal, Martha & Jacob Sturgis resid. legatees. Southy Simpson Exr. Witt: Anne Copes, William Parker - p. 88

HORNSBY, JOHN - 20 Sept.1765 - 29 Dec. 1767 - To wife whole est. during her wid. To son Elisha Hornsby, my Manner Planta. cont. 100 A. adj. my bro. James Hornsby. To son John Hornsby the remaining part of my land. Son Eli Hornsby. Bal. of est. to my 7 youngest children, Eli, Eburn, William, Laben, Mary, Ann & Comfort. Wife & sons Elisha & John Hornsby Exrs. Witt: Elisha Meers, John Hornsby, James Hornsby. - p. 90
In order. of prob: Elisha Hornsby heir at law to the testator. Mary Hornsby, wid. of the testator, qualified with Elisha & John Hornsby.

WINDOW, ELIZABETH - 14 Jan. 1765 - 29 Dec. 1765 - To Ann Watson. To John Window, Levin Window, Eli Watson each 20 s. 2 youngest sons Babel Window & Abel Window resid. legatees. Eldest son John Window Exr. Witt: Robert Wale, Daniel Twiford, Tamer Twiford - p. 92

TURLINGTON, THOMAS - 25 Oct. 1767 - 29 Dec. 1767 - Wife Sarah. Son James Turlington. Son Edmund Turlington. Dau. Comfort Warrington. Grandson James Wise. Son Edmund Exr. Witt: Elijah Addison, William Tizeker - p. 93

ALLEN, EDMUND - 14 Oct. 1767 - 26 Jan. 1768 - To dau. Margaret Allen whole est. both in Virginia & Maryland except the planta where I now live which I give to my wife Tabitha Allen during her wid. Should my dau. die without issue during the life time of Stephen, Edmund or John Allen, children of my bro. John Allen, then the est. left my dau. Margaret to be equally div. bet. them. Wife Exec. Witt: James Henry, James Berry, Major Gibbons. - p. 94

BAYLY, JOHN - 27 Dec. 1767 - 26 Jan. 1768 - To son Charles Bayly 636 A. where I now live. To dau. Mary. To son Laban Bayly. Son & dau. Laban & Mary resid. legatees. Neighbor John Finney, son Charles & dau. Mary Exrs. Witt: John Finney, Thomas Guy, John Saulsbury, Mary Guy - p. 96

FINNEY, JOANNA - 7 Jan. 1768 - 26 Jan. 1768 - To son Laban Stott. Grandaus. Joanna, Anne & Henrietta Stott, daus. of my son Jonathan (all under age). Grandson Jonathan Dolby Stott, son of my son Jonathan. Grandau. Bridget Burton. Grandau. Pegg Hudson. 6 grandaus. which is daus. to my sons Laban & Jonathan Stott, viz: Sarah, Bridget, Anne, Joanna, Anne & Henrietta, resid. legatees. Son Laban Stott & son in law John Finney Exrs. Witt: John Finney, Fairfax Only, Attalanta Finney - p. 97

WARRINGTON, WILLIAM -27 July 1767 - 26 Jan. 1768 - To wife Comfort the small planta. I leased of my son Alexander Warrington during the said lease. To son William Warrington. To son James Warrington. To wife Comfort 1/2 of personal est. during her wid. then to be div. between her 6 children, William, John, James Anne, Sally & Esther. To dau. Jane Benston. Dau. Mary Townsend. Bal. of est. to be div. bet. children now already mentioned, viz: Alexander, Josephus, Walter, Rachel, Elizabeth & Leah Warrington. Wife Comfort & her bro. Edward Thornton Exrs. Witt: Thomas Matthews, James Matthews, Joshua Matthews, William Warrington. - p. 102

COLLINS, JOSHUA - Not dated - 24 Feb. 1768 - Wife Mary. To son Stephen Collins my land & for want of heirs to my dau. Scarburgh Collins. Wife, son Stephen, dau. Scarburgh & unborn child resid. legatees. Bro. Thomas Collins Exr. Witt: Jacob Waterfield, Isaac Smith - p. 120

In order of prob: Littleton Dennis app. guardian to Stephen Collins, Inf't. heir at law to the testator.

SMITH, SUSANNA – 10 Jan. 1768 – 25 Feb. 1768 – To son George Smith whole est.   except clothing, & for want of heirs to those that bring him up. Bros. William Boggs & Mackemi Boggs Exrs & to bring up my son. Witt: John Boggs, William Smith. p. 131

WALKER, STEPHEN – 15 Mar. 1765 – 27 Feb. 1768 – To Charlotte Littleton, dau. of Comfort 5 S. Bal. of est. to Comfort Littleton & her 2 daus. Elizabeth & Margaret Littleton. Witt: Mark Littleton, William Littleton. – p. 137
In order of prob: John Young appeared and contested the said will and the recording thereof until next Court.   Ordered to be admitted to probate 29 Mar. 1768 – Comfort Littleton qualified.

JUSTICE, RICHARD, Sr. – 12 Feb. 1768 – 29 Mar. 1768 – To son Ralph Justice 450 A. where I formerly lived before I moved to Seaside. Wife Anne. To son Richard 87 A. where I live & 150 A. where my son William Justice did live adj. the land given my son Ralph, also 150 A. where he now lives, also 50 A. of swamp land. Wife & sons Ralph & Richard resid. legatees. Son Richard Exr. Witt: Thomas Crippen, James Crippen, Comfort Flemmons (Clemmons?) – p. 138
In order of prob: Ralph Justice heir at law to the testator.

WATSON, BARTHOLOMEW – 1 Feb. 1768 – 30 Mar. 1768 – Wife Sarah. To dau. Patty Watson land where I now live & for want of heirs to unborn child & should said child die to my bro. Jacob Watson. Wife & Thomas Hall Exrs. Witt: Ezekiel Watson, Director Watson. – p. 147
In order of prob: Littleton Dennis app. guardian to Bartholomew Watson, heir at law to the testator.

SCARBURGH, ELIZABETH – 18 May 1767 – 20 Apr. 1768 – To mother Allice Dunton. Bro William Scarburgh resid. legatee. Father in law Isaac Dunton Exr. Witt: Robert Wale, Edmund Scarburgh, Isaac Waterfield – p. 148
In order of prob: Isaac Dunton relinquished his right & Americus Scarburgh qualified.

SILL, GOWEN – 26 Nov. 1764 – 26 Apr. 1768 – To wife Christian Sill whole est. during her life & then to Elizabeth Jenkins my land. Bal. of est. to be div. bet. Elizabeth Huse & Elizabeth Jenkins, provided the said Elizabeth Jenkins never demands nor sues for any part of her father's est. Wife Exec. Witt: Littleton Scarburgh Major, Anne Kellam – p. 149
In order of prob: John Sill heir at law to the testator.

CLARK, ELIZABETH – 2 Aug. 1762 – 26 Apr. 1768 – Dau. Sophia West sole legatee & Exec. Witt: William Melson, Bridget Melson,

Thomas Batson. – p. 151
In order of prob: Sophia West "now Sophia Wessels" qualified, Elijah Wessels sec.

CUTLER, WILLIAM – 2 May 1767 – 26 Apr. 1768 – To Samuel Cutler, son of Richard Cutler, my kinsman, planta. where I now live near the New Church in the Parish of St. George, being 150.A. To Richard Cutler, the father. To kinsman & neighbor George Cutler. To Mary, dau. of George Cutler. To William, son of George Cutler. To friend Hugh Roberts. To Anne, the wife of John Harrison. To William Foster & Thomas Elliot. To Mary, the dau. of Major Ironmonger. George Cutler, Richard Cutler, the father, Samuel Cutler & Hugh Roberts resid. legatees. Friend Benjamin Bull & Richard Cutler, the father, Exrs. Witt: John Powell, John Beavans, Thomas Edmunds – p. 156
In order of prob: John Cutler heir at law to the testator cited to appear – Sheriff's return "Not found within this Bailiwick".

BELL, THOMAS – 12 May 1760 – 31 May 1768 – To son William Bell 250 A. where I now live. To son Thomas Bell 150 A. which I bought of George Green. To son Robert Bell. To dau. Mary Fisher. To dau. Sarah Gaskins. To son in law Thomas Fisher 100 A. on Hog Island. Sons William & Robert resid. legatees & Exrs. Witt: Arthur Upshur, Baily Harmon, Nathaniel Fosque. – p. 160
In order of prob: William Bell heir at law to the testator.

BYRD, EBURN – 18 Nov. 1766 – 31 May 1768 – Wife Mary. To son Jacob 90 A. adj. Thomas Hargress. Grandson Jacob Byrd. Grandson Levi Byrd 105 A. To dau. Mary Hornsby. Grandson Eburn Hornsby. Grandson Major Byrd. Son Jacob Byrd, grandson Levi Byrd & dau. Mary Hornsby resid. legatees. Son Jacob Byrd Exr. Witt: John Wharton, Elizabeth Wharton – p. 162
In order of prob: Littleton Dennis app. guardian of Levi Byrd, heir at law to the testator.

HICKMON, CHRISTIAN – Nunc. – Proved 29 May 1768 – Prob. 1 June 1768 – Son William Warner. Dau. Anne Groten. To dau. Christian Stakes' two daus. (under age) Grandau. Joyce Melson. To dau. Elizabeth "the remainder of her estate that she brought to Solomon Melson's" Proved by Smith Melson, Elizabeth Melson – p. 167
In order of prob: Solomon Melson qualified.

TURNER, ABRAHAM – 21 Mar. 1768 – 31 May 1768 – Dau. Rachel Turner. Wife Mary Anne to have use of remainder of est. during her wid., then to be div. bet. my said wife & all her children. Wife Exec. Witt: Thomas Riley, Major Rafield – p. 169

STOCKLY, THOMAS – 13 Apr. 1768 – 26 June 1768 – Wife Elizabeth. I give my land if my day. Tabitha Matthews should have a son & call him Thomas Stockly, to him & his heirs, but should she die without a son called by that name my land to be sold among the Stocklys & the

money div. bet. my daughters children. Son in law Southey Matthews. Cousin Alexander Stockly. Wife Elizabeth, Nehemiah Stockly & Alexander Stockly Exrs. Witt: Sarah Thornton, Rachel Vannelson, Elizabeth Gooddy. - p. 181
In order of prob: Tabitha Matthews, wife of Southey Matthews, heir at law to the testator.

BOGGS, MACKEMIE - 7 May 1767 - 28 June 1768 - Wife to have use of my land during her life, & then to my son Mackemie Boggs, provided he never marry an own cousin, & in the event he do then to my son William Boggs. To son Robert Boggs. Dau. Sarah. Dau. Betty. Grandson George Smith (under 21) Daus. Sarah, Susanna & Betty resid. legatees. Wife (no name) & son William Exrs. Witt: Edward Parker, William Parker, William Smith - p. 183
In order of prob: Robert Boggs heir at law to the testator. Sarah & William Boggs qualified.

BOOTEN, JOHN - Not dated - Partly proved 28 June 1768 - Prob. 29 June 1768 - Wife Polly Booten planta. where I live for life except she be with child, then the said child to have the aforesaid lands. Should said child die without heirs then I give the said land to my sister Elizabeth Booten at the death of my wife. Witt: James Selby, Sarah Taylor - p. 183
In order of prob: Joseph Houston & Anne his wife & Elizabeth Booten heirs at law to the testator. Joseph Feddaman qualified.

MEERS, ROBERT - 6 May 1766 - 26 July 1768 - To sister Sarah Duncan. To Rachel Meers, dau. of Jonathan Meers. To Leah Meers, dau of Jonathan. Bro. Jonathan Exr. & resid. legatee. Witt: Thomas Clark, Baily Baily, Thomas Baily - p. 190

FINNEY, ABEL - 15 Jan. 1768 - 26 July 1768 - To wife Elizabeth whole est. during her wid. To son William Finney land & planta. To dau. Polly. Son George. Unborn child. Children William Finney, Polley Finney, George Finney & unborn child resid. legatees. Wife Exec. Witt: Southey Simpson, William Finney - p. 191
In order of prob: Sebastian Cropper guardian to William Finney, Inf't. heir at law to the testator.

COLEBURN ELIZABETH - 21 Sept. 1768 - 29 Sept. 1768 - To son John Coleburn. Dau. Comfort Peal. Grandau. Anne Guy. Grandau. Margaret Nock. Grandson William Spires. Grandau. Patience Spires. Grandson John Spires resid. legatee & Exr. Witt: John Wharton, Scarburgh Miles. - p. 217

PARKER, LEVIN - 14 Aug. 1768 - Partly proved 26 Oct. 1768 - Prob. 28 Oct. 1768 - If my Exrs. think best my land to be sold for the payment of my debts, but should my land not all be sold I give the residue of same to my wife until my son John arrives to lawful age, then to my said son & for want of heirs to my dau. Elizabeth, & for want of heirs to Levin Parker, son of Phillip Parker, of Onancock. 2

children resid. legatees. est. to remain with my wife to bring them up & educate them till they arrive to age or marry. Wife Elizabeth & bro. Clement Parker & friend John Powell Exrs. Witt: Henry Scarburgh, Johannas Wise, Robert Boggs - p. 224

In order of prob: James Henry app. guardian to John Parker, heir at law to the testator.

WELBURN, FRANCIS - 8 Oct. 1767 - 31 Jan. 1769 - To son William Welburn planta. where I now live & also land which I bought of Thomas Welburn & Covington Corbin, except what I give my son Drummond Welburn. To son Drummond Welburn the house & orchard and about 6 A. of land, & for want of heirs to my dau. Barbara Welburn. To son Drummond all my swamp land. Bal. of est. to be sold & proceeds div. bet. my 3 children, William, Drummond & Barbara Welburn. To James Whealton 1 A. of land in the swamp adj. him, & for which he has a bond. All my wife's clothes to my dau. Barbara Welburn. Bro. in law George Corbin Exr. - Witt: William Burton, Charles Martial, Upshur Russell - p. 243

In order of prob: Littleton Dennis app. guardian to William Welburn, Inf't. heir at law to the testator.

JEFFREY, ALEXANDER, Merchant - 20 Oct. 1768 - 31 Jan. 1769 - 245 A. land & planta. which I purchased of John Milligan & also my rights on Wallops Island to be sold for the payment of my debts. To friend Agniss, wife of Edward Parrish. To Mary, the dau. of my friend James Henry. To Parker Barnes, my store-keeper. To friend David Bowman. To friend James Scott of Onancock. To friend Edward Ker of Andua. To friend James Henry. To Sarah Hook. Bal of est. to my Honored Parents, Francis & Marion Jeffrey of the City of Edenburgh during their lives & during the life of the survivor of them, such survivor to dispose of same to my brothers or their children, if any of my brothers be dead. Friends James Scott, Edward Ker, David Bowman & James Henry Exrs. Witt: Robert McClean, Euphamia McClean. John Matthews. p. 245

TOWNSEND, STEPHEN - 21 Dec. 1768 - 31 Jan. 1769 - To wife Mary whole est. during her wid. then to be div. 1/2 to my dau. Rachel Townsend. Wife & John Townsend Exrs. Witt: Ezekiel Broadwater, Covington Ewell, Thomas Townsend - p. 248

BUNDICK, JUSTICE - 15 Dec. 1768 - 1 Feb. 1769 - To Robert Jones. To Thomas Bloxom. To Richard Bundick. To Rachel Sandrews. 2 daus. Susannah & Beersheba Bundick resid. legatees. Thomas Crippen & Charles Bagwell Exrs. Witt: Richard Onions, John Riggs - p. 252

In order of prob: Richard Onions app. guardian to Tabitha Bundick, one of the co-heirs of the testator.

HORNSBY, JAMES - 2 Oct. 1768 - 28 Feb. 1769 - To son John Hornsby planta. where I live cont. 216 A. To son James Hornsby all the rest of my land. To son Argol Hornsby. To dau. Naomi Hornsby. To

dau. Rachel Hornsby. To daus. Elizabeth Downing & Esther Lecatt. Grandson Major Lecatt. Grandau. Leah Downing. Grandson John Downing. Dau. Tabitha Hornsby. To son Zorobabel Hornsby. Son Levi Hornsby. Son Ezekiel Hornsby. Wife Rachel & sons John & James Hornsby Exrs. Witt: Thomas Aimes, John Darby, John Kennahorn, John Meers (son of Elisha) - p. 266
In order of prob: John Hornsby heir at law to the testator.

CAIN, MARTHA - 29 Mar. 1768 - 28 Feb. 1769 - To son John Cain. To Anne Cain. Witt: William Selby, Priscilla Orrick, William Lewis - p. 269
In order of prob: William Cain qualified.

TURNER, RICHARD - 17 Feb. 1767 - 28 Feb. 1769 - To godson John Parkerson, son of John Parkerson & Mary his wife "that I now am informed liveth in Carolina" Land & planta. where I now live, being 100 A. provided he pay 20 s. yearly to the Churchwardens of this parish to be distributed to such persons as shall be in want of charity, & if no heir of the said John Parkerson or himself should come to take possession of the land, then my cousin Hillary Turner to have the same upon the same condition & for want of heirs to William Turner, the son of Abraham Turner & Mary his wife. To cousin Andrew Turner, son of Andrew & Sarah his wife land where he now lives which I bought of his bro. Abraham, cont. 50 A., he to pay 10 s. yearly to the Churchwardans, & for want of issue to George Turner, son of Abel Turner & Tabitha his wife. Clothing to Henry Clark & William Page. Wife (no name) bros. & sisters resid. legatees. Wife & cousin Andrew Turner Exrs. Witt: James Rodgers, Peter Watson, Rachel Turner. - p. 270
In order of prob: George Turner heir at law to the testator. Elizabeth Turner & Andrew Turner qualified.

KELLAM, WEST - 20 May 1768 - 28 Feb. 1769 - To son Scarburgh Kellam land where he now lives called Sarah's Neck, cont. (including the 50 A. formerly given him by deed) 200 A. To wife Elizabeth. To dau. Euphamla Major. To grandau. Catharine Kellam. Friend Edward Ker Exr. Son Caleb alias Laban Kellam, wife Elizabeth, son Scarburgh & 5 daus. Patience Chandler, Euphamia Major, Amey Colony, Tamar Darby & Seymour Kellam resid. legatees. Witt: John Rodgers, John Hutchinson, John Reid, Peter Rodgers - p. 272

COLLINS, MARY - 21 Feb. 1769 - 1 Mar. 1769 - To dau. Scarburgh Collins. Son Stephen Collins. Dau. Sarah Collins. To Anne Whaley. Children Scarburgh, Stephen & Sarah Collins resid. legatees. Bro. Thomas Collins. Witt: William Marshall, Esther Whaley, Elijah Blake - p. 276

SHEPHERD, JOHN - 17 Jan. 1769 - 20 Mar. 1769 - To dau. Elizabeth Shepherd. To dau. Sally Shepherd. To wife Lucretia Shepherd. Children Elizabeth & Sally Shepherd resid. legatees. Charles Bagwell Exr. Witt: William Nock, Lucretia Powell - p. 277

In order of prob: Lcretia Shepherd, wid. of the testator qualified.

STOCKLY, JOSEPH - 27 Mar. 1769 - 25 Apr. 1769 - To son Elijah Stockly. To dau. Naomi Stockly. To dau. Rachel Conquest. To dau. Rebecca Stockly. To dau. Sarah Stockly. To dau. Anne Hope. Daus. Rachel Conquest, Sarah Stockly resid. legatees. To Edmund Tunnell. Bro. Nehemiah Stockly & cousin Alexander Stockly Exrs. Witt: Major Davis, John Rowley - p. 280

DARBY, LITTLETON - 2 Mar. 1769 - 26 Apr. 1769 - To wife Susanna Darby 114 A. of land during her wid. then to my son William Darby (under 21) & for want of heirs to my cousin Margaret, the dau. of Leshe Darby, & if my sister Leah Darby should live longer than my wife or my son William, she to have a home on my said land. Wife & son William resid. legatees. Wife & John Milby Exrs. Witt: Francis Darby, Augustine Lecatt, John Darby. - p. 281
In order of prob: George Holden app. guardian to William Darby, heir at law to the testator.

WISE, WILLIAM, SR. - 16 Apr. 1768 - 26 Apr. 1769 - To son William Wise planta. where he now lives & for want of heirs to my son James Wise. To son James Wise 1 s. To son Thomas Wise 1 s. To grandson Smith Rodgers, heir of my dau. Elizabeth, 1 s. To dau. Mary Bonwell 1 s. To son John Wise. Dau. Susanna. To grandau. Hannah Wise. To grandau. Mary Rodgers. Daus. Susanna Wise & Scarburgh Parker Executrices & resid. legatees. Witt: John Bonwell, James Bonwell, Thomas Bonwell, Michael Budd - p. 283

SAVAGE, PATIENCE - 23 Oct. 1765 - 26 Apr. 1769 - To son William Hope Savage. To son Griffin Savage. Dau. Sarah Johnson. Dau. Patience Crippen. Grandaus. Anne & Esther Savage. Grandchildren Benjamin, Elizabeth & Sinah Riley. Bal. of est. to 4 children Anne Justice, Mary White, William Hope Savage & Sarah Johnson - Sons in law Richard Justice & William White Exrs. Witt: Baily Hinman, Anne Beech, Abraham Riggs - p. 285
In order of prob: William Savage qualified, the other Exrs. being both dead.

EVANS, LEVIN - 24 Sept. 1768 - 30 May 1769 - To son Nathaniel Evans 100 A. adj. Henry Fletcher & Robert Bayly, & for want of heirs to my son Arthur Evans, & for want of heirs to my son Littleton Evans. To son Nathaniel 25 A. of marsh in McKeels Neck. To wife Anne Mary Evans personal est. & planta. where I live during her wid. Wife Exec. To son Levin Evans (under 21) planta. where I now live except the 100 A. given my son Nathaniel, & 25 A. of marsh in McKeels Neck. To son John 100 A. on the South side of ths Longoes & 50 A. marsh in McKeels Neck. To dau. Aby 60 L- provided she makes her right over to John Wilkins of a certain tract of land cont. 25 A. which the said Wilkins now has in possession, & should she refuse to have no right or title to the legacies hereafter mentioned. Daus. Anne & Tabitha to be paid the legacy their grandfather left them which was 5 L each. Grandchildren Betty Matthews & Evans Matthews. Son John under 21. 6 children by my wife Anne Mary resid. legatees. John Watts, Henry Fletcher & Nehemiah Stockly Trustees. Witt: Francis Edwards, Martha March, John March, John Matthews - p. 294

WATKINSON, SUSANNA - 21 Mar. 1769 - 30 May 1769 - Dau. Bridget Chance. Grandau. Patience Savage. Grandau. Anne More. Dau. in law Tabitha Wilkinson. Grandau. Elizabeth Warrington. Grandau. Leah Warrington. Dau. Sarah Twiford. Dau. Bridget Chance resid. legatee & Exec. Witt: Thomas Meers, Sacker Taylor - p. 296

PEAL, COMFORT - 29 May 1769 - 31 May 1769 - Son William Spiers. Son Coleburn Peal. Son John Spires. Son Robert Spires. Son in law William Nock. Clothing to be div. bet. dau. Peggy Nock & Anne Guy. Sons William Spires & Coleburn Peal resid. legatees. Son John Spires Exr. Witt: John Coleburn, William Beech - p. 298

WILLIS, PETER - 21 May 1769 - 29 Aug. 1769 - To dau. Sarah Willis & for want of heirs to dau. Susanna Darmon & grandsons John & James Richardson. To son Zerrobabel Willis planta. where I now live at the death or marriage of my wife Rosanna Willis. Grandsons John & James Richardson & dau. Susanna Darmon resid. legatees. Son Zerrobabel Exr. Witt: Littleton Lecatt, Littleton Wyatt. - p. 332
In order of prob: Zerrobabel Willis relinquished his right & John Coleburn qualified.

TAYLOR, JAMES - 10 Mar. 1767 - 29 Aug. 1769 - To son Jacob & his wife negro for life, reversion to their dau. Scarburgh & should my grandau. marry an extravagant man or offer to sell the negro, then to fall to my grandson, her bro., James Taylor. To son James Taylor planta. where I live and part of the 100 A. I bought of my bro. Charles Taylor, lying on the West side of Wallops road, & should he marry any of his cousins to have the land for life & then to my son Jacob Taylor's son James Taylor. To son Shadrack Taylor the remaining part of the 100 A. purchased of my bro. Charles. To dau. Susanna. To dau. Sarah. Should my dau. Sarah marry Jesse Taylor the above legacy to be div. bet. my son Jacob Taylor, Mary Taylor & Susanne Taylor & Sarah to have 1 s. To dau. Mary Taylor. To dau. Esther Pilsher. Dau. Comfort Warrington. Grandson Teackle Warrington. Dau. Elizabeth Smith. Son Teackle Taylor. John Potter, William Whealton & Thomas Matthews to div. est. Son Jacob Exr. Witt: John Potter, John Shae, Nehemiah Howard - p. 343.
In order of prob: Shadrack Taylor heir at law to the testator.

TEACKLE, THOMAS - 9 Oct. 1763 - 26 Sept. 1769 - To wife Elizabeth 500 A. purchased of Jacob White for life. To son Caleb part of the tract of land where my son Thomas lives which formerly belonged to Richard Hill, & adj. the land that was lately devised to me by my bro. John Teackle, dec. To son Severn the land devised me by my bro. John Teackle. Caleb & Severn under age. To son Thomas the

246

residue of my lands with the reversion of the lands above given to my wife. Confirms gifts to 4 married children, Thomas, Susanna, Anne & Elizabeth. To children Caleb, Margaret. Leah, Severn & Sarah when Caleb comes to age of before if occasion require. Wife & 5 children last named resid. legatees. Bros. Levin & Upshur Teackle & friends Mr. Arthur Upshur, Mr. Peter Hack & Mr. John Finney to div. est. Wife guardian of children until they come to 18 or marry. Wife Exec. & son Thomas Exr. Witt: Americus Scarburgh, Thomas Jacob, Walter Jameson, Peter Hack.
Codicil; 21 July 1769 - Whereas in my will I made my dau. Margaret, since inter-married with Mr. George Hack, one of the resid. legatees, & since her marriage I have given her several slaves &c., My will is that the said slaves &c. shall be in full of that part devised to her in my said will. Witt: Walter Jameson, Peter Hack, Thomas Jacob - p. 347

MAHON, JOHN - 20 Mar. 1769 - 26 Sept. 1769 - Son John Mahon. Son Robinson Mahon. To Sarah Mahon. Dau. Mary Mahon. Dau. Margaret Mahon. Dau. Sophia Mahon. Wife Margaret Mahon & John Mahon Exrs. Witt: Charles Bayly, Sr., Zerrobabel Rodgers, Nathan Pearce - p. 350

BEECH, WILLIAM - 22 July 1769 - 26 Sept. 1769 - To wife Mary my land during her wid. & then to my son Ezekiel Beech. Bal. of est. to wife for life then to dau. Margaret Beech. John Ashby & Reuben Beech Exrs. Witt: John Spires, Scarburgh Miles, John Beech. - p. 351
In order of prob: Thomas Parramore app. guardian to Ezekiel Beech, heir at law to the testator.

BADGER, JOHN, SR. 26 Feb. 1766 - 1 Nov. 1769 - Wife Abigail. To dau. Sarah James. Dau. Polly Wharton. Son Nathaniel Badger. Dau. Tabitha Harrison. Son Abel Badger. Two youngest sons William & Jacob. Wife Abigal & her 6 youngest children, viz: Abel, Leanna, William, Jacob, Anne & Sinah Badger resid. legatees. Son Nathaniel Badger & Abel Badger Exrs. Witt: John Edwards, Caleb Chandler, Richard Rodgers - p. 356
In order of prob: Nathaniel Badger heir at law to the testator.

TAYLOR, TEACKLE - 10 July 1769 - 1 Nov. 1769 - Bro. in law Bayly Smith. Bro. James Taylor. Bro. in law James Hopman. Cousin Spencer Smith. Bro. in law Elijah Pilchard. To sister Susanna Taylor my land in Worcester County. Bro. in law James Hopman Exr. Witt: James Potter, Rebekah Vessels, Betty Smith. - p. 362.
In order of prob: Shadrack Taylor heir at law to the testator.

STOCKLY, NEOMY - 31 Aug. 1769 - 28 Nov. 1769 - To sister Rebecah Stockly. Bro. Elijah Stockly. Sister Ann Hope. Sister Sarah Stockly resid. legatee. Cousin Alexander Stockly Exr. - Witt: Nehemiah Stockly, William Hutson.

DARBY, JOHN - 30 Apr. 1769 - 26 Dec. 1769 - To son Benjamin Darby all my land, & for want of heirs to my dau. Ann Darby, & for want of heirs to my bro. Churchell Darby, & for want of heirs to my bro. Francis Darby. To bro. Churchell Darby 1/2 my water mill. Two children Benjamin & Ann resid. legatees. Bro. Churchell Exr. & guardian of my children. Witt: Bezaleel Watson, Mary Crafford, John Meers - p. 368
In Order of Prob: Luke Luker, guardian to Joshua Darby, heir at law to the testator.

KELLAM BABEL, ALIAS LABAN - 14 Aug. 1769 - 26 Dec. 1769 - To son West Kellam all my land, & for want of heirs to my dau. Catherine Kellam. Wife to have use of land until my son comes to age. Crops to be div. bet. my wife, mother & sister Semor. Should both my son & dau. die under age & without issue, I give my land to Upshur Colony. To wife (no name) all that will fall to her of her father's est. Wife & son resid. legatees. Should both children die without issue personal property to be div. bet. Littleton Colony's children & John Chandler's children & Semor Kellam. Wife & William Joyne Exrs. Witt: Ama Colony, William Coward, Richard Meers, John Meers - p. 369
In order of prob: Elizabeth Kellam, wid. of the testator. relinquished her right & William Joyne qualified.

BAYLY, RICHARD - 2 Oct. 1768 - 26 Dec. 1769 - Wife Betty. Dau. Sarah Gascoyne. Son John Bayly. Dau. Welthy. Son Ismey. Dau. Susanna. Dau. Elizabeth. I give 6 L cash to be equally div. bet. 6 of my children, viz: Richard, John, Ismey, Welthy, Susanna & Elizabeth. Son Edmund. Wife & 7 of my children, Richard, John, Ismey, Welthy, Susanna, Elizabeth Bayly & Sarah Gascoyne resid. legatees. Friends Isaac Durton & Americus Scarburgh Exrs. Witt: Thomas Jacob, Henry Gascoyne.

JUSTICE, JAMES - 31 Aug. 1769 . 26 Dec. 1769 - Wife Sarah. Should my wife be with child I give said child my planta. at Gartha & the planta. where I now live. To wife planta. called Garthia & the Lower Beech, her dower in Keccotank & wbole est. for life. To cousin Arthur Teackle planta. at Gargatha at the death of my wife. Remainder of est. to be div. bet. my 2 cousins John & Arthur Teackle. Wife Exec. Witt: Thomas Pettit, Robert James, Henry Custis. p. 373
In order of prob: Susanna Justice heir at law to the testator.

YOUNG, JOHN - 8 Aug. 1769 - 27 Dec. 1769 - Wife Comfort - To son John Young planta. where he now lives adj. where I live. To son George planta. where I now live at the death of his mother. To sons John & George my Island Ridges, that is the plantable land thereof. To sons John, George & Solomon all the marsh adj. the Ridges above mentioned. To son Solomon planta. I bought of Isaac Williams. Dau. Anne Hinman. Dau. Patience Wessels. Dau. Tabitha Young. Wife Exec. & 3 sons Exrs. Witt: William Young, Sr., Margaret Young. Southy Simpson - p. 374

RODGERS, JAMES - 7 Oct. 1769 - 27 Feb. 1770 - 100 A. where Laben Belote now lives to be sold for the payment of debts. Bal. of est. to wife till my sons Daniel & John Rodgers come to age, then to be div. bet. wife Patience, son Daniel Rodgers, John Rodgers, Csandrah Rodgers & Elizabeth Rodgers. Wife & 2 sons above named Exrs. Witt: Elie Window, Thomas Fox, John Belote - p. 387
In order of prob: Zerrobabel Rodgers app. guardian to Daniel Rodgers, heir at law to the testator.

WHEELTON, WILLIAM - 3 Sept. 1768 - 28 Mar. 1770 - Wife Mary Exec. & sole legatee. Witt: Edward Joynes, Charles Thornton, Elijah Collins, Caleb Townsend, Samuel Singleton. - p. 392
In order of prob: Nehemiah Wheelton heir at law to the testator.

WISE, JOHN - Not dated - 29 Mar. 1770 - Whole est. to wife Peggy Wise during her wid. "to my daughter Wise. To son Tully Robinson Wise land purchased of William Wise & "one half of my land & marsh known and Called by the Name of the Bayside hammock & Deeded to me by my ---- Not completed. In order of prob: Proved by James Henry & Tully Robinson Wise. John Wise. heir at law to the testator, app. guardian to Tully Robinson Wise. Peggy Wise qualified. - p. 393

MASSEY, JEAN - 10 Nov. 1769 - 24 Apr. 1770 - Dau. Jean Walker. Son Stephen Massey. Grandau. Neomy Massey, dau. of my son Stephen. Son Littleton Massey. Dau. Agnis Shipham. William Shipham, Jr. & his wife Agnis Exrs. Witt: Andrew Gootee, Robert Jenkinson - p. 394

ANDREWS, JACOB - 15 Feb. 1770 - 24 Apr. 1770 - Wife Margaret to have use of all my land being 286 A. during her wid. & then to my dau. Sarah Andrews (under 18) & for want of heirs I give the 200 A. my father gave me to Robert Andrews, son of my cousin William Andrews, & the 86 A. I bought of Littleton Darby to my wife Margaret. Wife & dau. resid. legatees. Wife Exec. & bro. in law William Joynes. Exr. Witt: Thomas Jacob, William Andrews, Henry Gascoyne - p. 395

FOSQUE, LUKE, Sr. - 27 Sept. 1766 - 24 Apr. 1770 - To dau. Sarah, wife of Littleton Savage, 50 A. on the South side of my land on the Main Branch of Pungoteague where the said Littleton has now built a house. To Elizabeth Savage, my dau. who was the wife of Nelson Savage, dec., 50 A. where she now lives adj. the land given my dau. Sarah. To dau. Rachel, the wife of Jacob Lurton 50 A. on the North side of my land. To dau. Mary, the wife of Solomon Richerson the remaining 50 A. of my land lying also on the North side thereof. Grandson Luk Fosque my heir at law. 4 daus. resid. legatees. Sons in law Jacob Lurton, Solomon Richerson & Littleton Savage Exrs. Witt: James Henry, John Nelson, Susanna Cutler. - p. 397
In order of prob: Littleton Dennis app. gdn to Luke Fosque, heir at

law to the testator.

LURTON, JACOB, Sr. - 8 Dec. 1769 - 24 Apr. 1770 - Wife Rachel. To son Jacob (under age) all my land, being 150 A. where I now live & 100 A. over the road where Benjamin Richeson now lives, & for want of heirs I give the 150 A. to Michael Bonewell, son of James Bonewell, and the 100 A. to be div. bet. Jacob Savage, son of Betty & Thomas Savage son of Sarah. To Solomon Richerson. To son Jacob negro, & for want of issue to Mary Bonewell, dau. of John. To Stephen Bonewell, son of John Bonewell. Sr. Wife & son Jacob resid. legatees. Witt: George Cutler, William McWilliams - p. 399

SAVAGE, GRIFFITH - 17 Mar. 1770 - 24 Apr. 1770 - To dau. Esther Savage 125 A. beginning at the Gleabe Branch & running to the main branch of Guilford Creek. To dau. Mary Savage 125 A. next to Davises land & 50 A. of marsh on Guilford Creek. To dau. Anne Savage my planta. & all my land not before given, together with the Water Mill. Dau. Elizabeth. Wife Esther. To dau. Sarah Savage 1/2 of an Island called Morrisses Island. To wife Mary Savage, Elizabeth Savage & Sarah Savage negroes. Wife & dau. Anne Exrs. Witt: William Young, Jacob Fitchett. - p. 400
Note: The bequest to wife Mary is undoubtedly an error & should be daughter Mary, as in the order of probate Littleton Dennis is app. guardian to Anne, Esther, Elizabeth, Sarah & Mary, co heirs to the decedent. Esther Savage, wid. of the testator, & Anne Savage qualified.

WARRINGTON, ALEXANDER - 11 Feb. 1770 - 24 Apr. 1770 - To friend Arthur Rowley 50 A., remainder of my land to my wife Marget during her wid. & then to my daus. Rebeckah & Rhoady Warrington. Wife & 2 daus. resid. legatees. Wife & William Patterson Exrs. Witt: Andrew Gootee, Edward Benson, Josephus Warrington - p. 403
In order of prob: Littleton Dennis app. guardian to Rebecca & Rhoda Warrington, Inf'ts. & co heirs to the testator.

RODGERS, ISAAC - 11 July 1769 - 29 May 1770 - To wife Mary Rodgers all my land during her life, & then to be equally div. bet. my 2 sons Leavin & Babel Rodgers. Dau. Agness Rodgers. Dau. Elizabeth Rodgers. Dau. Ann Rodgers. Wife & children resid. legatees. Wife Exec. - Witt: George Scott, Sarah Scott - p. 406

BUNTING, SMIIH - 6 May 1770 - 29 May 1770 - To son Levin Bunting all my land. Wife Eleshe. Bro. William Black Bunting. Daus. Bridget Bull, Neomy Poulson, Burton Ironmonger, Seymour Bunting, Nancy Bunting, sons Smith Bunting, Robinson Bunting, William Bunting, George Bunting & Kendal Bunting resid. legatees. Wife & bro. William Black Bunting Exrs. Witt: Tabitha Bayly, Elizabeth Bayly - p. 410
In order of prob: Levin Bunting heir at law to the testator.

TOWNSEND, JOHN - 30 Jan. 1770 - 29 May 1770 To sister Leah Townsend & Ann Cain my planta. for the space of 20 years to keep my 3 children Ann Townsend & Rebecker, excluding the house & 1 A. which I preserve for the use of my father & mother, and after their dec. to Leah Townsend & Ann Cain. Leah Townsend & Ann Cain Executrices. Witt: Michael Dickerson, Jacob Broadwater. - p. 411

COLLINS, ELIJAH - 29 Apr. 1770 - 26 June 1770.- To dau. Betty Collins 1 cow that I had of John Townsend & all her mother's wearing clothes. Dau. Peggy Collins. Bro. Joseph Collins. Daus. Peggy, Nancy & Salley Collins resid. legatees. Friend John Watts Exr. Witt: Joshua Broadwater, Thomas Tegel Townsend - p. 415

SCARBURGH, HENRY - Not dated - 26 June 1770 - To dau. Sarah Scarburgh, & for want of heirs to be equally div. bet. my other children. Land at Pungoteague to my 3 sons Henry, Bennett & George Scarburgh. Bal. of est. to wife (no name) during her wid. "without her commiting"---- Not completed - p. 417
In order of prob: "the above will was presented together with another writing dated 21 April 1764, and signed by the decedent, which being set aside the said within writing is adjudged by the Court to be the will of the said decedent" George Corbin, Jr. app. guardian to Henry Scarburgh, heir at law to the testator. George Parker qualified.

ROBERTS, ROSE - 20 Oct. 1767 - 31 July 1770 - Grandsons Edmund & Peter Watson. Grandau. Rose Green. Grandau. Priscilla Watson. Dau. Sabra Simpkins. Edmund & Peter Watson Exrs. Witt: Francis Savage, Jonathan Garrison, Archabel Garretson p. 422

COPES, PARKER - 15 May 1770 - 31 July 1770 - To wife Elizabeth whole est. during her wid. & then my land to my son Southy Copes. 4 youngest children Elizabeth, Beverly. Peter Parker & Rachel resid. legatees. Wife Exec. Witt: Southy Simpson. Jacob Sturgis. - p. 428
In order of prob: George Corbin, Jr. app. guardian to Southy Copes, heir at law to the testator.

MATTHEWS, WILLIAM - 9 Feb. 1767 - 28 Aug. 1770 - To eldest son William (under age) 310 A. where I now live, being all the land that my father gave me. To my 2nd son Joseph Matthews planta. cont. 200 A. purchased of Col. Robert King. Should either of my said sons die without issue his or their part to fall to my youngest son Meshack Matthews - Wife Esther. Dau. Sarah Matthews. Dau. Rachel Matthews. Dau. Esther Matthews. Bal. of est. to wife during her wid. then to be div. bet. all my children. Wife & son William Exrs. Witt: S: Feddiman, Elizabeth Massey. p. 434

KELLAM, WILLIAM, Sr. - 8 May 1770 - 28 Aug. 1770 - To wife Sarah the house where I live & 1/2 my land during her life, & the other 1/2 to my son Benston Kellam during his life & at the death of my wife her part to my grandson William Kellam & also Benston's part at his death to my grandson. Dau. Sarah Kellam. Dau. Mary Kellam.

Grandson William & 2 daus. Sarah & Mary Kellam resid. legatees. Neighbor Thomas Jacob Exr. Witt: Solomon Kellam, Jonathan Kellam, Absalom Sturgis. - p. 43_ (unclear)
In order of prob: Benston Kellam heir at law to the testator.

LEWIS, JOSIAH - 10 Aug. 1770 - 20 Aug. 1770 - To eldest son George Lewis 50 A. on Leep Creek. To 2nd son Abel Lewis 50 A. adj. his bro. George. Should both die without issue I give the land to my bro. of the half blood, Cornelius Ironmonger. Wife Joice Lewis. Cornelius Ironmonger Exr. Witt: Severn Guthridge, James Taylor, William E. Waggaman, John Walker - p. 438
In order of prob: Littleton Dennis app. guardian to George Lewis, heir at law to the testator.

ROBERTS, HUGH - 11 June 1770 - 25 Sept. 1770 - To my sister Mary Herring. To Charles Herring. To young George Cutler. To young Margaret Cutler. To Margaret Cutler, wife of George Cutler. To Thomas Bayly, son of Charles Bayly. To the 4 sons of George Cutler. To William Elliott, son of Thomas. To Capt. Rowland Savage. To Edmund Wise my hatt my Uncle left to me. To Euphamy James. To William Tilney. To Susanna Savage. To George Cutler, Sr. Charles Herring resid. legatee. George Cutler & Charles Herring Exrs. Witt: Rowland Savage, Comfort Savage, William Meers - p. 440

NIBLET, CALEB - Nunc. Proved 24 Aug. 1770 - 25 Sept. 1770 - Whole est. to John Niblet. Proved by Southy Tignal, Rachel Beech & Mary Niblet. - p. 441
In order of prob: John Niblet qualified.

BLOXOM, JOHN - 1 May 1770 - 25 Sept. 1770 - Son John Bloxom. To wife Tabitha Bloxom whole est. during her wid. Son Littleton Bloxom. Dau. Sarah Bloxom. Dau. Ann Bloxom. Bal. of est. to Sarah, Littleton & Ann Bloxom at their mother's death or marriage. Bro. Thomas Bloxom Exr. Witt: Stephen Bloxom, Woodman Bloxom - p. 441

HARMON, SIMON - 1 Aug. 1769 - 30 Oct. 177?0 - To wife Sarah whole est. for life during the time she sees fit to keep house & then to be div. bet. my wife & daus. Betty Ailor & Rachel Huff, Ezekiel Harman, Henry Harman & John Harman. Dau. Peggy Henderson. Dau. Rose Jackson. Grandson Robert Savage & cousin William Harmanson, Jr. Exrs. Witt: Arthur Robins, Richard Sturgis, John Sturgis - p. 452

BLOXOM NICHOLAS - 3 May 1770 - 30 Oct. 1770 - To son William Bloxom 100 A. where he now lives, provided he pay all demands which my cousin Richard Bloxom has against my est., & should he refuse my son Abbott Bloxom to have the said land. Wife Catharine Bloxom planta. where I live cont. 80 A. during her life or wid. then to my son William. Dau. Leah Bloxom. Bal. of est. to wife during her wid. then to be div. bet all my children except my son William. Wife & son William Exrs. Witt: Thomas Bloxom, Margaret Hinman - p. 454

In order of prob: William Bloxom heir at law to the testator.

LEWIS, WILLIAM - 1 Apr. 1770 - 30 Oct. 1770 - To wife Amey use of my land during her wid. Son William. Dau. Esther. Bal. of est. to wife during her wid. then to be div. bet. Robert Lewis, Mary Lewis, Amy Lewis, Isaac Lewis & Ann Tabitha Lewis. Wife Amey & Rodolphus Lewis Exrs. Witt: Thomas Ryley, Charles Snead - p. 456
In order of prob: Rodolphus Lewis heir at law to the testator.

AMES, JOSEPH, Sr. - 3 Feb. 1770 - 27 Nov. 1770 - To son Caleb 90 A. adj. where I now live. To son Joseph Ames 90 A. adj. to Thomas Ames. To son Levin 51 A. adj. Thomas Ames' line where he now lives. Dau. Anne Belote. Bal. of est. to wife Dorothy during her wid. then to my son Churchwell Ames. Sons Caleb & Joseph Exrs. Witt: Robert Watson, John Taylor, Sacker Taylor - p. 470
In order of prob: Caleb Ames heir at law to the testator.

GORE, DANIEL - 7 Nov. 1770 - 29 Nov. 1770 - To Benjamin Aydelott 100 A. land & marsh on Ashateague & Popes Island to be laid off from sea to bay with a parallel line with the Virginia line. To son John Gore all the rest of my land from Aydelott's line to John Smith's land. To son Thomas Teackle Gore all the remaining part of my land on Ashateague Beach. To son John land where I now live called Great Neck bounded by a branch dividing Great Neck from Little Neck. To son Thomas Teackle Gore land to the South of the said branch, also my water mill adj. the said land. To James Martin the land & mill I sold him in Worcester County, Maryland. To son Thomas Teackle Gore 48 A. bought of Stephen Taylor, also a piece of land I have entered on the Surveyor's book adj. the said 48 A. Should my 2 sons die without issue or without disposing of the above mentioned lands, then the same to be div. bet. my 4 daus. Mary, Elizabeth, Susanna & Ann. Wife Susanna. Wife, Littleton Dennis & Thomas Teackle Exrs. Witt: Daniel Mifflin, Skinner Martial, Shadrack Dennis. - p. 475
In order of prob: Littleton Dennis app. guardian to John Gore, heir at law to the testator.

PEAD, RICHARD - 21 Sept. 1770 - 29 Jan. 1771 - To wife Elizabeth whole est. during her wid. to bring up my children. To son John Read all my land & planta., he to pay my son William Read 60 £ current money within 2 years after said William arrives at lawful age, & should he refuse my son William to have that part of land belonging to me on the South-east side of the Main Road. Dau. Sarah Scarburgh Lecatt. Son Edmund Read my part of the water grist mill. Son Richard Read. Son Severn Read. Wife Exec. Witt: Joseph Aimes, William McWilliams, Elizabeth Clouds. p. 490
In order of prob: Littleton Dennis app. guardian to John Read heir at law to the testator.

PARRISH, EDWARD - 26 Mar. 1770 - 29 Jan. 1771 - To wife whole est. for life then 1/2, real & personal, I give to be at her disposal & the other 1/2 to my bro. Robert's son William & my bro. John's son

George, equally, & should either of them die before they arrive to age, I give the deceased's part to my bro. in law Frederick Philes son Thomas, & should he die before coming to age to my bro. Isaac's son Samuel. Wife (no name), friend John Watts & Stephen Collins, merchant in Philadelphia, Exrs. Witt: Johannes Watson, John White, James Sandford, Leah Abbott. - p. 492

In order of prob: Agnes Parrish, wid. of the testator qualified.

WIMBROUGH, JOSEPH - 9 Sept. 1767 - 29 Jan. 1771 - To dau. Patience Roach land where I now live for life, reversion to her dau. Mary Roach. Grandson Planner Roach. Grandau. Elizabeth Roach. Dau. Beersheba Bundick. Bal. of est. to dau. Patience Roach for life, reversion to my 3 grandchildren Elizabeth, Planner & Mary Roach. Patiance Roach Exec. - Witt: William Black Bunting, Alexander Roach, Betty Bunting. - p. 494

In order of prob: John Bundick, who intermarried with one of the heirs of the decedent, cited to appear & having nothing to object the said will was admitted to probate.

BUNCLE, ANNE - Wid. of Alexander Buncle, late of the Parish of Allhallows in the County of Worcestor, Province of Maryland - 27 Sept. 1770 - 27 Nov. 1770 - To son William Drummond all the upper part of Lot No. 11 in Snow Hill Town with the dwelling house lately possessed by John Chaillie. To son William all my part of the profits arising from the "Excutory" of my dec. husband Alexander Buncle's est. To son William all the tract of land called in the patent Water Lotts lying contiguous to Snow Hill Town. To Anne Drummond, dau. of my son George Drummond, dec. part of Lot No. 11 & for want of heirs to her bro. Richard Drummond, & should he die without issue or without disposing of same then to my son William Drummond. To the said Richard Drummond, son of my dec. son George, all my remaining part of Lot No. 11, reversion to his sister Anne Drummond, & for want of issue to my son William Drummond. Grandchildren Sally, Elizabeth, & George Drummond, children of my son William Drummond. Son William resid. legatee & Exr. Witt: Robert Evans, Polly Martin, Esther Adams - p. 507

In order of prob: Anne Bayly heir at law to the testatrix.

PARRISH, AGNES - 8 Feb. 1771 - 26 Mar. 1771 - To George Douglas Wise, son of Tully P. Wise, all my swamp land. Bal. of est. to be div. bet. my bro. in law's (Skinner Wallop's) 3 daus. Izabel, Peggy & Mary & my sister Peggy Wise's 3 daus. Kessey, Elizabeth & Mary. Bro. in law Tully Robinson Wise & friend John Watts Exrs. Witt: Edward Ardis, Abigail Sturgis, Leving Gooddy. - p. 512

In order of prob: Tully Robinson Wise on behalf of his wife, & Peggy Wise, sisters & co-heirs of the testatrix, appeared & having nothing to object the foregoing will was admitted to probate.

BRADFORD, JOHN - 11 June 1768 - 26 Mar. 1771 - To bro. Jacob Bradford whole est. he paying my 2 sisters Rachel & Peggy Bradford the sum of 40 L each, also to Abel Bradford's dau. I give 40 L Bro.

Jacob Exr. Witt: Arthur Upshur, Ezekiel Badger - p. 516

LINGO, LITTLETON - 25 Sept. 1770 - 26 Mar. 1771 - To wife Elizabeth whole est. during her wid. & then to my bro. Caleb Lingo all my land & planta. reversion to his son Littleton Lingo. Personal est. to wife during her wid. & at her marriage she to have 1/2 & the other 1/2 to be div. bet. my bros. John & Caleb Lingo. Capt. John Coleburn & Bro. John Lingo Exrs. Witt: William Polk, Charles Richardson - In order of prob: John Lingo heir at law to the testator.

STOCKLEY, ANNE - 20 May 1766 - 26 Mar. 1771 - To Robert James planta. where I live & all the balance of my est. Robert James Exr. Witt: Arnold Morgan, John Onions, Scarburgh Lewis. - p. 530 In order of prob: William Bradford heir at law to the testatrix.

MILNER, HENRY - 22 Nov. 1770 - 25 June 1771 - To wife Neomi land I bought of Middleton Melson during her life & then to be div. bet. my son Smith & Henry Milner. Should Smith die without issue his part to go to my son William Milner, & should Henry die without issue his part to go to my son Robert Milner. Bal. of est. to wife for life then to be div. bet. all my children. Wife Exec. Witt: William B. Bunting, Sebastian Cropper, Jr. - p. 537 In order of prob: Smith Milner heir at law to the testator.

SMITH, FAIRFAX - 1 Dec. 1770 - 26 June 1771 - Wife Mary Robinson Smith to have use of whole est. during her life to being up my 2 daus, then to my said daus. Molly & Sally Smith. To bro. Charles Bagwell. To each of my daus. six silver soup spoons marked "James Fairfax". Wife & Bro. Charles Bagwell Exrs. Witt: Johennes Watson, Lewis Algeo, James Taylor - p. 540

CORBIN, GEORGE - 31 Mar. 1771 - 30 July 1771 - Son Ralph Corbin. If George Thomas at his death should not devise unto his dau. Sarah Corbin an equal part of his est. with the rest of his children, then the said Sarah shall not enjoy any part of my est. I have here given to my son Ralph Corbin. To friend John Michael 90 A. of land & marsh that I bought of Levin Evans. Wife Mary Corbin. To son George Corbin planta. in Jollys Neck which I bought of William Savage, being 173 A. after the death of his mother, also 40 A. purchased of William Merril adj. the above. Dau. Polly Corbin. Wife Mary & son Ralph Exrs. Witt: James Richarson, William Burton, John Nicholson - p. 542

METCALF, THOMAS - 29 Dec. 1770 - 30 July 1771 - To son Charles, after his mother's death. To wife Elizabeth whole est. during her wid. Son John Metcalf. Slaves & personal est. at the death of my wife to be div. bet. all my children, viz: Charles, John, Gordon, Walter, Thomas, Anne & Rachel (children under age) Friends John Wharton & James Henry to div. est. To son Charles all my land & planta. & should he die without issue to my son John. Wife & son Charles Exrs. Witt: William Chandler, John Guy - p. 556 In order of prob: Charles Metcalf heir at law to the testator.

FITZGERRALD, JAMES - 17 May 1771 - 30 July 1771 - To son John Fitzgerrald my land & planta. during his life, reversion to my son Richard Fitzgerrald. To dau. Susanna Royal. Grandau. Susanna Churn. Dau. Susanna Royal & son Richard Fitzgerrald resid. legatees. Charles Bagwell Exr. Witt: Sarah Melson, Elizabeth Baker - p. 557 In order of prob: John Fitzgerrald heir at law to the testator.

POULSON, EDMUND - Not dated - 31 July 1771 - To wife whole est. during her wid. & then to be div. bet. my children. "Wife & my near friend George Parker to sell my lands & houses when they think fit & lay the money out as they think Best, and also to give my Boys such Education as their Estates will afford & then bind them out to any trade that they should think proper ----------------" Not completed - Proved by George Parker, William Riley & Abraham Outten. - p. 571 In order of prob: Anne Poulson qualified. 30 Apr. 1772, George Parker & John Poulson granted letters of adm. on the above est. unadministered by Anne Poulson.

WARRINGTON, TABITHA - 23 Mar. 1768 - 27 Aug. 1771 - Son George Warrington. Grandson Stephen Warrington. Grandson John Warrington. Grandau. Elizabeth Warrington. Dau. Nanney Warrington. To Molley Laws, dau. of Jonathan Laws. Grandson William Crippin. Grandau. Nanney Warrington. To Susanna Abbott, dau. of Robert Abbott. To Hannah Laws, wife of William Laws. Should my son George die without issue what I have devised him to be div. bet. my 4 grandchildren Stephen Warrington, John Warrington, Elizabeth Warrington & Nanny Warrington. Son George Warrington, John Watts & Charles Bagwell Exrs. - Witt: Arnold Morgan, Joseph Nock, Mary Nock - p. 574

GROTEN, WILLIAM - Not dated - 27 Aug. 1771 - Son Solomon Groten. Dau. Sarah Groten, alias Green. To wife Mary Groten all my lands & livings to her disposing. Son William Exr. Witt: Thomas Ames, John Taylor, William Taylor - p. 576 In order of prob: Solomon Groten heir at law.

WARRINGTON, BENJAMIN - 3 Apr. 1771 - 27 Aug. 1771 - To son George Warrington 87 A. where I now live, & for wamt of heirs to my son Benjamin, & for want of heirs to my son James. Wife Comfort. Dau. Comfort. Dau. Lishe Turlington. Son in law Edmond Turlington. Dau. Sarah. Dau. Mary. Bal. of est. to be div. bet. wife & all my children except George. Wife Exec. - Witt: Luke Luker, James Turlington, John Winder - p. 577 In order of prob: Thomas Parramore app. guardian to George Warrington, heir at law.

KELLAM, JOHN - 22 Sept. 1761 - 27 Aug. 1771 - To son Argil Kellam 150 A. on Matchapungo Creek, same land whereon my father Edward Kellam lived, he to pay my son John 15 L at my death or deliver the said land to the said John. To son Zorobable Kellam planta. where I now live cont. 130 A., he to pay my son John 10 L-current money or deliver the said land to him. To son John Kellam. Wife Ursilla Kellam. Sophia Bagwell to have my negro woman Dinah at the death of my wife. Bal. of est. to wife during her wid. & then to be div. bet. all my children, Argil Kellam, Zorobable Kellam, Susannah Savage, Ann Sinah Lecatt, Sophia Bagwell, Comfort Buntain, Adah Wyatt & John Kellam. Sons Argal, Zorobable & John Exrs. Witt: Thomas Parrmore, Ann Bagge, Cornelius Watkinson. - p. 579 In order of prob: Argal Kellam heir at law to the testator.

FITSGARRELL, RACHEL - 27 Mar. 1769 - 27 Aug. 1771 - To son Custis Watson. Bal. of est. to be div. bet. my 3 eldest daus., Sarah, Rachel & Agnes Watson. Edmund Watson Exr. Witt: Robert Drurey, John Henderson, Zorobable Watson - p. 581

DURTON, RACHEL - 27 Jan. 1771 - 27 Aug. 1771 - To son Jacob Lurton 50 A. my father gave me, & for want of heirs to my 3 sisters Mary Richardson, Sarah Savage & Elizabeth Vernelson. To Sarah Foster, wife of James Foster. Son Jacob resid. legatee, & for want of heirs to 3 sisters above named. Solomon Richardson to take care of my son & learn him his trade & give him a good education. Solomon Richardson & Littleton Savage Exrs. Witt: George Cutler, John Hannaford - p. 582

BULL, BENJAMIN - 16 Dec. 1770 - 27 Aug. 1771 - To wife Bridget whole est. during her wid. Son Major Bull. To son John Bull a linen wheel which was once the property of Rhody Melson. Bal. of est. to wife for life & then to be div. bet. my 3 sons, Benjamin, John & Major Bull. To son Richard Bull 1 s. To son Southy Bull 1 s. Friends James Henry & Thomas Parramore Exrs. Witt: Thomas Edmunds, Joyce Edmunds, Charles Smith - p. 590

BAGWELL, THOMAS, Gent: 18 Nov. 1770 - 28 Aug. 1771 - To wife Sophia Bagwell all my land, my 1/2 of the mill on Burton's Branch & all my right on Cedar Island until my son John attains his full age of 21, she to maintain, educate & bring up all my children. 100 A. at the head of my tract of land, 25 A. near George Garrison's & Negro Moll to be sold for the payment of debts. Sons John & Thomas, as soon as they have acquired education suitable, and have attained an age proper, to be put out to some trade. When my son John arrives at 21 years of age my wife to take her dower in my lands & 1/4 my personal est. & slaves. To son John all my land which shall remain after paying my debts, including my 1/2 of the mill on Burton's Branch, & all my right on Cedar Island, & for want of issue to my son Thomas, & for want of issue to my dau. Rachel. 2 younger children, Rachel & Thomas resid. legatees. Wife & friends John Wharton & James Henry Exrs. Witt: Aser Shield, William Spires. p. 607

BLOXOM, EZEKIEL - 15 Dec. 1770 - 24 Sept. 1771 - Wife Ann Bloxom to have use of all my land during her wid. Est. to be div. bet. my wife & children Ezekiel, Bable, Ann & John. Wife Exec. - Witt:

John Wharton, William Coleburn, Nash Kellam. Codicil: Should my son Southy Bloxom die without issue my land to descend to my son Ezekiel Bloxom, &. so to descend from child to child. Witt: John Wharton, Thomas Mason, Woodman Bloxom, John Bull, Richard Bull. – p. 612
In order of prob: Robert Pitt app. guardian to Southy Bloxom, Inf't. heir at law to the testator.

MATTHEWS, THOMAS – 3 Feb. 1771 – 24 Sept. 1771 – Wife Keziah – To sons James & Stayton Matthews all my land & planta. adj. my bro. John Matthews. Bal. of est. to wife for life then to my children James, Stayton, Sarah, Mary, Tabitha & Rebecca Matthews. Wife & son James Exrs. Witt: Nehemiah Stockly, Thomas Wheelton, James Henry. – p. 618
In order of prob: Samuel Matthews heir at law to the testator.

ARMITRADER, LITTLETON – 9 Oct. 1771 – 29 Oct. 1771 – To grandson Littleton Armitrader land where I now live, & for want of issue to my dau. Ann Bird. To son Archibold all the rest of my land I have in possession & for want of heirs to my dau. Euphamy Armitrader. Dau. Comfort Morgan. Dau. in law Comfort Armitrader. 4 daus. Comfort Morgan, Ann Bird, Sinah Hopman & Euphamy Armitrader resid. legatees. Son in law William Morgan Exr. Witt: Joseph Blake, Nehemiah Stockly. – p. 624
In order of prob: James Henry guardian to Littleton Armitrader, heir at law to the testator.

WHITE, HENRY, SR. – 11 Mar. 1768 – 29 Oct. 1771 – Son Nathan White. Dau. Salomy White. Grandson Southey White. Grandson Levin White. To my dau. Comfort Raifield's children. To my dau. Sarah's children. Dau. Salomy White & Grandson Southey White resid. legatees. Grandson Southey White & John Riley Parker Exrs. Witt: Nehemiah White, John Riley Parker, Elizabeth Turlington – p. 627

BELL, ROBERT, SR. – 9 Nov. 1771 – 26 Nov. 1771 – To son William Bell land where I live & for want of heirs to my son Robert Bell. Wife Scarburgh Bell. Son Levin Bell. Son John Bell. Dau. Leah Bell. Dau. Sarah Houston. Grandchildren Margaret, Sarah & Rachel McAllen. Children William, Robert, Leavin, John & Leah Bell & Sarah Houston resid. legatees. Wife Scarbrough Bell & William Bell Exrs. Witt: George Stewart, John Pitts, Margaret Smith – p. 636

REESE, EDWARD – 27 Sept. 1771 – 26 Nov. 1771 – To wife Tabitha whole est. in America during her wid. to bring up my child, then my whole est. in America to my dau. Mary Reese, & should my dau. die in the lifetime of her mother, she to have 1/3 of my est. & my son Deere Reese to have the other 2/3. Wife Exec. – Witt: Rosey Parker, Southey Simpson – p. 638

WALKER, DANIEL - 14 Sept. 1771 - 27 Nov. 1771 - Wife Jane. To son James planta. where I live when he comes to the age of 21. To wife Jane the planta. where Jacob Benston now lives. cont. 126 A, 46 A. of the said land lying in Maryland & the remainder in Accomack County, during her natural life, reversion to my dau. Ann Walker. Bal. of est. to my wife to bring up my children. Wife Jane & George Stewart Exrs. Witt: Shadrack Dennis, Skinner Marshall, Major Pettit, William Hill. p. 639
In order of prob: James Walker heir at law to the testator.

MORGAN, ARNOLD - 1 Dec. 1771 - 26 Feb. 1772 - Grandson John Glasby planta. where I live. To grandson William Glasby planta. purchased of Joseph Smith. Wife Mary to have use of land, if she remain a wid., until my grandsons come to age, provided she let my youngest dau. Sarah Morgan live with her, & to let my two grandsons live with her. Dau. Leah Cole. Bro. William Morgan & William Sacker James Exrs. Witt: Edward Gunter, Thomas Taylor, Mary Bennit. - p. 640
In order of prob: Leah Cole & Sarah Morgan, 2 of the co-heirs of the testator, appeared in their proper persons, Ann Hinman, the other co-heir not being found by the Sheriff to be cited. - Stephen Bloxom app. guardian to William Glasby, another of the heirs of the testator. Mary Morgan qualified.

WEST, JOHN - 16 Nov. 1770 - 25 Feb. 1772 - Dau. Ann West. Dau. Rachel West. Son Benjamin West. Dau. Betty West. Son Randal West, "now but twelve months old". Daus. Ann, Rachel & Betty West & son Randul West resid. legatees. Richard Bundick Exr. Witt: Elizabeth West, Aligal West, Benjamin West - p. 643
In order of prob: Zorobable Rodgers app. guardian to Benjamin West. Inf't. heir at law.

WATSON, BENJAMIN, SR. - 7 Apr. 1771 - 1 Jan. 1772 - Land which my bro. Moses Watson left me, being 36 1/3 A. to be sold, my bro. Mitchel Watson or my bro. Robert Watson to have the refusal of same, & the procceds div. bet. my children. Bal. of est. to wife Elizabeth during her wid. to bring up my children. Dau. Peggy Watson. Son Joshua Watson. Sons Moses, Revel & Benjamin Watson. Wife Elizabeth & bro. in law John Mears Exrs. Witt: George Henderson, Teackle Waltham, Benjamin Stringer - p. 649
In order of prob: William Bamfield Walker app. gdn. to Joshua Watson, heir at law to the testator.

CORMICK, JOHN, Shipright. 12 Feb. 1772 - 25 Feb. 1772 - To Mary Ironmonger. To Clement Cutler. To Thomas Cutler, son of Richard Cutler. To Major Ironmonger, son of Major Ironmonger, 10 L to put him to school. To Major Nelson. To Daniel Ironmonger 5 L. To Comfort Bell & Susanna Bloxom 5 L each. To Ann Benthal 5 L. To Provest Nelson, son of Major Nelson 15 L to be spent in schooling him. Margaret Griffin & Mary Benthal, John Smith & John Benthal resid. legagees. Witt: Major Ironmonger, George Booth - p. 650

KIRBY, WILLIAM - 30 Dec. 1771 - 25 Feb. 1772 - To 2 children Godfree & Elizabeth Kirby whole est. Hezekiah Holloway Exr. - Witt: Jeremiah Mason, Hezekiah Halloway, Thomas Holt - p. 651

TAYLOR, LEVEN - 10 May 1771 - 26 Feb. 1772 - To son Charles Bayly Taylor land I & my mother now live on cont. 110 A. & for want of heirs to my cousin Joshua Taylor, son of William Taylor, & for want of heirs to my 2 cousins Bartholomew Taylor, son of Bartholomew Taylor & Sacker Taylor, son of John Taylor, Cordwinder. Son resid. legatee. Bro. John Taylor & Charles Bayly, Sr., Exrs. Witt: Joseph Aimes, Joseph Roberts, James Broughton - p. 653

REW, COMFORT - 15 May 1771 - 25 Feb. 1772 - To son Woney Rew. Son Absalom Rew. 4 grandchildren Rubin, Comfort, Frances & Southey Rew. Dau. Tamer Middleton. Dau. Elizabeth Lewis. Thomas Copes, Sr., Exr. Witt: William Young, Sr., Mary Sturgis, Elizabeth Barnacasel - p. 656

BAGGE, WILLIAM - 3 Aug. 1769 - 25 Feb. 1772 - To Sarah Henry, Jr. To Mary Henry "a Tea table which Mr. James Henry presented me with". To Elijah Addison. To Peggy Williams. To John Addison, son of Elijah. To Bridget Addison. To wife planta. I now live on for life & then to John Addison. To wife 1/3 of my negroes for life & then to be div. bet. James Henry, John & Bridget Addison. To James Henry my planta. called Linseys & the other 2/3 of my negroes. Wife (no name) & James Henry Exrs. Not Witnessed. Proved by Samuel Bagge & George Holden - p. 657
In order of prob: Samuel Bagge heir at law to the testator.

FEDDEMAN, JOSEPH - 20 Feb. 1772 - 31 Mar. 1772 - To dau. Elizabeth planta. where I now live cont. 120 A. for 5 years. I lend 124 A. adj. the above land, which I purchased of Samuel Feddeman, to my dau. Ann for the term of 5 years. To my dau. Esther planta. now rented to Isaac Merril for the term of 5 years. At the expiration of the terms aforesaid, the said lands, together with the lands I bought of Samuel Wilson & the land now rented to Ezekiel Broadwater, with all my mills, to my son Faderick Feddeman. Bro. Meshack Feddeman & friend George Corbin & my son Faderick Exrs. Witt: Ezekiel Broadwater, William Merril. Ann Warrington.
Codicil: To dau. Esther part of the land now rented to Ezekiel Broadwater, adj. the lands before given her, for the term of 5 years, & my desire is that Ann Warrington live with my said dau. Ann for the term of 4 years to take care of her. The 124 A. lent to my dau. Ann to include the 14 A. to be conveyed to me by John Pitts. Witt: William Merril, Jabez Pitt, Ezekiel Broadwater - p. 673

PETTIT, JOHN, Jr. Nunc. - 24 Jan. 1772 - 31 Mar. 1772 - To son William Pettit. Bal. of est. to wife during her wid. then to be div. bet. my 2 daus. Proved by John Gootee & Betty Taylor - p. 676
In order of prob: Tropenny Pettit, wid. of the testator qualified.

HORNSBY, MARY - 17 Dec. 1770 - 31 Mar. 1772 - p. 676 - Sons John & Levin Hornsby. Sons Eli & William Hornsby. Daus. Mary, Anne & Comfort Hornsby. To my 8 children John, Eli, Mary, Ann, Comfort, Eburn, William & Laban Hornsny all the est. I got of my father & mother, dec. Sons Eli & John Exrs. Witt: Elisha Mears, John Mears, (Constable), Solomon Mears. Memo: Son John to take care of my son Laban & bring him up. - p. 676

GUNTER, MESHACK - 8 Feb. 1772 - 31 Mar. 1772 - Bro. Bednego Gunter 60 A. where I live. To Benjamin Gunter, son of Bednego. To Parker Savage, son of Abel. To John Savage, son of Abel. Wife Peggy. To my Mother. Wife resid. legatee. Wife & Bro. Bednego Exrs. Witt: Richard Rodgers, William Savage - p. 678

TUNNEL, WASHBURN - 23 Nov. 1771 - 28 Apr. 1772 - Should my wife have issue by me I beq. the whole of my est. to such issue, male or female, & in case of no such issue to my wife Rachel during her wid. & then whole est. to my bro. Charles Tunnel. Wife Exec. Witt: John Watts, Nehemiah Stockley, Jonathan Powell - p. 685
In order of prob: Scarburgh Tunnel heir at law to the testator.

MICHAEL, SUSANNAH - 19 July 1769 - 28 Apr. 1772 - After the est. of my late husband, Simon Michael, dec., shall be set apart pursuant to his will, I give to Anne, the wife of Samuel Mathews, dau. of my late dau. Anne Milburn, personalty &c. To son Joachim. Dau. Mary, Dau. Adrah, Dau. Elizabeth Abbott. Son John Michael. Children, Joachim, Mary & Adrah resid. legatees. Grandson Michael Milburn & grandson Joachim Milburn, sons of my dau. Anne above named. Daus. Mary & Adrah Exrs. Witt: William Bloxom, George Holden, Southey Northam - p. 689

BEACH, JOSEPH - 27 Aug. 1769 - 26 May 1772 - To son Kendal Beach land where I now live, & for want of issue land to be sold & the proceeds div. bet. my 3 daus. Sophia, Mary & Sarah. Grandson Abel Mears. Wife Mary & 3 daus. resid. legatees. Son & wife Exrs. Witt: John Spires, Robert Spires - p. 696

BAKER, WILLIAM - 6 Jan. 1769 - 26 May 1772 - To wife Elizabeth whole est. during her wid. To son Isaiah 100 A. of land adj. Joshua Bell on Wallops Road, the remainder of my land to be div. bet. my sons Salathiel & Hezekiah Baker. 4 sons William, Solomon, George & Leven Baker resid. legatees. Wife & son Hezekiah Exrs. Witt: Charles Bagwell, John Kitson, William Fitchet - p. 698
In order of prob: John Baker heir at law to the testator.

MAJOR, Littleton Scarburgh - 22 May 1767 - Wearing apparel & diet to be found for my son Frederick Major out of my est. by my grandson Littleton Major as long as my said son lives, & if my grandson re-fuses I give as much of my land as I bought of Nathaniel Milby to be rented out as will keep him in these things. To grandson Littleton

Major, after payment of debts & he complying with the gift to his uncle Frederick, whole est., real & personal, & to receive the same when he is 21 years of age. Thomas Hall Exr. Witt: William Coloney, Jane Hall – p. 705

WINDOW, JOHN – 13 Feb. 1772 – 26 May 1772 – To wife Sarah whole est. during her wid. To son John Window 96 A. where I now live & for want of heirs to my son. Robert, & for want of heirs to my son Able, & for want of heirs to my son Bable. To son Henry Window 60 A. Dau. Welthy Window. Dau. Sarah Window. Dau. Peggy Window. Wife & 8 children resid. legatees. Wife & Levi Window Exrs. Witt: Robert Parker, Selby Vernelson – p. 706
In order of prob: George Corbin guardian of James Window, orphan heir at law to the testator.

BRADFORD, MARY – 21 May 1771 – 26 May 1772 – Dau. Betty Bradford. Dau. Rachel. "I give unto Susannah Bradford, the wife of Edmond Bayly", for life reversion to her dau. Mary Bayly. Dau. Esther Bradford. Dau. Mary, wife of Caleb Harrison. Son Nathaniel Bradford, 6 L due me in the hands of Jesse Hunt of New York. After the will of my husband Fisher Bradford, dec., is fulfilled the remainder of my est. to be div. bet. my daus. Betty Bradford, Rachel Bradford & Esther Bradford. Son Nathaniel & son in law Edmond Bayly Exrs. Witt: William Polk, William Stockley – p. 709

PETTIGREW, JAMES – 20 Apr. 1771 – 26 May 1772 – Wife Leah to sell 50 A. of land purchased of Richard Hinman for the payment of my debts. To son "Pettigrew" the remaining part of said tract, being 50 A. To son John Pettigrew 300 A. purchased of William Andrews. Son Gavin Pettigrew (under age) resid. legatee. To son Gavin Pettigrew the legacies left me by my bro. William Pettigrew at the death of my two sisters Margaret Simpson & Agnes ____. Wife Exec. Witt: Robert Moore, Rebecca Walker – p. 713

RILEY, THOMAS, Sr. – 12 May 1772 – 28 May 1772 – To son William Riley 200 A. where I live beginning at the Creek. To son Thomas 100 A. purchased of Jacob Litchfield & Joseph Walker. To son John Riley 100 A. purchased of Thomas & William Simpson. To son Raymond Riley (under age), all the remainder of the tract of land where I live, & all my plantable land on "Shoarses" Island. To sons William, Thomas, John & Raymond the remainder of my Island. To 3 sons Thomas John & Raymond the land purchased of James Boyle & wife. To dau. Sarah Snead for life, reversion to her children except her son Bennet Riley. To grandson Bennet Riley (under 12) All my children William Riley, Jr., Thomas Riley, John Riley, Raymond Riley, & Sarah Snead resid. legatees & Exrs. Witt: Thomas Bayly, Richard Drummond, Catherine Grinnals – p. 718
In order of prob: William Riley heir at law to the testator.

WINDOW, ELI - Adm. his est. to Elijah Addison, Violetta Window, wid. of the dec. refusing to qualify - James Henry sec. - 27 Jan. 1774 - P. 19

NEWTON, ANDREW - Adm. his est. to David Bowman - Edward Ker sec. - 22 Feb. 1774 - p. 34

MARSHALL, DANIEL - Adm. his est. to Beautifila Marshall - George Marshall & Edward Ardies sec. - 22 Feb. 1774 - p. 40

PERRY, THOMAS - Adm. his est. to Abel Russell - William Crowson & Andrew Russell sec. - 22 Feb. 1774 - p. 42

HINMAN, GEORGE - Adm. his est. to Bayly Hinman - Drake Drummond sec. - 22 Feb. 1774 - p. 43

CRIPPEN, JOHN - Adm. his est. to Thomas Crippen & John Kitson - 22 Feb. 1774 - p. 45

MILLIGAN, JOHN - Adm. his est. to George Holden & Henry Fletcher - Thorogood Smith sec. - 24 Feb. 1774 - p. 70

JAMES, THOMAS - Adm. his est. to Thorogood Smith - George Holden sec. - 25 Feb. 1774 - p. 71

SMITH, WILLIAM - Adm. his est. to Elizabeth Smith - William Smith & Smith Snead sec. - 29 Mar. 1774 - p. 96

WINDOW, JOHN - Adm. his est. to Elijah Addison, unadministered by Eli Window dec. - 26 Apr. 1774 - p. 122

ROWLEY, WILLIAM - Adm. his est. to James Berry - Alexander Stockly sec. - 27 Apr. p. 137

RUSSELL, JOHN - Adm. his est. to Sarah Russell - John Custis (seaside) & John Bull, Jr. sec. - 29 Apr. 1774 - p. 169

OWIN, SAMUELL - Adm. his est. to Mary Owin - Skinner Wallop sec. - 28 June 1774 - p. 192

WATKINSON, TABITHA - Adm. her est. to Elizabeth Watkinson - Robert Coleburn sec. 28 June 1774 - p. 197

QUINTON, SOUTEY - Adm. his est. to Richard Cutler, Thomas Quinton bro. of the dec. having relinquished his right to qualify - George Cutlar sec. - 27 Sept. 1774 - p. 225

SAVAGE, ROBERT - Adn. his est. to Shady Savage - 25 Oct. 1774 - p. 271

BLOXOM, JOHN – Adm. his est. to Henry Fletcher – George Corbin sec. – 29 Nov. 1774 p. 280

ARDIES, WILLIAM – Adm. his est. to Edward Ardies – George Corbin sec. – 29 Nov. 1774 – p. 281

BLOXOM, LITTLETON – Adm. his est. to Lucretia Bloxom – George Corbin, Jonathan Meers & Robert Small sec. – 29 Nov. 1774 – p. 281

STEPHENS, JAMES – Adm. his est. to Thomas Stephens – John West sec. – 27 Dec. 1774 – p. 285

LEWIS, LABAN – Adm. his est. to William Parramore – Thomas Bayly sec. – 27 Dec. 1774 – p. 292

COPES, PETER – Adm. his est. to Jesse Copes – William Patterson sec. – 31 Jan. 1775 – p. 298

ROBINSON, JAMES – Adm. his est. to Catherine Bloxom – Bayly Hinman sec. – 31 Jan. 1774 – p. 300

MICHAEL, SIMON – Adm. his est. unadministered by Susanna Michael, his wid. & Exec., dec. to Adah Michael – George Corbin sec. – 28 Feb. 1775 – p. 318

THORNMAN, OBADIAH – Adm. his est. to Tabitha Thornman – Jonathan Scott, Walter Scott & Clement Parker sec. – 28 Mar. 1775 – p. 328

CHAMBERS, EDMUND – Adm. his est. to John West, Deep Creek – Smith Snead sec. – 29 Mar. 1775 – p. 336

BALDING, JOSEPH – Adm. his est. to Elizabeth Balding – John Morrison & John Benson sec. – 29 Mar. 1775 – p. 341

LITCHFIELD, EZEKIEL – Adm. his est. to Francis Litchfield – John Watts sec. – 26 Sept. 1775 – p. 384

NORTHUP, MANSFIELD TUCKER – Adm. his est. to Margaret Mehorn – Zerrobabel Rodgers sec. – 1 Nov. 1775 – p. 393

BANDY, MARY – Adm. her est. to Isaac Riggs – William Young sec. – 28 Nov. 1775 – p. 398

TOWNSEND, ELIZABETH – Adm. her est. to William Riley – Ezekiel Young scc. – 30 Nov. 1775 – p. 405

UNDERHILL, SALATHIEL – Adm. his est. to William Underhill – George Corbin sec. 27 Feb. 1776 – p. 408

TOWNSEND, THOMAS - Adm. his est. to Michael Robins - George Corbin sec. - 27 Feb. 1776 - p. 411

MEERS, WILL - Adm. his est. to George Meers - Augustine Lecatt sec. - 27 Feb. 1776 - p. 412

BLAXTON, WILLIAM - Adm. his est. to Sebastian Cropper, Jr. - George Stewart sec. 27 Feb. 1776 - p. 414

BLOXOM, ABBOTT - Adn. his est. to Isaac Waterfield - John Read, Jr. & Eli Hornsby sec. - 28 Feb. 1776 - p. 416

KELLAM, BENSON - Adm. his est. to Edmund Bayly - Nathaniel Bradford & Americus Scarburgh sec. - 26 Mar. 1776 - p. 431

IRONMONGER, JOHN - Adm. his est. to Philoclear Ironmonger - William Riley & Daniel Bull sec. - 25 June 1776 - p. 444

SIMPSON, SOUTHY - Adm. his est. to Selby Simpson - Alexander Stockly sec. - 30 July 1776 - p. 448

BENETT, GEORGE - Adm. his est. to Tabitha Bennett - Mary Beavans sec. - 30 July 1776 - p. 448

LATCHUM, GEORGE - Adm. his est. to George Latchum - Josenh Stockly sec. - 30 July 1776 - p. 453

DUNTON, ELIZABETH - Adm. her est. to Benjamin Dunton - James Henry sec. 30 July 1776 - p. 454

BISWICK, PRUDENCE - Adm. her est. to George Biswick - James Henry sec. - 24 Sept. 1776 - p. 465

RODGERS, JOHN - Adm. his est. to Nanny Rodgers - Robert Rodgers sec. - 26 Nov. 1776 - p. 478

MASSEY, STEPHEN - Adm. his est. to Anne Massey - Joseph Matthews & Francis Houston sec. - 26 Nov. 1776 - p. 479

BLAKE, CHARLES - Adm. his est. to Hannah Blake - John Burton & Joseph Matthews sec. - 26 Nov. 1776 - p. 479

ABBOTT, JOHN - Adm. his est. to his wid., Betty Abbott - Richard Justice (seaside), Robert Coleburn & Richard Abbott sec. - 31 Dec. 1776 - p. 486

BAYLY, HENRY - Adm. his est. to Sarah Bayly - Elisha Mears & Edmund Bayly sec. - 31 Dec. 1776 - p. 488

AIMES, ZERROBABEL - Adm. his est. to Elizabeth Aimes - Joseph Kellam sec. - 28 Jan. 1777 - P. 490

HARRISON, JAMES – Adm. his est. to Mary Harrison – Benjamin Floyd & Custis Rodgers sec. – 28 Jan. 1777 – p. 492

HARMAN, EZEKIEL – Adm. his est. to Rowland Savage – John Bagge sec. – 29 Apr. 1777 – p. 515

Wills &c. 1772-1777

VANELSON, ELIAS – 14 Sept. 1771 – 30 June 1772 – To wife Mary whole est. to bring up my children, then my land to my son William Vanelson & the bal. of my est. to be div. bet. the rest of my children. Witt: William Burton, Jesse Broadwater. – p. 1
In order of prob: George Corbin app. guardian to William Vanelson, heir at law to the testator. Mary Vanelson qualified. Children under age.

BRADFORD, LEVIN – 29 Oct. 1766 – 30 June 1772 – To wife Joana whole est. during her wid. to bring up my children, then to be div. bet. my children then living. Wife & Jacob Bradford Exrs. Witt: Arthur Upshur, William Bradford, Jacob Bradford. – p. 2
In order of prob: Zephaniah Bradford heir at law to the testator.

BLOXAM, SARAH – 18 Dec. 1771 – 30 June 1772 – Bro. Littleton Bloxam. Sister Nancy More. Cousin Southey Bloxam. Uncle Thomas Bloxam. Bro. Littleton Bloxam Exr. Witt: John Bloxam, Jr., Thomas Bloxam, Jr., Thomas Bloxam – p. 2

MEARS, ELISHA, Sr. – 21 Mar. 1772 – 1 July 1772 – Son Solomon Mears. Dau. Margaret Mears. To son John Mears 130 A. where I now live & 17 A. purchased of Josiah Harrison, Sr. Children John, Margaret & Solomon resid. legatees. Cousin John Mears, son of William & my son John Mears Exrs. Witt: Major Bayly, Edmond Heath. p. 11

BAYLY, CHARLES – Not dated – 28 July 1772 – Land where I now live cont. 845 A. to my 5 daus., Elizabeth Wise Bayly, Sarah Wyatt, Susannah Bayly, Ann Braughton, Margaret Bayly & my grandson Charles B. Taylor, to be equally div. in 6 parts. To wife Amey slaves for life, reversion to my 5 daus. & grandson. Bal. of est. to wife during her wid. then to my 5 daus. & my said grandson. Wife Amey, dau. Elizabeth & James Braughton Exrs. Witt: Benjamin Hutcheson, Luke Luker, Naomay Bradford – p. 12

BAYLY, PATIENCE – 25 Nov. 1771 – 29 July 1772 – To William Welch. To sister Sarah Bayly. Bro. Shadrack Bayly. William Welch Exr. Witt: Thomas Hickman, Hezekiah White, Sarah Crippen – p. 16

MUIR, ADAM – 2 Aug. 1770 – 25 Aug. 1772 – To wife Francina land where I now live, formerly purchased by her father George Hack, cont. 1416 A., to her & her heirs forever. To son Adam Muir. To daus.

Elizabeth, Ann, Sarah & Margaret. Bal. of est to wife to pay my debts, & the remainder to be disposed of as she thinks proper. Wife Exec. Witt: Baly Reade, Walter Hatton, Henry Martin - p. 18

CRIPPEN, PATIENCE - 23 July 1772 - 25 Aug. 1772 - Dau. Eliza: Evans. Dau. Sarah Evans. Dau. Scarburgh Stakes. Dau. Sophia Crippin. Son John Crippin. Grandau. Atterlanter Evans 4 L for her schooling, & if she dies before she is big enough to go to school, then to be div. bet. her bro. & sister John & Sarah Evans. Son William Crippin (under age) Dau. "Jacey" Crippen. Son Thomas Crippen (under age). Children William Jacey & Thomas resid. legatees - Charles Bagwell Exr. Witt: Sarah Wimbrough - p. 18

MATTHEWS, GEORGE - 16 May 1770 - 25 Aug. 1772 - To son Ephraim Matthews land purchased of William Blake, except 82 A. on the east side of said tract that is now held by Sarah Blake as her dower, which said 82 A. I give to my son William Blake, provided he pay my son Ephraim 10 L- 3 s. 7 d., & in the event of his failure to do so then I give the said 82 A. to my son Ephraim. I also give my said son 10 A. on the East side of the land that belongs to me in Pocomoke Swamp. To son George the remaining part of my land in Pocomoke Swamp, being 120 A., also all my right & title to what land I hold on Syexes Island. Dau. Hannah Blake. Bal. of est. to be div. bet, my wife Arcady & 4 children, Ephraim, George, Margaret & Comfort. Bro. Joseph Matthews & friend John Watts Exrs. - Witt: Washburn Tunnell, Scarburgh Tunnell, Nehemiah Whealton. - p. 19
In order of prob: Ephraim Matthews heir at law to the testator.

BELL, RACHEL - 17 Apr. 1769 - 25 Aug. 1772 - To son Joshua Bell. Dau. Easter Nock. Bal. of est. to 6 children Caziah Bundick, Stephen Bell, Sarah Bell, Leah Bell, George Bell & Southey Bell. Sons Stephen Bell & George Bell Exrs. Witt: Arnold Morgan, Mary Morgan - p. 22

RIGGS, JOSHUA - 19 July 1772 - 29 Sept. 1772 - To son Isaac planta. cont. 100 A. & 50 A. of marsh, being the marsh I bought of John Mackeel. To son Joshua Riggs 25 A. marsh. To dau. Mary Bandy 25 A. Marsh, she to have the use of about 2 A. that lies over the Gully next to John Riggs as long as she lives single. To son Isaac grist mill. Son Joshua & dau. Mary Bandy resid. legatees. Son Isaac Exr. Witt: William Young, Sr., George Churn, Ann Churn. - p. 26

HOWARD, AMBROS - 10 July 1772 - 29 Sept. 1772 - Wife Elenor Howard Exec. & sole devisee. Witt: Southy Lucas, Nehemiah Stockly - p. 27

MEARS, RICHARD - 22 Apr. 1772 - 27 Oct. 1772 - To son Richard 150 A. where I now live & for want of heirs to my son Daniel. To son William Mears 209 1/2 A. purchased of Joseph & Abel Kellam, & for want of heirs to my son Levi Mears. Sons Daniel & Levi to have each

2 years schooling out of my est. Dau. Tabitha Ames. To dau. Mary Mears, provided she never marry West Kellam, if she marry him to have no part of my est, not one farthing. To dau. Elizabeth Mears. Wife Tabitha Mears to take care of my 4 boys, Richard, William, Daniel & Levi. Bal. of est. to be div. bet. my wife & all my children except Mary if she marry West Kellam. Wife, Thomas Aimes, Jr. & John Meers, son of Elisha, Exrs. Witt: William Ward, John Meers, In order of prob: Luke Luker guardian of Richard Mears, heir at law to the testator.

THOMAS, GEORGE - 25 Jan. 1772 - 24 Nov. 1772 - To son John Thomas planta. where he lives that I bought of Jonathan More, cont. 150 A., also 100 A. purchased of Jonathan Edmonds. To son George Thomas planta. where I now live purchased of John Gibson, cont. 500 A., "and in case he should die & his daughter without having no heirs (but not cuting off his son if please God he should ever again marry & have one), then I give the above land to my son Levin Thomas". To son Levin Planta. at Pigg Point purchased of Jacob White cont. 300 A., & for want of heirs to my son John Thomas. To son in law John Tankard 20 s. Grandson Harrison Thomas, son of John Thomas 20 s. To Houson Mapp & Betty, his wife 50 I. current money. To Ralph Corbin & Sarah his wife the effects & money they have had of me in my lifetime to be accounted for in the division of the est as a part of their equal division. To Jedday Tunnel & Anne his wife, they to account for the effects they have already had. Should my dau. Anne, wife of the said Tunnell, die before her husband, the above negroes to be divided among her children. To dau. Rosannah. Wife Bridget to live with my son George, she to have her equal division of the est. & after her death to be div. among our children, George, Leven, Sarah, Anne & Rosannah. Wife & sons George & Leven Exrs. Witt: Jonathan Powell, Sarah Powell, William Fraser Ross - p. 39 In order of prob: John Thomas heir at law to the testator.

NELSON, JOHN - 28 Apr. 1771 - 24 Nov. 1772 - To grandson John Phillips, Jr. planta. where I live. Grandson Provess Nelson 120 A. purchased of Perry Leatherbury. Bal. of est. to 3 daus. Susanna Phillips, Sarah Hall & Sophia Hickman. Grandson John Phillips Exr. - Witt: John Smith, Major Ironmonger, William Tilney, John Cornick.- p. 44 In order of prob: George Corbin app. guardian to Proviss Nelson, heir at law to the testator.

FOSTER, WILLIAM - 4 Nov. 1772 - 24 Nov. 1772 - To wife Tabitha planta. where I now live during her wid. & then to my son John Fostsr. Son James Foster. Dau. Comfort Foster. To Levin Simson, the lad that lives with me, clothing. Bal. of est. to my wife during her wid. then to be div. bet. my 3 children, John, James & Comfort. Witt: John Finney, Ann Rodgers, Ann Bell. - p. 45 In order of prob: John Foster heir at law to the testator.

PITT, ANN – 23 Oct. 1761 – 24 Nov. 1772 – To be buried near my late husband. To son Robert (under age), the land I bought lying at the head of Pitts Creek adj. William Drummond's mill & for want of heirs to my dau. Anne Pitt (under age). To son John Pitt (under age). To my Aunt Buncle. Bal. of est. to be sold, & after payment of debts to pay off the estates of my 2 children Robert & Anne that shall be coming to them of their father's est., & the bal. to be div. between my 3 said children. John, Robert & Anne. George Holden, James Henry & William Drummond Exrs. Witt: Richard Benneston, Sabra Walker, Moses Virgin.
Codicil dated 23 Oct. 1779 refers to children as being "almost all of the age of 21 years – p. 46
In order of prob: The Exrs. named in the foregoing will relinquished their right, & Robert Pitt, Jr. qualified. John Pitt heir at law to the testator.

DRUMMOND, WILLIAM – 28 June 1772 – 29 Dec. 1772 – Wife Diadamia. Dau. Elizabeth. At the death or marriage of my wife dau. Elizabeth to have whole est., & for want of heirs my sister in law Bersheba Sturgis to have her choice of my negroes, & my 2 sisters Nanny Dix & Sarah Drummond to have all the rest of my negroes between them. Wife Exec. – Witt: Southey Simpson, Thomas Grinolds – p. 52
In order of prob: Littleton Dennis app. guardian to Elizabeth Drummond, heir at law to the testator.

DARBY, CHURCHIL – 31 Oct. 1769 – 24 Feb. 1773 – To John Darby, son of Francis Darby my 1/2 of the water grist mill & for want of heirs to the heirs of his father Francis Darby. I give my right of land where I now live to Benjamin Darby, son of John Darby, & for want of heirs to John Darby son of Francis Darby. To Churchill Aimes. To sister Dorothy Aimes. All my right of the negroes to be div. bet. Dorothy Ames, John Darby, Benjamin Darby & Ann Darby. Francis Darby, Ann Johnson, Dorithy Ames, Tabitha Mears resid. legatees. Friend Abel West Exr. & trustee over my nephews Benjamin Darby & Ann Darby. Witt: John Mears, John Hornsby, Babel Hornsby. – p. 58
In order of prob: John Coloney app. guardian to Benjamin Darby, heir at law to the testator.

McLAUGHLIN, WILLIAM, of Northampton County, Shopkeeper, but now in Philadelphia in Pennsylvania. – 4 June 1772 – 30 Mar. 1773 – To my father William, now living in the County of Dunegall in the Kingdom of Ireland, & to his children then surviving with him in Ireland 200 L Pennsylvania currency to be div. bet. them, only my sister Nancy McKee to have 10 L over & above the share of any of the other children, & in case of her death her share to be given to her children if any be then living, & in case of the death of my father the whole of the above sum to be div. bet. my mother & said father's children, my brothers & sisters in Ireland. To my uncle James McLaughlin, provided he be living, Ten Guineas or 10 L 10 s. English money. To Polly McLaughlin, dau. of my bro. James, 20 L Pennsylvania money. Bal. of est. to be div. bet. my bro. James McLaughlin of Philadelphia & Alexander McLaughlin of Somerset County, Maryland. Bro. Alexander to have my planta. in Northampton as his share of my est. Bros. James & Alenander & William Christian of Northampton Exrs. Witt: Francis Gurney, John Spence, Randle Mitchell, William Christian, Rachel Johnson, Hezekiah Pitts, Stewart James - p. 65

JAMESON, WALTER - 29 Sept. 1772 - 31 Mar. 1773 - To wife Sarah all the negroes that came by her, & in case of her death to be div. bet. the 2 boys she had by me, & should they die without issue to be div. bet. my other children I had by my 2nd wife. Lands on the Western Shore to be div. bet. Walter & James Jameson. Personal property to be div. among all my children. Friend Edward Ker & Samuel Heath Jameson Exrs. Not witnessed. Proved by James Henry & Walter Hatton - p. 69

TOWNSEND, LITTLETON - 28 Mar. 1773 - 27 Apr. 1773 - To be buried by my wife. Whole est. to bro Levin Townsend & son James Townsend except 5 L which I give to my bro. William Townsend's dau. Anne. Bro. William & friend William Drummond Exrs. Witt: John Montgomery, James Berry, Joseph Nock, Nathaniel Beavans - p. 72

MEERS, TABITHA, wid. of Richard Meers, dec. - 25 Feb. 1773 - 27 Apr. 1773 - Son Richard Meers. Son William Meers. Son Daniel Meers. Son Levi Meers one trunk that I had from Churchel Darby. To Mary Mears. Richard, Daniel & Levi Mears resid. legatees. John Mears Exr. Witt: West Kellam, Dorothy Ames - p. 73

KELLAM, JOHN - 20 Nov. 1772 - 27 Apr. 1773 - To wife Bridget whole est. during her wid. to bring up my younger children, daus. Peggy, Betty & Susey Kellam & son George Kellam. To grandchildren Peggy Budd, Edward Budd & Comfort Budd a bond of their father's, Thomas Budd for 17 L & interest. Edward Ker & wife Bridget Exrs, Witt: Hillary Green, Solomon Kellam, William "Buddle" Hughes. - p. 74 In order of prob: Littleton Dennis app. guardian to George Kellam, heir at law to the testator.

PETTIGREW, LEAH - 18 Mar. 1773 - 27 Apr. 1773 - To James Henry full power to sell 50 A. willed to me by my husband for the purpose of paying his debts. Son John Pettigrew to have the management of his brother's est. provided he will bring him up, giving him sufficient English schooling & clothing. James Henry trustee to see my will performed. Son Gauven Pettigrew. To Sarah Johnson, wife of Shadrack Johnson (Indian). James Henry Exr. & if he should die Littleton Dennis or Edward Ker. Witt: Thomas Bloxam, Jonathan Fitchet - p. 83
In order of prob: John Pettigrew heir at law to the testatrix.

DICKERSON, DAVID – Not dated – 27 Apr. 1773 – Bro. Elisha. Wife Hannah to have 1/2 of the wheat now growing in my brother Jesse Dickerson's plantation, with all the oats that is now in the Barn _____ these and all other Articles which have been already mentioned I do give & _____ Not completed. Proved by William Smith who wrote the said will & John Montgomery who was present when the same was read to him – p. 84
In order of prob: Hannah Dickerson qualified.

PARKER, SARAH – 22 Nov. 1772 – 27 Apr. 1773 – Should my dau. Mary marry with her first or own cousin she to have no part of my est. that I shall hereafter give her, but to be div. bet. my son William Parker & my 3 grandchildren Henry, John & Thomas Parker. To dau. in law Betty Parker till my grandson John Parker comes to age. To Betty or Elizabeth Riley that lives with me. Son William & dau. Mary resid. legatees. Est. to be div. by George Parker, Upshur Teackle & Smith Snead. George Parker, John Finney & dau. Mary Exrs. Witt: Richard Parker, William Tizeker, John Finney – p. 88

STURGIS, SUSANNAH – 22 Oct. 1772 – 27 Apr. 1773 – To 2 youngest daus. Mary & Leuranah Sturgis whole est., they to be my Executrices. Witt: Thomas Crippin, Margaret Sturgis – p. 90

STOCKLEY, NATHANIEL – 31 Nov. 1772 – 26 May 1773 – Son Nathaniel Stockley. Dau. Comfort Stockley (both under age) – Should both die without issue their negroes to be div. bet. my 2 children Joseph & Leah Stockley. Grandau. Sarah Samuels & for want of heirs to my grandson Stockley Samuels. To son Kendal Stockley. To wife Leah Stockley. Son Joseph & dau. Leah resid. legatees. Son Kendal & friends Nehemiah & Alexander Stockley Exrs. Witt: George B. Corbin, Polly Corbin, Susanna Parks – p. 97

SMITH, ISBELL – 16 Apr. 1773 – 29 June 1773 – Grandson George Smith Savage. Grandson Smith Kellam. Dau. Elizabeth Smith. Dau. Mary Savage. Dau. Ann Kellam. Grandau. Susana Kellam. Grandau. Adah Savage. Grandau. Mary Savage. Daus. Elizabeth Smith, Mary Savage & Anne Kellam resid. legatees. Son in law William Savage & Dau. Elizabeth Smith Exrs. Witt: John Darby, William Joyne, Billy Jacob – p. 100

BARNS, WILLIAM – 5 Feb. 1773 – 27 July 1773 – Wife Susannah Barnes. Son George. Son Parker. Dau. Susannah & for want of heirs to my dau. Bridget. To son John Sacker Barns the whole of my land, mill & still. To grandau. Leah Simpson. Grandson John Hickman. To dau. Esther Simpson. Son John Sacker Barns Exr. Witt: Ambrose Willit, William Bishop, Thomas Willet – p. 103
In order of prob: John Sacker Barnes heir at law to the testator.

KELLAM, ELIZABETH – 23 Sept. 1772 – 31 Aug. 1773 – To dau. Semor Biles, & for want of heirs to my grandau. Eufame Chandler. To dau. Eufame. To dau. Patience Chandler. Dau. Ame Coloney. Dau.

Tamer Darby. Grandau. "Nanney Redefas Dua". Dau. Semor Biles resid. legatee. James Boils (Biles) & John "Folla" Exrs. Witt: John Mears, Constable, Able West - p. 109

FOSTER, JOSHUA - 5 Aug. 1773 - 1 Sept. 1773 - To son Absalom Foster planta. where I live for life, reversion to my 2 grandsons Joshua Foster, son of my son Absalom Foster, & Joshua Hickman, son of my dau. Peggy Hickman. To Custis Hickman. The land I bought of Jemima Booth lying over the road to return from whence it came after the crop is taken off. To Jemima Booth negro during her wid. then to return to my est. 3 Daus. Betty, Peggy & Siner resid. legatees. Mekeel Bonwell, Sr. Exr. Witt: Thomas Foster, Levener Foster, Mekeel Bonwell - p. 115
In order of prob: Absalom Foster heir at law to the testator.

WHEELTON, JAMES - 9 Sept. 1772 - 28 Sept. 1773 - To wife Rhoda Wheelton use of whole est. during her wid. To son Arthur Wheelton planta. where I now live, & for want of heirs to my son William. Dau. Joyce Wheelton & for want of heirs to my dau. Nanne Wheelton. 3 youngest children William, Scarbrough & Nanne Wheelton resid. legatees. Wife Exec. Witt: William Hargis, Elijah Townsend, Isaac Hill. - p. 116
In order of prob: Arthur Wheelton heir at law to the testator (under age)

DARBY, FRANCIS - 13 Aug. 1773 - 28 Sept. 1773 - To wife Elizabeth Darby. To son John Darby land where I now live cont. 120 A., my said son to find a maintenance for Leah Darby. Dau. Mary Darby. Dau. Tabitha Darby. Dau. Ann Poulson. Wife son John Darby & daus. Mary & Tabitha Darby resid. legatees. Wife & son John Darby Exrs. Witt: Joseph Aimes, Churchel Aimes, Mary Crofford - p. 118

WALTHAM, JOHN - 5 May 1773 - 28 Sept. 1773 - To son Teackle Waltham all my land & my 1/2 the grist mill that is between William Joyne & myself. Son John Waltham. Son Stephen Waltham. Son William Waltham. Son Charlton Waltham. To wife Sarah Waltham household goods, cattle &c. I had with her when I intermarried with her & what Henry Gascoynes owes me for the maintenance of Elizabeth Gascoynes. Wife & sons John, William & Charlton resid. legatees. Wife & son Teackle Exrs. Witt: Issac Dunton, Samuel Jameson, Edmond Bayly -
Codicil: 8 May 1773 - I give the tuition of my son Charlton to my son Teackle Waltham - Witt: Isaac Dunton, John Mears - p. 123

MIDDLETON, GEORGE - 24 Feb. 1769 - 28 Sept. 1773 - To wife Tamer whole est. during her wid, then Southy Simpson to div. my land as he thinks just bet. my 2 sons George & Riley. Bal. of est. to be div. bet. all my daus. Wife Exec. & son George Exr. Witt: Southey Simpson, John Dix - p. 127
In order of prob: George Middleton heir at law to the testator.

GROTEN, SHADRACK – 5 Sept. 1773 – 28 Sept. 1773 – To bro. William Groten. Bro. Edmund Groten (under age) Bro. Major Groten. Bro. Zorobabel Groten. Bro. Jonathan Groten. To sister Margaret Hutchison. To sister Patience Groten. To my mother. To friend John Rowles. Bros. Jonathan & Edmund & sisters Patience & Amey resid. legatees. Friend Levin Joyne Exr. – Witt: William Banfield Walker – p. 127

BOGGS, MAKEMIE – 7 Aug. 1773 – 26 Oct. 1774 – To wife Jean Boggs whole est. during her wid. then to my son William Boggs, & for want of heirs all the est. that came by my wife Jean to go to John Smith, Shipcarpenter. Wife Jean & John Arlenton Exrs. Witt: William Crowson, William Parker, Revil Custis – p. 131

REESE, TABITHA – 16 Aug. 1773 – 26 Oct. 1773 – To dau. Mary Reese whole est. & for want of heirs to my daus. Agnes White & Margaret Allen & grandau. Elizabeth Taylor & Margaret Burton. Son John Burton Exr. Witt: Rosey Parker, Southey Simpson – p. 131

STURGIS, ABSOLUM – 28 Apr. 1773 – 26 Oct. 1773 – To son Americus Sturgis at his mother.s death. To dau. Fanney Sturgis. Wife Easter Sturgis. To dau. Mary Sturgis. To son John Sturgis. Wife & children resid. legatees. Dau. Fanny Sturgis & son Americus Sturgis Exrs. Witt: Edmund Heath, Mary Sill – p. 132

HORNSBY, JOHN, Sr. – 4 Apr. 1773 – 26 Oct. 1773 – To dau. Susannah Hornsby 216 A. where I live, Moveable est. to wife Keziah Hornsby during her wid. & then to my dau Susannah. At the death of my wife my bro. Argol Hornsby to take my dau, Susannah and her est. Should my dau. die without issue moveable est. to bros. Argol & Babel Hornsby. John Mears, son of William, Exr. Witt: John Hornsby, Rachel Hornsby, Peggy Watson – p. 133

BADGER, ABBEGAL – 28 Oct. 1772 – 26 Oct. 1773 – Dau. Sinoe. Dau. Leaner East. Daus. Sarah James & Polley Warrington. Son Nathaniel. Son William Badger. Son Abel Badger. Dau. Nancy Badger. Dau. Tabltha Harrason. Daus. Leaner, Nancy & Sinor resid. legatees – Son Abel Exr. – Witt: George Cutler, Margaret East – p. 135

HARMON, WILLIAM – 23 Sept. 1773 – 30 Nov. 1773 – Wife Rachel Harmon. Son Patrick Harmon. Dau. Ader Harmon. Dau. Tamer Harmon. Son Bayly Harmon. Son John Harmon. Son Henry Harmon. Son Littleton Harmon. Dau. Lendor Dunton. Wife Rachel, son Patrick & daus. Ader & Tamer resid. legatees. Grandson William Harmon Exr. – Witt: John Kellam, Viana Widgion, Ann Widgion – p. 136

WEST, JOHN, of Andua – 29 Feb. 1772 – 30 Nov. 1773 – To son Anthony personalty &c. on Deep Creek planta. To son Abel land & planta. on Deep Creek, he to pay to each of my grandaus. Anne & Elizabeth Rowles 10 L. To son John land & planta. on Merry Branch which I lately recovered at law of Mr. George Holden & others. A ditch lying at Deep Creek Mill to divide the lands of my two sons Abel & John. To dau. Agnes 1/2 doz. silver tea spoons markes "A.W." &c. To dau. Rachel Gascoyne. To dau. Nanney. Dau. Susanna. Grandson Jonathan Rowles. 5 children Abel, John, Agnes, Nanney & Susanna resid. legatees. Sons Anthony & Abel Exrs. Witt: Thomas Teackle, Absalom Sturgis, William Puezey, Argil Kellam, John Rowles – p. 137

CARUTHERS, ROBERT – 3 Sept. 1773 – 1 Dec. 1773 – To wife what she had at her marriage; land to be sold & wife to have 1/3 of the proceeds & my 2 sons William & John Caruthera to have the other 2 parts. To son James as much of my est. as will make him equal with my sons William & John. Four daus. Sarah, Mary, Elizabeth & Margaret resid. legatees. Sons to be bound to some good trade & have what schooling my Exrs think proper. Isaac Smith & Ezekiel Young Exrs. Witt: Thomas Lilliston, Jr., Edmund Allen.
In order of prob: James Henry app. guardian to William Caruthers, heir at law to the testator.

WYATT, WILLIAM, Sr. – 26 Nov. 1773 – 25 Jan. 1774 – To son Joshua Wyatt land where I now live. To dau. Margaret Cuttler. Wife Susannah Wyatt. To son Kendall Wyatt land purchased of John Lingo cont. 65 A. Youngest son Thomas (under age) To 5 last children Kendal, Arthur, George, Thomas & Mary 5 L each. Wife & all my children except Joshua, viz: Margaret, Nanne, Joyce, John, Kendal, Arthur, George, Thomas & Mary resid. legatees. Sons George & Thomas to be bound out to trades. Son Joshua & George Cutler Exrs. Witt: Arthur Roberts, William Wyatt, William F. Ross, Solomon Groten. – p. 141

CUSTIS, EDMUND – 15 Nov. 1773 – 25 Jan. 1774 – Bro. Levin Custis. Father Thomas Custis Exr. & resid. legatee. Not witnessed. Proved by Thomas Custis & Robert Spires. – p. 143

RIGGS, SARAH – 19 May 1771 – 25 Jan. 1774 – Dau. Betty Riggs sole legatee. Dau. Betty & Joshua Riggs, Sr. Exrs. Witt: William Young, Sr., Robert Moore, Thomas Young – p. 143

SILL, JOHN – 16 Dec. 1773 – 25 Jan. 1774 – Land where I live to be div. bet. my 2 daus. Ann Ritter Hinmon & Mary Boggs. To America Sturgis a part of my land adj. Peter Hack's line to my old orchard & adj. Christian Sill's line. To John Pitts the remainder of my land adj. America Sturgis. To William Pitts. Ann Ritter Hinman, Mary Boggs & John Pitts resid. legatees. Abel West Exr. Witt: Elizabeth Only, Thomas Only – P. 144
In orber of prob: Abel West relinquished his right & John Boggs qualified.

WESSELLS, EPHRAIM – 21 Dec. 1773 – 25 Jan. 1774 – Wife Ann Wessells. To son Arthur Wessells 16 A. adj. where he lives. To son

274

Ephraim Wessells my planta. & all the land belonging not before given. To dau. Creshe Parks Wessells. To dau. Rebeccah Wessells. To dau. Rachel Wessells. To son Ephraim Wessells 16 A. that I hold of William Young, Jr., & 20 A. of land & marsh being part of the land & marsh that was William Young Sr's. on France Creek. To son Ephraim Wessells land purchased of Robert Justice & Joseph Webb until my son John comes of age. Dau. Ann Wessells. Bal. of est. to wife during her wid. Daus. Rebecca, Rachel & Ann resid. legatees. Wife & son Ephraim Exrs. Witt: William Young, Sr., David Lewis, Solomon Ewell p. 145
In order of prob: James Wessells heir at law to the testator.

PITT, JABEZ – 1 Nov. 1773 – 25 Jan. 1774 – To son John Pitt & dau. Esther Pitt all my lands, negroes & moveable est. To my other children I give 1 s. sterling each. Son Jabez to take their estates & maintain them well on it. Witt: Francis Houston, Esther Hill, Michael Robins – p. 147
In order of prob: Jabez Pitt qualified.

SMITH, JOHH – 6 Nov. 1773 – 25 Jan. 1774 – To son John Smith land in Chingoteague Neck, also 50 A. near Horn Town. To son James Smith land where my father, dec., lived, with the water mill & also the land I hold in the Province of Maryland in Worcester County (except 150 A.) To wife Tabitha 150 A. in Worcester County, Md. called the Landing Plantation during her wid. then to my son John Smith. Sons John & James resid. legatees. Friends Ayres Gillett & George Stewart Exrs. Witt: William Parradise, Charles Thornton, Thomas Alexander – p. 148
George Corbin app. guardian to John Smith heir at law to the testator.

WATSON, MITCHEL – 16 Feb. 1773 – 25 Jan. 1774 – To son Americus Watson 100 A. adj. John Taylor & William Garrison. Son David. Son Jessy (under age) Wife Neomy. Wife & sons Americus, David & Jessy Watson resid. legatees. Benjamin Stringer & son Americus to bring up my sons David & Jessy until they arrive at the age of 19. Benjamin Stringer & wife Neomy Exrs. Witt: Major Savage, Zerobabel Ames – p. 150

DUNTON, ISAAC – 11 Oct. 1773 – 25 Jan. 1774 – To wife the sum of 60 L, she to make over her right of dower in my lands to my Exrs. Bal. of est. to be sold & the money loaned; slaves to be hired & land rented for the support of my children until my eldest surviving child arrive to lawful age, then to be div. bet. all my children then living (children under age). To son George all my lands, & should he die before arriving at lawful age land to be rented until my next surviving son arrives to age, then if I have more than one son living land to be sold & the money div. bet. all my sons then living. Wife (no name), Luke Luker, George Corbin & William Seymour Exrs. Friends Isaac Smith & Tully R. Wise to settle my Sheriff's books. Witt: Jacob Watson – Further proved by Edward Ker & Charles Snead – p. 151

GRINALDS, RICHARD - 1 Jan. 1772 - 25 Jan. 1774 - To son Richard 50 A. where he now dwells. Dau. Elizabeth, Son William. Son Southy. Wife to have use of the rest of my land & whole est. during her wid. & then to my son Richard planta. where I now live cont. 54 A. Bal. of est. to be div. bet. all my children. Wife & son Richard Exrs. Witt: Jacob White, Joyce White, Rachel White - p. 152 In order of prob: Mary Grinalds & Richard Grinalds qualified.

FITCHETT, SALATHIEL - 13 Jan. 1767 - 26 Jan. 1774 - To wife Shady Fitchett land & planta. during her wid. then to my son William Fitchett land where I now live. Dau. "Cleartrouen" Fitchett. Daus. Shady, Siner & Anariter Fitchett. Sons Salathiel, Thomas & Jonathan Fitchett, Severn Fitchett, unborn child. All my children except William resid. legatees. Wife & son William Exrs. Witt: William Young, Sr., George Young, Mary Young - p. 154

SAUNDERS, RACHEL - 2 Nov. 1766 - 22 Feb. 1775 - To dau. Keziah Sparrow for life, reversion to her children. To dau. Catherine Ingerson for life, reversion to her children. 2 daus. Keziah & Catherine resid. legatees. Sons in law John Sparrow & Samuel Ingoson Exrs. Witt: William Young, Sr., Margaret Young, William Young, Jr. - p. 157

HOLDEN, GEORGE - 14 Sept. 1768 - 23 Feb. 1774 - Whereas I promised my wife Anne that if she should consent to dock the entail of the lands at Matchatank of which she was seized as tenant in fee tail at the time of our marriage, & having docked the same & got the fee simple thereof vested in me & my heirs, that she should in case she survived me enjoy the profits of the said lands for & during the term of her natural life &c., I therefore give & beq. the said lands to my wife Anne & her assigns during the term of her natural life -- Not witnessed - p. 161
In order of prob: George Holden, only son & heir at law to the testator qualified.

TAYLOR, JOHN - 22 Jan. 1774 - 29 Mar. 1774 - To wife personal est. during her wid. To son Benjamin Taylor 75 A. being part of the planta. where I now live adj. my son Reubin, & for want of heirs to my son John Taylor (under age) & for want of heirs to my son Reubin Taylor Shield. To daus. Polly & Adar. To my grandson, son of Kendal Richeson & my dec. dau. Betty. To my grandson by Moses Taylor. Wife Tabitha. To son John Taylor his chest "if he dies or don't return to my son Benjamin". Thomas Custis, planter at the head of Matchapongo, Exr. Witt: William F. Ross, Robert Spires, John Lingo. p. 165
In order of prob: James Henry app. guardian to Scadia Taylor to contest the proof of the within will, & having nothing to object same was admitted to probate.

SCARBURGH, AMERICUS - 10 July 1773 - 29 Mar. 1774 - To wife slaves &c. To son Americus. To son John. Bal. of est. to wife during her wid. then to be div. bet. my 2 sons Edmund & Charles.

Son Americus to have the tuition of my 2 youngest sons & their estates. Son Americus Exr. Not witnessed. Presented & proved by Edward Ker, Gent: – p. 172

BRADFORD, LABEN – 30 Aug. 1772 – 29 Mar. 1774 – To Robert Bradford. To Arter Bradford. Witt: Levi Kellam, Joacam Roberts – p. 173
In order of prob: Robert Bradford qualified.

BROADWATER, WILLIAM – 1 Nov. 1773 – 20 Apr. 1774 – Son William Broadwater. Dau. Susannah Broadwater. Dau. Ann Broadwater. Son Jesse Broadwater. Wife Bridget Broadwater. Children Susanna, Ann & Jesse Broadwater resid. legatees. Wife (no name) Exec. Witt: Caleb Broadwater, William Burton, Jacob Broadwater – p. 185

LUKER, LUKE – 17 Dec. 1773 – 26 Apr. 1774 – To wife Susannah Luker planta. where I now live cont. 400 A. which I bought of Dr. William Williams, stock, slaves &c during her wid. to bring up my children, & should my wife marry my Exrs. to sell my planta. & the money to be equally div. bet. my 5 daus., Elizabeth, Rose, Anne, Sarah & Susanna Luker, reserving 1/8 part for my wife. My Exrs. to sell my 1/2 the mill held & occupied by the heirs of John Revil, dec. & myself, if they think it best for the benefit of my children. 5 daus. aforesaid resid. legatees. Wife & friend Isaac Smith Exrs. Witt: Levin Window, David Watson, Robertson Mahorn p. 188

WINDOW, BABEL – Not dated – 26 Apr. 1774 – Bro. Abel Window. Bros. Levin, Eli & Abel Window to have proceeds from my crop of tobacco &c. To Elizabeth Luker. To John Window, son of Abel. Sister Ann Watson. 3 bros. & sister aforesaid resid. legatees. To godson Babel Window 5 L. Bro. Abel Exr. Witt: Nathan Addison, Edward Revell, Southy Rayfield – p. 190

GITTINS, SOUTHY – 6 Feb. 1774 – 26 Apr. 1774 – To wife Sarah Gittins whole est. during her wid. & then to be div. bet all my children. Wife Exec. Witt: William Phillips, Abbott Bloxom, Littleton Lurton – p. 192

LUCAS, JABEZ – 13 Jan. 1773 – 29 Mar. 1774 – To son William Richard Lucas my land cont. 38 A. & for want of heirs to my son Luke Lucas. 2 sons resid. legatees. Wife to have use of whole est. during her wid. Wife Elizabeth Exec. Witt: Joseph Blake, Nathaniel Howard, Jacob Bird – p. 198

TEACKLE, UPSHUR – 10 Nov. 1773 – 31 May 1774 – Son William Teackle. Est. to be div. between my wife & son William. Wife & son William Exrs. Witt: James Turlington, Francis Boggs. – p. 199

METCALF, ELIZABETH – 24 Apr. 1774 – 31 May 1774 – To dau. Tabitha Metcalf. Son Mark Metcalf & dau. Tabitha Metcalf resid.

legatees & Exrs. Witt: John Wharton, Elizabeth Wharton, Briget Bird – p. 200

MELSON, SOLOMON – 8 Dec. 1773 – 31 May 1774 – Wife (no name) to have use of whole est. for life & then to be div. bet. all my children. To son Isaac (under 21) my planta. where I now live cont. 50 A. To son Daniel all the rest of my land cont. 60 A. Wife Exec. Witt: Jacob White, Betty Melson, John Melson – p. 200

ADDISON, ELIJAH – 27 Oct. 1773 – 1 June 1774 – Son Nathan Addison. Dau. Jemima Parker Addison, Dau. Bridget Addison, Son John Bradford Addison. Son Nathaniel Addison. Grandson John Purnal Outten. Dau. Catherine Addison. Dau. Violater Window. Children Jemima Parker Addison, Nathaniel Addison, Catherine Addison & Grandson John Purnal Outten resid. legatees. Friends Michael Bonnawell, Jr. & John Sharlock Exrs. Not witnessed – p. 201
In order of prob: The Exrs. named refused to act & Nathan Addison, son & heir to the testator qualified.

CAINE, WILLIAM – 2 Jan. 1773 – 28 June 1774 – To dau. Martha Caine & for want of heirs to my wife Leah. Wife resid. legatee & Exec. Friend David Garret Exr. Witt: Andrew Gootee, John Cain, John Pitt, Joseph Waggoman – p. 209

BELL, ELIZABETH – 25 Mar. 1770 – 31 May 1774 – Grandau. Sarah Wats Houston sole devisee & Exec. Witt: John Smith, Jr., John Sandrews – p. 210

TILNEY, WILLIAM – 26 May 1774 – Partly proved 2 June 1774, prob: 29 June 1774 – To wife Neomy. To William Harrison. To Mary Guy, wife of Thomas Guy. To Philip Harrison, son of John Harrison. To Ufamy Harrison. Land & remainder of est. to be sold – John Spiers, Robert Coleburn & Robert Spiers Exrs. Witt: Littleton Wyatt, Jr., Henry Harmon, Robert Spiers – p. 211
In order of prob: The citation sued out against John Harrison, heir at law to the testator, being returned by the sheriff that he was beyond seas, the same was admitted to record.

WISE, JOHN – 26 May 1766 – 26 July 1774 – To wife Brooks Wise whole est. during her wid., then to be div. bet. my children born of my said wife. Wife Exec. – Witt: Adah Parker, Philip Parker, George Parker – p. 212

BELOTE, CALEB – 13 June 1774 – 26 July 1774 – Dau. Sarah Garret Belote 30 L provided my wife Fanny be not with child, but should she be with child the said child to have 15 L of the said sum. To wife Fanny whole est. real & persons. Wife & friend Edward Ker Exrs. Witt: Joseph Aimes, William Kellam, Susanna Darby – p. 212

HORNSBY, RACHEL – 28 Dec. 1772 – 26 July 1774 – Son Argil Hornsby. Son Zorobabel Hornsby. Son John Hornsby. Dau. Rachel Hornsby.

278

Son Levi Hornsby. Argil Hornsby, Babel Hornsby, Levi Hornsby & Rachel Hornsby resid. legatees. Son James Hornsby, Dau. Neomy Watson. Dau. Tabitha Heath. Dau. Elizabeth Downing. Dau. Esther Lecatt. Son Argil Hornsby Exr. Witt: John Hornsby, James Bonwell – p. 214

THOMAS, GEORGE – 5 Mar. 1774 – 27 Sept. 1774 – To mother Bridget Thomas. To bro. Levin Thomas 100 A. of land & marsh on Wallops Island purchased of William Kendall, he to pay to each of my sisters 10 L. Sisters Mary Tankard, Elizabeth Mapp, Sarah Corbin, Roscana Marshall & Ann Tunnell. Bal. of est. to bros. John & Levin Thomas, they to be my Exrs. Witt: John Watts, Sarah Cade – p. 230

BAILY, WILLIAM – 5 Oct. 1773 – 27 Sept. 1774 – To son Sacker Baily all my land & planta. Dau. Elizabeth Baily. Should my son Sacker die without issue land to be sold & 1/2 the proceeds to be paid my dau. Elizabeth Baily & the other 1/2 div. bet. my other 2 daus., Tabitha & Patience Baily. To son Charles Baily 1 s. 4 children Sacker, Elizabeth, Tabitha & Patience resid. legatees. Dau. Elizabeth Exec. – Witt: Jacob Bird, Levi Bird – p. 231

WATT, JAMES – 18 July 1774 – 27 Sept. 1774 – Wife Rachel Watt. That part of my land on the South side of the Branch to be sold. Dau. Nancy Watt to have the remaining part of my land & planta. Wife to have use of same during her wid. to bring up my children. Should my dau. die without issue I give my said land to my cousin Southy Broadwater, son of my sister Susanna Broadwater. Wife & friend John Watts Exrs. Witt: William Downing, Nimrod Powell, Elizabeth Fletcher. – p. 233

SAVAGE, JONATHAN – 24 July 1774 – 27 Sept. 1774 – Planta. & 4 negroes to be rented for 4 years beginning the first of Jan. next & the money to be applied to the payment of my debts. At the expiration of the 4 years I give my planta. & negroes to my wife Susanna. Wife resid. legatee & Exec. Isaac Smith Exr. Witt: Selby Hickman, Susanna Hickman, Solomon Willis – p. 234

TALER, WILLIAM Sr. – 23 Mar. 1772 – 27 Sept. 1774 – To son Southey Taler 50 A. land & marsh beginning near the Island Creek. To son Richard Taler my house & orchard & the remaining part of my land & marsh. Moveable est. to be div. bet. all my children. Sons Charles, Southey & Richard Exrs. Witt: William Young, Sr., William Starling, William Taler, Jr. – p. 235

SMITH, WILLIAM – 14 Sept. 1774 – 25 Oct. 1774 – To son George Smith planta. where he now lives cont. 125 A. for life, reversion to my grandson William Smith & for want of heirs to my grandson Elisha Smith. To grandau. Scarbrough Luker. Dau. Peggy Smith resid. legatee. Son George Exr. – Witt: John Hutchinson, Sovereign Bunting, Kendall Stockly – p. 248

RICHARDSON, WILLIAM - 29 Dec. 1769 - 25 Oct. 1774 - To wife
Elizabeth Richardson whole est. during her wid. & should she marry to
have 1/3 of my estate. To son William Richardson my land & planta.
where I now live cont. 75 A. after his mo- ther's death or marriage.
Dau. Sarah. Dau. Comfort Meers. Grandson Severn Mears. 3 children
William, Comfort & Sarah resid. legatees. Wife & Littleton Meers
Exrs. Witt: Major Meers, John Ashby - p. 249

GROTEN, WILLIAM - 24 Sept. 1774 - 29 Nov. 1774 - To son William
Groten planta. where I now live, also the planta. I bought of Charles
Lecatt, cont. together 227 A. To son Edmund Groten (under age). To
son Major Groten my two plantations commonly called Johnsons &
Belotes, cont. 200 A. To son Zorobabel Groten (under age) my planta.
called Turlingtons, cont. 184 A. To son Jonathan (under age) my
planta. called Niblets, cont. 175 A. Dau. Margaret Hutchinson. To
dau. Patience Groten. Dau. Amy Groten. Wife Amy Groten to have
use of bal. of my est. during her life & then to be div. bet. my 6 children, viz: Margaret, Patience, Zerrobabel, Jonathan, Amy & Edmund.
Wife Amy & friend William Joyce Exrs. Witt: William Welsh, Levin
Joyne, John Rowles - p. 256

BLAKE, JOHN - ___ ___ Nov. 1774 - 29 Nov. 1774 - Sloop to be sold
for payment of debts. Sister Ann Welborn. To John Welborn. To
Mary Laws. To John Laws. To Martin Laws. Levinah Nock resid.
legatee. Robert Moore & Joseph Blake Exrs. Witt: Thomas Hope,
Thomas Lowell - p. 258

KELLAM, EDMUND - 1 Feb. 1771 - 29 Nov. 1774 - To son John
Kellam planta. where I now live cont. 100 A., also 20 A. bought of the
Exec. of James Rodgers. To son Edmund Kellam the remaining part
of the land bought of the Exec. of James Rodgers held for 80 A. Wife
Mary. Dau. Molly Kellam. Wife & 6 children, John, Nanny, Molley,
Betsey, Edmund & Susannah resid. legatees. Wife, William Seymour
& Luke Luker Exrs. Witt: William Brice, Babel Window - p. 262

PARKER, ROBERT, Sr. - 5 Aug. 1774 - 29 Nov. 1774 - To wife Peggy
negroes & personalty during her wid. To son Samuel Parker. To son
John Parker planta. where I live, & for want of heirs to my son Ander-
son Parker. To son John 2 pewter dishes marked "J.P." To son
Robert Parker. To son Anderson Parker 2 pewter dishes marked
"A.P." Dau. Scarbrough Parker, 2 pewter dishes marked "S.P." & one
pine chest called her mother's. To dau. Catherine Parker 2 pewter
dishes marked "C.P." &c. Dau. Molly Parker. Dau. Peggy Parker.
Dau. Esther Parker. Wife, John Parker, Anderson Parker, Scarbrough
Parker, Catherine Parker, Charles Parker, Molly Parker, Peggy Parker,
Samuel Parker & Esther Parker resid. legatees. Wife to be guardian
to my son Samuel & dau. Esther. William Crowson guardian to daus.
Molly & Peggy Parker. Son Anderson Parker & John Riley Parker
Exrs. Witt: Abel Savage, Sheabe Savage - p. 263
In order of prob: John Parker heir at law to the testator.

RICHARDSON, DANIEL – 9 Oct. 1774 – 27 Dec. 1774 – To wife Comfort Richardson all my land during her natural life & then to my son John Richardson 50 A. on the South end of my land & all the rest of my land to my son Charles Richardson. Wife Comfort resid. legatee & Exec. Witt: Charles Taylor, Levin Claywell, William Turlington – p. 271

PARRAMORE, THOMAS – 8 May 1773 – 27 Dec. 1774 – Son William Parramore. To son John Parramore my planta. in Maryland. To son Thomas Parramore 100 A. of marsh which I bought of John Michael, my lease Hold Estate which I bought in Bradford's Neck, as also the time to come, which shall be the season after my death, in the Lease I have from Sacker Shield where my son William now lives. Son in law Ezekiel Young. Son in law Major Guy. To grandau. Anne Abbott, wife of Richard Abbott. Grandchildren John & Sarah Stran. Grandsons John & Robert Purnell. To Ann Holland, dau. of my son in law William Holland. Grandau. Mary Holland, dau. of William. Grandson William Stran. To son William Parramore 100 A. land & marsh on the Beach which I bought of Mr. William Burton, dec. Son William my heir apparent. Daus. Sarah Guy & Elizabeth Guy. Sons William, John & Thomas, dau. Mary Holland & the children of Sinah Stran, dec. resid. legatees. Sons William, John & Thomas Parramore Exrs. Witt: Samuel Long, Henry Heath, George Bell – p. 272

MOORE, ROBERT – 3 Dec. 1774 – 27 Dec. 1774 – To son James Moore whole est. & for want of heirs to my sister Agness Moore & bros. William, Major & Joseph Moore. Father Joseph Moore & George Corbin Exrs. Witt: Mary Hampton, George Warrington. p. 275

BAGGE, SAMUEL – 30 Jan. 1774 – 27 Dec. 1774 – Son William Bagge (under age). Bal. of est. to be div. bet. the remainder of my children which is eight, & unborn child. Wife (no name) Exec., she to pay my children their estates when they come to age or marry. Not witnessed. Proved by James Henry & William Polk, Gent: p. 276

FOSTER, ANNE, 17 Dec. 1774 – 27 Dec. 1774 – Dau. Betty Poolman. Dau. Pegey Hinmon. Dau. Siner Foster. Dau. Absalom Foster. Daus. Betty, Pegey & Siner resid. legatees. – Son Aboalom Exr. Witt: John Foster, Jacob Bell, Michael Borwell – p. 279

DRUMMOND, ANNE – 15 Feb. 1774 – 27 Dec. 1774 – To son Richard Drummond all my interest in the lands left me by my dec. husband Spencer Drummond's will, at or near Mesongo. Dau. Sarah Drummond. Dau. Elisha. Grandson Richard, son of my son Spencer Drummond. Dau/ Elisha, posthumous child. Dau. Esther & grandau. Nancy, dau. of my son Spencer, resid. legatees. Friends James Henry & Thomas Bayly Exrs. Witt: George Knight, Isaac Henry – p. 280

TAYLOR, THOMAS TEACKLE, of Newport in the County of Newport, in the Colony of Rhode Island & Providence Plantations, in New England, Merchant – __ __ 1769 – Recorded in the Town Council

Book of Newport No. 14 Pages 171 & 172, Newport April 2, A. D. 1774
- Prob. in Accomack County 27 Dec. 1774 - To wife Patience Taylor
my lot & dwelling house where I now live, together with the lot lately
purchased of Stephen Wanton, during her life in lieu of dower. To son
Edward Taylor all my lands in the Colony of Virginia & marsh cont.
200 A. adjoining my homestead Farm in Virginia, he paying to my
wife 20 L each year during her life. To my daus, namely Elizabeth
Taylor, Catherine Tillinghast, Margaret Taylor & Mary Waite, after
the dec. of my wife, all my lot of land & dwelling house aforesaid in
Newport (except such part as is hereafter disposed of). To daus.
Elizabeth & Margaret Taylor all that South-West part of my dwelling
house in Newport cont. a shop, a back room, an entry room & garret,
being the whole of the addition I made to the said house, & is known
by the name of the Shop Port, together with the land the same stands
upon, also all my land to the South of said addition. Grandau Sarah
Johnson $50. at the age of 21 or marriage. To Samuel Johnson of
Newport, To wife Patience Taylor 1/3 of the residue of my personal
est. & to my son Edward Taylor & my 4 daus. the other 2/3. To son
Edward the rest of my real estate not disposed of. Son Edward resid.
legatee. Wife Patience Taylor, friend George Holden, Son Edward
Taylor & son in law Nicholas Tillingast Exrs. Witt: Willan Howard,
Sarah James, Mary Wanton - p. 281

CHANCE, ELIJAH - 28 Oct. 1774 - 31 Jan. 1775 - To wife planta.
where I now dwell during her wid. to bring up my children & then to my
son Elijah Chance. To dau. Nanney chest that was my mother's.
Daus. Nanney, Fanny & Patience Chance resid. legatees. Spencer
Coleburn Exr. Witt: Littleton Wyatt, Jr., Meshack Watson, Arthur
Trader - p. 289
In order of prob: Leah Chance, wid. of the testator relinquished her
right & Spencer Coleburn qualified.

SPARROW, John - 24 Jan. 1771 - 31 Jan. 1775 - To wife Keziah
Sparrow use of my est. during her wid., & at her death or marriage to
be div. bet. all my children. Wife & Richard Bundick Exrs. - Witt:
William Young, Sr., Jacob Mason, Abel Wright. - p. 290

GIDDENS, RUBEN - 21 Jan. 1775 - 31 Jan. 1775 - To wife Athaliah
Giddens 100 A. near Deep Creek until my son Kendal Giddens arrives
at lawful age, except my wife marry, & then I give the said land to
him. Dau. Peggy Giddens. Unborn child. Wife & bro. John Giddens
in Northampton Exrs. Witt: Joseph Aimes, William Ward, Mary
Watson. - p. 290

BENSTON, NATHANIEL - 27 Dec. 1774 - 31 Jan. 1775 - To cousin
William Benston planta. where I now live, also part of the land I
bought of Daniel Toles. To cousin James Benston all the rest of the
land I bought of Toles. To cousin Margaret Benston. To Nathaniel
Benston, son of my cousin William Benston. Cousins William
Benston & James Benston resid. legatees & Exrs. Witt: Meshack
Feddiman, Joseph Boggs - p. 293

HORNSBY, ARGALL – 27 Oct. 1773 – 31 Jan. 1775 – To wife Leah Hornsby whole est. during her wid. & at her death or marriage I give the land I bought of Thomas Hargrass, cont. 50 A., to my son Major Hornsby, To son John Hornsby negro boy Levin, he paying my son Bagwell Hornsby (under 21) 20 L when he arrives to age. 4 daus. Peggy, Susannah, Betty & Anne Hornsby resid. legatees. Charles Bagwell Exr. Witt: Sarah Cole, Elizabeth Baily – p. 294
In order of prob: Major Hornsby qualified.

SCOTT, GEORGE – 23 Apr. 1773 – 28 Feb. 1775 – Whereas I did join with Tully Robinson Wise in the purchase of a tract of land of a certain Robert Snead, part of which said land I now live on, which was conveyed by the said Snead to the said Wise, & my part has not been conveyed by the said Wise to me, & whereas I have since sold the said Wise 100 A. of my 1/2 of the said land, my desire is that all the remainder of my 1/2 of said land be conveyed by the said Wise to my 2 sons Walter & Jonathan during their lives, & at their death to Charles Scott, son of Walter Scott & Thomas Scott, son of Jonathan Scott. Exrs. to sell my right to the land commonly called the Lease Land now in the possession of William Foster, Jamima Booth & Joshua Foster, & the proceeds of sale I give to my sons Walter & Jonathan Scott, they paying my daus. 20 s. Grandson Severn Scott. Grandau. Catherine Scott. Son Jonathan resid. legatee & Exr. Witt: Tully Robinson Wise, Cason Beasley – p. 301

MARSHALL, DANIEL – 23 May 1774 – 28 Feb. 1775 – To wife Sarah 1/2 my lands & houses out of every child's part that I shall hereafter mention during her natural life or wid. To son Daniel Marshall all the land my father John Marshall gave me where I now live on the Seaside. To dau. Sarah Marshall all my land between Thomas Marshall & Peter Marshall till death or marriage, reversion to my son Peter Marshall for life & then to his son, if any, & for want of such son to my son Daniel Marshall. To son Skinner Marshall all the land whereon my son John Marshall formerly lived for life, reversion to his son, if any, & if not to my son Stephen Marshall. To son Stephen Marshall 100 A. where he now lives. To dau. Sarah Marshall 1/2 the land that I bought of Levin Taylor. To dau. Esther Dennis the other 1/2 of the said land. I give all my lands on Assateague to be div. bet. my surviving children. Son Daniel Exr. Witt: Samuel Warren, Ezekiel Delastatius, Charles Marshall – p. 302
In order of prob: Daniel Marshall heir at law to the testator.

JOYNE, WILLIAM – 30 Jan. 1775 – 28 Feb. 1775 – To wife Margaret the 4 slaves which were hers before our marriage, also the use of the planta. where I now live during her wid. To my son Levin Joyne planta. where I now live. Son Levin resid. legatee & Exr. Witt: Henry Gascoyne, Jonathan Roles, Teackle Waltham – p. 303

GIDDENS, JOHN – 7 Feb. 1775 – 28 Feb. 1775 – To wife Lishea whole est. until my son William Giddens comes to the age of 21, then to be div. bet. my wife & all my children here mentioned, Peggy West, John Giddens, Thomas Giddens, Ismay Giddens, Custis Giddens, Sarah Giddens, William Giddens, Elizabeth Giddens, Michael Giddens & Ishmael Giddens. Wife Exec. Witt: Henry Scott, Jacob Turlington, John Chandler – p. 304

MIFFLIN, MARY – 18 June 1772 – 28 Mar. 1775 – To my son Samuel Mifflin's two children Edward & Mary Mifflin whatever is due me from the est. of Samuel Mifflin, dec., & should both die to go to my grandsons Warner Mifflin & Daniel Mifflin & my great-grandson Daniel Nock, son of James Nock. To great-grandau. Mary Mifflin, dau. of Southy Mifflin, dec., "I give & bequeath unto the Monthly Meeting at Little Creek. Kent County on Dellaware Bay, Pensylvania, of the People called Quakers, 30 L Pennsylvania currency to be disposed of as the members of that Meeting shall see fit" Great-grandson Charles Mifflin, son of George Mifflin. To Ann Roberts. To Stephen Maxfield & Susannah Beary. Great-grandau. Mary Mifflin, dau. of Warner Mifflin. To Susannah Nelson. Son Daniel Mifflin resid. legatee. Son Daniel & grandson Warner Mifflin Exrs. Witt: George Stewart, Annabellah Willet – p. 312
In order of prob: Daniel Mifflin, one of the Exrs. named in the foregoing will, being of the People called Quakers, qualified.

STERLING, WILLIAM – 30 May 1771 – 28 Mar. 1775 – To son William Sterling 50 A. in Forked Neck on the South side of my land, & should he offer to sell the same then to go to my son Richard. To son Richard the remaining part of my land, & should he offer to sell then to my son Southy Sterling. Son Richard to school my son Southy, or the land devised Richard to be rented out for that purpose. To dau. Catherine Sterling. Dau. Ann Temperance Sterling. To wife Sarah Sterling 1/3 of my est. real & personal during her wid. Children Ann Temperance, Catherine, Richard, William & Southy Sterling resid. legatees. Wife Sarah & son Richard Exrs. Witt: William Broadwater, William Burton – p. 314
In order of prob: Richard Sterling heir at law to the testator.

MEERS, THOMAS – Not dated – 28 Mar. 1775 – To son Southy Meers planta. where I now live for life, reversion to my grandson Covington Mears. Cousins John Meers & George Meers to rent out my land I bought of Garret Kitchens until my debts are paid, then I give the said land to my grandson Thomas Meers. Cousins John & George Meers Exrs. Witt: Francis Savage, Solomon Groten, Custis Groten – p. 315
Southy Meers heir at law.

WATSON, ZERROBABEL – 27 Nov. 1774 – 28 Mar. 1775 – To wife Keziah planta. where I now live & my marsh on the Bayside during her wid. then to my son Arthur. In case Southy Meers do not take the land at Occahannock I leave it to be sold by my Exrs., & the money to pay for the land I now live on. Dau. Adah & unborn child resid. legatees. Wife & Edmund Core Exrs. Witt: George Warrington, Scarburgh Broadwater – p. 316

FLETCHER, TABITHA – 28 July 1774 – 28 Nov. 1775 – Son John Fletcher. Grandau. Esther Walter. Dau. Tabitha Handcock. Dau. "Riddagail" Savage. Dau. Elizabeth Addison. Grandau. Rachel Walter. Son Richard Walter. Son John resid. legatee & Exr. Witt: Joseph Aimes, Josiah Herson, Leah Fuollud – p. 317

PHILLIPS, JOHN – son of Thomas – 2 Apr. 1774 – 30 May 1775 – To wife planta. where I live during her wid. then to my son Thomas Phillips. Dau. Elizabeth Phillips. Dau. Susannah Phillips. Unborn child. Daus. Elizabeth, Susannah & unborn child resid. legatees. Wife Exec. (no name) Witt: Major Ironmonger, John Hannaford – p. 332
In order of prob: Catherine Phillips, wid. of the testator qualified.

HASTING, RICHARD – 21 Dec. 1773 – 30 May 1775 – To wife Scarburgh Hasting whole est. during her wid. to bring up my children, & at her death or marriage to my son Rich: Salvy Hasting all my land, & for want of heirs to my son Major Hasting, & for want of heirs to my daus. Susanna, Ann & Kesiah Hasting. Children Susanna, Ann, Kesiah, Thomas, Richard Selvy & Major Hasting resid. legatees. Wife Scarburgh & dau. Susanna Exrs. Witt: William Young, Sr., Ralph Justice, Nancy Britt – p. 327

HINMAN, RICHARD – 8 Jan. 1774 – 30 May 1775 – To dau. Leah Hinman 100 A. where I live. To dau. Rachel Hinman & dau. Elizabeth Hinman all the remainder of my land. To sister Ann Hinman use of planta. where I live for life. 3 daus. Leah, Rachel & Elizabeth Hinman resid. legatees. Mr. James Henry & dau. Leah Hinman Exrs. Witt: Wlliam Young, Sr., John Fitchett, Joshua Fitchett – p. 328
In order of prob: Hannah Hinman, wid. of the testator, relinquished any benefit under said will.

BAKER, JOHN – 30 Jan. 1775 – 30 May 1775 – Dau. Mary Baker. Son Levin Baker. To wife Mary Baker whole est. during her wid. Son William Baker, George Baker, dau. Elizabeth Baker & Mary Baker & Levin Baker resid. legatees. Son William Exr. Witt: Robert James, Abel Wright, William Taylor – p. 330

HINMAN, JOHN – 20 Mar. 1775 – 27 June 1775 – To Susanna Riggs. Dau. Bethany Hinman resid. legatee. Moses Hinman & Nehemiah Stockley Exrs. Witt: Samuel Warren, Moses Hinman – p. 343

WARRINGTON, GEORGE – 20 Feb. 1775 – 27 June 1775 – To my housekeeper, Patience Bishop, negro, 100 L cash, personalty, provided she shall not claim any right, title or demand whatsoever on the remainder of my est, if she do I give the said legacies to my cousins Elizabeth & Nancey Warrington, but if the said Patience accepts the same I give the aforesaid legacies to her for the support & maintenance of a child she now has by me & another unborn child. To James Bishop, son of the aforesaid Patience. Cousins Nancey & Elizabeth Warrington resid. legatees. James Henry & George Corbin Exrs.

Witt: Samuel Warren, Patience Bishop, Elizabeth Bishop - p. 344

DOO, SAMUEL - 10 Nov. 1774 - 28 June 1775 - To 2 sisters Nelle & Margaret Doo planta. where I now live & all the remaining part of my est. Mickeel Bonwell Exr. & trustee. Witt: George Poulson, Southey Bull - p. 346

COTTINGHAM, THOMAS - 26 June 1775 - 29 Aug. 1775 - To wife planta. cont. 84 A. & whole est. during her wid. & should she marry then to my 2 girls, Nancy & Salley. Witt: Hallaway Bunting, Mason Watt - p. 349
In order of prob: Susanna Cottingham qualified.

SCARBURGH, DOROTHY - 20 July 1775 - 29 Aug. 1775 - To grandson Andrew Steward. To Americus Scarburgh use of my negro boy Babel until my grandson Henry Custis arrives to the age of 21 years, then to my said grandson, & in case of his death before lawful age to Americus Scarburgh. To Elizabeth Steward. To Sarah Scarburgh Thorowgood. To John Scarburgh. To Americus Scarburgh. To Dorothy Wainhouse Walker. To Sarah Steward. Dau. Sarah Jamison resid. legatee & Exec. Witt: Caleb Teackle, Adah Jacob - p. 350

MORGAN, MARY - 26 June 1775 - 29 Aug. 1775 - To Leah Tatham. To Mary Bennet, wife of William Bennet. To Jacob Bell & Ann Foster, son & dau of my cousin William Bell. To Elizabeth Redding. To John Glasby. Thomas Tatham resid. legatee & Exr.- Witt: Thomas Bloxom, Stephen Bloxom - p. 351

BONWELL, JOHN - 22 Sept. 1774 - 29 Aug. 1775 - To wife Mary whole est. during her wid. for the maintenance & education of my 5 children, to-wit: Charles, Hannah, Arthur & Smith Bonwell & unborn child, & for the boarding of all my other children. Should my wife marry or die before my 5 children be educated equal to my elder children, then my son James Bonwell to take my est. into his possession & fulfil this my will. Sister Leah Bonwell. Bal. of est. to be div. bet. my wife & chiidren except James when my youngest child arrives to the age of 12 years. To son James Bonwell my planta. where I now live, also my land & marsh on or near Gilford Creek, also the moiety of a water grist mill I now hold in part with Major Ironmonger, lying on the South branch of Onancock. Son Thomas Bonwell. Wife Mary, James Bonwell & Thomas Bonwell Exrs. Witt: John Smith, Mikeel Bonwell, James Bonwell, William Kennahorn - p. 353

TAYLOR, LEVIN - 9 May 1775 - 29 Aug. 1775 - To wife Mary Taylor 15 A. during her wid. to raise Levin, George & Lizebeth, & should she marry said tract to be rented out for 10 years to raise these 3 children. At the expiration of 10 years I give the said land to my son Jesse Taylor upon condition that he pay George Taylor 50L & should Jesss offer to sell the said land the same to fall to my son Levin, & should Levin offer to sell to fall to George. Bal. of est. to wife for life then to my dau. Leath Taylor & Anne Taylor & Levin Taylor & George

Taylor & Lezebeth Taylor. Wife Mary & son Jesse Exrs. Witt: Lisney Gootee, Polley Broadwater - p. 355

HANDCOCK, WILLIAM - 10 Feb. 1775 - 26 Sept. 1775 - Son Elijah Handcock. Dau. Elizabeth Handcock. Bal. of est. to wife Elizabeth for life & then to be div. bet. my son Elijah & dau. Elizabeth Handcock. Son George Handcock 5 L at the death of my wife. Son in law Peter Savage. Friend Solomon Richardson Exr. Witt: Joseph Aimes, Elijah Aimes, John Hornsby - p. 356

JAMES, WILLIAM SACKER - 16 Feb. 1775 - 26 Sept. 1775 - To eld. son Delight James. Dau. Elizabeth James. Son Spencer James. Son William Sacker James. Son "Jammy" James. Wife Leah James & 3 children Spencer, William Sacker & Jemmy James resid. legatees. Robert James & Shadrack Bayley Exrs. Witt: Edward Gunter, George Wimbrough, Mary Hampton - p. 357
In order of prob: Littleton Savage app. guardian to Delight James, heir at law to the testator.

MARSHALL, SKINNER - Not dated - 26 Sept. 1775 - To wife Sarah land where I live for life then to my 2 daus. Susanna Marshall & Phame Marshall & should both die without heirs I give the said land to my wife at her own disposal. To wife all my personal est. for life & if she marry again to have 1/3. I give the other 2/3 to my 2 daus. above named _ _ _ _ _ Not completed. Not signed. Proved by George Stewart, Benjamin Royal - p. 358

HALL, THOMAS - 27 Jan. 1770 - 31 Oct. 1775 - Dau. Jean Hall. Dau. Tabitha Hall. To dau. Margaret Fisher the articles I bought out of Francis Roberts' estate & left on said Roberts' planta. Grandson Thomas Hall Parker. Grandson Thomas Hall Fisher. Bal. of est. to be div. in 5 parts, 1/5 to dau. Anna Maria Andrews; 1/5 to dau. Jean Hall; 1/5 to dau. Tabitha Hall & 1/5 to my grandau. Elizabeth Roberts, & the other 1/5 to my grandchildren Sarah Roberts, Margaret Roberts, Edmund Roberts, Arthur Roberts, Thomas Hall Fisher & Obediah Fisher. Planta. to be div. in 3 equal parts, the 2 lower parts I give to my dau. Anna Maria Andrews & Jean Hall, the 3rd & upper part I give to my dau. Margaret Fisher for life, reversion to my grandson Thomas Hall Fisher & for want of heirs to my grandson Arthur Roberts. To dau. Tabitha Hall planta. called Sambo's. To grandau. Elizabeth Roberts house & lot in the town of Portsmouth. William Andrews Exr. Witt: Edward Ker, Obadiah Johnson, John Coloney, Thomas Jacobs, Richard Cutlar - p. 363

WINDOW, JOHN - 26 Sept. 1775 - 31 Oct. 1775 - To wife Ann all my land during her wid. Wife & children resid. legatees. Anderson Parker & Selby Vannelson Exrs. Witt: Caleb Parker, Robert Window - p. 364

DRUMMOND, WILLIAM, son of Spencer - 24 July 1775 - 31 Oct. 1775 - All my lands, negroes & personal est. except what is hereafter given to unborn child, & for want of issue to my bro. Richard Drummond. Wife Ann Robertson all the negroes I got by her & 1/3 of my land during her wid. Unborn child resid. legatee, & for want of heirs to my wife & bro. Richard Drummond. Friend Thomas Bayly Exr. Witt: John Drummond, Raymond Riley, Charles Drummond - p. 365

TIGNAL, DENNIS - 26 Nov. 1774 - 31 Oct. 1775 - To wife Mary Tignal the dwelling house commonly called my son Southy Tignal's & 1/3 of my lands during her life. Should I have a child by my said wife said child to have all that I got by my aforesaid wife at our marriage. To son Philip Tignal planta, where I live including all my land. Grandson Dennis Tignal, son of Philip. Son Southy Tignal. To dau. Sarah Bayly & to her dau. Pegga Bayly. Dau. Tabitha Turner. To dau. Comfort Martain for life, reversion to her dau. Betty Martain. My forner wife's side saddle &c. to my son Major Tignal, reversion to his children. Children, except Philip, resid. legatees. Son Philip & wife Mary Exrs. Witt: William Banfield Walker, John Belote - p. 366

WILKERSON, THOMAS - 1 Feb. 1774 - 31 Oct. 1775 - To wife Elizabeth Wilkerson all my est. during her wid. To son William the planta. where I now live. Dau. Elizabeth Wilkerson resid. legatee. Wife Elizabeth & son William Exrs. Witt: William Selby, Thomas Merrill, Sarah Taylor - p. 368

AIMES, THOMAS, Sr. - 8 Feb 1775 - 31 Oct. 1775 - To son Levi Aimes 100 A. on the South-west side of the Chestnut Ridge Road, adj. the land of Joseph Aimes. To wife Lisha Aimes. To son Shadrack Aimes 100 A. purchased of William Aimes, Jr., & adj. the land of William Aimes, Sr. To son Zerrobabel Aimes all the remaining part of my land. Son Thomas Aimes. Wife Elisha & son Shadrack Aimes & son Levi Aimes resid. legatees & Exrs. Witt: Joseph Aimes, Caleb Aimes, John Aimes - p. 368

KELLAM, Benston - 11 Mar 1775 - Proved 31 Oct. 1775 - Prob. 26 Mar. 1776 - To 2 sons Joseph & Abel Kellam. Dau. Peggy. Dau. Comfort. Daus. Polly & Fama. Son William. Bal. of est. to wife (no name) for life & then to be div. bet. my 6 children Peggy, Fama, Joseph, Comfort, Abel & Polly Kellam. Wife Exec. - Witt: Edmund Bayly, Levi Beaucham.
In order of prob: Edmund Bailey qualified, the executrix named in said will being dead without having qualified.

WEST, BENJAMIN - 8 May 1774 - 29 Nov. 1775 - To dau. Comfort Collen 25 A. at Hills Branch, & for want of heirs to dau. Elizabeth West. To son Benjamin all the rest of my land that is over Hill's Branch during his natural life, reversion to my grandson Thomas West. To daus. Elizabeth & Abigail West all the remainder of my land till my grandson Kendall West comes to age to bring my said grandson up, & then I give the land to my said grandson. Daus. Elizabeth & Abigail West resid. legatees & Exrs. Witt: William Young, Sr., William Hickman, Richard Justice - p. 379

In order of prob: George Corbin app; guardian to the heir at law – (Benjamin West heir at law - Order of probate in Order Book

KELLAM, SCARBURGH – 11 Dec. 1773 – 27 Feb. 1776 – To dau. Patience Laylor all the estate she has received, & at her mother's death I give her my boy called Babel, &c. To wife land where I live during her wid, but should she marry to have only her third. Son Severn (under age). Wife & son resid. legatees. Wife guardian to my son until he comes to age. Wife (no name) Exec. Witt: Abel West, Willaim Ward, John West. – p. 380
In order of prob: George Corbin app. guardian to Severn Kellam, heir at law to the testator. Keziah Kellam, wid. of the testator qualified.

BENSON, JONAS, Sr. – 23 Dec. 1775 – 27 Feb. 1776 – To son Moses planta. where I now live cont. 218 A. To son John 100 A. on the South side of Pratts Branch adj. to me. To dau. Comfort. To dau. Sarah. To Leshy Lingo, my dau. in law. Children Moses, John, Comfort, & Sarah resid. legatees. Son Moses Exr. Witt: Jonathan Addison, Benjamin Stringer, William F. Ross – p. 381
In order of prob: Moses Benson heir at law to the testator.

TAYLOR, JOSEPH – 3 Nov. 1769 – 27 Feb. 1776 – To son Elijah Taylor planta. where I now live. Wife Ann. 5 youngest children Tabitha, Nathan, Levin, William & Weltha to live with my son Elijah until they come to lawful age or marry. To son Abel all that I have lent or given him. To dau. Sophire Allen all that I have lent or given her. 6 children Elijah, Tabitha, Nathan, Levin, William & Whealthy resid. legatees. Son Elijah Exr. Friends John Watts, William Whealton & Skiner Wallop & Washbourn Tunnell, or any 3 of them, to div. est. Witt: John Watts, Thomas Slocomb, Rachel Warrington – p. 382
In order of prob: Abel Taylor heir at law to the testator – Sheriff's return "not found within my Bailiwick".

289

WILLS AND ADMINISTRATIONS,

ACCOMACK COUNTY, VIRGINIA
1663–1800

VOLUME II

GROTEN, MARY - 4 July 1775 - 27 Feb. 1776 - To grandau. Mary Groten 45 A. of my land adj. Solomon Groten's line, she to pay William Groten's est. 3 L To son Solomon Groten the remainder of my land being 45 A., he to pay 3 L to William Groten's est. Sabra Lurton, Rachel Trader, Charles Groten, Margaret Groten & Jonathan Groten, son & dau. of Jonathan Groten, resid. legatees. - To son William Eyrss 1 s. To dau. Sarah Green 1 s. To dau. Mary Townsend 1 s. Cousin Argol Kellam Exr. & grandau. Mary Groten Exec. - Witt: William Taylor, Levi Kellam - p. 389
In order of prob: Solomon Groten heir at law to the testatrix.

PARKER, EDWARD - 16 Oct. 1775 - 27 Feb. 1776 - Est. to be div. bet. wife Scarburgh Parker & 4 daus. Nancy, Molly, Susey & Mary Parker. Wife Exec. - Witt: Thomas Bayly, Drake Drummond, George Russell - p. 390

BUNTING, ELISHE, wid. of Smith Bunting - 30 Oct. 1775 - 27 Feb. 1776 - To son Pearce Chapman. To dau. Leah Bird. To son Thomas Edmunds. To son John Edmunds. To Sarah Edmunds, dau. of my son John Edmunds. To Nancy Bird, Leah Bird & Sally Bird, daus. of Jacob Bird. To Nanney Edmunds, dau. of Thomas Edmunds. 4 children Pearce Chapman, Leah Bird, Thomas Edmunds & John Edmunds resid. legatees. Jacob Bird Exr. Witt: Naney Bunting, Robert Davidson - p. 391

PARKS, BENJAMIN - 6 Mar. 1776 - 26 Mar. 1776 - To son Benjamin Parks my land & water mill &c. To dau. Rachel Hickman all the things I have lent her. Daus. Nanney, Elizabeth & Tabitha Parks resid. legatees. Son Benjamin Parks & Solomon Ewell Exrs. Witt: William Young, Sr., John Evans, William Ewell - p. 395

TATHAM, THOMAS - 4 Nov. 1775 - 26 Mar. 1776 - To son Ezekiel Tatham land purchased of Joseph Tunnel. Wife Tabitha to have use of planta. where I now live & all the rest of my est. during her wid, except the planta. I gave my son Ezekiel. To dau. Esther. To dau. Comfort. To dau. Rachel. To dau. Molly. To dau. Leah the use of my negro boy Daniel during her life, reversion to my grandson Airs Tatham. To grandau. Tabitha Watson. Grandau. Lurcretia Watson. To grandson Prieson Watson. 6 Daus. Sarah, Leah, Molly, Rachel,

Esther & Comfort resid. legatees. Wife Tabitha & son Ezekiel Exrs.
Witt: Nehemiah Stockley, Elijah Stockley - p. 410

PARKS, MARK - 24 Nov. 1775 - 26 Mar. 1776 - To wife whole est.
during her wid. & then to my son John Parks all my land. Bal. of est.
to be div. bet. the rest of my children, Mark, Rachel, Ann, Tabitha,
Solomon, Comfort Sacker. Wife (no name) Exec. Witt: Robert Turnal, John Only, Ezekiel Young. - p. 412
In order of prob: John Parks heir at law appeared by James Henry, his
guardian. Tabitha Parks, wid. of the testator qualified.

EVANS, JESSE, Sr. - 3 Feb. 1776 - 26 Mar. 1776 - Wife (no name) to
have use of whole est. for life. To son Jesse. To dau. Mary. To
daus. Leah & Susannah. Children Jesse, Mary, Leah, Susannah & Ann
resid. legatees. To son William 1 s. To son Thomas 1 s. & all my
wearing clothes. Thomas Hickman Exr. Witt: Charles West, Hezekiah White - p. 413

LEATHERBURY, PERRY - 17 Mar. 1776 - 26 Mar. 1776 - To son
William Leatherbury 25 A. on Gargothy Road. To son George Leatherbury 75 A., being the remaining part of 100 A. before beq. to my son
William. To wife Sarah Leatherbury the stock which she had with her
& 1/3 part of the land where I live during her life. To dau. Elizabeth
Leatherbury. To dau. Comfort Parker. To son Edmund Leatherbury
negro Dublin until my youngest dau. comes to age upon condition that
he school & bring up my 4 youngest children, & when the youngest
child arrive to lawful age Edmund to pay the value of the aforesaid
negro to be div. between my 6 children, Edmund, Elizabeth, Elliner,
William, George & Patience. To grandau. Betty Leatherbury 10 L. to
bring her up. 6 children Edmund, Elizabeth, Ellinor, William, George
& Patience resid. legatees. Son Edmund & wife Sarah Exrs. Witt:
Abraham Outten, Jemimy Outten, Elizabeth Belote - p. 414
In order of prob: Edmund Leatherbury heir at law to the testator.

COLEBURN, JOHN - 24 Feb. 1776 - 26 Mar. 1776 - To son Thomas
Coleburn part of my land I bought of Stratton Burton, beind the mannor
Planta. as far as the road &c., also 25 A. of land on Sedar Island, also
1/2 my mill I bought of James Henry, & for want of heirs to my son
Isaac Coleburn. To son George Coleburn land adj. that given my son
Thomas & 25 A. on Sedar Island, & for want of heirs to my son Samuel
Coleburn. To son John Coleburn the remaining part of my land I
bought of Stratton Burton, also 25 A. on Sedar Island, & for want of
heirs to my son Isaac Coleburn. To son Isaac water mill I bought of
Henry Heath & Elijah Chance, & for want of heirs to my son Samuel. I
also give my son Isaac 25 A. on Sedar Island. To son Samuel 25 A.
on Sedar Island &c. To dau. Elizabeth Coleburn. To dau. Ann Coleburn. To wife "Catrin" Coleburn. To son Robert Coleburn negro & 1/2
the book accounts, clothing & all the money due me for the old sloop
between me & Robert Coleburn; one sloop to be sold to the highest
bidder & 1/3 of the money to my son Robert Coleburn. Thomas, John,

George, Isaac, Samuel, Elizabeth & Ann Coleburn resid. legatees. Robert Coleburn, Thomas Coleburn &'John Spiars Exrs. Witt: Thomas Johnson, James Spiars, John Spiars. - p. 415
In order of prob: Robert Coleburn heir at law to the testator.

MONTGOMERY, Dr. JOHN, - Nunc - 8 Mar. 1776 - 26 Mar. 1776 - Wife to have best bed & furniture; clothes to be div. bet. my 3 bros. Should my wife be with child est. to be div. bet. wife & child. Should my wife not be with child I give 1/2 my est. to my wife & the other 1/2 to my father if he should be alive, & if not to my bro. Archibald Montgomery to be div. bet. all my bros. & sisters. James Henry & Thomas Bailey to settle my est. Proved by Mary Harris & Thomas Bailey. - p. 417
In order of prob: Patience Montgomery, wid. of the testator qualified.

WATSON, PETER - 24 Feb. 1776 - 26 Mar. 1776 - To son Zerobabel Watson my manor planta. cont. 166 A., he to bring up my son Peter Watson until he arrive at lawful age, & should he refuse 1/2 my planta. to be rented and the proceeds applied to the maintenance & education of my son Peter. To son John Watson (under age) 100 A. purchased of John Parkerson, & for want of heirs to my 3rd son Caleb Watson. Son John to take & bring up my son Benjamin until he arrive at lawful age, & should he refuse 1/2 the said land to be rented until my said son arrive at lawful age, & the proceeds applied toward educating or learning him the trade of a Taylor. To dau. Peggy Lilleston for life, reversion to her children. 5 sons Zerobabel, John, Caleb, Benjamin & Peter & my dau. Sally Watson & Peggy Lilleston resid. legatees. William Banfield Walker & Edward Ker & son Zerobabel Watson Exrs. Witt: Phillip Tigner, Mary Laurence, Abel Hawley - p. 418
In order of prob: Zerobabel Watson heir at law to the testator.

GARRISON, WILLIAM, Sr. - 1 Apr. 1776 - 25 June 1776 - To wife Agnes Garrison. To dau. Fillice Garrison. To dau. Elizabeth Garrison. To son William Garrison 240 A. of land, reversion to my grandson John Garrison. To son John Garrison. To dau. Fanny Garrison. To grandson Burton Silverthorne. To grandau Ann Silverthorne. Dau. Tabitha Silverthorne 1 s. Children John, Fillace, Elizabeth & Fanny Garrison resid. legatees. Sons William & John Exrs. Witt: Joseph Aimes, Jonathan Garrison, Solomon Groten - p. 420

SILVERTHORN, LEAVIN - 11 Jan. 1775 - 25 June 1776 - To wife Tabitha whole moveable est. during her wid. to bring up my children. Land & mill to be sold for the payment of my debts, & should there be anything over the same to go to my wife in the same manner as the rest of my est. John Watts & Isaac Smith Exrs. Witt: Littleton Wyatt, Jr. John Fortesque, Finley Rodgers. - p. 421
In order of prob: John Powell app. guardian to Burton Silverthorn, heir at law to the testator.

COLONY, BENJAMIN – 12 Apr. 1775 – 25 June 1776 – To son Major Colony land where I now live. To son John. To son William Colony. To dau. Susanna Colony. To grandson Joshua Darby. 4 children Major, William, John & Susana Colony resid. legatees. Sons Major & William Exrs. Witt: Abel West, Upshur Colony, Ann Coloney, Laban Chandler – p. 422

TAYLOR, TEACKLE – 1 Apr. 1776 – 25 June 1776 – To wife all the furniture in general belonging to her at the time of her marriage or since that is now in my possession. To son Abraham Taylor negro man Sam, personalty &c. that I had with my former wife, the dau. of Frances Milby. To my present wife Susanna. To son Bailey Taylor 1 pr. silver shoe buckles & knee buckles. To wife Susanna one diamond ring. To bro. Joshua. Friends John Milby, Joshua Taylor & Zerobable Rodgers Exrs. Witt: John Read, John Rodgers, Salathiel Milby – p. 424

CROPPER, SEBASTIAN, Jr. – 18 Mar. 1776 – 25 June 1776 – To wife Sabra Cropper. To son John Cropper negroes after his mother's death or marriage. To son Thomas Cropper negroes at his mother's death or marriage. To son Covington Corbin Cropper. Bal. of est. to be sold & what remains to be div. bet. wife & 3 sons. Mr. George Corbin & son John Cropper Exrs. Witt: James Arbuckle, John Nicholson – p. 427

KELLAM, JOHN – Adm. his est. with will, will annexed, unadministered by Bridget Kellam, dec., the late Exec., to William Ward, Edward Ker, the other Exr. named in said will refusing to act. Meshack Watson & John Bagge sec. – 30 July 1776 – p. 429

LEWIS, DANIEL – 1 Apr. 1776 – 30 July 1776 – To wife Sabrah Lewis use of my planta. & mill during her wid. & at her death to my son John Lewis 30 A. of my land at the head of my land, also my mill. To son Levin Lewis the remainder of my land. To son Liddy Lewis. To son Daniel Lewis. Bal. of est. to wife & at her death or marriage to be div. bet. Betty Lewis, Mary Lewis, Daniel Lewis, Elishe Lewis, Ritter Lewis, Rachel Lewis, Hetty Lewis & Rodolphus Lewis. Wife Sabrah Lewis & John Lewis, my bro., Exrs. Witt: Thomas Riley, Robert Parks, Lisey Rew – p. 429
In order of prob: John Lewis, heir at law to the testator.

MATTHEWS, SOUTHY – 13 Aug. 1775 – 30 July 1776 – To son Charles Stockly Matthews 155 A. adj. my water grist mill, likewise my said mill. To son William Matthews my swampy land. To son Thomas Stockly Matthews. Bal. of est. to wife Tabitha Matthews during her wid. & then to be div. bet my 3 children & unborn child, namely Charles Stockly Matthews, William Matthews, Mary Matthews & unborn child. Wife Exec. & cousin Alexander Stockly Exr. Witt: Edward Thornton, Joseph Matthews, Hannah Blake – p. 430
In order of prob: Thomas Stockly Matthews heir at law to the testator.

LAWS, JOHN – 12 Oct. 1775 – 30 July 1776 – To wife Elizabeth. Son William resid. legatee. Bro. William Laws Exr. & wife Exec. Witt: Joshua Wishart, William Ewell, Jr., Edward Thornton – p. 431

WHARTON, JOHN – 29 May 1772 – 30 July 1776 – To son John all my lands & for want of heirs to my son Bagwell Wharton (under age); John to pay to my son Bagwell when he arrives to lawful age, the sum of 26 L current money of Virginia, & should he refuse Bagwell to have the said land. To wife Elizabeth negroes during her wid. & then to be div. bet. sons Bagwell & William Wharton. Wife & 3 children Tabitha, Bagwell & William resid. legatees – Wife Exec. Not witnesses. Proved by James Henry & William Parramore – p. 432

BRATTEN, WILLIAM – 3 Feb. 1776 – 30 July 1776 – To wife Sophia all my land during her wid. & then to my sons Nehemiah Bratten & James Bratten. Should Nehemiah pay his bro. James 36 L current money of Virginia he to have the whole tract. Personal est. to wife during her wid. & then to my dau. Leady & unborn child. Wife Exec. Witt: Lisney Gootee, John Benson – p. 433
In order of prob: Sophia Bratten, wid. of the testator, guardian to Nehemiah Bratton, heir at law to the testator.

RODGERS, SARAH – 14 Jan. 1774 – 30 July 1776 – To son James Twiford. To dau. Margaret Wise. To grandau. Sarah Wise. To grandau. Sarah Twiford. To grandson Henderson Rodgers 18 s., the same to be put in a pair of shoe buckles for him. To grandson Robert Rodgers. To daus. in law Anne Twiford, Dorothy Rodgers & Elizabeth Rodgers. Sons John & Robert Rodgers & dau. Margaret Wise resid. legatees. Sons John & Robert Exrs. Witt: John Wharton & Elizabeth Wharton – p. 435.
In order of prob: John Wharton, one of the witnesses, since deceased.

RODGERS, BABEL – 28 Mar. 1774 – 27 Aug. 1776 – To son Gilbert Rodgers (under age) negroes, & for want of heirs to my 2 sisters Elizabeth Rodgers & Anne Finney. Exr. to sell my land and residue of est. toward the payment of debts. John Finney & Charles Bagwell Exrs. Witt: William Parker, John Parker – p. 437
In order of prob: George Corbin app. guardian to Gilbert Rodgers, heir at law to the testator.

WATTS, JOHN – 6 July 1776 – 27 Aug. 1776 – Wife Rebecca to be whole Exec. To son David Watts 18 A. on Pungoteague which I purchased of Henry Scarburgh. Wife to be guardian of my children Henry, David, William & Rebecca. To son William Watts the land purchased of David Walker & the land I bought of William Blake, cont. 82 A. To dau. Anne Downing. In case of the death of my wife my son in law William Downing to be my Exr. Children resid. legatees. Witt: Skinner Wallop, James Drummond, William Fosque – p. 438
In order of prob: James Henry app. guardian to David Watts, heir at law to the testator.

DRUMMOND, WILLIAM, of Assawoman - 28 Feb. 1773 - 27 Aug. 1776 - To wife Sarah use of whole est. until my son John Drummond comes to the age of 21 years & then she to have 1/3 of my Manner Plantation & 1/3 of my Messongoe lands, being 250 A. & after my son John comes to age wife to have the use of all my lands hereafter devised to my son George & all the slaves which I shall bequeath to my son John until my son George attains the age of 21 years, & after that time to have 1/3 of my lands & slaves & a child's part of my personal est. & should my wife marry before my son George becomes 21 then to have what the law allows her. To son John my Mannor planta. where I now live cont. 521 A. & the tract of land in Massongo Swamp supposed to cont. 250 A., slaves, &c. To son George planta. at Pocomoko cont. 400 A. with the mills thereto belonging & the remainder of my Messongo lands cont. 500 A. on the North side of Persimaon Gut adj. Spencer & George Drummond's lands, negroes, &c. To daus. Elizabeth & Sally Drummond the residue of my slaves & their increase when my dau. Elizabeth attains the age of 21 years or marriage. Should all my children die without issue in the lifetime of Tabitha, the dau. of my bro. in law James Henry, I devise in that case my Manor planta. where I live which came by the said Tabitha's Aunt, my first wife, unto the said Tabitha & her heirs, & should all my children die without issue in the lifetime of my bro. Spencer Drummond's sons Charles & Richard, or the lifetime of either of them, in that case I give all the residue of my lands beside the Manor planta. to the said Charles & Richard Drummond. To my 2 daus. aforesaid all my right, title & interest to lands & houses in the Town of Snow Hill. Bal. of est. to be div. between my children aforesaid. Son John Drummond & bro. in law James Henry Exrs. Witt: William Williams, John Montgomery, William Underhill, Littleton Townsend - p. 445
In order of probate - John Montgomery & Littleton Townsend, two of the witnesses, since deceased.

VESSELS, ANN - 19 July 1776 - 24 Sept. 1776 - To son in law Ephraim Vessells. To dau. Amey Vessells. To dau. Ann Vessells. Ephraim Vessells Exr. Witt: William Young, Sr., Sinah Justice, Rebecca Vessells - p. 454

KNIGHT, GEORGE - 10 Sept. 1776 - 29 Oct. 1776 - To Betsy Hack, dau. Peter Hack, Sr. all my negroes, personalty &c., she to give to Rachel Bunting such cloaths as she pleases. Medicines & books to be sold, book accounts made out & the money I give to Betsey Hack. Friends James Arbuckle, Dr. William Williams & Peter Hack, Jr. Exrs. Witt: Henry Custis, George Hack, John Tompkins - p. 358

ROWLEY, ARTHUR - 2 Aug. 1776 - 30 Oct. 1776 - Personal est. to wife during her wid. To son Henry Rowley planta. purchased of Charles Blake & for want of heirs to my dau. Comfort Rowley. To dau. Comfort land purchased of Alexander Warrington, cont. 50 A. on the North-west side of Wallops Road. To dau. Sarah Westerhouse. To son Henry 30 L. Virginia current money to be laid out for him in education. Children Sarah Westerhouse, Comfort & Henry Rowley resid. legatees. Wife Rachel to be guardian of my son Henry, & should my wife die in the minority of my son John Kendall to be his guardian. Wife Exec. Friends John Kendall, son of Lemuel, & Charles Ewell Exrs. Witness: George Corbin, William Ewell, Sackar Parker - p. 459

SPARROW, MARY - 8 May 1775 - 30 Oct. 1776 - To grandson Scarburgh Sparrow. Dau. Susannah Riggs resid. legatee. Isaac Riggs Exr. Witt: William Young, Sr., John Lewis, Anne Hinman - p. 462

WYATT, KENDALL - 12 Mar. 1776 - 26 Nov. 1776 - Whole est. to be put to the use of bringing up my children, Adah & John. Wife Mary to bring up my children. Bro. Joshua Wyatt Exr. Witt: Major Savage, Arthur Wyatt - p. 464

NOX, ELIJAH - 22 Nov. 1774 - 26 Nov. 1776 - To son Nehemiah Nox. To dau. Esther Nox. To son George Nox. "unto my third son the younger Solomon Nox" Wife Elizabeth & bro. Solomon Nox Exrs. Witt: Ayres Gillet, Stephen Marshall, Richard Mariner, John Gillett - p. 468
Note: Should be "NOCK" Indexed "Nock" - "Nock" in order of prob: & other records.

SEYMOUR, WILLIAM - 9 Nov. 1776 - 31 Dec. 1776 - Land purchased of Luke Luker to be sold. To son George Seymour (under age) my land adj. on the Eastward side of the Main County Road, cont. 450 A., also 1/2 of the watergrist mill. To wife Leah Seymour. Bal. of est. to be div. bet. Wife Leah & 4 children, Elizabeth, Rose, William & Leah. Wife, Thomas Teackle & Levin Joyne Exrs. Witt: Arthur Teackle, John Sharlock, Levin Window - p. 469
In order of prob: Isaac Smith app. guardian to George Seymour, heir at law to the testator.

CHURN, GEORGE - 30 Mar. 1776 - 31 Dec. 1776 - To dau. Mary Churn her mother's chest & clothes. To dau. Susannah Churn. To dau. Tabitha Churn. To wife Ann Churn all the remainder of my est. during her wid., & at her marriage or death to my son Thomas Churn. Daus. Mary, Susannah & Tabitha resid. legatees. Wife Anne Churn & William Young, Jr. Exrs. Witt: William Young, Sr., Isaac Riggs, Salathiel Fitchit.

MEARS, LITTLETON - 7 Nov. 1776 - 31 Dec. 1776 - Land to be rented out, except my wife's dower, for 8 years following my death, the profits to maintain my 2 youngest children Sarah & Shadrack Mears. To son John Mears planta. where I now live, including all my lands. To wife Naomi what she brought with her when I married her. 8 children, Levin, Littleton, Severn, Kendall Mears, Sophia Martin, Betty & Sally Mears & son Shadrack Mears resid. legatees. Wife & William Banfield Walker Exrs. Witt: Philip Tignal, Kendall Savage - p. 473

TEACKLE, WILLIAM - 19 Dec. 1776 - 28 Jan. 1777 - To mothor Margaret Teackle planta. where James Wise now lives, she to sell the said planta. if she choose to pay my debts. Mother resid. legatee. Cousin John Teackle Exr. Witt: John Smith & John Arrington - p. 474
In order of prob: Thomas Teackle heir at law.

HORNSBY, JAMES - 5 Dec. 1776 - 28 Jan. 1777 - Land that formerly belonged to Abel Kellam to be sold. To wife Ester Hornsby. To sister Tabitha Heath. To James Hornsby, son of Argil Hornsby, 5 L. John Meers, son of William, to keep it until he comes to age, & should James Hornsby die without heirs then to his sister Tabitha Heath. To bro. Zerobabel Hornsby what money is left, & if he die John Meers, son of William, to take the said money & give it to such people in the County as he thinks need it most. "My Desire is that he Shudent have the money till he comes out of the service & that John Meers, son of William, should keep it in his hands tel he does come out" Friend John Meers, son of William Exr. Witt: John Hornsby, John Watson, William Meers - p. 481

EDMUNDS, THOMAS - 22 Nov. 1776 - 28 Jan. 1777 - Wife to have use of whole est. during her wid. To son John Edmunds the planta. I now live on including 150 A. next to Richard Bull's. To son William Edmunds 50 A. next to Robert Bull. Negroes & all personal est. at the death of my wife to be div. bet. all my children. Wife Joyce Exec. - Witt: George Cutler, John Edmunds - p. 482

MILBY, JOHN - 2 Dec. 1776 - 28 Jan. 1777 - To son Salathiel Milby 150 A. & for want of heirs to my son Solomon Milby. To son Salathiel Milby my Water Mill on Pungoteague. To son John Milby 100 A. starting at a place called the old Wading Place, & for want of heirs to my son Gilbert Milby. To son Gilbert Milby Water Mill & land adj. it on the head of Occahannock, & for want of heirs to son Solomon Milby. To dau. Tabitha Milby. To grandson Abraham Taylor & for want of heirs to my dau. Tabitha Milby. To wife Patience Milby all the est. I had by her at our marriage. Should my wife be with child I give said child negro boy called Cuff. Children Salathiel, Tabitha, John, Solomon & Gilbert Milby & unborn child resid. legatees. Wife Patience, son Salathiel & friend Augusten Lecat Exrs. Witt: Joseph Ames, Caleb Ames, Edmund Poulson - p. 484

WATSON, EDMUND - __ __ 1776 - 29 Jan. 1777 - To wife Newberry Watson 3 negroes until my son Edmund Watson comes to the age of 22 years, then they & their increase to be div. bet. my sons Edmund Watson, James Watson & Caleb Watson. To son Elijah Watson 350 A. of land. To son Levin Watson 50 L cash. To dau. Agnes Nock & John Nock, her husband, reversion to their children. To dau. Sarah Watson. To dau. Unice Watson. 3 youngest sons Edmund, James & Caleb Watson resid. legatees.
Wife & son Elijah Watson Exrs. Not witnessed. Proved by Daniel

RIGGS, ISAAC – 17 Feb. 1777 – 25 Mar. 1777 – To dau. Nancy Riggs all my land & mill, & for want of heirs to unborn child, & should my wife not be with child to descend to my cousin Sally Bandy & for want of heirs to my bro. Joshua Riggs. To John Riggs. Wife Susana & dau. Nancy Riggs resid. legatees. William Young, Jr. Exr. Witt: John Riggs & Leviner Melson – p. 499

GUTTERIEDGE, SEVERN – 7 Feb. 1777 – 25 Mar. 1777 – Exrs. to sell all my land on the West side of the Court House Branch up to Doe's old field toward payment of my debts, except my houses & garden & about 1 1/2 A. where Coxwell lives, & should the land not be enough to pay my debts then to sell the house & lot. To wife Attalanta Gutteriedge all my lands which shall not be sold during her wid., then to my son Littleton in fee simple. Wife to bring up my children I had by her with the profits & give them reasonable schooling, & should Littleton die under age & without issue all my lands at the death or marriage of my wife to be sold & the money equally div. bet. such of my daus. as may then be living. Wife & children resid. legatees. Wife & friends David Bowman & James Henry, or either of them, Exrs. Witt: William Arbuckle, James Henry, Thomas James – p. 499
In order of prob: George Corbin app. guardian of Littleton Gutteriedge, Inf't. heir at law to the testator.

HARMAN, LITTLETON – 24 Oct. 1775 – 25 Mar. 1777 – To wife Sophia Harman. To bro. John Harman. To bro. Henry Harman. To my little godson Littleton Harman my silver shoe buckles, knee buckles, stock buckles & sleave buttons. To godson Ephraim Watson my planta. in the woods & stock thereon except what I have given my bro. John. Wife resid. legatee. Wife & bros. Henry & Ephraim Exrs. Not witnessed. Proved by John Harmon, Asher Shield. – p. 503
In order of prob: Bayly Harmon heir at law to the testator.

BARNS, JOHN SACKER – 29 Feb. 1776 – 25 Mar. 1777 – To son William Barns planta. where I now live. To dau. Anne Barns. Son William & dau. Anne resid. legatees. Charles Bagwell Exr. Witt: Benjamin Peck, Susannah Barns.
In order of prob: Charles Bagwell, the Exr. named in the foregoing will refusing to act. Parker Barnes qualified.

GROTEN, MAJOR – 19 Feb. 1777 – 29 Apr. 1777 – To bro. Edmund Groten my tract of land cont. 200 A., my mother to have use of same until my son arrives to the age 16 yers & should die without issue to fall to my bro. Zerrobabel Groten. To bro. Jonathan Groten. To sister Amey Groten. To John Rodgers, son of James Rodgers all the crop he makes upon my planta. this year, he paying my sister Amey Groten 8 L. To son William Groten. Friend Benjamin Hutchenson Exr. Witt: John Rowles, Amy Groten – p. 510

BALDWIN, JOSEPH – Adm. his est. to John Mills – 27 May 1777 – p. 2

GAULT, PATRICK – Adm. his est. to Thorowgood Smith – Littleton Savage sec. – 27 May 1777 – p. 3

HALL, ASA – Adm. his est. to Anne Hall – George Corbin & Ralph Corbin sec. – 29 July 1777 – p. 11

MIDDLETON, GEORGE – Adm. his est. to Catherine Middleton – John Custis (seaside) & Cornelius Ironmonger sec. – 29 July 1777 – p. 13

JACKSON, ARCHIBALD – Adm. his est. to Jenny Jackson – William Young, sec. – 29 July 1777 – p. 14

COLONY, JOHN – Adm. his est. to Elizabeth Colony – John Custis & John Parker (Matty) sec. – 31 Sept. 1777 – p. 27

NOCK, JOHN – Adm. his est. to Lucretia Nock – John Teackle sec. – 25 Nov. 1777 – p. 36

BUNTING, WILLIAM BLACK – Adm. his est. with will annexed to Thomas Bayley, Jr., the Exr. therein named refusing to qualify. William Young & William Downing sec. – 25 Nov. 1777 – p. 36

AIMES, JOSEPH – Adm. his est. to Elizabeth Ames – Edmund Poulson & Leavan Aimes sec. – 27 Jan. 1778 – p. 49

DAVIS, HENRY – Adm. his est. to Keziah Davis – John Ashby & Rowland Savage sec. – 27 Jan. 1778 – p. 50

EWELL, JAMES – Adm. his est. to Solomon Ewell – George Hope Ewell sec. – 27 Jan. 1778 – p. 53

EVANS, THOMAS – Adm. his est. to Thomas Hickman – George Hickman sec. – 27 Jan. 1778 – p. 53

BURTON, JOSHUA – Adm. his est. to Thomas Burton – John Parker & Levi Nock sec. – 25 Feb. 1778 – p. 60

SAVAGE, MAJOR – Adm. his est. to Peggy Savage – Zorobabel Kellam & George Garrison sec. – 31 Mar. 1778 – p. 67

DRUMMOND, JAMES – Adm. his est. to John Drummond – William Young sec. 31 Mar. 1778 – p. 69

KELLAM, JONATHAN – Adm. his est. to Francis Kellam – Edmund Bayly & John Bagge sec. – 26 May 1778 – p. 78

WILLIS, SOLOMON - Adm. his est. to William Mister - Charles Bayly sec. - 26 May 1778 - p. 83

PEIRCE, NATHAN - Adm. his est. to Elizabeth Peirce - John Reid sec. - 26 May 1778 - p. 83

POWELL, THOMAS - Adm. his est. to Comfort Powell - Sackar Parker sec. - 30 June 1778 - p. 94

MARTIN, EDWARD - Adm. his est. to George Hack - Abraham Outten sec. - 30 June 1778 - p. 94

HICKMAN, WILLIAM - Adm. his est, to Isaiah Hickman - Thomas Hickman sec. - 28 July 1778 - p. 169

LAWRENCE, JOSEPH - Adm. his est. to Joshua Lawrence - Abel Savage & Jonathan Mears sec. - 25 Aug. 1778 - p. 186

KENDALL, JABEZ - Adm. his est. to John Kendall - James Henry & George Corbin sec. - 28 Oct. 1778 - p. 247

UPSHUR, CALEB - Adm. his est. to John Upshur & Abel Upshur - John Teackle & Thomas Teackle sec. - 24 Nov. 1778 - p. 255

COLEBURN, SPENCER - Adm. his est. to Abel Upshur & Arthur Teackle - John Teackle & John Upshur sec. - 24 Nov. 1778 - p. 255

COWLEY, LEAH - Adm. her est. to Elizabeth Cowley - William Emmerson sec. - 24 Nov. 1778 - p. 257

LEWIS, Spencer - Adm. his est. to Mary Lewis - Jonathan Willet & Thomas Lewis sec. - 25 Nov. 1778 - p. 262

WILLIS - SOLOMON - Adm. his est. to William Willet - Jonathan Willet & John Chandler sec. - 23 Feb. 1779 - p. 322

POWELL, ROBERT - Adm. his est. to Elizabeth Powell - Thomas Bayley Sec. - 29 Apr. 1779 - p. 350

BLOXOM, LEVI - Adm. his est. to Athalia Bloxom - William Andrews & Daniel Kelly sec. - 29 June 1779 - p. 379

KELLAM, WILLIAM - Adm. his est. to Sarah Kellam - John Warrington sec. - 27 July 1779 - p. 395

KELLAM, LEVI - Adm. his est. to Argol Kellam, Sr - Custis Groten sec. - 27 July 1779 - p. 396

RODGERS, LEVIN - Adm. his est. to Thomas Bayly & William Tizaker - John Custis & Benjamin Peck sec. - 26 Oct. 1779 - p. 443

WHEALTON, NEHEMIAH - Adm. his est. to Rachall Whealton - John Finney & Ephraim Millman sec. - 30 Nov. 1779 - p. 466

ADDISON, JEREMIAH PARKER - Adm. his est. to Nathan Addison - William Polk & Reuben Joyne sec. - 2 Dec. 1779 - p. 473

PELCERF, FRANCIS - Adm. his est. to Francis Barboutin - David Bowman sec. - 2 Dec. 1779 - p. 474

MEARS, BARTHOLOMEW - Adm. his est. to James Duncan, unadministered by Rachel Mears, dec. - 25 Jan. 1780 - p. 486

SHAE, WILLIAM - Adm. his est. to Edmund Scarburgh - Thomas Custis sec. - 29 Feb. 1780 - p. 505

Wills &c - 1777-1780

KELLAM, SOLOMON - 15 Aug. 1768 - 27 May 1777 - Wife Matilda Kellam sole legatee & Exec. Witt: Littleton Scarburgh Major, Leven Green - Proved by Andrew Stewart, both witnesses being dead - p. 13

READ, JOHN - 11 Mar. 1777 - 29 July 1777 - To son Charles Read (under age) planta. where I now live being 200 A. To son Caleb Read planta. where my bro. Solomon formerly lived cont. 138 A., to begin at Southy Read's line and across to John Read's line, also a gun that was my father's. To dau. Tabitha Read. To dau. Elizabeth Read. Wife Elizabeth Read to have use of whole est. to bring up my children, she to have same until the year 1782. Wife & daus. Tabitha & Elizabeth resid. legatees. Wife Elizabeth & bro. Solomon Read Exrs. Witt: John Rowles, Robert Hutchinson, William B. Walker - p. 14
In order of prob: Thomas Teackle app. guardian to the heir at law.

BEAVANS, JOHN - 10 Mar. 1775 - 29 July 1777 - To mother Mary Beavans whole est. during her life & after her death I give to my nephew, Walter Beavans, son of my bro. Nathaniel Beavans, 200 A. on Pocomoke adj. to Samuel Beavans & the heirs of William Beavans, dec., also my part of the marsh on the Bayside which my father William Beavans, dec., devised to me, 1 pr. of paste knee buckles set on silver & one stock buckle silver. To nephew William Henry Beavans, son of my aforesaid bro. Nathaniel Beavans, all the remaining part of my est. to pay my debts. Mother Mary Beavans & bro. Nathaniel Beavans Exrs. Witt; Betty Abbott, John Abbott - p. 15
In order of prob: John Abbott, one of the witnesses to the foregoing will now deceased.

CUSTIS, LEAVEN - 1 July 1777 - 29 July 1777 - To wife Leah Custis whole est. during her wid., should she die my wid. whole est. to my dau. Elizabeth, & if she marry one half my est. until her death & then to my said dau., & should my dau. die without issue to my sister Leah Custis. To Andrew Stewart, son of Leven Stewart. To George

Stewart, son of Leven. Bro. Thomas Custis Exr. To my loving father. Witt: Thomas Custis, Leven Stewart, Ann Custis - p. 17

BURTON, ABNER - Not dated - 30 July 1777 - To wife Susannah Burton my land & planta. & personal est. during her wid. To son Caleb Burton all that I have lent him. To son Benjamin Burton all that I have lent him. To dau. Sarah Burton one chest marked B/T with lock & key. To dau. Comfort Burton. To son John Burton all my land which I now live on, & for want of heirs to my grandson Jacob Burton. 4 children, Benjamin, Sarah, Comfort & John Burton resid. legatees. Son Benjamin Exr. Witt: Ezekiel Ross, Jacob Ross, Joseph Ross - p. 20
In order of prob: The Exr. named in the foregoing will being absent, Susanna Burton qualified.

SAVAGE, WILLIAM - 21 Mar. 1777 - 30 July 1777 - To wife the use of whole est. during her wid., but should she marry to have such part as the law directs, & at her death or marriage my land to be sold & the money equally div. bet. all my children. Wife Sarah & George Cutler Exrs. Witt: John Warrington, Zerobabel Edwards - p. 23

JENKINSON, ROBERT - Not dated - 26 Aug. 1777 - To son Custis Jenkinson my now dwelling planta. & 20 L-cash. To son Robert Jenkinson all the lands I bought of James Hutchison & 20 L- cash. Bal. of est. to be div. bet. my other 6 children, Nancy, Peggy, Ralph, Thomas, James & Sally. Witt: Leah Brittingham - proved by George Corbin, Kendal Stokely & Leah Brittingham - p. 25
In order of prob: Mary Ann Jenkinson qualified.

GROTON, SOLOMON - 10 Oct. 1776 - To son John Groton planta. where my father William Groton formerly lived, cont. 90 A., his wife to have 1/3 of it after his death during her wid., and after my said son John's death to go to his son John. To son Custis Groton the planta. & tract of land I bought of Arthur Trader where I now live cont. 60 A. Wife & 4 children Sevron, William, Thomas & Nanney Groton resid. legatees. Wife Ann & son Custis Groton Exrs. Witt: Henry Davis, William B. Walker, Leah Taylor - p. 25

BELL, SCARBROUGH - 28 Dec. 1772 - 26 Aug. 1777 - To son George Smith. To son John Smith. To dau. Mary Satchell. Son George Smith resid. legatee. Witt: George Stewart, Sophia Bell, Ruth Holston. - p. 26
In order of prob: George Smith qualified.

RUSSELL, SOLOMON - 13 July 1777 - 26 Aug. 1777 - To son George Russell & son Solomon Russell all my land & marsh to be equally div. bet. them, Personalty &c. Bal. of est. to wife Mary Russell. Wife & sons George & Solomon & daus. Jemimea & Mary Russell & James Nelson resid. legatees. Sons George & Solomon Russell, William Young, Jr. & Richard Young Exrs. Witt: Jonathan Willit, Rachel Parks. - p. 27

ELLIOT, THOMAS – 28 Oct. 1775 – 26 Aug. 1777 – To son John Elliot my land & planta. cont. 70 A., he to maintain my dau. Peggy Elliot till she arrive to the age ot 18. Daus. Esther & Peggy Elliot to have their homes in the house till they marry. 9 children, Leah, Betty, Thomas, Levinah, Leavin, William, Teackle, Easther & Peggy Elliot resid. legatees. Son in law Goldin Fox & Major Ironmonger Exrs. Witt: Major Ironmonger, Jenny Haden, Margaret Doe – p. 28

PARKER, ROBERT – 23 Sept. 1776 – 26 Aug. 1777 – To sister Betty Parker negroes, provided she never marry into the name or family of a Gutler or Leatherbury, & should she marry either of the above names the said negroes to descend to my bro. John Parker. Sister Betty Exec. Witt: Clement Parker, Edmund Wise, Wise Middleton – p. 29

WALTHAM, TEACKLE – 14 May 1777 – 26 Aug. 1777 – to son John Waltham, alias Heath, my planta. & all belonging to it, all my slaves & moveable est., & for want of heirs to my 2 bros. John & William. Bro. John Exr. & to be guardian to my son. Witt: Thomas Jacob, Patiance Heath, Edward Ker – p. 30

KIPP, BENJAMIN – 3 May 1777 – 31 Sept. 1777 – To wife Elizabeth Kipp. To dau. Curnela Kipp. Bal. of est. to be sold & wife to have 1/3 & dau. 2/3 of the proceeds. Neighbor Edmund Bayley Exr. & guardian of my dau. Curnela. Witt: Henry Minson, William Kellam, Zephaniah Bradford – p. 31.

CUSTIS, BAGWELL – 7 Nov. 1774 – 31 Sept. 1777 – To goddau. Peggy Custis, dau. of Thomas Custis, Sr. 10 L current money of Virginia. To sister Elizabeth Garrison 1 s. To eldest bro. John Custis 20 L – Youngest bro. William Custis resid. legatee & Exr. Not witnessed. Proved by William Riley – p. 31

FISHER, SHADRACK – 18 Dec. 1776 – 31 Sept. 1777 – To bro. Isaac Fisher 1/2 my est. and to my sister Sally Walker the other 1/2 "if I never return". Witt: Solomon Johnson, Robert Small, Elijah Bird – p. 32.
In order of prob: Salathiei Fitchet qualified.

GROTEN, JOHN – 24 Dec. 1776 – 31 Sept. 1777 – "I John Groten Soldier in the Sarvice of the United States in the Ninth Regiment of Virginia Forces, being called to the field of Battle & not knowing but a Random Shot may take my life I ordain this my last Will and Testament" To wife Margaret Groten my planta. on Mattchapungo during her life or wid. & then to my son John Groten. Wife, dau. Betty & son Kendall resid, legatees. Wife Margery Groten & Tully Robinson Wise Exrs. Witt: William Parramore, Thomas Parramore, Charles Snead – p. 33

FOSQUE, NATHANIEL – 27 Feb. 1777 – 25 Nov. 1777 – To wife Ann Fosque. To son John Fosque. To son Nathaniel Fosque. To dau.

Ann Fosque. To dau. Elizabeth Fosque. To dau. Mary Smith. Wife & 5 children resid. legatees. Wife Ann & John Smith Exrs. Witt: Baley Harmon, William Harmon – p. 35

GROTEN, WILLIAM – 6 June 1777 – 25 Nov. 1777 – To bro. Zerobabel Groten planta. where my mother & I live, cont. 175 A. To bro. Jonathan Groten my planta. called Charles Lecates, cont. 102 A., Zerobabel Groten to pay his bro. Edmund Groten 40 L & Jonathan to pay his bro. Edmund 20 L, which said sums make up the amount I was to pay by my father's will. The public house with the privileges now belonging to be enjoyed by Benjamin Hutcheson for the present year & the year following, he accounting for it at the rate he now gives of 30 L per year, & the money & the 50 L owing me by Major Colony & all my corn to be sold & the money to be div. bet. my 3 sisters, Margaret Hutcheson, Patience Rodgers & Amy Groten. My mother to enjoy all the houses where she now lives durihg her nat. life. To friend John Rowles. Bro. Zerobabel Groten resid. legatee. John Rowles & Benjamin Hutcheson Exrs. Witt: Edward Ker, John Watson, Robert Andrews, Annamariah Andrews – p. 36
In order of prob: Heir at law to the testator under age.

COWARD, WILLIAM – 30 June 1777 – 25 Nov. 1777 – To son Samuel Coward 68 A. purchased of Thomas Kellam. To wife Margaret Coward the use of all the rest of my est. during her wid. then to be div. bet. my children Amy, Adah & Samuel Coward. Wife & Thomas Jacob Exrs. Witt: Margaret Joyne, John Roose, John West – p. 38
In order of prob: Thomas Teackle App. guardian to the heir at law.

FITZHUGH, WILLIAM – 22 Dec. 1776 – 26 Nov. 1777 – To wife whole est. Jacob Bird Exr. Witt: Major Bayley, Susannah Hornsby – p. 39

BUNTING, WIILIAM B. – 20 Dec. 1776 – 28 May 1777 – To sons Charles & William B. Bunting my land & mill, & should either die their part to the survivor, & shouid both die to fall to my grandson William Crippen. To my love begotten son Edward Phillips 20 L for his maintenance. Bal. of est. as follows: To son John Selby Bunting 2 shares & Charles, William & Betty Cropper 1 share. Sons Charles & William to maintain my son Selby. Spencer Bagwell & sons William & Charles Exrs. Not witnessed: Proved by Isaac Smith & Spencer Bagwell – p. 39
In order of probate: The Exrs. named in the foregoing will refused to act. & Thomas Bayley, Jr., granted letters of Adm. with will annexed.

MEERS, BARTHOLOMEW – 7 Mar. 1777 – 27 Jan. 1778 – To grandson John Meers 45 A. & my great house. To wife Easter Meers my kitchen & 3 A., also 42 A. more adj. the above gift, 1/3 of moveable est. & all the things she brought with her, negroes for life, reversion to my grandson John Meers. To son Elijah Meers the remaining part of my land for life, reversion to his son John Meers, & for want of heirs to Bartholomew Meers, son of Elijah. To grandau. Catharine Kellum, & for want of issue to be div. bet. all the children of Elijah Meers.

Southy Meers, Elijah Meers & John Meers, my grandson, to take care of Catharine Kellam & his est. until she comes to age or marries. To William Meers the son of Kendal Meers, my grandson 10 L & if he dies before he comes to age to my grandson John Meers, Elijah Meers' children resid. legatees. Grandson John Meers, wife Easter Meers & John Meers, son of Elisha Meers, Exrs. Witt: John Meers, son of William, Mary Meers, Reubin Kellam - p. 48

RILEY, WILLIAM, Jr. - 5 Nov. 1777 - 27 Jan. 1778 - To son William Riley all my land where I now live with the mill thereon, & all the lands & marsh on "Shoures Island". To son Thomas Riley. To dau. Elizabeth Riley. Wife Elizabeth Riley to have use of whole est. until my youngest child comes to the age of 14 years. Wife, William Riley, Thomas Riley & dau. Elizabeth Riley & unborn child resid. legatees. Wife & friend Zerobabel Rodgers Exrs. Witt: Thomas Bayly, Thomas Lilleston, John Riley - p. 50

LITCHFIELD, FRANCIS - 19 Mar. 1777 - 24 Feb. 1778 - Land bought of Midleton Mays (Mason) to be sold for the payment of debts. Mother to have the land she now lives on for life. Wife to have planta. where I now live during her wid. To son Zadock Litchfield land where my mother lives beginning at the corner tree of Levin Gale's land. To son Francis Litchfield 100 A. to begin at the head of my land, & for want of heirs to my sons John & Zadock Litchfield. To son John Litchfield all the remainder of my land, & for want of heirs to my son Francis. To wife Elizabeth all my est. during her wid, & then to be div. bet. my 6 children John, Zadock, Nancy, Bettey, Mary & Francis. Wife Elizabeth & Henry Fletcher, Sr., Exrs. Witt: Solomon Johnson, Nathan Riggan, Betty Boston — p. 51
In order of prob: Wife Elizabeth relinquished her right, & William Young, Jr. qualified - George Corbin app. guardian to the heir at law to the testator.

WHITE, HEZEKIAH — 17 Dec. 1776 - 24 Feb. 1778 - To Thomas Hickman 25 A. adj. the land I have already sold him. To Thomas Hickman all the rest of my land to be sold for the payment of debts. Dau. Famey White resid. legatee. Thomas Hickman Exr. Witt: John Riley, Richard Drummond, Spencer Drummond - p. 53
In order of prob: James Taylor app. guardian to the heir at law to the testator.

PHILLIPS, MATTHIAS - 5 Jan. 1771 - 24 Feb. 1778 - Wife Rachel Phillips sole legatee & Exec. Witt: Jacob Rodgers, David (blank), John Spiers - p. 53
In order of prob: William Parramore qualified, the Exec. named in the foregoing will being lately deceased.

CRIPPEN, WILLIAM — 28 July 1776 - 25 Feb. 1778 - To sister Jaca Crippen. To bro. John Crippen. Bal. of est. to be div. bet. John, Elizabeth, Scarbrough & Sophia. Jesse Hickman Exr. Witt: Jesse Hickman, Sarah Melson, Elizabeth Mendoum - p. 54

In order of prob: The Exr. named in said will refusing to act, William Young, Jr. qualified.

RICHARDSON, CHARLES - 2 Dec. 1776 - 31 Mar. 1778 - To wife Elizabeth whole est. real & personal until such time (if she should have a child by me) that the said child shall come to the age of 21 years, & if she have no child to possess the said est. during her wid. & should the said child die before the age of 21, the whole est. to my bro. William Richardson, & for want of heirs to my bro Daniel Richardson, & for want of heirs to my bro Zerobabel Richardson, & for want of heirs to my bro. Kendal Richardson. Uncle John Mears Exr. Witt: William Townsend, Robert Davidson, Meshack Matthews - p. 66

FLUD, KEZIAH - 24 Feb. 1778 - 31 Mar. 1778 - To son in law John Kelly. To Susannah Barns. To Bettey Bonwell. To son Abane Flud. To son in law John Richardson. To Cate Bonwell, dau. Mikeel Bonwell. To Leah Parker Richardson. To dau. Ann Richardson. To Nanny Flannagen. Dau. Ann Richardson & son Abane Flud resid. legatees. Mekeel Bonwell & son Abane Flud Exrs. Witt: John Parker. p. 67

PHILLIPS, RACHEL - Nunc. - Reduced to writing in less than 24 hours after her death. Proved 21 Feb. 1778 - Prob: 31 Mar. 1778 - To Jacob Phillips the still which my husband desired he should have. To Jacob Badger. To Ann Chandler. To Thomas & William Parramore. To Margerit Buntain. To Abel Buntain. To Jonathan Groton, "all my husband's clothes & my husband's chest, 1 pair silver buttons". To Sarah Shield. To Susannah More. To Leah Chandler. To John Phillips, son of John. Margeret Buntain, Ann Chandler, Jonathan Groton & Susannah More resid. legatees - William Parramore to have the care of Susannah More's est. Proved by Leah Chandler who first relinquished her legacy in said will. William Parramore qualified.

ROBINS, SPENCER - 4 Dec. 1776 - 31 Mar. 1778 - To cousin John Robins, son of Michael Robins, 40 A. of land "provided I never return from the Wars". Witt: John Pitt, Robert Pitt, Mark Robins - p. 70

AILWORTH, JAMES - 9 June 1777 - 26 May 1778 - To wife Susanna all my land for life then to my sons Ezekiel Ailworth & James Ailworth, & for want of heirs 1/2 my land to my wife & the other 1/2 to my sister Rachel Justice during her life, & then to my cousin Beathfamy Justice. Wife Susanna & Thomas Kelly Exrs. Witt: Kesiah Sparrow, Barshiba Bundick - p. 71

GUY, WILLIAM - 17 Mar. 1778 - 26 May 1778 - To wife whole est. during her wid. To son John Guy my land. To Peggy Guy. To dau. Ann Guy. 3 children, Ann, Peggy & John resid. legatees. Wife (no name) & John Spiers Exrs. Witt: Henry Harmon, Benjamin Nock, Peggy Watson.
In order of prob: Nancy Guy & John Spiers qualified.

FISHER, JOHN – 12 May 1764 – 26 May 1778 – To dau. Susannah Phillips. To wife Mary Fisher bal. of est. for life. To dau. Susannah Fisher 1/2 my land & marsh for life, reversion to my grandson Charles Phillips. To grandson James Fisher the other 1/2 of my land & marsh & for want of heirs to my grandson Charles Phillips. Dau. Susannah Phillips resid. legatee. Wife & Banjamin Phillips Exrs. Witt: Upshur Teackle, William Smith, Makemie Boggs, Elijah Phillips, William Smith, Levin Smith – p. 81
In order of prob: Littleton Savage app. guardian to James Fisher, heir at law to the testator.

POWELL, NATHANIEL – 16 Dec. 1776 – 26 May 1778 – To bro. Laban Powell. To my father & mother. Sisters Anaritta Powell & Elisha Powell. Bros. Nicholas, Peter & Isaac Powell resid. legatees. Bro. Laban Powell & William Riley, Jr., Exrs. Witt: Jonathan Willet, Agnes Willet – p. 99

PARKER, ANDERSON – 4 Dec. 1774 – 26 May 1778 – To bro. John Parker. Sisters Scarbrough Parker & Catharine Parker resid. legatees. Bro. John Parker & John Brickhouse, Sr., Exrs. Witt: John Riley, Parker, Smith Martain, Charles Parker – p. 100

ANDREWS, WILLIAM – 31 Mar. 1777 – 30 June 1778 – To wife Anna Maria plantation where I live during her wid. The land I bought of Col. Thomas Hall to my wife to remain at her own disposal, notwithstanding any Act of Assembly which may be made to the contrary. To son Robert Andrews my manor planta. & lands on Puncoteague & Tangier Island. Wife to have use of whole est. to bring up my children until my son comes to age or one of my daus. marry, & she still to enjoy the younger children's estates until they come to age or marry. When my son comess to age or one of my daus. marry, residue of slaves to be div. bet. all my children & personal est. bet. my wife & son & 7 daus. Wife & friends Nathaniel Bradford, Thomas Hall Parker & Edward Ker Exrs. Witt: Augustine Lecatt, Benjamin Hutchinson, Walter Jameson – p. 110

STOCKLY, NEHEMIAH – 10 May 1778 – 22 July 1778 – Land to be div. beginning at Sacker Parker's line on the Road leading from Atsawaman Church to Mrs Holden's &c., son Airs Stockly to have his first choice of said land & I give my other part of the land to my son William Stockly. If my son Charles Stockly had rather have the land given Airs Stockly than his water grist mill, then he is to have it, provided he make over the said mill to my son Airs. To wife pewter, &c. for life, reversion to my dau. Tabitha Stockly. Bal. of pewter to my wife (no name) & 5 children, Charles, Comfort, Airs, Tabitha & William Stockly. Wife & son Charles Exrs. Witt: Alexander Stockly, Hannah Blake – p. 111
In order of prob: Ann Stockly, the executrix named in the foregoing will, qualified.

STOCKLY, ELIJAH – 26 May 1778 – 22 July 1778 – To sister Rebecca Matthews planta. where I now live, likewise negro boy Isaac that was given her by my father. To sister Ann Hope negro Kissiah given her by my father. Sisters Rachel Conquest & Ann Hope resid. legatees. Bro. in law Joseph Matthews Exr. Witt: Major Davis, William Hinmon, Alexander Stockly – p. 114

HICKMAN, JESSE – 20 Dec. 1777 – 28 July 1778 – To son John Hickman (under age) planta. where I now live & for want of heirs to be div. bet. my bros. Richard & George Hickman & my sister Bridget's son John Scofield. "To the son of Selby Hickman, Richard Hickman. To my housekeeper Sarah Melson. Son John resid. legatee. Bros. Richard & George Exrs & guardians of my son John. Witt: William F. Ross, George Bundick, Jacob Sturgis – p. 116

KELLUM, COMFORT – 22 May 1777 – 25 Aug. 1778 – To son Custis Dormon Kellam, sole legatee. Bro. West Kellam Exr. Witt: Abel West, Argal Kellam – p. 124

SCOTT, JAMES – 19 July 1778 – 25 Aug. 1778 – To wife Catharine my lots & houses on the South side of Onancock Town where I now dwell, also the lot before the dwelling house lately taken up, to her & her heirs forever, also 103 A. forever, being the land I bought of Charles West, also the slaves I had by her & the slave willed her by Stephen Horsey. To John Revill, son of John Revill of Pungoteague, dec., the lots & houses lying on the North side of the town of Onancock & occupied by William Riley Parker. 1/2 of lot & storehouses held in joint tenancy with Edward Ker to be sold. To James Revell Corbin, son of Col. George Corbin, negro Phillip, alias Pompy, as also my library except the large bible & prayer books belonging to my wife. To Agnis Drummond Corbin. To Sarah Revel, dau. of John Revel, dec. To William Revell, son of John Revell, dec., To Edward Revell. To Margratt Ker, dau. of Edward Ker 300 L current money. Wife Catharine resid. legatee. Wife & Col. George Corbin & Edward Ker Exrs. Witt: Anthony West, John Parker, Mary Gunter, Elizabeth Parker – p. 124

WHITE GEORGE – 20 May 1778 – 25 Aug, 1778 – Should my wife be with child I give my whole est. to said child, but if not, or if said child should die under the age of 21 years without heirs, I give to my nephew, George White Burton all my land & planta. where I now live. To my wife all my negroes & their increase that I had with her. To nephew George White, son of William. To nephew George Finney, & for want of heirs to his sister Mary Finney. Wife to have use of planta. for life. To Mary Russ 1 bed. Wife Agnes White & friend John Burton Exrs. Witt: Thomas Crippen, Comfort Roberts, Luraner Sturgis – p. 140

WISE, TULLY ROBINSON – 30 Apr. 1778 – 25 Aug. 1778 – To son John Wise all my ready money & debts due me at my death, all my right, title & interest in & to the salt works on Jingoteague Island, all

my interest in a sloop called the *Supply* lately built & now lying in Jingoteague Creek. Bal. of est. to wife for life or wid. & then to my son Tully the whole of the planta. where I now live & the planta. purchased of Robert Sneed, & for want of heirs to my son John, & for want of heirs to my son George. To son George all my lands & marshes on Wallops & Jingoteague Islands. 3 sons aforesaid resid. legatees. Div. to be made by my friends Anthony West, John Custis of Deep Creek & Thomas Custis. Wife (no name) & son Tully Exrs. Witt: Luther Martin, Cassey Wisc, Ann West. p. 141
In order of prob: Tabitha Wise & Tully Wise quaiified.

HORNSBY, LEVI – 5 Dec. 1776 – 25 Aug. 1778 – Wife Hannah Hornsby sole legatee & Exec. Witt: Richard Bull, Ruth Bull – p. 143

SAVAGE, FRANCIS – 13 Nov. 1776 – 29 Sept. 1778 – Wife Rose to have use of whole est. during her wid. To son Richard Savage land & planta. where I now live cont. 160 A. To son John Savage 85 A. adj. John Smith & Major Savage. To son Francis Savage. Should either my sons Richard or John die without issue the land to go to my son Francis Savage. To dau. Betty Bell. To dau. Matilda Benson. 5 children Richard Savage, John Savage, Francis Savage, Betty Bell & Matilda Benson resid. legatees. Sons Richard & Francis Exrs. Witt: George Garrison, Isaac Garrison. Nanney Garrison – p. 160

CORBIN, COVENTON – 8 Mar. 1777 – 29 Sept. 1778 – To grandson Coventon Corbin planta. purchased of George Dukes lying in Worcester County, Maryland & the 100 A. on Gingoteague Island, also that parcel of land purchased of John Robins lying in Worcester County, Maryland. Crops on the Dukes planta. to be sold for the education of my said grandson, & what I have given him to be rented & laid out for his education until he is 21 years of age, then to take possession of said lands. Should my said grandson die before the age of 21 I give the lands given him to Thomas Cropper, all the rents &c. for his education till he is 21, & should he also die before the age of 21 I give the said lands to my grandau, Agnis Corbin, dau. of my son George. To grandson John Cropper. To grandson Thomas Cropper 2 A. at the lower end of Horntown, being part of the land purchased of John Dubberly. To son George Corbin all my other lands which I have a right to either on the Islands or on the main not before devised. Son George resid. legatee & Exr. Witt: Shadrack Dennis, Smith Melvin, Jemimah McCredy, John Field – p. 161

WATSON, LEVI – 20 Dec. 1776 – 27 Oct. 1778 – To sister Rosey Watson 13 A. adj. the place called Belhaven. Bro. in law Churchill Ames Exr. Witt: John Meers, Richard Meers, Daniel Meers – p. 172

HARDY, PETER – 2 Oct. 1778 – 27 Oct. 1778 – To friend Mary Slaver whole est., real & personal. Friend John Wise on Onancock Exr. Witt: Clement Parker, John Neill, John Wise – p. 175

CROPPER, SEBASTIAN, Sr. - 24 Sept. 1778 - 27 Oct. 1778 - To son Sebastian Cropper. To son Bowman 100 A. at the upper part of my planta. To dau. Leah Blaxton negroes, reversion to my grandau. Elizabeth Blaxton. To dau. Leah Blaxton during her life or wid. 5 A., together with the houses & a quarter of the orchard where Smith Milliner now lives. To dau. Bridget. To dau. Sophia. Bal. of est. to be div. bet. all my children except Rachel Evans, she having received her est. Sons Sebastian & Bowman & friend James Arbuckle Exrs. Witt: Charles Taylor, Mary Simpson, William Arbuckle, John Custis - p. 182
In order of prob: Sebastian Cropper heir at law to the testator.

CUTLAR, THOMAS - 11 Sept. 1777 - 24 Nov. 1778 - To son Thomas Fletcher Cutlar planta. cont. 150 A., & for want of heirs to my dau. Margaret Cutlar, & for want of heirs to my bro. Richard Cutlar. Wife Sarah. Dau. Margaret resid. legatee. Father Richard Cutlar, Father in law John Arlington & wife Exrs. Witt: John Folio & Sarah Harison.
Codicil: 11 Sept. 1777 - Should my wife be with child I give that child my planta. before my bro. Richard Cutlar, & if my wife be not with child the gift to stand good to my bro. Cutlar. - Witt: John Folio, Sarah Harison - p. 184

NELSON, PROVOST - 21 Dec. 1776 - 24 Nov. 1778 - To sister Betty Harman my land & planta. cont. 125 A. To my aunt Susannah Philips & the dau. of John Philips named Catherine, all the money in the hands of John Spiers, Const., due me for rent. Major Ironmonger Exr. Witt: Major Ironmonger, Mary Ironmonger.
In order of prob: John Harman qualified.

WEST, Anthony - 18 Apr. 177- - 24 Nov. 1778 - To son John West planta. where I live being 300 A. To my grandchildren Charles & Abel West, sons of Richard West. To son Richard West planta. in the woods where he now lives. To dau. Anne Fosque. To dau. Matilda Rodgers. To grandchild West Rodgers. To dau. Comfort Scarburgh. To grandsons Edmund & Charles Scarburgh. To son Jeremiah West. To dau. Elizabeth Riley. To grandchildren William & Thomas Riley. To grandson Anthony West. To grandson John West. To grandson Nathaniel Fosque. Bal. of est. to be div. bet. my children John. Ann, Matilda, Jeremiah & Elizabeth & my grandchildren Abel & Richard West & my 2 grandchildren Edmund & Charles Scarburgh, their 1/7 to be received by their mother. Sons John & Jeremiah Exrs. Witt: Edward Ker, Abel West, John West - p. 186

TUNNEL, WILLIAM - 28 Sept. 1778 - 24 Nov. 1778 - To wife Mary whole est. during her wid. to being up my children. To son Nathaniel to have as good learning as my wife can give him. To son Nathaniel planta. where I now live cont. 170 A., & for want of heirs to my dau. Elizabeth Tunnel; my land to be valued & my dau. Elizabeth to pay the worth of said land to every dau., namely Sarah Tunnel, Esther Tunnel & Marget Tunnel according to appraisement. 4 children Elizabeth, Sarah, Esther & Marget resid. legatees. Wife Exec. Witt:

HAYSLOP, WILLIAM - 4 Dec. 1777 - 24 Nov. 1778 - To dau. Hannah Hayslop that end of my land where I formerly lived & for want of heirs to my grandau. Comfort Meers. Son in law John Meers. To dau. Betty Taylor all my land not before given during her life & then to her heirs, & for want of heirs to my dau. Ziller Meers. Dau. Hannah Hayslop resid. legatee. Friend William B. Walker & dau. Hannah Exrs. Witt: William B. Walker, George Meers - p. 205

BRADFORD, EZEKIEL - 13 Mar. 1777 - 29 Dec. 1778 - To my bro. John Bradford my right of 400 A. in Bradford's Neck in Accomack County. "I give one half of this said 400 A. of land unto my son Kendell Bradford supposing my brothor Should Get it for Trying for it". Witt Rand: Clark, Richard Bull, Ruth Bull - p. 217
In order of prob: David Bowman app. guardian to the heir at law to the testator.

RODGERS, PETER - 11 Dec. 1778 - 26 Jan. 1779 - To wife Peggy Rodgers use of land cont. 260 A. during her wid., reversion to my son Peter Rodgers (under age). To dau. Polley. To son John Rodgers. To son Levi Rodgers (under age). To dau. Margret Rodgers. William Coloney & son Peter Exrs. Witt: William Moore, Isaac Starling, Willlam Coloney - p. 217
In order of prob: Peter Rodgers heir at law to the testator.

WEST, ISAAC - 3 May 1777 - 27 Jan. 1779 - "Being about to take a Cruize to Sea in the Privateer Called the *Northampton*". To sister Sarah West. To sister Ann West. To sister Elizabeth West. To sisters Bridget & Yearly West. My 5 sisters Sarah, Anne, Elizabeth. Bridget & Yardly to bear in equal proportion the payment of my debts, and upon their refusal, or their guardians for them, to forfeit any claim to my est. Uncle Isaac Smith Exr. Witt: Elizabeth Smith, Charles Snead - p. 238
In order of prob: Jonathan West qualified.

SATCHELL, HENRY - 13 Nov. 1778 - 27 Jan. 1779 - To wife whole est. during her wid. To son Southy planta. where I live, he to pay his sister Anne 1/2 of the value of the negro Philip. To dau. Susannah Rodgers. To dau. Anne. To dau. Molly. To dau. Elizabeth Bonnewell, she to pay 1/2 of the value of the negro Sybal to my dau. Esther. Children resid. legatees. Wife (no name) & son Southy Exrs. Witt: David Bowman, William Steavans, Phillip Parker West - p. 239
In order of prob: Rachel Satchell & Southy Satchell qualified.

SIMPKINS, SABRAH - 18 Dec. 1778 - 27 Jan. 1779 - To dau. Patience Roberts & Arthur Roberts, my son in law. Dau. Sabrah James & Hezekiah James, my son in law. To 2 grandchildren John & Sarah Stott 8 negroes, & their increase to be div. in 3 parts, 1/3 to Patience Roberts & Arthur Roberts, her husband & their children, 1/3 to Sabrah James & Hezekiah James & their children, & the other 1/3 to be equally div. bet. John Stott & Sarah Stot & their heirs, & should they die under age without issue to my dau. Patience Roberts & Arthur Roberts, & Sabra James & Hezekiah James. Daus. Patience & Sabra resid. legatees. Caleb Smith Exr. Witt: Joshua Wyatt, Joakim Roberts, Nancy Roberts - p. 241

WISE, SAMUEL - 12 Nov. 1778 - 27 Jan. 1779 - To wife whole moveable est. during her wid. & then to be equally div. bet. my 4 daus. To son Thomas Wise 300 A. where I live & 2 mills. To dau. Susanna Wise 50 A. of land on the North side of my mill dam. Wife (no name) Exec. - Witt: Charles Snead, Thomas Lillistone, Ezekiel Young - p. 231
Susanna Wise, the Exec. named in the foregoing will qualified.

BELL, GEORGE - 23 Dec. 1776 - 23 Feb. 1779 - To sister Esther Hack 1 s. To bro. Stephen Bell. My 2 bros. & 3 sisters hereafter named resid. legatees; Keziah Bundick, Stephen Bell, Sarah Bell, Leah Bell & Southy Bell. Bros. Stephen & Southy Exrs. - Witt: Stephen Bell, Leavin Taylor, Leah Bell - p. 244

STRINGER, FEREBY - 25 Mar. 1776 - 23 Feb. 1779 - To wife Rachel use of planta. where I live, also my planta. adj. Hillery Stringer & William Garrison until my son comes of age, if she remains my wid. Wife Exec. To son Sacker planta. where I live. To dau. Comfort. To son John planta. cont. 100 A. adj. Hillery Stringer & William Garrison. Children Sacker, Comfort & John resid. legatees. Rowland Savage, Jr. & Jacob Watson guardians to my estate. Wife to bring up my children & give them proper education provided she remain my wid, & in case of her death or marriage the guardians above named to take them and their estates under their care. Witt: William F. Ross, Benjamin Stringer, Americus Watson - p. 287

BAGWELL, SPENCER - 23 Sept. 1778 - 23 Feb. 1779 - To wife Sophia use of all my lands & water mill during her wid, then my son John Bagwell to have the planta. where I live cont. 120 A. & my water mill, also my right on Cedar Island. To son Heli Bagwell land at Folly Landing which I leased to Thorowgood Smith for a term not yet expires, & for want of heirs to my son John. To son Heli 26 A. in the woods purchased of Thomas Hargriss. Clothing to be div. bet. 3 sons, John Heli & William. Bal. of est. to be div. bet. all my children except John, viz: Betty Bonnewell, Sarah, Anne, Heli & William Bagwell at their mother's death or marriage. Children to live with their mother, she to give them good learning & to bind out my younger sons to trades as she conveniently can. Wife & son John Exrs. Witt: James Henry, Elizabeth Fitzhugh - p. 291
In order of prob: John Bagwell heir at law to the testator.

TAYLOR, CHARLES - 5 Mar. 1779 - 28 Apr. 1779 - To wife Elizabeth use of all my land till my son Charles comes to lawful age, & then to my said son Charles. To wife 1/2 my est. & all the crop that is on the ground this year. Children John, Elizabeth, Mary, Rebecca,

Charles, Leah & William Taylor resid. legatees. Wife & John Kilmon Exrs. Witt: William Young, Jr., Richard Taylor, Mathew Killman - p. 338
In order of prob: John Taylor heir at law.

HOPE, GEORGE - 28 Oct. 1778 - 28 Oct. 1779 - To son George Hope 150 A. at the head of the land where I now dwell & where the said George now dwells. To son John the remainder of the said tract. To dau. Elizabeth Nock. To dau. Johannah Hope. To dau. Nancy Hope. To son Henry Hope. To dau. Peggy Hope. To son Reuben Hope. To unborn child. To son Thomas Hope 1 s. To wife Rachel Hope negroes for life, then to be div. bet. the children begotten of her by me. To Nancy & Anabeller Hope, daus, of Kendall Hope, dec., & Leah his wife. Wife Rachel & 7 children Elizabeth Nock, Johanna, Nancy, John, Henry, Peggy & Reuben Hope resid. legatees. Wife & Ezekiel Young Exrs. Witt: Custis McCland, Thomas Evans, Elizabeth Cowly - p. 339
In order of prob: Thomas Hope heir at law to the testator.

TAYLOR, JOHN, bricklayer - 9 Apr. 1779 - 25 May 1779 - To wife Sophia all my land where I now live till my son George comes to lawful age, then the land to my said son George. To wife all the household goods she brought with her from her father's. To son Thomas Taylor. To son Peter Taylor. Dau. Sophia Custis. Wife & 3 children, Thomas, Peter & Sophia resid. legatees. Wife & George Cutlar Exrs. Witt: Richard Rodgers, Caleb Chandler, William Sacker Chandler - p. 344

DOWNING JOHN ROBINS, Yeoman - 25 Mar. 1779 - 25 May 1779 - To son John Downing land where I live, also 25 A. of swamp land which I bought of Col. Rule. To son Francis Downing 81 A. which I bought of John Savage of Northampton. To wife Sophia Downing. To dau. Peggy negro for life, reversion to her dau. Rachel. My desire is that my nephew John Pits shall have schooling as high as the Rule of three. To dau. Nancy Downing. Wife Sophia, dau. Leah, Rachel, John, Nancy & my son Francis resid. legatees. Wife & James Henry Exrs. Witt: James Robinson, John Smaw, John Mears - p. 349
In order of prob: George Corbin app. guardian to John Downing, Jr., heir at law to the testator.

SIMPSON, SOUTHY - 15 Oct. 1778 - 25 May 1779 - To son Selby Simpson silver watch & 1000 L current money to be paid immediately after my death. Bal. of est. to my wife during her wid, & at her death or marriage all my lands & marshes, also my water grist mill to be sold & 250 L of the proceeds to my grandau. Elizabeth Simpson Marshall, & the remainder, together with the bal. of my est. to be div. bet. my 6 children, Leah, Sarah, John, Southy, Elijah & George. Wife (no name) son in law John Parker, sons Southy, Elijah & George Exrs. Not witnessed. Proved by James Arbuckle, George Corbin, Thomas Bayly & Henry Gustis, Gent: - p. 351
In order of prob: Selby Simpson heir at law to the testator. Comfort

Simpson, John Parker & Southy Simpson, the executors named in the foregoing will qualified.

SAVAGE, ESTHER - 9 June 1778 - 25 May 1779 - To dau. Mary Finney. To grandson Savage Crippen. To grandau. Tabby Custis. To dau. Betsey. William Vere Exr. Witt: William Savage, Jemimah Parks - p. 352

PITT, JOHN - 14 Nov. 1778 - 25 May 1779 - To sister Ann Pitt & bro. Robert Pitt all my land & marshes where I live to be div. bet. them. To Joshua George a piece of ground cleared by Howell Gladen at the upper end of my land. Friends William Selby & George Stewart Exrs. Witt: William Selby, Michael Robins, Joseph Waggaman - p. 353

FREEMAN, MOSES - 16 July 1774 - 25 May 1779 - To youngest son John Freeman. To Ann Freeman 10 L 10 cash. To youngest son John. Thomas Crippin Exr. Witt: Joshua Laws, William Laws, William Sacker James, Robert James - p. 354

SMITH, JOHN - 18 Feb. 1779 - 29 June 1779 - To wife Susannah Smith Dau. Anne. son John. Grandau. Elizabeth Smith Hack. Dau. Sarah Lyon. To dau. Nancy. Exrs. to sell my lots in Onancock for the payment of debts. Daus. Sarah & Anne, son John & grandau. Elizabeth Smith resid. legatees. Dau. Elizabeth Hack. Cousin George Parker & Mr. Peter Hack, Jr., Exrs. Witt: William Finney, John Finney, Elizabeth Finney - p. 371

MILLINER, AMEY - 25 Oct. 1778 - 1 July 1779 - To son Smith Milliner. To son William. To son Robert. To son Southy 20 L cash. To dau. Rachel. To dau. Betty. To daus. Laney Melson & Anne Milliner. Bal. of est. to be sold & div. bet. my children. James Arbuckle Exr. Witt: George Arbuckle. - p. 373
In order of prob: The Exr. named in the foregoing will refusing to act William Milliner granted letters of administration.

MARSHALL, CHARLES - 27 Apr. 1779 - 27 July 1779 - To wife Rosannah Marshall 1/3 of all my land during her natural life. To unborn child all my land if a son, but if a dau. I give my land to my dau. Bridget Marshall. To dau. Elizabeth Simpson Marshall. Daus. Elizabeth Simpson Marshall, Bridget Marshall & unborn child resid. legatees. Wife Exec. Witt: Thomas Marshall, George Marshall, Levin Marshall - p. 393

BONWELL, JAMES - 31 Mar. 1779 - 27 July 1779 - To son John Bonwell enough of my est. to have him kept at school, gold sleeve buttons, silver stock buckle & knee buckles. To unborn child, if a boy, enough of my est. to keep him at school for 7 years. Bal. of est. to be div. bet. wife & children when my son John comes to lawful age. Wife Margaret Exec. Witt: Parker Barnes, Elizabeth Cooke - p. 395

GILLETT, AYERS - 24 Apr. 1771 - 29 June 1779 - All my land & planta. to be rented out for the support of my sons John Gillet, Ayers Gillet, Joseph Gillet, James Gillet & dau. Nancy Gillet until my son John comes to the age of 21. To son John land where I now live. To son Eyers Gillet 2 tracts of land in Worcester County, Maryland, one called "Macker" & the other called "Level Ridge Enlarged". To son Joseph Gillet land purchased of James Thompson in Accomack County, & all the land I bought of William Wise adj. the above tract. To son James Gillet 150 A. on Morrisses Island. To dau. Nancy Gillet. Son James & dau. Nancy resid. legatees. Son John Gillet & bro. in law John Smith Exrs. Witt: John Ramsey, Mary Goodin, Esther Savage - p. 395
In order of prob: Will contested & the Court is of the opinion that the same as to the land is good, and ordered to be recorded, but as to the personal est., it appearing to the Court that the testator after making his will married a second wife & had 3 children by her now living, & from sundry declarations in his life time of his intention to provide for them, it is also their opinion that he did not continue in the same mind till his death, and that the same amounted to a revocation, & on the motion of John Gillet certificate is granted him for letters of administration.

HARMON, JOHN - 13 Dec. 1778 - 31 Aug. 1779 - To wife Rachel Harmon, she not to be disturbed of all the houses where I live during her wid. To grandson John Harmon, son of Kendal Harmon land & planta. where I live after his father's death, but my son Cornelius Harmon to have the use of my land & planta. as the fence runs between the horse pound & peach orchard for the term of 10 years next ensuing after my death. To son Kendal Harmon 6 s. To son Zorobabel Harmon. To son Edmond Harmon. Bal. of est. to be div. bet. my 3 children, viz: Susey Holds two children, Rachel & Reubin to have 1 part & John & Cornelius Harmon the other two parts. Sons John & Cornelius Exrs. Witt: John Ashby, Nickolas Shield, James Ashby - p. 413

GORE, EDMUND - 23 Aug. 1779 - 26 Oct. 1779 - To son Levin Core planta. where I live. To wife (no name) use of negro Leah during her life. To dau. Ader Core. To son Babel Core. Wife & 2 children Ader & Babel resid. legatees. Wife & Alexander Stockly Exrs. Witt: Henry White, Joseph Stockly, Edmund Powell - p. 431
In order of prob: Sarah Core, the Exec. named in the foregoing will qualified.

MEERS, RACHEL - 9 Sept. 1778 - 26 Oct. 1779 - To son Jonothan 1 s. To son Meshack 1 s. Clothing to be div. bet. my 5 daus. To Jonathan Chandler. Daus. Rachel, Elizabeth, Leah & son Shadrick resid. legatees. Son Shadrach & Isaiah Baker Exrs. Witt: Southy Bell, Elijah Bloxom - p. 432

BELL, ROBERT - 5 June 1779 - 28 Sept. 1779 - To wife Elizabeth Bell whole est. during her wid. To son Thomas Bell all my land. To dau. Polly Bell. Dau. Rosey Bell, 4 children Robert, Savage, Polly & Rosey Bell resid. legatees. Wife & her bro. Richard Savage Exrs. Witt: William Dunton, James Kelly – p. 433

TWIFORD, DANIEL – 17 May 1774 – 26 Oct. 1779 – To son Bartholomew Twiford. As much of my est. to be sold as will pay my debts. Bal. of est. to be div. bet. my 4 children, Robert, George, Bartholomew Twiford & Margaret Window. William Seymour & son Robert Exrs. Witt: David Watson, William Welsh – p. 451

LEWIS, THOMAS – 26 Aug. 1779 – 26 Oct. 1779 – To wife Bettey all my land on the North side of the cross road where my dwelling house stands during her wid, meaning the road that leads from Onancock town down to William Parramore's, & at her death to my son Thomas all my lands, cont. by est. 100 A., he to take possession of the land on the South side of the road immediately after my death, & the remainder at the death of my wife. To son Richard Lewis 1 s. To son William Lewis. Wife & 3 sons Thomas, William & Isaac Lewis resid. legatees. Wife & son Thomas Exrs. Witt: William Gibb, James Twiford – p. 451
In order of prob: The Exrs. names in the foregoing will refusing, Benjamin Peck qualified.

BELL, WILLIAM – 9 Sept 1779 – 30 Nov. 1779 – To friend Custis Raphield 50 L current money of Virginia. To Nancy Raphield 30 L. To William Raphield 10 L. To friend Holbard Raphield 9 L. To Sarah Mason, Mulato a bed quilt. William Scarburgh Exr. Witt: William Scarburgh, Edmund Heath, Custis Raphield – p. 466

MARCHANT, CATHRIN – 18 Oct. 1779 – 30 Nov. 1779 – To Robert Dennis, son of John Dennis. To my half bro. Spencer Evans. To my bro. Zorowbale Marchant. Bro. John Marchant. Bros. Zorowbale & John Marchant resid. legatees – Friend William Selby Exr. Witt: Joseph Waggaman, Dixon Hall – p. 471

TAYLOR, JAMES – 27 Sept. 1779 – 30 Nov. 1779 – To John Pepper, son of Margaret Pepper, 1/2 of the planta. where Argalus Taylor & Pharaoh Taylor now dwell. To my son Joseph Pepper the other 1/2 of the planta. Planta. to be rented & money div. bet. John. Joseph & Esther Pepper until the said John becomes 21. Bal. of est. to be sold & the money given to Esther Pepper when she arrives at age. To son Stephen Taylor 1 s. Nephew William Taylor Exr. Witt: Jessey Wilkerson, Joshua Wilkerson, Joseph Feddeman – p. 474
In order of prob: Stephen Taylor, heir at law to the testator, appeared & contested the said will. 1 Dec. 1779 – William Taylor, the Exr. named in said will relinquished his right to qualify. 2 Dec. 1779 – Will proved & ordered to be recorded – Stephen Taylor qualified.

BUTLER, JUDAH – 16 Dec. 1779 – 26 Jan. 1780 – To grandson Elemewill Butler whole est. Est. to be sold & money put out at interest. John Taylor Exr. If he never returns to be left to John Taylor &

Howsen Mapp. Witt: John Taylor, Abraham Kellam, Howsen Mapp –
p. 491

DIX, SOLOMON – 7 June 1779 – 26 Jan. 1780 – To wife Leah Dix all
my land during her wid. & then to my son Preson Dix, but should he
offer to sell the said land then to descend to my son Caleb Dix, &
should he offer to sell or mortgage to descend to my 2 daus. Mary &
Santer Dix. Mary & Santer Dix resid. legatees. Charles Bagwell Exr.
Not witnessed – Proved by Selby Simpson & John Dix, Sr. – p. 492
In order of prob: Leah Dix qualified.

EMMERSON, WILLIAM – 24 July 1779 – 29 Feb. 1780 Wife Hannah
Emmerson to have the use of whole est. until my children arrive at
lawful age or marry, she to bring them up. When my son comes to
age I give him the planta. where I now live. Wife & 2 children Arthur
Emmerson & Anne Emmerson resid. legatees – Wife Exec. Witt:
John Teackle, Jenny Collins – p. 502

TIZEKER , ELIZABETH – 21 Jan. 1780 – 29 Feb. 1780 – To dau.
Mary Tizeker. To Thomas Chandler. Husband William Tizeker Exr.
Witt: Littleton Lurton Leatherbery, Southy Coloney – p. 513

BIRD, NATHANIEL, Sr. – 30 Dec. 1778 – 29 Feb. 1780 – To son Jacob
Bird a parcel of land that the wid. Harmon now lives on cont. 60 A. To
bro. Solomon Bird land he now has in possession. To dau. Sarah Bird
during her single life 1/3 of the land where I now live & 1/3 of my old
orchard & the house I now live in, she not to lease or sell the same to
anybody but her bro. Nathaniel Bird. To dau. Rachill Johnson. To
grandau Elizabeth Bird, dau. of Nathaniel Bird. To dau. Charity Rigin.
To son Nathaniel Bird all the remainder of my land. Daus. Sarah Bird
& Rachill Johnson & grandau Cherity Rigin resid. legatees. Son
Nathaniel Exr. Witt: Henry Fletcher, Joseph Smith, Charles Broadwater, Oliver Bell, Nathaniel Bird – p. 514
In order of prob: Nathaniel Bird heir at law to the testator.

WALKER, WILLIAM BANFEILD – 3 Feb. 1780 – 28 Mar. 1780 – To
wife Sarah whole est. until my son Hugh Walker arrives to the age of
12 years, then my wife to take the land I bought of Luke Luker &
James Broughton during her life & she to have the management of my
2 children Hugh & Anne Robertson Walker until Hugh arrives to the
age of 12 years. To son Hugh the land given me by my grandfather
John Branfeild & the land before given to my wife at her decease. In
case both my children should die without heirs, then I give to my bro.
Levin Walker the land given me by my grandfather & to my wife Sarah
the land purchased of Luke Luker & James Broughton – Bal. of est. to
be div. bet. wife & 2 children when my son arrives to the age of 12
years. Wife Sarah & Thomas Jacob Exrs. Witt: Richard Mears,
Teackle Heath – p. 529
In order of prob: George Corbin app: guardian to the heir at law.

STEVENS, WILLIAM – Adm. his est, to William Scott & Thomas Stevens – John Sherlock & Smith Snead sec. – 7 Mar. 1780 – p. 4

LEWIS, JOHN – Adm. his est. to Elizabeth Lewis – James Arbuckle & Thomas Copes sec. – 30 May 1780 – p. 30

HICKMAN, GEORGE – Adm. his est. to John Parker (Matompkin) – John Dix sec. – 31 May 1780 – p. 37

COX, JOSEPH – Adm. his est. to Tully Wise, Gent: – John Custis, Gent: sec. – 28 June 1780 – p. 65

SAVAGE, ROWLAND – Adm. his est. to Elizabeth Savage – Moses Benston & John Mears sec – 26 Sept. 1780 – p. 91

LEWIS, JOHN – Adm. his est. to Benjamin West – Willet Lillaston sec. – 28 Sept. 1780 – p. 103

ANDREWS, EBENEZER – Adm. his est. to Benjamin Peck & John Lyon – Abram Outen & Robert Coleburn sec. – 28 Nov. 1780 – p. 108

McCLAIN, ROBERT – Adm. his est. to Euphamy & John McClean – George Corbin & William Williams sec. – 27 Feb. 1781 – p. 127

WILKENSON, JACOB – Adm. his est. to John McClain – John Gootee sec. – 28 Feb. 1781 – p. 129

MAJOR, LITTLETON – Adm. his est. to Sarah Major – Nathaniel Bradford & Thomas Bayley sec. – 28 Feb. 1781 – p. 129

JUSTICE, RALPH – Adm. his est. to John Lewis – Andrew Russel & Arthur Russel sec. 28 Feb. 1781 – p. 130

TAYLOR, WILLIAM – Adm. his est. to William Garrison – Joshua Wyatt & John Spiers sec. – 27 Mar. 1781 – p. 136

MEARS, SOUTHY – Adm. his est. to William Taylor – Argol Kellam, Sr. sec. 27 Mar. 1781 – p. 138

GRINALDS, SOUTHY – Adm. his est. to Richard Grinalds – John Riley sec. – 25 Apr. 1781 – p. 149

ROBINSON, JAMES – Adm. his est. to Babel Kellam – Levin Stewart sec. – 29 May 1781 – p. 153

EWELL, WILLIAM – Adm. his est. to Charles Bagwell, Gent. – Thomas Evans sec. – 28 Aug. 1781 – p. 159

MINSON, HENRY. Adm. his est. to Elizabeth Minson - Edw. Ker James Dorman sec. 25 Sept. 1781 - p. 165

BOOTH, JAMIMAH - Adm. her est. to Mordecaia Booth - Banjamin Peck & George Cullar sec - 25 Sept. 1781 - p. 165

HUNTINGTON, SAMUEL - Adm. his est. to John Grannis - James Bonewell, Jr. sec. - 30 Oct. 1781 - p. 171

MELSON, GEORGE - Adm. his est. to Thomas Bayley - Drake Drummond sec. - 27 Nov. 1781 - p. 173

RAMSEY, JOHN - Adm. his est. to Peter Marshal - George Corbin sec. - 27 Nov. 1781 - p. 174

MELSON, WILLIAM - Adm. his est. with will annexed to Southy Satchell & Susanna Melson - Andrew Russell & Absalom Rew sec. - 27 Nov. 1781 - p. 174

TUNNEL, MARY - Adm. her est. to Thomas Abbot - Jabez Pitt sec. - 29 Jan. 1782 - p. 176

CLERK, RAND - Adm. his est. to John Bradford - William Gibb sec. - 30 Jan. 1782 - p. 179

BAYLEY, SHADRACK - Adm. his est. to Sarah Bayley - Thomas Evans & George Savage sec. - 26 Mar. 1782 - p. 215

SNEAD, CHARLES - Adm. his est. to Charles Snead, Sr. - George Stewart sec. - 1 May 1782 - p. 219

BRADFORD, ABEL - Adm. his est. to George Hyslop - "Henry" sec. - 1 May 1782 - p. 222

WHITE, ROBERT - Adm. his est. to Elizabeth Badger - Robert Boggs sec. - 25 June 1782 - p. 255

MELSON, WILLIAM - Adm. his est. to Adah Melson - George Oldham & Willet Lillaston sec. - 26 June 1782 - p. 268

KELLY, WILLIAM - Adm. his est. to Elizabeth Kelly - Woodman Bloxom & Daniel Kelly sec. - 30 July 1782 - p. 277

FINNEY, JOHN - Adm. his est. to Anne Finney, Abram Outten & Charles Bagwell - John Custis, Zorobabel Rodgers & Michael Bonewell sec. - 30 July 1782 - p. 285

BROADWATER, THOMAS - Adm. his est. to John Hickman - Isaiah Hickman & Thomas Hickman sec. - 30 July 1782 - p. 286

WEST, MAJOR – Adm. his est. to Peggy Willis – Jonathan Willet & William Willet sec. 30 Oct. 1782 – p. 386

MAHOM, JOHN – Adm. his est. to Solomon Reid – 31 Dec. 1782 – p. 398

MOORE, WILLIAM – Adm. his est. to Ezekiel Tatham – Henry Heath sec. – 25 Feb. 1783 – p. 439

DUNTON, JOSEPH – Adm. his est. to Richard Bundick – Robert Drummond & John Young sec. – 25 Mar. 1783 – p. 494

EVANS, NATHANIEL – Adm. his est. to Arcadia Evans & John Mathews – Joseph Staton & John Kendal sec. – 30 Apr. 1783 – p. 523

KELLAM, WILLIAM – Adm. his est. to Nathaniel Kellam – John Walker & William Scarbrough sec. – 30 Apr. 1783 – p. 524

LEWIS, WILLIAM – Adm. his est. to Richard Lewis – Nash Kellam & John Elliot sec. 27 May 1783 – p. 537

HOPE, KENDAL – Adm. his est. to Robert James, the heir at law refusing to qualify – 27 May 1783 – p. 537

Orders – 1783-1784

MARRET, NIMROD – Adm. his est. to Samuel Marret – John Marret sec. – 29 May 1783 – p. 3

CUSTIS, JOSEPH – Adm. his est. to James Twiford – Thomas Stringer sec. – 1 Aug. 1783 – p. 66

HINMAN, THOMAS – Adm. his est. to Nanny Hinman – Skinner Wallop & William Andrews sec. – 27 Aug. 1783 – p. 79

PIERCE, MICHAEL – Adm. his est. to Ebenezer Wheeldon – Jonathan Mears sec. – 29 Aug. 1783 – p. 100

WYATT, LITTLETON, Sr. – Adm. his est. to William Wyatt – Robert Twiford & Abraham Kellam sec. – 30 Sept. 1783 – p. 104 (See Page 483.)

WILKINSON, LEVIN – Adm. his est. to Hannah Wilkinson – William Patterson & Samuel Henderson sec. – 28 Oct. 1783 – p. 126

KELLAM, WILLIAM – Adm. his est. to Mary Kelly – Richard Kelly & John Kelly sec. 25 Nov. 1783 – p. 159

JAMES, THOMAS – Adm. his est. to Sarah James – Nathaniel Badger sec. – 26 Nov. 1783 – p. 171

DELASTATIUS, WILLIAM - Adm. his est. to Peter Delastatius - George Corbin sec. - 24 Feb. 1784 - p. 179

ROYAL, BENJAMIN - Adm. his est. to Anne Royal - John Riggs & George Young sec. - 24 Feb. 1784 - p. 180

HARRISON, LITTLETON - Adm. his est. to Edward Ker - Eli Hornsby sec. - 24 Feb. 1784 - p. 180

SCOTT, JOHN - Adm. his est. to Thomas Snead - John Custis, Bayside, sec. - 24 Feb. 1784 - p. 180

REVEL, WILLIAM - Adm. his est. to George Dunton - Ezekiel Young & John Roles sec. 24 Feb. 1784 - P. 186.

SPIERS, ROBERT - Adm. his est. to Newbury Spiers   Babel Laylor & Argol Kellam sec. - 24 Feb. 1784 - p. 188

WISE, THOMAS - Adm. his est. to Rachel Wise - Richard Grinalds sec. - 24 Feb. 1784 - p. 189

HINMAN, WILLIAM - Adm. his est. to Richard Bloxom - William Andrews & Major Cole sec. - 24 Feb. 1784 - p. 189

WEST, SCARBOROUGH - Adm. his est. to Leah West - Michael Budd sec. - 26 Feb. 1784 - p. 211

WILLIS, WILLIAM - Adm. his est. to Molly Willis - Mickall Budd sec. - 26 Feb. 1784 - p. 211

JOHNSON, PATIENCE - Adm. her est. to Daniel Mifflin - 31 Mar. 1784 - p. 226

MARSHALL, NEHEMIAH - Adm. his est. to Tabitha Marshall - George Corbin sec. - 31 Mar. 1784 - p. 226

SANDFORD, JOHN - Adm. his est. to Thomas Sandford - William Broadwater sec. - 25 May 1784 - p. 305

HORNSBY, EBEN - Adm. his est. to Elisha Hornsby - Eli Hornsby sec. - 25 May 1784 - p. 306

MICHAEL, JOHN - Adm. his est. to Adriana Michael - Custis Jenkinson & Thomas Sandford sec. - 25 May 1784 - p. 307

SPIERS, NEWBERRY - Adm. his est. to Littleton Ward - Thomas Stringer & William Garrison sec. - 25 May 1784 - p. 309

HOWARD, NEHEMIAH - Adm. his est. to John Howard - Eli Shay sec. - 25 May 1784 - p. 311

HINDLEY, JOHN – Adm. his est. to Richard Parker – John Wise sec. – 25 May 1784 – p. 313

COLE, ISAIAH – Adm. his est. to Edmund Leatherbury – John Hannaford sec. – 25 May 1784 – p. 314

WARRINGTON, COMFORT – Adm. her est. to William Badger – Henry Heath & William Polk sec. – 26 May 1794 – p. 320

HATTEN, WALTER – Adm. his est. to Abraham Outten – William Snead & John Gootee sec. – 26 May 1784 – p. 321

RODGERS, JACOB – Adm. his est. to William Waterfield – Samuel Beavans & William Patterson sec. – 29 June 1784 – p. 343

LEGATTE, LITTLETON – Adm. his est. to Shadrack Lecatte – Joshua Taylor sec. – 29 June 1784 – p. 348

CHANCE, ELIAS – Adm. his est. de bonis non, unadministered by Spencer Coleburn sec. to Arthur Teackle – George Corbin sec. – 30 June 1784 – p. 361

BRADFORD, JOHN – Adm. his est. to James Bradford – William Bell sec. – 30 June 1784 – p. 364

HUFF, JOSEPH – Adm. his est. to George Bundick – John Bundick sec. – 27 July 1784 – p. 371

CUTLER, SAMUEL – Adm. his est. with will annexed to Richard Cutler – Zerobabel Kellam sec. – 27 July 1784 – p. 371

KELLY, DANIEL – Adm. his est. to Scarborough Kelly – Stephen Bloxom & Richard Bloxom sec. – 31 Aug. 1784 – p. 405

CUSTIS, ROBINSON – Adm. his est. to Revel Custis – Henry Custis sec. – 1 Sept. 1784 – p. 411

BADGER, JOHN – Adm. his est. to Elizabeth Badger – James Kellam sec. – 26 Oct. 1784 – p. 493

COPES, JESSE – Adm. his est. to Rachel Copes – Thomas Marshal sec. – 26 Oct. 1784 – p. 501

BARCLAY, JOHN – Adm. his est. to William Barclay – George Corbin sec. – 27 Oct. 1784 – p. 503

Wills – 1780-1784

COX, JOSEPH – 23 Mar. 1780 – Proved 30 May 1780 – Prob: 28 June 1780 – To son Joseph Cox. To dau. Mary Cox. Son Joseph Cox, John

Bloxom & dau. Mary Cox resid. legatees – Ezekiel Young & Tully Wise Exrs. – Witt: Jacob Ayres, John McMath, Thomas Baily – p. 24

MATHEWS, ROBINS KENDALL – 9 Apr. 1778 – 27 June 1780 – To bro. Joseph Mathews all my land & slaves which were left me by my Honored Father "but which he reserved a reversion unto some of my Relations, as I am advised the devise over of this land and slaves upon failing heirs of my body is void, my will is that my said brother Joseph should have the said Land and Slaves as an acknowledgment, the only one I can make, for his Tenderness to me in my sickness" Bro. Joseph resid. legatee & Exr. – Witt: Comfort Parker, Coventon Broadwater, William Leatherbury – p. 29

HARDING, JONATHAN – 9 Sept. 1779 – 28 June 1780 – To wife Jenney Harding whole est. Wife Exec. Witt: Jabez Pitt, Baily Hinman, Nancy Flanegan – p. 30

JUSTIS, ROBERT – 1 Dec. 1777 – 28 Mar. 1780 – To Robert Webb 1/2 my estate & for want of heirs to be div. bet. his mother & Sarah, the dau. of Isaiah Justis. To Elizabeth Young's 3 children the other 1/2 of my estate. Isaiah Justis to have the use of my lands during his life & then to his dau. Sarah. Jacob White, Sr., & Isaiah Justis Exrs. Witt: Robert Parks, Anne Ewell – p. 31
In order of prob: Richard Justis, Sr., heir at law to the testator.

TAYLOR, SAMUEL – 25 Apr. 1780 – 25 July 1780 – To son Ezekiel Taylor. To grandson Alexander Taylor all my land, but should he offer to sell same I give it to his bro. Hezekiah Taylor. To son George Truit Taylor. To Esther Anderson. Son George Truit Taylor Exr. Witt: John Hoult, Robinson Johnson, John Cord, John Johnson – p. 32
In order of prob: Ezekiel Taylor heir at law to the testator.

KELLY, HENRY – To son Nicholas Kelly. To dau. Nanny Kelly. To dau. Sabe Kelly. To wife Comfort Kelly the use of my land & planta. during her life & then to my dau. Sabe Kelly – Wife & Joshua Wyatt Exrs. Witt: George Meers, Peggy Mears – p. 33

BURDETT, WILLIAM – 7 Aug. 1780 – 30 Aug. 1780 – Whole est. To wife Elizabeth & children (no names) Col. George Corbin & Mr. John McClain Exrs. Witt: John L. Fulwell, William Manhall, George Bull – p. 41

TAYLOR, JOHN – 2 Nov. 1773 – 30 Aug. 1780 – To wife Bridget & sons William & Abraham Taylor, they to be my Exrs. Wife to have use of whole est. during her wid. To daus. Tabitha & Leah Taylor. To dau. Patience Taylor. To son William planta. where I now live & for want of heirs to my son Abraham. Witt: William Garrison, Arthur Roberts, William McWilliams – p. 42

WARREN SOPHIA – 25 Apr. 1780 – 30 Aug. 1780 – To James Hinman. To Betty Hinman. Capt. John Burton & Capt. William Nock Exrs.

326

Witt: Betty Perry, Ann Stockely - p. 49

BENSON, MASSAY - 24 Aug. 1780 - 26 Sept. 1780 - To sons Major & George Benson all my lands until the youngest of my said sons arrive at lawful age, then all my land to my son Major. To dau. Rebeckah Benson. To dau. Nancy Benson. Bal. of est. to be div. bet. all my children. Son Massey Benson Exr. Witt: John Taylor, Samuel Melvin, Arthur Hill - p. 58
In order of prob: The Exr. named in the foregoing will refusing to act, Ezekiel Benston qualified.

EVANS, MARK - 9 May 1780 - 31 Oct. 1780 - To wife all my land & planta. during her wid. then to my son Jacob Lurton Evans, & for want of heirs to my son Henry Evans. To dau. Agnes Evans. Wife to have use of whole est. during her wid. then to be div. bet. all my children. Wife (no name) & Solomon Ewell Exrs. Witt: Jacob White, Dolly Husk, Richard Justice - p. 72
In order of prob: Sarah Evans qualified.

POWELL, JONATHAN - 20 Dec. 1778 - May Court 1780 - To wife Sarah whole est. during her wid., she to bring up & school my children. To son John Powell that part of the planta. where I now live below the main road. To son Joseph Powell that part of my planta. above the main road. To son George land bought of William Chandler. To sons John, Joseph & George land & marsh on Wallops Island. To dau. Agnes. To daus. Famey, Agnes & Sally. Bal. of est. to be div. bet. all my children - Wife Exec. Witt: William Williams, Joshua Wishart, Levin Thomas - p. 75
In order of prob: George Corbin app. guardian to the heir at law to the testator.

SNEAD, JOHN - 28 Sept. 1780 - 28 Nov. 1778 (obviously an error - should be 1780) To wife Scarburgh Snead. To son Charles Snead. planta. where I now live cont. 500 A., he to make good his right & title to the land now in dispute to my son Thomas Snead should the same be recovered of my bro. Smith, if not to pay to my son Thomas 100,000 pounds. To son Thomas land now in dispute with my brother Smith Shead should it be recovered by law, land purchased of Thomas Webb lying in the woods, cont. 100 A. To son Thomas negro Milly in trust for my grandau. Sarah Stewart, & for want of heirs to the next child of my dau. Anne, if any, & for want of such issue to my grandson James Stewart. To dau. Mary Wise, reversion to her children. To dau. Catharine Snead. To dau. Scarburgh. Children Mary, Thomas, Catharine, Scarburgh & Tully resid. legatees. Wife, Charles Snead, Thomas Snead & Tully Snead, my sons, Exrs. Witt: Peggy Gillet, Anne West, David Bowman - p. 87

HUTCHINSON, BENJAMIN - 14 Oct. 1780 - Partly proved 31 Oct. 1780 - Prob: 28 Nov. 1780 - Wife Margaret. To son William. To dau. Susanna Hutchinson. To dau. Peggy Hutchinson. To dau. Eunice Hutchinson. Exrs. to sell my 1/4 part of the Schooner Friendship to settle my debts. Bal. of est. to be div. bet. all my children when my son William arrives to the age of 21 years. Wife Exec. Bro. in law Zorowbable Groten Exr. Witt: John Hutchinson, Jr., Edmund Read, Benjamin Darby. Codicil: To my wife Margaret – Personalty – Witt: John Rodgers, Robert Hutchinson – p. 91

DOBINS, LEONARD – 26 Oct. 1780 – 28 Nov. 1780 – Friend Leonard Vallum of Prince Georges County, Maryland sole legatee & Exec. – Witt: Thomas Copes – Benjamin Turlington Hugh Gillins – p. 94

HILL, ELIZABETH – 1 Mar. 1776 – 28 Nov. 1780 – To son Arthur Hill planta. where I now live cont. 100 A. with all the whole lands in Maryland & Virginia, he to pay my debts & to pay his bro. William 20 L, & should he refuse my son William to have the said land. Should all my sons die without male issue my eldest dau. Leah Broadwater to have the said land. To son Zorowbable Hill. Bal. of est. to be div. bet. my several daus. Son Arthur Exr. Witt: Lisney Gootee, Masey Benson, Rebecker Benson, Mary Melvin – p. 95
In order of prob: Zerobable Hill qualified.

CHANDLER, JOHN – 6 Feb. 1781 – 27 Mar. 1781 – To son Mitchel my young peach orchard & old apple orchard. Remainder of my land to my wife during her wid. To son Mitchel all my land where I now life. To son Thomas Chandler. To dau. Catey Chandler. Wife Patience. To son Littleton 25 A. at the White Marsh. Bal. of est. to be sold & money div. bet. sons Laban, Thomas & Littleton & dau. Catey. To my 5 grandchildren John Chandler, son of Mitchel, also Milly, Thomas, Mitchel & Rosey, children of Mitchel. To Comfort Scott. Wife Patience, son Mitchel & John Custis Exrs. Wife guardian of dau. Caty until she come to age of 21 years. Witt: Thomas Doe, Severn Scott, Susanna Doe – p. 115

RICHARDSON, WILLIAM MARTIAL – 29 June 1780 – 27 Mar. 1781 – To wife Rachel all my lands & 2 plantations & 1/3 of personal est. during her wid., she to bring up my Jacob Richardson & my 3 youngest children Leah, Ralph & John Richardson. To son Jacob planta. where I now live on the unpassable branch. To son John planta. adj. the above. To dau. Mary Brown. To dau. Barsheba Brown. To dau. Rachel Benston. To dau. Scarbrough Richardson. To son Skinner Richardson (under age). To dau. Susanna Richardson. Bal. of est. to be div. bet. my last wife's children. Sons Jacob & John under age. Wife Rachel & son in law James Benston Exrs. Witt: Smith Melvin, William Merril, Sr. – William Scott Merril – p. 117

SAVAGE, WILLIAM – 9 Oct. 1778 – 27 Mar. 1781 – To son George planta. where I now live cont. 212 1/2 A. To son William Hope Savage land where he now lives cont. 100 A. To wife Elizabeth. To dau. Mary James for life, reversion to her children. To son Griffin. To dau. Elizabeth Savage. To son Richard Rodgers Savage. To dau. Ann Savage. Wife Elizabeth & 5 children, Mary James, Griffin, Elizabeth, Richard Rodgers & Ann Savage resid. legatees. – Wife

Elizabeth & son George Exrs. Witt: John Powell, Mary Copes - p. 119

BEECH, TABITHA - 9 Mar. 1780 - 27 Mar. 1781 - To dau. Anne Elliot. To dau. Susanna Ashby. Grandau. Elizabeth Elliot. Dau. Seymore Beech resid. legatee. William Stokely & dau. Seymore Exrs. Witt: William Stokely, Peggy Stokely, Peter Dolby - p. 121

YOUNG, WILLIAM, Sr. - 10 Mar. 1781 - 25 Apr. 1781 - To son William Young all the land over the Gut where the mill stands, that side next the Warehouse. To wife Margaret. To son George Young. To dau. Anne Savage. To dau. Mary Savage. To son Thomas. To son James the remaining part of my land where I now live. To son Ezekiel land next to my son William. Wife to have use of my water mill during her wid., reversion to my sons William, Ezekiel & James. To sons William, Ezekiel & James 50 A. of marsh on Guilford Creek. To my 4 grandchildren Peggy & Anna Bella Stokely & William Young Burk & Scarburgh Stokely. To son Thomas 50 A. of Marsh on France Creek. Sons Richard, William, George, Ezekiel & James Young & daus. Mary Savage & Anne Savage resid. legatees - Son William Exr. - Witt: Parker Parradice, Peggy Hickman, Robert Joins - p. 122
In order of prob: Richard Young heir at law to the testator.

TURLINGTON, WILLIAM - 29 Apr. 1780 - 29 May 1781 - To son Peter Turlington the South & Western end of my land. To son William the remaining part of my land. Wife to have the use of land & personal est. during her wid. To daus. Margaret & Anne Turlington. William, Margaret & Anne Turlington resid. legatees. Peter & William Turlington Exrs. Witt: William Coleburn, Levin Rodgers, James Lurton - p. 125
In order of prob: Anne Mary Turlington relinquished what benefit she might claim under the will of her late husband, William Turlington

STRINGER, SMART - 27 Nov. 1780 - 27 Feb. 1781 - Grandau. Sarah Stringer. Grandau. Peggy Smart Stringer. To son John Floyd Stringer. Grandson Thomas Stringer. Grandson William Floyd Stringer. To son James Stringer. To son Thomas Stringer. To William Downs. 6 grandchildren above named resid. legatees. Son Thomas Stringer & John Smith Exrs. Witt: John Smith, Jonathan Garrison, Jr. - p. 126

WELCH, WILLIAM - 7 Mar. 1781 - 29 May 1781 - To wife Bridget planta. where I now live until my youngest son arrives to the age of 21, provided she remains my wid. & if not I give my planta. to my son William. To youngest son Wally. Wife & 2 children resid. legatees. Friends Mr. Abram Outten & Mr. Ephraim Watson & wife Bridget Exrs. Witt: Robert Walker, Joseph Heath, William Beloate - p. 129

PEARCE, EDWARD - 26 Nov. 1777 - 24 Apr. 1781 - To sister Mary Ozn. Sister Rachel Richardson. Sister Sarah Dunton. Wife Scarburgh Pearce resid. legatee. Witt: William Marshal, Jacob Rodgers, Sarah

MILLENER, ROBERT - To bro. William Millener my land. To bro. Southy Millener. To bro. Smith Millener. William & Smith Millener Exrs. Witt: William Arbuckle, John Bagwell, George Monger, Israel Watson, Levin Prewit - p. 133

HENRY, WILLIAM BLAIR - 17 June 1781 - 28 Aug. 1781 - To wife Elizabeth land purchased of Custis Rodgers. Wife resid. legatee & Exec. Edward Ker & Zorobable Rodgers Exrs. Witt: Revill Custis, Margaret West, John West, Peter Hack, Sr. - p. 134
In order of prob: George Corbin app. guardian to the heir at law to the testator.

MILLENER, ELIZABETH - Not dated - 28 Aug. 1781 - Sister Rachel Millener. Bro. William Millener. Neice Betsey Millener, dau. of Smith Millener. Bro. Smith Millener & sister Rachel Millener Exrs. Witt: Elizabeth Warner, Thomas Evans - p. 136

BLOXOM, WOODMAN - 13 Mar. 1778 - 28 Aug. 1781 - To son Stephen Bloxom. To son William. To son Margaret Siimpson Bloxom. To dau. Patience Hinman. To dau. Elizabeth Bell. To son in law Richard Bloxom. To son Thomas Bloxom. To son Simpson Bloxom. To dau. Rachel Bloxom. 6 children Sarah Johnson, Patience Hinman, Elizabeth Bell, Margaret Simpson Bloxom, William Bloxom & Stephen Bloxom resid. legatees. Son William Bloxom & Richard Bloxom Exrs. Witt: Southy Simpson, William Fitchet, Salathiel Fitchett, John Burton - p. 138

CROPPER THOMAS - 14 July 1780 - 28 Aug. 1781 - To grandson Edmund Cropper my manor planta. To son John Cropper the residue of my planta. & all other lands I have any claim to not already given, slaves, negro Tobit, he to give a moderate hire for him until the youngest of my son Nathaniel's children be brought up, the said sum to be div. bet. my son Nathaniel's children. To grandau Ann Cropper, dau of Nathaniel. To grandau Sarah Cropper, dau. of Nathaniel. To grandau Betty, dau. of Nathaniel. Estate given my son John & grandson Edmund to be subject to the payment of two years schooling to William Cropper, son of Elijah Cropper; one years schooling to a bastard of my son Elzee Cropper, & one years schooling to a bastard son of my son Levin Cropper by one of the Bakers. Dau. in law Delany Cropper to have the use of my grandson Edmund's est. till he arrive to 21 years, provided she bring up my said grandson & lives Nathaniel Cropper's widow. Friend Col. John Cropper & son John Cropper Exrs. Witt: John Abbott, John Cropper, Jr., Henry Custis, Smith Millener - p. 139

BAYLEY, THOMAS - 18 June 1781 - 25 Sept. 1781 - To wife Elizabeth. To son Thomas. To dau. Priscilla Bayley. Wife to keep the land & all my est. during her wid. to bring up my two children till one of them arrives to age or marries. "I give (in case my half brother

Henry Custis should not again return from sea to this country, the two negroes he has given me in his will, to-wit: Shadrack & Babel) to John Custis (Allens) during his natural life" & I then give Shadrack to his son John Montgomery Custis & Babel to his son Thomas Custis. Wife Elizabeth Exec., James Arbuckle & John Cropper, Jr. Exrs. Witt: Phillip Parker West, Anna M. Ardrews, Charles Parker - p. 141

BOOTH, JAMIMAH - Not dated - 28 Aug. 1781 - To son Mordecai & 4 daus., Anne, Mary, Elizabeth & Scarbrough whole est. Son Mordecai & friend James Taylor Exrs. Witt: Griffin Stith, Jabez Pitt, John Harris - p. 146

WATSON, JOSHUA - Nunc - Proved 1 July 1781 - Prob: 25 Sept. 1781 - Whole est. to wife Mary Watson to bring up my children. Proved by William Davis, James Wise, Ritter Lewis - p. 146

FITZGERALD, JOHN - 22 June 1781 - 30 Oct. 1781 - To wife Mary. To sons Shadrack & Purnal Fitzgerald (under age) the bal. of my est. To dau. Esther Harman's children 1 s. Wife Exec. & neighbor Nathaniel Bevans Exr. Witt: Mathew Northam, Leah Abbott, Zadock James - p. 149
In order of prob: The Exrs. named in the foregoing will relinquished their right & Richard Abbott qualified.

MORGAN, WILLIAM - 22 Oct. 1781 - 27 Nov. 1781 - To son William Morgan planta. where I now live up to Wallop's Road, wife Betty to have use of same until my said son arrives to the age of 21 years. To son John Morgan all my land lying over Wallop's Road. Wife to have use of same during her wid. To dau. Rebeccah Moore. To son Joseph Morgan. To dau. Sinah Morgan. To son Littleton Trader Morgan. 5 children Joseph, William, John, Sinah & Littleton Trader Morgan resid. legatees. Wife Betty & William Nock Exrs. - Witt: Stephen Bloxom, Levin Bloxom - p. 156

MATHEWS, JOHN - 23 Aug. 1777 - 27 Nov. 1781 - To eldest son William 160 A. where he now lives, being the same land purchased of William Vannelson. To son John Mathews 200 A. where he now lives adj. land where I now live. To son Thomas Mathews planta. where I now live cont. 200 A. for life, reversion to his son John. To eldest dau. Mary Ewell, wife of Coventon Ewell. Dau. Anne Staton, wife of Thomas Staton. Dau. Rebecca Riggin. Dau. Scarbrough Staten, wife of Joseph Staten. Grandau. Rebecca Staton, dau. of Scarbrough Staton. To Joseph Staton, son of Scarbrough Staton. Grandau. Anne Staton, wife of George Staton. Grandau. Rebecca Taylor, wife of Elijah Taylor. To Naomi, dau. of Thomas Mathews. To grandau. Anne Mathews, dau. of Thomas Mathews. To Staten Mathews, son of William Mathews. Grandau. Betty Mathews, dau. of John Mathews. To Susanna Lucas "that lives with me". To son William Mathews' wife. Sons John & Thomas Exrs. & resid. legatees. Witt: Staton Mathews, James Mathews, William Burton - p. 152
In order of prob: William Mathews heir at law to the testator.

331

MELSON, WILLIAM — 1 Nov. 1781 – 27 Nov. 1781 – To dau. Bridget Satchell, wife Susanna. Dau. Easther Melson. Dau. Sarah Melson. Dau. Shady Melson. Son George Melson. Wife & children resid. legatees. Wife Susanna & Southy Satchell Exrs. Witt: William Strann, Richard Bundick, Benjamin Parks – p. 160

WARRINGTON, GEORGE, Ship Carpenter – 6 Jan. 1782 – 29 Jan. 1782 – To bro. Benjamin Warrington. To Teackle Shrieves. To "Neffew" Esther Wise. To my two "Neffews' Susanna & Sarah Turlington. Sisters Sarah Wise & Mary Warrington. Bro. Benjamin Warrington resid. legatee. Witt: John Dix, Sr., William Dix, William Shrieves, John Dix – p. 161

WISE, WILLIAM – 13 Jan. 1782 – 29 Jan. 1782 – To dau. Anne Wise. Dau. Hannah Taylor. Dau. Mary Mathews. Grandson William Wise Taylor. Daus. Susanna, Scarbrough & Tabitha Wise resid. legatees. Dau. Susanna Exec. Witt: John Gillet Whitely Hatfeld, Nimrod Powell – p. 161
In order of prob: John Mathews qualified.

WISE, JOHN, Sr. – 14 Sept. 1776 – 29 Jan. 1782 – To wife Margaret all my land until my son George Arrives to age of 21. To son Solomon Wise 100 A. including the house where I now live. To son William the remaining part of my land adj. Kiely Bonewell and the house where my father lived. To son Charles Wise. Dau. Margaret. Dau. Anne Wise. Grandau. Mary Wise. Grandau Ann Wise Belote. Bal. of est. to children & grandchildren, to-wit: Charles, Margaret, George & Anne each 1/5 & my 2 grandchildren to have 1/2 between them, to-wit: Mary Wise & Anne Wise Belote, & should either of my children die their part to go to my grandau. Sally Scarbrough Wise. Son Solomon & wife Margaret Exrs. Witt: John Carss, Caleb Broadwater, Jonathan Chambers – p. 165 –
In order of prob: Solomon Wise heir at law to the testator.

JOHNSON, JOSHUA — 23 Aug. 1781 – 26 Mar. 1782 – Land to build a church at Bloxom's Bridge. To wife Patience land during her wid. To son Crippen Johnson my planta. cont. 99 A. & for want of issue to my wife Patience Johnson. "My father in law Isaiah Johnson to let my wife Patience keep my son Crippen Johnson till he arrive to the age of 16". Father in law Isaiah Johnson Exr. Witt: Solomon Johnson, John Brimer, George Northam – p. 170

BLOXOM, MOSES – 14 Mar. 1776 – 26 Mar. 1782 – To wife Rachel whole est. during her wid., then to be div. bet. all my children – Son Stephen. Stephen Bloxom, Sr., wife & son Stephen Bloxom Exrs. Witt: Thomas Bloxom, Shadrack Fisher – p. 171

FITCHETT, JOHN — 13 Oct. 1781 – 26 Mar. 1782 – To dau. Anne Howard & dau. Esther Silverthorn 10 A. of Marsh on the South side of Messongo Creek, reversion to Betsey Churn. Grandau. Betsey Churn resid. legatee. Dau. Ann Howard & William Young Exrs. Witt: William Young, Thomas Young - p. 173

BULL, DANIEL - 3 Dec. 1781 - 27 Mar. 1782 - To son Tobias Bull 100 A. where I now live. To son Daniel Bull all the remainder of my land. To son Spencer Bull. To dau. Fanney Bull. Son William Bull. Son Ezekiel Bull. 3 sons Spencer, William & Ezekiel & dau. Fanney resid. legatees. - To Ezekiel Young negro James to hire out for the support of my 4 youngest children - Witt: Thomas Lillaston, William Lillaston, Robert Bull - p. 175
In order of prob: Tobias Bull qualified.

BAYLEY, ROBERT - 2 Feb. 1782 - 30 Apr. 1782 - Sister Sarah Smith. Niece Peggy Tankard. Niece Narcissa Bayley. Niece Anna Bella Bayley. Sister Sarah Bayley resid. legatee. Friend Thomas Crippen & sister Sarah Bayley Exrs. Witt: William Hickman, Peggy Tankard - p. 176

AYRES, JACOB - 25 May 1778 - 1 May 1782 - To son George 100 A. being part of the planta. where I now live adj. Ezekiel Young's land. To son Richard 100 A. being part of the planta. where my father lived adj. his bro. George. To son Francis 100 A. adj. his bro. Richard. To dau. Sally. To son Levin. To son Edmond. 4 children Sally, Levin, Tabby & Edmund resid. legatees. Wife to have use of their estates till they come to age or marry or during her wid. Wife (no name) & sons George & Richard Exrs. Witt: William T. Ross, John Riley, John Only - p. 177
In order of prob: George Ayres heir at law to the testator.

IRONMONGER, MAJOR - 29 Jan. 1780 - Proved 27 Nov. 1781 - Prob: 1 May 1782 - To wife Catherine whole est. which belonged to her before her marriage. Personal est to wife during her wid., then to my two children I had by her. To dau. Mary my 1/2 the water mill. To dau. Peggy 1 black cloak which belonged to my first wife &c. To son Edward planta. where I now live. To dau. Betsy. Bal. of est. to daus. Molly, Peggy & Betsy. George Cutlar Exr. & wife Exec. Witt: William Gibb, Cornelius Ironmonger, William Townsend.
Codicil: 14 Feb. 1780 - John McLean & Benjamin Peck Exrs. should George Cutlar refuse to act. - Witt: George Cutlar, George Ironmonger - p. 179
In order of prob: Benjamin Peck qualified.

TUNNELL, SCARBROUGH - 22 Oct. 1781 - 28 May 1782 - To son William Henry Tunnell planta. where I now live & for want of heirs to my bro Elias Tunnell. To wife Catherine Tunnell. To Nathaniel Hall 5 L to educate him. Bal. of est. to wife during her wid. then to my son William Henry Tunnell. Bro. Elias Tunnell & friend John Kendall Exrs. Witt: John Nicholson, William Ewell, John Holt, Sr. - p. 184

BLAKE, JOSEPH - 17 Apr. 1779 - 25 June 1782 - To wife Sophia land purchased of John Howard cont. 60 A. Wife resid. legatee & Exec.

Witt: John Howard, William Henderson, Littleton Trader - p. 185

WILLET, THOMAS - 24 Sept. 1780 - 25 June 1782 - All my land to Abbott Aires, son of Richard Aires. To Elizabeth Willet. Father Ambrose Willet resid. legatee. Richard Aires Exr. Witt: Charles Bagwell, Caesar Evans - p. 187

JOYNE, ABEL - 18 Dec. 1781 - 30 July 1782 - To wife Anne use of land where I now live for 5 years according to a contract I have with Arthur Downing, Jr., & use of personal est. for 5 years to bring up my children. To Priscilla, the wife of Jesse Watson. At the end of 5 years whole est. to be div. bet. wife & 3 children, Susanna, Margaret & Mary. Wife Anne, Arthur Downing & Elijah Watson Exrs. Witt: Thomas Underhill, Eleazer Core - p. 217

CROPPER, BOWMAN - 8 May 1782 - 30 July 1782 - To nephew John Blackstonc. To nephew Bowman Blackstone as much as will defray the expense of schooling him 4 years. Witt: William Bunting, Purnal Belk - p. 218
In order of prob: Sebastian Cropper qualified.

TOPING, SAMUEL - 30 July 1781 - 30 July 1782 - To wife Robinson whole est. during her wid. then to be div. bet. all my children that are unmarried "to make them equal with them that have already had". Wife Exec. - Witt: Charles Snead - p. 219

SNEAD, SMITH - 31 May 1771 - 24 Sept. 1782 - To wife Sophia. To son Charles planta. on Mary Branch given me by my mother. Son William Snead. To wife lots & houses in Onancock Town during her wid., then to my son William. To son Smith planta. purchased of William Fitzgerald & Peter Fitzgerald. To son George planta. that my cousin Robert gave. To dau. Cathey. Dau. Elizabeth. Wife & children resid. legatees. Wife Exec. Witt: Sarah Eashon, John Poulson, William Waggaman - p. 225
In order of prob: Proved by Charles Snead, son of John, & by Thomas Snead. Charles Snead, son of Smith, heir at law to the testator qualified.

KELLAM, EAZER - 16 June 1782 - 24 Sept. 1782 - To father Zorobable Kellam. To wife Ann whole est. during her wid. To son Zorobable Kellam 100 A. purchased of Edmond Bradford in Bradford's Neck. To unborn child all my personal est. Custis Kellam & wife Anne Exrs. Witt: John Spiers, Ann Spiers, Edmond Bradford - p. 226

BAILY, CHARLES - 13 Mar. 1782 - 24 Sept. 1782 - To son Thomas all my land in the lower end of the Neck. To son John Baily land beginning at the mouth of Salsburys Gutt & on Finney Creek. To wife Mary land where I live for life. Dau. Susanna Baily. Dau. Sarah Baily. Dau. Nancy Baily, Dau. Peggy Baily, Dau. Betsey Baily. Dau. Mary Baily. Bal. of est. to be sold for debt & the remainder div. bet. my 6 daus. Wife, son Thomas & John Baily Exrs. Witt: Abraham

Outten, Edmond Leatherbury - p. 228
In order of Prob: Thomas Baily heir at law to the testator.

KELLAM, JOHN - 27 July 1776 - 24 Sept. 1782 - To father & mother,
Jonathan & Easter Kellam, his wife, whole est. for life, then to be div.
bet. West Kellam & Frederick Kellam, Comfort Kellam & Ann Beau-
chum, my 2 bros. & 2 sisters. Bro. Frederick Exr. - Witt: Zorobabel
Hornsby, William Kellam - p. 240
NOTE:
The following certificate of John Kellam is recorded 27 Apr. 1785 in
Deed Book No. vi - p. 213:
"August 5th 1783, Brooklen. Long Island.
   This is to Certifie all persons that this is my own handwriting,
and still am yet alive and doth disannul the Will I left when I left
Virginia, and all other Wills that hath been produced in my Absence,
and doth impower my brother Frederick Kellam to take upon himself to
settle all accounts belonging to me as my Attorney, to pay and receive
all accounts with being attested to and my receipts and taking the
same, and his receipt shall stand good in my behalf.
Teste: Francis Savage, Edmund Read, John Haggoman, Custis Kellam. (Signed) John Kellam"

KELLY, TIMOTHY - 22 Oct. 1780 - 25 Sept. 1782 - Land to be div.
bet. my two sons, William & Charles Kelly, reversion to my grandsons Timothy & Stephen Kelly. To dau. Kettey Kelly. To wife Sophia
Kelly bal. of est. for life & then "the 3 children that is now with me to
have as much of the moveables as them that is gone from me, Isaiah
Kelly & Anne Kelly, and the remainder to be equally divided bet. them
all five children" - Wife & son William Exrs. - Witt: Robert Rodgers,
Dorothy Rodgers - p. 241
In order of prob: Isaiah Kelly heir at law.

TEACKLE, MARGARET - 8 Apr. 1782 - 30 Apr. 1782 - To be buried
in the graveyard where my first husband lies. To dau. Anne Handy & 2
grandaus. Margaret Custis Beavans, dau. of Nathaniel Beavans, &
Tabitha Custis Scarburgh Beavans. To dau. Margaret Downing, dau.
of William Downing. To Elizabeth Boggs, dau. of Robert Boggs. To
Tabitha Custis Beavans my mother's picture. To "two daughters
children Ann Handy Tabitha Custis Beavans, namely Thomas Henry &
Elizabeth Handy & William Henry Walter & Margaret Custis & Tabitha Custis Scarburgh Beavans, to be equally divided between them".
Son in law Nathaniel Beavans Exr. - Witt: Charity Smith, John Arlington, Jr. - p. 242

KITTSON, JOHN - 8 June 1780 - 29 Oct. 1782 - To wife Elizabeth all
my land above the main road during her wid. To grandson John Crippen. Grandson Thomas Crippen. Grandson Thomas Evans. Grandson
Charles Bagwell. Grandau. Grace Simpson. Grandson John Kittson
Evans. Son in law Charles Bagwell. To Richard Bundick. Two sons
in law Charles Bagwell & Thomas Crippen Exrs. Witt: Robert James,
Thomas Taylor, Rebecca Warrington - p. 244

EDWARDS, JOHN - 31 May 1781 - 27 Nov. 1782 - To wife Betty Edwards 50 A. for life then to my son Zorobable Edwards. Grandau. Molly Edwards. Son in law Isaac Lewis. Son in law Richard Lewis. Son in law William Lewis. Son in law Thomas Teackle Taylor. 5 youngest children William, Labin, John, Abel & Famey Edwards resid. legatees. Son Zorobable Edwards Exr. Witt: Littleton Lurton, Mary Rodgers, Fanney Tailor - p. 254
In order of prob: Elizabeth Lewis, widow of the testator relinquished her right & Isaac Lewis qualified.

BERRY, JAMES - 11 Mar. 1782 - 31 Dec. 1782 - To John Berry, alias Hickman, son of Sarah Hickman 4 A. To friend Levin Hoynes. Bal. of est. to be sold & proceeds div. bet. sisters Rebeckah & Allah, daus. of William Berry of the Parish of Burt & County of Donnegal in Ireland, & eldest son of my uncle Thomas Berry. Clothing to be div. bet. John Berry, Alias Hickman, & Nathaniel Polk. Friend Levin Joynes, David Bowman & Alexander Stockly Exrs. Witt: Joseph Matthews, Henry White - p. 282
In order of prob: No heir at law within the United States.

BAKER, WILLIAM - 1 Feb. 1782 - 26 Mar. 1782 - To dau. Kesiah Baker all my lands & for want of heirs to my natural dau. Sarah Shipham, dau. of Susannah Shipham, for life, reversion to my bro. Levin Baker. Dau. Kesiah resid. legatee. Neighbor John Teackle Exr. Witt: Zadock Nock, William Bishop, William Taylor - p. 283
In order of prob: Mary Baker, wid. of the testator qualified.

CRIPPEN, THOMAS - 7 Nov. 1782 - 28 Jan. 1783 - To wife Anne planta. where I now live, she to school my 4 small children. To son Samuel Crippen water grist mill & 30 A. adj. called Little Neck. To son Thomas land where I live except the above 30 A., same cont. 337 A. Son Savage Crippen. Son James Crippen. Dau. Esther Crippen. Should my wife die my son Thomas to school & bring up my 4 small children. Bal. of est. to wife Anne & 3 small children Esther, Samuel & James. Wife, friend Daniel Mifflin & son Thomas Exrs. Friends William White, Parker Barnes & Thomas Evans to appraise & divide est. Witt: Sarah Baily, Betty Nock, Thomas Evans - p. 284

MATTHEWS, EPHAIM - 20 Dec. 1781 - Proved 31 Dec. 1782 - Prob: Jan. Court, 1783 - To son George Matthews 111 A. where I now live, also 10 A. in Pocomoke on the South side of my tract where Littleton Townsend now lives. To son Levin the residue of my land in Pocomoke. To wife Anne whole est. during her wid. to bring up my sons George & Levin. Sons George & Levin resid. legatees. Wife & William Downing Exrs. Witt: John Nicholson, John Evans, Elizabeth Nicholson - p. 297
In order of prob: Anne Matthews, wid. of the testator, relinquished her right & William Shipham qualified.

MILLINER, WILLIAM – 4 Apr. 1782 – 28 Jan. 1783 – To wife whole est. during her wid. Should unborn child be a son I give him the houses where I live with 30 A. adj. To dau. Betsey, should unborn child be a dau., I give the above houses & 30 A. Bal. of land & personal property to be sold & proceeds to be div. bet. my said children. Bro. Smith Millener Exr. Witt: David Bowman, Rachel Milliner, Elizabeth Lewis – p. 298

DUNTON, WILLIAM – 24 Feb. 1783 – 25 Feb. 1783 – Nunc. To dau. Peggy Bal. of est. to be sold & a small sum paid toward bringing up my youngest child Susey, bal. to be div. bet. Isaac, Major & Susey (all under 21) – Jacob Bird & bro. in law Major Guy Exrs. Proved by Jacob Bird & Major Guy – p. 310

CRIPPEN, ANN – 18 Mar. 1783 – 25 Mar. 1783 – To son James Crippen 100 A. adj. Mark Littleton & John Taylor's heirs. & my part of the land on Morrises Island & Assateague Island. To son Savage Crippen the remainder of my planta. in the woods, cont. 150 A. with houses & mill & 1/2 the land I hold on Morrises Island & Assateague Island. To son Samuel Crippen. Daus. Esther & Peggy Crippen. Dau. Peggy resid. legatee & for want of heirs to dau. Esther Crippen. Friends William White, Daniel Mifflin, Thomas Crippen & Parker Barns Exrs. Daniel Mifflin to have charge of my children & their estates. Witt: Esther Custis, Thomas Crippen, Parker Barnes. – p. 318

SHAY, DANIEL – 12 Feb. 1783 – 25 Mar. 1783 – To wife Comfort land & planta. during her wid. To son Eli Shay 75 A. where I now live. To dau. Betty Trader. To dau. Nancy Northam. Bal of est. to wife during her wid. reversion to my 4 children, Teackle Shay, Elijah Shay, Molly Shay & Kesey Shay – Son Eli Exr. Witt: Solomon Johnson, Susannah Howard, Nanney Coock – p. 320
In order of prob: Pielee Shay qualified.

HOPE, LEAH – 11 Dec. 1781 – 25 Mar 1783 – To Jamey James. To Spencer James. To William Sacker James. 6 children Spencer James, William Sacker James, Jamey James, Nancy Hope, Annabella Hope & John Hope resid. legatees, Robert James Exr. Witt: Robert James, William Hope Savage – p. 325

COWDRY, SAVAGE – 14 Feb. 1783 – 29 Apr. 1783 – To wife Mary Cowdry whole est. except mare called Fly which I give to my son Henry Barlow Cowdry. Wife Exec. Witt: Thomas Marshall, George Marshall, John Morison – p. 331

READ, ABSABETH – 13 Feb. 1783 – 30 Apr. 1783 – To dau. Sarah Lecatt. Son William Read. Son Edmund Read. Son Richard Read. Son Severn Read. 5 children above named resid. legatees. Sons William & Edmund Read Exrs. Witt: Nathan Addison, Henry Window, Levin Rodgers – p. 337

PARKER, CLEMENT – 2 Apr. 1783 – 30 Apr. 1783 – To son Thomas part of my land adj. me & William Coard. Remainder of my land to my 3 sons James, Clement Deshsild & George Parker. Dau. Rosy. Dau. Nancy. Son Thomas to have the tuition of my 2 youngest sons until they come to the age of 16. 6 children above named resid. legatees. Son Thomas & friend Thomas Bayley Exrs. Witt: Charles Snead, Jacobus White, Rachel Booth – p. 340

ROBESON, THOMAS – 28 Mar. 1783 – 1 May 1783 – Wife Patience sole legatee'. Wife & Robeson Custis Exrs. Witt: Jabez Pitt, Richard Drummond, Sophia Drummond – p. 347

CULLAR, WILLIAM – 29 June 1777 – 30 Apr. 1783 – To bro. John Cullar, & in case my bro. is dead to be div. bet. my sisters Fanny McClain & Elizabeth Monger's children. George Bonewell Exr. & if he should die William Richardson & Clement Parker Exrs. Witt: Thomas Chandler, John Scott, Ephraim Hall, William Richardson – p. 348

BONEWELL, JOAKIM MICHAEL – 18 Jan. 1783 – 27 May 1783 – To son Michael Bonewell land where I live & all my marsh on Gilford. To dau. Sarah Russell, To dau. Betty Bonewell. To dau. Peggy. To son Thomas "but should my said son never return from sea I give my said negroes to be equally div. bet. my dau. Scarburgh Bonewell & my two sons Elijah & Southy Bonewell" Children Sarah, Betty, Peggy, Scarburgh, Thomas, Elijah & Southy resid. legatees. Friends Mr. Thomas Bailey, George Parker, Sr. & George Parker, Jr. to divide est. Son Michael Bonewell Exr. Witt: George Parker, Sr., Sarah Parker, Elizabeth Poulson – p. 351

ALEXANDER, THOMAS – 2 Apr. 1783 – 27 May 1783 – To wife Elizabeth. Son Thomas Alexander. Dau. Ann Alexander. Son Thomas & Thomas Marshall Exrs. Witt: William Welbourn, Abel Taylor – p. 353

COLLINS, JAMES – 21 Oct. 1781 – 27 May 1783 – To wife Martha 1/2 my dwelling planta. during her wid. To son Thomas Collins. To son James Collins 1/2 the planta. where the house stands at the death of my wife. To son Sterling Collins the other 1/2 my dwelling planta. To dau. Sally Collins. Bal. of est. to 5 children Jenny, Rachel, James, Sally & Sterling. Wife Martha & son James Exrs. Witt: Samuel Beavans, William Taylor, John Smith – p. 361

TURNALL, TABITHA – 24 Feb. 1771 – 27 May 1783 – To son Edmund Melson. Son Shadrick Melson. Dau. Elizabeth Melson resid. legatee & Exec. Witt: Thomas Riley, Robert Turnal – p. 363

POWELL, ANARITTA – Nunc. 5 Apr. 1783 – Prob: 28 July 1783 – "half a negro man named Moses to Peter Powell" Proved by Sinah Rew – p. 379

GUNTER, ADRAH - 8 May 1783 - 30 July 1783 - Henry Heath Exr. Grandson Joseph Gunter (under 21). Grandson Benjamin Gunter. Grandau. Nancy Gunter. To Sarah Gunter. To Abigail Melson. To Mary & Francis Melson. Witt: Gabriel Purse, Betty Edwards - p. 382

TURNAL, ROBERT - 8 Apr. 1782 - 26 Aug. 1783 - To son Thomas land where I live. Bal. of est. to wife & 4 daus. Dau. Nancy to have 2 years schooling. Wife (no name), son Thomas & friend Richard Bundick Exrs. Witt: Solomon White, Ezekiel Young. - p. 385 In order of prob: Susanna Turnal & Thomas Turnal qualified.

MERRILL, WILLIAM - 20 Jan. 1783 - 26 Aug. 1783 - To wife Elizabeth whole est. during her wid. then to son Joseph planta. where I live when my youngest child is 16, which I reserve to raise & school my youngest children. To dau. Nancy Merrill. To dau. Sally Merrill. To dau. Leah Merrill. 3 youngest daus. Nancy, Sally & Leah Merrill resid. legatees. Wife Elizabeth Exec. Witt: Jacob Broadwater, Mary Delastatius - p. 386

BROADWATER, WILLIAM - 19 June 1783 - 26 Aug. 1783 - To son William Broadwater. To son John Broadwater. To son Ephraim Broadwater. To dau. Mary Broadwater. To dau. Ann Broadwater. To dau. Susanna Broadwater. To son Henry Broadwater (under 21). To wife Comfort Broadwater all her est. she had before I married her. Aforesaid children resid. legatees. Son William & wife Comfort Exrs. Witt: Jacob Broadwater, William Broadwater - p. 388

HINMAN, THOMAS - 8 Oct. 1777 - Proved 25 Mar. 1783 - Prob: 27 Aug. 1783 - To wife Nanney Hinman land, water mill & personal est. until my son George Hinman arrives to the age of 21 years, then my wife to have 1/3 of my est. To son George land & planta. cont. 200 A. & water mill, & for want of heirs to my dau. Ann, & for want of heirs to my dau. Peggy. Daus. Anne & Peggy Hinman resid. legatees. Cousin William Hinman & Solomon Johnson Exrs. Witt: Solomon Johnson, Bayley Hinman, Margaret Hinman - p. 394

PRATT, MOSES - 27 Mar. 1782 - 26 Aug. 1783 - To wife Comfort whole est. during her wid. To son Scarbrough Pratt at his mother's death or marriage. To son Levin Pratt at his mother's death or marriage. Bal. of est. to my 5 children at their mother's death of marriage, viz: Babel, Spencer, William, Scarbrough & Levin Pratt. Wife Comfort & son William Pratt Exrs. Witt: John Ashby, Philip Tignal.

JOHNSON, JOHN - 2 June 1783 - 30 Sept. 1783 - To wife Famy Johnson. Dau. Sarah Johnson. Dau. Ann Johnson. Son Isaiah Johnson. Youngest dau. Ewfamy Johnson. Wife & 4 children resid. legatees. Wife & father, Isaiah Johnson, Exrs. Witt: William Young, Thomas Fisher, Mills Northam - p. 399

TOWNSEND, CALEB - 5 Mar. 1770 - 28 Oct. 1783 - Wife Attalanta to have use of whole est. to bring up & educate my children, then to be

div. bet my children then living. Wife & Arthur Rowley Exrs. Witt:
William Sturgis, John Cord, Adam Watt - p. 411

BIRD, JACOB - 2 Jan. 1783 - 28 Oct. 1783 - To wife Leah Bird. To
dau. Nancy Bird, wife of Levy Bird. To dau. Leah Bell, wife of Jonn
Solby Bell. To son Jacob Bird planta. where I now live. To son Ebron
Bird (under 21). Wife Leah, daus. Nanny Bird & Leah Bell & son
Ebron Bird resid. legatees. Son Jacob & Levy Bird Exrs. Witt:
Joseph Fitzgerald, Mekeel Bonwell, Major Bayly, Joseph Fitzgerald -
p. 414

TAYLOR, SAMUEL, Sr. - 23 Sept. 1783 - 26 Nov. 1783 - To wife
Molly Taylor my planta. during her wid. & if she marry to fall to my
two youngest sons Elias & William Taylor. To son Samuel Taylor.
To son John Taylor. To dau. Rachel Taylor. To grandson Edward
Ewell. To dau. Molly Collins. To grandson Robert Watson. To dau,
Leah Walters. Wife & son Elias Exrs. Witt: John Holt, Sr., Joseph
Collins - p. 450

RICHARDSON, ZOROBABEL - 16 Oct. 1780 - 26 Nov. 1783 - To bro.
William Richardson. To bro. Daniel Richardson. To bro. Kendal
Richardson. Friend Zorobabel Rodgers Exr. Witt: Matildah Rodgers,
Zorobabel Rodgers - p. 452

RUSSELL, GEORGE - 17 July 1782 - 26 Nov. 1782 - Wife Sarah to
have use of whole est. during her wid. & then to be div. bet. my dau.
Peggy Russell & my son Robert Russell. To son Isaiah Russell all
my land & marsh. Joakim McKiel Bonewell, Sr. Exr. Witt: Drake
Drummond, Richard Young, Leah Drummond - p. 453

PARKER, PHILLIP - 17 Jan. 1781 - 24 Feb. 1784 - To son Richard
Parker all my lands & marsh cont. 400 A. To grandson Leven Parker.
To grandson James Parker, son of Richard. To grandson George
Powell (under 21). To 3 daus. Scarburgh, Anne & Patience. Wife
Anne, son Richard & 3 daus. above named resid. legatees. Son Rich-
ard & son in law John Drummond Exrs. Witt: William Gibb, Elijah
Stakes - p. 454

SAVAGE, CHARLES - 16 July 1783 - 24 Feb. 1784 - To wife Molly
use of my land & planta. during her wid. & then to my son Robert
Savage. To son Charles (under 21). To son Joseph Savage. To daus.
Patience, Elizabeth & Sally Savage. Children resid. legatees. Wife &
son Robert Savage Exrs. Witt: John Smith, John Kellam - p. 459

BRADFORD, NEOMY - 4 Feb. 1784 - 24 Feb. 1784 - To dau. Keziah
Bradford. To dau. Jemyah Heath. Children Thomas Bayly Bradford,
Charles Bradford & Kessiah Bradford resid. legatees. Son Thomas
Bayly Bradford Exr. - Witt: Zorobabel Rodgers, James Broughton - p.
460

KITSON, ELIZABETH – 2 Oct. 1783 – 24 Feb. 1784 – To Mary Gladding. To Rebecca, dau. of Mary Gladding. To Thomas Crippen "A large gold ring that was his grandfathers" To Grace Simpson. To John Kitson Evans. To Thomas Nock. To William Laws. To Rachel Thornton. Abel Right & William Laws Exrs. Witt: John Fitzgerald, William Vere.
Codicil; All my clothes to be div. bet. Rebecca Nock & Rachel Thornton. Witt: John Fitzgerald, William Vere – p. 463

BRADFORD, JACOB – 4 Sept. 1778 – 24 Feb. 1784 – To wife Betty Bradford all my land during her natural life, & then to return to Brown Bradford. Bal. of est. to my wife during her wid. then I give 150 L to be div. bet. Susey Bradford, Rachel Boggs, Esther Long, Cearse Johnson & Charles Hannaford. To cousin Brown Bradford. Wife Betty Exec. Witt: Littleton Lurton, Sarah Parker – p. 465
In order of prob: Brown Bradford qualified.

SMITH, WILLIAM – 4 June 1783 – 24 Feb. 1784 – To grandson George Smith all my land & marsh I ever owned on Pungoteague Creek in Slutgill Neck. To dau. Elizabeth Boggs. To dau. Peggy Boggs. To son Solomon Smith. To grandson William Smith (under 21). To Henry Trader (under 21). To grandson Smith Aimes. Bal. of est. to be div. bet. Betty, Peggy, Solomon, William & George. John Arlington & son Solomon Exrs. Witt: John Smith, Levin Boggs – p. 466

SMITH, THOMAS – Not dated – 24 Feb. 1784 – To dau. Nanny chest that was my wife's & my wife's wearing apparel. To bro. Richard Smith. To sister Ruth Smith. Bal. of est. to be sold & the money to my dau. Nanny, & for want of heirs to my bros. that are living & my sister. John Hornsby Exr. To Peggy Hargis my wife's riding saddle in part for keeping my child. Witt: William Arbuckle, Lante Guttery – p. 468

KELLAM, RICHARD – 26 Feb. 1784 – 30 Mar. 1784 – To Elsy Only – To Elsy Only, dau. of Elizabeth, wid. of Thomas Only. Elsy Only & Patience White resid. legatees. Mr. Edward Ker Exr. Witt: John Martin, constable, Severn Kellam – p. 474

CUTLAR, GEORGE – 7 Nov. 1780 – 30 Mar. 1784 – To wife whole est. for life or wid. then to my son Smith Cutlar the land on the South side of the branch that runs through my planta. cont. 127 A. adj. a former line between my uncle Williams' land & the land my father bought. To son Joshua all the land on the North side of the said line cont. 175 A. & a gun that was my son George's. To son Smith the gun that was my son Clement's. To dau. Mary Bird for life, reversion to her children. Rest of my negroes to be div. bet. my 3 children Margaret, Nanny & John. Bal. of est. to be div. in 4 parts, to dau. Mary Bird 1/4 for life, reversion to her children, & the other 3 parts to my children Margaret, Nanny & John. Youngest children to have schooling out of my est. Wife Margaret Cutlar & Mekeel Bonewell "the Clark of the Church", Exrs. Witt: William Gibb, John Warrington.

Codicil: 13 Jan. 1783 - My dau. Anne to have my negro Darky. Abraham Outten to qualify as an Exr. Witt: William Gibb, John Warrington - p. 475

UPSHUR, ARTHUR - 5 Sept. 1781 - 30 Mar. 1784 - To wife 1/3 of planta. where I now live for life, negroes, cattle &c. To son Littleton Upshur 500 A. in Church Neck in the Parish of Hungars, County of Northampton, also a tract of land in the County of Lunenburg which was bought of Col. David Garland, cont. 1350 A. called the Manner Planta., & also 521 A. in said county purchased of Mr. John Garland adj. the said Manner Planta., all the negroes on the Hungars or Church Neck planta. & on the home planta. To nephew Arthur Upshur, son of my bro. John, 370 A. in the County of Lunenburg called the Quarter planta. purchased of Col. Garland. To son Abel Upshur planta. where I now live & all negroes & personal est. not before given. Should my son Abel die without issue male, my son's estates to change, Abel's to go to Littleton & Littleton's to go to Abel's female issue; should both die without male issue their estates not to change. Wife & 2 sons Abel & Littleton Exrs. Witt: John Core, Caleb Harrison, Thomas Teackle - p. 477

BUNDICK, JOHN ABBOTT - 13 July 1780 - 30 Mar. 1784 - To wife Bridget Bundick. To son George Bundick planta. where I now live cont. 200 A. To sons John Abbott Bundick & William Bundick my swamp land & marsh. To dau. Anne. To dau. Shady. To grandson John, son of George. Wife Bridget, daus. Ann, Santer, Shady, Leah & sons John & William resid. legatees. Wife & 3 sons George, John & William Exrs. Witt: Spencer Barnes, Jacob Sturgis, John Barnes - p. 480

PARKER, WILLIAM - 17 Aug. 1781 - 30 Mar. 1784 - To dau. Ruth Boggs. To dau. Frances Read. To grandaus. Elizabeth & Sarah Nelson. To Elizabeth Taylor all my right & title of a negro boy called Israel. To dau. Mary Boggs. To son Robert Parker (Watts Island), hand mill &c. To Son Michael Parker. To son John Parker 100 A. where he now lives. To dau. Sarah Smith. Son John Parker & William Crowson Exrs. Witt: Barth: Taylor, John Smith, Zorobabel Hornsby - p. 483

WATSON, BENJAMIN - Nunc. Died 19 Feb. 1784 about 1 o'clock in the afternoon at the house of Phillip Tigner. Proved 24 Feb. 1784 - Prob: 30 Mar. 1784 - To youngest bro. & sister, Caleb & Sally Watson, whole est. Bro. John Watson. Proved by Ann Tigner, Leah Tigner, Dennis Tigner - p. 485

DAWSON, MARGARET - 2 Sept. 1778 - 30 Mar. 1784 - To dau. Ritter Mason. To dau. Charity Kellam. To dau. Sarah Turlington. Son Smith Martin resid. legatee & Exr. Witt: Littleton Lurton, Parker Savage - p. 486

SIMPSON, COMFORT - 15 Jan. 1775 - 30 Mar. 1784 - Dau. Mary Parker Copes sole legatee & Exec.   Witt: Southy Simpson, John Simpson - p. 487

DUNTON, PHILENDER - 25 May 1783 - 28 Apr. 1784 - To sons Meshack & Ephraim Watscn.   To dau. Elishe Larrence.   Son Southy Dunton resid. legatee. Ephraim Watson & Southy Dunton Exrs. Witt: Robert Spiers, Newberry Spiers - p. 490

LEWIS, JAMES - 21 Apr. 1784 - 29 Apr. 1784 - To son Planer William Lewis (under 21) planta. where I live. To daus. Margaret & Sarah Lewis.   To Reuben Wise, orphan of James Wise.   Friend James Bonwell, son of James, John Bull, son of Benjamin, Thomas Chandler & my bro. Levin Lewis Exrs. Witt: Elijah Fitzgerrald, Joseph Fitzgarrald, Abel Janney - p. 491

VERNELSON, SELBY - 23 Nov. 1783 - 27 Apr. 1784 - To wife Elizabeth all my house - hold goods during her life then to be div. bet. my 4 children Rachel, Elizabeth, William & Nanny Vernelson. To son Thomas Vernelson 50 A. purchased of Jacob Lurton.   To son in law Jacob Savage. 4 children before mentioned resid. legatees.   Friends Zorobabel Rodgers & Jacob Lurton Exrs.   Witt: Thomas Savage, William Savage, Matildah Rodgers - p. 493

Orders-1784-1786

EWELL, SOLOMON - Adm. his est. to Absalom Rew - Benjamin West sec. - 30 Nov. 1784 - p. 3

CHANDLER, THOMAS - Adm. his est. to Edmund Custis & Mitchel Chandler - Thomas Snead sec. - 30 Nov. 1784 - p. 7

MERRILL, LEVIN - Adm his est. to Rebecca Merrill - Stephen Marshall sec. - 30 Nov. 1734 - p. 8

PECK, BENJAMIN - Adm. his est. to Sarah Peck - Thomas Custis & John Gootee sec. 25 Jan. 1785 - p. 49

WISE, JOHN, son of Johannes Wise dec., Adm. his est. to John Riley & John Guy - Thomas Riley sec. - 25 Jan. 1785 - p. 50

KELLY, GEORGE - Adm. his est. to William Thornton - William Andrews & James Young sec. - 25 Jan. 1785 - p. 50

SAVAGE, KENDAL - Adm. his est. to Joshua Taylor - Bartholomew Taylor sec. - 20 Jan. 1785 - p. 52

HEMMONS, JOSEPH - Adm. his est. to James Holston - John Gootee sec. - 27 Jan. 1785 - p. 69

SCOTT, DANIEL ROE - Adm. his est. to William Harman - Nathaniel Bell sec. - 27 Jan. 1785 - p. 70

EWELL, WILLIAM WHITTINGTON - Adm. his est. to Anne Ewell - Levin Evans sec. - 22 Feb. 1785 - p. 78

COPES, JONATHAN - Adm. his est. to Thomas Snead & Solomon Read - John Gootee & John Speirs sec. - 22 Feb. 1785 - p. 83

VANNELSON, PARKER - Adm. his est. to Henry Heath - John Spiers sec. - 22 Feb. 1785 - p. 85

HINMON, JOHN - Adm. his est. to William Bundick - John Burton sec. - 22 Feb. 1785 - p. 86

GUNTER, ZACHARIAH - Adm. his est. to James Warrington. Zorobable Chandler sec. - 23 Feb. 1785 - p. 92

LYON, JOHN - Adm. his est. to Sarah Lyon - Levin Joynes sec. - 27 Apr. 1785 - p. 109

WHELDON, EBENEZER - Adm. his est. to John McLane - George Corbin sec. - 28 Apr. 1785 - p. 151

DELASTATIUS, EZEKIEL - Adm. his est. to George Corbin - John McLane sec. - 28 Apr. 1785 - p. 165

BIGGABY, FRANCIS - Adm. his est. to Susanna Biggaby - John Rodgers sec. - 1 June 1785 - p. 171

MELSON, JOHN - Adm. his est. to John Barnes - Richard Grinalds sec. - 1 June 1785 - p. 171

WHITE, MICHAEL - Adm. his est. to Amos Underhill - Thomas Stringer sec. - 6 June 1785 - p. 199

WHELDEN, EBINEZER - Adm. his est. to David Whelden - Skinner Wallop sec. - 28 June 1785 - p. 212

COLE, ISAIAH - Adm. his est. to Thomas Snead _ Edmund Wise - Elisha Mears sec. - 28 June 1785 - p. 220

DICKERSON, GEORGE - Adm. his est. to Leah Dickerson - Robert Pitt & John Joynes sec. - 26 July 1785 - p. 258

SAVAGE PARKER - Adm. his est. to Sally Savage - John Martin sec. - 26 July 1785 - p. 259

BADGER, WILLIAM - Adm. his est. to John Smith, Pungo: - Severn East & William Polk sec. - 27 July 1785 - p. 266

MURRAY, DAVID - Adm. his est. to William Marshall, Jr. - William Ward sec. - 31 Aug. 1785 - p. 299

STEWART, GEORGE - Adm. his est. to Mary Stewart - George Wise, Charles Snead, son of John & Zorobabel Rodgers sec. - p. 299

SAVAGE, JOHN - Adm. his est. to Betty Savage - Hilmon Lawson sec. - 31 Aug. 1785 - p. 300

STANTON, LEMUEL DELASTATIUS - Adm. his est. to Williams Turner - Richard Grinalds & William Rolly sec. - 31 Aug. 1785 - p. 300

ABBOTT, GEORGE - Adm. his est. to Sarah Abbott - Henry Custis, seaside, & John Burton sec. - 1 Sept. 1785 - p. 306

TURLINGTON, WILLIAM - Adm. his est. to Thomas Guy - Shadrack Dawson sec. - 27 Sept. 1785 - p. 322

DOLBY, NICHOLAS - Adm. his est. to Peter Dolby - William Stockley sec. - 28 Sept. 1785 - p. 324

BOLING, JAMES - Adm. his est. to Nicholas Nock - James Smith & Coleburn Long sec. - 25 Oct. 1785 - p. 333

SNEAD, CHARLES, Jr. - Adm. his est. unadministered by Charles Snead, Sr., dec., to Preeson Snead - John Cropper & Jacob Sherwood sec. - 25 Oct. 1785 - p. 335

GILLEN, HUGH - Adm. his est. to Preeson Snead - John Cropper & Jacob Sherwood sec. - 25 Oct. 1785 - p. 335

ABBOTT, ROBERT - Adm. his est. to Caleb Broadwater - Ezekiel Tatham sec. - 29 Nov. 1785 - p. 362

SNEAD, SOPHIA - Adm. her est. to Smith Snead - George Corbin sec. - 29 Nov. 1785 - p. 367

SNEAD, CHARLES - Adm. his est. to William Snead - Levin Joynes sec. - 27 Dec. 1785 - p. 393

BONEWELL, ELIJAH - Adm. his est. to Mickeel Bonewell - John Bull sec. - 27 Dec. 1785 - p. 394

WATSON, MESHACK - Adm. his est. to John Beech & Frederick Beech - William Ward & William Bull sec. - 31 Jan. 1786 - p. 436

FISHER, THOMAS - Adm. his est. to Shadrack Mears - William Andrews sec. - 31 Jan. 1786 - p. 439

ARBUCKLE, GEORGE – Adm. his est. to Tabitha Arbuckle – George Corbin sec. – 2 Feb. 1786 – p. 453

WARRINGTON, JOSEPHUS – Adm. his est. to William Warrington – Nehemiah Broughton & William Patterson sec. – p. 466

HINMAN, "THANY" – Adm. his est. to Southy Silverthorn – William Stockley sec. – 1 Mar. 1786 – p. 477

RICHARDSON, SUSANNA – Adm. her est. to Wilson Brown – Solomon Bunting sec. – 28 Mar. 1786 – p. 479

WATSON, SHADRACK – Adm. his est. to Robert Twiford & Zorobabel Chandler – Zorobable Rodgers sec. – 28 Mar. 1786 – p. 482

CRIPPEN, THOMAS – Adm. his est. to John Custis – John Parker (Matompkin) sec. – 28 Mar. 1786 – p. 484

SNEAD, SMITH – Adm. his est. unadministered by Charles Snead, dec., who was Exr. of the said Smith Snead, to William Snead – Thomas Snead sec. – 29 Mar. 1786 – p. 488

BAGWELL, JOHN & STEPHEN BAGWELL – Adm. their estates to John Arlington & Rosey his wife – William Mears sec. – 26 Apr. 1786 – p. 499

SMITH, RICHARD – Adm. his est. to Edmund Wise – Southy Tallent sec. – 26 Apr. 1786 – p. 500

TURLINGTON, LABAN – Adm. his est. to Major Chambers – Jonathan Scott sec. – 26 Apr. 1786 – p. 501

BUNDICK, ABBOTT – Adm. his est. to Richard Baker – Hezekiah Baker sec. – 26 Apr. 1786 – p. 501

BUNTING, SMITH – Adm. his est. to "Hyatinca" Bunting – John Cropper, Sr. sec. – 26 Apr. 1786 – p. 502

DRUMMOND, JAMES – Adm. his est. unadminstered by his former Exrs., to William Drummond – Elijah Grinalds sec. – 26 Apr. 1786 – p. 503

Wills &c. – 1784-1787

FITCHETT, JACOB – 19 Dec. 1773 – 25 May 1784 – To wife Comfort whole est. Wife & Solomon Young Exrs. Witt: William Young, Sr., Sarah Hinman, John Fitchett – p. 5

FITCHETT, COMFORT – 12 Apr. 1784 – 25 May 1784 – To son John Fitchett. To son William Fitchett. Dau. Comfort Fitchett. Dau.

Mary Marriner. Dau. Comfort & sons John & William resid. legatees, they paying 5 L tc Tabitha Fitchett. Son John & bro. Solomon Young Exrs. Witt: William Young, Ann Royall, Rachel Royall - p. 5

TURLINGTON, PETER - 20 Sept. 1783 - 25 May 1784 - To wife Leah whole est. for life or wid. Son John my land. Dau. Rachel resid. legatee. Wife & Abraham Taylor Exrs. Witt: William Coleburn, William Turlington, Preeson Melson - p. 9 (children under age)

STEWART, LEVIN - 25 Jan. 1784 - 25 May 1784 - To son Andrew the Northward part of my land, also 25 A. on Cedar Island, & for want of heirs to my son James. To son George the remainder of my land, being the lower end, also 25 A. on Cedar Island, & for want of heirs to my son Charles. To son John the remainder of my land not before given during his life, reversion to my son Levin Custis Stewart. Wife to have use of same until my son Levin comes to lawful age. To dau. Sarah. Wife & sons James, Levin & Charles resid. legatees. Wife to have use of whole est. until children come to age. Wife Exec. (no name) Nathaniel Beavans & Charles Snead Exrs. Witt: Thomas Collins, Sabra Coleburn, Scarburgh Snead - p. 12

KELLY, THOMAS - 23 Jan. 1781 - 29 June 1784 - To dau. Tabitha C. Hinman 1/2 of my land where I now live & 1/2 my marsh on Guilford Creek. To wife Tabitha Kelly the remaining 1/2 of my land & marsh for life, reversion to my dau. Mary Kelly, George Clayton Hinman to have a road along the creek out. To dau. Keziah Hinman all my marsh in Fishers Marshes & Nock's Marshes. Grandau. Tabitha Churn. Grandson Thomas Churn. To goddau. Anne Fitchett 100 A. bought of Lishe Elliot lying in Sussex County. George Cleyton Hinman Exr. Witt: William Young, Jr., Clemmons Free, Richard Hickman - p. 20

CUTLER, SAMUEL - 5 May 1784 - 25 May 1784 - Prob: 27 July 1784 - To bro. Richard Cutler all my land that I bought of my bro. George Cutler, cont. 18 A., also all my land that my uncle William Cutler gave me cont. 75 A. To cousin John Cutler. To cousin Betty Cutler. Bro. Richard resid. legatee & Exr. Witt: William Colony, George Hack - p. 31
In order of prob: The heir at law to the testator summoned - Sheriff's return "not found within my Bailiwick".

CHANDLER, THOMAS - 11 June 1784 - 29 July 1784 - Land, planta. & negro Southy to be sold & proceeds div. bet. my friends Esther Snead, Mitchell Chandler, Laban Chandler, Littleton Chandler & Katy Chandler - 1/2 the bal. of my est. to be div. bet. the children of my half bros. & sisters. 1/2 the remainder to my friend Esther Snead, & the remainder to my friends Patience Chandler & her children, viz: Mitchel, Laban, Littleton & Caty Chandler - To friend Edmund Custis. Friends Esther Snead, Mitchell Chandler & Edmund Custis Exrs. Witt: Thomas Parker, Jr., Southy Bull - p. 44

TALLOR, PHARAOH - 4 Jan. 1775 - 31 Aug. 1784 - To dau. Esther Taylor & for want of heirs to Argales Taylor's daus. Sally, Mathew & Sophia. 2 sons Littleton & Charles Taylor resid. legatees at my wife's death of marriage - Wife Elizabeth & Bro. Argales Taylor Exrs. Witt: John Gillett, Giles Copes, Southy Taylor -p. 46

CORE, LEVI - 21 June 1784 - 31 Aug. 1784 - To bro. Zorobabel Core all my lands &c. To sister Adah Laws. To cousin Leven Core. Alexander Stockly Exr. Witt: William Cowley, Joseph Stockley - p. 47

WARNER, SOPHIA - 24 Nov. 1783 - 1 Sept. 1784 - To husband Isaac Warner land where I now live, formerly belonging to Joseph Blake, being 60 A. Witt: John Howard, Nancy Blake, Polly Howard - p. 48
In order of prob: Isaac Warner qualified.

BUNDICK, ABBOT - 7 Mar. 1784 - 1 Sept. 1784 - To wife Kesiah Bundick my planta. during her wid., reversion to son Elias Bundick & for want of heirs to my 5 daus. Rachel, Leah, Tabitha, Patience & Keziah Bundick. Personal est. to wife for life & then to my 5 daus. Wife & Stephen Bell Exrs. Witt: Robert James, Thomas Taylor, William Taylor - p. 48

WARRINGTON, JAMES - 23 Sept. 1784 - 28 Sept. 1784 - To grandson James Warrington 100 A., being part of the land where he & his mother now live, he not to disturb his mother during her life, & provided he do not claim any part of his father's est. from the rest of his bros. & if he should the land to be equally div. bet. the 3 bros. To Grandson William Savage the remaining part of my land. To wife Mary all the estate I had by her. To grandson Abel Savage. To grandson John Edwards. To grandson James Warrington Belote. Dau. Bridget Edwards & Handcock Pelote resid. legatees. Friend Zorobabel Rodgers & James Warrington Exrs. Witt: William Belote, Thomas Elliott, Zorobabel Rodgers, Siner Rodgers - p. 49

HYSLOP, HANNAH - 22 Apr. 1784 - 28 Sept. 1784 - To Comfort Mears, dau. of John Mears the land where I now dwell. To William Mears, son of John. To Zilla Mears. Aby Mears resid. legatee, she to take Peggy Bloxom & bring her up. Bro. in law John Mears Exr. Witt: Elisha Mears, Babel Savage, Nathaniel Johnson - p. 51

SLOCOMB, THOMAS - 31 July 1784 - 28 Sept. 1784 - "My will is that as much of the estate of Samuel Wise, dec., be said as will pay his three daughters, & then the remainder of my estate I give to my wife and my two children to maintain & educate them". To son William. To dau. Salley. Wife Susanna & friend Charles West Exrs. Witt: Elijah Lillaston, William Slocomb - p. 52

TEACKLE, THOMAS - 18 Sept. 1781 - 28 Sept. 1784 - To son John Teackle planta. where I now live including Milboy's 500 A. To son

Thomas Teackle the 200 A. formerly belonging to Col. West, together with part of the 19 A. I purchased of Littleton Major. To son George Teackle planta. purchased of Margaret Teackle on the head of Pungoteague. Wife (no name) & children resid. legatees. Wife to have children's estates until they come to age or marry for their support. Abel Upshur & Littleton Upshur Exrs. Not witnessed. Proved by Levin Joynes & Littleton Upshur - p. 52

In order of prob: The Exrs. named in the foregoing will refusing, John Teackle, Jr. & John Boisnard qualified.

TAYLOR, JOHN - 14 Aug. 1784 - 29 Sept. 1784 - To wife my planta. during her wid. to bring up my youngest child called Hessey & my dau. Seymour to have her home on the planta. until she is 21 or marries. To son Selby Taylor. To Abel Barnes. Land to be sold at the marriage of my wife or when my dau. Hessey comes to lawful age, & the money to be div. bet. all my children, Nevir, Selby, Severn, Purnal, Seymour & Hessey. Friends Charles Bagwell & Charles West Exrs. Witt: John Parker, Levi Dix - p. 54

GASCOYNES, HENRY - 17 Sept. 1784 - 26 Oct. 1784 - To Susanna West, Sr., upon Andua, 170 A. on Occohannock Creek where I now live which she is to pay 450 L for. To sister Susanna Dunton & her children. To Ann West, Sr., upon Andua, negroes for which she is to pay 90 L. To Abel West, Sr. Wife Rachel Gascoynes resid. legatee & Exec. Witt: Elizabeth Colony, Bridget Custis Glofflin - p. 56

BEAVANS, MARY - 24 Sept. 1784 - 26 Oct. 1784 - To grandson William H. Beavans. To grandau Mary Stevens. To grandson Walter Beavans. To grandau. Tabitha Custis Scarburgh Beavans. To grandau. Molly Upshur 3 silver spoons marked WBM. To grandson William Turpine. To Betty Fooks, dau. of Daniel Fooks & Sarah his wife. To 3 daus. Elizabeth Turpine, Anne Upshur & Rachel Stevens. To grandson Nathaniel Beavans. Grandchildren Walter & Tabitha Beavans resid. legatees. Son Nathaniel & grandson John Upshur Exrs. Witt: Siner Foster, John Burton - p. 57

SANDREWS, AMEY - 4 Dec. 1782 - 26 Oct. 1784 - To son Samuel Sandrews 90 A. where I live, he to give my son Richard Sandrews 1 years schooling. To dau. Elizabeth Sandrews. Son Thomas Sandrews. Dau. Rachel Sandrews. Bal. of est. except the crop to 4 children, Elizabeth, Thomas, Rachel & Richard Sandrews & the crop to be div. bet. my 5 children, Samuel, Rachel, Thomas, Elizabeth & Richard. Son Samuel Exr. Witt: Solomon Johnson, Robert Small, Richard Abbott - p. 59

KELLAM, ARGOL - 2 Oct. 1784 - 26 Oct. 1784 - To son Hezekiah & grandson Argol planta. where I now live cont. 150 A. To grandson Argol "in the way of his father's est". To wife Margaret. To grandson Housen Kellam. To dau. Nanny Taylor. Wife, son Hezekiah, dau. Nanny Taylor & grandson Argol Kellam resid. legatees. Son in law William Taylor Exr. - Witt: John Smith, Mary Rodgers - p. 64

BLOXOM, THOMAS - 18 Aug. 1784 - 26 Oct. 1784 - To son John Bloxom personalty &c. "and that is due from the United States on account of his brother Thomas his Services or Depreciation". Planta. where I now live to be sold & he to have 1/2 the profits, & my wife Patience the other 1/2. To dau. Levinah Kelly. Dau. Susanna Reed Evans. Son John Exr., James Duncan & Thomas Fletcher to audit & settle my est. Witt: Woodman Bloxom, William Bloxom, Richard Bloxom - p. 65

MARSHALL, DANIEL - 7 Sept. 1784 - 26 Oct. 1784 - To wife Sophia negroes & 1/2 my land during her nat. life. To son Daniel Jenepher Marshall planta. where I now live that my father left me, and part of the land I got by my wife, also a piece of land in the Swamps, also 75 A. now in the possession of my bro. Peter Marshall, lent him during his life by my father, Daniel Marshall, also all my lands on Wallops Island except 25 A. To dau. Betsey Marshall the other part of my land I got by my wife, also a small planta. in the Swamps cont. 40 A., also 25 A. on Wallops Island. Wife & 2 children resid. legatees, & in case of the death of both my children without issue, wife to have whole personal est. & the land I got with her, & at her dec. the land I got by my father, Daniel Marshall, to my bro. Peter & my bro. Stephen & my 2 sisters Sarah & Esther, to be equally div. bet. them. Wife Sophia Exec. Witt: Robert Foreman, William Hill, Thomas Waters - p. 75

PARKER, GEORGE - 13 Aug. 1784 - 27 Oct. 1784 - To wife Sarah 1/2 the planta. where I now live on Onancock Creek during her wid., also a child's part of my slaves during her life, then to be div. bet. my children except my son Thomas, also a child's part of my personal est. in lieu of dower. To son George Parker the other 1/2 of my land & the reversion of the half given my wife. To son John Andrews Parker. To son Jacob Parker. To dau. Sarah Parker. Wife Sarah & son George Exrs. Witt: Levin Joynes, Elizabeth Poulson, Jabez Taylor. (John, Jacob & Sarah under age)

JUSTICE, RICHARD - 10 May 1784 - 27 Oct. 1784 - To son William Justice (under age) planta. where I live cont. 98 A. & for want of issue to be div. bet. my sons John & Thomas Justice. To sons John & Thomas (under age) 300 A. on the Bayside to be equally div. bet. them. To dau. Amey Justice. Bal. of est. to wife for life or wid. To grandson Solomon Justice "a gun that was called his father's." Wife (no name) & 4 youngest children William, John, Thomas & Amey Justice resid. legatees. Thomas Riley Exr. Witt: John Parks, Robert Parker, John Lewis - p. 79

BROADWATER, CALEB - 15 Nov. 1784 - 30 Nov. 1784 - To wife Esther Broadwater 125 A. purchased of William Harris during her wid., & then to my 2 sons Joseph & Ezekiel Broadwater, they paying my youngest son Edward Broadwater 7 L 10 s. To son Elias Broadwater. Dau. Mary Sterling. Son Caleb Broadwater. Dau. Martha Broadwater. Son Elias Exr. Witt: Jacob Broadwater, William Burton. Codicil -

Children Elias Broadwater, Mary Sterling, Caleb, Joseph, Martha, Ezekiel & Edward Broadwater resid. legatees. - p. 80

SAVAGE, JACOB - 18 Oct. 1782 - 30 Nov. 1784 - Wife to have use of whole est. during her wid. To grandson Robert Savage. To Kesiah Richardson, dau. of Solomon. To Grandsons Robert & Arthur Savage. To grandson Robert Savage planta. where I now live. Neighbor John Smith & grandson Robert Savage Exrs. Witt: John Smith, Charles Richardson - p. 82

MARSHALL, PETER - 4 Oct. 1784 - 30 Nov. 1784 - To dau. Polly Marshall. To dau. Scarbcrough Moore. To wife Patience negroes & 1/3 of personal est. during her life. Should both my daus. die without issue, whole est. to Skinner Marshall, son of Stephen Marshall. Wife Patience & bro. Stephen Exrs. Witt: Joseph Allen, John Welburn, William Holt - p. 82

BIRD, SOLOMON - 28 Sept. 1784 - 30 Nov. 1784 - To dau. Esther Bird. To dau. Rebecca Bird. To 3 daus. Esther, Rebecca & Scarbrough Bird the bal. of my est. Witt: James Duncan, Major Bird, Jesse Duncan, Nathaniel Bird - p. 83
In order of prob: Esther Bird qualified.

HICKMAN, RICHARD, Sr. - 5 Oct. 1784 - 30 Nov. 1784 - To son Arthur Hickman all my land cont. 119 A. & for want of heirs to my son Richard Hickman except 30 A. which I bought of Charles Camperson, which I give to my dau. Comfort Hickman. To wife Adah Hickman & 2 children Comfort & Arthur resid. legatees. Son Richard & friend Charles Bagwell Exrs. Witt: Richard Hickman, Joakim White - p. 84

DRUMMOND, JOHN - 12 Oct. 1779 - 30 Nov. 1784 - To son John Drummond 85 A. land & marsh where I now live. To son Stephen Drummond 50 A. lying bet. William Drummond's land, dec., & my bro. William Drummond, it being part of the land I took up. To son John 32 A. adj. Thomas Bayley's land. To dau. Comfort Drummond. To son William Drummond. To dau. Sophia. To son Ezekiel Drummond. To son Richard Hill Drummond. To son William my part of the boat that is between my son John & myself. Wife to have use of whole personal est. during her wid., & when my youngest child comes to age or at her death or marriage, to be equaliy div. between all my children except my son John Drummond. 2 youngest sons Ezekiel & Richard Hill Drummond. Wife Sarah Drummond, John Drummond & William Drummond Exrs. Not witnessed - Proved by John Custis & John Drummond - p. 85
In order of prob: William Drummond, Jr., qualified.

ANDREWS, MARGARET - 28 Apr. 1784 - 1 Dec. 1784 - To grandchild Jacob Parker my land on Occahannock purchased of Levin Joynes, & should he die before he is 21 to my Grandson John A. Parker, & for want of heirs to my dau. Sarah Parker. To grandau Sarah Parker. 3 grandchildren Sarah, John A. & Jacob Parker resid. legatees & should they all die before they arrive at age to enjoy the said property, then to my dau. Sarah Parker. Dau. Sarah Exec. - Witt: John Darby, Sarah Darby - p. 86

TOWNSEND, JOHN, Sr. - 17 Oct. 1784 - 1 Dec. 1784 - To son Richard Townsend. To dau. Elizabeth Townsend. To youngest son George Townsend. Bal. of est. to be div. bet. the rest of my children, Teackle Townsend, Rachel Collins, John Townsend, Betty Townsend, Leah Collins, Richard Townsend & George Townsend. Also my desire is that those 3 children my last wife had before I was married to her, viz: Isaiah Jester, Peggy Jester & Jedediah Jester to have 15 s. each. Sons Teackle & John Exrs. Witt: John Holt, Sr., William Holt, James Douglass - p. 87

KELLY, RICHARD - 7 Aug. 1784 - 1 Dec. 1784 - To son John Kelly the land where he now lives. To son William Kelly land adj. his bro. John, & 1/2 of my boat called the Dolphin. To dau. Mary Kelly 2 A. adj. Oliver Bell. To son Jacob Kelly all the remainder of my land where I now live & 1/2 my boat called the Dolphin. To dau. Nanny Kelly. Bal. of est. to wife Nancy during her wid. & then to my 3 daus. Mary Kelly, Elizabeth Only & Nancy Kelly. Son Jacob Exr. Witt: Solomon Johnson, Elijah Bird, Rachel Johnson - p. 88
In order of prob: John Kelly heir at law to the testator.

READ, ANN - 24 Nov. 1784 - 1 Dec. 1784 - To son John Read. To son Henry Read. Dau. Tabitha Read resid. legatee. Neighbor John Read Exr. Witt: Southy Read, Zorobabel Read - p. 90

SNEAD, CHARLES - 1 Dec. 1784 - 29 Dec. 1784 - To wife whole est. for life & then to son Bowdian Snead my land, he to pay to my sons Robert, Preeson, George & Levin Snead 5 L each, & to my grandsons John Henry Snead & George Snead the sum of 10 L to be paid in schooling. To dau. Mary Snead - Sons Robert, George, Levin & my daus. Laney Cropper & Fanny Sharrod & Mary Snead & "grandsons George Levie White" resid. legatees. Wife (no name) & Charles Snead Exrs. Son John Snead. Witt: Solomon Wise, William B. Bunting. - p. 94
In order of prob: Robert Snead heir at law to the testator. Arabella Snead qualified.

RILEY, JOHN - 2 Dec. 1784 - 25 Jan. 1785 - To wife whole est. during her wid. to maintain & educate my children. Wife to sell the planta. I lately purchased on the Western Shore & any part of the residue of my est she may think fit for the payment of my debts. At the death or marriage of my wife est. to be div. bet. my 2 children Tabitha Robinson Riley & Thomas Robinson Riley - Wife & Tully Wise Exrs. - Witt: John Custis, Robert Drummond, George Turnal, Rosah Parker, Anne Young. - p. 95
In order of prob: Anne Robinson Riley, wid. of the testator qualified.

MEARS, JOHN - 17 Dec. 1784 - 25 Jan. 1785 - To son Richard 100 A.
To son Abel Mears the remainder of my land cont. 50 A. Wife Molly
Mears. To son John Mears. To son Robert Mears. To son William
Mears. To son in law Frederick Beech. Wife Molly Mears, John
Mears, Polly Mears, Robert Mears, Betsy Mears, Patience Mears,
Adah Mears, Peggy Mears, James Mears & William Mears resid.
legatees. Kendal Beech & John Spiers Exrs. Witt: John Elliot,
Robert Guy. - p. 99

SAVAGE, ROWLAND - 14 Nov. 1784 - 25 Jan. 1785 - To son Kendal
Savage 44 A. adj. Hannah Hyslop, also 10 A. on the South end of
Cedar Island. To son Robinson Savage all the remainder of my land.
To grandau. Peggy Savage. To son Babel Savage. To dau. Nanny. To
dau. Susanna Davis. Son in law George Ashby. Children resid. lega-
tees. Sons Kendal & Robinson Exrs. - Witt: William F. Ross, Isaac
Waterfield - Isaiah Kelly - p. 100

MARSHALL, THOMAS - 9 Dec. 1784 - 26 Jan. 1785 - To wife Peggy
Wise Marshall whole est. to maintain & school my children until they
come to age, then to my son John Marshall 230 A. as the tract leads
from the Salt Bay. To son William Walton Marshall 1/3 part of the
remainder of my land near Horntown, & the other 2 parts of my land
be equally div. bet. my 2 daus. Elizabeth & Mary Marshall. Wife &
bro. Jenefer Marshall Exrs. Witt: William Walton, Thomas Wooldridge, Shadrack Dennis - p. 105
In order of prob: George Corbin app. guardian to the heir at law.

LEATHERBURY, EDMUND - 23 Jan. 1785 - 22 Feb. 1785 - To wife
Peggy the use of my land & planta. until my son John arrives to lawful
age & then to possess 1/2 of the land during her wid., & then to my
son John Leatherbury. To dau. Betsey. Children John, Betsey, Rosey
& Gilbert resid. legatees. Wife, Edmund Wise & Thomas Snead Exrs.
Witt: Thomas Snead, Noah Belote, Richard Parker - p. 108

RICHARDSON, JOHN - 4 Sept. 1784 - 22 Feb. 1785 - To son Kendall
Richardson 100 A. at the North end of my land where I now live for
life, reversion to my son James Richardson for life, & then to the
survivors of my sons during their natural lives. To son John Richardson 26 A. where he now lives for life & then to my son William during
his natural life. To son William Richardson the remainder of my land
during his life, & then to my son John Richardson during his natural
life & then to the survivors of my sons during their natural lives &
after the death of all my sons to be equally div. bet. my two grandsons
Severn Richardson, son of Kendall Richardson, & William Richardson,
son of William. Friends Littleton Wyatt Exr. Witt: Littleton Wyatt,
Custis Willis, Susanna Lingo - p. 110
In order of prob: Kendall Richardson heir at law to the testator.

MEARS, SABRA - 20 Apr. 1784 - 22 Feb. 1785 - To son John Mears.
To son Spencer Mears. To grandau. Creshe Bradford. To son Zorobabel Mears. To grandau Polly Mears. To dau. Elizabeth Bell. Sons &

daus. William Mears, Levin Mears, Zorobable Mears, Spencer Mears, Margaret Richardson, Rose Harmon & Siner Bradford resid. legatees. Sons John & Spencer Exrs. Witt: John Spiers, Richard Mears, John Elliot - p. 111

ARBUCKLE, JAMES - 26 Oct. 1773 - 23 Feb. 1785 - To son Edward (under age) 100 A. where the schoolhouse stands & for want of issue to son James, & if my son George should die without heirs then my son Edward to inherit the land whereon I now live on Metompkin, & the above 100 A. to my son James. My Exrs. to purchase the schoolhouse at a reasonable rate and have it repaired & kept so. Exrs. to sell my planta. at the bayside & after payment of debts the bal. to be div. bet. my 5 children, Katharine, Margaret, Edward, Mary & James (all under age) Bal. of est. to be div. bet. all my children when my youngest child comes to the age of 18. Wife (no name), Mr. David Bowman, Mr. Samuel Wilson, Mr. Tully Robinson Wise, Mr. Luther Martin & Dr. William Williams Exrs. & guardians to my dear little children. Whole est. to my wife during her wid. Witt: John Montgomery, Pa: Jeffrey. Proved by William Williams & George Corbin - In order of prob: Tabitha Arbuckle qualified.

HALL, DANIEL - 4 June 1784 - 23 Feb. 1785 - To dau. Susanna Kennet. To son Henry Hall the land I now live on. To grandau. Sally Hall. To grandau. Catron Hall. To bro. Ephraim Hall. To son Dixon Hall 200 A. where he now lives. To grandson Bennet Hall. To grandau. Abigail Hall, dau. of Dixon Hall. Son Dixon Hall resid. legatee. Son Henry Hall, Henry Fletcher, Sr. & Thomas Fletcher Exrs. Witt: Spencer Drummond, John Cox, Susanna Fletcher. - p. 115 In order of prob: Henry Hall heir at law to the testator.

HALLOWAY, HEZEKIAH - 18 Feb. 1785 - 27 Apr. 1785 - To son Hezekiah Halloway. To grandson John Halloway. To son William Halloway. 5 children Nancy, John, Hezekiah, Sarah & William Halloway resid. legatees. Ezekiel Tatham Exr. Witt: Richard Justice, Samuel Church - p. 117

POWELL, NICHOLAS - 13 Feb. 1785 - 27 Apr. 1785 - To son Laban Powell 100 A. where he now lives for life, reversion to my grandson George Powell, & for want of heirs to my son Peter Powell. To son Nicholas Powell 150 A. where I now live, & for want of heirs to my sons Peter & Isaac Powell (Isaac under age) - Nicholas to give my son Isaac 8 years schooling. To dau. Elisha Hickman. To wife Elisha Powell. To dau. Bridget Dix a bond of 20 L which I have of George Dix. Son Peter & dau. Elisha Hickman resid. legatees. Sons Laban & Nicholas Exrs. Witt: William Young, Thomas Hickman - p. 122

BIGARBY, FRANCES - 10 June 1775 - proved 27 Apr. 1785 - Prob: 1 June 1785 - Whole est. to be equally div. bet. my dau. Susanna Bigarby & her son Levin Bigarby. Witt: Levin Joyne, Augustine Lecatte - p. 123

In order of prob: Susanna Bigarby qualified.

PETTIT, JOHN – 20 Dec. 1784 – 27 Apr. 1785 – To son Thomas Pettit. Wife Mary & 4 children Rachel Wright, Mary Pettit, George & Thomas Pettit resid. legatees. Wife Mary & son in law Henry Wright Exrs. Witt: Charles Bagwell – p. 126

BRADFORD, NATHANIEL – 15 Jan. 1785 – 28 Apr. 1785 – To eldest son Thomas Hall Bradford my manor planta. where I now live. To son Nathaniel (under age) all my lands in Watchapungo Neck, reserving 7 years of Samuel Long's lease, & for want of heirs to my youngest son Severn Bradford. Wife Jenny Bradford to have whole est. to bring up the little children until my son Thomas Hall Bradford arrives to the age of 18 years. Elizabeth Bradford, Annamariah Bradford, Caleb Bradford, Nathaniel Bradford & Severn Bradford resid. legatees. Col. Levin Joynes Exr. Witt: Andrew Bagge, Anne Bagge, Elizabeth Mears – p. 130

SNEAD, ROBERT, Sr. – 3 Jan. 1785 – 28 Apr. 1785 – To wife Ester Snead all my right, title & interest to lands, Islands &c., to her & her heirs forever. Wife resid. legatee & Exec. Friend Edmund Custis Exr. Witt: Edmund Custis, Southy Bull – p. 131
In order of prob: William Snead heir at law to the testator.

MEARS, NATHAN – 20 Aug. 1784 – 1 June 1785 – Wife Elizabeth. To dau. Leah "born of my wife Elizabeth before our marriage was solemnized agreeably to the laws of men, but after the same was confirmed before God". Bro. William Mears resid. legatee – Friend George Corbin Exr. Witt: George Corbin, James Thornton, William Thornton – p. 133

COPES, THOMAS, Sr. – 19 Jan. 1784 – 1 June 1785 – To sons Handcock & Levin planta. where I live. To grandson Thomas Simpson. Bal. of est. to wife during her wid. then to be div. bet. my sons & grandson. Wife (no name) & sons Exrs. Witt: Charles Mitcalf, Beverly Copes, Southy Copes. – p. 134
In order of prob: Edmund Bayly guardian to Hancock Copes, heir at law to the testator. Susanna Copes qualified.

TURLINGTON, WILLIAM – 3 Feb. 1785 – 1 June 1785 – To my wife all my land during her wid. then to my bro. Peter Turlington's two children, John & Rachel Turlington. Wife (no name) resid. legatee. William Coleburn, Exr. Witt: William Coleburn, Rachel Bundick, Mary Groten – p. 135
In order of prob: Zorobabel Groten guardian to the heir at law.

MELSON, ISSAC – 5 June 1784 – 1 June 1785 – To my wife my land during her wid. to raise my 4 youngest children. To son Levin Melson. To dau. Nancy. To dau. Betty. To dau. Caty. To dau. Polly. 4 smallest children resid. legatees. Charles Bagwell Exr. Witt: Pegg Melson, Anne Melson, William Arbuckle – p. 136

In order of prob: McKeel Bonewell, Clerk, qualified.

HARRIS, JOHN – Nunc. – Proved 26 Jan. 1781 – Pro. 31 May 1785 – George Oldham to settle est. Whole est. to Betty Booth, dau. of Jemima Booth except 100 L to Littleton Guttridge, son of Severn Guttridge, dec. – Proved by William Chord & Whitimore Prideaux – p. 137
In order of prob: George Oldham qualified.

THOMAS, LEVIN – 12 Apr. 1785 – 28 June 1785 – To son George Douglas Thomas (under age) 500 A. near Assawoman, 100 A. on Wallops Island & 300 A. at Pocomoke. Dau. Peggy Thomas resid. legatee. Wife Peggy to have Pocomoke lands during her wid. Wife, John Thomas & Ralph Corbin Exrs. Witt: John Chord, John Field – p. 138

MUIR, FRANCINA – 10 Dec. 1783 – 28 June 1785 – To 3 daus. Elizabeth, Anne & Sarah Muir the use of the land where I now live during their natural lives, being the tract of land formerly possessed by my father George Hack, cont. 1416 A., & after the death of my said daus. to my grandson Walter Hatton. Grandson, when he arrives to the age of 21, to convey to William Drummond the lots in Onancock Town, to whom I have sold them. To grandau. Margaret Hatton. To grandau. Anne Hatton. To James Muir son of Adam Muir. 3 daus. Elizabeth, Anne & Sarah Muir resid. legatees. 3 daus. Executrices. Witt: Edward Ker, Zorobabel Hornsby, Hilsmon Lawson – p. 139
In order of prob: James Muir, orphan of Adam Muir, heir at law to the testatrix, appeared by George Corbin, his guardian. Francina Muir wid. of Adam Muir.

BISHOP, JOHN – 11 Sept. 1783 – 28 June 1785 – To wife Betty whole est. Wife Exec. Witt: Elisha Hornsby, Josiah Harrison, John Mears. Codicil: – 9 Jan. 1785 – To dau. Leviner Shiles 1 s. To dau. Mary Jarvis 1 s. To dau. Elizabeth Wimbrough 1 s. To dau. Dolly Millener 1 s. Witt: Elisha Hornsby, William Darby – p. 143

BRADFORD, WILLIAM – 31 Jan. 1784 – 28 June 1785 – To son in law William Polk & my dau. Sabra Polk all my land & planta. (except my wife's dower therein) until my grandson Nathaniel Polk comes to the age of 21 years, & then that part of the land where I live, being 275 A. to my said grandson, & the remainder of the land where my son in law William Polk & my dau. Sabra now live I lend to them for life & at their death to my grandson James Polk. Should my grandson Nathaniel Polk die before he arrives to lawful age & without issue, I give his land to my grandson Robert Polk. Wife Sarah Bradford. To grandau. Bridget Polk. To grandau. Martha Polk. To grandau. Margaret Polk. To great grandson William Polk Lurton. To goddau. Leah Savage. Wife to have 1/3 of the bal. of my est. & son in law William Polk the other 2/3. Abel Upshur & Nathaniel Bradford Exrs. Witt: Samuel Long, Henry Townsend, Jacob Lurton – p. 144
In order of prob: Nathaniel Polk heir at law to the testator.

356

HUTSON, WILLIAM - 21 Sept. 1781 - 28 June 1785 - To dau. Scarburgh Hutson 25 A. in the field called the Lime Hill Field. To grandson Raymond Gorse Hutson 125 A. where I now live, & for want of heirs to my grandson Ishmael Hutson. To Southy Northam 1 s. To son Kelly Hutson 1 s. Dau. Scarburgh Hutson & Esther Lucas resid. legatees. Henry Fletcher & Solomon Johnson Exrs. Witt: Solomon Johnson, Archibald Trader, Elizabeth Trader - p. 145
In order of prob: Elijah Lucas, heir at law to the testator, qualified.

COLEBURN, ROBERT - 15 Mar. 1785 - 28 June 1785 - To my wife Tabitha Coleburn. To son James Coleburn land at Matomkin & for want of heirs to my son William Coleburn. To son John Coleburn land where I now live & for want of heirs to my son William. To son William land where my mother in law Catharine Coleburn now holds for her thirds. To dau. Elizabeth Coleburn. To dau. Sarah Coleburn. Children James, Elizabeth, John, William & Sarah resid. legatees - Wife, Thomas Coleburn & John Spiers Exrs. Witt: Levin Rodgers, Isaac Waterfield, Ruth Smith - p. 148
In order of prob: George Corbin app. guardian to James Coleburn, heir at law to the testator.

RICHARDSON, SOLOMON - 21 Apr. 1781 - 26 July 1785 - To wife Mary 1/2 my land for life. To dau. Elizabeth Richardson. To son Charles Richardson the other 1/2 my planta. & at his mother's death the whole of my land. To dau. Kesiah Richardson. 2 daus. Kesiah & Elizabeth resid. legatees. Son Charles Exr. Witt: John Smith, Peter Savage, George Hancock - P. 154

PARKER, SARAH - 5 Feb. 1785 - 26 July 1785 - To son Joshua Taylor my land & planta. together with my part of the water grist mill. To grandson LeviN Taylor. To grandson Severn Savage. To grandau Sarah Hutchinson. Dau. Elizabeth Taylor resid. legatee. Son Joshua Taylor Exr. Witt: John Read, Abigail Armitrader, Coleburn Guy - p. 155
In order of prob: Zorobable Rodgers guardian to Charles Bayly Taylor, heir at law to the testatrix.

EDMUNDS, JOHN - 3 Dec. 1784 - 27 July 1785 - To son George Edmunds planta. where I live & for want of heirs to my son Thomas Edmunds. 3 children Sarah, Polly & Thomas Edmunds resid. legatees. Wife Tabitha to have use of whole est. during her wid. Wife Tabitha & John Arlington, Sr. Exrs. Witt: McKeel Bonewell, Mark Metcalf, Sarah Mathews - p. 156

RIGGS, ABRAHAM - 24 Sept. 1783 - 30 Aug. 1785 - To wife Mary whole est. during her wid. To son George 1 s. To 4 children William, Abraham, Esther & Leah Riggs all my lands & all the rest. of my est. to be equally div. bet. them. Wife Mary Exec. Witt: Solomon Johnson, Benjamin Royall, John Fitchett - p. 165
In order of prob: William Riggs heir at law to the testator.

WHITE, SOLOMON - 25 Oct. 1784 - 31 Aug. 1785 - To son Solomon White 70 A. adj. John Dix, Sr. & Richard Grinalds. To son William White 10 A. adj. the above. To son Levin White the remaining part of my land. To son Galen White. To son George White. Daus. Susanna, Lucretia & Annabella White resid. legatees. Dau. Susanna to have the care of my son George's money until he comes of age. Son Solomon & dau. Susanna Exrs. Witt: Thomas Evans, William Grinalds - p. 170

FORSTER, JOHN - 2 Dec. 1784 - 1 Sept. 1785 - To 4 eldest daus. Anne, Salley, Elizabeth & Tabitha planta. where I now live for the term of 7 years, they to care for the rest of my younger children, & after the said 7 years I give to my son William Forster the said planta. & all the rest of my land. Bal. of est. to be div. bet. all my children except my son William, viz: Anne, Salley, Elizabeth, Tabither, John, Sefier, James, Absalom, Levi & Polly. Witt: John Kelly, Absalom Forster, Comfort Forster - p. 174
In order of prob: William Bell & John Bull qualified.

BROADWATER, JESSEE - 15 Nov. 1784 - 27 Sept. 1785 - 2 sisters Susanna & Ann Broadwater sole legatees. Friend William Burton Exr. Witt: Jacob Broadwater, William Selby, Jr. - p. 176

SHIELD, RICHARD - 18 Aug. 1785 - 27 Sept. 1785 - To Leah Abbott planta. where I live. To Jene Shield. Leah Abbott resid. legatee & Exec. Witt: Zadock Jones, Miles Northam, Nathaniel Beavans - p. 177

TAYLOR, BARTHOLOMEW - 14 May 1785 - 22 Sept. 1785 - To wife Patience Taylor planta. where I now live on Pungoteague cont. 100 A. during her wid., also 70 A. I bought of Isaac Waterfield, reversion to my son John Taylor (under age) To wife all my negroes to dispose of as she sees proper during her wid. to bring up my children. To son George Taylor (under age). To son Major (under age). To dau. Margaret Taylor (under age). George, Major & Margaret Taylor resid. legatees. Wife Patience Taylor, Shadrack Lecatte & Major Taylor Exrs. Witt: Zorobabel Hornsby, George Twiford, Patience Kennihorn - p. 177

MOORE, JOSEPH - 31 May 1785 - 27 Sept. 1785 - To wife Ann Moore the whole est. she brought here, & 1/4 of my personal est. during her wid. Grandau. Elizabeth Moore. To son John Moore. To dau. Agnes Right. To son Joseph Moore (under age). To James Moore. Son John & Elijah Right Exrs. Witt: Solomon Johnson, Joseph Moore, Richard Sanders - p. 181

AIMES, WILLIAM - 25 Nov. 1784 - Partly proved 27 Sept. 1785. Prob: 25 Oct. 1785 - To wife Mary whole est. during her wid. & then personal est. to be div. bet. my children & the representatives of those which are dead, that is to say in 6 parts. To sons John & Elijah Aimes all my lands, particularly the planta. where I live "which was sold to him

13 April 1771" Sons John & Elijah Aimes Exrs. Witt: William Mears, Jr., Charles Gunter, Rachel Downing - p. 186
In order of prob: Kendal Aimes heir at law to the testator.

LITTLETON, COMFORT - 25 July 1782 - 25 Oct. 1785 - To dau. Peggy Littleton. To grandau Betty Crippen. To grandson John Williams Littleton. To grandson "Littleton Littleton". To niece Sally Walker. To dau. Betty Crippen. Betty Crippen, William Crippen, John W. Littleton & "Littleton Littleton" resid. legatees. Dau. Peggy Littleton Exec. - Witt: Parker Barnes, William Bundick - p. 187

WARRINGTON, SOUTHY - 21 Apr. 1784 - 25 Oct. 1785 - To son George Warrington. To 3 sons Abbott, Walter & Shadrack. To wife Comfort land where I now live during her wid. Personal est. to be div. bet. wife & 7 children, Ann, George, Rebecca, Abbott, Walter, Shadrack & Caty. To son Teackle Warrington at his mother's death land where I now live. Wife & son George Exrs. Witt: Elijah Northam, James Jester, Henry Fletcher, Sr. - p. 187

WRIGHT, HENRY - 18 Apr. 1785 - 25 Oct. 1785 - To son George Wright. To son Isaac Wright - Bal. of est. to wife Susannah during her wid. & then to 5 children George, Isaac, Peggy, Scarburgb & Rachel Wright. Solomon Johnson & Elijah Wright Exrs. Witt: Solomon Johnson, James Wise, Elijah Wright - p. 189

BENSTON, SAMUEL - 17 June 1781 - 29 Nov. 1785 - To wife Anne whole est. during her wid. to bring up my children & then to be div. bet. my wife & children Azariah, Anne, Joy, Comfort & Amos. Wife Anne Exec. - Witt: Thomas Underhill, Susanna Underhill, Elizabeth Pearson - p. 190

DIX, GEORGE - 23 Aug. 1784 - 29 Nov. 1785 - To wife Bridget Dix all my land during her wid. & then to my son Richard Dix. To son Isaac Dix. To dau. Elizabeth Dix. Children, except eldest son Richard, resid. legatees. George Savage & son Richard Exrs. Witt: John Young, William Hope Savage, Naomi Young - p. 191

SAVAGE, WILLIAM - 18 Sept. 1785 - 29 Nov. 1785 - To wife the use of all my lands during her wid. & then to my son George Smith Savage. Dau. Nancy Savage. To grandson William Mears, & for want of heirs to my dau. Adah Mears. 3 children George Smith Savage, Mary Savage & Adah Mears resid. legatees. Wife (no name) & son George Smith Savage Exrs. Witt: John Smith, George Smith, John Fosque - p. 198

KELLAM, JOHN - 13 Sept. 1783 - 27 Dec. 1785 - When my son Hutchinson Kellam arrives to the age of 21 negroes to be div. bet. my 3 children, Hutchinson, Custis & Betsy. I give all my wife's clothes to my dau. Betsy. 3 children above named resid. legatees. John Smith, Richard Savage & John Fosque Exrs. Witt: John Smith, William Savage, Robert Savage - p. 202

TATHOM, ESTHER - 5 May 1783 - __ Dec. 1785 - To Lucretia Watson. To James Tathom Watson. To sister Comfort Dicks. To Henry Tathom, son of Rachel Tathom & for want of heirs to Tabitha Watson. To sister Sarah Watson. To bro. Ezekiel Tathom. To Ears Tathom. To Sally Watson & Tabitha Watson, daus. of Johannis Watson, Sarah Watson & Elizabeth Moore, dau. William Moore & Molly Moore & Peggy Dix, dau. William Dix & Comfort his wife. Sisters Molly Moore & Leah Tathom resid. legatees.
Witt: Johannis Watson, William Smith Custis, Lucretia Watson - p. 203

WHITE, CHARLES - 19 Dec. 1783 - 31 Jan. 1786 - To wife Catharine White all my land during her wid. & then to son George White 33 1/2 A. To son Levin White 33 1/2 A. 3 daus. Betty, Lishey & Charity White resid. legatees. Wife & son Joakim White Exrs. Witt: Richard Bundick, John Young - p. 206

GLADDEN, HOWEL - 10 Nov. 1785 - 31 Jan. 1786 - To son John Gladden - To son Jehu Gladden. To son Jessee Gladden. To son Preeson Gladden. To son James Gladden. To son Sacker Gladden. Sons John, James, Jessee, Jehu & Preeson Gladden resid. legatees. (all under age). Son John & friend Joseph Waggaman Exrs. Witt: Jeminah Spalding, Robert Pitt, Elizabeth Lewis - p. 206

STRINGER, RACHEL - 11 July 1782 - 31 Jan. 1786 - To son Sackar Stringer. To son John Stringer. To Custis Watson. Son Sackar Stringer & John Stringer & Custis Watson resid. legatees. John Smith (Justice of peace on seaside) Exr. Witt: Americus Watson, Benjamin Stringer, Jacob Stringer - p. 207
In order of prob: Jacob Stringer qualified.

CLEMMONS, STEPHEN - 16 Feb. 1782 - 31 Jan. 1786 - To daus. Siner & Bridget Clemmons 50 A. on Wallops Road. To son Stephen Clemmons bal. of my land. Wife Susannah to have the use of 1/2 my land during her wid. To son Peter Clemmons. To dau. Mary Hooten. To dau. Nanny Rodgers Mason. 3 children Stephen, Siner & Bridget Clemmons resid. legatees. Wife & son Stephen Exrs. Witt: Thomas Crippen, Sr., Anne Crippen, Thomas Crippen, Jr., Thomas Evans, Levi Hudson - p. 208

LURTON, JACOB - 3 Oct. 1785 - 31 Jan. 1786 - To wife Sally whole est. until my dau. Betsy comes to age of 16, then my wife to have 1/2 the land during her life. To dau. Betsy all my lands & for want of heirs to my wife Sally. To Nancy Shield White, dau. Levin White. Should both my wife & dau. die without heirs then whole est. to be div. bet. the children of William Polk, father of my wife Sally. Wife & Levin White Exrs. Witt: John Hannaford, William Townsend, Henry Townsend - p. 209

TWIFORD, JAMES - 12 Oct. 1785 - 1 Feb. 1786 - To wife Amey Twiford 1/2 my planta. for the term of 2 years. To son John Twiford (under age) my planta. including 6 A. purchased of Smith Kellam. To dau. Nancy Twiford. To dau. Mary Dix. Children, except John, resid. legatees. Friend Thomas Burton to be guardian of my 3 youngest children & friend Edmund Custis to be guardian of my son John Twiford. Friends John Bull & Edmund Custis Exrs. Witt: Smith Kellam. Codicil: 3 Dec. 1735 - To son John an equal share with the rest of my children of my personal est. Witt: Robert Rodgers, Reubin Wise, Edmund Custis - p. 210

OUTTEN, ABRAHAM - 6 May 1785 - 2 Feb. 1786 - To wife Mary whole est., but if she be with child est. to be equally div. bet. my wife & said child, & if said child should die under the age of 21 unmarried, wife to have the whole. Wife & Levin Joynes Exrs. Proved by Thomas Custis, Thomas Snead & William Gibb - p. 211
In order of prob: John Wise guardian to John Wise Outten, Inf't. heir at law.

GROTEN, CUSTIS - 23 May 1784 - 28 Feb. 1786 - To bro. Severen Groten. To my mother "the whole land and living" & at her death to Seyeren, provided he pay to William, Nancy & Thomas 20 L. Should Severen die without issue the whole land & living to William. Bro. William Groten Exr. Witt: Joshua Taylor, William Taylor - p. 212
In order of prob: Severn Groten qualified.

SILVERTHORN, JOHN - 18 Dec. 1785 - 28 Feb. 1786 - To wife Abey land & planta. purchased of Jonathan Mears & Daniel Hall & 4 A. of the land where I now live adj. the same, being 204 A. lying on Pocomoke River, for life, she to keep my son John Silverthorn & educate him until he arrive to 16 years of age, then the said land to my son John, & for want of heirs to my son Henry Silverthorn. To son Joshua Silverthorn land on Pocomoke River cont. 225 A. To son William all the land where I now live during his life, provided he give my Exrs. bond for the bringing up of my son Henry Silverthorn from 7 years until 16 years, & give him a good education; to my son William's first male heir the land where I now live cont. 221 A. & for want of such heir to Joshua Silverthorn. Daus. Nancy & Tabitha Silverthorn. Wife Aby, unborn child, Nancy, Tabitha, John & Henry Silverthorn resid. legatees. Wife, John Silverthorn & Solomon Johnson Exrs. Witt: Arthur Silverthorn, Thomas Sandford, Ann Sandford - p. 212

BOWMAN, DAVID - 15 Oct. 1785 - 28 Feb. 1786 - To wife the planta. where I now live to do with as she sees fir for her & my children's interest, also my lot in Onancock. Bal. of est. to wife, & after payment of debts the residue to be div. bet. all my children. My wife & my other Exrs. to empower my friends Patrick Jeffery or James Balfour, writer, in the City of Edenburgh, or either of them if alive, & in case of the death of both any other person they may think fit, to sell & dispose of my houses &c. in KerkaldieFifeshire, as also to receive what money will become due to me at the death of my mother in Law, also my 1/3 part of the personal est, all of which to be applied to the payment of my debts. Wife & friends Edward Ker, Charles Bagwell & Americus Scarburgh Exrs. Not witnessed. Proved by Edward Ker & George Corbin.

In order of prob: George Corbin app. guardian to James Oswell Bowman, heir at law to the testator. Katharine Bowman granted letters of adm. with will annexed, on the est. of David Bowman.

WRIGHT, MACK WILLIAMS - 15 Oct. 1766 - 28 Feb. 1786 - To wife Elizabeth the use of my planta where I live and all my personal est. during her wid. then the planta. where I live to my son Elijah Wright & for want of heirs to my son Abel Wright. To son Jacob Wright planta. where he lives & 60 A. of land during his natural life, reversion to my son George Wright, & for want of heirs to my son Abel Wright. To son George the remaining part of my land, being 40 A. Dau. Elizabeth Wright, son Abel Wright, son Henry Wright, dau. Rachel Wright, dau. Sinah Wright & dau. Leah Wright resid. legatees. Wife Elizabeth & son Elijah Exrs. Witt: William Young, Sr., Margaret Young, George Young - p. 215

WINDOW, LEVIN - 22 Feb. 1786 - 28 Mar. 1786 - To wife 1/2 of my whole est. Bal. of est. to my children - Dau. Rachel to have 10 L less than my other children. Friend Edward Ker Exr. Witt: Solomon Smith, John Savage, Edward Ker. - p. 217

POWELL, JOHN - Nunc. Proved 15 Mar. 1786 - Prob: 28 Mar. 1786 - He gave to his bro. Joseph Powell the planta. whereon his mother now lives, exclusive of the dwelling house which he gave to his mother during her life. Mother Sarah Powell. To sister Betsy Powell. To sister Frances Godwin & to her son John Godwin. Bal. of land & personal property to mother Sarah & sisters Sarah, Agnes & Elizabeth Powell to be div. bet. them. Mother Sarah Exec. Proved by Jacaman Milligan, William Hickman - p. 217

DAVIS, MAJOR - 31 Mar. 1782 - 28 Mar. 1786 - To son William my land provided he pay my son Thomas & my dau. Agnes the sum of 50 L. Sons William & Thomas & dau. Agnes resid. legatees & Exrs. - Witt: William Matthews, Joseph Matthews - p. 218

CUTLER, JOHN - 20 Feb. 1786 - 28 Mar. 1786 - To wife Polly whole est. to bring up my children till they come to the age of 14, & then to be equally div. bet. my wife Polly & 3 youngest children George, Peter & Rosanna. Wife Polly, father Richard Cutler & John Rodgers Exrs. Witt: Richard Cutler, Betty Cutler, Richard Cutler & Betty Bishop - p. 219

WATSON, ROBERT - 1 Feb. 1781 - 28 Mar. 1786 - Land to be equally div. bet. my 2 sons John & Robert Watson. Wife Betty, John Watson, Robert Watson & unborn child resid. legatees. Wife Exec. - Witt: Levin Marshall, John Taylor - p. 219

LILLASTON, THOMAS - 8 Dec. 1785 - 28 Mar. 1786 - To son Tully Lillaston all my land except that part that I laid off for my son Thomas. To son Thomas land I laid off for him. To grandson James Snead. Son Tully resid. legatee. Sons Tully & Thomas Exrs. Witt: Willet Lillaston, Tobias Bull, Thomas Lillaston, Sr. - p. 222

RILEY, THOMAS - 20 Mar. 1786 - 26 Apr. 1786 - To son Henry (under age) planta. where I now live & the marsh at Shores Island. Wife Ann to have use of my dwelling house until my son Henry comes to lawful age or marriage, provided she remain my wid. To wife Ann the use of all the estate I had with her, she to bring up my youngest child, & then to be div. bet. my children at the discretion of my wife. If my wife should have a child or children, they to inherit the est. I had with her by marriage. Bal. of est. to be div. bet. my 5 children, Elizabeth, Thomas, Ramon, Anney & Susannah Fletcher. Henry Fletcher, Sr. & Thomas Fletcher Exrs. Witt: Charles Bagwell, Solomon Gray - p. 227

KELLAM NASH - 9 Mar. 1781 - 26 Apr. 1786 - To wife Elizabeth an equal share with my children of personal est. & 1/3 of my land for life. To son James Kellam land adj. James Twiford. To son Spencer the remaining part of my land. Should James or Spencer die without issue their land to descend to my son John Kellam. Bal. of est. to be div. bet. all the rest of my children, John, Thomas, Patience, Mary, Betty & Nancy. Levin Stewart Exr. Witt: Levin Stewart, John Fitchett, Timothy Kelly - p. 227

TAYLOR, MOLLY, wid of Samuel Taylor - 13 Mar. 1786 - 27 June 1786 - To Sophia Ewell, wife of Edward Ewell. Two sons Elias & William Taylor resid. legatees. Son Elias Taylor Exr. Witt: John Gillett, William Marshall, Jr., Peggy White - p. 234

PARKER, SUSANNA - 23 Nov. 1785 - 27 June 1786 - To sister Mary Parker. To Bridget Wise. Sister in law Molly Parker & my sister's child Rosey Patterson Bonewell, all the remaining part of my est. to be equally div. bet. them. Robert Drummond Exr. Witt: Charles Snead, Johannis Wise - p. 234

HICKMAN, CUSTIS - 1 May 1786 - 27 June 1786.- Two daus. Sally Hickman & Susy Hickman sole legatees. George Garrison Exr. Witt: Robert Snead, William Arbuckle. - p. 235

HARMAN, RACHEL - 19 Oct. 1786 - 31 Oct. 1786 - Son Cornelius Harman. Grandau. Rachel Shield. To Sarah Watson's dau. Susey. To grandau. Catharine Harman. To grandau. Leah Harman. To Frances Harman. To son John Harman. To son Kendall Harman. Sons Zorobabel Harman & Edmund Harman resid. legatees. Ephraim Watson Exr. - Witt: John Shield, Isaiah Beach, Sarah Watson - p. 290

SPIERS, WILLIAM - 24 Mar. 1786 - 1 Nov. 1796 - To wife Margaret all my land for the term of 15 years to bring up her children, & then to my son Thomas Spiers. To dau. Anney Spiers. To dau. Elizabeth Spiers. To dau. Margaret Spiers. Wife & her children Agnes Spiers, Matilda Spiers, Mary Spiers & Sally Revel Spiers resid. legatees. Zerobabel Rodgers & John Spiers Exrs. Witt: George Snead, Custis Kellam, Joy Bradford - p. 298

YOUNG, EZEKIEL - 20 Mar. 1784 - 26 Dec. 1786 - To son Thomas Young 150 A. where I live, also 1/2 of my marsh & Islands. To son John Young all the remaining part of my land & marsh. To daus. Mary Millener, Peggy Young, Ann Young & Tabltha Young. Bal. of est. to be div. bet. all my children. Children to be in the care of my Exrs. David Bowman, Thomas Parramore & William Stran Exrs. Witt: Thomas Lilleston, Henry Fitzgarald, Peter Melson - p. 306
In order of prob: Thomas Evans app. guardian to the heir at law to the testator.

CHANDIER, CALEB - 13 Mar. 1786 - 26 Dec. 1786 - To wife Sarah whole est. during her wid. & then to be equally div. bet. my wife & children except Charles Chandler, he to have my land. Son Caleb Chandler. Son William Chandler. To dau. Peggy Chandler 3 ℒ that her uncle Sacker left her. Wife Sarah, daus. Peggy, Sophia, Sarah & Mary Wise & sons Caleb & William resid. legatees. George Taylor Exr. - Witt: Sophia Taylor, John Phillips - p. 307

TIZEKER, WILLIAM - 17 Nov. 1786 - 27 Dec. 1786 - To dau. Mary Tizeker all my lands & personal est., & for want of heirs I give the planta. where I now live to my friend Joseph Hanaford; to my friend George Hanaford the upper part of my planta. cont. 145 A; to my friend James Hanaford my land called Linses, all on proviso that my dau. die without issue. To friend William Hanaford. To friend William Boggs. To friend John Hanaford, Jr. To friend Sarah Savage. To friend Elizabeth Mahoon. To friend Edmund Turlington. To Edmund Turlington, Sr. Should my dau. die without issue the bal. of my est. to be equally div. "amongst my friends the children John Hanaford had by his first wife. Friends Zorobabel Rogders, Sr., Zorobabel Rodgers, Jr. & John Boggs Exrs. Zorobabel Rodgers, Sr. guardian of my dau. Mary Tizeker - Witt: William Leatherbury, George Leatherbury. p. 308

MARSHALL, WILLIAM - 5 Dec. 1786 - 30 Jan. 1787 - To son William Marshall land & planta. where I now live cont. 315 A. To son Solomon Marshall land cont. 300 A. lying bet. the land of William Patterson & Edward Ardis. To dau. Rhoda Harrison 100 A. adj. the land that belonged to Samuel Taylor, dec. & for want of heirs to my son Solomon. To dau. Fanny 175 A. adj. the land of Samuel Taylor's heirs & James Watts' heirs, & for want of heirs to my dau. Famey Marshall. To dau. Famey Marshall 140 A. near Swanzygut Creek, & for want of heirs to my dau. Fanny. All my Island land to be equally div. bet. my children William, Solomon, Rhoday, Famey & Fanny. Solomon, Famey & Fanney resid. legatees. Sons William & Solomon Exrs. Son William guardian of my daus. Famey & Fanney. Witt: William Waterfield, Mathias Taylor, Jacob Waterfield - p. 309

LEWIS, JOHN - 13 Jan. 1786 - 30 Jan. 1787 - Wife to have use of my land until my youngest child comes to lawful age. Wife (no name) resid. legatee & Exec. - Witt: Bridget Justice, Mary Lewis - p. 311
In order of prob: Betty Lewis qualified.

KELLY, JOHN - 5 Oct. 1786 - 30 Jan. 1787 - To wife Susanna Kelly all my lands during her life & then to my son George Kelly planta. where I live. Son Richard Kelly. Witt: Major Bayley, Caleb Mears, Sarah Bayley - p. 312
In order of prob: Susanna Kelly qualified.

RODGERS, RICHARD - 17 Apr. 1785 - 30 Jan. 1787 - To wife Esther land purchased of Nicholas Shield and 1/3 of land where I now live during her wid. & whole personal est. for life. To son Smith Rodgers land where I live. Dau. Mary Rodgers. (Esther step-mother of Smith) To dau. Dorothy Phillips. To dau. Peggy Rodgers. To son James Rodgers land purchased of Nicholas Shield. To dau. Elizabeth Darby Rodgers. Wife & son Smith Rodgers Exrs. Witt: William Coleburn - p. 312

WEST, JONATHAN - 9 June 1786 - 1 Feb. 1787 - To son John (called Great John) all the lands adj. the lands he now has in possession, up the Creek to a gut called Salt Pond Gut, adj. the land of Tully Wise. To wife the lands lying bet. the lands devised my son John & the lands which I gave my son Thorowgood, during her wid. in lieu of dower. To son Jonathan (under age) the land which I have given my wife for life, & for want of heirs to my son Thomas. To sons Kendal & Jonathan my Island called Tobacco Island. To son Charles. To dau. Bridget. Dau. Elizabeth. Daus. Sally, Nancy, Betsey & Bridget to pay their proportionate part of their bro. Isaac's debts out of their part of my est. Son Charles Exr. Witt: James Snead, John Wise - p. 316

BUNTING, SOLOMON - 28 Sept. 1781 - 1 Feb. 1787 - To son William, who is now beyond Sea & has been for the space of 4 years now last past, if he should be living & return to Northampton, my planta. in Neswaddes Neck in Northampton County cont. 176 A., together with the water grist mill upon it for life, reversion to my son Solomon Bunting & his heir of the name of Solomon, but should he not have an heir of that name, then after the death of my son Solomon I give the said planta. & mill to the heir of my son William of the name of Solomon, & if he have no heir of that name then to the heir of my son Holloway by the name of Solomon, & should he have no heir of that name then to the heir of my son Jonathan by the name of Solomon, & if he should have no heir of that name then to the male heir of my body forever. To wife Peggy negroes & all the rest of my personal est. in Accomack during her wid. Sons Holloway & Jonathan resid. legatees. I leave the care of my son Jonathan & the management of his tuition to my friend James Taylor of Northampton. Wife Peggy, son Solomon & William Satchell Exrs. Witt: Esther Coxwell, John

Custis, Benjamin Darby, William Garrison, William Chord, Robert Coxwell.

9 Apr. 1784. Since making the above will having a dau. by my wife named Peggy Marshall, my will is that she have an equal share with my wife & children, & to be supported by my wife & my estate until she comes to age. Witt: William F. Ross, Kendal Savage, John Rose - p. 319

In order of prob: Holloway Bunting & Levin Bunting qualified.

SNEAD, THOMAS - 16 Mar. 1787 - 25 Apr. 1787 - I lend to my wife Elizabeth Snead my houses & lotts in Onancock Town, the land I bought of Edmund Custis, & one moiety of a water mill bought of James Bonewell until my son John Smith Snead arrives to lawful age, he to be educated as my friends William Gibb, Tully Snead & Levin Joynes may approve. Land I bought of Smith Snead to be sold for the payment of debts. To son John Smith Snead all my lands, negroes &c. I have lent my wife when he attains full age or at the death of his mother. Should my said son die under age & without lawful issue I give 1/2 my whole est. to my wife Elizabeth Snead during her life, & at her death to my sister Mary Wise's children, & the other 1/2 to my bro. Tully Snead. Wife Elizabeth, bro. Tully & friend William Gibb Exrs. Witt: Ann West, Sarah Oldham, Levin Joynes - p. 338

MAPP, LABAN - 7 Feb. 1787 - 25 Apr. 1787 - To dau. Betsy. To dau. Peggy. To dau. Rachel Waterson. To son John. To goddau. Tamer Harman. Whole est. to wife Rachel to bring up my children, & at her death or marriage to be equally div. bet. my children. William Harman Exr. - Witt: Nathaniel Bell, Jr., Rachel Fitchriald, Sally Harman - p. 339

STOCKLY, ALEXANDER - 3 Aug. 1783 - 25 Apr. 1787 - To son Joseph all my lands, houses &c. To dau. Mary Stockly spoons marked "M.S." To dau. Catharine Stockly. Nephew Charles Stockly Exr. Witt: Thomas Bates. Proved by Charles Stockly & John Burton - p. 340

In order of prob: The Exr. named in the foregoing will refusing to act, Thomas Teackle qualified.

HICKMAN, RICHARD - 21 Nov. 1786 - 26 June 1787 - To son Hampton Hickman. To dau. Elizabeth, the wife of Isaiah Hickman. To wife all the remainder of my est., real & personal, during her wid., & then to my son Hampton Hickman all my lands & the remainder of my personal est. to my dau. Elizabeth. Wife (no name) & son Hampton Hickman & Isaiah Hickman Exrs. Witt: George Bundick, Tubitha Bundick, Thomas Hickman - p. 375

In order of prob: Anne Hickman, Isaiah Hickman & Hampton Hickman qualified.

JOYNES, EDWARD - 3 June 1787 - 26 June 1787 - To dau. Rhodah Joynes 100 A. next to the schoolhouse. To dau. Mary Mears 20 A. adj. Capt. William Drummond. To 2 sons John & Edward Joynes the remainder of my land. To dau. Esther Lamberson negroes for life, reversion to her children. To George Warrington Joynes. To dau. Sarah Huggins. Dau. Rhoda Joynes to keep my dau. Betty until her death or marriage. John, Edward & Rhoda Joynes resid. legatees. John Chord & dau. Rhoda Exrs. Witt: John Holt, Sr., Jeremiah Taylor, Ezekiel Taylor – p. 376

JAMES, ROBERT – 18 Jan. 1787 – 26 June 1787 – To wife dur. her wid. all my lands & water grist mill. Daus. Elizabeth, Nancy & Mary. To son William 200 A. on the North side of my planta. where I now live, also my water grist mill. To son David (under age) planta. which I bought of George Colony. Should unborn child be a boy I give said child the residue cn the South side of the planta. where I now live, but if a girl, or being a boy should die before arriving at 21 years in the life time of my son David, then I give the said residue of my planta. to my son David, & if said child should be a boy & my son David should die before he comes to the age of 21 in the life time of my now unborn child, he being a boy, then after the death of my said son David my said child the planta. I purchased of George Colony & which I have above devised to my son David. Wife to bring up & educate my children. Wife Mary & friend George Savage Exrs. Witt: Thomas Evans, Thomas Holt – p. 378

CORBIN, GEORGE BONNEWELL – 7 June 1787 – 31 July 1787 – Land where I now live to be equally div. bet. my 2 sons Ralph & Coventon Corbin (both under age). 2 daus. Pamela & Nancy Corbin resid. legatees. Wife to have use of whole est. during her wid to bring up my children. Wife (no name) & William Downing Exrs. Witt: Polly Delastatius, Scarburgh Broadwater – p. 390
In order of prob: Sarah Corbin qualified.

HALEY, BENJAMIN – 6 May 1787 – 31 July 1787 – To son William Haley planta. where I now live. Son William & Spencer Kellam Exrs. Witt: Peter Wise, Robert Haley. p. 421

MELVIN, SMITH – 27 Oct. 1786 – 2 Aug. 1787 – To wife Mary planta. where I now dwell during her natural live & then to my son James Melvin. I lend to my son James Melvin 100 A. in Worcester County, Maryland, being part of a tract called Chance & part of a tract called Partnership, during his mother's life, & at her death to my son Smith Melvin. To son Walker Melvin (under age). To son Obadiah Melvin. To son John Melvin. To dau. Nancy Melvin. Wife Mary resid. legatee & Exec. Witt: Arthur Whealton, James Benson, Betty Owen – p. 422

HENRY, JAMES – 12 Feb. 1787 – partly proved 27 Feb. 1787 – Prob: 25 Sept. 1787 – To wife Susannah land where I now live forever. To mother Sarah Darby, wid. of John Darby of the State of Maryland. To bro. Isaac Henry & to his son Hugh Henry. To cousin Handy Harris. To my sister Nancy Polk. To sister Elizabeth Henry, wid. of William B. Henry. Wife Susannah resid. legatee. Edward Ker & Col.

John Darby Exrs. Witt: Amos Underhill, Christopher Satchell, Charles Carpenter - p. 433

STERLING, RICHARD - 27 Jan. 1787 - 25 Sept. 1787 - Manor planta. cont. 147 A. to be sold & the money equally div. bet. my children, viz: Rebecca, Harry & Richard Sterling. To wife Mary Sterling personal est. during her wid. & then to be div. bet. my 3 children aforesaid. Caleb Broadwater, Jr. Exr. Witt: Elias Broadwater, William Sterling - p. 434

WALTER, RICHARD - 27 Aug. 1786 - 25 Sept. 1787 - To son Richard Walter land cont.   104 A. adj. the lands of Hillary Stringer. To son Thomas Walter planta. where I now live cont. 50 A. Should my 2 sons die before they arrive at lawful age land to be div. bet. my younger sons Solomon, John & Abel, if they live. To wife Peggy use of whole est. during her wid. to bring up my children & to find Keziah Clark a sufficient maintenance. Children Rachel, Tabitha, Solomon, John & Abel resid. legatees. If Keziah Clark outlives her sister Peggy, she to be maintained by my son Richard's planta. Wife Peggy & friend Peter Savage Exrs. Witt: Upshur Folio, William Watson, John Folio - p. 435

READ, TABITHA - 9 Jan. 1787 - 25 Sept. 1787 - To father in law Levin Rodgers during his natural life negro, reversion to my sister Elizabeth Conaway. To bro. Caleb Read. Father in law Levin Rodgers Exr. Witt: Peter Wise, John Edmunds - p. 436

BROADWATER, WILLIAM - Not dated - 26 Sept. 1787 - To wife Sally Broadwater 1/2 my est. for life then to be div. bet. all my children, James, Caty & unborn child. James & Caty to have 1 years schooling each between 12 years old & 20 years old, & also that John Corbin, son of my wife Sally, one year at the same age. I give my land to my 2 children, & if they die without issue wife to have whole est. for life & 1/5 part forever, & the remainder to be div. bet. my 3 bros. & sister, viz: Jacob Broadwater, Caleb Broadwater, Coventon Broadwater & Esther Fitzgerald. Wife Sally & Jacob Broadwater Exrs. Not witnessed & not signed. Proved by George Corbin & Kendal Stockly - p. 438

BLADES, JESSE - 4 Oct. 1787 - 30 Oct. 1787 - To Children Charlotte Blades, Susanna Blades, Benjamin Blades, Winney Blades, William Blades & Caleb Blades by my late wife Rebecca Blades, 1 s. each. Bal. of est. to my wife Eleanor. Wife Eleanor Blades Exec. Witt: William Finney, Andrew Martin, Shadrack Dawson - p. 447

LURTON, LITTLETON - 24 Aug. 1786 - 30 Oct. 1787 - To son Laban Lurton 30 A. where he now lives adj. Henry Window & Severn East. To son John Lurton 30 A. adj. the above. To dau. Tabitha Mahorn 1 s. To dau. Semor Elliott 1 s. To wife Patience Lurton. 2 children James & Peggy Lurton resid. legatees. Son James & Zorobabel Rodgers Exrs. Witt: Z: Rodgers, Zorobabel Rodgers - p. 450

RAYFIELD, PETER - 7 May 1787 - 26 Dec. 1787 - To wife Sinah Rayfield whole est. during her wid. & then 1/2 to her forever, & the remaining 1/2 to be div. bet. my cousin Jenny Rayfield & Nathaniel B. Addison. Friends Zorobabel Rodgers, Severn East & wife Sinah Exrs. Witt: Nathaniel Addison, Anne Badger - p. 459
In order of prob: Sarah Rayfield qualified.

HUTCHINSON, JOHN - 2 Sept. 1787 - 25 Dec. 1787 - To son Robert Hutchinson 250 A. that formerly belonged to Littleton Wyatt. To son Levi Hutchinson planta. where I now live & all the remaining part of my land cont. 312 A. & for want of heirs to my son Jessee Hutchinson (under age) & for want of heirs to my son Stephen Hutchinson (under age). To dau. Sarah Hutchinson. To wife Sarah Hutchinson the whole of my est. during her wid., & then to be div. bet. my children then living. Zorobabel Hornsby & wife Sarah Exrs. Witt: Peter Rodgers, Levin Rodgers & John Downing - p. 460
In order of prob: Robert Hutchinson heir at law to the testator.

Orders - 1787-1790

ADDISON, JOHN - Adm. his est. to John Rodgers & Susanna Addison - Levin Rodgers sec. - 25 Sept. 1787 - p. 29

EWELL, SETH - Adm. his est. to Margaret Ewell & Robert Twiford - Henry Scarburgh, John Savage, John Read & Levin Rodgers sec. - 26 Sept. 1787 - p. 35

PLANNER, WILLIAMS - Adm. his est. to William Gibb - George Parker sec. - 30 Oct. 1787 - p. 44

MATHEWS, THOMAS - Adm. his est. to William Mathews, Sr. - Jabez Pitt & Robert Pitt sec. - 31 Oct. 1787 - p. 45

WATTS, ESTHER - Adm. her est. to Mason Dodd - James Collins & James Howard sec. 26 Dec. 1787 - p. 85

BLAKE, SARAH - Adm. her est. to Jacob Dunstan - James Douglass & David Watts sec. 29 Jan. 1788 - p. 93

COLLINS, PHILBE - Adm. his est. to George Collins - George Wallop sec. - 29 Jan. 1788 - p. 95

HOWARD, NATHANIEL - Adm. his est. to Keziah Howard - Isaac Warner & John Moore sec. - 30 Jan. 1788 - p. 101

MELSON, ADAH - Adm. her est. to Southy Satchell - Smith Milliner & John Cropper, Sr. sec. - p. 102

MATHEWS, JOSEPH – Adm. his est. to Neil Laferty – William Welburn & John Wise sec. 26 Feb. 1788 – p. 109

MASON, WILLIAM – Adm. his est. to James Benston, Peggy Mason, wid. of the dec. relinquishing her right to qualify – Jabez Pitt & Thomas Sandford sec. – 26 Feb. 1788 – p. 110

WINDOW, ABEL – Adm. his est. to Robert Twiford – Margaret Window sec. – 26 Feb. 1788 – p. 110

KELLAM, EZAR – Adm. his est. unadministered by Custis Kellam, dec., to Zorobabel Groten – James Spiers & John Watson sec. – 30 Apr. 1788 – p. 154

COLLINS, MARTHA – Adm. her est. to James Collins – Edward Joynes & John Joynes sec. – 29 Jul 1788 – p. 217

WISE, RACHEL – Adm. her est. to Richard Grinalds – John Parker sec. – 1 Aug. 1788 – p. 228

BULL, BENJAMIN – Adm. his est. to John Bull. Betty Bull, wid. of the dec., relinquishing her right to qualify – Thomas Custis sec. – 1 Oct. 1788 – p. 256

MERRILL, WILLIAM SCOTT – Adm. his est. to William Merrill – Elijah Townsend & Jacob Richardson sec. – 28 Oct. 1788 – p. 264

DICKENSON, JESSE – Adm. his est. to Leah Dickenson – John R. Parker & Thomas Fletcher sec. – 28 Oct. 1788 – p. 264

RODGERS, RICHARD – Adm. his est. with will annexed to John Rodgers – Solomoon Read & Robert Twiford sec. – 20 Dec. 1788 – p. 283

BULL, JOHN – Adm. his est. to Bridget Bull – John Cropper sec. – 30 Dec. 1788 – p. 283

PARKS, ROBERT – Adm. his est. to John Evans – William Stran & Elijah Colony sec. – 30 Dec. 1788 – p. 284

ONLY, FAIRFAX – Adm. his est. to John Savage – Robert Twiford & Littleton Savage, Sr. sec. – 30 Dec. 1788 – p. 285

LUCAS, ELIJAH – Adm. his est. to Isaac Warner – George Warner & John Howard sec. 30 Dec. 1788 – p. 285

KITSON, ELIZABETH – Adm. her est. to John Laws – George Laylor sec. – 27 Jan. 1789 – p. 294

HUTSON, LEVIN – Adm. his est. to Hannah Hutson – John Taylor & Levin Evans sec. 28 Apr. 1789 – p. 326

LAWS, JONATHAN - Adm. his est. to John Laws - William Davis & John Moore sec. - 29 Apr. 1789 - p. 333

CUTLAR, EBENEZER - Adm. his est. to Rachel Cutlar - James Broadwater & Jacob Broadwater sec. - 29 Apr. 1789 - p. 333

PITT, JOHN - Adm. his est. unadministered by George Stewart, dec., to Robert Pitt - Jabez Pitt sec. - 29 Apr. 1789 - p. 334

LOWELL, THOMAS - Adm. his est. to Thomas Bagwell - John Poulson sec. - 29 Apr. 1789 - p. 334

TATHAM, JAMES - Adm. his est. to James Tatham - Robert Twiford & Phillip Tignor sec. - 30 June 1789 - p. 380

CORGAN, NEIL - Adm. his est. to Thomas Burton - George Coleburn sec. - 28 July 1789 - p. 397

POULSON, GEORGE - Adm. his est. to John Custis (seaside) - Southy Satchell sec. - 28 Aug. 1789 - p. 418

GROTON, EDMUND - Adm. his est. to Zorobabel Groten - George Coleburn sec. - 29 Sept. 1789 - p. 426

TAYLOR, WILLIAM (Blacksmith) Adm. his est. to Rachel Taylor & Samuel Henderson - Joseph Feddeman & William Downing sec. - 27 Oct. 1789 - p. 460

DUNCAN, ELI - Adm. his est. to Jessee Duncan - Southy Northam & Jacob Kelly sec. 27 Oct. 1789 - p. 461

COPES, JOSHUA - Adm. his est. to Isaac Williams - Thomas Evans sec. - 29 Dec. 1780 - p. 481

BUNTING, TINCEY - Adm. her est. to John Cropper - Thomas Cropper sec. - 29 Dec. 1789 - p. 483

EVANS, JOHN - Adm. his est. to Lucretia Evans - Johannis Watson sec. - 29 Dec. 1789 - p. 484

ABBOTT, RODGER - Adm. his est. to Richard Bundick - John Lundick & Parker Parradice sec. - 29 Dec. 1789 - p. 484

TAYLOR, EDWARD - Adm. his est. to Deidamia Taylor - Charles Bagwell & John Burton sec. - 30 Dec. 1789 - p. 488

RILEY, RAYMOND - Adm. his est. with will annexed to Tully Wise - William Gibb sec. 1 Jan. 1790 - p. 496

BOWMAN, CATHERINE – Adm. her est. to Oswald Bowman, Edward Ker & Americus Scarburgh – John Wise & Edmund Bayly sec. – 26 Jan. 1790 – p. 498

STATEN, GEORGE – Adm. his est. to Anne Staten – Warrington Staten & Samuel Beavans sec. – 26 Jan. 1790 – p. 499

DRUMMOND, EZEKIEL – Adm. his est. to Sarah Drummond – William Drummond & John Custis (seaside) sec. – 29 Jan. 1790 – p. 508

PIELEE, GILBERT – Adm. his est. to John Cropper, Jr. – Thomas Cropper sec. – 23 Feb. 1790 – p. 516

TURNAL, THOMAS – Adm. his est. to Argol Bloxom – Jacob White sec. – 24 Feb. 1790 – p. 518

SHIELD, ASA – Adm. his est. to Peter Shield – Levin White sec. – 24 Feb. 1790 – p. 519

BOWMAN, DAVID – Adm. his est. to Edward Ker – 25 Feb. 1790 – p. 520

FOREMAN, ROBERT – Adm. his est. to Edmund Bayly, Jr., the wid. relinquishing her right to qualify – Thomas Bayly & Thomas Cropper sec. – 1 Apr. 1790 – P. 537

NOTTINGHAM, ABEL – Adm. his est. to Elizabeth Nottingham – William Gibb sec. – 27 Apr. 1790 – p. 563

BRADFORD, ZEPHENIAH – Adm. his est. to Elizabeth Bradford – John Mears, son of John, Robert Twiford, Robinson Savage & William Polk sec. – 29 Apr. 1790 – p. 566

BOOTH, JOHN – Adm. his est. to John McLean – William Warrington sec. – 29 Apr. 1790 – p. 566

HOTTEN, WALTER – Adm. his est. to Walter Hotten – John McLean & Robert Pitt sec. 29 Apr, 1790 – p. 567

Orders – 1790–1793

BROADWATER, CALEB – Adm. his est. to Rachel Broadwater – Jacob Broadwater sec. – 29 June 1790 – p. 6

OLDHAM, GEORGE – Adm. his est. to John Custis & John Poulson – Elijah Grinalds & Southy Satchell sec. – 30 June 1790 – p. 8

HARVEY, JONATHAN – Adm. his est. to John Cropper, Jr. – John Cropper, Sr, sec. – 28 July 1790 – p. 16

WARRINGTON, JOHN - Adm. his est. to Stephen & Elizabeth Warrington - John Bayly & James Spires sec. - 28 Sept. 1790 - p. 39

THOMSON, JOHN - Adm. his est. to Tabitha Thomson - Revil Watson & Robert Twiford sec. - 29 Sept. 1790 - p. 45

SPIRES, WILLIAM - Adm. his est. to John Spires & John Guy - John Bull & George Coleburn sec. - 29 Sept. 1790 - p. 45

DAVIS, WILLIAM - Adm. his est. to Sally Davis - John Burton & Richard Drummond, Sr. sec. - 26 Oct. 1790 - p. 51

LEATHERBURY, CHARLES - Adm. his est. to Sarah Leatherbury & Noah Belote - John Custis (Bayside) sec. - 26 Oct. 1790 - p. 56

RUSSELL, THOMAS - Adm. his est. to Southy Silverthorn - Richard Taylor & John Fitchett sec. - 30 Dec. 1790 - p. 77

CORE, CHARLES - Adm. his est. to Zorobabel Core - William Wyatt & Ismael Wyatt sec. - 25 Jan. 1791 - p. 87

CUSTIS, REVEL - Adm. his est. to Levin Ames - Southy Satchell & Revil Custis sec. 22 Feb. 1791 - p. 119

ABDEL, EZEKEL - Adm. his est. to Jesse Watson - Robert Twiford & Zorebable Henderson sec. - 22 Feb. 1791 - p. 121

JOHNSON, JOHN.- Adm. his est. to William Johnson - John Bowles & Michael Dickerson sec. - 22 Feb. 1791 - p. 121

TAYLOR. NATHAN - Adm. his est. to Abel Taylor - James Benston & Peter Delastations sec. - 22 Feb. 1791 - p. 126

RAYFIELD, PETER - Adm. his est. to Robert Twiford - George Scarburgh & Thomas Coleburn sec. - 23 Feb. 1791 - p. 127

YOUNG, JAMES - Adm. his est. to William Young - Crippen Taylor & John Moore sec. 27 Apr. 1791 - p. 161

ONLY, ALLIS - Adm. her est. to John Martin - Andrew Stewart & Betty Martin sec. 27 Apr. 1791 - p. 164

ABBOTT, ROBERT - Adm. his est. to George Truet Taylor - John Teackle, Sr. sec. - 26 July 1791 - p. 196

MELVIN, JOHN - Adm. his est. to William Harman - Elijah Aimes & Levin Aimes sec. 27 July 1791 - p. 198

TAYLOR, JOHN - Adm. his est. to George Corbin - John Wise sec. - 27 July 1791 - p. 201

KELLAM, CUSTIS - Adm. his est. to John Kellam - Coventon Broadwater & George Coleburn sec. - 28 July 1791 - p. 202

LINGO, ROBERT & Ralph Lingo - Adm. their estates to John Lingo - James Bradford & George Hyslop sec. - 28 July 1791 - p. 204

PARKER, JOHN - Adm. his est. to William Bull, Sr. - Michael Bonwell, Sr. & John Moore sec. - 27 Sept. 1791 - p. 265

ABBOTT, JOHN - Adm. his est. to Richard Bundick - William Grinalds & Spencer Hickman sec. - 27 Sept. 1791 - p. 265

WILLIAM, ISAAC - Adm. his est. to Sophia Williams - Spencer Hickman sec. - 27 Sept. 1791 - p. 266

COLEBURN, THOMAS - Adm. his est. to Sabra Coleburn - Jesse Kellam & John Kellam & Southy Satchell sec. - 27 Sept. 1791 - p. 266

HOPE, JOHN - Adm. his est. to Charles Hope - John Moore & George Hope sec. - 27 Sept. 1791 - p. 269

FIDDEMAN, ISAIAH - Adm. his est. to Meshack Fiddeman - John McLean & Revel Copes sec. - 25 Oct. 1791 - p. 275

REVEL, EDWARD - Adm. his est. to George Ker, John Shepherd Ker & Samuel Galt - John Teackle, Sr. sec. - 28 Dec. 1791 - p. 300

HICKMAN, WILLIAM, Sr. - Adm. his est. to John Abbott Bundick - John Moore & George Wright sec. - 28 Dec. 1791 - p. 301

FREE, CLEMENS - Adm. his est. to John Wise - John Custis & William Gibb sec. - 31 --- 1792 - p. 302

RUSSEL, ANDREW - Adm. his est. to Ephraim Vessels - William Young sec. - 31 Jan. 1792 - p. 303

GLADDING, MILLY - Adm. her est. to John Gladding - Coventon Broadwater sec. - 31 Jan. 1792 - p. 304

PATTERSON, WILLIAM - Adm. his est. to William Patterson - John Logan & Samuel Henderson sec. - 1 Feb. 1792 - p. 308

OWEN, SAMUEL - Adm. his est. to John Thornton - Arthur Whittington & Elisha Whealton sec. - 28 Feb. 1792 - p. 316

KENDAL, JOHN - "Ordered that the Sheriff take into his possession the estate of John Kendal, dec., and make sale thereof" 28 Feb. 1792 - p. 319

TAYLOR, JOHN - Adm. his est. to George Corbin - Thomas Cropper & Thomas Evans sec. - 1 Mar. 1792 - p. 325

MARSHALL, JENEPHER - Adm. his est. to John Holland. William Welburn & Thomas Gore sec. - 25 Apr. 1792 - p. 360

MAXWELL, JOHN - Adm. his est. to Nicholas Knox - John McLean & Thomas Hargis sec. - 25 Apr. 1792 - p. 361

COLONY, ELIZABETH - Adm. her est. to Bennett Scarburgh - Solomon Read & Garrett Topping sec. - 25 Apr. 1792 - p. 362

MEARS, WILLIAM - Adm. his est. to Charity Mears - John McLean sec. - 25 Apr. 1792 - p. 363

STURGIS, JACOB - Adm. his est. to Selby Simpson - William Drummond sec. - 25 Apr. 1792 - p. 365

WEST, EDMUND - Adm. his est. to John Simpson - John Moore & Southy Simpson sec. - 26 Apr. 1792 - p. 365

LITTLETON, WILLIAM - Adm. his est. to Mark Littleton - John Burton sec. - 26 Apr. 1792 - p. 376

FLUHART, JOHN.- Adm. his est. to John Boisnard - Esther Hickman relinquishing her right to qualify. George Simpson sec. - 26 June 1792 - p. 405

DOLBY, PETER JOHN - Adm. his est. to Eleshe Dolby - Jacob White & Theophilus Bagge sec. - 26 June 1792 - p. 409

DIX, COMFORT - Adm. her est. to John Cropper - Southy Satchell & Garrett Topping sec. - 26 June 1792 - p. 409

TAYLOR, WILLIAM - Adm. his est. to Elisha Mears, Nanny Taylor, wid. of the dec. relinquishing her right to qualify. Archibald Garrison, Nathaniel Aimes & Robinson Savage sec. - 31 July 1792 - p. 413

JOHNSON, ISAIAH - Adm. his est. to Sarah Johnson - Crippen Taylor sec. - 25 Sept. 1792 - p. 463

BENSTON, JAMES - Adm. his est. to Rachel Benston - Jacob Richardson & William Benston sec. - 28 Jan. 1793 - p. 496

MEARS, LEVI - Adm. his est. to William Mears, son of Richard - John Rodgers & Thomas Aimes sec. - 28 Jan. 1793 - p. 497

NELSON, Spencer - Adm. his est. to John Abbott Bundick - George Wright & Levin Copes sec. - 28 Jan. 1793 - p. 498

BENSTON, ELEAZER - Adm. his est. to Charles Richardson. Eli Hornsby sec. - 29 Jan. 1793 - p. 500

RODGERS, ZOROBABEL - Adm. his est. to John Wise p Mary Rodgers, wid. of Zorobabel relinquishing her right to qualify. John Custis & Noah Belote sec. - 29 Jan. 1793 - p. 501

WISE, PETER - Adm. his est. to William Haley - Jesse Kellam sec. - 29 Jan. 1793 - p. 503

Wills - 1788-1794

DOE, ALEANOR - 25 Aug. 1786 - 29 Jan. 1788.- To McKeel Bonnewell, son of James, all the land devised me & my sister Peggy by our bro. Samuel Doe, cont. 35 A. McKeel Bonnewell resid. legatee & Exr. Witt: Major Bayly, Caleb Mears, Caleb Bonnewell, John Bull, Jr. - p. 1

WEST, RICHARD - 18 Jan. 1787 - 29 Jan. 1788 - To wife Ann West 1/3 of my est. during her wid. To son Salathiel Milby West planta. where I now live. Dau. Comfort Mears. Dau. Rachel West. Son Charles West. Son Abel West. Daus. Comfort Mears & Rachel West resid. legatees. Son Salathiel Milby West & son in law Elisha Mears Exrs. Witt: John Ashby, Nathaniel Aimes - p. 6

WILKERSON, MARY - 29 Oct. 1787 - 29 Jan. 1788 - To son Jesse Wilkerson land & planta. where I now live & for want of heirs to Joshua Wilkerson. To Anne Gillett. To grandau. Fanney Wilkerson. Sons Jesse, Jehua & Joshua Wilkerson resid. legatees. Son Jesse Exr. Witt: William Selby, Joseph Fiddeman, Samuel Taylor - p. 13

HOLDEN, ANNE - 15 Nov. 1787 - 29 Jan. 1788 - I give all my lands on Matchtank known as Fookes Neck to John, Francis & Joseph Boggs. I give 100 A. purchased by my dec. husband King to Thomas & John Sandford. To Betty Sandford. To Ann Sandford, widow. To Ann Sandford dau. of the wid. To Esther Benston. To Dr. William Williams. 20 of my slaves to be div. bet. the children of Ann Whittington, Elizabeth Whittington & Jacoman Milligan, except Elizabeth Nichols, each to have 1/3 part. "I give the two pictures of father & Mother to Samuel Wilson". To Col. William Selby. To Rev. Jacob Ker. To Rev. Samuel McMaster. To John Milligan & Mary Milbourn land & planta. where I now live, also my marsh land at or near Saxes Island. Should John Milligan die without issue I give his part to Arthur Whittington. John Milligan son of Jacoman Milligan. To Millison Gladden. To Peggy Milligan. Bal. of est. to be sold & money div. bet. Ann Whittington, Elizabeth Whittington & Jacoman Milligan. Dr. William Williams, Col. William Selby, Samuel McMaster & Elijah Milbourn Exrs. Witt: Peter Delastatius, Charles Drummond, Joaikim Milbourn, Comfort Drummond, George Corbin, Thomas Evans - p. 16

HOWARD, NATHANIEL – 9 Jan. 1788 – 29 Jan. 1788 – Land where I live to be sold & when the money is collected I give to my son Daniel Howard when he arrives to 20 years of age 6 L. Bal. of est. to be div. bet my 5 children, Leah, Mary, Caziah, Catron & Daniel Howard. Isaac Warner Exr. Witt: Isaac Warner, John Howard – p. 18
In order of prob: Isaac Warner relinquished his right & Keziah Howard qualified. John Howard app. guardian to the heir at law to the testator.

HALL, THOMAS – 27 July 1787 – 26 Feb. 1788 – To dau. Rebecca Hall. To dau. Betty Hall. Son Nathaniel Hall resid. legatee & Exr. Witt: William Downing, David Watts, William Beavans – p. 28

BELL, JACOB – 8 Jan. 1788 – 27 Feb. 1788 – Whole est. to wife Levinah during her wid. then to John Elliott for the maintenance of my 3 children, Jacob, Sophia & Thomas Bell. Wife & John Elliott Exrs. Witt: Joshua Cutlar, Thomas Rodgers, Absalam Foster – p. 34

WARD, ISAAC – 19 Dec. 1787 – 30 Apr. 1788 – Exr. to lay out the money due me in Somerset in land & I give the said land to my dau. Sarah Ward & for want of issue to my son Stephen Ward. Bal. of est. to wife Mary until Stephen comes to age of 21 & then to be div. bet. my wife & 2 children, Stephen & Sarah. Wife Exec. Witt: Charles Bagwell, Joice Fitchett – p. 37

SAVAGE, SARAH – 19 Oct. 1786 – 30 Apr. 1788 – "In the name of God Amen, I Sarah Twiford" (Signed "Sarah Savage" – S.N.) To Sally Savage. To Mary Savage & her 2 daus. Patience & Sally Savage. Robert Savage, son of Charles, Exr. Witt: Patience Savage, Peggy Savage, Joshua Wyatt – p. 37

LANE, ISRAEL – 24 Apr. 1787 – 30 Apr. 1788 – To wife Jane Lane planta. where I now life during her wid. reversion to daus. Zilpah Lane & Polly Lane. Daus. resid. legatees. Wife Jane Exec. Witt: Samuel Pane, Polly Massey – p. 38

LINGO, JOHN – 20 June 1781 – 30 Apr. 1788 – To wife Rachel Lingo 1/2 my land during her wid., then my whole land to my son Robinson Lingo & for want of male heirs to be div. bet. Joice Lingo & Sally Fisher, & for want of heirs to return to Robinson Lingo's heirs. Dau. Rachel. Dau. Joice Lucas. To Peggy Hickman. Son Robinson Lingo, Rachel Richerson & Sarah Spiers resid. legatees. Wife Rachel, Robinson Lingo & Robert Spiers Exrs. Witt: Thomas Custis, Levi Beachum, Anne Glenn – p. 39

RIGGS, JOHN – 29 Dec. 1787 – 1 May 1788 – To wife Sarah Riggs use of my land for life, then 1/2 to my son George Riggs & 1/2 to my son Joseph Riggs. To wife Salady Riggs personal est. for life then to be div. bet. my 2 sons, George & Joseph. Wife & Henry Fletcher, Sr., Exrs. Witt: William Young, John Fitchett, Parker Paradice – p. 39
In order of prob: Sarah Riggs qualified.

OUTTEN, SAMUEL - 21 Jan. 1788 - 24 June 1788 - To son William Outten 200 L. To dau. Tabitha Outten 100 L. To wife Ann Outten. bal. of est. during her wid. & then to be sold & the money div. bet. my son William & dau. Tabitha Outten, & should they die before lawful age wife to have whole est. at her will. Wife Anne & John R. Parker Exrs. Witt: Henry Parker, John Parker - p. 57

UNDERHILL, DANIEL - 19 Nov. 1787 - 24 June 1788 - Land to be div. bet. sons James & William. Negroes to be div. in 3 parts, 1/3 to dau. Polly, 1/3 to dau. Betsy & 1/3 between my 2 sons James & William. Wife's clothing to be div. bet. my daus. Polly & Betsy. Sister Bullock to continue in the family as a guide to my children until James comes to age. Bros. Thomas & Amos Underhill Exrs. Witt: John Thompson, Elijah Watson, Athaliah Bullock - p. 58

MEARS, JOHN (son of William) 9 Dec. 1784 - 24 June 1788 - To son William planta. where I now live. To son Richard my part of the sloop. To dau. Polly Mears. dau. Elizabeth Mears. Dau. Peggy Mears. Dau. Elishe Mears. Wife Mary Mears negro for life, reversion to my son William. All my children, William, Richard, Polly, Elizabeth, Peggy & Elishe Mears resid. legatees. Sons William & Richard & bro. Elisha Mears Exrs. Not witnessed. - Proved by Edward Ker, Thomas Jacobs, Benjamin Darby & Argil Kellam - p. 59

GARRISON, WILLIAM - 8 Dec. 1787 - 25 June 1788 - To wife Betty whole est. for the term of 10 years to bring up our younger children, & then to be equally div. bet. my children Tabitha, Joshua, Betsy, William, Bagwell, Edmund & Rose & my said wife. Wife & son John guardians of all my children under age. Friend Thomas Custis (Folly) Exr. Witt: Fanny Garrison. John Garrison, Edward Ker - p. 63

ARDIS, EDWARD - 25 Jan. 1788 - 29 July 1788 - To son James Ardis the Manor planta. where he now lives after raising two younger children to the age of 16 years., & for want of heirs to my son Daniel. To son Daniel the land my father Robert Ardis gave me, & for want of issue to my son James. Dau. Leah Ardis. Dau. Betty Ardis. Dau. Nanny Ardis. 4 children James, Daniel, Leah & Betty resid. legatees. Son James & Nehemiah Tunnell Exrs. Witt: William Taylor, James Howard, Elijah Townsend - p. 68

HINMAN, BAYLY - 15 Jan. 1788 - 29 July 1788 - To wife Sarah my dwelling house during her wid. Dau. Margaret Hinman to have a home at said house as long as she remains single. To son Argol Hinman all the land my father gave me, the land I now live on, for 200 A. As much of my est. to be sold as will make 10 L for my grandson Ralph Hinman, for money that I made use of out of his est. Dau. Margaret resid. legatee. Son Argol Exr. - Witt: William Young, Jonathan Mears, Argol Bloxom - p. 84

GRAY, SOLOMON - 9 May 1788 - 31 July 1788 - To son Solomon Gray 60 A. at the Northwest end of my planta. Remainder of my land

to my two daus., Tabitha & Ann Gray, & for want of heirs to my dau. Sarah Gray. To son Thomas Gray, he to have liberty to get timber to support & supply the seaside planta. which he is heir to. William Thornton & Parker Paradise Exrs. Witt: Benjamin West, Richard Sparrow. p. 91
In order of prob: John Burdick qualified.

GIDDENS, THOMAS - 23 Nov. 1787 - 28 Oct. 1788 - To sister Elizabeth Giddens land where I now live. Bal. of est. to be sold & money div. bet. my bros. John, Ishmael, William & Kiely Giddens & sisters Margaret Willet, Sarah Willet & Elizabeth Giddens. Bros. John & William Giddens Exrs. Witt: John Smith, Sarah Oldham. p. 105

COLLINS, THOMAS - 22 Aug. 1786 - 29 Oct. 1788 - To son Philby Collins. To son George Collins. Dau. Pheby Fletcher. "to all my grandchildren". Son John Collins resid. legatee & Exr. Witt: David Whelden, William Collins - p. 107

ADDISON, NATHAN - 22 Aug. 1788 - 30 Dec. 1788 - To wife Elizabeth. Dau. Bridget. To son William Bradford Addison. Godson Elijah Addison White. To Zipporah Twiford. Bal. of est. to be sold & after payment of debts residue div. bet. wife Elizabeth, Bridget Addison & William B. Addison. Levin Joynes, Levin White, Robert Twiford Exrs. Witt: John Savage, Daniel Twiford, Caty Addison - p. 117

IRONMONGER, EDWARD - Nunc. - 27 Nov. 1788 - 30 Dec. 1788 - Land to go to John Major Monger, son of George Ironmonger, & for want of heirs to George Monger, father of the said John Major; Sally, his sister, to have his chest & all the money due him from his uncle Cornelius Monger/ Proved by Elizabeth Warrington, Peggy Warrington & Rachel Warrington - p. 119
In order of prob: John Hannaford qualified.

BLOXOM, WOODMAN - 24 Oct. 1788 - 31 Dec. 1788 - To son Jacob Bloxom land & planta. where I now live. Dau. Mary Bloxom. Dau. Esther. To son Joshua Bloxom the land he now lives on. To son Severn Bloxom all the remainder of the land. To son Severn. To Griffith Bishop. To son in law George Young. 6 daus. Elizabeth Riley, Scarburgh Kelly, Comfort Young, Nancy Kelly, Esther Harman & Mary Bloxom & Griffith Bishop resid. legatees. Sons Jacob & Severn Exrs. Witt: John Riley, Sarah Riley, Isaiah Johnson, William Bloxom - p. 129

GARRISON, JONATHAN - 18 Jan. 1789 - 29 Jan. 1789 - To son Archibald Garrison land where I now live cont. 200 A., also the land on Rodgers Island I bought of William Bell. To wife Susannah Garrison. To grandau. Nancy Dunton Garrison 20 L to be deposited in the hands of Dicky Dunton until she arrives at the age of 18 or marries. To sons Abel, George, & Isaiah Garrison. To wife Susannah 1/7 of my personal est., the bal. to be div. bet. my son Isaiah Garrison & grandau.

Peggy Satchell Garrison. Son Archibald Garrison & Isaiah Garrison Exrs. Witt: John Smith, Richard Savage, Joshua Wyatt - p. 132

BLACKSTONE, LEAH - Not dated - 27 Jan. 1789 - To son John Blackstone. Dau. Elizabeth Blackstone. Son Bowman Blackstone. Sebastian Cropper, John Blackstone & John Cropper, Jr., Exrs. - Witt: John Cropper, Jr., Sebastian Cropper, Thomas Cropper - p. 133

GROTEN, AMEY - 6 Feb. 1788 - 27 Jan. 1789 - (Wid. of William Groten) - To son Zorobabel Groten. To son Jonathan Groten. To dau. Amey Milby negro Polly, she to pay Amey Rodgers, dau. of John Rodgers & my grandau., the sum of 12 L. Grandau. Peggy Hutchinson. To son Edmund Groten. Son Zorobabel Groten & Jonathan Groten Exrs. Witt: John Read, John Mears, son of William - p. 134

RODGERS, ZOROBABEL - 2 Aug. 1787 - 28 Jan. 1789 - To wife Matilda Rodgers whole est. during her wid. & then to son Zorobabel Rodgers planta. where I now live & should both he & my son Thomas Wise Rodgers die without heirs then to my godson John Robison Waddy. To son Thomas Wise Rodgers 100 A. which I bought of Parker, & should both he & his bro. Zorobabel die without heirs to my cousin George Radmond Riley, also the land I hold on Cedar Island. To son Zorobabel 21 A. in Penny Swamp. Sons Zorobabel & John Wise Rodgers resid. legatees, & for want of heirs to my sister Elizabeth Waddy's children. Wife Matilda & sons Zorobabel & Thomas Wise Rodgers Exrs. Not witnessed. Proved by Joshua Taylor & Robert Twiford - p. 135

RILEY, RAYMOND - 30 Aug. 1785 - 29 Jan. 1789 - My Island to be sold for payment of debts. Bro. Thomas Riley. To my bro. John Riley's two children. To my sister Sarah Snead's dau. Betsy. To my bro. William Riley's son George R. Riley. Elizabeth Drummond, wife of Richard Drummond & Thomas Custis, son of John Custis resid. legatees. Friends John Custis & Tully Wise Exrs. - Witt: Bridget Giddens, John Custis - p. 138
In order of prob: Proved by John Custis, the other witness being now dead.

LINGO, CALEB - 16 Jan. 1789 - 29 Jan. 1789 - Thomas Aimes & Abraham Taylor Exrs. To Thomas Aimes land where I now live to rent out as long as Joice Lewis lives, & at her death I give the said land to my son Thomas Lingo for life, reversion to my grandson Robert Taylor. To son Thomas Lingo, Dau. Sarah Lingo, dau. Leah Lingo & Robert Taylor the rent of my land as long as Joice Lewis lives. Bal. of est. to be div. bet. Thomas Lingo, Sarah Lingo, Leah Lingo & Robert Taylor. To dau. Susy Lingo 50 A. on the head of Matchpungo & she shall never inherit it as long as Littleton Wyatt lives, & should she die without heirs to be div. bet. my daus. Sarah & Leah. Witt: Levi Nock, Abraham Taylor, Argil Kellam - p. 139

ROBINS, MICHAEL – 28 Feb. 1789 – 29 Apr. 1789 – To wife Leah Robins. To son Michael Robins. To dau. Sarah Robins. Dau. Susanna Robins negro after the death of David Garrett & his wife Bridget Garrett. Son John Robins. Dau. Mary Wilkerson. Grandson John Wilkerson. 5 children resid. legatees. Jesse Wilkerson & Walter Bayne Exrs. Witt: Lisney Gootee, John Morrison, Nehemiah Broghton, Hannah Morrison – p. 142

BLOXOM, WILLIAM – 15 Nov. 1788 – 29 Apr. 1789 – To wife Mary Bloxom 1/3 my land during her wid. To son Richard Bloxom land where I now live & 20 A. purchased of Salathiel Fitchett that he had of Thomas Bloxom, & for want of heirs to my son Nicholas Bloxom. To son Nicholas Bloxom land where my mother in law now lives & for want of heirs to my son Richard Bloxom. To my 2 youngest sons George & Abbott Bloxom nine months each schooling out of my est. Wife Mary & 6 children Naomi Baker, Robert Bloxom, Francis Bloxom, Rebecca Bloxom George Bloxom & Abbott Bloxom resid. legatees. Son Robert & wife Mary Exrs. Witt: Solomon Johnson, Scarburgh Bloxom, Solomon Johnson, Jr. – p. 147

HARMAN, HENRY – 16 Feb. 1789 – 29 Apr. 1789 – To son Littleton Harman 25 A. of my land. To son John Harman the remainder of my land. To wife Sinah Harman. To son George Harman (under age). To dau. Tabitha Harman. To son Thomas Harman. Bal. of negroes to wife for life, reversion to my 3 smallest children, George, Tabitha & Thomas Harman. Wife Sinah & children Littleton, George, Tabitha & Thomas Harman resid. legatees. Wife Sinah, John Harman, Littleton Harman & Thomas Burton Exrs. – Witt: John Spiers, Anne Guy, Patience Savage – p. 150

ELLIOTT, WILLIAM – 25 Apr. 1788 – 26 May 1789 – To bro. Teackle Elliott. To sisters Esther & Margaret Elliott. To Elizabeth Metcalf & Levin Elliott. Bros. & sisters resid. legatees. Teackle Elliott & John Elliott Exrs. Witt: Richard Jones, Thomas O. Bryan, Daniel Sturgis, Teackle Elliott – p. 155

SHIELD, WILLIAM S. – 5 Jan. 1784 – 30 June 1789 – To bro. Peter Shield 150 A. where I now live for life, reversion to his son Aser Shield. To bro. Aser Shield the remainder of my land cont. 150 A. for life, reversion to his son William Sackar Shield. To bro. Aser Shield's children, except William Sackar Shield, & to bro. Peter Shield's children, except Aser Shield, the bal. of my est. Aser Shield, Sr. & Peter Shield Exrs. Witt: Nash Kellam, John Badger, Levin Stewart. – p. 156
In order of prob: Proved by Charles Snead, Levin Stewart who wrote & witnessed the said will since dec., & the other witness thereto being also dead.

KELLAM, JOSEPH – 18 Jan. 1788 – 30 June 1789 – To grandau. Margaret Savage. Whole est. to be div. bet. John Kellam's children,

Mary Savage, Elizabeth Aimes & Keziah Davis, John's children to have their father's part excepting this legacy, remainder to be div. bet. the four. Grandson Robert Savage & Abel West Exrs. Witt: Richard Savage. - p. 157
In order of prob: Robert Savage, Jr. qualified.

JOYNES, REUBEN - 3 Nov. 1785 - 30 June 1789 - To son William Joynes my lands. Dau. Sarah Joynes. Dau. Tabitha Joynes. Dau. Elizabeth Joynes. Son Elias Dunton Joynes. To each of my sons 50 L to be applied to their education. Wife to have the use of whole est. during her wid. Children resid. legatees. Wife Margaret & friend Levin Joynes Exrs. - Witt: Theophilus Nugent - p. 164
In order of prob: Proved by John Cropper, the witness Theophilus Nugent being beyond seas. The Exrs. named in the foregoing will refusing to act Thomas Underhill qualified.

GILCHRIST, GEORGE - 14 Aug. 1789 - 29 Sept. 1789 - All my slaves in Virginia & Maryland to be free at the age of 21. To Polly Rees. To son Andrew Gilchrist (under 21) whole est. & for want of heirs to the children of my sister Bundick - William Bundick Exr. Witt: Levin Walker, Sarah Peck - p. 218

EDWARDS, DAVID - 31 Mar. 1789 - 29 Sept. 1789 - To sons John & Sacker Edwards all my lands. Son John to pay Jacob Edwards 6 L & if he refuse Jacob to take 6 A. of the land I gave him. Sacker Edwards to pay my son David Edwards 6 L or David to take 6 A. of the land I gave him. Dau. Betty Edwards. Dau. Nancy Edwards. Dau. Rachel Edwards. Jacob, David, Betty, Nancy & Rachel Edwards resid. legatees. Sons John & Sacker Exrs. - Witt: Smith Kellam, Zorobabel Edwards, John Edwards - p. 218

SHEARWOOD, JACOB - 9 June 1789 - 29 Sept. 1789 - Wife to have whole est. during her wid. & then lands to be equally div. bet. her 3 children, William, Revel & George Satchell & the bal. of my est. to Levin Satchell. Should either of her said sons die without issue her son Levin to have their part of the land. Wife Anne & Southy Satchell Exrs. Witt: William Arbuckle, Esther Wimbrough, Levin Melson - p. 224

DIX, WILLIAM - 10 May 1789 - 1 Oct. 1789 - To wife Comfort whole est. during her wid. & then to be div. bet. all my children, Thomas, Peggy, William, Tabitha & Esther Dix. House & lot in Drummond-town to be sold to pay debts. Bro. Levin Dix & Edward Arbuckle Exrs. Witt: Peggy Allen, Aires Tatham - p. 226
In order of prob: John Cropper, Jr. qualified.

KELLAM, ABRAHAM - 4 Sept. 1788 - 29 Dec. 1789 - To son Shadrack Kellam 150 A. where I & my said son now live, he to take my bro. Moses Kellam to live with him. Son Levin Kellam resid. legatee. Sons Shadrack & Levin Exrs. Witt: Joshua Taylor, William Taylor - p. 254

HORNSBY, ARGAL - 29 Nov. 1789 - 29 Dec. 1789 - Land to be rented for payment of debts & then I give the same to my son James Hornsby. Bal. of est. to wife for life & then to my 3 daus. Elizabeth, Mary & Margaret. Bro. Zorobable Hornsby & Edward Ker Exrs. Witt: Margaret Budd, Margaret Savage, William Budd - p. 255

COVERLY, NATHANIEL, Sr. - 12 Oct. 1789 - 29 Dec. 1789 - To son Nathaniel Coverly all my lands. 2 sons Nathaniel & Thomas resid. legatees. Witt: John Dix, Sr., Hancock Simpson, James Poulson - p. 256
In order of prob: Nathaniel Coverly qualified.

SHREAVES, WILLIAM - 15 Oct. 1789 - 29 Dec. 1789 - Wife Annabella Shreaves to have the use of 1/2 my planta. during her wid., reversion to my son William Shreaves. To son Jacob Shreaves. Son Teackle Shreaves. Son Stafford Shreaves. Dau. Molly Shreaves. Son Levin Shreaves. Son Thomas Shreaves. If my son Teackle marry with Bridget Dix he to have no part of my est. Children above named resid. legatees. Wife & son Jacob Exrs. Witt: Charles Bagwell, George Savage. Parker Paradice - p. 256

GARRISON, GEORGE - 20 Mar. 1789 - 29 Dec. 1789 - To son Thomas planta. where I now live, being the land I bought of Dennard Turpin & Thomas Upshur, & for want of heirs to my son George Smith Garrison (under age) Son Thomas to pay George Smith Garrison the sum of 8 L per year for five years for the use of schooling. To son James Garrison the planta. I bought of William Metcalf & the land I bought of Patience Taylor, the whole cont. 172 A., & for want of heirs to my son George Smith Garrison., James to pay George Smith Garrison 8 L per year for five years for schooling. To son Abel Garrison planta. I bought of George Oldham, cont. 100 A., & for want of heirs to my son George Smith Garrison, Abel to pay 5 L per year for five years to my son George Smith Garrison for schooling. To son George Smith Garrison grist mill I bought of James Ashby, also 25 A. I bought of John Fosque. To dau. Betty Garrison. Dau. Rachel Floyd 15 L. Rest of my negroes to be div. in 3 parts, dau. Susanna Garrison to have 1/3, dau. Betty Garrison 1/3 & the other 1/3 to my 3 grandchildren Peggy Floyd, Leah Garrison Floyd & Betty Floyd. Bal. of est. to be div. in 5 parts, wife Rachel to have 1 part. dau. Susanna 1 part; Betty 1 part; George Smith Garrison 1 part and the other 1/5 part to be div. bet. my 3 grandaus. above named. Wife & 2 sons Thomas & James Exrs. - Witt: Littleton Wyatt, Benjamin Gunter, Susanna Lingoe - p. 258

TUNNEL, Joseph, Sr. - 27 Nov. 1789 - 30 Dec. 1789 - To wife Rachel whole est. during her wid., then to my son John Tunnell I give 44 A. of land & the remainder to my son Joseph Tunnell, Jr., & should either offer to sell or rent except to the other, they shall loose their rights & the said land to go to Isaiah Tunnell. To son James Tunnell 40 s. Joseph Tunnell, Jr. & John Tunnell Exrs. Witt: Ezekiel Tatham, Aires Tatham, William Stevens - p. 260

CHANDLER, PATIENCE – 7 Feb. 1789 – 30 Dec. 1789 – To dau. Caty Chandler – Son Michael Chandler. Son Littleton Chandler. Son Michael Exr. – Witt: Thomas Parker, Jr. – Mordecai Booth – p. 261 In order of prob: Caty & Littleton Chandler qualified.

STEVENS, JOHN – 21 Apr. 1789 – 31 Dec. 1789 – To wife Mary whole est. for life reversion to all my children. Witt: Daniel Melson, Molly Grinalds – p. 262 In order of prob: Mary Stevens qualified.

ADDISON, JONATHAN – 16 Mar. 1784 – 26 Feb. 1790 – To son John (under age) planta. where I now live, he to pay to my 3 youngest children 15 L each, viz: Esther, Betsy & William, when they come to lawful age or marry. To wife Comfort all her est. not yet received from her mother. Dau. Peggy. Dau. Sarah. Dau. Comfort. Wife & 5 daus. & little son, viz: Peggy, Sarah, Comfort, Esther, Betsy & William resid. legatees. Wife & friend Thomas Underhill Exrs. Witt: Thomas Underhill, Joshua Lawrence, Benjamin Stringer. Codicil: To dau. Susanna that was not born when this will was made 15 L & an equal share with all the rest of my children. Witt: Moses Benston, George Melvin. – p. 267

METCALF, TABITHA – 2 Nov. 1788 – 26 Jan. 1790 – To John & Thomas Metcalf, the sons of MarK Metcalf. To sister in law Sarah Metcalf, wife of Mark Metcalf. John & Thomas Metcalf, sons of Mark Metcalf, resid. legatees. Bro. Mark Metcalf Exr. Witt: Mark Metcalf, Isaiah Bagwell, Tabitha Bundick. – p. 269

WHITE, JACOB – 8 Apr. 1788 – 26 Jan. 1790 – To dau. Joyce White 1 A. at the East corner of my planta. during her single life. To 2 daus. Rachel & Tabitha the use of my planta. where Joshua Melson formerly lived cont. 8 A. during their lives. To Elizabeth Hinman. To Laban White. To son Jacob White my planta. cont. 150 A. 4 children Jacob, Joyce, Rachel & Tabitha resid. legatees. Son Jacob Exr. Witt: Charles Bagwell, Thomas Hickman, Argal Bloxom – p. 271

ELLIOTT, THOMAS, SR. – 19 Nov. 1784 – 27 Jan. 1790 – To wife whole est. during her wid., then to sons John, Thomas, William & Charles Elliott all my lands to be equally div. bet. them. 6 children John, Thomas, William, Charles Elliott, Anne Bell & Hannah Kelly resid. legatees. Sons John & Thomas Exrs. Witt: Zorobabel Rodgers, Fosque Savage. – p. 375

SIMPSON, WILLIAM – 8 Feb. 1785 – 28 Jan. 1790 – To son William land cont. 25 A. till he marries with Betty Prewit, & at his death or marriage to her "I give to his son William the land mentioned to him & his heirs forever". To son Richard 25 A. for life, reversion to his son Southy. To son Charles all the rest of my land cont. 50 A. Bal. of est. to wife (no name) for life or wid. & then to my 2 daus. Anne & Tabitha. Son Charles Exr. Witt: Jacob White, Joakim White,

Charles White. – p. 276
In order of prob: Proved by Joakim White, Jacob & Charles White being since dead.

GARRISON, GEORGE – 19 Mar. 1788 – 23 Feb. 1790 – To wife Sarah whole est. during her wid. to bring up unborn child, then said child (if alive) to have whole est. & should the said child die to be div. bet. Mary Garrison, dau. of Archibald & Phillis Garrison, dau. of Abel, & Peggy Garrison, dau. of Nancy Garrison. Wife & Francis Savage Exrs. Witt: Isaiah Garrison, John Churn – p. 277 In order of prob: The Exrs. named in the foregoing will relinquished their right & Dickie Dunton qualified

STOCKLY, WILLIAM – 15 Feb. 1790 – 23 Feb. 1790 – Wife Peggy sole legatee & Exec. Witt: Zorobabel Kellam, Thomas Garrison, Francis Savage. – p. 278

SHIELD, NICHOLAS – 25 Apr. 1789 – 24 Feb. 1790 – To wife Becky Shield whole personal est. forever, also the use of the land where I live during her wid. & then to my sister Sarah Rodgers, wife of James Rodgers – Witt: Robert Nock, Robert Harris, Becky Riggs – p. 284
In order of prob: Becky Shield qualified.

WHITE, JOACHIM – 24 July 1789 – 26 Feb. 1790 – Whole est. to wife Nancy during her wid. & then to be equally div. bet. my children – Wife Exec. Witt: Southy Satchell, William Satchell – p. 292

NOCK, ELIJAH, Sr. – 15 Mar. 1790 – 29 Apr. 1790 – To son Zadock Nock 50 A. of my planta. where I now live on the North side. To son William Nock the remainder of my land where I live cont. 300 A. To son John Nock 100 A. of marsh on Birds or Johnsons Marshes. To wife Susanna Nock. "Whereas I have heretofore given unto my 3 eldest sons & my dau. Comfort Drummond as much of my estate as I am desirous they should possess" &c. 4 youngest children John, Elizabeth, Littleton & Peggy resid legetees. Son William Exr. Witt: John Teackle, Sr., Solomon Lucas, William Mason – p. 298

DELASTATIUS, MARY – 26 Feb. 1789 – 29 Apr. 1790 – To son James Smith 1/2 of the houses & lot in Horntown, & the other 1/2 to my dau. Elizabeth Delastatius, & for want of heirs to Euphamy Marshall, dau. of Jenepher Marshall. Son George Jackson. Son James Smith Exr. Witt: James McReady, James Smith, John McLean – p. 299

EVANS, ISAIAH – 5 Oct. 1780 – 29 Apr. 1790 – To sister Sarah Evans land given me by the last will of my bro. Zoroball Evans, together with the land I purchased of Maj. William Young & George Savage. To my mother. To bro. William Evans. Mother & sister resid. legatees. Sister Exec. & friend George Corbin to advise & assist her. Witt: George Corbin, John Wise – p. 301
In order of prob: Proved by George Corbin, John Wise the other witness since dec. William Wise & Sarah, his wife, qualified.

BUNDICK, RICHARD – 19 Feb. 1789 – 29 Apr. 1790 – To wife Suke whole est. during her wid., then to my son George Bundick the use of the planta. where I live during his life & then to be sold & the money to be div. bet. such of my children & grand children as shall be alive, viz: son Richard Bundick, John Bundick, William Bundick Abbott Bundick, Justice Bundick, Susanna Bundick, Sally Bundick & my grandchild Richard Bundick, son of my son George. To bro. John Bundick the planta. where he now lives which was conveyed to me by his wife Sarah, which was the widow of James Foster. Grandau. Nancy Garrett, dau. of John Garrett. 3 grandaus., the daus. of Richard Garrett, viz: Tabby Garrett, Betsy Garrett & Thomas Garrett. Wife & son William Exrs. Friend Charles West overseer. Witt: Moses Hinman, William Hinman, son of Moses, John Rigges – p. 306
In order of prob: George Bundick, heir at law to the testator. Luke Bundick & William Bundick qualified.

WARRINGTON, JOHN – 1 June 1790 – Proved 29 June 1790 – Prob: 28 Sept. 1790 – To son John Warrington 50 A. adj. the middle or Gargathy road. To son Thomas all the remaining part of my land. Wife Elizabeth slaves for life, reversion to my 5 younger children, John Burton Warrington, Elizabeth, Susy, Joshua & William Burton Warrington. To son Stephen Warrington & dau. Sally Mears. Dau. Nancy Taylor. Dau. Peggy. Dau. Rachel. Wife & children Peggy, Rachel, Thomas, John, Elizabeth, Susy, Joshua & William resid. legatees. Wife, son Stephen & son in law John Mears Exrs. Witt: William Gibb, Samuel Wise – p. 310

WHITE, GALEN – 8 Dec. 1789 – 29 June 1790 – To sister Lucretia White. To bro. George White. To sister Annabella White. Wife Ann resid. legatee. Wife & bro. Solomon White Exrs. Witt: John Dix, Jr., Levin White – p. 312

SHAY, JOHN – 23 Sept. 1788 – 29 June 1790 – To grandson John Shay Hall 83 A. where I now live. To dau. Mary Hall negroes for life, reversion to my grandaus. Tabitha & Mary Hall. To grandau Margaret Hall. To friend Isaac Warner. Isaac Warner Exr. Witt: John Howard, William S. Christopher, Mary Howard – p. 312

PHILLIPS, JACOB – 15 Mar. 1786 – 29 June 1790 – To wife Pricilla Phillips my land & planta. for life, reversion to my son Mathias Phillips, & for want of heirs to my son Jacob Phillips. Dau. Mary Phillips. Bal. of est. to wife for life then to be div. bet. all my children now living, Peggy, Mary, Jacob, William & Mathias. Sons Jacob & Mathias Exrs. Witt: Joseph Garrett, John Bull, Jr. – p. 313

EVANS, JOHN – 22 Feb. 1790 – 29 June 1790 – To son John Evans land adj. the land where Robert Parks lately lived. The remainder of my land to be sold & the money div. bet. my children Susanna Evans, Rachel Evans, William Evans & Levin Evans. Friends William

Strann & Charles Bagwell Exrs. – Witt: John Parks, Joyce Lewis – p. 314

COPES, SOUTHY – 25 May 1790 – 29 June 1790 – To son Thomas 150 A. adj. Indian Town Branch where I now live. To dau. Comfort Copes 50 A. adj. Sophia Vessells land. Dau. Leah Parker Copes. Dau. Ritter Copes. Dau. Catey Copes. 5 children resid. legatees. Johh Cropper, Jr., Thomas Evans & Southy Satchell Exrs. Witt: Fenwick Fisher, Hancock Copes, Levin Copes – p. 315

COPES, GILES – 11 Mar. 1790 – 27 July 1790 – To grandau Mary Johnson Copes. Grandson Parker Copes. Son Major Copes. Wife Sally Copes. To son Revel Copes the planta. where my father, Robert Copes, formerly lived, adj. the planta. where I now live. To son Giles Copes planta. where I now live. Dau. Polly Copes. Son John Copes. Wife Sally. Sons Revel & Giles & dau. Polly Copes resid. legatees. Son Revel Exr. Witt: Stephen Marshall, Joseph Gillett, John Gillett – p. 320

WATSON, AMERICA – 5 Dec. 1789 – 28 Sept. 1790 – Wife Elizabeth. To John Kennihorn the use of 6 A. of my land during the life of he & his wife on condition that he take my wife & family for 2 years. To son Isaac Watson my land & planta. Wife & Benjamin Stringer Exrs. Witt: George Mears, Coventon Mears, William Taylor – p. 329

DARBY, OWEN – 2 Apr. 1785 – 26 Oct. 1790 – To wife Tamer negroes for life, reversion to my son Owen Darby. To dau. Susanna negro Leah, "and if the said Susanna has no lawful heir of her body then the said negro to her daughter Nancy Boggs". Dau. Tamer. Dau. Zilliah Bunting. Wife & children resid. legatees. Wife & Edmund Bayly, Sr., Exrs. Witt: John Major, Stephen Taylor – p. 343

SPEIRS, LEAH – 25 Aug. 1790 – 27 Oct. 1790 – Whereas there has been an exchange of land by my husband & me in his lifetime with my bro. Levin Bell, he to have my right to the part to the North-east of a line drawn between him & my bro. John Bell-------- and as there has not been a division, I desire that a just division be made, the land sold & the money div. bet. my 7 children, William, Sally, Comfort, John, Mary, Ann & Henry Spiers. Friend Daniel Mifflin Exr. Witt: John Bell, Levin Bell, Daniel Mifflin, Henry Johnson – p. 346

WHITTINGTON, SOUTHY – 3 Aug. 1789 – 27 Feb. 1790 – Whole est. to my wife Ann until my son George arrives at 26 years of age, & I give to my son Arthur Whittington 120 A. adj. the land where I now live, & for want of heirs. or if he should attempt to sell, the land to go to my son George. To son George the remainder of my land; being 280 A. & for want of heirs to my son Arthur. To dau. Elizabeth Nicholson negro Moll & increase, reversion to her two eldest daus. Ann & Arcadia Nicholson. Dau. Hannah Blake. Bal. of est. when my son George arrives to the age of 26 years to be div. bet. my wife Ann & my 3 children George, Gartrude & Arthur Whittington. Wife & son George

Exrs. Witt: Thomas Abbott, William Ewell, Jr., Edward Taylor - p. 347
In order of prob: Proved by William Ewell, Jr., Edward Taylor being since dec.

COLEBURN, WILLIAM - 27 Nov. 1790 - 28 Dec. 1790 - To friend Betty Burton. To son George Coleburn part of my land starting at a red oak at Spiers line. To son William Coleburn the remaining part of my land. Son James Coleburn. Dau. Nancy Coleburn. James & Nancy Coleburn resid. legatees & Exrs. Witt: Thomas Coleburn, Isaac Powell, Benjamin Bradford - p. 350

WEST, BENJAMIN - 6 Dec. 1790 - 28 Dec. 1790 - To Arabella White & Lucretia White. Bal. of est. to my son John West, & should he die under the age of 21 & without issue to my bro. Randall West. Richard Bundick & Levin White Exrs. Witt: Benjamin Parks, Elijah Colony - p. 351

EWELL, WILlIAM - 10 Dec. 1790 - 25 Jan. 1791 - To wife Peggy all the est. I hold by her intermarriage during her wid. & then to my dau. Rebecca Ewell, & for want of heirs to my son William Ewell. To sons Charles & William Ewell the lower part of my planta. from the water upwards. To son Solomon Ewell the head of my land to be cut off from Mathews line with a straight line to Whittington's land, cont. 120 A., & for want of heirs to be div. bet. the surviving bros. Rebecca Ewell resid. legatee. Sons Charles, Solomon & William Exrs. Witt: William Downing, George Whittington, Arthur Whittington - p. 353

MEARS, SOUTHY - 11 Nov. 1790 - 25 Jan. 1791 - To son Armstrit Mears land I bought of John Bayly & land I bought of Richard Mears in the swamp for timber, land where I now live & grist mill to son Armstrit "this land and Mill that came by his mother". Remainder of land bought of Richard Mears to my son Asa Mears. Dau. Mary Mears. Dau. Deborah Mears. Children Armstrit, Mary, Deborah & Asa Mears resid. legatees. Son Armstrit Exr. Witt: Richard Mears, Sarah Mears, Frances Bull - p. 354

JOYNES, MARGARET - 14 Mar. 1787 - 25 Jan. 1791 - To goddau. Margaret Mears, dau. of my bro. John Mears. Bro. Solomon Mears to have whole est. until my son William Joynes comes to 21 years of age to bring him up, give him schooling & pay my debts. Whole est. to son William Joynes, & for want of heirs to my bro. Solomon Mears. To 2 goddaus. "Margaret Mears, Daughter of my Brother John and John Mears, son of William, his Daughter" Solomon Mears Exr. Witt: John Mears, son of Elisha, Sally Mears - p. 356

TATHAM, MICHAEL RICKARDS - 1 Apr. 1790 - 26 Jan. 1791 - To friend George Ker. Should there be any money left after the payment of my debts, the same to be div. bet. Catharine Scarburgh, dau. of Edmund, & Anne Ker, dau. of George. Friend George Ker Exr. Witt: William Seymour, Hugh Ker, Edward Ker - p. 357

LILLISTON, ELIJAH – 9 Jan. 1791 – 26 Jan. 1791 – To Charles West about 4 A. adj. the land the said West bought of Riley Middleton. Wife Elizabeth to have use of whole est. during her life & then I set all my negroes free, & my land to the children of John West, alias Lilliston, who is called John Lilliston, to be div. bet. them "I not knowing their names". Bal. of est. to be sold & after payment of debts to be div. bet. my friends John Custis (Seaside) & Charles West. John Custis (Seaside) & Charles West Exrs. Witt: Thomas Hickman, Sr., George White, Kelly Lewis – p. 358

BROADWATER, WILLIAM – 24 Nov. 1790 – 22 Feb. 1791 – To wife Esther all my land where I now live during her wid., & then to my son Savage Broadwater. My interest in the land where James Warrington now lives to be sold for the payment of my debts. Bro. John Broadwater Exr. Witt: Elias Broadwater, Martha Pitt – p. 361

HORNSBY, ELISHA – 21 Dec. 1790 – 22 Feb. 1791 – To wife Siner Hornsby. To eldest son John Hornsby the whole of my land I now live on, John to pay my 2nd son Elisha 20 L and should he refuse Elisha to have 1/2 the land. Dau. Sally East & youngest son Elisha Hornsby resid. legatees. Friend Jeremiah West, William Hornsby & wife Exrs. Witt: John Teackle, Andrew Turner, Mary Watson – p. 365

ARMITRADER, ARTHUR – 20 Jan. 1791 – 27 Apr. 1791 – To wife Catherine whole est. during her wid. to bring up my child, then to my dau. Ann Burton Armitrader. Bro. Henry Armitrader, Samuel Armitrader & wife Catherine Exrs. Witt: John Spiers, Littleton Trader, Elizabeth Nock – p. 372
In order of prob: Henry Trader & Catherine Trader qualified.

ROBERTS, JOAKIM – 10 Feb. 1791 – 28 June 1791 – To son John Roberts all my land & planta. reserving 3 A. for my 2 daus. Mary Bagwell Roberts & Rachel James Roberts & for Mary Rodgers, dau. of Margaret Kellam, as long as they live single. Son John to keep & maintain my 2 youngest sons, Arthur & Joshua Roberts until they arrive to the age of 16 years. Son John to pay to my 3 sons Francis Roberts, Arthur Roberts & Joshua Roberts 15 L each when they come to lawful age. To wife Sarah Roberts. Wife & children (excepting John) resid. legatees. Wife, John Bradford & Charles Taylor Exrs. Witt: Patrick Casy, Archibald Garrison, Margaret Kellam – p. 377

WYATT, THOMAS – Not dated – 28 June 1791 – To bro, Arthur Wyatt 1/3 of my whole est. To sister Mary Churn 1/3 of my est. To my mother 1/3 of my est. Friends William Wyatt & John Churn Exrs. Witt: John Walker, Jr., John Wilkins – p. 379

BONEWELL, JACOB – 23 Apr. 1791 – 28 June 1791 – After payment of debts est. to be div. bet. my 4 children, subject to the provision which the law makes for my wife. Friend Levin Bloxom Exr. Witt: John Teackle, Sr., Southy Bishop, Esther Bishop – p. 379

BUNTING, TINEY - Nunc - Proved 30 Nov. 1789 - Prob: 28 June 1791 - "That she have the one half of all her estate after paying her just debts to Jonathan Tarp" Proved by Richard Young & Reubin Young - p. 1789
In order of prob: John Cropper, Jr., qualified.

NOCK, BENJAMIN - 23 Dec. 1790 - 26 July 1791 - To son Thomas Nock all the land on the North side of the branch & also a small strip that lies on this side of the branch, & for want of heirs to my son Solomon Nock. To son George Nock the remaining part of my land. Dau. Sophia Nock. Wife to have use of negroes during her wid. Wife Elizabeth, Thomas Nock, Solomon Nock & Sophia Nock resid. legatees. George & Thomas Nock Exrs. Witt: John Speirs, Fletcher Heath, Sarah Clark - p. 381

TATHAM EZEKIEL - 27 Jan. 1791 - 26 July 1791 - To negro woman Mathew, once my slave but now free, 5 A. during her natural life. To dau. Tabitha Tatham whole estate. John Teackle Exr. Witt: Nathan Tunnel, Jediah Tunnel - p. 382
In order of prob: John Teackle relinquished his right & Southy Grinalds qualified.

LATCHUM, GEORGE - 21 Aug. 1790 - 27 July 1791 - Wife Elizabeth to have all the goods she was possessed of before I married her. Daus. Sally & Mathew Latchum. Sister Sarah Latchum. Wife & daus. Sarah & Mathew Latchum resid. legatees. Sacker Parker & Nathaniel Beavans Exrs. Witt: Sinah Foster, Walter Beavans, Margaret Custis Beavins -
"Memo: I hereto annex the ages of my two Daughters that no dispute hereafter may arise, viz: Sally Latchum born'd May 4th 1774, Mathew Latchum January 3rd 1779" - p. 382

NOCK, WILLIAM, Sr. - 12 June 1790 - 27 July 1791 - To son Thomas Nock all my land where I formerly lived, being all which I have title to. Son Benjamin Nock. Sons John, Thomas & Benjamin Nock resid. legatees. Son Thomas Nock Exr. Witt: John Teackle, Sr., John Moore, Delight James - p. 389

BENSTON, MOSES - 15 May 1790 - Partly proved 26 Oct. 1790 - Prob: 27 July 1791 - To son John Savage Benston 168 A. being part of the tract where I now live. To son James Benston 100 A. adj. the above. Wife Matilda. Dau. Rose Bensston. Dau Margaret Benston. Dau. Mary Benston. Dau. Joyce Benston. Wife & 6 children, John, James, Rose, Margaret, Mary & Joyce resid. legatees. Wife Exec. & friend Francis Savage Exr. Witt: John Smith, Richard Savage, Charles Richardson - p. 398

HORNSBY, JOHN - 10 Jan. 1791 - 28 July 1791 - To son Edward Hornsby land which my father gave to my bro. Elisha. Remainder of my land to my son William Hornsby, To son Ebron Hornsby. Wife

Sarah & Zorobabel Hornsby Exrs. Witt: Samuel Galt, Thomas Aimes, Levi Mears - p. 400

KELLAM, ZOROBABEL - 12 Feb. 1791 - 28 July 1791 - To wife Mary negroes for life. Grandson Zorobabel Kellam. Wife to have use of my planta. during her wid., reversion to my son Thomas in case he ever returns home, but if he does not return then to my son John Kellam for life, & then to my grandson Thomas Kellam, son of the said John, said planta. being 130 A. To dau. Sabra Coleburn, wife of Thomas Coleburn, 50 A. adj. the South-east part of Thomas Garrison'a planta. To son John Kellam planta. where he now lives cont. 291 A., also 60 A. on Cedar Island. To grandson Zorobabel 50 A. which I bought of Edmund & Thomas Bradford, adj. his own land in Bradford's Neck. To grandson Ezer Kellam. Wife Mary & son John, son Thomas (if he returns), & dau. Sabra resid. legatees, reserving to my grandson Zorobabel Kellam 1/2 share. Wife, son John & Thomas Coleburn Exrs. Witt: Theophilus Bagg, Babel Savage, Josiah Larke - p. 400

WISE, JAMES - 14 Nov. 1790 - 28 July 1791 - To wife Sarah whole est. for life. To my dau. Esther Sparrow, wife of Richard Sparrow, my riding chair. Children Esther Sparrow, William Wise, James Wise & George Wise resid. legatees. Wife Sarah & Richard Sparrow Exrs. Witt: Parker Paradice, Samuel Sanders - p. 403

ALLEN, MOSES - 26 May 1790 - 27 Sept. 1791 - To wife Elizabeth whole est. for life then to be div. bet. all my children. Wife & son Joseph Allen Exrs. Witt: Ralph Corbin, George Mathews, Keziah Taylor - p. 421

SMITH, GEORGE - 30 Nov. 1788 - 27 Sept. 1791 - To son Custis Smith planta. where I now live. To son Isaac Smith. To dau. Nancy Moore. To dau. Susanna Bunting. To wife Rebecca Smith. 3 youngest sons, George, Elisha & Caleb resid. legatees. Wife Exec. - Witt: Jacob Broadwater, Jonathan Bunting, George Bunting - p. 422

BUNTING, JONATHAN - 12 Mar. 1791 - 27 Sept. 1791 - To wife Betty whole est. during her wid. To son in law Nathaniel Smart. To son Jonathan Bunting. To son George Bunting. Children Severn, Jonathan, Ishmael. William, Thomas & Thamer & Euphamy resid. legatees. Son Severn & wife Betty Exrs. To son George planta. where I now live. Witt: Arthur Watson, John Sickels, Isaac Smith - p. 423

MARSHALL, PATIENCE - 23 June 1790 - 27 Sept. 1791- To dau. Polly Marshall debt due me from Stephen Marshall, Exr. of my dec. husband Peter Marshall. Children Polly Marshall, Betsy Alexander, Rebecca Merril & Esther Fiddeman resid. legatees. To son John Taylor. Son in law Thomas Alexander Exr. Witt: George Corbin, George Johnson - p. 423

RODGERS, JOHN. Sr. - 16 Feb. 1791 - 27 Sept. 1791 - To wife the use of my land for the term of 7 years to bring up my small children.

To son James Rodgers 1/2 my land & the other 1/2 to my son John & for want of male heir to John to fall to Laban, his bro., & so from Laban to Daniel & George. Dau. Betty Philips. Dau. Ann Rodgers Forten. Dau. Peggy Rodgers. To James Cruthers. To William West. Bal. of est. to be div. bet. wife & own children that the land is not left to. "Peggy and James Cruthers and William West is to have after their mother's death their Portion falls to them, the first children, that is Betty and Laban and Ann Rodgers is to have their part at my death". Son John Rodgers & wife (no name) Exrs. Witt: Severn East, Zoro: Chandler, Elizabeth Tunnel - p. 424
In order of prob: Elizabeth Rodgers & John Rodgers qualified.

BEAUCHAMP, John, formerly of Accomack, but now of Somerset County, Maryland - 27 Apr. 1791 - Proved in Maryland 31 May 1791 - Admitted to record in Accomack 28 Sept. 1791 - To wife Mary Ann Beauchamp 15 1/4 A. in Accomack which I purchased of John Bell. To daus. Peggy & Leah Beauchamp, to unborn child & to my said wife all the remainder of my lands in Accomack County during the wid. of my wife, & at her death or marriage to be div. bet. my 3 said children. Wife & Thomas Benston Exrs. Witt: Samuel Smith, Amely Benston, William Curtis. - p. 437

RILEY, WILLIAM - 18 Sept. 1785 - 28 Sept. 1791 - To dau. Sarah Riley planta. in the woods during her single life, reversion to my son John Riley. To son John land & marsh where I now live, except 200 A. in Mesongo, said 200 A. to be div. bet. my grandchildren. To grandau. Sarah Evans. To grandchildren Sally Mason, Zadock Mason, Susanna Mason, William Mason & Mary Riley Mason, John Mathews & Annie Mathews. Son John, dau. Sarah & grandchildren already named resid. legatees. Son John & dau. Sarah Exrs. Witt: William Young, Isaiah Johnson - p. 439

BEAVANS, WILLIAM - 24 Sept. 1789 - 25 Oct. 1791 - Land now in the possession of my mother to be div. bet. my 2 sons Thomas & William Beavans at my mother's death. 3 children Thomas, William & George resid. legatees (except what the law gives my wife (no name)) Friend John Gillett Exr. Witt: William Marshall, John Watson - p. 446

BELL, OLIVER - 22 Nov. 1781 - 25 Oct. 1791 - To son William Bell (under 14) all my land where I now live, being 50 A., & for want of heirs to my 4 children Elizabeth, Mary, Rachel & Sally. Wife Elizabeth to have use of land & personal est. to being up my children. Wife Exec. Witt: Solomon Johnson, Charles Broadwater, Ezekiel Howard - p. 447

TEACKLE, ARTHUR - 12 Jan. 1791 - Partly proved 27 Apr. 1791 - Prob: 2 Dec. 1791 - To wife Elizabeth during her wid. my interest in the lands where my father & myself now reside, & all my personal est. to raise & educate my children, then the land to be div. bet. my 2 sons James Justice & Edwin at the direction of my bro. John Teackle & my friend George Parker. To sons James Justice & Edwin, daus. Harriott & Anne Parker Teackle, the residue of my est. Bro. John Teackle & friend George Parker Exrs. Witt: Levin Teackle, Ann Teackle, Nancy Wharton, John Teackle, Sr. - p. 448

COLE, PETER - 29 Oct. 1791 - 27 Dec. 1791 - To my two half brothers John & James Cole all my interest in & to the reversion or remainder of my lands which my father holds for life, to be equally div. bet. them at his death, John Cole to have that half which lies next to Kegotank Branch. To William Cowley. To my half sister Sally Cole. Father Major Cole Exr. Witt: John Teackle, Major Cole - p. 449
In order of prob: Major Cole, Sr. qualified.

SAVAGE, GEORGE - 4 Dec. 1791 - 27 Dec. 1791 - To sister Ann Bunting 40 A. adj. Henry Wright's planta. To son Zorobabel Savage 100 A. adj. the above. To eld. son Robert Savage the remainder of my land. 4 daus. Elizabeth, Mary, Sarah & Rachel Savage resid. legatees. Bro. Richard R. Savage & Jacob Broadwater Exrs. Witt: Ezekiel Young, Thomas Young, Griffin Savage - p. 450

FEEHARY, JAMES - 29 Apr. 1791 - 27 Dec. 1791 - To wife Rachel whole est. for ever. Friend Zorobabel Hornsby & wife Rachel Exrs. Witt: Walter Jameson, John O. Twiford, Teackle Heath - p. 450

SAVAGE, WILLIAM HOPE - 23 Nov. 1791 - 31 Jan. 1792 - To wife Ann Savage use of land & whole est. during her wid. to bring up my children, then to my son George 50 A. over the Gully next to Hampton Hickman's - The remainder of my land this side the Gully next to my bro. George Savage to my son William Savage. Daus. Sally, Annabeller & Peggy Savage resid. legatees. Bro. George Savage Exr. Witt: William Young, Thomas Young - p. 451
In order of prob: Richard Rodgers qualified.

FINNEY, WILLIAM - 13 May 1789 - 31 Jan. 1792 - To son William planta. where I now live cont. 300 A., he to convey the land in the woods which comes by his mother to my dau. Sarah Finney. To dau. Sarah land in the woods to be conveyed to her by my son William when he comes to age, cont. 125 A. & should he refuse to convey said land Sarah to have the land before given William. Bal. of est. to be div. bet. son William & dau. Sarah after my wife's dower is laid off. Friends Charles West, John Abbott Bundick & Richard Jacobs Exrs. Witt: George Finney, William Parker, John Abbott Bundick - p. 452

BEAVANS, NATHANIEL - 29 Dec. 1786 - 31 Jan. 1792 - To son William Henry Beavans planta. where I now live, 138 A. where John Fields now lives, 100 A. called swamp planta., & 50 A. where John Small lives at Messongoes, also my right & title to Birds Marsh, the above land being devised me by my father & fell to me by my mother, also negro which fell to him by his grandmother Margaret Teackle. To son Walter Beavans planta. & marsh left him by his uncle John Beavans. To dau. Tabitha Custis Scarburgh Beavans. To dau. Margaret Curtis Beavans. Children to be paid out of my est. their respective parts left them by their grandmothers Margaret Teackle & Mary Beavans. Daus. Margaret & Tabitha resid. legatees. Son William Henry Beavane & friend Thomas Evans, Esq. Exrs. Not witnessed. Proved by John Wise & William Gibb – p. 459

DARBY, TAMER – 16 Jan. 1791 – 1 Feb. 1792 – To dau. Zillah Bunting my part of the riding chair that is between myself & Kendal Bunting. Dau. Susanna Martin. Dau. Tamer Bunting. Grandau. Nancy Darby. Son Owen Darby. Friend Kendal Bunting Exr. Witt: Levin Bunting, West Kellam – p. 467

ASHBY, JOHN – 16 Jan. 1792 – 1 Feb. 1792 – To wife Rachel that part of my land I bought of Elisha Mears for life, negroes &c. then personal property to be div. bet. all my children, John, Sam, Ezekiel, William, David, Elizabeth Ashby & Sally Aimes. To son John all the lands that joins the land of Francis Downing, and the land I lent his mother after her dec. To sons Sam Ashby & Ezekiel Ashby the remaining part of my land to be div. bet. them. Sally Aimes, William Ashby, David Ashby & Elizabeth Ashby resid. legatees. John Ashby Exr. Witt: Elisha Mears, Fenwick Fisher, David Ashby – p. 468

RICHARDSON, WILLIAM – 30 Nov. 1791 – 1 Feb. 1792 – To son John Richardson planta. where I now dwell. To dau. Peggy Richardson. To son William Richardson. To dau. Elizabeth Richardson. Wife Tabitha Richardson. Wife & 3 small children, Tabitha, Peggy, William & Elizabeth Richardson resid. legatees. Wife & son John Exrs. Witt: Elisha Mears, John Ashby, Dennis Tignal – p. 469

HARMAN, BAYLY – 10 Feb. 1792 – 28 Feb. 1792 – To son George Harman land & planta. & marsh adj. Nathaniel Bell's land & near Matchpungo Creek. To son William Harman all the residue of my land. Should my son William refuse to let my son George have the 75 A. that his grandfather William Harman gave him a deed for, then George to have 75 A. out of the land I have given my son William. Bal. est. to be div. bet. wife Mary Harman, William Harman, George Harman & Rachel Fitzgerald. Sons William & George Exrs. Witt: John Smith, William Mears, Patrick Harman, Kendall Wyatt – p. 474.

UPSHUR, LEAH – 26 Nov. 1790 – 5 Apr. 1792 – (Wid. of Arthur – p. 623) To 2 daus. in law Elizabeth & Ann Upshur. To grandson Caleb Upshur. To grandau. Juliet Upshur. Grandau. Nancy Upshur. Grandson Abel Upshur. To Caleb Harrison. Son Littleton Upshur resid. legatee & Exr. Witt: John Nathaniel Harden, Ann C. Wise – p. 522

GILLETT, JOHN – 19 May 1790 – 25 Apr. 1792 – To bro. James Gillett all my lands, water mill &c. where I now live, also the swamp land which my father bought of Custis Rodgers. 100 A. on Assateague Inland to be div. bet. my bros. Ayres Gillett & Joseph Gillett. To nephew William McMaster planta. where Joseph Baldwin formerly lived that I bought of Daniel Welburn. To bro. in law George Gillett planta. where William Paradise formerly lived that I bought of Daniel Welburn. Bal. of est. to be div. bet. my bro. in law William Gillett & my sister in law Tabitha Gillett. Bro. Joseph & bro. in law Samuel McMaster Exrs. Witt: Hannah Taylor Samuel Henderson, David Whelden, Thomas W. Burdett – p. 530

PARKS, CHARLES – 3 Apr. 1792 – 25 June 1792 – To wife Sally the use of my whole est. till my children come to lawful age or marry. To son John Parks planta. where I now live & for want of heirs to my 2 daus. Elizabeth & Peggy Parks. Wife to have her 1/3 for life. The 25 A. bought of Mr. Waggoman to be sold & the money div. bet. my 2 daus. Should all my children die without issue est. to be div. bet. my wife Sally Parks & my sister Elizabeth Massy. Wife Exec. – Witt. Walter Bayne, Joseph Waggoman, John Massy – p. 539

BELL, GEORGE – 26 Nov. 1791 – 25 June 1792 – To Jedediah, son of my bro. William Bell, whole est., real & personal, except the following legacy: To Molly Turner, dau. of Atha Turner, a love begotten child, 20 L. Bro. William Bell & friend Francis Savage Exrs. Witt: William Gibb, John Kellam, Thomas Nere, Joshua Cutlar – p. 540

DARBY, BENJAMIN – 12 Nov. 1791 – 26 June 1792 – To wife Polly my planta. for the term of 16 years & all personal est. to bring up my children, then personal est. to be div. bet. my 2 daus. Ann Crippen Darby & Esther Darby & wife Polly. To son Edmund Darby that part of my land where my dwelling house stands, also my grist mill. All the remaining land to my son Shadrack Darby. Wife Polly & Major Colony Exrs. Witt: William Mears (son of John), Major Colony, Jr., Levin Biggaby – p. 555

DAVIS, AGNES – 3 Aug. 1790 – 26 June 1792 – To bro. William Davis' children, Elizabeth, David & Nancy the 50 L cash left me by my father & now in the estate of my bro. William. To bro. Thomas Davis. To niece Peggy Davis. Niece Elizabeth Davis. Niece Nancy Davis. Bro. Thomas Davis & my bro. William's children resid, legatees. Bro. Thomas & sister in law Sarah Davis Exrs. Witt: Joseph Matthews, William Hinman – p. 556

HOFF, CATY – 2 July 1791 – 26 June 1792 – To Nancy Copes, my sister's dau. To Peggy Copes, my sister's dau. To Sophia Vessels. To sister Peggy Copes. To my sister Nancy Bundick's children. To Levin Copes, son of Peggy. Peggy Copes, Nancy Copes, Levin Copes & Savage Copes, my sister's children, resid. legatees. Thomas Copes Exr. To Elizabeth Broadwater. Witt: John Parker, Beverly Copes – p. 559

BEECH, JOHN – 5 Oct. 1737 – 26 June 1792 – To wife Amey Beech whole est. during her wid. To son Frederick Beech my land & planta. where I now live, he to find his sister Rachel Beech a home during her life. To son Isaiah Beech. 3 children Leah Watson, Isaiah Beech & Rachel Beech resid. legatees. Son Isaiah Exr. Witt: David Ashby,

Robert Guy, John Ashby, John Ashby, Ezekiel Ashby. - p. 563

SAVAGE, JOHN - 30 Mar. 1792 - 31 July 1792 - To wife Margaret my Metompkin planta. & 10 negroes in lieu of dower in the rest of my land & slaves during her wid, she to bring up & educate my children. To son William Savage. To son Thomas Waters Savage. To son George Savage. To son Severn Eyre Savage. To son Charles Savage. To son Joseph Savage. To dau. Anne Savage. Bal. of est., real & personal, to be sold except the planta. I bought of James Henry, which I leave to bring up my children until the youngest arrives to the age of 18 years, & then to be equally div. bet. all my children. Wife Margaret Exec. Friends John Stringer of Northampton & George Waters of Somerset County, Maryland, Exrs. Witt: William Gibb, William Bowman, George Corbin, Tully Snead, William Parker - p. 593
In order of prob: 26 Oct. 1801 - On the motion of Margaret A. Custis, Adm. with the will annexed, granted her on the estate of John Savage, dec. William Custis, Thomas Custis & John Custis, (S.S.) sec.

AMES, JOHN - 30 Dec. 1791 - 25 Sept. 1792 - I lend to Elizabeth Ames all my land & negroes, she to hold the same until Babel Ames comes to the age of 20 years, & then I give my land to my bro. Babel Ames. Two sisters Nancy Kellum & Elizabeth Ames resid. legatees. Elizabeth Ames & bro. Babel Ames Exrs. Witt: Thomas Bayly, Laban Johnson, Richard Mears - p. 617

TAYLOR, JACOB - 2 Feb. 1792 - 25 Sept. 1792 - To wife Nancy Taylor. To son William Taylor. To dau. Polly Taylor. To son Sackar Taylor. Nancy Taylor, my wife, resid. legatee. Witt: Isaiah Mears, Levin Hickman - p. 639

FEEHARY, RACHEL - 15 May 1792 - 30 Oct. 1792 - To bro. John Downing & cousin Elizabeth Hornsby Savage. To uncle Zorobabel Hornsby. To aunt Sarah Hornsby. To sister Peggy Mears. Cousin Rachel Marshall. Cousin Rachel Mears. Uncle Zorobabel Hornsby Exr. Witt: William Davis, Samuel Ashby, Major Lecatte - p. 643
In order of prob: Robinson Savage qualified.

BROADWATER, CALEB - 8 July 1792 - 30 Oct. 1792 - 10 A. now in the possession of Elias & Esther Broadwater to be sold to pay my debts. Wife Anne Broadwater Exec. Witt: Elias Broadwater, William Sterling.

TURLINGTON, ANN - 15 Jan. 1788 - 30 Oct. 1792 - To dau. Nancy Tignal whole est. Abel Savage & John Savage, son of Abel Savage, sole Exrs. Witt: George Taylor, Sophia Taylor, James Coleburn - p. 645
In order of prob: Isaac Powell qualified.

CONQUEST, WILLIAM - 19 Sept. 1792 - 30 Oct. 1792 - To wife negro Isaac for life, reversion to my son James. To dau. Peggy Conquest. Dau. Nancy. Dau. Keziah. Wife (no name) & children resid. legatees.

William Conquest & Thomas Jones Exrs. Witt: Thomas Jones, Daniel Godwin, William Conquest - p. 646

KELLAM, MATILDA - 8 Aug. 1792 - 30 Oct. 1792 - To son Andrew Stewart. To dau. Elizabeth. To dau. Sarah. To dau. Nancy. To son Scarburgh. To dau. Susanna. To son Charles Kellam. To son James. Sons Charles & James resid. legatees. Son Charles Kellam Exr. Witt: Keziah Kellam, Abel Kellam, John Walker, Sr. - p. 655

LUCAS, WILLIAM RICHARDSON - 6 Oct. 1790 - 30 Oct. 1792 - To bro. Luck (Luke) land beq. me by my father Jabez Lucas where my mother now lives, cont. 41 1/2 A. Eli Shay Exr. Witt: William Downing, William Hutson, Isaac Warner - p. 655

DRUMMOND, ROBERT - 29 Oct. 1792 - 25 Dec. 1792 - To wife Anariter Drummond the use of all my lands during her wid., reversion to my son George Drummond. To son Henry Drummond. To dau. Elizabeth Drummond. To dau. Elisha Drummond. To dau. Rosey Drummond. To dau. Nancy Drummond. To son James Drummond. To son Richard Drummond. To dau. Peggy Drummond. Grandchildren Solomon & Betsey Melson. To wife 1/3 of personal est. in lieu of dower. Dau. Sarah Garrat. Children George, Sarah, Elizabeth, Henry, Elisha, Rosey, Nancy, James, Richard & Peggy Drummond & Solomon & Betsy Melson resid. legatees. Wife Anariter, George & Henry Drummond Exrs. Witt: William Drummond, Smith Melson, Jr., Thomas Johnson - p. 656

SHARLOCK, JOHN - 27 Mar. 1792 - 28 Jan. 1793 - To dau. Betsy Bell. Dau. Charlotte Sharlock. To Fanny Carmine my land from Fosters Bars through the Waterhole to Bonniwell's line, all that part to Bell's Bridge for life, but in case she suffer her sister Tabitha Carmine to dwell with her more than one month at a time to forfeit the said land. Dau. Betsy Bell to have all the land Eastward of the land that William Bell purchased of William Snead, together with the reversion of the land given Fanny Carmine. Bal. of est. to be sold & after payment of debts to be div. bet. my 2 daus., Betsy Bell & Charlotte Sharlock. Levin Joynes & William Gibb Exrs. Witt: Josi: Larke, John Guy - p. 657

BAYLY, RICHARD - 2 Apr. 1792 - 29 Jan. 1793 - To wife Mary during her wid. land at the head of Craddock Creek until my son Thomas Bayly arrives at the age of 18 years, & then to my son Thomas. To dau. Mary Bayly. Son Thomas & dau. Mary resid. legatees. Friends Americus Scarburgh & Bro. Edmund Bayly Exrs. - Witt: Elizabeth Bayly, Jane Herbert, Rachel Watson - p. 684

HICKMAN, RICHARD - 16 Dec. 1791 - 29 Jan. 1793 - To son William planta. where I now live "And I leave him no part of my est. if Daniel should die under age" To sister in law Rebecca Bird. To son Thomas. Son Daniel resid. legatee, he to be free at 18. Son Thomas Exr. Witt: Parker Barnes, Santer Evans - p. 695

In order of prob: William Hickman qualified, Thomas relinquishing his right.

DIX, AMAZIAH (Azariah?) – 20 Feb. 1790 – 26 Feb. 1793 – To wife Scarburgh planta. where I live to bring up my children, or until my son John is old enough to be bound out or get his own living. To eldest son Neddy Dix 2/3 of my land during his mother's life & then to have the remaining 1/3. To dau. Grace Dix. Daus. Patience & Esther Dix & son John Dix resid. legatees. Bro. Levi Dix & friend John Poulson Exrs. Witt: John Poulson – Levi Dix – p. 698

TOWNSEND, JOHN – 9 Feb. 1793 – 30 Apr. 1793 – All my lands that I bought of Thomas Cropper to be sold. To my wife, after the payment of debts, all the remainder of my est. during her life to bring up my children & then to be div. bet. all my children. Wife Peggy Exec. – Witt: John Burton, Joseph Powell, William Cowley – p. 711
In order of prob: Peggy Townsend qualified.

SELBY, WILLIAM, Sr. – 9 Nov. 1792 – 30 Apr. 1793 – The house & lot I sold to Sally Gladdin, wife of John Gladdin, Sr., to contain 1 A. To dau. Tabitha Tunnel during her life the planta. I bought of Michael Robins & the planta. I bought of Joseph Tilghman, reversion to my grandson Charles Tunnel of 150 A., being part of the land purchased of Joseph Tilghman, & to Grandson William Tunnel the planta. purchased of Michael Robins & 65 A. of the land purchased of Tilghman. To son William Selby 1/2 the Mills & land I hold with Col. George Corbin, also during his life the planta. where I now live, also the marsh lands I purchased of John Milligan & Mrs Holden, & then to my grandson George Selby after the death of his father William. To son William the planta. I lately purchased of Thomas Custis, Esq., with all my right, title & int. to the lands on Chincoteague Island, also the planta. I purchased of Francis Houston during his natural life, & then to my grandson Gorey Waugh Selby after the death of his father, William. To grandau. Molly Tunnel. Son William resid. legatee & Exr. Witt: Walter Bayne, Sally Bayne – p. 712

BLOXOM, WILLIAM, Sr. – 26 Mar. 1792 – 30 Apr. 1793 – To son Azariah Bloxom part of land bought of Thomas Bayly cont. 60 A. To son Solomon Bloxom part of same tract cont. 55 A. To son Levin Bloxom the remainder of said tract, together with the land purchased of John Evans cont. 130 A. To dau. Rachel Bloxom. To 3 sons Azariah, Levin & Solomon 10 A. purchased of John Fitchett. To dau. Mary Ann Bloxom. To dau. Nanny Bloxom. To dau. Sally Bloxom. Bal. of est. to wife Sarah in lieu of dower during her wid. & then to be div. bet. my children Azariah, Levin, Solomon, Rachel, Mary Ann, Nanny & Sally. Sons Azariah & Levin Bloxom Exrs. Witt: James Duncan, Sr., James Duncan, Jr, Meshack Duncan – p. 713

LEATHERBURY, GEORGE – 2 Mar. 1793 – 24 June 1793 – To wife Ann Leatherbury whole est. during her wid. & then to my son Perry Leatherbury, & for want of issue to my wife all my lands during her life, & then to descend to my goddau. Elizabeth Leatherbury for life, reversion to her bro. Samuel Leatherbury. Wife Anne Exec. Witt: Noah Belote, William Leatherbury, Robert Parker – p. 748

PARKER, THOMAS, son of Clement – 5 Apr. 1793 – 24 June 1793 – The land that falls to me by the death of my bro. Clement Parker to be sold & after paying 1/4 of his expenses for his last sickness & funeral expenses in Philadelphia, the bal. to be applied toward the payment of my debts & a bond due to the Exr. of George Parker, dec., which George Poulson is liable for, being my security. Friend John Custis (B.S.) Exr. Witt: John Finney, Sarah Smith – p. 748

SAVAGE, LITTLETON, Sr. – 4 Dec. 1792 – 24 June 1793 – To son John. To son Thomas. To son Jacob. To dau. Peggy. To Betty Powell. Son John Exr. Witt: Josi: Larke, John Fosque, William Only – p. 749

BAGWELL, CHARLES – 26 Aug. 1792 – 24 June 1793 – To son Charles Bagwell the use of the planta. I bought of James Arbuckle with my two mills for life, & then to be equally div. bet. all his children, & should they die before 21 years without issue then the land on the North side of Little Back Creek, alias Timber Creek, to be div among the children of my son in law Thomas Evans, namely John, Ned & Thomas, & all the land on the South side of the said Creek, with my 2 mills, to be div. bet. the children of Sally Cropper Mears. To negro Daniel his freedom & 6 A. in Robins Hole for life. To Esther Carter 1 A. in Robins Hole where she now lives. To Sally Cropper Mears all the rest of my land in Robins Hole including the land given Daniel after his dec., for the term of her natural life, reversion to her son Revil Mears. Son Charles resid. legatee. Son in law Thomas Evans, son Charles Bagwell & Thomas Evans' 3 sons, John, Ned & Thomas Exrs. Not witnessed. Proved by John Burton & Edmund Bayly, Jr. – p. 751

BAYLY, JOHN, of Ocoahannock Creek – 22 July 1792 – 29 July 1793 – To son Charles Land & mill to be sold to pay my debts & bal. div. bet. my 2 children Mary & Charles. Isma Bayly & Christopher Satchell Exrs. Not witnessed – Proved by John Martin & William Mears – p. 755

CUSTIS, HENRY – 3 Nov. 1792 – Partly proved 4 June 1793 – Prob: 30 July 1793 – To nephew Thomas Abbott. To nephew James Justice Abbott. To wife Matilda Custis all my slaves for life & then to go free. To wife whole est. for life & then to be sold & the money div. bet. the children of my sister Anne West & my sister Sarah Grinalds. Wife & friend John Cropper Exrs. Witt: Levin Core, Peggy Allen. p. 757

HEATH, TEACKLE – 30 Mar. 1793 – 31 July 1793 – To wife land bought of Robert Twiford during her wid. & then to be sold & the money div. bet. my 3 children, William, Arody & Teackle Heath.

Personal est. to be sold & money div. bet. wife & 3 children. Wife
(no name) & friend John Read, Sr. Exrs. Witt: Edmund Heath,
Thomas B. Bradford, Mary Calyhann – p. 765
In order of prob: Wife Jamimah qualified.

ARLINGTON, JOHN – 9 Feb. 1791 – 30 Sept. 1793 – To son John
Arlington. To grandson Thomas Bagwell Arlington 1/2 the bal. of my
est. to my son John Arlington, & the other 1/2 to my dau. Sarah Meers
during her life, reversion to her children. Neighbor Levin Joynes Exr.
Witt: William Boggs, James Badger – p. 767

BLOXOM, RICHARD – 1 Feb. 1786 – Partly proved 31 Oct. 1786 –
Prob: 30 Sept. 1793. To wife Margaret Simpson Bloxom whole est
during her wid. then the land where I live to be div. bet. my 2 sons
Major Simpson Bloxom & Richard Bloxom. (Richard under 21) 4 chil-
dren Major, Siner, Nancy & Johannah Stacks Bloxom resid. legatees
(all under age). Wife Margaret Simpson Bloxom, Major Bloxom &
Johanna Stacks Bloxom Exrs. Witt: Solomon Johnson, Joseph Kelley,
Josua Bell – p. 773

POWELL, PETER – 22 Sept. 1793 – 28 Oct. 1793 – To wife Amey all
my negroes to bring up my children, & at her death or marriage to be
div. bet. my children James Powell & unborn child. Wife & children
resid. legatees. Bro. Nicholas Powell Exr. – Witt: William Stran,
Richard Dix, Ritter Melson, Isaac Dix – p. 779

CORBIN, GEORGE – 24 Sept. 1793 – 29 Oct. 1793 – To dau. Agnes
Drummond Ker whole est. provided if she have a son that my son in
law John Shepherd Ker call such son George Corbin, to which said son
I will my Chingoteague planta., Island & swamp land. To friend
Catherine Scott for life my planta. at Onancock, & my dau. Agnes
Drummond Ker to pay her 50 L annually. To Catherine Parker 25 L
annually as long as she continues in Mrs Scott's family. To friend
Revil Horsey & wife, of Somerset. To John Read & William Hill, my
tenants in Horntown. To Mrs Barbary Knox. To nephew John Wel-
burne. To George Corbin, son of my cousin Ralph Corbin, Jr., my
planta. on Pocomoke, being the lands that were my grandfathers. To
William & Drummond Welburne lands purchased of William Broad-
water's Exrs., also 50 A. purchased of Ralph Corbin & my 1/2 of the
lands & Mills held in partnership with William Selby. Nephew John
Cropper & son in law John Shepherd Ker Exrs. Witt: George Ker,
Peter Delastatius, Samuel Henderson.
Codicil: The lands directed to devolve on my grandson to be called
George Corbin to include all the lands on Chingoteague, Assateague &
Wallops Islands, the lands bought of Risdon Moore & Scarburgh, his
wife, being 37 1/2 A., the lands on Wolf's Ridge, being 150 A., also
Joynes cont. 100 A. & no other – p. 782

WEST, JEREMIAH – 16 Oct. 1791 – 29 Oct. 1793 – To son William
West. To son John West. To dau. Polly. Bal. of est. to 6 children,
Polly, William, Fanny, Sarah, Ann & John. John Read & bro. John

West Exrs. Witt: Andrew Turner, Elisha Hornsby, Tabitha Turner – p. 785

DUNTON, GEORGE – 24 Sept. 1792 – 25 Nov. 1793 – To son Isaac land where I now live. Bal. of est. to 3 daus. Leah, Caty & Nancy. Should my wife be with child said child to share equally with my 3 daus. Wife to have use of whole est. to support my children during her wid. Friend Christopher Satchell & bro. Carvey Dunton Exrs. Witt: Thomas Parker, Edmund Scarburgh, Charles Scarburgh – p. 786

JOHNSON, AZARIAH – 27 Oct. 1793 – 30 Dec. 1793 – To son John Johnson all my lands, & for want of heirs to my son William Johnson, & for want of heirs to my son Caleb Johnson. Should my 3 sons die without issue to my 3 daus. Sally Ardis, Betsy Copes & Peggy Johnson. Bal. of est. to wife Leah Johnson for life then to my 2 sons, William & Caleb Johnson & my 3 daus. above named. Wife Leah Exec. Friend William Marshall to assist her. Witt: Solomon Marshall, Thomas Boniwell, Sebastian Delastatius – p. 791

WYATT, JOSHUA – 10 Dec. 1793 – 30 Dec. 1793 – Whole est. to wife during her life or wid., then my land to my son William Wyatt, he to pay my son Ismey Wyatt 50 L & to my son John Wyatt 50 L & to my son Joshua 50 L, & should he refuse the land to be sold & the money div. bet. my 4 sons, William, Ismey, John & Joshua. Bal. of est. to be div. between my 4 sons & my 4 daus, Tamer Savage, Peggy Floyd. Joyce Joynes & Nancy Wyatt. Wife & sons William & Ismey Wyatt Exrs. Witt: John Smith, Richard Savage, Archabel Garretson – p. 791 (See page 483.)

LONG, SAMUEL – 10 Oct. 1793 – 30 Dec. 1793 – To wife Margaret 1/3 of my land during her life. To son William Coleburn Long all my lands Negro Edmund to be sold, & out of the proceeds I give my dau. Esther Long 30 L in lieu of 30 L left her by her uncle Jacob Bradford, & the bal. to be div. bet. my 4 children, Esther, Mary, John & Leannah. To my bro. John Long's 3 children Elizabeth, Sarah & Samuel Long 6 L each Maryland money. Children resid. legatees. Friends William Floyd, Frank Savage & Thomas Bagwell Exrs. Witt: Peggy Bagwell, William Parramore, Peter Shield, James Wharton, Joseph Lisle – p. 794

TURLINGTON, JAMES – 31 Aug. 1792 – 30 Dec. 1793 – To wife Ann. To dau. Ann Parker. To grandchildren William Custis Savage & Peggy Savage. To son James Turlington. To dau. Comfort Martin. To grandau. Betty Martin. To grandson James Martin. To dau. Catharine Watson. To son Arthur Turlington. To dau. Margaret Turlington. Wife Ann & children Catherine Watson, Arthur & Margaret Turlington & James Turlington resid. legatees. Wife Ann Exec. Witt: John Savage, George Scarburgh, Leah Savage – p. 795

FEDDERMAN, MESHACK – 20 Nov. 1793 – 31 Dec. 1793 – To son Joseph Feddeman planta. where I now live. To grandson Henry

401

Feddeman at 21 100 A. at the west end of my land, 3 daus. Mary, Betty & Ann to have use of said 100 A. until my grandson is 21, & should he die before then I give the land to his bro. William, To son William Feddeman the bal. of the land where I now live, together with all the land I bought of George Corbin. To dau. Mary Feddeman 50 A. purchased of Joseph Gillett & William Selby. To dau. in law Ester Feddeman negro Alexander for 10 years for the support of her children, & then to my grandson William Feddeman. 3 daus. above named resid. legatees. Sons Joseph & William Exrs. Witt: Mary Melvin, John Login, Nathaniel Benson - p. 799

WINDOW, VIOLATER - ___ ___ - 1793 - 31 Dec. 1793 - To John Addison White, son of Levin & Bridgett, my small piece of land that I call mine, reversion to Elijah Addison White. Son John Purnell Outten. Not witnessed. Proved by Ephraim Watson, William White & Betsy Parker - p. 800
In order of prob: The foregoing will contested by John Purnell Outten, heir at law to the testatrix, but by the Court admitted to record.

GUNTER, EDWARD - 19 Jan. 1793 - 31 Dec. 1793 - To son Labin Gunter all my lands, not disturbing my son Steven in the land he now holds during the life of the said Steven, son Labin to pay at the end of 5 years to my grandson Stephen Gunter, son of Levin, 5 L; 5 L to my grandson Steven Gunter, son of Stephen at the end of 7 years; 5 L to my grandson Purnal Lurton, son of Labin Lurton at the end of 7 years. 1/3 of the bal. of my est. to my dau. Mary Gunter, 1/3 to my dau. Rachel Gunter & the other 1/3 to be div. bet. my grandchildren Euphamy & Edward Gunter, children of Stephen Gunter. Friends Isaiah Bagwell & William Cord Exrs. Witt: Isaiah Bagwell, Thomas Scott, Major West - p. 800

CUSTIS, ELIZABETH - 24 Nov. 1788 - Partly proved 28 Feb. 1792 - Prob: 27 Jan. 1794. To son Robertson Custis all the land devised to me by my father Jacob Dunton, he to support & maintain my son John Montgomery Custis in such manner as my son in law Henry Custis may think necessary, & should he refuse I give the said land to my son John Montgomery Custis & his heirs. To dau. Elizabeth. To son William. 3 children Anne, Thomas & William resid. legatees. Son in law Henry Custis Exr. Witt: Littleton Savage, Abel Upshur, Bowden Kendall - p. 801

ANDREWS, ISAMAEL - 22 Aug. 1792 - 28 Jan. 1794 - To sister Molly Mason. Wife to have no part of my est. unless the law directs it. Whole est. to my dau. Catherine Gibbons Schoolfield Andrews at the age of 18 or marriage, then to pay to my sister Rachel Andrews 30 L. Should my dau. die before 18 or marriage I give the bal. of my est. to my sister Rachel Andrews. Wearing apparel to my father William Andrews & my youngest bro. Jacob Andrews & cousin Robert Andrews. John Wharton Exr. Witt: Thomas Cropper, Preson Snead, Joseph Moore - p. 808

THOMAS, BRIDGET - 18 July 1789 - 24 Feb. 1794 - To dau. Sarah Corbin. Dau. Ann Tunnell. Dau. Betty Mapp. Grandau. Polly Corbin. Grandson George Tunnell. Daus. Sarah Corbin & Ann Tunnell resid. legatees. Son in law Ralph Corbin Exr. Witt: Joachim Milbourn, Coventon Broadwater - p. 809

ONLY, JOHN - 25 Sept. 1793 - Partly proved 30 Dec. 1793 - Prob: 24 Feb. 1794 - To son Jesse Only land & planta. where I now live. Wife Nancy Only. To son John Only & dau. Molly Only all my negroes. Dau. Nancy Only. Wife Nancy, son John, dau. Molly & dau. Nancy resid. legatees. To dau. Betsy Groten 1 s. To dau. Salley Only 1 s. Elijah Meers & John Rodgers Exrs. Witt: Custis Willis, Francis Savage - p. 809

TAYLOR, DANIEL - 12 Oct. 1793 - Partly proved 28 Jan. 1794 - Prob: 24 Feb. 1794 To son Severn Taylor land where I now live, & should he offer to sellor mortgage the land, or should he die without issue, I give the said land to my other son Savage Crippen Rigs (both under age). Should both sons die without issue to James Tunnell, son of Elias Tunnell. Son Severn resid. legatee, & should he die without issue before coming to lawful age to my son Savage C. Rigs. Friend Elias Tunnell & Peter Delastatius Exrs. Witt: William Downing, Daniel Spalding - p. 827

District Court Order Book - May 12, 1789 to May 18, 1797

RAMSEY, SAMUEL - Adm. his est. to Edmund Bayly, Jr. - William Gibb & John Custis, (B.S.) sec. - 17 Oct. 1796 - p. 458

GALT, AZEL - Adm. his est. to Samuel Galt - John Shepherd Ker & Thomas Custis sec. 15 Oct. 1794 - p. 350

District Court Records - W. D. 1789 - 1799

KER, EDWARD - 17 May 1786 - 18 Oct. 1790 - To wife planta. where I live cont. 550 A. for life & then to my son George. To son George planta. bought of Thomas H. Parker, cont. 175 A. To son John Sheppard 300 A. of the land bought of James Cox, the line dividing him & his bro. Hugh to be the branch running into the head of Pungoteague. To son Hugh all the land bought of James Broughton as contained in 3 deeds, being 109 A., & all the surplus of 300 A. of the land bought of James Cox, supposed to be 98 A., also the land & planta. bought of Michael R. Tatham. To son Edward all the land I now hold or may die possessed of in the County of Northampton, & the lands in Accomack bought of John & Littleton Harmon & Edmund Polson. To 3 daus. Jean Scarbrough, Catharine Christian & Ann Revell the lands 1 hold in Gloucestor, cont. 243 1/4 An. To dau. Elizabeth Ker 500 L to be paid in 2 negro girls & 1 negro boy & in stock & household furniture. To dau. Isabel 500 L to be paid in like manner. Remainder of my land to be sold, & the proceeds, together with the residue of my est. to be div. bet. my 4 sons George, John Shephard, Hugh & Edward. Wife (no name) Exec. Sons George & John Shephard Exrs. Codicil No. 1 – I revoke the 5th gift to my son Hugh, & in lieu thereof give to the said Hugh all the land & planta. near the Court House bought out of the estate of Severn Guttridge, with the lots in the Court yard, also the lots held in joint tenancy with Catharine Scott. In lieu of the lands bought of John & Littleton Harmon & Edmund Polson, I give to my son Edward Ker the land & planta. bought of Michael Rickets Tatham on the North side of Andua. To son John Sheppard the remainder of the land purchased of John Cox, being about 98 A. and 13 A. lying below the main road purchased of James Broughton. Dau. Margaret to have her board with either of my sons she may incline to live with, & should she choose to board elsewhere I bequeath her 12 L per annum while she remains single to be paid by my 4 sons, 3 L each. I desire that the representatives of my dec. dau. Ann Revell should have an equal share with my daus. Jean Scarburgh & Catherine Christian. The land purchased of John & Littleton Harmon & of Edmund Poulson I beq. to my 4 sons – Dated 28 Sept. 1788 – Witt: Reavel Watson, George Pearson, Rosy Harman. Will proved by John Wise, Jabez Pitt, Edmund Bayly, Jr. Codicil proved by Revill Watson & Rosy Harman – p. 20

DRUMMOND, RICHARD, Jr. – 6 June 1794 – 16 Oct. 1794 – Personal property to wife Esther until my son George arrives to the age of 21 years, then to said George, if he shall be the only child she shall have living by me at that time, or if she have more children living by me at that time to be equally div. get. them. In case of the death of my children wife to have personal property. Should my wife have another son by me I beq. said son my Back Creek planta, cont. 250 A., the Meeting house field & land adj. thereto, 2 half acre lots in the Town of Drummond with a double house thereon, & one half acre lot with a single house thereon adj. Fisher's lots, & my Exrs. to purchase for him about 50 A. of land if it can be done convenient. & if not I give my said son 150 L to be placed at interest. In case my wife should have a dau. I beq. said dau. my Back Creek planta. aforesaid, & my Exrs. shall endeavor to purchase my said dau. 50 A. of land, & if it cannot be done she to have 50 A. of land where Elijah Booth lives, & 2 half acre lots in the Town of Drummond with double house thereon. To Patience Robinson during her natural life, the grass Lot at present in her tenure adj. the County Road, Potters Lot & Simpsons Lot in Drummond Town, reversion to my son George Drummond. To son George all the residue of my lands & lots. Slaves to be free after specified terms of service. Should all my children die without issue before they arrive to lawful age, I give to George Drummond Wilkins, my nephew & godson, my whole est., real & personal before given to my son George Drummond, the 50 A. where Elijah Booth lives, the Meeting house field & the land adj. thereto on the Western side of the Middle Road, the 2 half acre lots & double house thereon in Drummond Town and the 50 A. intended to be purchased by my Exrs, or if not purchased the 150 L in lieu thereof. To all the children of my sister Anne Wilkins, except George Drummond Wilkins. 60 A. of my Back

Creek planta. to Richard, son of my cousin Richard Drummond. 40 A. to Richard, son of my cousin Anne Bayly, & the residue of said planta. to Richard, son of my cousin Spencer Drummond. To the children of my dec. sister Susanna Townsend the residue of my personal est. Should George Drummond Wilkins die before lawful age; the est. given him to go to the children of my sister Wilkins equally. John Cropper, Jr. to be guardian to my son George Drummond & to such other child or children as I may hereafter have. John Cropper, Jr. Exr. Witt: George Corbin, Edward Fisher, Jemima Kelley – p. 102

LILLISTON, ELIZABETH – 26 Aug. 1794 – 16 Oct. 1794 – To Kendle Melson. To John Cord, son of William. To George Melson, son of Kendle. Kendle Melson resid. legatee. Col. John Cropper Exr. Witt: John Dix, Levin Ayres, John Bonwill – p. 108

DRUMMOND, DRAKE – 14 Feb. 1793 – Partly proved 17 Oct. 1794; Further proved 18 Oct. 1794; Prob: 20 May 1795 – Land to pay my debts, & after the payment of debts to David Drummond & his wife during their lives & after their death to John Drummond, son of David, 100 A. land & marsh. "I give to my son one Yoke of Stears" To grandson John Drummond. To dau. Patience. Dau. Mary Drummond resid. legatee, she to have whole est. during her single life. Son David Drummond Exr. Witt: Daniel Melson, Daniel Drummond, Robert Drummond – p. 109

DRUMMOND, RICHARD, Sr. – 28 Feb. 1795 – 14 May 1795 – To son Richard Drummond planta. where I live. To sons Thomas & William (under age) my Mesongo Land. To dau. Sarah Ann Drummond 200 L that remains in Mr. Walter Bayne's hands, said sum to be put on interest for her. To wife Elizabeth use of personal est. until my son Richard arrives to the age of 21 years, then to be div. bet. my wife & her 4 children before mentioned. Wife Elizabeth & bro. Spencer & friend Edmund Bayly, Jr. (or son of Thomas) Exrs. Witt: Edmund Custis, Fenwick Ficher, William East, Elijah Grinnalds – p. 114

PARKER, ELIZABETH – 20 Feb. 1795 – 14 May 1795 – Whole est. to my only child Elizebeth Parker. Friend John Custis guardian to my said child. John Custis Exr. Witt: Southy Satchell, George Poulson – p. 117

LEWIS, ABEL – 5 Mar. 1794 – 16 May 1795 – Whole est. to dau. Phamy Lewis, & should she die before 21 or marriage my land to descend to my bro. George Lewis after the death or marriage of my wife (no name) John Custis Exr. Witt: Severn Willis, Southy Walker East, John Custis – p. 129

ROBINSON, PATIENCE – 3 Jan. 1791 – 20 May 1795 – To sister Mary Drummond & to Betty Jillings. To Betty Clayton (a free black woman) & her 2 children my common Corse clothing. Bal. of est., real & personal, to my bro. David Drummond except a negro woman Sinah, whom I set free, & charge the estate given my bro. David with her

405

maintenance during her life.   John Cropper, Jr., & bro. David Drummond Exrs. - Witt: John Wise, Archibald Forsyth, Hugh Ker - p. 137

KELLAM, SEVERN - 16 Nov. 1794 - 20 May 1795 - "I lend the use of my land for 10 years to my sister Adah Kellam for her to find a home and cloath and school Susanah Andrews on" and if my sister refuse supplying the said Susannah Andrews the said land to be rented for 10 years & Susannah Andrews to have the rent.   Rosey Ross to have the use of my negro Nathan for 4 years & then the said Nathan to be free. I also lend Rosey Ross my negro girl Beck until she is 21 years old, at which time she is free by my father's will.   At the expiration of 10 years my land to be rented out annually until a child called Severn Ross, but not baptised, which I had by Rosey Ross shall marry & have a child to live to be a month old, & should that period ever arrive I give the said Severn my land forever; if the said Severn be alive at the end of 10 years he to have the rents of my land during his life in case he dies before the gift takes place, & should he die before the gift takes place Susannah Ahdrews to have the rents of my land during her life or until she marries & have a child to live to be a month old, at which time I give her my land forever.   Bal. of est. to be sold, & what remains after payment of debts to be lent out, & should Susannah Andrews or Severn Ross live to marry I give them 1/2 of it, & if tho other be dead the whole.   Should both die whole est. to my sister Adah Kellam.   James Powell & Hezekiah Pitts Exrs.   Witt: John White, William White - p. 139

MACKMATH, JOHN - 9 Dec. 1794 - 16 May 1796 - To my natural son John Mackmath Melson whole est. & for want of heirs to Elizabeth Melson, dau. Elizabeth & Jenny Mackmath, dau. of Fanny, & for want of heirs to the children of my sister, John Powell & Elijah Powell in Maryland.   Friend John Cropper, Jr., Exr.   Witt: Thoman Iron Monger, John Cropper - p. 152

SAPPINGTON, HARTLY - 12 Oct. 1796 - 17 Oct. 1796 - To Dr. F. Fisher $300.   To Edmund Bayly, Jr. $150.   To Rosey Flannegal, dau. of Betsy, 40 L. To Joseph Moore $100.   To William Ardis $100. Rosey Flannegan resid. legatee.   Dr. F. Fisher & Edmund Bayly, Jr. Exrs. Witt: John Cole, Richard Grinalds - p. 170

WEST, PHILLIP PARKER - 12 Sept. 1793 - 18 Oct. 1796 - "In case my son Scarburgh West shall save the 50 A. of land bequeathed by Southy Copes to his daughter Comfort, now the wife of the said Scarburgh, for which there is a suit at law depending against the said Scarburgh & Comfort", in that case I beq. to my son Alexander West the planta. where I now live, including the land I purchased of John Cropper. Jr.   Wife Elizabeth to have her maintenance on same during her wid.   My said planta. to be subject to the payment of 30 L. to my son Phillip Parker West when he attains the age of 21 years.   In case my son Scarburgh saves the land above mentioned, I beq. to my son John West the land I purchased of Johannes Watson, 25 A. more or less; in case my son Scarburgh shall loose at law the land above mentioned, I beq. to the said Scarburgh the planta. where I now live, my said planta. to be subject to the payment of 30 L to my son John West when he attains the age of 21 years, & to my son Phillip Parker West 30 L when he attains the like age. In case my son Scarburgh takes the land where I now live I give the land purchased of Johannes Watson, 25 A. more or less, to my son Alexander West. To wife Elizabeth negroes until my dau. Leah arrives to the age of 15 years for the purpose of maintaining herself & the younger children Phillip Parker, Adah, Leah. To Mary Satchell (daughter - p. 206) Bal. of est. to be div. bet. wife & children except that child that takes the planta. where I live. Wife Elizabeth & sons Scarburgh & Alexander Exrs. Witt: John Cropper, Jr., Richard Jacobs, Sebastian Cropper - p. 179

READ, CALEB - 6 Mar. 1797 - 16 May 1797 - I give the planta. where my father lived which descended to me by the death of my bro. Charles Read, to my sister Elizabeth Conway. To Levin Rodgers the planta. in the woods which my father gave me. Father in law Levin Rodgers Exr. - Witt: Robert Twiford, Edmund Bayly - p. 202

WHITE, WILLIAM - 24 Mar. 1792 - 18 May 1797 - To 5 sons Arthur, William, George, James & John all my lands to be equally div. bet. them. To dau. Easther 150 L. 5 sons resid. legatees. Friends John Poulson, John Burton & Parker Barnes Exrs. & to divide my land. Witt: Mary Poulson, Leah P. Copes - p. 220
In order of prob: Proved by Leah R. Copes, the other witness being dead.

HARRISON, CALEB - 16 Jan. 1797 - 17 Oct. 1797 - Planta. where I now live to be sold & the proceeds equally div. bet. my children Elizabeth, Caleb, James, Benjamin, Leah & Thomas Harrison. 6 children resid. legatees. Son Caleb Harrison & Francis Savage Exrs. Witt: Branson Dolby, John Carr, Peggy Rodgers - p. 245

HYSLOP, GEORGE - 7 Apr. 1797 - 17 Oct. 1797 - To wife Joice Hyslop all the est. that she received out of her mother Joice Lewis' est. To son William Hyslop planta. where I now live being 50 A., he to pay my son George Hyslop 15 L when said George arrives to the age of 21 years, & also to my son Smith Hyslop 15 L when he comes to the age of 21 years. Dau. Molly Hyslop. Son George, dau. Betsy, & son Smith Hyslop resid. legatees - Francis Savage Exr. Witt: James Lewis, John Lurton - p. 248

GRINALDS, SOUTHY - 20 Apr. 1798 - 20 Oct. 1798 - To wife Sarah Grinalds. To bro. Elijah Grinalds. To son in law Tommey Abbott. To John Grinalds. To Thomas Grinalds six silver tea spoons marked "T.G." &c. To nephew William Grinalds. To nephew Southy Grinalds 6 silver tea spoons marked "S.S.G." &c. Stock not already given to be div. bet. my wife & mother Catharine Grinalds. Wife & bro. Elijah to settle my est. Not witnessed. Proved by John Teackle, Sr. & Charles Stockly - p. 337

RAYFIELD, MAJOR – 10 Oct. 1797 – 20 Oct. 1798 – To son William Rayfield. To son Major Rayfield. Real & personal est. to be div. bet. 4 children William, Elizabeth, Major & Mary. To Thomas Bayly Sr. the lands I bought of William Bull & Dianiah his wife & the lands bought of Levi Annis & Peggy his wife, which will appear by their deeds to me, provided the said Bayly pays the sum of money that I was to give for the said lands which will appear by said deeds. Sons William & Major Exrs. Witt: William Rolley, Asia East, Rachel Darby.
Codicil: My 2 sons William & Major to have one barrel of Brandy as well for their trouble, saving the drink out of the crop of Brandy – Witt: Elijah Grinnalds – p. 339

WALKER, LEVIN – 21 Oct. 1798 – 22 Oct. 1798 – To wife Elizabeth Walker. All my lands to my son John B. Walker. Charles Stockly Exr. Witt: Matthias Outten, William Robinson Custis, William T. Peck – p. 341

WEST, SCARBURGH – 2 Apr. 1799 – 15 May 1799 – To wife Comfort planta. & negroes during her wid. to support & educate my children, & at her death or marriage to be div. between my 2 children Tabby West & Kessey West. John Cropper, Jr. Exr. Witt: Thomas Cropper, Jacob Lilliston, Alexander West – p. 373

POULSON, JOHN – 9 Apr. 1799 – 18 Oct. 1799 – My Exrs. hereafter named to bring up & raise all my children from the profits arising from my whole est. until my son Erastus Poulson arrives to lawful Age & then to son Erastus all the land & planta. where I now live, together with 50 A. in Hack Swamp. To son John Poulson my water grist mill & saw mill. To son Thomas all that tract of land where Joseph (free negro) now lives. To dau. Polly Poulson $1000. Should my son Erastus die before arriving to lawful age or marriage, the land & other things given him to descend to my next eldest son, & that part of my est. given to my son who may survive the said Erastus to descend to the survivor or survivors of my said other children. To dau. Polly all her mother's wearing apparel. To Zadock Poulson 1/9 of all the crop that is made on my planta. this year, provided he continues on said planta. & does his duty as a Crops man. All the remainder of my est when my son Erastus arrives to lawful age to be equally div. between the survivors or survivor of my children, except the one who may own the planta. where I now live. Children to be kept together until Erastus arrives to lawful age, & that with their grandmother Nancy Dix if she choose to take them & remains single. Friends George Bagwell, James Poulson & Parker Barnes Exrs. – Witt: John Burton, John Teackle, Sr., Thomas Evans – p. 441

Orders – 1793-1796

FOSQUE, WILLIAM – Adm. his est. to Leah Fosque – William Dickerson & Thomas Massey sec. – 25 Feb. 1793 – p. 3

BELL, OLIVER - Ordered that the Sheriff take into his possession the est. of Oliver Bell & make sale thereof agreeable to law - 26 Feb. 1793 - p. 5

SHARROD, HENRY - Adm. his est. to John Sharrod - Levin Gray sec. - 30 Apr. 1793 - p. 43

YOUNG, WILLIAM - Adm. his est. to Benjamin Mills - Samuel Henderson & Revil Patterson sec. - 30 Apr. 1793 - p. 45

WINDOW, MARGARET - Adm. her est. to Robert Twiford - Joseph Heath & Solomon Smith sec. - 1 May 1793 - p. 49

EVANS, ARCADIA - Adm. her est. to George Matthews - John Evans & Joakim Milbourn sec. - 24 June 1793 - p. 68

CARSS, JOHN - Adm. his est. to Thomas Custis, Betty Carss, wid., relinquishing her right to qualify - John Wise sec. - 30 July 1793 - p. 75

BUNTING, WILLIAM BLACK - Adm. his est. to John Cropper, Jr. - Thomas Cropper sec. 30 July 1793 - p. 77

JOHNSON, WILLIAM - Adm. his est. to Covington Broadwater - William Henry Beavans sec. - 30 Sept. 1793 - p. 94

WINDOW, VIOLETTA - Adm. her est. to John Purnal Outten - Levin Joynes sec. - 30 Sept. 1793 - p. 95

SAVAGE, GRIFFIN - Adm. his est. to William Young - Joseph Kelly sec. - 30 Sept. 1793 - p. 95

GUNTER, ESTHER - Adm. her est. to Joseph Garrett - Jacob Bird sec. - 28 Oct. 1793 - p. 100

TATHAM, JAMES - Adm. his est. to Patience Tatham - Elijah Hancock sec. - 30 Dec. 1793 - p. 121

SILVERTHORNE, ARTHUR - Adm. his est. to Joshua Silverthorne - Isaac Warner & John Moore sec. - 27 Jan. 1794 - p. 127

COLE, MAJOR - Adm. his est. to John Finney - John Teackle, Jr. sec. - 27 Jan. 1794

COPES, THOMAS - Adm. his est. to Southey Satchell - John Custis, bay side, sec. - 27 Jan. 1794 - p. 128

NOCK, THOMAS - Adm. his est. to George Nock & John Walker - John Walker, Sr. sec. with Levi Hutchinson - 24 Feb. 1794 - p. 134

LEWIS, BETTY - Adm. her est. to John Lewis - William Strann & Robert Russell sec. - 26 Feb. 1794 - p. 153

WRIGHT, HENRY - Adm. his est. to Henry Wright - Thomas Hickman, Constable, & William Evans sec. - 27 Feb. 1794 - p. 157

HINMAN, JOHN - Adm. his est. to Moses Hinman - John Burton & John Moore sec. - 1 Apr. 1794 - p. 163

DIX, GEORGE - Adm. his est. to Levi Dix - Southy Satchell sec. - 4 Apr. 1794 - p. 172

STEWART, GEORGE - Adm. de bonis non to Charles Snead, James Stewart relinquishing his right to qualify - John Custis. B. S., Levin Joynes & William Gibb sec. - 29 Apr. 1794 - p. 180

CARY, JAMES - Adm. his est. to William Downing - William Young sec. - 30 Apr. 1794 - p. 182

PITT, ROBERT - Adm. his est. to John Burton - John Custis, Thomas Custis, John Wise, Thomas Evans & Edmund Bayly sec. - 30 Apr. 1794 - p. 182

FULLER, ASA - Adm. his est. to John Walker, Jr. & John Philips, son of William. Salathiel West & William Philips sec. - 30 June 1794 - p. 201

GAY, THOMAS - Adm. his est. to Thomas Metcalf - Nathaniel Badger sec. - 30 June 1794 - p. 201

TOWNSEND, JAMES HENRY - Adm. his est. to Southy Broadwater - John Wallop & Mary Beavans sec. - 30 June 1794 - p. 202

SINGLETON, RICHARD - Adm. his est. to Robinson Custis - John West sec. - 28 July 1794 - p. 204

SAVAGE, JOHN - Adm. his est. to Leah Savage - Robert Twiford, William Drummond & Isaiah Beech sec. - 29 July 1794 - p. 205

ASHBY, THOMAS - Adm. his est. to James Ashby - Charles Snead & George Coleburn sec. 29 July 1794 - p. 208

RODGERS, ROBERT - Adm. his est. to Abel Rodgers - John Bull & Michael Bonwell sec. 29 Sept. 1794 - p. 241

JOHNSON, LABAN - Adm. his est. to Hannah Johnson & John Martin. Noah Belote, Robert Twiford & Smith Melson, Jr. sec. - 27 Oct. 1794 - p. 244

WILKERSON, JESSE - Adm. his est. to Mary Wilkerson - Isaac Boston & Jehu Wilkerson sec. - 28 Oct. 1794 - p. 246

JOHNSON, WILLIAM, JR. - Adm. his est. to William Welburn - George Marshall & Charles Stockly sec. - 28 Oct. 1794 - p. 248

JOYNES, LEVIN - Adm. his est. with will annexed to John Smith, John Custis & John Wise. - John Burton, Peter Hack & Edmund Bayly, Jr. sec. - 28 Oct. 1794 - p. 248

FOSTER, JOSHUA - Adm. his est. to John Poolman - John Moore sec. - 18 Nov. 1794 - p. 251

SIMPSON, SOUTHY - Adm. his est. to John Parker - John Poulson sec. - 18 Nov. 1794 - p. 261

EWELL, EDWARD - Adm. his est. to John S. Ker - Edmund Bayly, Jr. sec. 18 Nov. 1794 - p. 262

GROTEN, ZOROBABEL - Adm. his est. to Anne Groten - Carvey Dunton & John Milby sec. - 29 Dec. 1794 - p. 265

WHITE, NATHAN - Adm. his est. to Elizabeth Badger - William Gibb & Thomas Badger sec. - 29 Dec. 1794 - p. 265

WALKER, WILLIAM - Adm. his est. to Elizabeth Walker - George Fisher, Edmund Powell & William Hickman sec. - 29 Dec. 1794 - p. 266

TOWNSEND, HENRY - Adm. his est. to Sally Townsend - William Polk & William Townsend sec. - 29 Dec. 1794 - p. 266

ABDELL, ELISHA - Adm. his est. to Abg: Abdell - Kendal Bunting, Philip Fisher & George Ker sec. - 29 Dec. 1794 - p. 266

HINMAN, MOSES - Adm. his est. to Scarburgh Hinman - Joachim Milburn & Major Hinman sec. - 29 Dec. 1794 - p. 266

HUTSON, RAYMOND - Adm. his est. to John Wharton - Edmund Bayly. Jr, sec. - 29 Dec. 1794 - p. 267

BISHOP, WILLIAM - Adm. his est. to Anne Bishop - William Hinman & William Northam sec. - 29 Dec. 1794 - p. 267

LEWIS, HENRY - Adm. his est. to John Darby - John S. Ker sec. - 30 Dec. 1794 - p. 268

AYRES, RICHARD - Adm. his est. to Francis Ayres - Thomas Bayly & Levin White sec. - 30 Dec. 1794 - p. 270

CHANDER, HATHAN - Adm. his est. to Henry Custis - Southy Satchell sec. - 30 Dec. 1794 - p. 270

TWIFORD, BARTHOLOMEW - Adm. his est. to Robert Twiford - John Gootee & James Twiford sec. - 30 Dec. 1794 - p. 270

WILLETT, THOMAS - Adm. his est. to John Walker, Jr, - John Phillips sec. - 26 Jan. 1795 - p. 273

WHITE, LEVIN - Adm. his est. to Ephraim Watson - John Walker, Jr. & Robert Walker sec. - 26 Jan. 1795 - p. 273

BAYLY, NEOMY - Adm. her est. to Margaret Ewell & John Walker, Jr. - John Walker, Sr. & Ephraim Watson sec. - 26 Jan. 1795 - p. 274

DUNTON, MAJOR & Isaac Dunton - Adm. their estates to Major Guy - Southy Satchell sec. 26 Jan. 1795 - p. 274

BURDETT, THOMAS W. - Adm. his est. to Tabitha Burdett, John Wallop & William Wallop - George Wallop & James Ardis sec. - 27 Jan. 1795 - p. 277

SANDFORD, ANN - Adm. her est. to John Sandford - Thomas Bunting & Elias Broadwater sec. - 27 Jan. 1795 - p. 277

WHITE, ROBERT - Adm. his est. to Elizabeth White & George Wallop. - William Wallop, John Wallop & Spencer Waters sec. - 27 Jan. 1795 - p. 278

STEVENS, MOLLY - Adm. her est. to Southy Satchell, with will annexed. McKeel Bonwell & John Moore sec. - 28 Jan. 1795 - p. 281

WHARTON, JAMES - Adm. his est. to Susanna Wharton - William Floyd & James Wharton sec. - 24 Feb. 1795 - p. 288

MORGAN, WILLIAM - Adm. his est. to William Bell, Sr. - John Moore & Edward Bell sec. - 24 Feb. 1795 - p. 288

NOCK, WILLIAM - Adm. his est. to Elijah Nock, Jr. - John Poulson, Zadock Nock, Isaac Warner & Aires Tatham sec. - 24 Feb. 1795 - p. 288

HEWET, ROBERT - Adm. his est. to John Custis (S.S.) Robert Twiford sec. - 25 Feb. 1795 - p. 293

TAYLOR, DUDIMIA - Adm. her est. to John Poulson - John Teackle, Sr. sec. - 30 Mar. 1795 - p. 295

OLDHAM, ANN - Adm. her est. to Robinson Custis - Thomas Custis sec. - 30 Mar. 1795 - p. 296

TAYLOR, MATHEW - Adm. his est. to Spencer Waters - George Wallop & Solomon Mears sec. - 27 Jan. 1795 - p. 298

LITCHFIELD, WILLIAM – Adm. his est. to John Wharton – Edmund Bayly, Jr. sec. – 31 Mar. 1795 – p. 301

KELLY, JEREMIAH – Adm. his est. to John Moore – John Custis sec. – 28 Apr. 1795 – p. 312

LEATHERBURY, GEORGE – Adm. his est. to William Leatherbury – Thomas Phillips & Samuel Parker sec. – 28 Apr. 1795 – p. 312

GRINALDS, THOMAS – Adm. his est. to Elijah Grinalds & Southy Grinalds – Charles Stockly sec. – p. 312

MATHEWS, THOMAS – Adm. his est. to Anne Mathews – John Mathews & William Hickman sec. – p. 314

COLLINS, JOSEPH – Adm. his est. to Levina Collins – William Downing & Nehemiah Mathews sec. – 29 June 1795 – p. 340

DIX, LEVIN – Adm. his est. to Barshiba Dix – John Bundick & Beverly Copes sec. – 29 June 1795 – p. 343

MELSON, LEVIN – Adm. his est. to Nanny Melson – Major Guy & Benjamin Burton sec. – 29 June 1795 – p. 347

ASHBY, RACHEL – Adm. her est. to John Ashby – James Spiers sec. – 29 June 1795 – p. 347

BRADFORD, JACOB – Adm. his est. to Benjamin Floyd – Berry Floyd & Francis Savage sec. – 27 July 1795 – p. 348

COLEBURN, JAMES – Adm. his est. to Charles Stockly – John Custis (B.S.) & John Burton sec. – 28 July 1795 – p. 352

EVANS, WILLIAM – Adm. his est. to Sebastian Cropper – John Cropper, Jr. & Thomas Cropper sec. – 1 Sept. 1795 – p. 366

MILBURN, JOAKIM – Adm. his est. to John Logan – John Burton. Thomas Custis & William Gibb sec. – 3 Sept. 1795 – p. 372

AIMES, ELIZA, Wid. of Babel – Adm. her est. to George Kellam & John Milby – William Bell & Custis Willis sec. – 28 Sept. 1795 – p. 377

WHEALTON, ELISHA – Adm. his est. to Anne Whealton – William Downing & George Mathews sec. – 28 Sept. 1795 – p. 379

MARSHALL, LEVIN – Adm. his est. to Esther Marshall – John McLean & Stephen Marshall sec. – 28 Sept. 1795

FLETCHER, NATHAN – Adm. his est. to George Wallop & Phebe Fletcher – David Watts & Spencer Watts sec. – 28 Sept. 1795 – p. 379

LAFFERTY, Neil - Adm. his est. to William Turner - Stephen Drummond & Samuel Russell sec. - 28 Sept. 1795 - p. 380

STOCKLY, KENDALL - Adm. his est. to Nancy Stockly - Custis Jinkins & Robert Jinkins sec. - 29 Sept. 1795 - p. 382

TRADER, HENRY - Adm. his est. to Samuel Trader - Thomas Jacob & Zerobabel Hornsby sec. - 29 Sept. 1795 - p. 383

TAYLOR, HARMON - Adm. his est. to Elisha Mears - Salathiel West sec. - 26 Oct. 1795 - p. 386

GARRISON, ARCHIBALD - Adm. his est. to Jonathan Garrison & Benjamin Floyd - Thomas Aimes & Custis Willis sec. - 26 Oct. 1795 - p. 387

DRUMMOND, ELICIA - Adm. her est. to Annaretter Drummond - Smith Melson, Jr. & Stephen Drummond sec. - 27 Oct. 1795 - p. 389

ASHBY, SARAH - Adm. her est. to James Ashby, Sr. - John Read sec. - 28 Oct. 1795 - p. 394

BEAVANS, SAMUEL - Adm. his est. to William Waterfield - Isaac Marshall sec. - 30 Nov. 1795 - p. 398

SATCHELL, WILLIAM - Adm. his est. to Mary Satchell - Alexander West & Phillip Miles sec. - 28 Dec. 1795 - p. 405

BAGWELL, HELE - Adm. his est. to Nancy Bagwell - John Custis (B.S.) & Thomas Cropper sec. - 28 Dec. 1795 - p. 406

DRUMMOND, ALLAS SHEPHERD, DRAKE - Adm. his est. to Phillip Miles - James Rooks sec. - 29 Dec. 1795 - p. 408

VERMILLION, FRANCIS - Adm. his est. to Southy Bloxom - Jesse Kellam & Thomas Bagwell sec. - 25 Jan. 1796 - p. 411

MEARS, PEGGY - Adm. her est. to James Mears - Robinson Savage & Custis Bradford sec. - 25 Jan. 1796 - p. 411

RIGGEN, JOHN - Adm. his est. to William Coton - Richard R. Savage & Jacob Broadwater sec. - 25 Jan. 1796 - p. 415

WILSON, EPHRAIM - Adm. his est. to Samuel Wilson - Benjamin Marshall & Thomas Bunting sec. - 25 Jan. 1796 - p. 414

BENSTON, STURGIS - Adm. his est. to Thomas Hargis - John S. Ker sec. - 25 Jan. 1796 - p. 414

PHILLIPS, JACOB - Adm. his est. to John Cropper, Jr. - Edmund Bayly, Jr. & Southy Satchell sec. - 29 Jan. 1796 - p. 422

MELSON, KENDALL - Adm. his est. to John Cropper, Jr. - Edmund Bayly, Jr. & Southy Satchell sec. - 29 Jan. 1796 - p. 422

MEARS, WILLIAM - Son cf Richard Mears - Adm. his est. to Richard Mears - William Mears, Solomon Read & John Arlington sec. - 29 Jan. 1796 - p. 422

Wills &c. - 1794 - 1796

JOHNSON, SOLOM - 30 June 1790 - 29 Apr. 1794 - To son Solomon Johnson all my lands & Water Mills, Mills &c., he to pay my son Zadock Johnson 100 L. To son Zadock all my bills, bonds, notes &c. Sons Solomon & Zadock resid. legatees. (both under age) - Son Solomon & Jacob Kelly Exrs. Witt: Bennet Mason, Teackle Bird - p. 3

TROY, BRIDGET - 25 Sept. 1793 - 26 May 1794 - Whole personal est. to be sold except my pewter, fire tongs &c., which I deposit in the hands of George Truet Taylor for my son John when he comes to lawful age; proceeds of said sale to be left in the hands of Solomon Marshall until my son John Troy comes to lawful age. George Truet Taylor to have the use of my house & ground until my son John comes to lawful age. To son John all the land I bought of George Matthews with one A. I bought of Gilbert Morris, & for want of heirs to my bro. George Truet Taylor's dau. Polley Taylor. George Truet Taylor Exr. Witt: Caleb Massey, John Thornton. p. 4

FISHER, PHILIP - 18 Mar. 1786 - 27 May 1794 - To wife Marthew Fisher planta. where I now live during her wid., reversion to my son George Fisher during his life & then to my grandson George Fisher, son of the aforesaid George. To dau. Nanney Fisher. Bal. of est. to my wife for life & then to my children & grandson, viz: John Fisher, Robertson Fisher, Sarah Sharply, Nancy Fisher, Lisey Walker, Comfort Mears & grandson Major Copes. William Walker Exr. Witt: John Burton, Mary Burton, Margaret Burton - p. 5

FOX, MARY - 16 Oct. 1788 - 29 Apr. 1794 - To my mother Sarah Hawley planta. where I now live for life & then to my half brother Henry Hawley. Father Abel Hawley Exr. Witt: John Rodgers, John Watson, Scarburgh Pratt - p. 6

POTTER, NICHOLAS - 26 May 1789 - 26 May 1794 - To dau. Vianna Potter land where I now live. To son Custis Potter. To son. Labin Potter 1 s. To son John 1 s. Custis Potter & Vianna Potter resid. legatees. Sons John Potter & John Spiers Exrs. Witt: William Nock, Littleton Wyatt, Peter Dolby, Branson Dolby, Littleton Armitrader - p. 7

SPIRES, COMFORT - 5 Jan. 1793 - 28 July 1794 - To dau. Rachel Spires. To dau. Suffiah Potter. To dau. Rachel bal. of est. & for want of issue to be div. bet. Labin Potter's children. Friends William Haly & Thomas Bagwell Exrs. Witt: Thomas Bagwell, Peggy Bagwell – p. 24

EWELL, GEORGE H. – 7 Oct. 1793 – 28 July 1794 – To son Mark Ewell land where he now lives adj. the land of Ephraim Vessels & John Young & James Vessels, also the 1/4 part of my Marsh at Shores Island. To sons George & James Ewell that part of my land where I now live & 1/2 my marsh on Shores Island. To son Solomon Ewell land & marsh I bought of George Young & the 1/4 part of my marsh on Shores Island. To son Solomon 8 A. adj. Mark Ewell, &c. To dau. Comfort. To dau. Ann Parks. To grandau Tabitha Ewell Taylor. Dau. Comfort Kilman & grandau. Taby Parks resid. legatees. Comfort Kilman to have 8 A. of land for life. Cattle to be div. bet. Son Mark Ewell, son George Ewell, son James Ewell, son Solomon Ewell, dau. Comfort Kilman & dau. Ann Parks. Sons Mark & George Exrs. – Witt: William Young, Southey Taylor – p. 25

RODGERS, JOHN, son of John Rodgers – 26 Jan. 1794 – 30 July 1794 – I beq. the reversion, remainder, expectancy &c. in 1/2 the land left me by my late father, John Rodgers, dec., cont. by est. 50 A., near or adjoining the White Marsh, to my dau. Elizabeth Rodgers. Wife Peggy Rodgers to have the use of same until my dau. arrives to 18 years of age. To bro. Labin Rodgers. Wife resid. legatee & Exec. Witt: John Spires, Ezekiel Beach, Elijah Chance – p. 28

PITT, ROBERT – 19 Jan. 1794 – 29 Apr. 1794 – To dau. Ann Hack Pitt during her life all the lands I am now possessed with, & should she have issue to dispose of same as she shall think fit. To wife (no name) personalty, my black mare that I had of Thomas Custis &c. Should my dau. die without issue my relation Samuel Wilson Pitt to have all my lands, & should they offer to sell or mortgage the same Robert Pitt, the son of Jabez Pitt & his heirs to enjoy the same. My desire is that my Exr. get Robert Conner Pitt & John Corbin Pitt bound in Philadelphia to a trade. To my Exr. 50 L for his services. Friend John Burton Exr. Witt: William Downing, Dixon Hall – p. 29

SCARBURGH, HENRY – 11 Mar. 1789 – Partly proved 29 Dec. 1789 – Prob: 29 Sept. 1794. To bros. Bennett & George Scarburgh whom I constitute my Exrs., all my lands that I now possess. To my mother Elizabeth Colony my 1/2 of a grist mill & a riding chair that Levin Rodgers is to make for me during her life, reversion to my aforesaid bros. To sister Sarah Scarburgh 250 L to be paid her by my Exrs. To my half bro. William Smith 30 L. To my half sister Catharine Colony 30 L. Witt: John Arlington, Moly Boags – p. 30

MEARS, SPENCER – 25 May 1794 – 29 Sept. 1794 – To wife Margaret land where I now live for 8 years to bring up my small children & then to my son James. To son Calep Mears. Children James, Rachel, Sally, Rosey, Calep, Robert, Frances, Elizabeth & Nancy Mears resid. legatees. Wife Margaret & Robert Bradford Exrs. Witt: Elisha

CUTLER, RICHARD - 2 July 1793 - 29 Sept. 1794 - To wife Rosanna Cutler whole est. during her life & then to my grandson Richard Cutler, son of John Cutler, all my lands, being 250 A., upon the conditions hereafter named, said land adj. George Hack, Peter Rodgers & William Colony, & should he offer to sell or mortgage the said land then to fall to the next male heir, to one George Cutler, he to pay to his 2 bros. & sister, George Cutler, Peter Cutler & Rosanna Cutler 20 L each when they arrive at 28 years of age; should Richard Cutler die without issue then I give the said land to my grandson George Cutler, & if he offer to sell or mortgage the said lands then to fall to the next male heir, Peter Cutler, & should Peter offer to sell or mortgage the said lands or die without issus, I give the aforesaid land to my son Richard Cutler, the land not to be divided but fall to the male heir, & if no male heir then to the eldest female heir, & if there should be no male or female heir the said land to be kept for a free school for the poor people in this Neck. To grandson Thomas Fletcher Cutler. To grandau. Margaret Mears. Dau. Susanna Hornsby & son Richard Cutler resid. legatees. Sons Richard & Major Hornsby Exrs. Wife Exec. - Not witnessed - Proved by George Hack, John Savage & Eli Hornsby - p. 32

HEATH, JANE - 22 Sept. 1794 - 29 Sept. 1794 - To dau. Tabitha Heath. To dau. Jane. To son Major. Husband Henry Heath to have use of all my property during his life as long as he remains single. To son Joseph. Sons Joseph & Major resid legatees. Witt: Levin Walker, Southy Copes, Elizabeth Flanagan - p. 34

BIRD, JACOB - 4 Mar. 1794 - 29 Apr. 1794 - To eldest son Nathaniel Bird land whcre I now live cont. 60 A. To my second son Eborn Bird. To youngest son Jacob Bird 25 A. purchased of a tract of land called Gales Land. To eldest dau. Sarah Bird. To youngest dau. Satharine Bird. 4 children Eborn, Jacob, Sarah & Catharine Bird resid. legatees. Friend Bennett Mason Exr. Witt: George Bush, Solomon Boston, James Duncan, Jr.
Codicil: Should youngest son Jacob die before arriving to the age of 21 years, my second son Eborn to fall heir to his land. Witt: James Duncan, Solomon Boston, George Bush - p. 35

RICHARDSON, JACOB - 19 Feb. 1794 - 29 Sept. 1794 - As much of my land & personal property as will pay my debts to be sold, & the remaining part of my land & planta. I lend to my mother during her natural life, provided she lay no claim to my lands that I have heretofore sold, & at her death all my land not sold to be equally divided between my bro. Isaac Richardson, bro. Edward Richardson, Bro. Ralph Richardson & sister Rachel Benston. Bro. Edward Richardson & sister Rachel Benston Exrs. Witt: James Melvin, William Benston, Polly Bell - p. 37

MONGER, CATHARINE - 5 Oct. 1794 - 27 Oct. 1794 - To son Thomas Phillips. To grandson John Phillips. To Catharine Phillips. To Sally Monger. Daus. Susanna Wise, Catharine Phillips & Sally Monger resid. legatees. Bro. John Hanniford Exr., & if he refuse Joseph Hanniford to act in his stead. Witt: Stephen Warrington, Susanna Phillips - p. 38

JOYNES, LEVIN - 15 Dec. 1793 - Proved 27 Oct. 1794 - Prob. 28 Oct. 1794 - To wife Ann the use of my respective children's legacies until my sons arrive at 14 years of age & my daus. at 18 years or marriage. To son John Joynes the planta. where I now live cont. by estimation 318 A. & for want of issue to my son Levin Joynes. To son Levin Joynes the land I hold under 2 several deeds from Thomas Grinalds & John Smith, together with 34 A. purchased of the heirs of Clement Parker, Jr., & for which no deed has been executed, containing in the whole 334 A., & for want of heirs to my son Thomas Robinson Joynes. Should Levin inherit the land devised my son John, in that case this dividet of land shall likewise go to my son Thomas Robinson & his heirs. To son Thomas Robinson Joynes my houses & lots in the town of Onancock, 108 A. adjoining the lands of Boniwell, Gibb, Lewis, Ames & Elliott, 200 A. in Guilford Neck & 100 A. on Hog Island, should he die under age & without issue, or should he inherit the lands devised to my son Levin, then I leave this. dividet of land & lots to be sold and the money equally div. bet. my daus. Susanna Joynes, Anne Smith Joynes & Sarah Joynes. Wife Anne Exec.
Codicil: I desire within 5 years from this time my State Bounty Lands wherever located may be sold on a long credit, & the money equally divided between my son Thomas Robinson & my 3 daus. Susanna, Anne Smith & Sarah, & as to my United States Bounty Land I give to my son Levin (as of the same name with myself) not for value thereof, but to remind him of the Honorable cause in which I earned it in the late Revolution. Not witnessed - Proved by George Parker, Thomas Evans & William Gibb. - p. 39
In order of prob: Wife Anne relinquished her right to qualify & appointed John Custis (B.S.), John Wise & John Smith Exrs.

MEARS, MESHACK - 3 Feb. 1790 - 27 Oct. 1794 - To wife Susanna whole est. during her wid. if she remain single until my son Meshack Mears come to the age of 21 years, & then my wife to have her legal part of my est. To sons John & Meshack Mears all my lands to be div. bet. them; should either die their part to the survivor. To 2 daus. Rachel & Leah Mears. Daus. Nancy Bundick, Rachel & Leah Mears resid. legatees. - Wife Susanna & James Duncan Exrs. Witt: William Warner, Elijah Baker, Salathiel Baker - p. 42

SMALL, ROBERT - 10 Sept. 1791 - 27 Oct. 1794 - To son Levi Small all my freehold estate with the water mill & stones & 1 A. recovered of the heirs of Richard Bloxom. To son Robert Small. To dau. Ann Small. To 2 grandaus. Polly & Lucreshe Bloxom. Bal. of est. to wife Canady for life & then to be div. bet. my 2 children Levi & Ann Small. Witt: James Duncan, Sr., Stephen Riggin, Griffin Kelley - p. 45

RAYFIELD, JOHN – 1 Oct. 1794 – 28 Oct. 1794 – To kinsman William Kinihorn, whom I make my Exr. all my property except such legacies as I shall hereafter leage. To Bennett Scarburgh 15 L – Witt: Polly Millman, Elizabeth Joynes – p. 46

JUSTICE, RALPH – 31 Dec. 1792 – 28 Oct. 1794 – To my wife the mare which she owned when I married her & also the 2 colts she has since brought. To son William Justice 200 A. on the South edge of where I now live adj. Scarburgh Hastings, Mary Riggs & my own land. To son James all my lands lying Southerly & Easterly of the line mentioned for my son William, supposed to contain 20 A. adj. my wife's land. All my other lands to be div. bet. my 4 daus. Negroes to be div. bet. my 6 children, the 1/3 allotted to my wife as her dower shall be the full part of the 2 children I had by her. Son William Exr. Witt: John Teackle, Sr., Joshua Bell, Meshack Mears – p. 47

KELLAM, SHADRACK – 3 Mar. 1794 – ____ 1794 – To wife Leah Kellam use of 2 negroes during her life then to my son Thomas Kellam. To son Thomas. To dau. Caty Kellam. I give all my land to my son Thomas Kellam. 1/2 of the bal. of my est. to my dau. Caty & the other 1/2 to be div. bet. my wife & son Thomas. Wife & Samuel Mapp Exrs. Witt: John Smith, Housen Mapp, Jr., Joshua Taylor, Houson Mapp, Sr. – p. 50

WALKER, WILLIAM – 22 Aug. 1794 – 29 Dec. 1794 – To wife whole est. during her life or wid. To dau. Elizabeth Walker. To son Littleton Walker. To son William Walker. To daus. Comfort & Nancy Walker. To 2 sons John & Southy Walker. Witt: John Burton, George Fisher, Thomas Hinman – p. 57
In order of prob: Elizabeth Walker qualified.

SAVAGE, ABEL – 28 Jan. 1793 – 29 Dec. 1794 – To son William Savage 75 A., wife to have use of same for 10 years. To son John 75 A. adj. the above. To grandson Abel Savage, son of Parker Savage, 40 s. Bal. of est. to wife Nanny Savage, sons John, William & Jacob Savage & daus. Betsy, Nancy Savage & Sally Savage. Son John & wife Nanny Exrs. Witt: Abel Savage, Jr., son of William, Littleton Savage, William Only – p. 60

SHIPHAM, WILLIAM – 3 July 1794 – 30 Dec. 1794 – To wife Agnes Shipham whole est. during her life then to my dau. Euphemy Atkins Shipham, otherwise Euphamy Atkins Mathews for life to raise & school her children, & at her death to be div. bet. her children. Son in law Elias Mathews & Zadoc Allen Exrs. Witt: Samuel Henderson, Levin W. Dallener, Jean Henderson – p. 61

DIX, LEVI – 1 Dec. 1794 – 30 Dec. 1794 – To wife Treffey Dix whole est. during her wid. Then I beq. my land to my son Levi Dix. Bal. of est. to be div. bet. my 5 children, Elizabeth, Rosey Gootee Dix, Isaac, Levin, Patty Dix. John Poulson, Sr. Exr. Witt: John Moore, Preson

SANDFORD, THOMAS - 19 Aug. 1794 - 30 Dec. 1794 - To mother Ann Sandford whole est, during her life & then to my bro. John Sandford 30 A. adj. him. To sister Elizabeth Sandford 45 A. where my dwelling house stands. Sister Ann Sandford to have her home in my dwelling house until she marries. To sister Ann Sandford 25 A. adj. Elizabeth's land. I give the marsh to my 2 sisters Ann & Elizabeth. Remainder of my lands to my sister Esther Benson. Bro. John & 3 sisters Elizabeth, Ann & Esther resid. legatees. To bro. John Sandford & John Benson wearing apparel. John Benson & John Sandford Exrs. Witt: William Downing, ____ Darby, Thomas Fletcher - p. 63

SANDFORD, ANN - 6 Oct. 1794 - Proved 30 Dec. 1794 - Prob: 27 Jan. 1795 - To daus. Elizabeth & Ann Sandford. To son Thomas Sandford personalty, reversion to my dau. Ann. Bal. of est. to be div. bet. all my children. Son John Sandford Exr. Witt: Elih Shay, William Downing, Jr. - p. 65

MARSHALL, WILLIAM - 7 Nov. 1793 - 30 Dec. 1794 - To son John Marshall all my plan. except 60 A. which I give to my dau. Betsy Marshall. To son William land & planta. purchased of Jabez Pitt. To dau. Polly Marshall planta. purchased of Joshua Dickerson in Worcester County, Maryland. To dau. Peggy Marshall 1/2 of all my moveable est. after my wife has her part. 5 children above mentioned resid. legatees. Bro. Solomon Marshall & wife Peggy Exrs. Witt: William Waterfield, Reavel Copes, Thomas Bonewel - p. 65

SANDRES, JOHN - 18 Nov. 1794 - 26 Jan. 1795 - To William & Esmey Wyatt. To Anne Wyatt. William Wyatt resid. legatee & Exr. Witt: Arthur Robins, Sr., Southey Dolby - p. 69

SAVAGE, ABEL - 8 Oct. 1794 - 26 Jan. 1795 - To wife Peggy. To son Nathaniel. To dau. Katty. Bal. of est. to wife during her life or wid. then to be div. bet. my wife & all my children, Nathaniel Katty & unborn child. Wife & bro. Peter Exes. Witt: George Craik, John Read, John Fletcher - p. 70

BRADFORD, SARAH - 3 Oct. 1794 - 26 Jan. 1795 - To grandau. Milly Polk. To Betsey Lurten. To Scharbrough Polk Townsing. To Peggy Townsing. Grandaus. Sally Townsing, Ginney Polk, Patty Polk & Milley Polk resid. legatees. Patty Polk's est. to remain in the hands of Henry Townsing until she comes to the age to receive it, & in case she dies before that age I give the said est. to my grandau Sally Townsing. Milly Polk's est. to remain in the hands of my grandau. Jinny Polk until she come to age to receive it, & in case she die before that age I give the said estate to my grandau Ginny Polk. Henry Townsing & Levin White Exrs. Witt: James Bradford, Zerobabel Harmon. - p. 71
In order of prob: William Polk qualfied.

ARMEY TRADOR, WILLIAM - "Armitrader" in order of prob: Signed "Trader" - 6 Jan. 1794 - 30 Dec. 1794 - To son Sacker Trador planta. where I now live & 10 A. of Marsh purchased of Abner Burton. To son William Armey Trador 1 s. To dau. Comfort Trador. To dau. Agnes Shay. To grandau. Peggy Trador. To dau. Ommey? Young 1 s. To son George Trador. Bal. of est. to be div. bet. children Elizabeth Lucust, Susannah Fisher, Near Taylor, Comfort Trador, Agnes Shay. William Morgan Exr. Witt: Richard Kelly, Archibald Trador, Major Hinman - p. 72

POWEL, NICKLESS - 21 Jan. 1795 - 26 Jan. 1795 - 1/2 my land to Laban Powel until Gim Powel, the son of Peter Powel, comes to age, & then to him & his heirs forever, & for want of issue to go to Laban Powel's children. The other 1/2 of my land to Isaac Powel until his son John comes of age, & then to him & his heirs forever, & for want of heirs to Laban's children. To bros. Laban Powel, Isaac Powel & Briget. To Betty Boswill 10 L. To Breget Dix 10 L. Isaac & Laban Powel resid. legatees. Bro. Laban Powel & John Bundick Exrs. Witt: Daniel Melson, Johannas Wise, Teagle Sreves - p. 73

THORNTON, EDWARD - 2 Jan. 1782 - 26 Jan. 1795 - Wife Rachel Thornton Exec. To wife whole est. during her wid. To son Henry Thornton the place where I now live, & should he offer to sell the land my son John to have it; my desire is that it shall continue in the same name, and for my son John to bequeath it to his proper heirs. 2 sons Henry & John resid. legatees. Should my wife be with child that child to have things equal in value to what I have left my son John, & the rest of my est. to be div. bet. all three. Witt: John Warrington, William Burton, Rachel Thornton - p. 74
In order of prob: "Mary" Thornton qualified.

MARRINER, GEORGE - 14 Jan. 1795 - 26 Jan. 1795 - To wife Sarah 1/3 of my whole est. the other 2/3 to be equally div. bet. my 4 children Levin, George, Major, Hastings, wife Sally & my youngest child Euphamy Mariner - Son George Exr. Witt: John Mclean, Wise Hargis, Thomas Hargis - p. 75

MARRINER, SARAH - 18 Jan. 1795 - 26 Jan. 1795 - To dau. Euphamy Marriner whole est. except my clothing which I give to my sister Suphier Brittingham. Should my dau. Euphamy die without issue whole est. to my said sister. Thomas Hargis Exr. Witt: John Marshall, Elizabeth Ardis - p. 76

KELLUM, SOLOMON - 4 Nov. 1794 - 27 Jan. 1795 - To son in law John Bell 4 L 10 s. that I lent him. To son John Kellam 4 L 10 s. To dau. Molley Kellum 4 L 10 s. To son George Kellum 5 L 4 children Rosannah Bell, John, Molly & George Kellum resid. legatees - Thomas Burton Exr. Witt: John Spiers, John Burton - p. 82

BELL, JOHN SELBY - 13 Dec. 1794 - 26 Jan. 1795 - To wife Sinah Bell negroes for life & then to my son William Bell. John Cropper,

Jr. & Jacob Bird Exrs. Witt: Smith Melson, William Pielee - p. 82

BRADFORD, BROWN - 2 Dec. 1794 - 27 Jan. 1795 - To wife Peggy whole est. during her wid, to school & bring up my children. Children to be bound out to learn a trade. Should my son John Brown Bradford live to lawful age I give him my land & should he die under age to my son Ezra Bradford, & should both die before they are of age & my unborn child should live to lawful age, I give the said child my land, & should they all die before age or marriage then to be div. bet. my bros. Ezra & Littleton Bradford & my sister Susannah Bradford. Should my wife marry all my property except my land to be div. bet, my wife & children, my eldest excepted. Bro. Ezra Bradford Exr. Witt: Hezekiah Pitts, William James - p. 83

GOOTEE, LISNEY - 17 Nov. 1794 - 27 Jan. 1795 - To son John Gootee all the lands that I have any title to & for want of issue to be div. bet. my 2 daus. Hannah & Elizabeth Gootee. Daus. Hannah & Elizabeth resid. legatees. Bro. John Gootee & friend Revel Patterson Exrs. Witt: Charles Beard, George Marshall, Ephraim Melvin, Reabeack Marshall - p. 86

STEPHENS, MOLLY - Not dated - 27 Jan. 1795 - To dau. Nancy Stephens 20 A. of land more or less & all the remainder of my est. Elisha Stephens Exr. Witt: George Bull, Elizabeth Bull, Daniel Melson - p. 87

HORNSBY, BAGWILL - 17 Nov. 1794 - 28 Jan. 1795 - To sister Nancy Hornsby the whole of my est. Bro. Major Hornsby Exr. "As witness my seal in the Burough of Norfolk" Witt: Robinson Custis, John Joynes, John Cook - p. 87

BELL, THOMAS - 13 Dec. 1794 - 28 Jan. 1795 - Bro. Roben Bell Exr. & sold heir of my landed estate lying upon the seaside adj. Mr. John Custis' planta. To Miss Leah Custis my mare. Sister Rosie Bell resid. legatee. Witt: James Garrison. Hutchinson Kellam - p. 88

MEARS, GEORGE - 22 Dec. 1794 - 23 Feb. 1795 - To son John Mears all my land. Moveable est. to be div. bet. wife Peggy Mears, Charles Mears, Moley Tignal, Milley Mears & Nancy Mears. Friend Thomas Ames & son John Mears Exrs. Witt: Elisha Mears, Rickets Tatham, Jesse Ames - p. 92

GRINNALDS, THOMAS - 29 Jan. 1795 - 23 Feb. 1795 - Whole est. to be div. bet. my bros. Elijah & Southy Grinnalds. To nephew John Grinnalds my horse saddle & bridle. To nephew Thomas Grinalds my silver watch & gun. Slaves to serve my bros. until 21, then to be free. Charles Stockly Exr. Witt: Caleb Dix - p. 93

YOUNG, JOHN - 2 Dec. 1794 - 23 Feb. 1795 - To wife Annabella Young. To son Bagwill Young. To dau. Elizabeth Colemons. To dau. Mary Bishop. Dau. Mary Bishop & son Bagwill Young resid. legatees

- Charles Stockly Exr. Witt: William Wise, John Perry - p. 94

GARRETT, HENRY - 8 Feb. 1795 - 23 Feb. 1795 - Friend Southy Bull to have the use of my negroe George for the support & maintenance of my children Susey & Henry for so long as he shall keep them. Should my wife be with child the said child to have 1 s. only of my est. Children Caty, Robert, Susanna, Henry & Elisha resid. legatees. Friends Tully Wise & Southy Bull Exrs. Witt: Tully Wise, Mitchel Chandler, Susannah Hall - p. 95

RODGERS, JOHN - 20 Jan. 1795 - 23 Feb. 1795 - Planta. & mill adj. to be rented until the year 1800, with my slaves for the said term, and the profits to be applied to the support of my 2 daus. Amy & Betsey, & at the expiration of that time the said slaves to be free. To dau. Amy all the land that I die possessed of, including the water grist mill adj. thereto, provided she do not demand anything from my est. anything given her by her grandmother, or any claim she may have by the death of Edmund Groten, exclusive of her proportion of the said Edmund's land held jointly with my dau. Betsy. Should my dau. Amy make such claim against my est. she to forfeit to my dau. Betsey my water grist mill. To dau. Betsey the whole of my est. not before given. Friend George Ker guardian to my 2 daus. until they arrive to 18 years of age. Friend George Ker Exr. Witt: Levin Ames, Nathaniel Ames, Samuel Galt - p. 96

BRADFORD, THOMAS BAILY - 1 Sept. 1794 - 25 Sept. 1795 - To wife Amy whole est. during her wid. to bring up my children, & at her death or marriage my lands to be rented out until my son Charles Baily Bradford arrive to lawful age, & the profits to be equally divided between my 3 children Bridget, Charles & Leah. I give my land to my son Charles Baily Bradford. Witt: William Leatherbury, Daniel Richerson, William Trador - p. 98
In ordor of prob: Amy Bradford qualified.

PARKER, PEGGY - 28 Dec. 1789 - 23 Feb. 1795 - To grandau. Peggy Parker, dau. of Samuel Parker 24 A. more or less adj. Abel Savage & William Nelson, Samuel Parker to have the use of same during his life. To grandau. Esther Carlisle Parker, dau. of Molly Carlisle 12 A. adj. Edward Peall, Benjamin Warrington & Zerobable Rodgers, which land I lend to my dau. Molly Carlisle during her life. To grandau. Margaret Luker Hickman, dau. of Peggy Hickman, 24 A. adj. Edward Revel & John Fosky, which land I lend to my dau. Peggy Hickman during her life. To son Samuel Parker. To son George Parker. To grandau. Catey Hickman. Grandau. Rose Hickman. Grandau. Susannah Hickman. Grandau. Sally Hickman. Son Samuel Parker, Molly Carlisle, & Peggy Hickman resid. legatees. Neighbor Levin White & John Read Exrs. Witt: Major Taylor, Henry Read, Margaret Read - p. 99

GROTEN, JONATHAN - 1 Dec. 1794 - 23 Feb. 1795 - Wife Joyce to have the use of my land & planta. during her natural life provided she be not with child, but if she be with child at my death my said wife to have the use of said land for only 4 years, after which I give the said land to that infant. Wife resid. legatee. Wife & father in law, Levin Ames, Exrs. Witt: John Rodgers, Levin Nock, Mary Ames - p. 101

WEST, ANTHONY - 5 Feb. 1795 - 23 Feb. 1795 - To bro. Abel West land & planta. on Andua Creek where he now lives cont. 500 A., he to make over his right of all the land he has on Deep Creek to the said Anthony & which the said Anthony now has in possession. To bro. Abel West all the right & title I have to the land that Henry Gasquine gave to Susannah West. To son Revel West the land where I now live & the land my bro. Abel has given to me agrreable to my will, the said Revel to pay 360 L to his brothers & Sisters George, Isaac, John, Ann, Elizabeth, Agnes. Margaret & Rachel, & should he refuse I give 1/2 the land to George, Isaac, Ann, Elizabeth, Agnes, Margaret & Rachel. Wife Elenor to have use of my lands during her wid. Bal. of est. to my wife during her wid. then to be div. bet. my 8 children George, Isaac. John, Ann, Elizabeth, Agnes, Marget & Rachel West. I give my part of Tangears Island to my 3 sons George, John & Isaac West. Sons George & John Exrs. John West, son of Jona: John Groten - p. 102

ASHBY, GEORGE - 23 Mar. 1794 - 23 Feb. 1795 - To wife Nancy personalty & negroes during her wid. then to be equally div. bet. all my children. To sons James & George Ashby. Children James, George, Keaty Ashby & unborn child. Custis Willis Exr. Witt: Elisha Mears, David Ashby, William Groten - p. 104

PREWIT, WILLIAM - 18 Jan. 1795 - 30 Mar. 1795 - To son John Prewit 4 A. on the North side of the Church Road adj. the land of Thomas Bayly, Levin White & Levin Ayres. To son Benjamin all the remaining part of my land not before given to him. To dau. Catey Holston. Wife Abigail Prewit. Children Catey Holston, Peggy, Nancy, William, Tabitha, Rachel, Agness & Betsey Smith Prewit resid. legatees. Friend William Drummond Exr. Witt: Smith Melson, Kendall Middleton, Major Middleton - p. 121

BRITTINGHAM JOHN - 13 Sept. 1794 - 28 Apr. 1795 - To son James Brittingham when he arrives at lawful age, the planta. purchased of Margaret Townsend, reserving his mother's dower in said land, & also that he will find a home for his sisters Elizabeth & Sally until their marriage; should James die under age I give the said land to my son John (under age). Daus. Betsy & Sally & son John resid. legatees. Wife Marey to have use of whole est. to bring up my children. Should all my children die before coming to lawful age my sister Mary Brittingham to have the lands before given. Wife Mary Exec. Witt: Nehemiah Tindell, Bettey Melvin - p. 122

WEST, GEORGE - 25 Mar. 1795 - 28 Apr. 1795 - To my sister Ann West 18 L. Bal. of the money due me & in my possession at my death to be equally div. bet. my bros. & sisters Elizabeth, Agnes,

Isaac, John, Margaret & Rachel. Bros. Isaac & John West to have that part of Tangear Island given me by my father. McKeel Wise to pay $20. for my 1/2 the schooner that we have in partnership, & that he have my 1/2, & if he refuse my 1/2 to be sold by my Exrs. Friend John Custis Exr. Witt: John Groten, Charles Crowson – p. 123

ROBINS, JOHN, Jr. – 2 Mar. 1795 – 28 Apr. 1795 – To my sister Polly Wilkerson, wife of Jesse Wilkerson dec. To sister Susanna Robins. To cousin John Wilkerson. Mother in law Leah Evens. To my 1/2 bro. Mickel Robins. Witt: Joseph Fiddeman, Teagle Taylor, Elijah Fitzgerald – p. 124
In order of prob: Proved by Elisha Garrett, one of the witnasses – John Logan qualified.

SAVAGE, ROBERT (son of Major) – 15 Sept. 1794 – 28 Apr. 1795 – To mother Peggy Savage. To bro. Arthur Savage all my land & for want of heirs to be equally div. bet. Abel Garrison, son of George, & Abel Burton, son of Thomas Burton. Bro. Arthur Savage resid. legatee. Bro. Arthur Savage & neighbor John Smith Exrs. Witt: Archibald Garretson, George Craik, George Nottingham – p. 126

RODGERS, JAMES – 10 Apr. 1795 – 28 Apr. 1795 – To wife whole est. during her wid. then to be equally div. bet. my son Ruben Rodgers, Richard Highland Rodgers & Mathew Rodgers – Wife (no name) Exec. – Witt: William Andrews, Robert Davis, Crippen Johnson – p. 126
In order of prob: Sarah Rodgers qualified.

SMITH, ELIZABETH – 4 Oct. 1794 – 28 Apr. 1795 – To sister Mary Savage. To Polly Heath. To George Smith. To Charles Smith. To John Smith, Sr. To John Smith, Jr. To Elizabeth Smith. To George Smith Savage. To Elizabeth Kellam. To Nancy Kellam (both under 18). To John Joynes. To Nancy Joynes. To Sarah Joynes. To Susanna Joines. To Smith Joines. To John Joines, Jr. To Robert Andrews Joines. George Smith & John Joines Exrs. To Elizabeth Lawrence. To Nancy Darby. To Susanna Martin. To Polly Kellam. Witt: Charles West, Ezekiel Ashby – p. 126

SALISBURY, JOHN – 26 Jan. 1789 – 28 Apr. 1795 – To wife Jenny whole est. during her wid. to bring up my children, then to be div. bet. all my children except my dau. Sally. To dau. Sally Topping. Wife & son Thomas Exrs. Witt: John Wise, Peggy Gillett – p. 128

CHANDLER, LEVY – 26 June 1794 – 28 Apr. 1795 – Land to be sold by my Exr. To wife Agnes Chandler proceeds of my land & all the rest of my est. during her wid. to bring up my children, then to be div. bet. my 3 children & my wife. John Spiers Exr. Witt: Connelus Wadkins, Levin Hargas, George Taylor – p. 129
In order of prob: John Bull qualified.

WAGGAMAN, JOSEPH – 24 Mar. 1795 – 29 Apr. 1795 – To wife Elizabeth 1/3 of all my moveable est. forever & 1/3 of the lands hereafter left to my son Hezekiah & my son Ephraim Waggaman during her natural life in lieu of dower. Daus. Polly, Nancy, Betsy & Sally to have homes on the lands left my sons during their single lives. To son Hezekiah Waggaman all the land & planta. where I now live cont. 200 A. & for want of heirs to my son Ephraim. To son Ephraim land lying near Pocomoke Church cont. 230 A., & for want of heirs to my 4 daus. Daus. resid. legatees. Wife Elizabeth & friend Walter Bayne Exrs. Witt: William Watts, William Downing - p. 129

MASSEY, NANNEY - 21 Jan. 1795 - 29 June 1795 - To son Caleb Massey land where he now lives cont. 100 A. To son Atkyns Massey land where ne how lives cont. 30 A. To son Thomas Massey land where he now lives cont. 30 A. Son Thomas resid. legatee. Witt: William Downing, Ephraim Broadwater, Nancy Burton - p. 131
In order of prob:. Caleb Massey qualified.

TAYLOR, BARTHOLOMEW - 11 Mar. 1783 - 29 June 1795 - To wife Tabitha Taylor the use of the land I now live on during her wid., then to be div. bet. my sons Jeremiah Taylor & Selby Taylor. To wife whole personal est. during her wid., then to be div. bet. my daus. To son John Taylor the land where he now lives. Dau. Rachel Taylor to have a home with my wife during her single life. Wife Exec. Witt: William Downing, Southey White, Caleb Massey - p. 131

DRUMMOND, SPENCER - 19 May 1795 - 29 June 1795 - To son Richard Drummond 100 A. where my dwelling house stands. To son Spencer Drummond 100 A. adj. Henry Hall's land & the land given my son Richard. To son Charles Drummond all the remainder of my Mesongo land. To sons Richard & Spencer my marsh on the South side of Mesongo by the name of Times Island. To sons William & George (under age) my Guilford land. To son William Drummond. To son Spencer Drummond 1/4 of my schooner Lisbon; 1/4 to my son Charles, 1/4 to my son Richard & the remaining part of my schooner to my dau. Nancy Drummond. To dau. Elizabeth Drummond. To dau. Sally Drummond. To wife Comfort Drummond. Bal. of est. to wife until my son George comes to the age of 21 years, then to be div. bet. my 5 sons & 3 daus, Richard, Spencer, Charles, William & George Drummond, Nancy, Elizabeth & Sally Drummond. Wife Comfort, Richard, Spencer & Charles Drummond Exrs. Witt: Thomas Fletcher, Joseph Conquest, Benjamin Marshall - p. 132

MERRIL, WILLIAM - 26 Jan. 1795 - 29 June 1795 - To son George Merril. To son Maximilian Merril the planta. where my son George Merril now lives lying in Somerset County on Planners Creek, known by the name of Scotland, & also a piece of swamp land called Merril's Folly adj. the above planta. To dau. Asenath Merrill. To dau. Mary Merril. Son Maximilian Merril & daus. Asenath & Mary Merril resid. legatees - Son Maxililian Exr. Witt: James Melvin, Nathaniel Benston, William Benston - p. 137

426

BOGGS, JOSEPH - 22 Sept. 1792 - 23 Apr. 1795 - To wife Mary Boggs whole est. during her wid. To son Francis Boggs planta. where I now live. To dau. Mary Boggs. To dau. Naomi Boggs. Daus. Mary & Naomi resid. legatees. Wife Mary & son Francis Exrs. Witt: Teackle Shay, John Benston, Thomas Sanford - p. 139

CONQUEST, ANN - 24 Apr. 1794 - 29 June 1795 - To son James Conquest. To dau. Nancy Conquest. To dau. Keziah Conquest. To grandau. Nancy Warner. To dau. Peggy Conquest. To dau. Polly Taylor. To Keziah, Nancy, James & Peggy Conquest the crop now growing for their support. Betsy Warner, Keziah Conquest, Polly Taylor, Nancy Conquest & Peggy Conquest resid. legatees. William Conquest & James Conquest Exrs. Witt: James Stanton, Joseph Conquest - p. 144

BRADFORD, ROBERT - 26 Nov. 1794 - 28 Apr. 1795 - To wife the use of my lands & personal est. during her wid. To Robert Mears, son of Spencer, all my lands except 5 A. where James Lurton now lives, which I give to my negro Tomny & negro Saul, to be given to them at my death. All my slaves to be free. Robert Mears & James Chandler, son of Zerobabel, resid. legatees. To John Kellam. Arthur Bradford & John Kellam Exrs. Witt: William Leatherbury, Judea Only, Peggy Only - p. 145

REW, ABSALOM - 24 Apr. 1794 - 29 June 1795 - To wife Sarah Horsey Rew whole est. during her wid., & at her death or marriage to my son John Rew my whole planta. that I now live on. To dau. Elizabeth Ewell. To son Charles Rew. To dau. Nancy Rew. To grandson Laban Powell. Sons John & Charles Rew & daus. Elizabeth Ewell & Nancy Rew resid. legatees. Sons John & Charles Rew Exrs. Witt: William Young, Woney Rew, Reuben Rew - p. 146

KELLAM, SACKER - 24 Feb. 1795 - 29 June 1795 - To wife Charity Kellam whole est. during her wid. To sons Smith & Revel Kellam all my lands adj. the lands of Robert Nock & James Rodgers. To son Custis Kellam. To dau. Rachel Kellam. To dau. Nancy Kellam. To dau. Betsey Kellam. To dau. Susah Kellam. To dau. Leah Kellam. To dau. Peggy Kellam. Wife Charity Kellam & daus. Betsy, Susah, Leah & Peggy Kellam resid. legatees - Wife & George Taylor Exrs. Witt: Smith Martin, Robert Nock - p. 153
In order of prob: Charles Kellam qualified.

BADGER, NATHANIEL - 14 Sept. 1793 - 29 June 1795 - To son Nathaniel Badger all the land I now live on cont. 125 A., the said Nathaniel to maintain & educate my son Thomas Wyatt Badger (under 15) & should he refuse Thomas to have 1/2 the said planta. To son John Badger 50 A. on Wallops Island. Bal. of est. to wife Joyce Badger during her wid. & then to be div. between the rest of my children then living. Wife Joyce & son James Exrs. Witt: Josi: Larke, Smith Beasly, James Edmunds - p. 154

EAST, SOUTHY – 6 Apr. 1793 – 29 June 1795 – To wife Scarbrough East whole est. during her wid. To son William land where I now live. To son Severn East. To son Southy East ground to set a house & shop upon on the South-west corner of the land if he should want it on Deep Creek Road. To son Asia East. To son Richard East. To dau. Mary East. To dau. Sarah. To son Nehemiah East. Bal. of est. to wife Scarbrough to distribute among the children as she thinks most convenient. Witt: Thomas Metcaff, Peggy Metcaff, Elizabeth Ross – p. 156
In order of prob: Robinson Custis qualified.

ELLIOTT, ANN – wid. Thomas Elliott, dec. – 10 July 1793 – 29 June 1795 – To grandau. Sally Kelly. To grandau Farney Mears. To grandau Ann Parker. To my grandson in law Samuel Parker. To grandau. Nancy Elliott, dau. of Charles Elliott. To grandau. Ann Mary Elliott. To grandau. Nancy Elliott, dau. of Thomas Elliott. To grandson John Elliott. To dau. in law Keziah Elliott. 4 sons John, Thomas, William & Charles Elliott & my dau. Nancy Bell resid. legatees. To sister Suffia Kelly. Son William Elliott & son in law William Bell Exrs. Witt: Abel Savage, Katron Monger, Geodiah Bell – p. 177

MELSON, LEVIN – 31 Mar. 1795 – 29 June 1795 – To wife Nanny Melson whole est. during her wid. To son Noah Wyatt Melson a small piece of land adj. Tully Lillaston, to include the house where Rachel Melson now lives. Rest of my land to my son James Milliner. Bal. of est. to son Noah Wyatt Miliner & my dau. Amey Melson, Bridget Melson & Rachel Melson. Wife Nanny Exec. – Witt: Southy Satchell, Susanna Lilleston, Jacob Lillaston – p. 184

COLEBURN, CATHARINE – 29 May 1795 – 27 July 1795 – To son Samuel Coleburn whole est. Son Samuel Exr. Witt: John Coleburn, Sarah Powell, William Coleburn – p. 199

WATSON, ZEROBABEL – 6 Feb. 1795 – 27 July 1795 – To wife Susanna Watson whole est. during her wid. to bring up my children. The negroes that came by my wife to be at her disposal. To son John Mar Watson the whole of my land. Witt: Ephraim Watson, Peggy Willis – p. 199
In order of prob: Proved by Ephraim Watson, the other witness being since dead. Susanna Watson qualified.

STURGIS, RICHARD – 24 Apr. 1795 – 28 July 1795 – To wife Peggy Sturgis whole est. during ner wid. to raise my children & then to be div. bet. my children. To dau. Salley. To godson John Sturgis. John Sturgis, Sr., Exr. Witt: Revel Sturgis, Polly Core – p. 208

MARSHALL, SOPHIA – 17 Aug. 1795 – 28 Sept. 1795 – To dau. Betsy Piper the whole of her est. that was devised her by her father Daniel Marshall, & also that I purchased of her. To Daniel Jenepher Marshall the whole of the est. devised him by his father Daniel Marshall. Son & dau. above named Exrs. Witt: George Corbin, John McLean – p.

SAVAGE, Abel – 18 Apr. 1795 – 28 Sept. 1795 – To Goddau. Peggy Townsend 4C s. Bro. John Savage resid. legatee & Exr. Witt: Custis Willis – p. 218

ABBOTT, ELIZABETH – 6 Feb. 1795 – 28 Sept. 1795 – To sister Margaret Townsend. To Ann Samson "my lite Chince gown with a vine running throw it which William Cowley brought Philadelphia". To niece Hester Broadwater. To Elizabeth Broadwater. To Lidy Hope. To sister Rachel Broadwater. To Anabella Hope. To nephew Robert Townsend. To bro. William Cowley. Rachel Broadwater, Margaret Townsend resid. legatees. Witt: William Adair, Rebecka Walker – p. 219
In order of prob: William Cowley qualified.

THORNTON MARY – 24 Apr. 1795 – 29 Sept. 1795 – To son Edward Fiddeman Thornton whole est. except such as is devised hereafter, & for want of heirs 1/2 of said est. to my sister Elizabeth Feddeman & 1/2 to my sister Ann Feddeman. To Esther Feddeman, wid. of Isaiah. To Elizabeth Feddeman, dau. of Joseph, To Mary Houston Feddeman, dau. of William. To Polly Fiddeman, dau. of Isaiah. To Catherine Fiddeman, dau. of Joseph. Joseph & William Fiddeman Exrs. & guardians to my son Edward. Witt: William Adair, Rachel Moses, Joshua Thornton – p. 234

COPES, HANCOCK – 24 Mar. 1795 – 29 Sept. 1795 – To wife Elizabeth whole est. during her wid. to being up my 2 children. Planta. to maintain & school my son Henry Savage Copes until he arrives to the age of 21 or marriage, & then I give him 50 A. to be laid off as my son John Custis Copes shall see proper. To son John Custis Copes all the rest of my land. Should both my sons die without issue, then to my wife Elizabeth for life, reversion to Crittey Copes, dau. of Levin Copes. Son Henry Savage Copes resid. legatee. Wife, John Custis (seaside) & friend Southy Satchell Exrs. Witt: Levin Copes, Jacob Taylor, Francis Taylor – p. 235

PHILLIPS, BENJAMIN, SR. – 16 Jan. 1795 – 29 Sept. 1795 – To wife Susanna Phillips whole est. for life & then to my son Jonathan Phillips, & should William Phillips Topping live to come to lawful age, my son Jonathan Phillips to pay him the sum of 10 L. Witt: John R. Parker, Ruth Parker.
Codicil: To son Benjamin Phillips all my land where I now live at his mother's death. Same witnesses – p. 236
In order of prob: Jonathan Phillips qualified.

BRADFORD, JAMES – 17 Nov. 1794 – Partly proved 29 June 1795 – Prob: 26 Oct. 1795. To son John Bradford all my land & planta. in Bradford's Neck on the Broadwater side cont. 200 A. To son William Mears Bradford a tract of land lying in the swamp adj. Kendall Beech, Arthur Bradford & Kendall Richardson, cont. 50 A. I give all the

remainder of my lands to my son John Bradford. To wife Lucresha whole est. for life to bring up my children. To my 2 daus. Rachel & Nancy Bradford. 4 children John, William, Rachel & Nancy Bradford resid. legatees. Levi Long & Lucresha Bradford Exrs. Witt: Littleton Wyatt, Isaiah Kelly, George Bradford – p. 236
In order of prob: "John Bell & Lucretia, his wife, qualified.

KELLUM, MARGARET – 8 Aug. 1795 – 26 Oct. 1795 – To son Arthur Rodgers. 2 daus. Molly Rodgers & Nancy Rodgers resid. legatees. Arthur Roberts Exr. Witt: William Roberts, Frances Roberts – p. 242

GARRISON, JOHN, JR. – 6 July 1795 – Partly proved 27 July 1795 – Prob: 26 Oct. 1795 – To bro. William Garrison land where I now live. To bro. Joshua Garrison the use or said land for the term of 4 years, he giving my bro. William 25 L per year, also giving him his home for the said 4 years. To sister Betsy Garrison. To bro. Bagwell Garrison. To bro. Edmund Garrison. To sister Rosey Garrison. Francis Savage Exr. Witt: Berry Floyd, Sarah Floyd, Charles Savage – p. 243

ROBERTS, SARAH – 21 Aug. 1795 – 26 Oct. 1795 – To son Francis Roberts. To dau. Mary Roberts. To dau. Rachil James Roberts. To son John Roberts. Sons Arthur & Joshua Roberts resid. legatees (both under age) – Son Francis Exr. – Witt: William Roberts, Arthur Roberts, Jr., Nancy Roberts – p. 244

BLOXOM, JOSHUA – 4 May 1788 – 27 Oct. 1795 – Wife Leah solo legatee & Exec. – Witt: James Hopman, Jacob Bloxom, Archabel Armatrader, Levin Bloxom – p. 245

DRUMMOND, HENRY – 7 Nov. 1795 – 28 Dec. 1795 – To son John Drummond land & planta where I now live lying on Merry Branch. To son Thomas Bonwell Drummond, & for want of heirs to my 3 children John, Peggy & unborn child. Should my unborn child die without issue whole est. given it I give to my wife Esther Drummond. Wife to have all that she had before I married her. Dau. Peggy to have 6 silver tea spoons & sugar tongs marked "F.M." and "R" William Gibb Exr. Witt: M. Bonwell, Sr., John Boisnard, Robert Bonwell – p. 256

BUNDICK, WILLIAM – 31 Oct. 1795 – 28 Dec. 1795 – To wife Agnes Bundick whole est. during her wid. to bring up my 3 children Lewis, George & William. Unborn child to be brought up & educated as my other children. At the death of my wife est. to be equally div. between my 3 sons above named & unborn child. Wife Exec. Witt: George Wright, Major Hinmon, Charles Stockly – p. 257

DRUMMOND, DAVID – 24 Oct. 1795 – 28 Dec. 1795 – To son John Drummond planta. that my father left me during his natural life, & at his death to his children, & for want of heirs to my unborn child for life & then to his or her heirs, & for want of heirs to my dau. Sarah Robinson Drummond & her heirs, & for want of heirs to the hereafter children of my said wife if any she should have, & if none John

Drummond & his children to equally inherit the said plantation. To wife Sophia Drummond the planta. where I now reside which I purchased of Johannes Wise, to her & her heirs forever. To dau. Sarah Robinson Drummond the houses & lot in Onancock Town that was formerly held by Patience Robinson, dec. Wife Sophia & friend Levin Walker Exrs. Witt: George Simpson, John Parker, Jr., Leah Dix - p. 258

DIX, JOHN - 4 Dec. 1793 - 29 Dec. 1795 - To wife whole est. during her wid., she to school my son James. To son James Milby Dix all my lands. Son James & dau. Mary Poulson resid. legatees. Wife (no name) Exec. & John Poulson & John Teackle, Merchants, Exrs. Witt: Parker Barnes, Betsey Copes - p. 260
In order of prob: Anne Dix qualified.

RICHARDSON, RACHEL - 23 Mar. 1795 - 29 Dec. 1795 - To dau. Peggy Mears Richardson whole est., & should she die without issue to my goddau. Rachel Edwards. McKeel Bonwell, Sr. Exr. Witt: William Bell, Sr., William Bell, Jr., Mary Budd, McBonwell - p. 260

RICHARDSON, WILLIAM - Not dated - 29 Dec. 1795 - To son William 25 A. at that end of my land adj. Perry Leatherbury, orphan. To eldest son Major the rest of my land. To wife Elizabeth. 2 sons Major & William resid. legatees. Friend William Gibb & Stephen Warrington Exrs. Witt: William Leatherbury, Thomas Phillips, Susanna White - p. 261

HASTINGS, SCARBURGH - Nunc. Died 23 Sept. 1795 - Proved 24 Sept. 1795 - To grandau Nancy Young whole est. - Proved by Richard Young, Sr. & Ann his wife. - p. 293
In order of prob: Richard Young qualified.

METCALF, MARK - 5 Dec. 1794 - 25 Jan. 1796 - Planta. where Thomas Metcalf now lives at the head of the Creek to be rented till my son John Metcalf comes to 21 years of age, & the money to be used for the schooling of all my children. To son John when he comes to age the above planta. cont. 100 A. & for want of issue to my son William Metcalf. To son Thomas Metcalf (under 21) 100 A. where I now live & for want of heirs to my son Samuel Metcalf (under 21). To wife Sarah Metcalf planta. where I now live until my son Thomas comes to the age of 21. To dau. Elizabeth Metcalf. Wife & children resid. legatees. Friend Jessey Kellum & Thomas Bagwell Exrs. Witt: Parker Copes, Sarah Edmunds - p. 303

SANFORD, ELIZABETH - 11 Nov. 1795 - 25 Jan. 1796 - To Cemmey Benston, son of John Benston, 10 A. of my land adj. John Sandford - Sister Ann Sandford to have the use of said land for 7 years. All the remainder of my land & marsh to my sister Ann Sandford. To Hettey, Nanney, Betsey & John Benson, children of John Benson. To John Benson. To bro. John Sanford. Sister Ann Sanford resid. legatee. Bro. Thomas Sanford. Ann Sanford Exec. - Witt: Thomas Fletcher, Tabi-

tha Silverthorn.
In order of prob: Selby Lucas qualified – p. 304

SPIERS, JOHN – 14 Nov. 1795 – 25 Jan. 1796 – Whole est. to my wife during her wid. then my land & planta. to my son James Spiers, he paying 40 L to the estate. To son John Spiers. Bal. of est. to my 6 children, Sarah Spiers, Ann Beach, Catharine Spiers, Elizabeth Spiers & Leah Spiers & John Spiers. Sons James & John Spiers Exrs. Witt: Thomas Burton, Peggy Knox – p. 305

CROPPER, SEBASTIAN – 26 Mar. 1795 – 25 Jan. 1796 – To son Sebastian Cropper (under age) my planta. except 100 A. next to small beer branch, & should he die before he is 21 to William Drummond Cropper. To son William Drummond Cropper the 100 A. above referred to, & for want of heirs to my son Sebastian Cropper. To dau. Betty Cropper. To dau. Mary Cropper. To dau. Sabra Cropper. Wife Barbara Cropper to have use of whole est. until my children come to lawful age, she to keep & educate them. William Welburn, Drummond Welburn & John Cropper, Jr. Exrs. Witt: John Cropper, Jr., John Snead, Jr. – p. 306

ASHBY, DAVID – 9 Jan. 1796 – 25 Jan. 1796 – To David Ashby, son of John Ashby, all the land that I bought of Isaack Massey in "Shatim" County on White Oak Creek. All the remainder of my lands lying in said county on Bresh Creek that I bought of Joseph Wilsa to be div. bet. George Ashby, son of George Ashby, & Luther Mears, son of Elisha Mears. To Ezekiel Ashby. To John Ashby. To William Ashby. To Samuel Ashby. To Ezekiel Beach. To sister Susanna Ashby the bal. of my est. John Ashby Exr. Witt: Elisha Mears, Salathel West, John Mears – p. 308

BUNTING, KENDALL – 7 Jan. 1796 – 25 Jan. 1796 – Wife to have use of whole est. during her wid. to suppprt & educate my children & then to be equally div. bet. all my children then living. Friend Severn Kellam Exr. Witt: Americus Scarborough, George Bunting, Andrew Turner – p. 310

HAWLEY, ABEL – 1 Oct. 1795 – 25 Jan. 1796 – To son Henry Hawley. Son Henry & wife Sarah resid. legatees. Son to be at age at 18. Neighbor John Read, Sr. Exr. Witt: Ephraim Watson, Levi Hutchinson – p. 310

MEARS, JONATHAN – 2 Feb. 1796 – 29 Feb. 1796 – To dau. Ziporah Mears land purchased of Joseph Killey. To son Robert Mears land bought of Bird, Fitchett & Bell & adj. the above. To son Jonathan Mears all my land to the South of the great ditch down to Gilford Branch, also the land bought of Parradice cont. 75 A. on Assatigue Island & all the money due me from the Western Shore. To cousin Shadrack Mears. To grandson Robert Wheelton. To grandau. Joice Wheelton. To son Bartholomew Mears. To son Mecajah Mears. Children Micajah Mears, Bartholomew Mears & Leah Collins resid.

legatees. Sons Barthomomew & Jonathan Exrs. Witt: Thomas Evans, George Young, Tabitha Fitchett - p. 325

BENSTON, JOHN SAVAGE - 4 Jan. 1796 - 29 Feb. 1796 - To bro. James Benston. To sister Marget Benston. Land & residue of est. to be div. bet. bros. & sisters Rosey Benston, Marget Benston, Marry Benston, James Benston & Joyce Benston - Uncle Richard Savage Exr. Witt: Revil Abdil. John Savage - p. 333

AMES, NATHANIEL - 23 Feb. 1796 - 29 Feb. 1796 - Wife Elizabeth to have use of land where I now live to bring up my 3 children James, John & unborn child until my son James comes of lawful age, then to go to my said son James. To son John the land where Hannah Johnson now lives. Wife Elizabeth & friend John Milby Exrs. Witt: Jesse Ames, Marget Mears, Molly Callahan - p. 334

MIFFLIN, DANIEL - 22 Dec. 1795 - 27 Apr. 1796 - Confirms to Levin Hickman 30 A. of land on Assateage Beach, being part of a larger tract purchased of Thomas Gore, to John Lewis & Arthur Cherix 80 A. of the above tract, & to John Blades 155 A. being part of two tracts of land one called Floyd's Lot & the other Mifflin's Purchase, situate in Pitts Creek Hundred in Worcester County, Maryland, not having given them deeds for the said land. To son Warner Mifflin 5 s. together with what he has already had I consider his full proportion of my estate. To son Daniel Mifflin 200 L. which with what he has already had I consider his part of my estate. To grandson Jonathan Walker Mifflin. To daus. Patience Hunn, Elizabeth Howell Eyre Mifflin, Rebecca Mifflin & my grandau. Ann Hunn the bal. of my est., real & personal. Refers to "my former wife Ann". Sons Warner & Daniel Exrs. Witt: John S. Ker, John Davis, William Booth.
Codicil - That part of my personal estate which is included in my wife's dower to be her own property and at her own disposal. Same witnesses - p. 365

TAYLOR, ALEXANDER - 10 Jan. 1796 - 27 June 1796 - To son Alexander Taylor land where I now live. To wife Ann Taylor. 4 children William Mathew Taylor, Nathaniel Taylor, Ann Taylor & Samuel Taylor resid. legatees. Wife Exec. - Witt: William Downing, Washburn Mathews, Zepheriah Taylor - p. 382

BAKER, SALATHEL - 12 June 1796 - 27 June 1796 - To son John Sheperd Baker land where I now live being 100 A. To son Solomon Baker. To dau. Ester Baker. To dau. Elizabeth. All my wife's wearing clothes to be div. bet. my daus. Ester & Elizabeth. 4 daus. Rachel, Suphia, Mary & Sarah Baker resid. legatees. Solomon Baker & Elijah Baker Exrs. Witt: William Andrews, Ezekel Baker, William Baker - p. 382

NORTHAM, JOHN - 6 Feb. 1796 - 27 June 1796 - To son John Northam land where I now live & 2/3 of the water mill, being 106 acres, during his life & then to his heirs. "one saddle that I had of John

Small", should my son John die without heirs the land to go to my son Custis Northam, & the personal property to my 2 children Custis & Betsy Northam. To son Custis Northam all the lands called Galloping Ridge cont. 60 A. To son in law Levin Lucas 1 s. & no more. To wife Rachel. To dau. Susannah Mears. To dau. Nancy Hinmon. To dau. Leah Northam. To Bagwell Nichalison. To dau. Ester Warrington 1 s. & no more. Friend James Duncas Exr. Witt: Meshack Duncan, Anne Duncan - p. 383

WALKER, JOHN, Jr. - 25 Nov. 1795 - 27 June 1796 - Wife to have use of my planta. for 5 years & then to be div. bet. my wife & son John S. Walker; wife to possess 1/2 for life in lieu of dower & at her death of marriage I give the whole to my said son John S. Walker, he paying to my estate 100 L. Children Ann, Sally, Elizabeth, Henry & James Walker resid. legatees. Levy Hutchinson & wife (no name) Exrs. Not witnessed. Proved by John Martin & West Kellam - p. 385 In order of prob: Elizabeth Walker qualified.

BRADFORD, JOHN - 16 Aug. 1794 - Partly proved 26 Jan. 1796 - Prob: 27 June 1796 - To son Custis Bradford planta. where I now live. To wife Sarah Bradford. To dau. Susannah Bradford. Custis William & son Custis Bradford Exrs. Witt: Peggy Mears, James Mears - p. 386

GILLETT, JOSEPH - 30 June 1788 - 27 June 1796 - To bro. James Gillett land which my father Ayres Gillett bought of James Thompson & William Wise, cont. 349 A. To George Gillett, William Gillett & Tabitha Gillett all the balance that will become due me of my father's estate. Bro. John Exr. Witt: Giles Copes, Neil Lafferty, William Hill - p. 387

MELSON, SMITH, Sr. - 4 Mar. 1796 - 27 June 1796 - To wife Betty whole est. during her wid. & at her death or marriage to my son Smith Melson 100 A. where I now live adj. the land of Sophia Drummond, Daniel Melson & Levin White & Thomas Bayly. All the remaining part of my land adj. the above I lend to my son Jonathan Melson during his natural life, reversion to my grandson Smith Melson, son of Jonathan. 4 daus. Abigil Prewit, Frances Melson, Mary Lewis & Tabitha Middleton resid. legatees. Wife & son Smith Melson Exrs. Witt: William Drummond, Edmund Only, Nancy Lewis. p. 387

KELLY, JOSEPH - 30 Sept. 1795 - 25 July 1796 - To wife Elizabeth whole est. during her wid. except the house, garden & potato patch where Jesse Mills now lives, he to have the same so long as my wife lives. To dau. Hessy Mills planta. where I now live & for want of heirs to my 2 youngest daus. Rachel Kelly & Famey Kelly. To my daus. Rachel & Famey 50 A. of land formerly called Joseph Bell's land. To James & Mary Riggs 20 s. cash. Wife & William Young Exrs. Witt: William Young, Sr., Jonathan Fitchett - p. 398

SAVAGE, ROBERT - 6 June 1796 - 25 July 1796 - To 3 sisters Peggy, Patience & Sally 2 A. of land adj. the land of Thomas Robins & Hutchinson Kellam - Bal. of my land to my bro. Joseph Savage, he to pay my debts & to claim no part of the estate my mother shall leave at her death, & he to build a sawed log house on the said 2 acres, & should he refuse the land to be sold except the said 2 A. & the money to be div. bet. my bro. & 3 sisters. William Harmon & bro. Joseph Savage Exrs. Witt: Patrick Casey, George Smith Savage, Richard Savage - p. 399

SAVAGE, CHARLES - 17 Aug. 1795 - 25 July 1796 - To bro. Joseph Savage. To each of my 3 sisters 4 L cash. To mother Mary Savage. Mother, bros. & sisters resid. legatees. Bro. Joseph Exr. Witt: George Savage, Patrick Casey, William Mears - p. 401

BAKER, JOHN SHEPERD - 28 June 1796 - 25 July 1796 - To bro. Solomon Baker planta. cont. 100 A. To sister Rachel Baker. To sister Mary Baker. To sister Sophia Baker. Richard R. Savage & Solomon Baker Exrs. Witt: William Wright, John Baker, William Baker - p. 403

HICKMAN, ANNE - 10 Sept. 1793 - 25 July 1796 - To son Hampton Hickman. Grandaus. Rebeckah & Peggy Hickman, daus. of Isaih Hickman. To my said grandaus. all the est. devised to their mothers by the last will of my husband, which est. was left in my care during my natural life. John A. Bundick & Parker Barnes Exrs. Witt: Leah Barnes, Susanna Barnes - p. 404

SEYMOUR, LEAH - 21 June 1796 - 25 July 1796 - Estate to be sold for the payment of debts. Children John Revell, Sarah Poulson, the heirs of Edward Revell, George Seymour & the dau. of Elizabeth Ker to share no part of my estate. Son William Seymour & dau. Leah Seymour to divide my whole est. between them. Son John Revell & son William Seymour Exrs. Witt: John Teackle, Jr., John Arlington, Hutchinson Kellam - p. 405

PARKER, CHARLES - 16 May 1796 - 26 July 1796 - To son Charles Parker. To wife Rebecca Parker whole est. during her wid. & then to be div. bet. my 3 children Elizabeth Deshield Parker, Charles Parker & Polly Parker - Wife Exec. - Witt: Levin Walker, Elijah Fitzgerald - p. 406

HORNSBY, ZOROBABEL - 15 May 1796 - 26 Sept. 1796 - To wife (no name) 3 negroes to be div. bet. Major Lecatt, John Downing, James Hornsby, Elizabeth Hornsby, Marah Hornsby, Margaret Hornsby. Dau. in law Leah Hutchinson. Eli Hornsby Exr. Witt: William Coloney, Jr., Robert Smith, Kendal Savage. - p. 427

AMES, CHURCHEL - 8 Feb. 1796 - 26 Sept. 1796 - To son Benjamin Ames. To dau. Rosanna Edwards. To son William Ames. To son Churchel Ames. To dau. Peggy Ames. To son Levi Ames. To dau.

Opansely Ames. Wife Peggy Ames resid. legatee. Levin Ames Exr. Witt: Major Ames, Thomas Fisher - p. 428

WALKER JOHN, SR. - 15 Feb. 1796 - 26 Sept. 1796 - To wife Elizabeth whole est. during her natural life. To son Levin Walker 25 A. on Wallop's Island. To grandson John Walker 25 A. on Wallops Island. William Waterfield to have free privilege to put creatures on that Island during his natural life. To son Robert Walker 35 A. where William White now lives, being part of the Manor planta. where I now live. To son in law Charles B. Taylor negroes, reversion to my 2 grandchildren Levin & Nancy Taylor. To grandau. Dolley Hutchinson. To grandau. Nancy Owens. To grandau. Nancy Walker, dau. of John Walker. To Sally Walker. To Betty Walker. To Henry Walker. To James Walker. Bal. of est. to be div. bet. my sons Levin Walker, Robert Walker, John Walker's children & Elizabeth Taylor's children. Sons Levin & Robert Exrs. Witt: Custis Willis, Elizabeth Perce - p. 429

BROADWATER, JACOB - 10 Aug. 1796 - 26 Sept. 1796 - Whole est. to be equally div. bet. all my children - Dau. Peggy & John Teackle, Sr. Exrs. Witt: John Baker, Willian Adair - p. 432

Orders - 1796-1798

SHIEID, WILLIAM - Adm. his est. to Solomon Read - Thomas W. Rodgers sec. - 25 Apr. 1796 - p. 40

BRADFORD, SABRA - Adm. her est. to Nancy Kelly - Levin Ames & Argil Kellam sec. 27 June 1796 - p. 76

GALT, SAMUEL - Adm. his est. to Thomas Parker - William Gibb sec. - 27 June 1796 - p. 80

NOTTINGHAM, ELIZABETH - Adm. her est. to William Gibb - Edmund Bayly, Jr. sec. - 25 July 1796 - p. 84

WARD, WILLIAM - Adm. his est. to Littleton Ward - Severn Kellam & George Nock sec. 26 July 1796 - p. 88

NOTTINGHAM, ABEL - Adm. his est. to William Gibb - John Wise & Thomas Evans sec. 26 July 1796 - p. 90

NOCK, THOMAS - Adm. his est. to Benjamin Nock - Richard R. Savage & John Glasby sec. - 27 Sept. 1796 - p. 135

AYRES, GEORGE - Adm. his est. to Mary Ayres - Robert Russell & Edmund Only sec. 27 Sept. 1709 - p. 137

HALL, GEORGE - Adm. his est. to John Cropper, Jr. - John Custis (B.S.) & John Moore sec. - 31 Oct. 1796 - p. 144

436

LECATT, AUGUSTINE - Adm. his est. to Thomas Parker - William Gibb & Edmund Bayly sec. - 28 Nov. 1796 - p. 151

WYATT, ADAH - Adm. her est. to Robert Twiford - John P. Outten sec. - 26 Dec. 1796 - p. 156

BUNDICK, AGNES - Adm. her est. to George Bundick - John A. Bundick & Americus Scarburgh sec. - 26 Dec. 1796 - p. 158

BAYLY, EDMUND - Adm. his est. to Americus Scarburgh & Richard Bayly, Elizabeth Bayly, wid., relinquishing her right - George Bundick & Samuel Trader sec. - 26 Dec. 1796 - p. 158

JUSTICE, RICHARD - Adm. his est. to John Cropper - Edmund Bayly sec. - 26 Dec. 1796 - p. 160

WHEALTON, ANNE - Adm. her est. to George Mathews - George Mathews, Sr. & Jediah Ewell sec. - 26 Dec. 1796 - p. 161

LEWIS, WILLIAM - Adm his est. to Tabitha Lewis - John Lewis & John Parks sec. - 26 Dec. 1796 - p. 162

WATSON, JOHN - Adm. his est. to Ephraim Watson - John Ashby & George Nock sec. - 30 Jan. 1797 - p. 164

MEARS, COVENTON - Adm. his est. to Nancy Mears - Arthur Roberts sec. - 30 Jan. 1797 p. 164

GLADING, SACKER - Adm. his est. to John Glading - Peter Delastatious & Elias Broadwater sec. - 30 Jan. 1797 - p. 165

MEARS, ROBERT - Adm. his est. to Bartholomew Mears & Jonathan Mears - Richard Sparrow sec. - 30 Jan. 1797 - p. 166

EVANS, ROBERT - Adm. his est. to Peter Delastatious - John Logan sec. - 30 Jan. 1797 - p. 166

PARKER, GEORGE - Adm. his est. to John Teackle, Sr. - Sacker Parker relinquishing his right. Richard Drummond sec. - 30 Jan. 1797 - p. 167

CHAMBERS, CALEB - Adm. his est. to Levin Rodgers - Revel West sec. - 31 Jan. 1797 p. 172

MATHEWS, JOHN - Adm. his est. to Evans Mathews - Thomas Jones & William Mathews sec. - 31 Jan. 1797 - p. 173

EAST, WILLIAM - Adm. his est. to William Gibb - Edmund Bayly sec. - 2 Feb. 1797 - p. 178

STURGES, ABRAHAM O. - Adm. his est. to Mary Sturges - John McLean & William Selby sec. - 27 Feb. 1797 - p. 184

JOHNSON, WILLIAM - Adm. his est. to James Duncan - John Northam & Jacob Northam sec. - 27 Feb. 1797 - p. 187

BURTON, NANCY & SUSANNA BROADWATER - Adm. their estates to Ephraim Broadwater - William Bruington & John Wilkins sec. - 27 Feb. 1797 - p. 189

SANDERS, SAMUEL - Adm. his est. to Keziah Sanders - William Hinman & Major Hinman sec. - 27 Feb. 1797 - p. 190

MATHEWS, JOSEPH - Adm. his est. to William Mathews - William Welburn & William Selby sec. - 27 Mar. 1797 - p. 207

MELVIN, OBEDIAH - Adm. his est. to James Melvin - Drummond Melburn & William Jones sec. - 26 June 1797 - p. 245

BUNTING, LEVIN - Adm. his est. to Samuel Coward - Adah Bunting, wid. relinquishing her right - Severn Kellam & George Coleburn sec. - 27 June 1797 - p. 250

OLDHAM, JOHN - Adm. his est. to George A. Wise - George Wise, son of John, sec. 31 July 1797 - p. 252

MILLS, BENJAMIN - Adm. his est. to John Gladin - Walter Bayne sec. - 31 July 1797 - p. 256

BELOTE, HANDCOCK - Adm. his est. to John Read, Mary Belote, wid. relinquishing her right - Edmund Read & Richard Read sec. - 31 July 1797 - p. 258

JAMES, DELIGHT - Adm. her est. to Robert Russell - Savage Crippen & Abel Wright sec. - 25 Sept. 1797 - p. 304

CUTLAR, PREESON - Adm. his est. to Rachel Cutlar - Isme Wyatt & John Wyatt sec. 26 Sept. 1797 - p. 306

TATHAM, Michael - Adm. his est. to Tabitha Tatham - Zorobabel Read & Shadrick Lecatt sec. - 26 Sept. 1797 - p. 309

DRUMMOND, WILLIAM - Adm. his est. to Anne R. Drummond - Thomas Waters & Robert Twiford sec. - 26 Sept. 1797 - p. 310

HICKMAN, HAMPTON - Adm. his est. to Isaiah Hickman & Seymour Hickman - John Parker & George Wright sec. - 30 Oct. 1797 - p. 320

HICKMAN, EDWARD - Adm. his est. to George Hickman, son of Edward - John Teackle, Sr. & Abel Wright sec. - 30 Oct. 1797 - p. 323

MELSON, SHADRICK - Adm. his est. to Daniel Melson - Stephen Drummond & Argil Bloxom sec. - 30 Oct. 1797 - p. 325

MC COLLOCK, WILLIAM - Adm. his est. to John Merchant, Betsy McCollock, wid., relinquishing her right - Robert Twiford & David Craton sec. - 31 Oct. 1797 - p. 326

BULL, SOUTHY - Adm. his est. to John Bull, Peggy Bull, wid., relinquishing her right - Thomas Cropper & William Gibb sec. - 28 Nov. 1797 - p. 340

BIGGABY, LEVIN - Adm. his est. to George Ker - Parker Barnes & William Gibb sec. - 25 Dec. 1797 - p. 343

BAGGE, WILLIAM - Adm. his est. to Isma Wyatt - John Addison, Sacker Stringer & Arthur Savage sec. - 29 Jan. 1798 - p. 346

PARKER, JOHN - Adm. his est. to Molly Parker - Benjamin Pruit & John Parker sec. - 29 Jan. 1798 - p. 350

TURLINGTON, JACOB - Adm. his est. to William Smith - Jonathan Phillips & Thomas S. Bayly sec. - 29 Jan. 1798 - p. 351

COLLINS, WILLIAM - Adm. his est. to William Downing - Peter Delastatious & Edmund Bayly sec. - 29 Jan. 1798 - p. 351

BLACKSTON, BOWMAN - Adm. his est. to Fenwick Fisher - Edmund Bayly sec. - 30 Jan. 1798 - p. 352

WYATT, THOMAS - Adm. his est. to David Bowman - John Arlington sec. - 30 Jan. 1798 - p. 352

WEST, JOHN - Adm. his est. to Jonathan West - Charles Snead sec. - 30 Jan. 1798 - p. 353

YOUNG, THOMAS - Adm. his est. to John Young - Robert Twiford & Smith Melson sec. - 30 Jan. 1798 - p. 354

KER, EDWARD - Adm. his est. to George Ker - Hugh Ker & David Bowman sec. - 30 Jan. 1798 - p. 355

PHILLIPS, WILLIAM - Adm. his est. to John Cropper, Jr. - Thomas Cropper sec. - 30 Jan. 1798 - p. 355

MELSON, CALEB - Adm. his est. to Tabitha Melson - Parker West & John West sec. - 26 Feb. 1798 - p. 357

TWIFORD, JOHN - Adm. his est. to William Mears - Richard Savage & John Wyatt sec. - 26 Feb. 1798 - p. 360

RUSSELL, JOSHUA – Adm. his est. to Charles Ewell – Charles Stockly & William Ewell sec. – 26 Feb. 1798 – p. 361

BEAVANS, MARY – Adm. her est. to Samuel Henderson – Walter Bayne sec. – 26 Feb. 1798 – p. 361

MEARS, CALEB – Adm. his est. to Michael Bonwell – Teackle Bull sec. – 27 Feb. 1798 – p. 365

TAYLOR, SAVAGE – Adm. his est. to Thomas Mears – Robinson Savage sec. – 1 May. 1798 – p. 407

KELLAM, BENJAMIN – Adm, his est. to George Kellam – John Milby & Edmund Scarburgh, Jr. sec. – 1 May 1798 – p. 407

POWELL, ISAAC – Adm. his est. to Polly Powell – Laban Powell sec. – 1 May 1798 – p. 410

BULL, ROBERT – Adm. his est. to John Bull, Jr. – Laban Gunter & Stephen Gunter sec. 1 May 1798 – p. 410

TURNER, WILLIAM – Adm. his est. to Betty Turner – Jonathan Willet & Thomas Evans sec. – 25 June 1798 – p. 440

HOFFMAN, JAMES – Adm. his est. to Andrew Hoffman – William Trader & Southy Northam sec. – 25 June 1798 – p. 440

MEARS, MICAJAH – Adm. his est. to Mary Mears – William Downing & Hezekiah Waggoman sec. – 25 June 1798 – p. 441

GUNTER, BENJAMIN – Adm. his est. to Joseph Gunter – Thomas Sturgis & William White sec. – 25 June 1798 – p. 443

MOORE, JOHN – Adm. his est. to Stephen Moore – Stephen Gunter & Custis Kellam sec. – 25 June 1798 – p. 446

TAYLOR, JOSEPH – Adm. his est. to William Taylor (carpenter) – Jacob Taylor sec. 25 June 1798 – p. 447

TUNNELL, JOSEPH – Adm. his est. to James Abbott – Samuel Johnson & John Moore sec. – 25 June 1798 – P. 451

KELLEY, CHARLES – Adm. his est. to Nanny Kelley – William James & Southy Bloxom sec. – 25 June 1798 – p. 451

DONE, NICHOLAS – Adm. his est. to John Bull – Smith Melson & Stephen Gunter sec. – 25 June 1798 – p. 451

SMART, NATHANIEL – Adm. his est. to Thomas Jenkins – Robert Jenkins & Nicholas Knox sec. – 30 July 1798 – p. 457

BLOXOM, CATHARINE – Adm. her est. to John Johnson – William Stephens & Selby Delastatious sec. – 30 July 1798 – p. 459

PARKER, REBECCA – Adm. her est. to John Boisnard – John Custis (B.S.) sec. – 31 July 1798 – p. 467

Wills &c. – 1796–1798

TAYLOR, EZEKIEL – 19 ____, 1795 – 26 Sept 1796 – To Iffeniah Taylor planta. where I now live, but should he offer to sell or lease the said planta then to go to Alexander Taylor, son of Alexander, & his heirs, & for want of heirs to my son Samuel Taylor. To daus. Edey & Sally, Sidney, Rebecca & Polley the balance of my est. – To son Alexander Taylor. Son Iffeniah Exr. Witt: John Gladding, Jr., Jesse Gladding, Walter Bayne – p. 2

JACOB, THOMAS, Sr. – 5 Oct. 1796 – 31 Oct. 1796 – To grandson Thomas Jacob all lands on Craddock Creek where I now live, he to give bond for the payment of 25 L each to my 2 daus. Peggy Parker & Susannah Ivy within 2 years after he has taken possession of the land, & also giving bond for the payment of 50 L to my grandson Thomas Jacob Parker 5 years after my death. To dau. Peggy Parker & her husband Thomas Hall Parker 88 A. near Pungoteague Church adj. the lands deeded to Thomas Jacob, Jr., which land formerly belonged to Thomas H. Parker and is at present in possession of Thomas Jacob, Jr. To dau. Susannah Ivy & her husband negroes &c. To grandson Thomas Ivy. To grandson Hugh Walker if he shall live to be 21 30 L cash. To grandson Henry Jacob. To 3 grandaus. Caty, Rosah & Peggy Bayly, daus. of Isma Bayly 70 L cash or good bonds, also the bond I have against their father Isme Bayly of about 30 L. Daus. Peggy Parker & Susannah Ivy resid. legatees – Friend Americus Scarburgh & son in law Thomas H. Parker Exrs. Witt: Severn Kellum, George Kellum – p. 3

JAMES, WILLIAM – 14 May 1796 – 31 Oct. 1796 – Whole est. to be div. bet. my 4 sisters Elizabeth Coulburn, Nancy James, Mary James & Hetty James. Bro. in law Capt. William Coulburn. John Teackle, Sr. Exr. – Witt: Zadock Nock – Samuel Lippincot, Rebecca Walker – p. 7

MILES, PARKER – 26 May 1796 – 31 Oct. 1796 – To wife Tabither Miles – To son John Miles. To dau. Molley Miles. To son Parker Miles. To son Jessey Miles – To grandau Nancy Miles, Thomas Fletcher to have her money in keeping until she comes to lawful age or marriage. Sons & daus. George, Jesse, John & Parker Miles, Elizabeth Marshall, Rebekah Wallis, Tabitha Taylor & Molley Miles resid. legatees. Son George Miles & John Miles Exrs. Witt: Thomas Fletcher, Thomas Marshall – p. 7

WEST, BEMJAMIN - 21 Jan. 1794 - 1 Nov. 1796 - To son Parker West 3 A. and the house thereon which I have already laid off for him adj. William Riley's land. I lend the use of the rest of my land to my 2 sons Parker & Benjamin West during the life of my wife Elizabeth West & no longer, & at the death of my said wife I then lend the use of the same to my son John West during his life, & at his death I lend the use of the said land to my son Parker West, & at his death I lend the use of the said land to my son Benjanin West, & at the death of the aforesaid persons I give the said land to the heirs of my son John West. To son Benjamin 15 L cash - negroes - To son John West personalty, provided he does not disturb my son Parker West in the possession of the land &c. 3 children Parker West, Tabitha Melson & Benjamin West resid. legatees - Sons Parker West, Benjamin West & Caleb Melson Exrs. Witt: William Drummond, William Willets - p. 9

CHANDLER, MITCHEL - Not dated - 1 Nov. 1796 - To son Mitchel & dau. Milly the use of all my lands whereon I now live and the planta. I bought of the heirs of Clement Parker, dec., until my dau. Betsey arrives to the age of 20 years to maintain & bring up my 3 yougest children. viz: Patience, Amey & Betsey until they arrive to the age of 20 years, respectively, & I then give the said land to my son Mitchell, he paying the sum of 25 L to be equally divided amoung the rest of my children. To dau. Rosey. To son Thomas. All my wife's wearing apparel to be divided equally between my 3 youngest children, Patience, Amey & Betsey. Bro. Littleton Chandler & friends Robinson Custis & Tully Wise Exrs. Witt: Elijah Fitzgerald, Comfort West, Sophia Fitzgerald - p. 10

STEPHENS, JOHN - 1 Mar. 1796 - 1 Nov. 1796 - To bro. William Stephens my Land & Livings, estate not to be sold, but that he may enjoy it during his life. John Parker Exr. Witt: Daniel Melson, Charles Simpson - p. 12

SNEAD, ELLZABEIH - 13 Apr. 1796 - 1 Nov. 1796 - "I give & bequeath unto my natural Born Child which I call Elizabeth Smith" negro boy Ephriam &c. & should she die before she arrives to the age of 18 negro to my son John Snead - Witt: Sally Ironmonger, Molly Scott, William Gibb.
Codicil - Should my son John Snead die before he arrives to lawful age the said negro to belong to my sister Bridget West - Same witnesses - p. 13

DRUMMOND, COMFORT - 29 Sept. 1796 - 28 Nov. 1796 - p. 58 - To dau. Ann Drummond. To Zadock Nock. To 4 children Ann, Elizabeth, Sarah & George Drummond the bal. of my estate. Son Richard Drummond & Charles Drummond, Sr. Exrs. Witt: William Drummond, Elias Nock, Comfort Drummond - p. 58

CROWSON, WILLIAM - 8 Nov. 1796 - 26 Nov. 1796 - To 2 daus. Peggy & Agnes Crowson. To dau. Susannah Boggs all my land where I

now live, she paying each of her 4 sisters 15 L current money, & upon her refusal the land to go to my dau. Catherine Brittingham upon the same condition. 4 daus. Sarah Boggs, Catherine Brittingham, Peggy Crowson and Agness Crowson resid. legatees. Daus. Susannah Boggs & Catherine Brittingham Executrices. Witt: John R. Parker, Kendall Ames, Francis Boggs. p. 59
In order of prob: William Boggs qualified.

SPALDING, George - 19 Feb. 1796 - 26 Nov. 1796 - To wife Martha Spalding whole est. Witt: William Selby, Euphamy Dickerson - p. 60
In order of prob: Martha Spalding qualified.

BAGWILL, JOHN - 25 Apr. 1795 - 26 Dec. 1796 - To wife Ann Bagwell whole est. until my son Henry Bagwell comes to the age of 14 years to bring my two sons up on, then I give to my said son Henry Bagwill 50 A. adj. John Young. To son John Young Bagwill the balance of my land, being 100 A. more or less. Sons John & Henry resid. legatess. Wife & friend Isaac Bagwill Exrs. Witt: William Drummond, Francis Ayres, Henry Beasly - p. 61
In order of prob: John Bagwell qualified.

SAVAGE, NANCY - 20 June 1796 - 26 Dec. 1796 - To son in law John Savage my part of land that was given me for a term of years to bring up my youngest son Abel Savage, & if my son Abel should die before the term of years are run out, then the place to be rented out for the remainder of the term & the money div. bet. John Savage, William Savage, Nancy Savage & Jacob Savage. To son Abel Savage cow & calf for his half bro. to keep it to raise him on. Dau. Nancy Savage. William Savage, Nancy Savage, Jacob Savage & Abel Savage resid. legatees. John Savage of Abel Exr. - Witt: Zorobabel Chandler, John Kellum, Mary Beloat - p. 62

SCARBURGH, CHARLES - 25 Nov. 1796 - 26 Dec. 1796 - To wife Bridget Scarburgh. To my mother. To my nephew Major S. Pitts. Bro. Edmund Scarburgh resid. legatee & Exr. Witt: Hezekiah Pitts, George Riley - p. 64

BENSON JONAH - 10 Mar. 1796 - 26 Dec. 1796 - To wife Elizabeth. To dau. Betsey "the wheel that was her mother's". To dau. Nancy Benson. To dau. Salley. 6 children Betsey, Nancy, Sally, William, Samuel & Ester. My first wife's clothes to be div. bet. my 3 daus. Betsey, Nancy & Sally. Bal. of est. together with my land to be sold & after the payment of debts remainder to be div. among my children & wife. Capt. Arthur Robins Exr. Witt: Isma Wyatt, Betsey Benson - p. 64

CUSTIS, HENRY, SR. - 8 Apr. 1795 - 30 Jan. 1797 - To son William all the land lying above Doll's Road. To son Henry all the remaining part of the lands which I possess. To dau. Sarah Custis. To wife Polly Custis use of whole est. during her wid., she to bring up my children in a decent & cleaver manner, then to have 1/3. Should my 3 children die without issue Henry Custis, son of Revell Custis, dec., to have the land I bought of John Savage, also 10 A. lying above Doll's Road, & if the said Henry be found wasting his estate the said land to be sold & the money equally div. bet. the children of the said Revel Custis, dec. To John Custis, son of my bro. William Custis, all the remaining part of my lands. To Robert Russell. Bal. of personal est. to be sold & Elizabeth Leatherbury to have 7 L & the remainder div. bet. the children of my bro. Revel, except Henry, Thomas Poulson & Elizabeth Drummond, dau. William Drummond. Wife Polly Exec. & Revel West & John Revell Exrs. Witt: William Seymour, Charles Taylor - p. 99

SHRIEVS, WILLIAM - 13 Dec. 1796 - 30 Jan. 1797 - To bro. Teackle Shrievs. To wife Anna Shrievs the remainder of my est. except my land, during her wid., & then to my son Billy Shrievs. To my son Billy Shrievs my land & should he die without issue to my bro. Teackle Shrievs. Parker Paradice Exr. Witt: Benjamin Parks, Kendall Coloney, Williams Thorns - p. 100

MARSHALL, STEPHEN - 27 Nov. 1796 - 30 Jan. 1797 - To wife Tabitha 1/3 of my land in lieu of dower for life. To son John Marshall all my lands my father Daniel Marshall purchased of Thomas Welburn, he to pay my son Skinner Marshall 100 L when the said Skinner comes to the age of 21, & should he fail to do so then I leave the said Skinner 50 A. of the aforesaid land. To son James Marshall all the land that lays between Rachal Beanson's & Arthur Wheelton except 10 A. lying at the North-west end of the said tract, which said 10 A. I give to my son Stephen Marshall. To dau. Polly Marshall. To dau. Leah Marshall. Son John Marshall Exr. Sons Skinner & Stephen resid. legatees. Witt: John Collins, James Watt, Esther Marshall, Masen Dod, Daniel J. Marshall - p. 101

BRADFORD, KENDALL - 14 Sept. 1796 - 30 Jan. 1797 - Wife Elizabeth to have the use of whole est. during her wid. To son Abel Bradford planta. where I now live. Dau. Nancy Bradford resid. legatee. John Phillips, son of William, Exr. Witt: Francis Savage, Custis Willis - p. 102

BROADWATER, JAMES - 9 Jan. 1797 - 30 Jan. 1797 - Land to be div. bet. my 2 sons George & Henry Broadwater. To dau. Ann Finney. Son James Broadwater, in Worcester County, Maryland, Rachel Cutlar & the children of my dec. dau. Leah Parker, formerly the wife of Robert Parker on Watts Island, resid. legatees. - Wife Elizabeth Exec. Witt: M. Beard, Stephen Beard, Joseph Merril - p. 124
In order of prob: William Corbin qualified.

ASHBY EZEKIEL - 11 Mar. 1793 - Partly proved 29 Apr. 1795 - Prob: 30 Jan. 1797 - Bro. David Ashby sole (unclear) Elisha Mears. John Ashby, Samuel Ashby. - p. 126

TIGNAL, PHILLIP – 12 Nov. 1795 – 31 Jan. 1797 – To wife Elizabeth use of all my land during her life & at her death to my son Dennis Tignal. To wife all the est. she had before I married her. To dau. Leah. To dau. Tabitha. To dau. Rachel. To dau. Catharine. To dau. Elizabeth. To dau. Rosey. Elijah Hancock Exr. Witt: Margaret Hancock, Susanna Waterfield – p. 127

CUSTIS, ONLY – 19 July 1795 – 1 Jan. 1797 – Whole est. to wife Patience Custis during her wid. in lieu of dower, then to my 5 children John, Thomas, Nancy, William & Henry Custis. Wife Patience & friend John Read Exrs. Witt: Obediah Thornman, Patience Thornman – p. 128

FOSTER, LEAH – 5 Aug. 1796 – 1 Feb. 1797 – To sister Catey Foster wearing apparel, Robert Snead to take care of them & let her have them at his discretion. To Robert Snead 1/6 part of the undivided land which fell to me by the death of my bro. Joshua Foster. Robert Snead resid. legatee & Exr. Witt: McBonwell, Sr., Preson Snead, Susa White – p. 129

UNDERHILL, THOMAS, SR. – 12 July 1796 – 30 Jan. 1797 – To wife Susannah whole est during her life, then personal est. to. be div. bet. my then surviving children, Thomas Underhill excepted. To son Thomas after his mother's death all my land where I now live. Son Thomas Exr. Witt: John R. Parker, Kendall Ames, Levin Smith – p. 138

ASHBY, NANCY – 24 Feb. 1795 – 27 Feb. 1797 – To son James Ashby 1 large trunk & 1 waistcoat that was his uncle's. To son George. To unborn child. To my aunt Elizabeth Ames 1 black cloak that was my mother's as long as she lives, & then to return to my children. Custis Willis Exr. Witt: Levin Ames, Elisha Mears – p. 140

THOMAS, SUSANNA – 14 Dec. 1796 – 27 Feb. 1797 – To William Thomas. To Marget Thomas. To Mehala Evans. To my sister Sarah Evans. To the 2 children of my sister Sarah, viz: Mehala & Levin Evins. To Harrison Thomas. To Bridget Dickson. All the cash which is due me from my father's est. which is in the hands of Harrison Thomas to pay my debts. Bro. in law Levin Evins Exr. Witt: Levin Delastatious, Ann Delastatious – p. 141

WEST, ELIZABETH – 22 Feb. 1797 – 27 Feb. 1797 – To son Benjamin West. To son John West personalty during his life reversion to my grandson John West. To dau. Tabitha Melson Bal. of est. to be div. bet. all my children. Witt: Elijah Grinnalds, Jacob Matthis – p. 142.
In order of prob: Parker West & Babel Melson qualified.

ACKWORTH, PATIENCE – 27 Nov. 1790 – 27 Feb. 1797 – To grandau. Elizabeth Arlington, & should she die before me to be div. bet. Elizabeth Ward & Sophia Nock. Two grandchildren Thomas Bagwil

Arlington & Elizabeth Arlington resid. legatees. Son in law John Arlington Exr. Witt: Cornelius Harman, Francis Harman - p. 143

DELASTATIOUS, SEBASTIAN - 24 Jan. 1797 - 27 Feb. 1797 - To son David land where I now live. To 2 daus Nancy & Jinne Delastatious my personal est.. Friend William Brewington Exr. Witt: Gehu Wilkerson, Susana Wilkerson - p. 144

ELLIOTT, JOHN - 26 Jan. 1797 - 27 Feb. 1797 - To son John 75 A. where I now live, & for want of heirs to my son Levin Elliott. To dau. Sally Elliott. To dau. Elizabeth Lewis. To Sally Bradford 3 L cash, personalty. 3 children, Elizabeth Lewis, Levin Elliott & Sally Elliott resid. legatees. Friends Teackle Elliott, George Taylor & Thomas Elliott Exrs. Witt: Caty Mears, George Taylor, Caleb Bonwell, William Bonwell - p. 145

LITTLETON, MARK - 10 June 1796 - 27 Feb. 1797 - I lend to my wife Raner Littleton my whole est. during her wid. To son George Littleton 4 A. in the North-east corner of my land adj. the land of Hezekiah Baker & Robert Davis, remainder of my land to be div. bet. my 2 sons Southey Littleton & James Littleton. 3 sons to be at age at 18. Daus. Sarah & Susanna & son George resid. legatees. Wife Raner & son Southey Exrs. Witt: Parker Barnes, George Snead, James Ailworth - p. 146

WINDOW, ROBERT - 31 Jan. 1797 - 27 Feb. 1797 - To son George my land. To dau. Leah all her mother's clothes &c. To son John (under age). To dau. Betsy. Bal. of est. to be div. bet. all my children. Friend David Bowman & John Read Exrs. Witt: William Leatherbury, Henry Window, Zorobabel Chandler - p. 147

BRADFORD, ABSALOM - 18 Aug. 1796 - 28 Feb. 1797 - To wife Mary Bradford whole est. during her wid., but if she marry to be equally div. bet. William & George Hyslup, the sons of George Hyslup, Sr. Wife Mary Exec. Witt: Theophilus Bagge, George Hyslup, Levy Ames - p. 148
In order of prob: Joshua Taylor qualified.

SMITH, BAYLY - 29 Sept. 1796 - 27 Feb. 1797 - To wife Elizabeth all my lands during her wid. To son Spencer Smith 100 A. adj. the land of Mr. Henry Fletcher on the West & upon Ann Holden on the North & Walter Bayne on the East. To son Ralph Smith 100 A. adj. the above, To Zorallingtine Smith all the remainder of my land adj. the Creek. To dau, Ann Smith. To dau. Nancy Smith - Witt: Elijah Northam, Elijah Pilsheard, Thomas Wheelton - Will not signed.
In order of prob: Spencer Smith qualified.

TUNNELL, NEHEMIAH - Nunc. "Died 23 December 1795 at sea & was then a Marriner on board the Schooner Fair American of the Port of Folly Landing, William Wallop Commander, & that after his death they put back into the Island of Jamaica and buried him". Proved 24

Jan. 1796 – Prob: 27 Mar. 1797 – To wife two negroes Southey & James & whole est. during her life & then the negroes to be free & what remains of my est. to be div. bet. them. It is my desire that none of my relations have anything to do with my est. Proved by Edward Joynes & William Ramsey, "who made oath that they arrives in Chingattage the 23rd day of January, 1796 from Jamaica & attested to the within before me the day & month written" – p. 174 William Downing.

BULL, JOHN – 18 Feb. 1797 – 24 Apr. 1797 – To wife Tabitha whole est. except wearing apparel which I give to William Chance Ardis. Witt: Southey Broadwater, William Hill – p. 175
In order of prob: John S. Ker qualified.

TAYLOR, SAMUEL – 22 Aug. 1794 – 29 May 1797 – Whole est. to wife Margaret Taylor. Wife Exec. If anything remains of my est. at the death of my wife I give the same to Selby Ewell. Witt: William Johnson, Edward Taylor, Thomas Walters – p. 176

FOLIO, JOHN – 20 Jan. 1797 – 26 June 1797 – To wife Pearcy Folio, she to pay Peggy Harrison 30 s. cash. Bal. of est. to be sold & after payment of debts to be div. bet. William Folio, Upshur Folio, Margaret Copes & Pricy Pewzicy. Son Upshur Folio Exr. Witt: George Gibson, Solomon Mears – p. 178

KELLAM, JOHN, son of Solomon – 13 Mar. 1797 – 26 June 1797 – To bro. George Kellam & sister Mary Kellam whole est. George Taylor Exr. Witt: George Taylor, Robert Nock – p. 179

PILCHER, PEGGY – 18 Dec. 1796 – 26 June 1797 – To dau. Nancy Groton 1 s. To grandau. Elizabeth Wills 1 s. Dau. Esther Watson Edwards resid. legatee & Exec. Witt: John Mears, Sophia Custis, George Taylor – p. 180

SAVAGE, WILLIAM – 19 Mar. 1797 – 26 June 1797 – Should wife be with child I give my whole est. to said child after the payment of my debts. Wife Elizabeth to have use of whole est. during her life. If my wife should not be with child I give my land to William Warrington, son of James. John Elliott Exr. Witt: Benjamin Gunter, John Edwards, William Beloate – p. 181

BULL, RICHARD – 19 June 1796 – 26 June 1797 – To wife Bridget Bull whole est. during her wid. reversion of my land to my 3 daus. Molly, Betsey & Sally Bull during their single lives. To son Teackle Bull 95 A., being part of the planta. where I now live. To son Tobias Bull 50 A. where he now lives, being part of my aforesaid planta. To son Richard Bull 50 A. adj. the above, he to be at age 18. Grandaus. Kitty Bonwill & Nancy Bloxom. 4 daus. Peggy Bayly, Molly, Betty & Sally Bull resid. legatees. Wife & sons Teackle & Tobias Exrs. Witt: McKell Bonwell, Sr., Major Budd, Caleb Bonwell – p. 181

HYSLOP, SMITH - 29 Feb. 1797 - 31 July 1797 - To wife Leah Hyslop land purchased of Levin Walker during her wid. then to be sold & the proceeds div. bet. James Tygner & Nancy Martin. To bro. Kendal Hyslop. Wife Leah & bro. Kendall Exrs. Witt: Custis Willis, Joshua Taylor - p. 202

STRINGER, BENJAMIN - 12 July 1797 - 31 July 1797 - To bro. Jacob Stringer whole est. Witt: John Stringer, Comfort Aderson, Moses Savage - p. 203 In order of prob: Jacob Stringer qualified.

WHITE, SARAH - 23 Dec. 1796 - 31 July 1797 - To dau. Margaret Lingo. To son Jacob White. To grandchildren George Lingo & Caty Lingo. Witt: Theophilus Bagge, Absalom Bradford, Nancy Bagge - p. 203
In order of prob: Robinson Lingo qualified.

BAGWELL, SOPHIAH - 4 June 1797 - 31 Aug. 1797 - To grandson Hele Bagwell. To grandson Henry Bagwell. To grandson Jesse Bonewell. To grandau. Nancy Bonewell. To Sarah Lileston. To Molly Smith. To Nancy Holeston. Sally Bull resid. legatee. Witt: Jacob Ross, - Sarah Lileston - p. 204
In order of prob: Isaiah Bagwell qualified.

KILMAN, JOHN - 18 May 1795 - 28 Aug. 1797 - To wife Elizabeth whole est. during her life. To eldest son William Kilman all my lands, & for want of heirs to my son Samuel. Children William, Samuel, Sarah, Betsey, Abba & Mary Kilman resid. legatees - Witt: Ephrim Vessels, James Vessels - p. 242
In order of prob: Elizabeth Kilman qualified.

DRUMMOND, WILLIAM - Not dated - 28 Aug. 1797 - Whole est. to wife Anne Robinson Drummond for life. My Messongo lands & mill to be sold & the money to remain in my wife's hands until her death. To son William S. Drummond my Hunting Creek land. To dau. Ann Temperance Drummond. To dau. Betsey silver spoons marked "W.D." Dau. Betsey to be in the care of Sophia Melon. To dau. Catharine Scarburgh Drummond. To son Richard Hill Drummond. At the death of my wife est. to be div. bet. Betsy, Nancy, Catharine & Richard Drummond. Friend Thomas Fletcher Exr. Witt: Henry Hall, Charles Drummond, George Miles - p. 243

DRUMMOND, DUBLIN, a free negro - 1 Oct. 1794 - 25 Sept. 1797 - To friend Walter Bayne 10 A. on the North side of the tract purchased of Isaac Warner for the purpose of paying the said Warner the balance I owe him, and also a balance due the said Walter Bayne for store dealings. To dau. Hannah 7 A. adj. William Lucas & the residue of the lands for 3 years. Should either of my sons obtain their freedom the residue of my land to be equally div. bet. them, & in case none of them get free the residue of my lands to be rented out & the money to be equally div. bet. my children that are slaves. Horse to be sold & the money applied to the payment of a debt due Spencer Drummond &

my other just debts I owe. Friend Walter Bayne Exr. Witt: Colmor Bayne, Woodman Bloxom, Peter Delastatius - p. 255

ALLEN, ZADOCK - 31 Jan. 1797 - 26 Sept. 1797 - To wife Elizabeth whole est. during her wid. to raise her children, then whole est. to be sold & the money divided between my 4 children John, Thomas, Zadock & Mary Allen - Wife Elizabeth Exec. Witt: George Mathews, Edward Evans - p. 256

JINKINS, MARY ANNE - 31 Mar. 1797 - 26 Sept. 1797 - To dau. Nancy Stockly. To Sally Ewell negro for life, reversion to my grandau Nancy Ewell. To son James Jinkins. To son Robert Jinkins. "four of my children & grandchildren, namely Custis Jinkins, Robert Jinkins, Ralph Jinkins & Peggy Silverthorne's children" resid. legatees. Witt: Charles Ewell, Solomon Ewell, Benjamin Holland. - p. 256
In order of prob: Custis Jinkins qualified .

TATHAM JOHN - 20 Apr. 1797 - 26 Sept. 1797 - To son James (under age) whole est. Friend John Read Exr. Witt: John Mears, Tabitha Mears - p. 257

FLOYD, BERRY - Not dated - 30 Oct. 1797 - To wife whole est. until my eldest son Benjamin Floyd arrives to lawful age to bring up my children, then personal est. to my wife forever & the use of my land to my 3 sons Benjamin, Elijah & John Floyd until my son John comes to lawful age, then to be equally div. bet. my surviving children before named. Wife (no name) & Elijah Watson Exrs. - Witt: Burton Silverthorn, Caleb Harrison, Elizabeth Harrison, Fanny Harris - p. 294
In order of prob: Elijah Watson & Sarah Floyd qualified .

MATTHEWS, EZEKIEL - 22 July 1797 - 30 Oct. 1797 - To wife Betsy whole est. during her wid. then to be div. bet. my 4 children George, Polly, Charles & Betty Matthews. Babel Mason Exr. Witt: William Conquest, Elizabeth Sterling, Southey Stering - p. 294
In order of prob: Betsy Matthews qualified.

ASHBY, WILLIAM - 7 May 1797 - 30 Oct. 1797 - To bro. John Ashby. To bro. Samuel Ashby. To bro. Ezekiel Ashby. To bro. David Ashby. To sister Elizabeth Ashby. Bro. John Ashby Exr. - Witt: Elisha Mears, Sr., Sarah Hawley, Leah Scott. p. 295

GORE, THOMAS, of Worcester County, Maryland - 26 Aug. 1797 - Proved in Maryland 1 Sept. 1797 - Recorded in Accomack 30 Oct. 1797 - To dau. Comfort all my real estate, & for want of issue to my friend John Custis Handy, son of Samuel. To William Quinton, son of Phillip, my watch & wearing apparell. To Phillip Quinton, Jr., son of Phillip. John Custis Handy guardian to my dau. Comfort & Exr. of my estate. Witt: John Meill, Isaac Nicholson, Samuel Nicholson - p. 296

BENSON, JAMES - 5 June 1797 - 27 Nov. 1797 - To wife Scarburgh whole est. during her wid. To dau. Anne Benson planta. where I now live. To dau. Sally Northam negro for life, reversion to her son James Northam. To dau. Peggy Taylor's children. To dau. Sally Northam's children. Wife Exec. Witt: Arthur Watson, Henry Trader, William Chesher - p. 337

HENDERSON, LEMUEL - 5 Feb. 1797 - 26 Nov. 1797 - To son James Henderson planta. where I now live. To dau. Rhoda Tunnel during her natural life, & in case she should marry & have issue I beq. what I have lent her to such heirs, & for want of such issue I give the above articles to my grandau. Scarburgh Henderson. To wife Scarburgh Henderson. To grandson Lemuel Henderson. Wife & son James resid. legatees & Exrs. Witt: James Gillett, Isaac Marshall, Levin Marshall, John Johnson - p. 338

POWELL, JAMES - 17 Sept. 1797 - 25 Dec. 1797 - To dau. Nancy Wainhouse Powell. To dau. Hannah Powell. To dau. Mahala Powell. Thomas Parramore, Jr. & Thomas Parramore, Sr. Exrs. Witt: Richard Johnson. Nancy Abdell - p. 339

ROBERTS, ARTHUR, Jr. - 17 Sept. 1797 - 25 Dec. 1797 - To wife Elizabeth Roberts 100 A. of land adj. John Stringer until my dau. Marget Roberts arrives to lawful age or marries, then to my said dau., & should she die before lawful age or marriage I give the said land to my wife for life, reversion to my son Eldred Roberts. Wife to have use of whole est. to bring up my 2 children & to give my son Eldred Roberts 6 years schooling & my dau. Marget 3 years schooling. Wife & William Roberts Exrs. Witt: Nancy Roberts, John Roberts. Francis Roberts - p. 340

EVANS, JESSE - 4 Nov. 1797 - 29 Jan. 1798 - To wife Elizabeth whole est. during her wid. To dau. Anna. To dau. Peggy. To son William "chest that was his brother Levin's" To dau. Betsy Richardson. To son Goorge Crippin Evans. To dau. Mary Taylor. To dau. Suse Taylor. Bal. of est. after the death of my wife to be div. bet. all my children. Witt: William Hargis, Isaac Melvin - p. 349

CUSTIS, ROBINSON - 23 Nov. 1797 - 29 Jan. 1798 - Wife to have use of household goods & kitchen furniture during her wid. Bal. of personal property to be sold including my slaves, & after the payment of my debts the residue to be put out at interest. Wife to have use of bal. of property, real & personal during her wid. then to be div. bet. my 4 children Thomas, Peter, Fanny & Edmund whrn my son Edmund attains the age of 21, at which time the said real estate to be div. bet. my said 4 children. Son Peter to have out of his share of the profits of my estate a Latin education and to be brought up to one of the learned professions. To other children to have such education as their guardians shall think proper. Bro. John Custis guardian of my said children & Exr. of my est. Witt: John Wise, Thomas Custis, Samuel Waples - p. 350
In order of prob: John Custis (B.S.) qualified.

WILLIT, AMBROSE - 14 Apr. 1796 - 29 Jan. 1798 - To wife Susanna Willit my part of the planta. where I now live with the mill, houses &c. for life in lieu of dower, provided she claim no dower in the lands I purchased of Hezekiah White's representatives, cattle, personalty & "the Boy Thos until of age". To dau. Betsey Wise Willit a small parcel of land beginning at a marked post near the Main Road. To dau. Nancy Taylor & to her 2 children James & Thomas Taylor. To son George Willit the remaining part of the planta. purchased of Hezekiah White's representatives, likewise the reversion of the lands where I now live. Wife & dau. Betsy resid. legatees. Wife & son George Exrs. Witt: Parker Barnes, James Ailworth - p. 351

SAVAGE, PETER - 31 Dec. 1797 - 29 Jan. 1798 - To wife Redegil Savage whole est. during her wid. To dau. Elizabeth Savage personalty, "also one chest called her brother Peter's". To dau. Ann Garrison. To son William Fletcher Savage (under age) 4 A. adj. Richard Savage, he to have the said land at his brother's death or marriage. To son Francis Savage at his mother's death or marriage my whole land & planta. "I desire that all my children be made equal in legacies as my wife and Daughter Elizabeth would think equal with Abel Savage what he had when he went away". Son Francis Savage, William Savage, Elizabeth Savage, my grandau. Jane Savage & my dau. Ann Garrison to share half the remainder of my estate. My grandson Nathaniel Savage & grandau. Caty Savage to share the remainder. Sons Francis Savage & William Fletcher Savage Exrs. Witt: John Milby, Charles Richardson, Richard Cutlar - p. 352
In order of prob: Francis Savage, Jr. qualified.

MILMOND, EPHRAIM - 8 Feb. 1788 - 26 Feb. 1798 - To cousin in law Warrington Staton land where I now live adj. the land of William Taylor, Ralph Jinkins & William Bevans. To wife Rachel, whole personal est. Wife & Warrington Staton Exrs.
Codicil: To dau. Betsey Milmond 5 s. To dau. Kessey Staton 5 s. To dau. Mary Milmond 5 s. To dau. Nancy Milmond 5 s. To dau. Tabitha Milmond 5 s. Witt: Solomon Marshall, William Roley Taylor, Betsey Taylor, James Taylor - p. 379

EDWARDS, SACKER - 5 Nov. 1797 - 26 Feb. 1798 - To sister Nancy Mason & her husband Thomas Mason all my land for their natural lives , provided they pail my grave & keep it paild as long as they both live, to take my father & mother's graves in the pailing &c., reversion to their son William Mason. To sister Racher Wilber. To bro. John Edwards. To bro. Jacob Edwards. Bro. John Edwards & George Taylor Exrs. Witt: Zorobabel Edwards, Abel Badger, Ezekiel Hitchins - p. 380
In order of prob: Charles Elliott qualified.

BEAVANS, MARY - 13 July 1796 - Partly proved 9 Feb. 1798 - Prob: 26 Feb. 1798 - To dau. Tabitha Marshall 1 s. To my grandau. Nancy Drummond whole estate, same to remain in my Exrs. hands till she come to lawful age. Should my said grandau. die under age & without issue I leave said estate to my grandau. Sally Beavans, dau. of Thomas, & George Beavans, son of William. Samuel Henderson Exr. Witt: John S. Ker, Daniel Twiford – p. 382

READ, ZOROBABEL – 8 Feb. 1798 – 27 Feb. 1798 – I lend my houses, orchards, lands &c. to Rachel Hancock for 14 years, except 2 A. which I lend to Tabitha Tatham for the same term of years. At the expiration of 14 years all my lands to be equally div. bet. Edmond Hutchinson & William Tatham. To George Hancock. Rachel & Tabitha above mentioned resid. legatees. George Hancock Exr. Witt: Elijah Hancock, John Hancock, Mary Hancock – p. 384

DELASTATIOUS, ELIZA – 23 Dec. 1797 – 27 Feb. 1798 – To Mary Walton, dau. of William Walton. To Sakar Walton, dau. of William Walton, dec. To Esther Walton dau. of William Walton, dec. To Elizabeth Walton, dau. of William Walton, dec. To Elizabeth Delastatious, dau. of Joseph Delastatious. To Peter Delastatious. My part of the houses & lot where I now live to be sold for the payment of my debts, & should there be any residue same to be div. bet. Elizabeth & Edward Walton. Bro. Peter Delastaticus Exr. Witt: George Corbin, William Welburn – p. 385

WISE, JOHANNAS – 22 July 1796 – 27 Feb. 1798 – To son in law Robinson Topping. To my grandson Sollomon Wise the use of my lands for his natural life, & at his death to my great grandson John Wise, son of my grandson Sollomon, provided that my dau. in law Susanna Wise shall hold the houses & tenements with the orchards & other improvements upon it during her wid. To dau. Rachel. Bal. of est. to be div. in 5 equal parts, one of which I give to my dau. Rebecca; one to my dau. Frances; one to my dau. Abigail; one to my dau. Anne & the other part to the children of my dau. Bridget. Sons in law John & Robinson Topping & friend John Wise Exrs. Witt: John Wise, John Guy, Molly Bonewell, Henry Guy – p. 386

BELL, SAVAGE – 5 May 1797 – Partly proved 26 Feb. 1798 – Prob: 26 Mar. 1798 – To John Savage Abdle 100 L. To Polly Benson 100 L. To Elizabeth Custis Savage my land & planta. adj. upon John Custis, seaside, being 200 A., she paying the 200 L before given, & if she refuse the land to be sold for payment of same & the remaining money to the said Elizabeth Custis Savage. To Francis Savage, Sr. To John Savage. John & Francis Savage resid. legatees. Francis Savage Exr. Witt: Thomas Custis, Sr., Charles Savage – p. 453

DUNCAN, MESHACK – 28 Apr. 1797 – 25 June 1798 – To father James Duncan my part of the schooner &c. To bro. John Sandford. To bro. James Duncan my part of the lot in Port Royal if he will pay the money that was borrowed of Staton Trader, and also my Quodrant Spy glass, waggoner & chart if he will pay the note I gave to Solomon Lucas. To bro. Nathaniel Bird. To sister Rachel Duncan silver shoe buckles & chest. John Sandford Exr. Witt: Teackle Shay, Arthur Watson – p. 481.

OUTTEN, PURNAL - 18 Sept. 1796 - 25 June 1798 - To wife Elizabeth all my property in Accomack County during her wid., then to my
son John Houston Outten, Shadrack Outten, Joseph Outten & Molly
Outten. Land & marshes left to me by the death of my father to be
sold at the death of my mother & the money divided between my 4
children above named. George Ker & Joseph Outten, my bro., Exrs.
Bro. Joseph Outten to settle all my business in Somerset County &
George Ker to settle my business in Accomack County - Witt: William Coloney, Jr., Peter Hack, Jr., William Watson - p. 482
In order of prob: Elizabeth Outten qualified.

PHILLIPS, John (of Senr) 6 Jan. 1798 - 25 June 1798 - To son John
Phillips 1 s. To dau. Lusey Phillips 1 s. To son James Phillips 1 s.
To wife Nancy & her 3 children that I had by her whole est. real &
personal. George Taylor Exr. - Witt: John Kellam, Sophia Taylor -
p. 483

AYRES, RICHARD - 26 Mar. 1798 - Partly proved 30 Apr. 1798 -
Prob: 25 June 1798. To wife Elizabeth whole est. during her wid. then
to be equally div. bet. my 5 children Grace, Peggy, Jacob, Elizabeth
& Hepsey. Wife Elizabeth & Col. John Poulson, John Burton, Esq., &
John A. Bundick Exrs. Witt: John Wharton, William Wharton, Wil-
liam H. Beavans - p. 484

HENDERSON, SAMUEL - 18 Mar. 1798 - 25 June 1798 - Son Jackey
Henderson's education to be finished, & that he have a horse, saddle &
bridle & a set of good bocks. To dau. Jinny Gillett I leave all the
money that is due me from the partnership of Downing & Henderson in
the hands of William Downing for the term of 3 years free of interest,
after which my Exrs. to purchase with said money two tracts of land of
an equal value for my 2 sons William & Joseph. Wife Charlotte
Henderson to enjoy all the rest of my est. to bring up my children, &
as my daus., namely Sally, Betsy, Charlotte Rebeckah Henderson
marry, then for my wife to pay them each the amount of 200 L in
bonds or property, & after paying the portions of my said daus. my
wife to enjoy 1/3 of all my lands and those purchased for my 2 sons
William & Joseph, as well as all the balance of my est. during her
life. To son Samuel land where I now live beginning at Warner's
Branch. To son Richard all the rest of my land adj. the above. Wife
& son in law James Gillett Exrs. Witt: William Downing, John
Logan, William Adair - p. 485

BAGGE, ANN - 7 Nov. 1796 - Partly provrd 25 June 1798 - Further
proved 30 July 1798 - Prob: 31 Dec. 1799 - To son William Bagge 200
A. adj. the land of John Kellam & Thomas Hall Bradford, being the
land where I now live, provided he pay to his 3 daus. (being the children of his first wife), namely Nancy, Axy & Elizabeth, the sum of 35
L each as they arrive to the age of 21 years or marry. To son Luke
Bagge 100 A. adj. the above. provided he pay to my dau. Nancy Read
20 L & 30 L to my dau. Molly. To my son Theophilus Bagge 40 A.

adj. the land belonging to the heirs of Arthur Teackle & Kendall Beach for life. To son Samuel Bagge the remainder of my land including the 40 A. lent my son Theophilus, provided he pay to my 3 grandchildren Andrew Wyatt, Ismae Wyatt & Sally Wyatt, children of William Wyatt, the sum of 10 L as they severally arrive to the age of 21 years. To grandau. Sally Bunker. Sons William & Luke Bagge Exrs. Witt: William Gibb, John Bell Gibb, William Gibb, Jr. - p. 486
In order of prob: Thomas Smith qualified.

ROSS, EZEKIEL - 19 Oct. 1796 - Partly proved 30 July 1798 & ordered to be recorded. To son Absalom Ross land where I now live. To dau. Elizabeth Ross. Bal. of est. to wife Esther during her wid., reversion to my 2 sons Ezekiel & James Ross to be equally div. bet. them. Wife Esther Exec. Witt: William Drummond, John Drummond, Sarah Darby - p. 488
In order of prob: Fully proved by John Drummond, George Scarburgh & Thomas Cropper 31 Mar. 1818 - William Drummond & Sarah Darby the other two witnesses being dead.

RIGHT, JACOB - 16 Apr. 1798 - 30 July 1798 - To dau. Sally Pruit. To son William Right 1 s. 3 small children Rosey Right, Dennis Right & Nancy Right resid. legatees. William Pettitt Exr. Witt: Levin Copes, Typhina Dix - p. 488

HEATH, MARGARET - 15 Nov. 1797 - 30 July 1798 - To bro. Josoph Heath, he to pay my bro. Fletcher Heath 8 L if the said Fletcher be living. To Cessey Heath. To Betsy Heath. Joseph Heath Exr. Witt: Revel Twiford, Elijah Hancock - p. 489

SILLIVAN, DANIEL - 18 Aug. 1798 - 24 Sept. 1798 - To son William land & planta. where I now live. Dau. Susanna Sillivan. Son William & dau. Susanna resid. legatees. Friend Severn Kellam Exr. - Witt: West Kellam, Jr., John Martin, William Pusey - p. 513

BLOXOM, ARGIL - 3 July 1798 - 24 Sept. 1798 - Wife to have use of all my land to bring up my children, then to be equally div. bet. them. Witt: Sally Watson, Scarbrough Bloxom, Leah Bloxom - p. 514
In order of prob: Lucretia Bloxom qualified.

Orders - 1798-1800

CLEMMONS, STEPHEN - Adm. his est. to Elizabeth Clemmons - Abel Teackle & William Nock sec. - 24 Sept. 1798 - p. 1

HOLT, ELIJAH - Adm. his est. to John Holt - John Marshall & James Marshall sec. - 25 Sept. 1798 - p. 8

ONLY, EDMUND - Adm. his est. to John Custis - William Gibb & Levin Walker sec. - 25 Sept. 1798 - p. 9

MELVIN, JOHN – Adm. his est. to William Welburn – William Downing & Drummond Welburn sec. – 29 Oct. 1798 – p. 10

TAYLOR, MAJOR – Adm. his est. to Samuel Trader – David Bowman & John Taylor sec. – 29 Sept. 1798 – p. 13

TAYLOR, JACOB – Adm. his est. with will annexed to Teackle Taylor – William Porter & William Trader sec. – 30 Oct. 1798 – p. 15

KELLAM, CHARLES – Adm. his est. to James Poulson – Richard Bayly & Isma Wyatt sec. – 31 Dec. 1798 – p. 47

BULL, ELI & John Bull – Adm. their estates to John Bull (church) – John Custis (B.S.) & William Gibb sec. – 31 Dec. 1798 – p. 49

READY, JAMES M. – Adm. his est. to Smith Horsey – William Downing & William Welburn sec. – 31 Dec. 1798 – p. 49

GLADDING, JOHN – Adm. his est. to Sally Gladding – Nehemiah Broughton & Warrington Staton sec. – 28 Jan. 1799 – p. 55

READ, SEVERN – Adm. his est. to Anne Read – Thomas Smith & James Lewis sec. – 28 Jan. 1799 – p. 58

WHITE, Levin – Adm. his est. to Sally White – Francis Ayres & Edmund Ayres sec. – 28 Jan. 1799 – p. 58

POWELL, GEORGE – Adm. his est. to Laban Powell – Thomas Bayly sec. – 29 Jan. 1799 – p. 63

MARSHALL, GEORGE – Adm. his est. to Sarah Marshall – Drummond Welburn & James Abbott sec. – 25 Feb. 1799 – p. 63

WISE, SAMUEL – Adm. his est. to George A. Wise – Charles Elliott & Charles Snead sec. – 26 Feb. 1799 – p. 68

HOLSTON, JOHN – Adm. his est. to John R. Parker – George Ker sec. – 26 Feb. 1799 – p. 68

WEST, ELIZABETH – Adm. her est. to Alexander West – John Cropper, Sr. & Jacob Lilliston sec. – 29 Apr. 1799 – p. 103

OUTTEN, JOSEPH – Adm. his est. to Thomas Fletcher & Robert Corbin – John R. Parker & William Silverthorn sec. – 29 Apr. 1799 – p. 104

ANDREWS, WILLIAM – Adm. his est. to Thomas Fletcher – John R. Parker sec. – 29 Apr. 1799 – p. 105

CHAPMAN, WILLIAM – Adm. his est. to Mary Chapman – John McLean & Smith Horsey sec. – 24 June 1799 – p. 145

MARTIN, HENRY – Adm. his est. to Owen Darby – Americus Scarburgh & William Bunting sec. – 24 June 1799 – p. 145

HINMAN, NANCY – Adm. her est. to George Hinman – Richard Savage & Elijah Wright sec. – 24 June 1799

WEST, PARKER – Adm. his est. to Henry Hall – Jonathan Melson & Major Northam sec. – 24 June 1799 – p. 147

BELL, WILLIAM, Jr. – Adm. his est. to Thomas Custis – John Custis (B.S.) sec. – 24 June 1799 – p. 147.

MIFFLIN, MARY – Adm. her est. to Charles Stockly – John Teackle & Thomas Evans sec. – 30 Sept. 1799 – p. 198

PARKER, SACKER, Sr. – Adm. his est. to Sacker Parker, Jr. & William Turpin – Isaac Warner & Zadock Nock sec. – 1 Oct. 1799 – p. 202

WALLACE, JAMES – Adm. his est. to Teackle Elliott – Thomas Mason & Henry Custis sec. – 28 Oct. 1799 – p. 207

VESSELLS, SOPHIA – Adm. her est. with will annexed to John A. Bundick – Savage Crippen & John Dix sec. – 29 Oct. 1799 – p. 211

SCOTT, THOMAS – Ordered that his estate be taken by the Sheriff & sold – 30 Dec. 1799 – p. 222

KELLAM, JOHN – Adm. his est. to Zorobabel Kellam, Margaret Kellam, wid. of John, relinquishing her right – Samuel Coleburn & Richard Read sec. – 30 Dec. 1799 – p. 222

BIRD, LEVI – Adm. his est. to Nancy Bird – Ebern Bird sec. – 30 Dec. 1799 – p. 224

Wills &c. – 1798–1800

MILBY PATIENCE – 27 Sept. 1795 – 29 Oct. 1798 – To son Daniel Rodgers. To grandau. Amey Rodgers. To grandau. Elizabeth Rodgers. To nephew Isaac West. To nephews & niece James, Thomas, Morton, Daniel, John, Clement & Hannah Rodgers, sons & dau. of Daniel Rodgers all my est. not before given. Son Daniel Rodgers & friend George Ker Exrs. Witt: Revel Twiford, Tabitha Heath – p. 21

TAYLOR, JACOB – 13 Nov. 1797 – 29 Oct. 1798 – To son Henry Taylor 100 A. of the land where I now live, together with the houses where I now live adj. William Ewell on the South. The remainder of my land where I now live to my son Ayres Taylor. Sons Henry & Ayres to have equal profit of the Mill & Marsh pasture adj. said lands. To sons Henry & Ayres Taylor part of a tract of land I bought of Crippen Taylor. I give a tract of land called Parkeses to be equally div. bet. my dau. Susanna & my dau. Taylor beginning at the Creek running up to William Vesselses. To dau. Polly. To dau. Naomy Taylor bal. of land bought of Crippen Taylor. To dau. Scarburgh 50 A. I bought of James Justice during her natural life or wid., then to be sold and the money div. bet. all my children. To grandau. Nancy Taylor, dau. of Hezekiah Taylor. Children James, Teackle, Ayres, Henry, Susanna, Polly & Naomy resid. legatees. Sons Teackle & Ayres & friend William Downing Exrs. Witt: Benjamin Holland, Polly Taylor, Henry Taylor, George Warrington, Willabey Jordan - p. 22

BRADFORD, CUSTIS - 6 Sept. 1798 - 29 Oct. 1798 - To Francis Roberts, Sr. planta. where I now live being 100 A. To sister Susanna Bradford 20 L. To James Mears. To James Roberts, son of John. To Francis Mears, son of Spencer. John, Molly & Rachel Roberts resid. legatees. Friend Francis Roberts, Sr. Exr. - Witt: John Downing, Nanny Mears, Francis Savage - p. 39

MEARS, ELISHA - 10 Dec. 1798 - 31 Dec. 1798 - To son Elisha Mears planta. where I now live cont. 161 A. To son William Mears all the land I bought that belonged to Phillip Tignal, cont. 74 A. To sons James & Luther all the land I bought of Taylor & Ricketts Tatham, with both the mills & all the lands belonging to them. To wife Comfort Mears. William Mears, Mary Fosque Mears, James Mears, Luther & Elisha Mears, my 5 children, resid. legatees. William Mears, son of John, & son Elisha Mears Exrs. Witt: John Nathaniel Harden, Dennis Tignal, Isaac Melson. - p. 40
In order of prob: Thomas Cropper qualified.

ALLEN, JOSEPH - 15 Aug. 1798 - 1 Jan. 1799 - To wife Hannah Allen whole est. during her life then to my 4 children Moses Allen, Denward Allen, Caty Allen & Elizabeth Allen. Not witnessed. Proved by John McLean, John Moore & Nicholas Knox - p. 41
In order of prob: William Downing qualified.

POWELL, SARAH - 29 May 1795 - 1 Jan. 1799 - To Frances Godwin. To her dau. Sarah Godwin & to her son Littleton Godwin. To her son John Godwin. To her son Joseph & her dau. Mary Godwin. To dau. Agnel Powell. To son Joseph Powell. To dau. Elizabeth Powell. To grandsons Edmund & John Roberts (under 21). If Labin Godwin does not give my Exr. a receipt for the estate he had of his wife in full, then the legacy I gave his wife to be equally div. bet. my 3 youngest children, Agnes, Joseph & Elizabeth Powell. "The estate that Labin Godwin is to give my executors a receipt for is ths estate of Jonathan Powell, his wife's father, that he has received of Sarah Powell. Joseph Powell & Agnes Powell Exrs. Witt: Daniel Godwin, George Tunnell, Peggy Townsend - p. 42

BELL, ANER - 25 July 1798 - 1 Jan. 1799 - To dau. Cassey Sturgis Bell. To son Isaac Bell. Bal. of est. to be equally div. bet. all my

children. Friend Thomas Custis Exr. – Witt: M. Bonewell, Lizey Bell, Betsy Beasly – p. 45
In order of prob: William Bell qualified.

EDMONDS, GEORGE – 21 Jan. 1799 – 28 Jan. 1799 – To wife Nancy Edmonds planta. where I now live during her wid. then I give the said planta. to my bro. Thomas Edmonds. Wife & Thomas Bagwell Exrs. Witt: Parker Copes, Thomas Metcalf – p. 63

MAPP, HOWSON, SR. – 25 Mar. 1796 – 28 Jan. 1799 – To wife Betty Mapp whole est. during her wid. to bring up my children. To my son Howson Mapp, my heir at law, all my lands, he to pay to Hester Mapp, Peggy Mapp, George Mapp, Robins Mapp & John Mapp 20 L each, & should he refuse my land to be sold & div. among my children. To son George Mapp. To son Robins. To son John. To dau. Hester. To dau. Peggy. To dau. Bridget Willis. To dau. Salley Downing. "and what Custis Willis & John Downing has had of me not to be mentioned". Wife Betty & son Howson Exrs. Witt: Smith Hyslip, Kendal Hyslop – p. 64

BONWELL, JAMES, son of James – 11 Dec. 1798 – 28 Jan. 1799 – To wife Betty whole est. during her wid. To son Robert all my lands & marsh. Bal. of est. to be div. bet. all my children except Robert. Wife & son Robert Exrs. Witt: William Gibb, Sarah Rodgers, M. Bonawell – p. 65

CUSTIS, JOHN (Sailor) – 16 Nov. 1798 – 28 Jan. 1799 – To son William. To wife Elizabeth whole est. during her life & at her death the remainder to be equally div. bet. all my children. Friend & bro. in law George Annis Wise Exr. Witt: William Gibb, John Poulson – p. 66
In order of prob: Elizabeth Custis qualified.

BELL, NATHANIEL, Sr. – 10 Dec. 1796 – 25 Feb. 1799 – To wife Susanna negroes during her wid., then to be div. bet. my daus. Nancy Satchell & Susannah Palmer. To son Nathaniel Bell planta. where I now live upon condition that he does not bring any charge or claim against my est. for the 50 L legacy which was left him by his grandmother Mary S. Bell, & if he should bring such claim 600 L to be raised out of the above planta. & div. bet. all my grandchildren. To son Nathaniel a tract of land on Hog Island and all Sandy Island, and a tract of land called Cold Spring. I lend to Sally Bell, the wid. of Robert Bell, my son, the use of 1/3 part of the planta. where the said Robert died during her wid., reversion to the heirs of the said Robert Bell, viz: Peggy & Polly Bell, & the other 2/3 of the said planta. & negroes to my said grandaus. Peggy & Polly Bell, & should they die without issue the property to go to my son Nathaniel Bell, Nancy Satchell & Susannah Palmer. Wife & daus. Mary & Susannah resid. legatees. Wife Susanna & son Nathaniel Bell Exrs. Witt: Golding Ward, William Harmon, Littleton Ward – p. 80

CORBIN, RALPH, Jr. - 29 Mar. 1799 - 29 Apr. 1799 - I lend my wife Sarah Corbin all my personal estate & also the land to the Westward end of my planta. To son Ralph Corbin after my dec. & the dec. of his mother, a parcel of land lying to the West end, also the 1/2 of the woods on the East end. To son Savage Corbin the place where he now lives, at the dec. of his mother he to have the land on the Wastward adj. his bro. Ralph. To dau. Sabra Welburn. To son George Corbin. To dau. Polly Jinkins. To son William Corbin (under 18) To Nancy Delastatius, wife of Walter 8 s. & no more. Bal. of est. to be div. as follows: William to have 2/3 & the other 1/3 to my son Ralph. William Welburn & son George Corbin Exrs. Witt: Thomas Joynes, James Broadwater, Spencer Waters - p. 123
In order of prob: Ralph Corbin qualified.

ROSS, JOSEPH - 19 Sept. 1798 - 29 Apr. 1799 -. To son James 45 A. adj. my bro. Jacob Ross, & the bal. which is adj. Levy Bird I give to my dau. Susanna Ross, & for want of heirs to my son James Ross. Wife & 2 children to live together & be brought up by the profits of the land. Wife to have the management of my est. during her wid. or until my son James comes to the age of 18 years, & at the death of my wife, Tabbe Ross, the remaining part of my est. to be equally div. bet. my 2 children. Witt Absalom Ross, Polly Doe, Jacob Ross - p. 125

FLETCHER, HENRY, SR. - 27 Sept. 1794 - 29 Apr. 1799 - To my eldest son Thomas Fletcher land where I now live at Massongoes cont. 600 A. To son Henry Fletcher land where he now lives cont. 450 A. To grandson Henry Riley, son of Thomas Riley, dec. 6 L current money. My 4 dau. now living, viz: Elizabeth Parker, Leah Dickerson, Susanna Riley & Euphamia Finny and the 5 younger children of my dec. dau. Ann Riley, resid. legatees. Son Thomas Fletcher & son in law John Riley Parker Exrs. Witt: Spencer Drummond, Thomas Evans - p. 126

STEPHENS, RICHARD - 4 Nov. 1798 - 29 Apr. 1799 - To bro. Elisha Stephens all my land & all the rest of my est. Bro. Elisha Exr. Witt: Jacob White, John Pruit, Molly Parker - p. 189

TAYLOR, IFFINIAH - 20 Apr. 1798 - 30 Apr. 1799 - To Daniel Collins, son of my sister Lavinah Collins. To sister Lavinah Collins. To bro. Ezekiel Taylor all the land & planta. where I now live as all the lands now in the possession of my mother in law Rebecca Taylor, together with the remainder of my property. Bro. Ezekiel Taylor Exr. Witt: Walter Bayne, John Gladding, Jr., Benjamin Hatton - p. 130

MORRISON, JOHN - 2 Mar. 1799 - Partly proved 29 July 1799 - Prob. 26 Nov. 1799 - To dau. Hannah. To son John Morrison. "Land where I now live to be sold with all the appurtenances thereunto belonging and titles given to the said land by the Will of John Pitts deed." Proceeds to be equally div. bet. my 4 children, John, Hannah, Molly & Leah Morrison. William Downing & John Logan Exrs. Witt: Edward Jones, George Bonwell - p. 185

THORNTON, EDWARD – 22 Apr. 1799 – 29 July 1799 – To dau. Sally Thornton for life, but if she marries with Matthew Taylor, son of Parker, I give the above named property to my grandson John Thornton, son of John. To son Southy Thornton.   4 sons John, William, Southy & George resid. legatees. Son John Exr. Witt: David Watts, Simson Bloxom – p. 186

BELL, WILLLAM, Ockn. – 23 Jan. 1799 – 29 July 1799 – To wife Elizabeth whole est. during her wid. to bring up & education younger children, & at her marriage or death I give the land where I now live cont. 169 A. to my son Agrippa Bell, he to find my son Samuel Bell his home as long as he is single. Children Margaret Bell, Ecana Bell, Samuel Bell, Felix Bell, Elizabeth Smith Bell & ____. (blank with "nameless" written in).   Bro. Anthony Bell & George Kellam Exrs. Witt: Sacker Stringer, Thomas Henderson, Armstd Mears – p. 187

BEECH, EZEKIEL – 3 May 1799 – 29 July 1799 – Personal est. to be div. bet. 3 daus. Sarah, Mary & Catherine Beech after my wife Anna has her dower. To 3 daus. the whole of my land for the purpose of bringing them up until my youngest dau. Catherine comes to the age of 21 years, then to be div. bet. them.   Bro. in law James Spiers Exr. – Witt: William Gibb, Thomas Burton, Stephen Kelley – p. 188

LEATHERBURY, WILLIAM – 13 June 1799 – 29 July 1799 – To wife Anna whole est. during her wid. then to be div. equally bet. my survivors except my son Samuel, and to him I give the land.   Nephew John Leatherbury Exr. Witt: Sally Sturgis, Thomas Sturgis – p. 190

SIMPSON, SELBY – 20 Mar. 1795 – Partly proved 29 Apr. 1795 – Prob: 24 June 1799 – To wife whole est. until my dau. Betsy arrives to lawful age or marries, then to be equally div. bet. my wife, dau. Betsy & unborn child. Should my dau. Betsy & my unborn child die under the age of 21 & without heirs, wife to have whole est. forever.   Friends Thomas Evans, Esq. & John Abbott Bundick Exrs. Witt: John Wharton, Sally Taylor, John Burton – p. 191

BAYLY, ELIZABETH – 21 Dec. 1798 – 24 June 1799 – To bro. Isma Bayly. To sister Sarah Waltham.   To 2 nephews Richard & Charles Bayly. To nephew Richard a note I now have against him. Sister Sarah Waltham resid. legatee. Nephew Richard Bayly Exr. – Witt: Isaac Outten, Stephen Pusey, Robert Jenkins – p. 192

PAYNE, SAMUEL – 8 Jan. 1799 – 24 June 1799 – To wife Joyce Payne negroes until my son Levin Payne arrives to the age of 21, then to be his property to serve him until the negroes arrive to the age of 30, then to be free. To dau. Caty Payne. Son Levin & dau. Caty resid. legatees. Wife to have use of 1/3 during her wid.   William Hargis Exr. Witt: Scarburgh Whealton, James Nelson Hargis. – p. 193

KNOCK, ELIZABETH - 3 Feb. 1798 - 24 June 1799 - To grandau. Nancy Trader. To dau. Elizabeth Ward. Son Littleton Trader resid. legatee & for want of heirs to grandau. Nancy Trader. Son Littleton Trader Exr. - Witt: Custis Willis - p. 194

DIX, BERSHEBA - 26 Mar. 1799 - 24 June 1799 - To son William Dix planta. where I now live, together with all the rest of my est. for 7 years, provided he finds all my children a maintenance during that time, then I give him his choice to keep the lands forever on paying my children 100 L- each, or to sell the same & the money to be div. bet. all my children (himself included). To son William all my personal est. at the expiration of 7 years provided he schools my 2 youngest sons Levin & Thomas each one year. If my children refuse when they come to lawful age of giving up that piece of land (which is about 18 A. that my husband purchased of John Hickman) to my son William Dix, in that case my will is that they have but $5. of my estate. Son William Exr. Witt: Parker Barnes, John A. Bundick, Nancy Dix - p. 194
In order of prob: Parker Barnes qualified.

TAYLOR, ABEL - 19 Apr. 1799 - 30 Sept. 1799 - To son Abel Taylor lands where I now live. To son Gillet Taylor. To son Joshua Taylor. To wife Elizabeth. Taylor. Personal est. to be div. bet. children Mary Ann Owen, Essee Taylor, Gillet Taylor & David Taylor - Friend William Downing Exr. - Witt: Atkins Massey, William Watts, Samuel Downing - p. 252

CORE, ZOROBABEL - 28 July 1799 - 30 Sept. 1799 - To son Edmond Core lands & planta. where I lately lived situate on the head waters of Assawoman, he to release to my dau. Sally all interest in the land hereafter devised to my said dau., but should he refuse my said dau. to be entitled to 1/4 part of the lands which I give to my son Edmond. To dau. Sally all the lands & improvements which belonged to my wife & which was devised to her by her father. Dau. Sally resid. legatee. Bro. in law John Laws Exr. Witt: John Teackle, Sr., Levin Core - p. 253

BARNES, JOHN - 10 Sept. 1799 - 28 Oct. 1799 - To son Arthur Barnes land where I now live. To wife Tabitha Barnes all my remaining est. during her wid. then to be div. bet. all my children. Witt: Samuel Russell, Daniel Drummond, Elijah Grennalds - p. 254
In order of prob: Tabitha Barnes qualified.

VESSELS, SOPHIA - 3 Oct. 1799 - 28. Oct. 1799 - To son Elijah Vessels & Charles Copes, Sr. all the brandy, cider & corn & all that was made on the planta. in the year 1799 to be div. bet. them. Son Elijah resid. legatee. Witt: Hancock Simpson, Betty Groton - p. 255. In order of prob: John A. Bundick qualified.

RODGERS, TILNEY - 1 Oct. 1799 - 28 Oct. 1799 - I lend to Peter Shield negro Henry for 12 years, then the said Henry to be free. Bal. of

est. to be sold & the money equally div. bet. Susannah Hickman's children that she had by Selby Hickman, & Bridget Edwards' children that she had by Zorobabel Edwards, & Mary Rodgers to have one child's part & said Mary Rodgers' two children to share equal with the rest of the children. George Taylor Exr. Witt: William James, Patience James. p. 256
In order of prob: Charles Elliott qualified.

VESSELS, ELIJAH - 25 Sept. 1781 - Proved 24 Feb. 1794 - Prob. 28 Oct. 1799 - To wife Sophia Vessels whole est. during her wid., & should she die before the child she now goes with comes to lawful age my planta. on the Bayside to be rented out yearly for the maintenance of the said child, & should the aforesaid child be a boy he to have the said planta. To son Elijah the land where I now live at the death of my wife. Bal. of est. to be div. bet. my daus. Witt: Thomas Watson, Jacob Taylor, George Middleton. Wife Exec. - p. 257

SCARBURGH, BENNET - 14 May 1799 - 28 Oct. 1799 - To niece Elizabeth Parker Rodgers $200. to be raised out of my est. to be paid her by my Exr. when she reaches the age of 18 years, & should she die before she is 18 to my bro. George Scarburgh. To friend Solomon Smith my watch. Bro. George resid. legatee & Exr. Witt: William Kennahorn - John Brittingham - p. 258

WEST, JOHN - 1 Feb. 1799 - 29 Oct. 1799 - To dau. Catherine. To grandson Samuel Burton Garrison. Grandson John Garrison. To grandau. Catherine Garrison. To dau. Comfort Vear. To John Garrison. To son Anthony the land where I now live, also all my right of Tangear Island, the said Anthony to make over 100 A. to John Crocket, & should he refuse I leave the whole of the Island to be sold. To grandson John Fosque. Bal. of est. to be div. bet. Anthony, Catherine, Comfort & John Garrison's children to have their mother's part of 1/4 part. Son Anthony & Abel West Exrs. Witt: John West, Thomas W. Rodgers, Severn Kellam - p. 258

SCOTT, WALTER - 14 Jan. 1799 - 30 Oct. 1799 - To wife Mary whole est. during her wid. To son John Scott all my land and planta. where I now live, & for want of heirs to my 3 daus. Betsey, Polly & Peggy. 3 daus. aforesaid resid. legatees. Wife Mary & friend Tully Wise Exrs. Witt: Michel Bonnewell, Sally Scot, Betsy Scot - p. 260

PHILLIPS, SUSANNAH - 11 Sept. 1795 - 30 Dec. 1799 - To son Benjamin Phillips all right, title & interest in the lands I now hold that was given me by my father John Fisher. To dau. Margaret Mason. To dau. Mary Charnock. Son Benjamin Phillips, dau. Mary Charnock & dau. Margaret Mason resid. legatees. Son Benjamin Exr. Witt: John R. Parker, Francis Boggs, Kendal Ames - p. 335

CONQUEST, WILLIAM, Sr. - 6 Apr. 1799 - 30 Dec. 1799 - To grandson James Conquest & his male heirs the planta. where he now lives cont. 125 A. adj. Wallops road, & for want of such issue to my grandson Nathaniel Conquest. To the said James 50 A. of swamp land, & for want of male heirs to Joseph Conquest. To grandson Nathaniel the remainder of my swamp land. To son Richard Conquest the residue of my lands during his natural life, reversion to my grandson William Conquest. To daus. Tabitha & Sarah Conquest. To grandau. Leah Conquest. To Comfort Conquest. To Mary Duncan. To Joseph Conquest. To James Duncan. To Keziah Conquest. I give Sarah Midcalf, dau. of Keziah Matthews, dec., 10 L current money. To Sarah Lilleston, dau. of Jemimah Bloxom 10 L current money. To Keziah Bloxom, dau. of Jemimah Bloxom 10 L current money. To Polly Hollon, grandau. of Nathaniel Conquest 3 L current money. Son Richard Conquest, Tabitha Conquest & Sarah Conquest resid. legatees. Richard Conquest & William Conquest Exrs. Witt: James Staton, John Staton – p. 335

MEARS, WILLIAM, of John. – 22 Nov. 1799 – 27 Jan. 1800 – To wife Betsy Mears. To son Thomas Fosque Mears all my lands & my mill & water grist mill, Mare called "the flower of Dust". To dau. Catherine Mears. Ann Arlington Mears & Catherine Mears resid. legatees. – Wife & bro. Richard Mears Exrs. Witt: Nathaniel Fosque, Ezekiel Ashby, Richard Rodgers – p. 338

HINMON, GEORGE C. – 22 Dec. 1799 – 27 Jan. 1800 – To wife Tabitha Hinmon all the land I bought of William Young, Sr. during her natural life, then to my son Dennis C. Hinmon, he paying the sum now owing on same. Wife Tabitha & son Dennis Exrs. Witt: Thomas Evans, George Hope Young, Capt. Epheram Vessels – p. 339
In order of prob: Dennis Clayton qualified.

SCARBURGH, EDMUND, Sr. – 14 Sept. 1777 – Partly proved 31 Dec. 1799 – Prob: 27 Jan. 1800 – All my lands to be rented out & all my negroes hired out until my son Edward K. Scarburgh comes to lawful age, & I then beq. to my said son my Occahannock estate, cont. 927 A., as also the lands I bought of George Dunton cont. 109 A., & for want of heirs to my son William M. K. Scarburgh. To son William Mered: K. Scarburgh (under age) the residue of my lands supposed to be 104 A. lying on Cradock, & for want of heirs to my son Edward K. Scarburgh. To Alice Scarburgh, "then the rest to share equally after receiving 80 L each before Peggy Coward comes in, but no more to my daughter Alice". Friends Dr. John Tankard & Samuel Coward trustees. Witt: Nathaniel Brown, Caty Scarburgh, Leah Bagwell Dunton – p. 340
In order of prob: Proved by Nathaniel Brown & Leah Dunton, alias Kellam – Samuel Coward qualified.

MIDDLETON, JOHN – Not dated – 27 Jan. 1800 – To bro. George Middleton. To sister Elizabeth Middleton, Frances Melson resid. legatee & Exec. Witt: Nancy Lucas, Thomas Johnson – p. 366

ROBERTS, ARTHUR – 22 Nov. 1799 – 24 Feb. 1800 – To son William Simkins Roberts 200 A. being the remainder of the lands where I now live, as I have given my son William S. Roberts a deed of gift for the other part, he to pay my grandson Eldred Roberts 900 L. To grandau. Nancy Roberts. To dau. Peggy Bagwell Powell. To dau. Nancy Groten, wife of William Groten. To the children my dau. Nancy had by Coventon Mears. To grandau Peggy Roberts. To wife Patience Roberts. Residue of est. to wife for life then 1/2 to my dau. Peggy Bagwell Powell & the other 1/2 to my dau. Nancy Groten & my grandau. Nancy Roberts. To grandau. Elizabeth Rebecca Savage 6 s. Son William S. Roberts Exr. Witt: John Smith, Isaiah Garretson, Susana Fletcher, Adah Fletcher – p. 366

BELL, ELIZABETH – 31 Jan. 1800 – 24 Feb. 1800 – To Sally Mears, dau. of Littleton Mears. To John Bell's wife Lucretia. To Suffiah Kelly. To Elizabeth Mears dau. of John. To Hillary Mears. To Sally Dolby. To Rachel Bradford, dau. of James. Elizabeth Mears, dau. of Spencer, Elizabeth Mears, dau. of John, Elizabeth Mears, dau. of Arthur, Sally Dolby & Elizabeth Kelly (all under age) resid. legatees. Francis Savage & Alexander Morrison Exrs. Witt: William Bell, John Mears – p. 368

TAYLOR, TABITHA – 22 Dec. 1799 – 24 Feb. 1800 – To 2 sons Jeremiah & Selby Taylor the land where they now live, the same having been devised them by their father Bartholomew Taylor. To Sarah Gladding. 3 daus. Rebecca Hasey, Nancy Johnson & Margaret Thomson resid. legatees – William Thounton & Jeremiah Taylor Exrs – Witt: Thomas Jones, William Mathews, Ayres Taylor – p. 370.

MEARS, JAMES – 21 Dec. 1799 – 24 Feb. 1800 – To bro. Caleb Mears 200 A. at the North end of my land adj. Kendal Richardson, for life & then to be sold & the money div. bet. my 2 youngest sisters Frances Mears & Betty Mears. To sister Sally Mears 20 A, of land. Bal. of land to be sold & proceeds div. bet. my. sisters Frances & Betty Mears – 3 sisters Sally, Frances & Betty resid. legatees. Francis Roberts Exr. Witt: Custis Willis, John Kelley – p. 370

CORBIN, RALPH, SR. – 27 Jan. 1800 – 24 Feb. 1800 – To wife Rachel whole est. during her natural life. To son Robert Corbin planta. where I now live cont. 280 A. To sons George & Coventon planta. at Mesongo cont. 125 A. To dau. Susanna Croswell. To John Pitt Corbin, reversion to my grandau. Sally Williams Broadwater. To 4 daus. Leah, Elizabeth, Levinah & Rosannah. Bal. of est. to be div. bet. all my children & my grandau. Sally William Broadwater & John Pitt Corbin. Son Robert Exr. Witt: James Benston, James Jenkins, William Williams, Jr. – p. 371

TRADER, GEORGE – 15 Jan. 1800 – 24 Feb. 1800 – To son Parker Trader 14 A. adj. James Abbott, but if Parker Trader never returns then to my son George Trader. To wife 1/3 of my est. To dau. Grace Trader planta. where I now live to be sold. Children resid. legatees. Robert Russell & Savage Crippin Exrs. Witt: William Wise, John Hickman, James Rocks, William Warner – p. 373

PARKER, JOHN RILEY – 20 Nov. 1799 – 24 Feb. 1800 – To wife Elizabath whole est. during her natural life, should my said wife die before my son William Parker arrives to the age of 21 years, whole est. except the land to be sold on a credit upon interest until my said son arrives to the age of 21, & the lands to be rented out. To 2 daus. Elizabeth & Leah Parker. I give the planta. where I now live together with the Island marsh to my son Henry Parker. I give my land bought of Bennet & George Scarburgh cont. 90 A. to my son Charles Parker, also 25 A. purchased of Stephen Pusey. To Nancy Riley, dau. of Thomas. Dau. Euphamy Rodgers & daus. Elizabeth & Leah Parker & my son William Parker resid. legatees. I leave my son William in the hands of my wife Elizabeth & Thomas Fletcher & Henry Parker. William Finney, Edmond Bayly, John Bayly & George Scarburgh to appraise & divide estate. Wife Elizabeth, Thomas Fletcher, William Finney & Henry Parker Exrs. Witt: William Finney, George Dewey, Henry Custis – p. 374

BEAUCHAMP, ANN – 22 May 1797 – 24 Feb. 1800 – To Frederick Kellam's daus. To George Kellam. To Peggy Kellam. Custis Kellam resid. legatee & Exr. Witt: West Kellam, Salathiel West – p. 407

MARSHALL, POLLY – 20 Aug. 1799 – 28 Apr. 1800 – To Peter Marshall Alexander, son of Thomas. Polly Fiddeman, dau. of Isaiah & Euphamy Alexander, dau. of Thomas resid. legatees, & for want of heirs to their brothers & sisters at their mothers death, "the part of Polly among the surviving children of my sister Easter & the part of Euphamy Alexander among the surviving children of my sister Elizabeth Alexander." John Shepherd Ker Exr. Witt: Thomas Alexander, Edward Richardson – p. 408

LINGO, ROBINSON – 28 Feb. 1800 – 28 Apr. 1800 – To son John Lingo land where I now live when he arrives at tha age of 25 years – land to be rented until that time & the proceeds div. bet. my son William Lingo, dau. Caty Lingo & son David Lingo. To wife Margaret Lingo. 5 children Rachel Lingo, William, George, Caty & David Lingo resid. legatees. Francis Savage Exr. Witt: Laban Lewis, Nanny Lewis, Molly Hyslop – p. 409

JAMES, WILLIAM – 28 Jan. 1800 – 28 Apr. 1800 – To wife Patience whole est. during her wid. to bring up my children, then to my son Levin the North-east end of my land where I live. To son Thomas James all the rest of my land. Daus. Elizabeth & Susannah James resid. legatees. Wife Patience & George Taylor Exrs. Witt: Ayres Rodgers, John Turlington – p. 410

TAYLOR, JACOB – 7 Jan. 1799 – 28 Apr. 1800 – To wife whole est. during her wid. To son James that part of land I bought of Robinson Custis. To son Bagweill Taylor land bought of Elijah Simpson. To son Raymond Taylor the lands formerly belonging to John Taylor. To dau. Betsy Taylor land that formerly belonged to my son George

Taylor. To dau. Sally Taylor land I now live on and the land I bought of William Middleton & Thomas Wiat. To dau. Peggy Hickman. 3 sons James, Bagwill & Raymond Taylor Exrs. Witt: John A. Bundick, Molly Prawit – p. 411

INDEX

AIMES (continued)
295 302 Kendal 359 Leavan
302 Levi 288 Levin 373 Lisha
288 Mary 358 Nathaniel 375
376 Rachel 237 Sally 394
Shadrack 288 Smith 341
Thomas 244 288 375 380 391
414 Thomas Jr 268 Thomas Sr
288 William 138 358 William
Jr 288 William Sr 288 Zerrobabel 265 288

AINSWORTH, Jenne 123 William
123

AIRES, Abbott 334 Richard 334

ALASTON, Frances 70

ALEN, Edmund 181

ALEWORTH, Dorcas 14 John 77
84 Jonathan 14 William 14

ALEXANDER, Ann 40 47 338
Betsy 391 Elizabeth 338 465
Euphamy 465 James 20 40 45
Peter Marshall 465 Thomas
275 338 391 465

ALFORD, William 11

ALGEO, Lewis 255

ALLEN, Ana 56 Andrew 78 84 85
97 Ann 17 83 Ardrew 126
Bridget 85 Bridgett 84 85 Caty
457 Denward 457 Edmond 21
Edmund 17 29 46 53 113 136
142 160 236 239 274 Elizabeth
22 391 449 457 Esther 236
Hannah 457 Henry 22 Henry Jr
17 James 49 142 160 172 John
104 115 143 160 236 239 449
Joseph 59 351 391 457 Mar-
garet 53 239 273 Marget 85
Mary 449 Moses 391 457
Patience 49 Peggy 382 399
Sophire 289 Stephen 46 121 142
160 236 239 Tabitha 239
Thomas 44 449 William 183
Zadoc 419 Zadock 449

ALLENS, John 331

ALLFORD, David 41 William 11

ALLIN, Henry 17

ALWORTH, Elizabeth 181 John
181 Jonathan 181

AMBLER, John 221

AMES, 418 Anne 253 Babel 396
Benjamin 435 Caleb 253 300
Churchel 435 Churchill 312

AMES (continued)
Churchwell 253 Dorothy 253
270 Elizabeth 221 237 302 396
433 445 Ester 52 Esther 181
James 433 Jesse 422 433 John
204 396 433 Joseph 16 52 181
253 300 Joseph Jr 237 Joseph
Sr 237 253 Joyce 424 Kendal
462 Kendall 443 445 Levi 435
Levin 253 373 423 424 436 445
Levy 446 Littleton 204 Major
436 Mary 149 163 181 424
Nancy 396 Nathaniel 237 423
433 Opansely 436 Peggy 237
435 436 Rosanna 435 Siner 224
Tabitha 268 Thomas 52 189
253 256 422 Thomas Jr 181
Thomas Sr 181 William 108
435 Zerobabel 275

AMOS, Mary 31

ANDERS, Elizabeth 54

ANDERSON, Catherine 140 Comfort 9 20 30 158 Esther 326
Father 20 John 140 Mary 30 31
34 Mr 23 Naomi 30 31 Naomy
9 12 Patience 158 Ralph 135
Robert 76 Roger 113 William 6
9 12 13 20-22 25 30 34 38

ANDREW, Jedidah 38

ANDREWS, Andrew 133 143 Ann
87 Anna M 331 Anna Maria 287
310 Annamariah 307 Catherine
Gibbons Schoolfield 402
Dorothy 67 Ebenezer 321
Elizabeth 43 67 136 138 Isaac
67 Isamael 402 Ishmael 216
Jacob 138 249 402 Joyce 219
Leah 219 Marcus 53 88 Margaret 249 351 Mary 216 219
Molly 402 Nathaniel 67 Rachel
402 Robert 43 87 120 121 136
138 146 249 307 310 402 Sarah
133 143 249 351 352 Susanah
406 Susannah 195 406 William
8 87 101 103 109 110-113 138
139 172 175 191 209 216 249
262 287 303 310 323 324 343
345 402 425 433 455 William
Jr 169 170

ANGELO, James 131 Sarah 131
William 131

ANKERS, Joseph 193

ANNINGHAM, Walter 83
ANNIS, Levi 408 Peggy 408
ANNYHOM, Walter 83
ANSELLO, Catherine 130 William 130 131
ANSIL, Elizabeth 153
ANTHONY, George 60
AONINS, Ann 142
ARBUCKLE, Ann 147 161 Anne 229 Catherine 230 Edward 354 382 Euphamia 147 George 317 346 354 James 161 162 164 173 229-231 235 296 298 313 316 317 321 331 354 399 Katharine 147 354 Katherine 140 162 164 168 Margaret 354 Mary 354 Mrs James 354 Mrs William 161 Tabitha 346 354 William 95 106 112 113 115 128 133 135 137 140 147 159 161 164 230 301 313 330 341 355 363 382
ARBUCKLEY, Euphamia 164
ARDES, Robert 143
ARDIES, Comfort 106 Edward 106 263 264 Elizabeth 169 Hazard 106 James 106 169 Robert 104 106 107 147 165 William 264
ARDIS, Anne 237 Betty 378 Daniel 378 Edward 237 254 364 378 Elizabeth 421 James 378 412 John 237 Joshua 237 Leah 378 Nanny 378 Patience 237 Robert 35 62 134 159 190 237 378 Sally 401 William 406 William Chance 237 447
ARENTON, John 106
AREW, John 3 18 Thomas 18 Wony 18
ARICHARDS, James 109
ARLENTON, John 37 273
ARLINGTON, Charity 87 Elizabeth 445 446 John 112 313 341 346 400 415 416 435 439 446 John Jr 335 John Sr 357 Rosey 346 Sarah 400 Thomas Bagwell 400 Thomas Bagwil 445 446
ARMATRADER, Archabel 430
ARMEYTRADOR, William 421
ARMITRADER, Abgil 220 Abigail 135 357 Abigal 139

ARMITRADER (continued)
Ann 258 Ann Burton 389 Anne 213 Archibold 258 Arter 220 Arthur 104 114 142 220 389 Catherine 389 Comfort 105 231 258 Elizabeth 182 213 Euphamy 258 Henry 104 105 135 172 220 389 Israel 231 James 213 John 104 Liddleton 104 Littleton 139 140 171-174 209 220 231 258 415 Mathew 213 Patience 105 147 213 Richard 56 104 115 167 182 213 Robert 213 Rose 182 220 Roxe 104 Sabra 182 Sabrah 182 Samuel 220 389 Sinah 258 Stephen 213 Susanna 213 William 104 421
ARMITRADING, Henry 88
ARMSTRONG, Henry 18
ARNOLD, Lawrence 169
ARRINGTON, John 70 210 224 300
ARRINTON, John 70
ARUE, John 31
ASH, Bridget 109 Joseph 31
ASHBY, Bridget 212 Charles 107 127 134 David 219 394 395 424 432 444 449 Eleanor 107 Elizabeth 394 449 Ezekiel 156 161 219 394 396 425 432 444 449 463 George 219 353 424 432 445 James 219 318 383 410 424 445 James Sr 414 John 219 232 235 247 280 302 318 339 376 394 396 413 432 437 444 449 Keaty 424 Mary 219 Nancy 424 445 Rachel 137 163 238 394 413 Sally 394 Sam 394 Samuel 396 432 444 449 Sarah 107 219 414 Susanna 219 329 432 Thamar 219 Thomas 410 William 219 232 394 432 449
ASHBYE, Edward 13
ATKINS, Ann 37 Elizabeth 21 John 37 Joseph 37 Matilda 37
ATKINSON, Elizabeth 22 James 22 25
ATOLES, Stockly 37
ATTLE, Sarah 48
AUSTIN, Moses 175
AYDELOTT, Benjamin 253

AYDLOTT, Benjamin 191 Mary
191
AYELOTT, Benjamin 191 Esther
191
AYERS, Jacob 221
AYMES, Ester 61 Esther 108
James 61 108 Joseph 11 36
Mary 108 William 61 108
AYRES, Ann 35 61 68 Ann Fran-
cis 67 Ann Mary 27 32 35 61
Comfort 61 Daniel 21 Easter
67 Edmond 23 333 Edmund 32
35 61 333 455 Elizabeth 61 68
129 453 Esther 58 Frances 58
Francis 3 23 35 61 68 333 411
443 455 George 333 436 Grace
453 Henry 23 27 35 61 Hepsey
453 Huldah 61 Jacob 210 326
333 453 John 3 16 24 28 58 67
John Jr 23 Levin 333 405 424
Mary 23 58 67 436 Mrs Jacob
333 Patience 3 61 Peggy 453
Richard 23 35 58 67 68 128 333
411 453 Richard Hill 23 29 54
58 67 Sally 333 Tabby 333
Tabitha 32 35 61
BACOR, Lazarus 225
BADGER, Abbegal 273 Abel 132
247 273 451 Abigail 247 Abigal
247 Ann 168 Anne 152 247 369
Bridget 152 David 152
Elizabeth 322 325 411 Ezekiel
179 255 Frances 152 Jacob 99
131 132 136 138 152 168 247
309 James 400 427 John 99
152 168 325 381 427 John Sr
247 Joyce 427 Leaner 273
Leanna 152 247 Nancy 273
Nathaniel 50 152 247 273 323
410 427 Polley 273 Polly 247
Rachel 132 152 Rannals 70
Reginald 152 Sabra 152 Sarah
247 273 Sinah 247 Sinoe 273
Sinor 273 Tabitha 247 Tabltha
273 Thomas 411 427 Thomas
Wyatt 427 William 247 273
325 344
BADGERS, Leah 223
BAGG, Theophilus 391 W 79
William 38 131 179
BAGGALE, Gervis 31
BAGGALY, Gervas 22

BAGGE, Andrew 355 Ann 257 453
Anne 219 355 Axy 453
Elizabeth 453 Jeremiah 183
John 266 296 302 Luke 453 454
Molly 453 Mrs Samauel 281
Mrs William 260 Nancy 448
453 Samuel 183 219 260 281
454 Theophilus 375 446 448
453 454 W 65 66 101 103 105
121 179 William 107 114 119
132-134 144 150 155 179 183
187 204 207 214 215 260 281
439 453 454
BAGWELL, Adah 154 Alexander
14 42 Ann 14 18 48 103 142
154 160 443 Anne 230 315
Betty 315 Charles 103 140 170
171 204 230 231 235 237 243
244 255 256 261 267 283 297
301 320-322 334 335 349 351
355 362 363 371 377 383 384
387 399 Comfort 18 48 Edward
43 Elizabeth 18 48 60 71 103
113 154 Farncis 18 George 408
Hele 414 448 Heli 104 165 315
Hely 197 204 Henere 49 Henry
14 48 82 84 90 103 104 115 204
443 448 Isaiah 154 181 219 220
384 402 448 John 13 14 18 41
43 48 89 92 96 103 115 124 132
143 154 163 220 257 315 330
346 443 John Jr 114 John Sr
154 Keziah 92 Margaret 49 103
104 160 Mary 43 Mrs Thomas
48 Nancy 414 Patience 220
Peggy 401 416 Rachel 257
Rebecca 14 Rebeckah 17 Rose
220 Sabra 104 Sara 48 Sarah
219 220 315 Sophia 197 257
315 Sophiah 448 Spencer 104
120 204 307 315 Stephen 220
346 Susanna 48 Tabitha 60 96
103 154 160 Thomas 5 13 14
17 18 26 43 48 94 103 104 113
121 142 154 160 172 188 220
257 371 401 414 416 431 458
Valeance 18 William 18 26
139 143 154 315
BAGWILL, Henry 443 Isaac 443
John 443 John Young 443
BAILEY, Abbigale 76 Edmund
288 Richd 76 Thomas 295 338

BAILY, Baily 242 Betsey 334
Charles 55 279 334 Edith 55 60
Edmund 113 Elizabeth 55 279
283 Henry 114 John 39 55 334
Mary 55 334 Mrs John 55
Nancy 334 Patience 279 Peggy
334 Richard 94 111 Rose 114
Sacker 279 Sarah 334 336
Susanna 334 Tabitha 55 279
Thomas 242 326 334 335 Wil-
liam 279
BAINS, William 196
BAKE, Mrs Salathel 433
BAKER, 330 Ann 50 Comfort 50
David 198 Edward 1 Elijah 418
433 Elizabeth 1 50 256 261 285
433 Ester 433 Esther 237
Ezekel 433 George 261 285
Hezekiah 261 346 446 Isaiah
261 318 John 50 92 122 174
261 285 435 436 John Sheperd
433 435 Jonathan 106 109
Kesiah 336 Leven 261 Levin
285 336 Lishea 50 Mary 50 93
151 204 285 336 433 435
Naomi 381 Rachel 433 435
Richard 346 Salathel 433
Salathiel 261 418 Sarah 433
Sebrou 50 Solomon 261 433 435
Sophia 435 Suphia 433 Thomas
44 William 50 74 92 151 162
261 285 336 433 435
BALDING, Elizabeth 264 Joseph
264
BALDWIN, John 147 169 Joseph
302 394
BALEY, Edmund 76 Elizabeth
169 John 170 194 Levin 194
Margaret 169 Richard 51 210
Rosana 76 Thomas 194 221
BALFOUR, James 361
BALL, Alphonso 2
BALLARD, Charles 185 Henry
184 Jarvis 184
BALLY, Hannah 37 Rich 3
Richard 10 16 37 Richard Jr 20
Robert 41
BALY, Isaac 83 Robert 83
Rosaner 83
BANCKS, Abraham 31
BANDFIELD, John 140
BANDY, Mary 264 267 Sally 301

BANFIELD, John 100 219
BANKS, Abraham 31 Christopher
134 148 Margaret 31 Naomi
134 Sarah 31
BARBOUTIN, Francis 304
BARCLAY, John 325 William 325
BARINCASTLE, Jane 83
BARKER, Arthur 29 Bethula 29
Bethulia 29 Mary 173 Roger 2
William 220
BARLOW, John 235
BARLY, Robert 39
BARNACASEL, Elizabeth 260
BARNES, Abel 349 Ann 51 Arthur
461 John 44 50 51 90 159 342
344 461 John Jr 43 44 John
Sacker 209 John Sr 52 53 Leah
435 Mary 51 Parker 243 317
336 337 359 397 407 408 431
435 439 446 451 461 Sacker
201 Spencer 342 Susanna 435
Tabitha 461 Will 26 William
29
BARNS, 30 Abraham 184 Anne
301 Archibald 217 Arthur 116
188 Bridget 271 Easter 116
Elizabeth 180 188 Esther 116
119 236 271 Ezekiel 116
Frances 116 George 271 Henry
51 John 60 116 141 188 John
Sacker 271 301 Mary 141 184
Parker 271 301 337 Robins 116
Susannah 118 271 301 309
William 116 118 169 188 196
203 236 271 301
BARRY, Robert 152 154
BARTON, Robert 8
BATES, Thomas 366
BATSON, Thomas 199 200 218
241
BAUGH, Rowland 3
BAYLEY, Anna Bella 333 Charles
54 Dorothy 188 Dorothy
Wainhouse 188 215 Edmund
158 160 161 188 215 225 306
Edward 87 Elizabeth 225 330
331 Hancock 160 Isme 225
Ismy 160 John 15 54 101 160
188 225 Levin 160 Major 307
365 Mary 2 54 158 225 Nar-
cissa 333 Priscilla 330
Richard 2 7 225 Robert 333

471

BAYLEY (continued)
Rose 160 Rosey 188 Sarah 225
322 333 365 Shadarack 287
Shadrack 322 Susannah 225
Tabitha 160 Thomas 160 188
194 303 321 322 330 338 351
Thomas Jr 302 307 Welthy 225
Whittington 159 William 188
BAYLY, Amey 266 Ann 224 266
Ann Catherine 55 Anne 254 405
Bagwell 138 Betty 248 Caty
441 Charles 36 58 227 239 252
266 303 399 460 Charles Sr 232
247 260 Comfort 55 Edith 54
Edmond 37 262 272 465 Ed-
mund 37 47 50 55 57 58 65 83
123 131 136 174 248 265 288
302 355 372 397 407 410 437
439 Edmund Jr 372 399 403-
406 411 413-415 436 Edmund
Sr 387 Edward 55 121 138
Elizabeth 54 55 57 58 83 84
248 250 266 397 437 460
Elizabeth Wise 266 Hannah 55
Henry 37 76 83 84 265 Isma
399 441 460 Isme 441 Ismey
248 John 55 118 227 239 248
373 388 399 465 Johnson 206
Joyce 37 Laban 239 Lacey 37
Major 266 340 376 Margaret
266 Mary 58 227 239 262 397
399 Mrs Edward 55 Neomy 412
Patience 266 Pegga 288 Peggy
441 447 Prisilla 44 Rachel 55
Richard 10 37 76 83 84 237 248
397 405 437 455 460 460
Richard Jr 37 Robert 55 233
245 Rosah 441 Rosana 83
Rosanna 84 218 Sarah 248 265
266 288 Shadrack 266 Southy
83 Susanna 248 Susannah 262
266 Tabitha 57 58 250 Thomas
207 218 224 226 252 262 264
281 288 293 303 308 316 372
396-398 405 411 424 434 455
Thomas S 439 Thomas Sr 408
Ursilia 37 Welthy 248 Whitentun 94 Whittington 37 58 83 84
135 William 83
BAYNE, Colmor 449 Sally 398
Walter 381 395 398 405 426
438 440 441 446 448 449 459

BEACH, Ann 432 Benjamin 232
Ezekiel 416 432 Isaiah 363
John 219 Joseph 261 Kendal
261 Kendall 454 Mary 261
Rachel 229 236 Sarah 261
Sophia 261 Tabitha 232
BEACHUM, Levi 377
BEANSON, Rachal 444
BEARD, Charles 422 M 444
Stephen 444
BEARY, Susannah 284
BEASLEY, Cason 283
BEASLY, Betsy 458 Henry 443
Smith 427
BEAUCHAM, Levi 288
BEAUCHAMP, Ann 465 John 392
Leah 392 Mary Ann 392 Peggy
392
BEAUCHUM, Ann 335
BEAVANE, William Henry 394
BEAVANS, Ann Handy Tabitha
Custis 335 Anne 209 349
Elizabeth 128 229 349 George
229 392 452 John 241 304 393
Joshua 188 195 229 233 Mar-
garet 394 Margaret Custis 335
393 394 Mary 154 176 188 229
265 304 349 394 410 440 451
Mrs William 392 Nathaniel
270 304 335 347 349 358 390
393 Rachel 349 Sally 452
Samuel 128 198 208 209 304
325 338 372 414 Sophia 188
Tabitha 132 188 229 349 394
Tabitha Custis 335 Tabitha
Custis Scarburgh 335 349 393
Thomas 198 222 226 229 392
452 Walter 304 349 390 393
William 68 77 80 100 113 126
132 134 145 154 158 168 180
188 195 209 229 304 377 392
452 William H 349 453 Wil-
liam Henry 304 393 409 Wil-
liam Jr 120 142 145
BEAVENS, John 205 Mary 205
Nathaniel 205 Rachel 205
Samuel 205 Will 205 William
205
BEAVINS, Margaret Custis 390
BECH, Henry 22
BEECH, Amey 395 Anna 460
Anne 245 329 Ben 35

472

BEECH (continued)
Benjamin 80 Catherine 460
Ezekiel 247 460 Frederick 345
353 395 Hannah 80 Isaiah 395
410 John 247 345 395 Kendal
353 Kendall 429 Leah 395
Leaven 238 Luke 80 Margaret
247 Mary 219 247 460 Mrs
Samuel 35 Rachel 252 395
Reuben 247 Rubin 238 Sacker
238 Samuel 35 105 113 135 173
238 Sara 29 Sarah 238 460
Seymore 329 Susanna 329
Tabitha 329 Thomas 35 80
William 238 246 247
BELK, Purnal 334
BELL, 432 Agrippa 460 Aner 457
Ann 156 268 Ann Foster 286
Anne 146 384 Anseleta 232
Anthony 3 460 Athalia 118
Betsy 397 Betty 146 156 312
Bridget 206 212 Cassey Sturgis
457 Cohole 54 Comfort 195 259
Easter 267 Ecana 460 Edward
54 73 131 412 Elias 53 73 94
131 138 154 Elizabeth 131 138
142 154 198 278 318 330 353
392 460 464 Elizabeth Smith
460 Esther 315 Felix 460
Geodiah 428 George 156 219
267 281 315 395 Grace 195
Hannah 156 Isaac 457 Jacob
281 286 377 Jedediah 395
Jeodiah 105 156 John 120 131
138 198 258 387 392 421 430
464 John Selby 421 John Solby
340 Joseph 53 115 122 146 167
195 204 434 Joshua 261 267
419 Josua 400 Keziah 315
Leah 227 258 267 315 340 387
Leavin 258 Levin 227 258 387
Levinah 377 Lizey 458
Lucretia 464 Margaret 460
Mary 54 64 75 131 146 179 195
200 223 241 392 Mary S 458
Nancy 428 458 Nathaniel 35 64
75 146 223 344 394 458
Nathaniel Jr 366 Nathaniel Sr
458 Oliver 54 195 320 352 392
409 Peggy 458 Polly 319 417
458 Rachel 131 146 156 223
267 392 Roben 422

BELL (continued)
Robert 35 75 142 192 223 236
241 258 318 319 458 Robert Sr
258 Rosannah 421 Rosey 319
Rosie 422 Sally 392 458
Samuel 460 Sarah 54 105 156
227 241 258 267 315 Savage
319 452 Scarbrough 258 305
Scarburgh 258 Sinah 421 Sophia
305 377 Southey 267 Southy
315 318 Stephen 267 315 348
Susanna 131 458 Susannah 195
458 Tabitha 50 75 131 146 200
Thomas 3 19 35 36 53 75 241
318 377 422 Thomas Jr 54
William 35 58 64 75 131 138
139 142 156 198 200 206 212
235 236 241 258 286 319 325
358 379 392 395 397 413 421
428 458 460 464 William Jr
431 456 William Sr 412 431
BELOAT, Jonas 63 Mary 443
BELOATE, William 329 447
BELOTE, Abbigil 224 Abigil 224
Ann Wise 322 Anne 253 Betty
224 Caleb 278 Elisha 224
Elizabeth 224 294 Fanny 278
Hancock 224 Handcock 438
James Warrington 348 John
224 249 288 Laben 249 Labon
226 Mary 224 438 Noah 173
182 353 373 376 399 410
Rebecca 238 Sarah 224 227
Sarah Garret 278 Siner 224
Susanna 178 William 224 348
BELOTTE, John 226 Jonas 226
Laban 226 Leah 226 Noah 206
226 Sarah 206 Sarh 226
BENNESTON, Richard 269
BENNET, Ann 238 Elizabeth 104
143 John 143 Mary 196 286
Richard 105 Thomas 104 182
William 222 286
BENNETT, George 265 Tabitha
2665 Thomas 166
BENNIT, Mary 259
BENNITT, Ann 219 John 219
BENSON, Anne 449 Betsey 431
443 Comfort 289 Edward 250
Elizabeth 443 Ester 443 Esther
420 George 327 Hettey 431
James 367 449 Johannah 144

BENSON (continued)
John 124 264 289 297 420
Jonah 144 443 Jonas Sr 289
Joyce 221 Major 327 Martha
144 Mary 144 Masey 328 Mas-
say 327 Massey 165 167 327
Matilda 312 Moses 289 Nancy
327 443 Nanney 431 Nathaniel
402 Peggy 450 Polly 452
Rebeckah 327 Rebecker 328
Salley 443 Sally 443 450
Samuel 144 156 443 Sarah 144
289 Scarburgh 449 William 443
BENSSTON, Rose 390
BENSTEN, Alexander 100 126
Ambrose 100 Edward 126
Elizabeth 100 102 Ezekiel 180
Hannah 180 Hill 180 Isaish 180
James 100 102 John 100
Jonathan 100 Leah 180 Levin
126 Levineah 180 Mary 100
Micajah 180 Nathaniel 100 159
165 Rebeccah 100 Sarah 100
Tabitha 100 Zefeniah 180
Zepheniah 180
BENSTENE, Ambrose 102 Edward
141 Leah 141 Mary 141
BENSTINE, Jacob 159
BENSTON, Alexander 4 35 45 187
Ambrose 35 149 Amely 392
Amos 359 Anabell 93 Ann 52
62 93 211 Anne 359 Azariah
359 Benjamin 58 Catharine 149
Cemmey 431 Comfort 359
Daniel 93 Edith 71 Edward 187
Edy 211 Eleazer 375 Elizabeth
35 165 Ellener 58 Ester 35 Es-
ther 376 Ezekiel 211 327 Francis 45 52 58 71 88 165 Francis
Sr 32 Grace 58 88 211 Hannah
146 149 167 176 211 220 Hill
165 Holston 58 Jacob 93 259
James 48 58 112 211 282 328
370 373 375 390 433 464 Jane
239 Jesse 165 Joanna 33 John
33 58 93 167 180 187 211 427
431 John Savage 390 433
Jonathan 71 149 Joseph 58 71
149 165 187 Joshua 71 Joy 359
Joyce 390 433 Levinah 146
Margaret 282 390 433 Marget
433 Marry 433

BENSTON (continued)
Mary 4 187 211 390 Massey 187
Matilda 390 Micajah 208 211
Moses 321 384 390 Mrs
Ezekiel 211 Nathaniel 93 165
187 282 426 Rachel 328 375
417 Rebecca 35 169 Robert 58
88 Rosewell 149 Rosey 433
Samuel 33 106 359 Sturgis 414
Thomas 392 William 4 32 35
45 58 71 88 93 211 282 375 417
426 William Sr 35 Zepheniah
167
BENSTONE, Ezekiel 167 John
167
BENTHAL, Ann 259 John 259
Mary 259
BENTON, Leah 187 Samuell 16
BENTS, Elizabeth 32 Kanutus 32
Margaret 32
BERRIT, Thomas 9
BERRY, Allah 336 James 234 239
263 270 336 John 336
Rebeckah 336 Thomas 336
William 336
BETTS, John 6
BEVANS, Nathaniel 331 William
89 451
BEVINS, Nathaniel 223
BIDLE, Thomas 110
BIGARBY, Frances 354 Levin 354
Susanna 354 355
BIGEROA, William 150
BIGGABY, Francis 344 Levin 395
439 Susanna 344
BIGGERBY, Mrs William 237
William 237
BILES, James 272 Semor 271 272
BIRD, 432 Ann 201 258 Bridget 23
Briget 278 Catharine 417
Charity 320 Daniel 82 138 191
Ebern 456 Ebon 134 Eborn 79
82 136 417 Ebron 340 Edward
29 Elijah 232 306 352
Elizabeth 191 320 Esther 351
Frances 201 Jacob 182 235 277
279 293 307 320 337 340 409
417 422 Jane 23 29 John 29 82
Leah 293 340 Levi 279 456
Levy 340 459 Major 82 131 139
149 151 155 351 Margaret 138
191 Mary 143 191 341

BIRD (continued)
Nancy 293 340 456 Nanny 340
Nathaniel 82 103 212 214 222
320 351 417 452 Nathaniel Sr
320 Rachel 191 Rachill 320
Rebecca 351 397 Sally 293
Sarah 139 214 320 417
Satharine 417 Scarbrough 351
Scarburgh 191 Selv 232
Solomon 82 167 191 201 320
351 Susannah 191 Teackle 415
BISHOP, Amy 122 Anne 411 Betty
356 362 Dolly 356 Elizabeth
170 286 356 Esther 389 Griffith
379 Jacob 89 152 170 189
Jacob Sr 152 James 285 John
189 204 236 356 Leah 189
Leviner 356 Margaret 189 Mary
356 422 Muns 189 Patience
122 189 285 286 Southy 389
Temperance 189 William 271
336 411
BISWICK, George 265 Lewis 195
Prudence 265
BLACK, Margaret 115 Sarah 60
William 69 71 74 115
BLACKLOCK, Christian 8
Thomas 8 9
BLACKSTON, Bowman 439
BLACKSTONE, Bowman 334 380
Elizabeth 380 John 151 334
380 Leah 380
BLADES, Ann 146 Anne 148 Ben-
jamin 368 Caleb 368 Charlotte
368 Eleanor 368 Hannah 146
Jesse 368 John 433 John Jr
167 Joseph 182 Mary 146
Rebecca 368 Sophia 167 176
Susanna 368 Wiliam 368 Win-
ney 368
BLAIR, Ann 103 Anne 92 121
John 87 Thomas 91 93 103 121
Walter 121
BLAKE, Abigail 83 Ann 33 34 198
280 Arcadia 79 Bridget 44 226
Charles 44 78 96 265 298
Daniel 22 Dennis 33 71 74 97
175 186 198 Dianer 83 Dianer
Coley 83 Elias 22 33 44 226
Elijah 244 Elizabeth 83
Frances 186 Hannah 265 267
296 310 387 Isbella 22

BLAKE (continued)
Jabez 198 207 Jabis 166 Jane
22 27 44 John 22 26 78 79 112
113 139 172 186 193 198 280
Joseph 22 33 74 96 109 198
258 277 280 333 348 Mary 22
27 79 Nancy 348 Naomy 33
Rachell 33 Rebecca 79 97
Rebecka 22 Sarah 22 27 169
172 198 267 369 Slocomb 186
198 220 Sophia 333 Thomas 15
20 58 Tobis 186 William 19 22
27 44 169 226 267 297
BLARE, Agnes 58 Elizabeth 58
Fenton 58 Hanna 58 John 58
Margrett 58 Robert 58
BLAXTON, Ann Mary 179 Anne
149 Elizabeth 313 John 149
179 Leah 313 Mary 179 Wil-
liam 179 265
BLEAR, Barbary 64 Clark 64
Henry 64
BLOCKSOM, Ann 54 John 54
Mary 54 Mrs William 54
Richard 54 William 54
BLOCKSON, John Sr 35
BLOXAM, John 51 John Jr 266
Johnson 51 Littleton 266 Mary
51 Nancy 266 Nicholas 51
Richard 51 Sarah 266 Southey
266 Thomas 266 270 Thomas
Jr 266 William 51 Woodman
51
BLOXHAM, 31
BLOXOM, Abbott 252 265 277 381
Ann 252 257 Argal 384 Argil
439 454 Argol 372 378 Athalia
303 Azariah 398 Bable 257
Catharine 252 441 Catherine
264 Comfort 379 Elijah 318
Elizabeth 151 178 330 379 Es-
ther 379 Ezekiel 161 257 258
Fortain 151 Francis 381
George 381 Jacob 379 430
Jemimah 463 Johannah Stacks
400 John 151 214 252 257 264
325 326 350 Joshua 379 430
Keziah 463 Leah 252 430 454
Levi 303 Levin 331 389 398
430 Levinah 350 Littleton 252
264 Lucreshe 418 Lucretia 264
454 Major 400

BLOXOM (continued)
Major Simpson 400 Margaret
Simpson 330 400 Mary 151 379
381 Mary Ann 398 Moses 151
332 Nancy 379 400 447 Nanny
398 Naomi 381 Nicholas 137
151 252 381 Patience 330 350
Peggy 348 Polly 418 Rachel
330 332 398 Rebecca 381
Richard 137 151 252 324 325
330 350 381 400 418 Robert
381 Sally 398 Sarah 222 252
330 398 463 Scarbrough 454
Scarburgh 379 381 Severn 379
Simpson 169 175 330 Simson
460 Siner 151 400 Solomon 398
Southy 258 414 440 Stephen
231 235 252 259 286 325 330-
332 Stephen Sr 332 Susanna
Reed 350 Tabitha 252 Thomas
133 139 172 176 178 195 202
205 208 209 222 234 243 252
286 330 332 350 381 William
137 151 161 222 252 253 261
330 350 379 381 William Sr
398 Woodman 151 195 232 235
252 258 322 330 350 379 449
BLOXSOM, John 131 Tabitha 131
BOAGS, Moly 416
BOGGS, Alice 88 Betty 242
Elizabeth 82 335 341 Francis
182 277 376 427 443 462 Jean
273 John 222 223 240 274 364
376 Joseph 282 376 427 Leah
206 Levin 341 Mackemi 240
Mackemie 242 Makemie 273
310 Mary 274 342 427 Mrs
Mackemie 242 Nancy 387
Naomi 427 Peggy 341 Rachel
182 341 Robert 223 232 242
243 322 335 Ruth 342 Sarah
223 242 443 Susanna 242
Susannah 442 443 William 48
88 194 240 242 273 364 400
443 William Jr 232
BOGS, William 223
BOILS, James 272
BOISNARD, John 349 375 430 441
BOLES, Sarah 66
BOLING, James 345
BOLLS, Thomas 49

BONAWELL, Anne 105 M 458
BONEWEL, Thomas 420
BONEWELL, Betty 338 Elijah
338 345 Elizabeth 65 George
226 338 Jacob 389 James 20
25 65 238 250 366 James Jr
322 Jesse 448 Joachim
Mikeall 87 Joakim McKiel Sr
340 Joakim Michael 338 John
250 John Sr 250 Kiely 332 M
458 Mary 65 250 Mekeel 341
Michael 250 322 338 Michal
238 Mickeel 345 Molly 452
Nancy 448 Peggy 338 Richard
87 Rosey Patterson 363 Sarah
65 338 Scarburgh 338 Southy
338 Stephen 250 Susana 65
Thomas 83 87 338
BONIWELL, 418 George 87
Thomas 87 401
BONNAWELL, Michael Jr 278
BONNEWELL, Ann 192 Anne 148
Betty 236 315 Caleb 376
Elizabeth 314 George 173 Hannah 210 236 James 148 236
376 Jane 197 Joachim Michael
107 148 201 John 148 197 236
Leah 236 McKeel 376 Michael
206 236 Michel 462 Mickeel
236 Mrs James 236 Peggy 201
Rachel 148 210 236 Richard
148 236 Sarah 201 236 Thomas
135 169 192
BONNIWELL, 397
BONNWELL, Thomas 115
BONNYWELL, George 131 Han-
nah 131 James 131 Joachim
131 John 131 Richard 131
Thomas 131
BONWELL, Ann 87 Arabella 68
Arthur 286 Bettey 309 Betty
458 Caleb 446 447 Cate 309
Charles 286 George 61 68 459
Hannah 286 James 2 87 245
279 286 317 343 458 John 33
73 74 87 119 245 286 317 Leah
286 M Sr 430 Margaret 317
Mary 2 68 245 286 McKeel 412
McKeel Sr 431 McKell Sr 447
Mekeel 272 340 Mekeel Sr 272
Michael 410 440 Michael Sr

BONWELL (continued)
374 Mickeel 286 Mikeel 286
309 Mrs John 87 Robert 430
458 Sarah 87 Smith 286
Thomas 68 245 286 William
446
BONWILL, John 405 Kitty 447
BOOLES, Sarah 66
BOOTE, Ann 3 Nicholas 3
BOOTEN, Elizabeth 242 John 242
Polly 242
BOOTH, Ann 37 Anne 331 Betty
356 Elijah 404 Elizabeth 37
331 George 37 184 205 213 259
Isabell 37 Jamima 283
Jamimah 322 331 Jamimy 188
Jemima 164 184 213 272 356
John 9 10 37 184 372 Katherine
37 Martha 184 213 Mary 331
Mordecai 331 384 Mordecaia
322 Naomi 37 Rachel 338
Sarah 37 Scarbrough 331 Sophia
184 Wealthyana 34 Weltheana
37 William 433
BOOTHE, George 48 John 48
BOOTIN, Agnes 165 166
Elizabeth 166 Howel 129
Howell 68 73 92 93 129 John
165 166 Nanny 166 William
129 157 165
BOOTING, Howell 93
BORWELL, Michael 281
BOSTON, Betty 308 Isaac 410
Solomon 417
BOSWILL, Betty 421
BOTE, Ann 20
BOWEN, Criffith 80 Elizabeth 10
Elliner 10 John 10 28 35
Richard 10
BOWLES, Ann 7 Edward 7
Elizabeth 7 Jane 7 John 373
Robert 7 Thomas 7 37 William
7
BOWLS, Ann 44 Henry 44 Jeane
44 Thomas 44 Zacharias 44
BOWMAN, Catherine 372 David
228 243 263 301 304 314 327
336 337 354 361 362 364 372
439 446 455 Edm 2 Edmund 10
18 20 67 Elizabeth 2 Ellinor 18
Gertrude 2 20 21 James Oswell
362 Katharine 362 Mrs David

BOWMAN (continued)
361 Mrs Edmund 20 21 Oswald
372 William 396
BOYD, Daniel 43
BOYLE, James 262 Mrs James
262
BRADFORD, Abel 179 232 254
322 444 Absalom 446 448 Amy
423 Ann 155 Annamariah 355
Anne 105 219 Arthur 427 429
Bayly 105 Benjamin 388 Benson 221 Betty 219 262 341
Bridget 105 423 Brown 341 422
Charles 175 340 423 Charles
Baily 423 Creshe 353 Custis
414 434 457 Edmond 334 Edmund 391 Elizabeth 115 134
151 214 355 372 444 Esther
219 262 Ezekiel 314 Ezra 422
Fisher 105 113 145 219 262
Frances 222 George 430 Jacob
222 232 254 255 266 341 401
413 James 219 325 374 420
429 464 Jemima 214 Jemyah
340 Jenny 355 Joana 266 Joane
21 Johannah 223 John 36 37 45
105 135 150 219 222 254 314
322 325 389 429 430 434 John
Brown 422 John Fisher 105
Jonna 230 Joy 364 Kendall 444
Kendell 314 Kessiah 340
Keziah 214 340 Laben 277
Leagh 223 Leah 423 Levin 266
Littleton 422 Lucresha 430
Lucretia 430 Margaret 222
Martha 144 Mary 145 219 222
262 446 Mettelder 223 Nancy
430 444 Naomay 266 Naomi
175 214 Nathaniel 33 105 115
214 219 262 265 310 321 355
356 Neomy 340 Noah 134
Peggy 254 422 Rachel 219 222
254 262 430 464 Retter 223
Robert 277 416 427 Sabra 356
436 Sally 446 Sarah 105 214
356 420 434 Severn 355 Siner
354 Susanna 33 457 Susannah
219 262 422 434 Susey 341
Tabitha 33 Thomas 105 391
Thomas B 400 Thomas Baily
423 Thomas Bayly 340
Thomas Hall 355 453 William

CANE, Thomas 93
CANNADAY, Thomas 25
CAREE, Jonathan 160
CARLISLE, Molly 423
CARMINE, Fanny 397 Tabitha 397
CARPENTER, Charles 368 Mary 212
CARR, John 407
CARROTHERS, Tabitha 191
CARRUTHERS, John 124 179
    Leah Bagwell 179 Mrs Robert
    179 Robert 115 122 124 179
    180 Sarah Bagwell 124 Tabitha
    180
CARSS, Betty 409 John 332 409
CART, Monser 183
CARTE, William 24
CARTER, Esther 399
CARUTHERS, Elizabeth 274
    James 274 John 274 Margaret
    274 Mary 274 Robert 124 274
    Sarah 274 William 274
CARY, Betty 156 Dorrithy 23 Ed-
    ward 62 James 62 159 162 410
    Jeremiah 26 Jessey 162 John
    16 26 61 Margaret 62 Mary 62
    156 159 162 Solomon 26 83 156
    Tabitha 162 Timothy 62
CASE, Ezekiel 173 John 150
CASEY, Patrick 435
CASY, Patrick 389
CATHEEL, Jonathan 160
CATHELL, Jemima 159 Jonathan
    159
CAVE, John 206 Stakes 205
CHACE, Isaac 109 Mary 70
CHAILLE, Moses 183 Moses Jr
    183 Peter 183
CHAILLIE, John 254
CHAMBERS, Agness 203 Ann 189
    Anne 188 Caleb 437 Cathrine
    182 Edmund 207 217 264
    Frances 53 John 67 127
    Jonathan 52 112 226 332
    Katherine 207 Major 346 Mary
    127 Sarah 132
CHAMERS, John 53 Philocleare
    53
CHANCE, Bridget 246 Brigit 194
    Elias 325 Elijah 229 282 294
    416 Esther 84 Fanny 282

CHANCE (continued)
    Jacob 79 80 104 115 Joan 17
    Leah 282 Margaret 101 Mary
    49 58 Nanney 282 Patience 282
    Rhoda 101 Rose 115 Sophia
    Wise 167 William 24 46 52 59
    84 90 101 126 154 164 167
    William Jr 59 84
CHANDER, Hathan 411
CHANDIER, Caleb 364 Mary 364
    Peggy 364 Sarah 364 Sophia
    364
CHANDLER, Abigail 87 Agnes
    425 Amey 442 Ann 143 309
    Anne 187 213 Anne Jr 213 Bet-
    sey 442 Betty 187 Bridget 143
    187 Bridgett 87 Caleb 214 247
    316 364 Catey 328 Caty 328
    347 384 Charity 87 Charles 364
    Comfort 187 213 Elizabeth 214
    Eufame 271 George 187 213
    Hathan 214 Hathan Fettapace
    214 Hathen Fettaplace 87
    Jacob 187 James 427 Joanna
    86 John 86 87 147 214 248 284
    303 328 Jonathan 318 Katy 347
    Laban 296 328 347 Leah 309
    Levy 425 Littleton 328 347 384
    442 Mary 187 364 Michael 384
    Milly 328 442 Mitchel 328 343
    423 442 Mitchell 347 442 Mrs
    Hathan Fettapace 214 Mrs
    John 86 Patience 244 271 328
    347 384 442 Peggy 214 364
    Rachel 214 Rosey 328 442
    Sacker 364 Solomon 87 187
    Sophia 364 Susannah 143 187
    Thomas 320 328 338 343 347
    442 William 187 213 255 327
    364 William Sacker 214 316
    Zerobabel 427 Zerrobabel 214
    Zoro 392 Zorobabel 214 346
    443 446 Zorobable 344
CHAPMAN, Elizabeth 153
    Humphrey 139 Joshua 125 162
    Mary 64 139 153 175 455
    Pearce 293 Peine 181 Silas 64
    153 William 64 455
CHARLES, Ann 38 John 13 38
CHARLS, John 10
CHARLTON, Ann 8
CHARNOCK, Major 224 Mary 462

CHASE, John 11 William 8 111
175
CHERIX, Arthur 433
CHESHER, William 450
CHIRSTOPHER, Joseph 226
CHISLY, Elizabeth 83
CHORD, John 356 367 William
356 366
CHRISTALL, William 166
CHRISTIAN, Catharine 403
Catherine 404 William 270
CHRISTOPHER, Leady 226 William S 386
CHRYSTALL, James 166 William 166
CHURCH, Samuel 354 Thomas 41
CHURN, Ann 267 299 Anne 299
Betsey 332 George 267 299
John 385 389 Mary 299 389
Susannah 299 Tabitha 299 347
Thomas 299 347
CLAPTON, Thomas 188 189
CLARK, Ann 36 Blake 108
Bridget 78 David 78 Elizabeth
240 George 1 78 Henry 36 244
Isabel 78 James 78 John 78
Joseph 36 Keziah 368 Major 78
Mary 36 Patrick 66 Pattrick 67
Peggy 368 Rand 314 Rhody 202
Sarah 78 390 Sophia 240
Tabitha 108 Thomas 43 165
199 202 242 Weltheana 37
William 95 98
CLARKE, Henry 31 86 Joseph 31
William 185
CLAYTON, Betty 405 Dennis 463
CLAYWELL, Levin 281 Peter 76
CLEAVEL, Peter 51
CLEMENS, Ann 162 Jane Brooks
162 Stephen 162
CLEMENT, John 117
CLEMMONS, Bridget 360 Comfort
240 Elizabeth 454 Mary 360
Nanny Rodgers 360 Peter 360
Siner 360 Stephen 360 454
Susannah 229 360
CLERK, Rand 322
CLEVERDON, Deborah 19 William 19
CLIFT, John 59
CLOUD, Margaret 187
CLOUDS, Elizabeth 253

CLOVELL, Comfort 22 Elizabeth
22 Peter 22 Selbe 22 Thomas
22
CLUGSTON, Benjamin 40 45
COARD, William 224 338
COB, Sammwell 43
COBB, 52 Ingold 43 Samuel 58
Sarah 43
COE, Benjamin 54 89 Berry 88
John 17 Mary 89 Sarah 17 88
109 Timothy 12 17 42 51 73
161
COKE, Richard 218 Samuel 218
COLE, Adah 236 Isaiah 344
James 393 John 13 18 88 103
112 393 406 Leah 259 Major
324 393 409 Major Sr 393
Nancy 212 Peter 393 Phillis 89
Robert 89 131 Sally 393 Sarah
283 325 William 218
COLEBURN, Ann 177 294 295
Capt 154 Catharine 357 428
Catrin 294 Comfort 176 242
Elizabeth 187 242 294 295 357
Frances 29 George 230 294 295
371 373 374 388 410 438 Isaac
294 295 James 357 388 396
413 John 154 169 172 176 177
183 204 208 209 220 230 235
238 242 246 255 294 357 391
428 Mrs Robert 176 Nancy 388
Robert 29 78 104 105 106 108
113 114 120 124 132 150 153
154 176 233 234 263 265 278
294 295 321 357 Sabra 347 374
391 Samuel 294 295 428 456
Sarah 357 Spencer 177 282 303
325 Susannah 177 230 Tabitha
357 Temperance 177 209
Thomas 294 295 357 373 374
388 391 William 177 209 230
258 329 347 355 357 365 388
428
COLEBURNE, Rebecca 29 Robert
29 80
COLEMAN, Stephen 231
COLEMONS, Elizabeth 422
COLEY, Dianer 83
COLLEE, Abigail 63 Diana 63
Elizabeth 63 Job 63 Sylvanus
63
COLLEN, Comfort 288

COLLENS, Joshua 229
COLLIAR, Elizabeth 77
COLLIER, Elizabeth 95 Mary 67
95 Peter 95 184
COLLINGS, Anne 222 223 James
222 John 223 Joshua 207
Peggy 222 Thomas 222
Timothy 208 222 223 William
222
COLLINS, Anne 150 Betty 251
Bridget 25 46 130 Daniel 154
459 Elijah 249 251 Elizabeth
56 George 369 379 James 338
369 370 Jean 154 Jenny 320
338 John 46 65 109 130 379
444 Joseph 156 251 340 413
Joshua 239 Lavinah 459 Leah
352 432 Levina 413 Martha 338
370 Mary 63 65 239 244 Molly
340 Nancy 251 Peggy 251
Phebe 202 Phebee 156 Pheby
379 Philbe 369 Philby 379
Rachel 338 352 Robins 196
Sally 251 338 Samuel 65 Sarah
244 Scarburgh 239 244 Stephen
239 240 244 254 Sterling 338
Thomas 46 64 101 130 156 202
239 244 338 347 379 Uriah 97
William 130 163 379 439
COLLONY, Benjamin 54 Brian 23
54 Ester 23 George 199 Her-
man 199 Hester 54 Isabel
Repentans 54 Owen 23 54
Winifret 54
COLONEY, Ame 271 Ann 296
Floriana 132 John 269 287
Kendall 444 O'Bryan 132
Southy 320 William 262 314
William Jr 435 453
COLONY, Ama 248 Amey 244
Benjamin 296 Catharine 416
Elijah 370 388 Elizabeth 302
349 375 416 George 367 John
296 302 Littleton 248 Major
296 307 395 Major Jr 395
Susana 296 Susanna 296 Up-
shur 248 296 William 296 347
417
COLQUHOUN, Pat 227
CONAWAY, Elizabeth 368
Thomas 15
CONDER, Dorothy 3

CONELEY, Bryant 95
CONER, James 89
CONNAR, Denis 49
CONNER, Comfort 77 Francis 29
William 120 133
CONNOR, Anna Margareta 70
Anne Mary 70 Patrick 70
CONNOWAY, Thomas 25
CONNYER, John 119
CONQUEST, Ann 204 427 Comfort
463 Elizabeth 170 211 James
396 427 462 463 Joseph 426
427 462 Keziah 396 427 463
Leah 463 Mrs William 396
Nancy 396 427 Nathaniel 170
463 Peggy 396 427 Polly 427
Rachel 245 311 Richard 463
Sarah 463 Tabitha 463 William
138 396 397 427 449 463 Wil-
liam Sr 462
CONTY, Hannah 55
CONWAY, Elizabeth 407 Thomas
23
COOCK, Nanney 337
COOK, Edward 234 John 422
Rachel 223 Thomas 171 Wil-
liam 171 210
COOKE, Elizabeth 317 John 104
COOPER, Richard 99
COOPR, Richard 15
COPES, Ann 237 Anne 238 Betsey
431 Betsy 401 Beverly 251 355
395 413 Catey 387 Charles 198
Charles Sr 461 Comfort 127
387 406 Crittey 429 Daniel 228
Elizabeth 228 237 251 429 Es-
ther 237 Giles 59 66 67 127
228 229 237 348 387 434 Han-
cock 355 387 429 Handcock
355 Henry Savage 429 Jesse
228 264 325 John 233 387 John
Custis 429 Jonathan 139 344
Joshua 234 237 371 Leah 237
Leah P 407 Leah Parker 387
Levin 355 375 387 395 429 454
Major 387 415 Margaret 59 447
Mary 67 78 127 329 Mary
Johnson 387 Mary Parker 343
Mathias 59 Mrs Thomas 355
Nancy 395 Parker 171 198 202
209 251 387 431 458 Peggy 395
Peter 123 228 264

COPES (continued)
Peter Parker 127 198 251 Polly
387 Rachel 251 325 Reavel 420
Revel 374 387 Rhody 198 Ritter 387 Robert 165 228 387
Sally 387 Savage 395 Solomon
198 Southy 127 251 355 387
406 417 Susanna 355 Thomas
49 61 66 67 127 198 233 321
328 387 395 409 Thomas Sr
260 355
CORBIN, Agnes Drummond 400
Agnis 312 Agnis Drummond
311 Ann 130 Anne 208 Coventon 123 312 367 464 Covington
148 167 168 171 173 208 228
243 David 130 144 Elizabeth
464 George 139 243 255 260
262 264-266 268 275 281 285
289 296 297 299 301-303 305
308 311 312 316 320-322 324-
327 330 344-346 353-357 362
368 373 374 376 385 391 396
398 400 402 405 428 452 459
464 George B 271 George Bonnewell 367 George Jr 251
James Revell 311 John 368
John Pitt 464 Leah 130 144
464 Levinah 464 Mary 255
Mary Ann 130 144 Mrs George
Bonnewell 367 Nancy 367
Pamela 367 Polly 255 271 403
Rachel 464 Ralph 60 73 97 103
107 130 144 145 148 163 208
255 268 302 356 367 391 400
403 459 Ralph Jr 144 232 400
459 Ralph Sr 464 Robert 60 69
78 107 130 208 455 464 Rosannah 464 Sabra 459 Sarah 255
268 279 367 403 459 Savage
459 Scarburgh 130 144 Susanna
464 Susannah 130 144 Wealthy
130 144 William 444 459
CORD, Arthur 137 164 Esther 164
John 159 164 326 340 405
Joseph 137 William 85 98 164
168 402 405
CORDRY, Rachel 143
CORE, Adah 348 Ader 318 Babel
318 Charles 373 Edmond 461
Edmund 284 Eleazer 334 John
342 Leven 348 Levi 348

CORE (continued)
Levin 318 399 461 Mrs
Zorobabel 461 Polly 428 Sally
461 Sarah 318 Zorobabel 348
373 461
CORGAN, Neil 371
CORMICK, John 259
CORNICK, John 268
CORT, Jane 23
CORTNEY, Mary 191
COSTEN, Steven 49
COTON, William 414
COTTINGHAM, Nancy 286 Salley
286 Susanna 286 Thomas 286
COULBURN, Elizabeth 441
Frances 29 Rebecca 30 Robert
29 30 Temperance 230 Wil-
liam 441
COURTNEY, Charles 221
COVERLY, Mary 159 Nathaniel
220 383 Nathaniel Sr 383
Thomas 383
COWARD, Adah 307 Amy 307
Margaret 307 Peggy 463
Samuel 307 438 463 William
248 307
COWDERY, Benj 3 Josias 3
COWDRY, Henry Barlow 337
Mary 337 Savage 337
COWLEY, Elizabeth 303 429
John 220 229 Leah 189 303
Margaret 429 Rachel 429
Samuel 146 208 William 348
393 398 429
COWLY, Elizabeth 316 Mary 57
Samuel 57 84
COX, James 403 John 354 404
Joseph 107 217 321 325 Mary
325 326 Richard 2
COXWELL, 301 Esther 365
Robert 366
CRAFFORD, Mary 248
CRAIK, George 420 425
CRATON, David 439
CRAWFORD, Andrew 45 46
CRIDLEY, Mary 207
CRIPIN, Elizabeth 71
CRIPPEN, Ann 337 Anne 336 360
Betty 359 Catherine 82 Eliza
267 Elizabeth 57 82 104 308
Esther 336 337 George 82 112
178 Jaca 308 Jacey 267

CRIPPEN (continued)
James 178 235 240 336 337
John 43 82 104 178 263 267
308 335 Margaret 104 178
Margritt 50 Mary 178 Patience
245 267 Paul 103 104 140 166
178 Peggy 337 Robert 82 138
166 178 Samuel 336 337 Sarah
266 267 Savage 317 336 337
438 456 Scarbrough 308 Scarburgh 267 Sophia 267 303
Thomas 27 39 50 82 104 106
112 130 133 140 160-162 170
178 203 229 231 235 240 243
263 267 271 311 317 333 335-
337 341 346 Thomas Jr 360
Thomas Sr 360 William 82 104
106 140 267 307 308 359
CRIPPIN, Elizabeth 104 Robert
104 Savage 464 Thomas 16 104
William 256
CROCKET, John 462
CROCKETT, Joseph 225
CROFFORD, Mary 272
CROPPER, Ann 330 Anne 216
Barbara 432 Betty 218 307 330
432 Bowman 170 313 334
Bridget 313 Charles 307
Covington Corbin 296 Delany
330 Edmund 330 Edmund Bowman 21 61 65 67 110 Elijah
201 330 Elizabeth 110 Elzee
330 Ester 65 Esther 67
Gertrude 20 21 John 6 7 296
312 330 345 370 371 375 382
399 400 405 406 437 John Jr
330 331 372 380 382 387 390
405-409 413-415 421 422 432
436 439 John Sr 346 369 372
455 Laney 352 Leah 313 Levin
330 Mary 432 Nathaniel 21 330
Rachel 313 Rachell 65 Sabra
296 432 Sarah 201 330 Seb 38
58 Sebastian 21 65 87 83 173
194 208 234 236 242 313 334
380 407 413 432 Sebastian Jr
170 171 174 207 210 234-236
255 265 296 Sebastian Sr 313
Sophia 313 Thomas 172 179
199 201 207 296 312 330 371
372 374 380 398 402 408 409
413 414 439 454 457

CROPPER (continued)
Wid 330 William 307 330 Wil-
liam Drummond 432
CROSSLY, Henry 215
CROSTON, Francis 40 68 100
CROSWELL, Susanna 464
CROUCHER, Mary 46 61
CROWSON, Agnes 442 Agness
443 Betty 163 Catherine 443
Comfort 69 Peggy 442 443
Sarah 443 Susannah 442 443
William 234 263 273 280 342
442
CRUMP, George 2
CRUTHERS, James 392
CUDDY, Elizabeth 32 James 32
Jane 32 Martha 32 Mary 32
CULLAR, Elizabeth 338 Fanny
338 George 322 John 338 Wil-
liam 338
CUMMINS, Thomas 167
CUNNINGHAM, Walter 94
CUP, William 71
CURLE, Sarah 34
CURTIS, William 392
CUSTIS, Ann 57 63 67 93 98 99
103 120 121 305 Anne 217 220
223 399 402 Bagwell 229 306
Betty 98 229 Bridget 78 120
Bridget Jr 80 Bridget Sr 80
Casey 217 237 Col 11 Dorothy
Wainhouse 215 216 Edmond 67
Edmund 31 72 155 200 274 343
347 355 361 366 405 450 Edward 63 120 188 Elishe 194
Elizabeth 16 17 63 67 72 223
237 304 306 402 458 Esther
337 Fanny 450 Frances 16 17
29 63 98 Hancock 47 54 56 67
70 77 78 92 98 Henry 16 17 29
40 63 67 72 92 93 98 99 103
113 114 139 144 155 163 173
215 216 220 222 223 248 286
298 325 330 331 345 399 402
411 443-445 456 465 Henry Sr
443 Jane 63 Joanna Mary 78
John 13 31 34 36 56 67 72 80
81 92 93 98 110 162 174 179
216 217 220 223 229 232 263
302 303 306 312 313 321 322
324 328 331 346 351 352 365
366 371-374 376 380 389 396

485

DARBY (continued)
Daniel 13 17 21 39 41 53 93
Darmon 125 163 Dorithy 42
Dority 39 Dormand 41 Dormant
51 Dormond 41 Dormund 39
Dorothy 269 Edmund 395 Eliah
192 Elijah 194 Elishe 189
Elizabeth 192 194 272 Esther
395 Francis 33 39 93 189 245
248 269 272 George 41 42
George D 125 John 39 41 93
147 171 190 192 199 223 244
245 248 269 271 272 352 367
368 411 John Dormund 39 John
Jr 155 Joshua 248 296 Leah
189 245 272 Leshe 245 Lit-
tleton 177 189 224 245 249
Margaret 245 Mary 170 192 194
223 272 Nancy 387 394 425
Nathaniel 223 Owen 158 387
394 456 Polly 395 Pricila 39
Rachel 223 408 Sarah 41 189
194 352 367 454 Shadrack 395
Smith 41 42 Susanna 245 278
387 394 Tabitha 93 190 272
Tamar 244 Tamer 272 387 394
Unlce 189 William 39 41 53
122 189 245 356 Zillah 394
Zilliah 387
DARMON, Susanna 246
DARTER, Margaret 44 William
31 44 51 76
DASHAWLE, George 101
DASHIEL, Henrietta 187
DASHIELD, Charles 184
Elizabeth 184
DAVES, Margaret 83
DAVIDSON, Robert 293 309
DAVIS, Agnes 362 395 Ann 48 80
Anne 113 Arthur 36 Charles 48
112 126 Comfort 36 128 David
395 Easter 36 Elizabeth 36 38
182 395 Gean 36 Henry 48 72
91 302 305 Hopkin 19 James
36 48 72 91 98 112 Japhat 146
John 138 433 Jonas 89 Keziah
302 382 Lazarus 107 116 Major
80 137 152 173 200 245 311
362 Margaret 53 Mary 36
Nancy 395 Naomi 56 103 110
128 Patience 107 Peggy 395
Robert 35 36 138 425 446

DAVIS (continued)
Sally 373 Samuel 36 54 103 110
138 159 173 Sarah 36 48 395
Sebella 159 Susanna 353
Thomas 36 48 66 113 137 362
395 William 53 137 143 152
331 362 371 373 395 396
DAWSON, John 158 168 181 Mar-
garet 342 Shadrack 345 368
DAY, Edward 143
DAYSON, John 155 158 160
DEANE, John 27
DELANAWAY, Thomas 226
DELASTAIUS, Wlater 459
DELASTATICUS, Peter 452
DELASTATIONS, Peter 373
DELASTATIOUS, Ann 445 David
446 Eliza 452 Elizabeth 452
Jinne 446 Joseph 452 Levin
445 Nancy 446 Peter 437 439
452 Sebastian 446 Selby 441
DELASTATIUS, Ann 198
Elizabeth 385 Esther 128 218
Ezekiel 127 171 175 209 218
234 283 344 Joseph 218 Leah
145 176 Lemuel 145 176 Mary
145 176 198 339 385 Nancy 459
Peter 127 128 218 324 376 400
403 449 Phebe 145 176 Pheobe
72 Polly 367 Rhoda 176
Samuel 198 Sebastian 54 60 70
72 75 127 145 198 401 Sebas-
tian Jr 64 75 100 117 Sebastian
Sr 64 117 William 198 218 230
324
DELASTIONS, Batillina 39
Frances 39 Peter 39
DELASTIUS, Roda 39 Sebastian
39
DELIGHT, James 438
DENNIS, Esther 283 John 319
Littleton 169 172 174 181 190
207-209 217 219-221 225-227
231-236 240 241 243 249 250
252 253 269 270 Martha 22
Robert 319 Shadrack 253 259
312 353
DENNISON, Ann 32 William 16-
18 30 32
DENT, Joseph 44 Thomas 31
DERING, Osmond 5
DESHEL, Henrietta 187

DESHSILD, Clement 338
DEVENISH, John 10
DEWEY, George 11 94 465
DIAS, Phebe 145
DICKASON, Charles 148
DICKENSON, Jesse 370 Leah 370
    Michael 208
DICKERSON, Charles 203 David
    271 Elisha 271 Euphamy 443
    George 344 Hannah 271 Jesse
    271 Joshua 420 Leah 185 344
    459 Mary 170 185 235 Michael
    235 251 373 Sarah 170 185
    William 408
DICKESON, Abraham 176 Boyer
    176 Edward 121 175 176 179
    181 Elizabeth 100 George 176
    Jessie 181 Leah 181 Martha
    176 181 Mary 176 181 Michael
    176 Peter 104 Peter Jr 81
    Rachel 176 Sarah 176 181
DICKINSON, Richard 111
DICKS, Comfort 360 John 58
    Thomas 58
DICKSON, Bridget 445 Michael
    178
DIE, John 1 28
DIGGES, Richard 21
DIMZIE, John 35
DINE, William 11
DIX, Amaziah 398 Ann 204 An-
    nabella 16 Anne 431 Azariah
    398 Barshiba 413 Bersheba 461
    Breget 421 Bridget 120 354 359
    383 Caleb 320 420 422 Comfort
    360 375 382 Elizabeth 16 60
    165 198 202 204 211 217 359
    419 Esther 382 398 George 165
    202 354 359 410 Grace 398
    Griffin 202 Iassc 60 Isaac 3 13
    15 16 59 82 119 120 123 165
    172 359 400 419 Isaac Jr 112
    Isack 43 Jacob 59 James 431
    James Milby 431 John 16 53
    59 118 123 137 157 165 166
    177 198 201 204 211 272 321
    332 398 405 431 456 John Jr
    137 211 231 386 John Sr 320
    332 358 383 Leah 320 431 Levi
    349 398 410 419 Levin 204 382
    413 419 461 Levin Milby 211
    217 Margaret 43

DIX (continued)
    Mary 9 15 16 60 120 123 204
    211 217 230 320 361 431 Molly
    202 Mrs John 431 Nancy 408
    461 Nanny 198 201 202 211 217
    269 Neddy 398 Patience 60 398
    Patty 419 Peggy 360 382
    Preson 320 419 420 Richard 43
    165 198 202 359 400 Rosey
    Gootee 419 Sabra 204 211 217
    Santer 320 Sarah 177 Scarburgh
    398 Solomon 165 192 205 320
    Tabitha 382 Thomas 382 461
    Treffey 419 Typhina 454 Wel-
    thyanna 199 William 60 99 201
    332 360 382 461
DIXON, John 233
DIXY, Henry 25
DOBINS, Leonard 328
DOD, Masen 444
DODD, Mason 369
DOE, Alexander 376 John 191
    Margaret 306 Mary 52 Peggy
    376 Polly 459 Samuel 376
    Samuell 52 Susanna 328
    Thomas 328 Vallance 185
DOLBY, Ann 4 40 Benjamin 40
    Branson 407 415 Edward 4
    Eleshe 375 John 4 John Sr 4
    Margaret 4 Mrs John Sr 4
    Nicholas 179 345 Peter 4 7 329
    345 415 Peter John 375 Sally
    464 Southey 420 Thomas 222
DONE, Nicholas 440 Nickles 78
DONELSON, Alexander 215 John
    215 Rachel 215
DONNISON, William 29
DONNOIIOS, Timothy 107
DONOHO, Timothy 141
DONOHOE, Agnes 177 Mary 177
DONOS, Arthur 70 Mrs Arthur 70
DOO, Margaret 286 Nelle 286
    Samuel 286
DOOTE, William 231
DORMAN, James 322
DORTON, Bridget 160 161
DOUGLAS, Agnes 190 Ann 172
    190 201 Anne 116 171 190 Eliz
    190 George 72 82 84 95 98-107
    112-117 121 123 126 128 133-
    141 143 144 146 147 149 154
    159 164 168 186 190 202

DOUGLAS (continued)
James 201 Mrs George 116 190
191 Walter 171 172 190 201
Peggy 190 Tabitha 141 172 190
DOUGLASS, James 352 369
DOVE, Thomas 79
DOW, Ralph Jr 2
DOWNING, Anne 297 Arthur 80
334 Arthur Jr 334 Elizabeth
244 279 Frances 29 58 Francis
69 137 316 394 Hannah Scar-
burgh 195 John 29 173 232 244
316 369 396 435 457 458 John
Jr 316 John Robins 137 316
Leah 244 316 Margaret 335
Maru 58 Mary 133 Nancy 316
Peggy 316 Rachel 316 359
Robert 133 Salley 458 Samuel
461 Sophia 316 William 279
297 302 335 336 367 371 377
388 397 403 410 413 416 420
426 433 439 440 447 453 455
457 459 461 William Jr 420
DOWNS, William 329
DREWE, George 80
DREWITT, Benjamin 75
DRUMAOND, Hill 54 John 12 58
DRUMMOND, Abigail 142 143 163
Allas Shepherd Drake 414 Amy
65 163 Anariter 397 Ann 49 97
106 194 195 224 288 442 Ann
Temperance 448 Annaretter
414 Anne 97 106 194 228 254
281 404 405 Anne R 438 Anne
Robinson 448 Barbara 84 Betsey 448 Betsy 448 Catharine
448 Catharine Scarburgh 448
Charles 194 288 298 376 426
448 Charles Sr 442 Comfort
351 376 385 426 442 Daniel
405 461 David 405 406 430
Diadamia 269 Drake 23 49 65
91 139 140 163 186 263 293
322 340 405 Dublin 448 Elicia
414 Elisha 224 281 397
Elizabeth 62 84 97 137 143 194
254 269 298 380 397 405 426
442 444 Esther 281 404 430
Ezekiel 351 372 George 129
167 168 171 222 228 254 298
397 404 405 426 442 Georgs 97
Hannah 448 Henry 397 430

DRUMMOND (continued)
Hill 23 49 58 59 62 83 84 88
James 43 47 49 53 88 297 302
346 397 John 3 5 9 12 16 21-23
28 35 49 53 65 72 116 133 141
143 163 171 186 288 298 302
340 351 405 430 431 454 John
Jr 137 Katherine 137 224 Leah
340 Margaret 49 Mary 49 80
405 Mrs David 405 Mrs Henry
430 Nancy 281 397 426 448 451
Nanny 196 269 Patience 23 65
84 405 Peggy 397 430 R 80
Richard 3 28 46 47-49 61 62 69
72 74 75 80 84 88 97 104 106
137 144 194 207 224 228 254
262 281 288 298 308 338 380
397 405 426 437 442 448
Richard Hill 351 448 Richard
Jr 69 404 Richard Sr 373 405
Robert 46 49 163 171 323 352
363 397 405 Rosey 397 Sabra
84 Sabrah 59 Sabrath 101 Sally
254 298 426 Sarah 178 194 230
269 281 298 351 372 397 442
Sarah Ann 405 Sarah Robinson
430 431 Scarburgh 60 62 Sophia
338 351 431 434 Spencer 62 97
191 194 224 228 232 233 281
287 298 308 354 405 426 448
459 Stephen 46 163 351 414
439 Steven 23 Susanna 405
Tabitha 84 Thomas 405
Thomas Bonwell 430 William
97 160 161 163 167 170 194
196 201 205 228 231-233 254
269 270 287 298 346 351 356
366 372 375 397 405 410 424
426 434 438 442-444 448 454
William Jr 351 William S 448
DRUREY, Robert 257
DRYAS, Betty 119 Edward 119
Lydia 119 William 118 119
DUA, Nanney Redefas 272
DUBBERLY, Esther 159 Grace
110 John 110 312 Thomas 159
DUBERLEY, John 27
DUBERLY, John 62
DUER, James 24
DUEY, Beautyfiler 50 Elizabeth
50 Jacob 47 50 Matilda 50
DUGGAN, John 45

ELLIOTT (continued)
Thomas 155 252 348 384 428
446 Thomas Sr 384 William
252 381 384 428
ELLIS, Elizabeth 77 Henry 87
Love 224 Mary 77 Thomas 77
169 William 57
EMMERSON, Anne 200 205 206
208 320 Arthur 122 146 190 196
200 202 206 208 320 Hannah
320 William 303 320
ENGLISH, Andrew 132 138
ENIS, Nathaniel 14
ENSWORTH, Peter 107
ESHON, Daniel 11 John 156
EUSTACE, John 230
EVANS, Aby 245 Agnes 327 Anjeletter 177 Ann 203 294 Anna
450 Anne 172 245 Anne Mary
245 246 Anneletter 177 Arcadia
323 409 Arthur 76 77 245 Atterlanter 267 Betsy 450 Caesar
146 166 178 199 334 Cesar 125
130 Col 143 Edward 449 Eliza
267 Elizabeth 70 77 180 450
Goorge Crippen 450 Grace 203
Henry 327 Hillary 199 Isaiah
130 158 166 180 227 385 Jacob
Lurton 327 Jesse 294 450
Jesse Sr 294 Jestinian 119
Joane 4 Job 77 Jobe 76 John 4
22 70 74 76 77 93 96 153 162
166 172 177 178 180 203 210
225 230 245 246 267 293 336
370 371 386 398 399 409 John
Kitson 341 John Kittson 335
Kezia 199 Leah 294 Leaven 77
Levin 76 245 255 344 370 386
450 Littleton 245 Lucretia 371
Mark 70 230 327 Mary 70 76 77
96 119 148 166 203 230 294
450 Mehala 445 Mrs Mark 327
Nathaniel 245 323 Ned 399
Peggy 450 Rachel 230 313 386
Richard 70 Robert 254 437
Santer 397 Sarah 22 180 227
267 327 385 392 445 Spencer
319 Susanna 175 386 Susanna
Reed 350 Susannah 294 Suse
450 Tabitha 245 Thomas 51 60
65 84 96 119 123 166 171 175
177 180 199 203 294 302 316

EVANS (continued)
321 322 330 335 336 358 360
364 367 371 374 376 387 394
399 408 410 418 433 436 440
456 459 460 463 William 141
180 199 210 227 294 385 386
410 413 450 Zerrobabel 166
Zerrobable 227 Zerrubbabell
180 Zoroball 385
EVENS, Anow Bellow 73 John 51
Leah 425
EVERNDEN, Thomas 21
EVINS, Grace 48 John 48 Levin
445 Mehala 445 Sarah 48
EWELL, Ann 35 80 83 103 128
202 416 Anne 35 326 344 Arcadia 138 Charles 35 299 388
440 449 Comfort 35 56 70 77
83 103 416 Coventon 331
Covington 243 Edward 103 340
363 411 Elizabeth 80 131 132
147 427 Famey 202 George 35
83 202 203 416 George H 416
George Hope 70 80 176 202 213
302 James 8 35 80 302 416
Jediah 437 Jedidiah 128 138
Jedodiah 103 Levinah 125
Margaret 369 412 Mark 35 51
70 80 125 202 416 Mary 331
Mary Ann 103 128 Mrs Mark 80
Mrs Solomon 83 Nancy 449
Naomi 83 103 121 211 Naomy
128 226 Patience 35 Peggy 388
Rebecca 388 Rhoda 125 Sally
449 Sarah 80 118 190 202 Selby
447 Seth 369 Solomon 35 62 74
77 80 82 83 91 97 99 103 110
121 195 275 293 302 327 343
388 416 449 Sophia 363
Tabitha 125 202 203 William
103 139 202 226 293 299 321
333 388 440 456 William Jr
297 388 William Whittington
226 344
EYRE, Ann 129 Benjamin 15 22
Col 189 Elizabeth 42 43 Littleton 189 Martha 15 22 43
Regnald 35 Regnold 15 42
EYRES, Benjamin 12
EYRSS, William 293
FADDERSICK, Job 116
FADRE, Hilliard 65

FADREE, Elizabeth 136 Hillyard
  136
FAIRFAX, James 255
FALCONER, James 179
FARMER, George 45 46
FATHERLY, Elizabeth 103 Hil-
  liard 103 John 103
FAWSETT, Charles 6 Elizabeth 6
  John 2 6 Rodeah 6 Thomas 6
  William 6
FEDDAMAN, Joseph 77 242 Mary
  218
FEDDEMAN, Ann 260 402 429
  Betty 402 Elizabeth 218 260
  429 Ester 402 Esther 260 429
  Faderick 260 Henry 401 402
  Joseph 112 128 146 148 238
  260 319 371 401 402 429 Mary
  402 Mary Houston 429
  Meshack 128 218 237 260 401
  S 238 Samuel 128 129 148 201
  260 Shadrack 112 William 402
  429
FEDDIMAN, Elizabeth 175 Esther
  175 Joseph 168 170 175 211
  233 Meshack 171 175 232 282
  S 251 Samuel 127 167 175 176
  198 231
FEEHARY, James 393 Rachel
  393 396
FENN, Elijah 130 John 16 Mary
  131 Philip 130 131
FENTON, Margaret 58 Moses 58
  87
FEREFAX, James 25
FEWZICY, Pricy 447
FICHER, Fenwick 405
FIDDEMAN, Catherine 429 Esther
  391 Isaiah 374 429 465 Joseph
  376 425 429 Meshack 374
  Polly 429 465 William 429
FIELD, John 148 312 356
FIELDS, John 393
FILBEY, Mary 185
FILBY, Febe 129 George 129
  Mary 129 211 Stephen 129
FINN, Charles 131 Mary 130
FINNE, Andrew 4 Jane 4 Sarah 77
  William 54
FINNEY, A 66 Abel 126 138 159
  202 242 Andrew 117 118 126
  Ann 444 Anne 297 322

FINNEY (continued)
  Arthur 126 Athalia 118 Attalanta 239 Betty 126 Comfort
  70 128 Elizabeth 117 126 128
  207 230 242 317 Ester 128
  George 242 311 393 Hannah
  128 Joanna 239 John 169 215
  239 247 268 271 297 304 317
  322 399 409 Mary 128 231 311
  317 Naomy 128 Polley 242
  Polly 242 Sarah 77 126 393
  William 118 126 231 242 317
  368 393 465 William Jr 60 66
  171 173 207
FINNIE, Andrew 1 Sarah 6 William 6
FINNY, Abel 166 Agnes 227 Attalanta 227 Betty 227
  Elizabeth 227 Euphamia 459
  Joanna 227 John 227 Rachel
  227 Sarah 227 Tabitha 227
  William 227
FISH, John 68 107 225
FISHER, 404 Ann 233 Bally 44
  Bridget 49 Comfort 415 Daniel
  186 Edward 405 Elizabeth 44
  115 170 Ester 49 F 406 Fen-
  wick 387 394 439 George 411
  415 419 Grace 49 Isaac 306
  James 310 John 44 45 49 106
  115 233 310 415 462 John Jr
  233 Lisey 415 Margaret 287
  Marthew 415 Mary 44 157 241
  310 Nancy 415 Nanney 415
  Obediah 287 Philip 44 157 411
  415 Phillip 3 49 Robertson 415
  Sally 306 377 Sarah 415
  Shadrack 306 332 Susannah 310
  421 462 Thomas 170 173 214
  222 241 339 345 436 Thomas
  Hall 287 William 49
FITCHET, Elizabeth 225 John
  170 Jonathan 270 Salathiei 306
  William 261 330
FITCHETT, 432 Anariter 276 Ann
  333 Anne 332 Cleartrouen 276
  Comfort 346 347 Esther 332
  Jacob 227 250 346 John 84 227
  285 332 346 347 357 363 373
  377 398 Joice 377 Jonathan
  276 434 Joshua 285 Mary 227
  347 Mrs Weatherington 84

FITCHETT (continued)
Rachel 84 Rachell 71 Salathiel 276 330 381 Severn 276 Shady 276 Siner 276 Tabitha 227 347 433 Thomas 276 Weatherington 69 71 84 William 276 346 347 Witherinton 54 Withertun 227
FITCHGARELL, John 90
FITCHIT, Salathiel 299
FITCHRIALD, Rachel 366
FITSGARALD, Susannah 213
FITSGARRELL, Rachel 257
FITTCHGRALL, John 76
FITTIMAN, Elizabeth 32 Joseph 32 45 Mary 32 Meshack 32 Samuel 32 Shadrack 32
FITZGARALD, Bridget 213 Henry 364
FITZGARELL, Frances 100 John 45 100 Steven 100
FITZGAROLD, James 73 Mary 73
FITZGARRALD, Peter 226
FITZGARRELL, Elizabeth 15 John 15 68 Katherine 15 Mrs John 15 Thomas 15
FITZGEARLD, 189
FITZGERALD, Anne 132 Charles 184 185 Elijah 425 435 442 Esther 331 368 James 114 John 114 132 133 184 331 341 Joseph 340 Mary 114 133 331 Peter 132 334 Purnal 331 Rachel 184 394 Sarah 160 185 Shadrack 169 331 Sophia 442 Stephen 149 153 160 179 184 185 198 Susanna 184 Thomas 114 William 334
FITZGERRALD, Bridget 187 David 187 Elijah 343 James 256 John 113 256 Joseph 343 Mary 119 Peter 236 Richard 256 Stephen 106 171 180 181 Susanna 171 256 Susannah 214
FITZGERROLD, John 112
FITZGRALL, Thomas 71
FITZHUGH, Elizabeth 315 William 307
FLACK, Comfort 88 John 18 Robert 88
FLANAGAN, Elizabeth 417
FLANEGAN, Nancy 326

FLANNAGEN, Nanny 309
FLANNEGAL, Betsy 406 Rosey 406
FLANNEGAN, Rosey 406
FLEAR, Elizabeth 57 Heaster 57 William 37 43 57
FLEEK, Robert 59
FLEETWOOD, Charles 14 15
FLEMMONS, Comfort 240
FLENNE, Easter 45
FLESON, James 160
FLETCHER, Adah 464 Ann 459 Batterton 46 61 Brand 61 Brandon 46 61 93 213 Brenden 87 Comfort 213 Dorithy 46 Elizabeth 17 46 61 279 285 459 Euphamia 459 Frances 46 61 Henry 107 134 141 144 177 181 191 195 200 232 245 246 263 264 320 354 357 446 459 Henry Sr 308 359 363 377 459 Jean 213 John 234 285 420 Leah 177 200 459 Mary 46 61 Mathew 46 93 Matthew 61 Mrs Thomas 107 Nathan 413 Phebe 413 Pheby 379 Read 234 Riddagail 285 Rosanah 46 Rose 213 Sarah 93 Susana 464 Susanna 354 459 Susannah 363 Tabitha 120 285 Thomas 46 61 107 350 354 363 370 420 426 431 441 448 455 459 465 William 8 14 17 46 61 69 87 93 107
FLOWERS, Richard 28
FLOYD, Benjamin 266 413 414 449 Berry 413 430 449 Betty 383 Elijah 449 John 449 Leah Garrison 383 Mrs Berry 449 Peggy 383 401 Rachel 383 Sarah 430 449 William 401 412
FLUD, Abane 309 Ann 309 Keziah 309
FLUHART, John 375
FOGG, Aaron 49 Ann 49 Cannedy 80 Daniel 49 98 Elijah 223 Elizabeth 150 Esther 156 Grace 150 Grace Houseton 223 Jane 80 John 49 150 223 John Watts 49 125 150 Moses 49
FOLIO, John 313 368 447 Pearcy 447 Upshur 368 447 William 447

FOLLA, John 272
FOLLY, Thomas 378
FOOKES, Benjamin 71 Daniel 71
74 87 100 Elizabeth 71
Grandfather 9 James 71 Mary
71 Neomy 71 Rachell 71 Sarah
71 74 Thomas 17 71 William
71
FOOKS, Betty 349 Daniel 122 349
Elizabeth 122 Leah 122 Rachel
122 Sarah 122 349
FOREMAN, Robert 350 372 Wid
372
FORSTER, Absalom 358 Anne
358 Comfort 358 Elizabeth 358
James 358 John 358 Levi 358
Polly 358 Salley 358 Sefier 358
Tabitha 358 Tabither 358 Wil-
liam 358
FORSYTH, Archibald 406
FORTEN, Ann Rodgers 392
FORTESQUE, John 295
FOSCUE, Ann 57 John 42 57 75
95 117 Luke 60 Nathaniel 117
Simon 57
FOSKEY, George 223 John 223
Luke 223 Sarah 223
FOSKUE, John 143
FOSKY, John 423
FOSQUE, Ann 64 306 307 Anne
313 Barbara 147 Barbary 64
Elizabeth 43 57 249 307
George 147 John 64 79 147 306
359 383 399 462 Leah 408 Luk
249 Luke 57 64 147 216 249
Luke Sr 249 Mary 147 249 307
Nathaniel 147 241 306 313 463
Rachel 147 249 Sarah 64 230
249 William 297 408
FOSTER, Aboalom 281 Absalam
377 Absalom 272 281 Ann 286
Anne 281 Betty 272 281 Catey
445 Comfort 66 268 Elizabeth
20 58-60 James 235 257 268
386 John 58-60 88 198 235 268
281 Joshua 272 283 411 445
Leah 445 Levener 272 Pegey
281 Peggy 272 Sarah 235 257
386 Sinah 390 Siner 272 281
349 Tabitha 198 268 Thomas
20 272 William 59 60 66 241
268 283 William Shephard 58

FOULER, Catherine 75 Roger 75
FOUNTAIN, Nicholas 91
FOWKES, Amy 6 9 Thomas 6
FOX, Amy 161 Ann 161 Golden
161 Goldin 306 Jacob 124 161
Levin 161 Mary 415 Sarah 161
235 Thomas 161 235 249
FOXCROFT, Bridget 10 Isaac 21
Joseph 6
FOXE, Daniel 120
FRAME, Major 51
FRANKLIN, Joan 19 Richard 19
Thomas 17
FREE, Clemens 374 Clemmons
347
FREEMAN, Ann 317 Jane 46 John
317 Mary 46 Moses 317
Thomas 46 William 6
FRENCH, William 21
FRESHWATER, Elizabeth 11
George 11
FRITCHETT, Anne 347
FULLER, Asa 410
FULLING, Hugh 52 Sarah 52
FULWELL, John L 326
FUOLLUD, Leah 285
FURLONG, Edmond 2
FURNACE, Samuel 175
GALE, Betty 104 George 143 200
John 143 Leah 92 93 104 143
144 Levin 92 93 104 143 168
200 212 308 Margaret 196
Mathias 162 Matt 143 Matthias
144 168 Mrs George 143 Mrs
John 143 Mrs Matt 143 Sarah
104
GALT, Azel 403 Samuel 374 391
403 423 436
GARASON, Jonathan 102
GARDNER, Thomas 110
GAREITT, Elizabeth 72
GARLAND, David 342 John 342
GARRAT, Sarah 397
GARRET, Ann 37 David 278
GARRETSON, Archabel 251 401
Archibald 425 Isaiah 464 Rose
34
GARRETT, Betsy 386 Bridget 381
Caty 423 David 381 Elisha 423
425 Henry 423 John 386 Joseph
386 409 Nancy 386 Richard 386
Robert 423 Susanna 423

GARRETT (continued)
Susey 423 Tabby 386 Thomas
386
GARRIS, Thomas 233
GARRISON, Abel 379 383 385 425
Agnes 147 295 Ann 56 451 Archibald 375 379 380 385 389
414 Bagwell 378 430 Betsy 378
430 Betty 378 383 Catherine
462 Edmund 378 430 Elizabeth
41 295 306 Fanny 295 378 Fil-
lace 295 Fillice 295 Fillis 199
George 199 205 257 302 312
363 379 383 385 425 George
Smith 383 Isaac 312 Isaiah 379
380 385 James 383 422 John
295 378 462 John Jr 430
Jonathan 56 69 104 147 199
205 251 295 379 414 Jonathan
Jr 329 Jonathen 123 Joshua
378 430 Margaret 56 Mary 385
Mrs Richard 56 Nancy 385
Nancy Dunton 379 Nanney 312
Peggy 385 Peggy Satchell 380
Phillis 174 385 Rachel 205 383
Richard 41 56 221 Rose 56 378
Rosey 430 Samuel Burton 462
Sarah 385 Susanna 383 Susan-
nah 379 Tabitha 56 378
Thomas 383 385 391 William
41 149 174 199 275 295 315
321 324 326 366 378 430 Wil-
liam Sr 295
GARRITSON, Esther 221 Jonathan
221 Richard 221 Rose 41
GARY, Tabitha 108
GASCOIGNE, Harmon 150 Henry
171 Sarah 112 150 Thomas 112
171 William 150 William
Bradford 150
GASCOINS, John 74 Thomas 74
GASCOYNE, Elizabeth 238 Henry
218 238 248 249 283 Rachel
274 Sarah 238 248 Thomas 69
William 218 238 William
Bradford 105
GASCOYNES, Elizabeth 272
Henry 272 349 Rachel 349
Susanna 349
GASCOYNS, Elizabeth 201
Susanna 201 Thomas 201 Wil-
liam 201

GASKINS, Anne 147 John 117 147
Sarah 241 Thomas 117
GASQUINE, Henry 424
GAULT, Patrick 302
GAY, Thomas 410
GEMIMA, 160
GEORGE, Joshua 317
GERRAT, Ann 52 John 52
GESERAN, Lanse 183
GESERON, Lange 183
GIBB, John Bell 454 William 319
322 333 340-342 361 366 369
371 372 374 386 394-397 403
410 411 413 418 430 431 436
437 439 442 454 455 458 460
William Jr 454
GIBBENS, Major 234 Sarah 83
GIBBINGS, Tabitha 140 Thomas
140
GIBBINS, David 38 Ellinor 38
Frances 38 Henry 38 Henry Sr
38 John 38 Sarah 38 Thomas
38
GIBBONS, Major 239
GIBBS, Henry 94
GIBSON, Agness 159 George 447
James 110 135 138 159 John
268 Mrs 116 Sarah 83
GIDDENS, Athaliah 282 Bridget
380 Custis 284 Elizabeth 284
379 Ishmael 284 379 Ismay
284 John 173 282-284 379
Kendal 282 Kiely 379 Lishea
283 Margaret 379 Michael 284
Peggy 282 284 Ruben 282
Sarah 284 379 Thomas 284 379
William 283 284 379
GILCHRIST, Agnes 200 Agness
159 Andrew 138 159 194 200
226 382 George 200 382 John
114 119 159 Mary 159 Tabitha
188 200 226 William 69
GILETT, William 226
GILL, Charles 217 Zorobable 128
GILLEN, Hugh 345
GILLET, Ayers 318 Ayres 173
236 299 Eupheme 123 James
318 John 35 318 Joseph 318
Margaret 123 Nancy 318 Peggy
327 Samecl 123 Samuel 123
162 191 William 123 159
GILLETT, Ann 224 Anne 376

GILLETT (continued)
Ayers 318 Ayres 226 228 275
394 434 Eyres 224 George 394
434 James 394 434 450 453
Jinny 453 John 224 299 348
363 387 392 394 434 Joseph
395 394 402 434 Mary 224
Peggy 425 Tabitha 395 434
William 395 434
GILLINS, Benjamin Turlington
Hugh 328
GILLITT, Samuel 93
GIN, Thomas 70
GINKINSON, Comfort 55 Thomas
57
GINN, Sarah 34 Thomas 120
GINNE, George 11
GITTINS, Elisha 205 Jain 205
Jean 205 Margaret 205 Sarah
277 Southy 277 Susey 205 Wil-
liam 205 William Watson 205
GIVAN, John 184
GLADDEN, Howel 360 James 360
Jehu 360 Jessee 360 John 49
360 Millison 376 Preeson 360
Sacker 360
GLADDIN, Howell 67 68 John 67
John Sr 398 Mrs John 67 68
Sally 398 Thomas 67 68
GLADDING, Jesse 441 John 374
455 John Jr 441 459 Mary 341
Milly 374 Rebecca 341 Sally
455 Sarah 464 Solomon 178
GLADEN, Howell 317
GLADIN, John 438
GLADING, Ann 83 Elizabeth 55
George 83 115 Howell 49 John
14 41 68 136 437 Joseph 115
Leah 136 Sacker 437 Thomas
189
GLANNING, John 34 Sarah 34
GLASBY, John 259 286 436 Wil-
liam 259
GLENN, Anne 377 Catherine 22
James 20 22 23 27 Lazarus 20
GLOFFLIN, Bridget Custis 349
GODDING, Thomas 63
GODWIN, Daniel 397 457 Frances
362 457 John 362 457 Joseph
457 Labin 457 Littleton 457
Mary 457 Sarah 457

GOFFIGON, Betty 182 John Jr
149 Thomas 149
GOLDSMITH, Maj 2
GOODAY, Bridget 204 William
174 204
GOODDAY, William 229
GOODDY, Elizabeth 242 Leving
254
GOODIN, Mary 318
GOODMAN, John 19
GOOTEE, Andrew 209 231 249
250 278 Elizabeth 422 Hannah
422 John 208 260 321 325 343
344 412 422 Joseph 186 208
211 Lisney 208 211 287 297
328 381 422
GORBIN, Ralph 82
GORDING, George 9 John 9
Lenard 9 Margaret 9 Mrs John
9 Nathaniel 9
GORDON, Thomas 77
GORE, Ann 253 Comfort 449
Daniel 27 45 62 140 173 191
224 253 Edmund 318 Elizabeth
253 John 253 Joyce 62 Mary 62
253 Maxamillian 18 Maxi-
milian 24 27 Mrs Daniel 62
Mrs Edmund 318 Mrs
Maxamillian 18 Selby 62
Susanna 253 Thomas 375 433
449 Thomas Teackle 253 Wil-
liam 62 100 101 129 140
GORES, John 217
GORING, Leonard 20
GOSLE, John 26
GOSSLING, Elizabeth 7 John 7
GOUTEE, John 112 114
GOUTEY, Joseph 63
GOUTY, Elizabeth 86 John 86
Joseph 86 91 102 180 Mary 86
GOWERS, William 3
GOWTEE, Andrew 222 John 134
149 174 222 Joseph 149 169
222 Lisney 222 Mary 134 135
222 Trephina 222
GRAHAM, Bridget 206 George 206
Henry 145
GRANNIS, John 322
GRATE, Bernard 215
GRAY, Ann 379 Benjamin 199
Dorothy 61 Elizabeth 61 180

GRAY (continued)
Ester 61 James 13 16 31 61
118 John 180 Levin 199 409
Mary 61 185 Mary Ann 178
Priscilla 193 Rachel 199 204
Sarah 379 Solomon 118 178 225
363 378 Tabitha 83 91 379
Thomas 91 199 379 William
158 159
GREEN, George 111 124 241 Hillary 270 John 111 124 Leven
304 Mordicay 46 Rose 147 251
Sarah 35 256 293 Thomazine
46
GREENALDS, Catherine 170
Henry 168-170
GRENNALDS, Elijah 461
GREY, John 31
GRICE, Mary 16
GRIFFIN, Ann 103 Benjamin 103
144 Elizabeth 103 Emanuel
103 133 144 Hillary 65 Luke
103 Margaret 133 144 168 259
Susanna 103
GRIFFIS, Daniel 69 Mary 68
GRIFFITH, James 134 Oliver 139
GRIMES, Hanah 142 Sarah 129
GRINALD, Henry 75 Mary 75
Richard 75
GRINALDS, Catharine 407 Elijah
346 372 407 413 Elizabeth 276
John 407 Mary 276 Molly 384
Richard 125 164 167 276 321
324 344 345 358 370 406 Sarah
399 407 Southy 276 321 390
407 413 Thomas 407 413 418
422 William 276 358 374 407
GRINALL, Mary 90 Richard 89 90
GRINNALDS, Elijah 405 408 422
445 Henry 137 John 422
Richard 161 Southy 422
Thomas 422
GRINNALL, Richard 24
GRINNALS, Catherine 262
GRINNOLD, Richard 23
GRINOLDS, Thomas 269
GRONANS, Elizabeth 180
GROTEN, Amey 273 301 380 Amy
280 301 307 Anne 241 411
Betsy 403 Betty 306 Charles
293 Custis 284 303 361 Edmund 273 280 301 307 330 423

GROTEN (continued)
John 425 Johon 306 Jona John
424 Jonathan 192 203 273 280
293 301 307 380 423 Joyce 423
424 Kendall 306 Major 273 280
301 Margaret 273 280 293 306
307 Margery 306 Mary 256 293
355 Nancy 361 464 Patience
273 280 307 Peggy 192 203
Sarah 256 293 Severen 361
Severn 361 Seyeren 361
Shadrack 273 Solomon 256 274
284 293 295 Thomas 361 William 231 256 273 280 293 301
307 361 380 424 464 William
Jr 170 Zerobabel 307 Zerrobabel 280 301 Zorobabel 273
280 355 370 371 380 411
Zorowbable 328
GROTON, Ann 305 Betty 461
Custis 305 Edmund 371 John
305 Jonathan 309 Mary 108
Mrs John 305 Nancy 447 Nanney 305 Sevron 305 Solomon
305 Thomas 305 William 72
Williiam 305
GROWSON, Charles 425
GUNTER, Abednego 193 Abigal
193 Adiax 193 Adra 108 Adrah
339 Adria 193 Bednego 261
Benjamin 261 339 383 440 447
Charles 359 Edward 64 171 185
193 259 287 402 Edward Jr 220
Esther 409 Euphamy 402
Joseph 64 141 152 193 339 440
Laban 440 Labin 402 Mary 63
311 402 Meshack 261 Mesheck
193 Nancy 339 Ously 63 Peggy
261 Rachel 402 Sarah 64 193
339 Sheba 193 Stephen 402 440
Steven 402 Susanna 63 William 64 Zachariah 344
GURNEY, Francis 270
GUSTIS, Henry 316
GUTHREY, Severn 174 207
GUTHRIDGE, Severn 252
GUTLER, 306
GUTTERIEDGE, Attalanta 301
Littleton 301 Severn 301
GUTTERY, Lante 341
GUTTRIDGE, Littleton 356
Severn 356 404

497

GUY, Ann 124 147 210 309 Anne
212 242 246 381 Betty 182 234
Caleb 144 Catherine 124
Coleburn 357 Elizabeth 102
212 281 Henry 452 John 110
119 124 234 255 309 343 373
397 452 Major 124 140 192 281
337 412 413 Mary 239 278 Mrs
William 309 Nancy 212 309
Nicholas 109 122 124 Peggy
309 Robert 214 238 353 396
Sarah 216 281 Sarah Dunton
214 Thomas 239 278 345 William 102 124 212 234 309
HACK, Ann 2 47 56 Anne 36 115
Betsey 298 Betsy 298 Betty 47
Elizabeth 36 317 Elizabeth
Smith 317 Esther 315 Frances
36 Francina 47 266 356 Franciner 83 Francinia 75 Geo Nich
34 Geo Nicholas 20 George 2
36 47 105 200 247 266 298 303
347 356 417 George Nich 3 56
George Nicho 15 George
Nicholas 36 Margaret 247 Mary
Margaretta 36 47 Matilda 186
Mrs Peter 56 Peter 11 20 36 47
48 56 105 200 220 247 274 411
Peter Jr 298 317 453 Peter Sr
298 330 Sarah 47
HACKETT, Simon 1
HADDERSICK, Job 126 129
HADEN, Jenny 306
HAGGOMAN, John 335
HAILL, Henry 8
HAISLOP, William 232
HAIZLUP, William 68 115
HAKET, Frances 61
HALEY, Benjamin 367 Robert 367
William 367 376
HALL, Abigail 177 354 Adam
171-173 Ann 128 Anna Maria
287 Anne 302 Asa 302 Bennet
354 Betty 128 130 157 158 174
190 377 Catron 354 Comfort
158 190 Daniel 130 135 157
181 354 361 Daniel Rowles 185
Dixon 319 354 416 Elizabeth
128 200 Ephraim 338 354 Felia
205 George 28 436 Hannah 205
Henry 354 426 448 456 James
185 210 Jane 53 262

HALL (continued)
Jean 287 John 47 50 76 118 128
141 185 189 200 John Shay 386
Joshua 135 Katherine 39 Margaret 287 386 Martha 135 Mary
128 386 Michael 120 157 174
185 190 Mickal 76 Nathaniel
333 377 Rebecca 377 Sally 354
Sarah 185 268 Stephen 128
Susanna 354 Susannah 423
Tabitha 287 386 Thomas 2 46
52 53 76 138 154 174 185 186
210 226 240 262 287 310 377
HALLET, Francis 185 Santeke
185 William 185
HALLOWAY, Hezekiah 354 John
354 Nancy 354 Sarah 354 William 354
HALY, Elizabeth 213 William
416
HAMERIN, William 11
HAMILTON, A 38 Andrew 38 93
Ann 93 James 93 John 184
HAMLING, George 1
HAMMON, Ann 9
HAMON, Edward 9
HAMPTON, Mary 184 281 287
HAMRON, William 147
HANAFORD, George 364 James
364 John 364 John Jr 364
Joseph 364 William 364
HANCOCK, 117 Arthur 9 Edith 9
Elijah 409 445 452 454 George
357 452 John 9 452 Margaret
445 Mary 452 Rachel 452
HANDCOCK, Elijah 287 Elizabeth
287 George 287 Tabitha 285
William 287
HANDY, Anne 335 Elizabeth 335
John Custis 449 Samuel 449
HANNAFORD, Charles 341 John
257 285 325 360 379 John Jr
231
HANNIFORD, Catharine 418 John
81 418 John Sr 237 Joseph 418
HANSON, John 18
HARD, Mary 54
HARDEN, John Nathaniel 394 457
HARDING, Jenney 326 Jonathan
326
HARDY, Peter 312
HARGAS, Levin 425 Phillip 124

HARGES, Mrs Walter 19 Walter 19
HARGIS, James Nelson 460 Peggy 341 Thomas 375 414 421 William 272 450 460 Wise 421
HARGRASS, Rachael 227 Thomas 283
HARGRESS, George 136 Thomas 241
HARGRISS, Thomas 315
HARISON, Sarah 313
HARLEE, Peter 117
HARMAN, Ann 37 Anne 37 Barbara 106 Bayly 394 Betty 313 Catharine 363 Cornelius 37 363 446 Edmund 363 Elizabeth 37 Emanuel 121 Ephraim 301 Esther 331 379 Ezekiel 252 266 Frances 363 Francis 446 George 217 381 394 Hannah 37 Henry 211 252 301 381 John 252 301 313 363 381 Kendall 363 Lacy 84 Leah 363 Littleton 301 381 Mary 37 394 Patrick 394 Rachel 363 Rosy 404 Sally 366 Sarah 37 Simon 58 Sinah 381 Sophia 301 Symon 37 Tabitha 381 Tamer 366 Thomas 381 William 37 58 64 84 112 344 366 373 394 Zorobabel 363
HARMANSON, Argail 101 Argill 98 Barbara 98 101 Benjamin 101 George 98 101 Gertrude 101 John 196 212 Sister 26 William 142 William Jr 252
HARMON, Ader 273 Baily 241 Baley 142 307 Barbara 147 Bayly 273 301 Betty 252 Cornelius 318 Edmond 318 Henry 273 278 309 John 142 211 273 301 318 403 404 Kendal 318 Lendor 273 Littleton 273 403 404 Patrick 273 Peggy 252 Rachel 252 273 318 Rose 252 354 Sarah 252 Simon 138 252 Susey 318 Tamer 273 Wid 320 William 95f 273 307 435 458 Zerobabel 420 Zorobabel 318
HARPER, Mary 1 Robert 2 Sarah 2

HARRASON, Tabltha 273
HARRIS, Handy 367 John 135 331 356 Mary 45 295 Robert 385 Tabitha 140 Thomas 81 140 William 350
HARRISON, Alexander 40 81 107 199 207 Ann 40 199 Anne 241 Arcabl 205 Arnold 23 41 Benjamin 407 Caleb 262 342 394 407 449 Elizabeth 166 207 212 213 407 449 Elizabeth Sr 212 Esther 181 Euphamy 199 Fanny 449 Flowerdew 62 James 201 266 407 John 81 134 199 241 278 Joseph 11 166 Josiah 356 Josiah Sr 266 Josias 166 Leah 407 Littleton 324 Margaret 199 Mary 201 262 266 Matilda 62 Matillda 11 Mattilah 17 Peggy 447 Philip 278 Phillip 199 Rhoda 364 Sarah 58 166 199 Sisceley 62 Stephen 136 152 166 201 Susanna 81 166 210 Susannah 212 Tabitha 166 212 247 Thomas 407 Ufamy 278 Welthyanna 199 William 161 166 195 278
HARRISTON, Esther 110 John 110
HARROD, Sarah 15
HARTFEILD, Elias 174
HARVEY, Jonathan 372
HARWOOD, Daniel 12 Sarah 12
HASEY, Rebecca 464
HASLES, Moses 172
HASTING, Ann 285 Kesiah 285 Major 285 Richard Salvy 285 Scarburgh 285 Susanna 285 Thomas 285
HASTINGS, Dorothy 67 113 John 113 Richard 285 Scarburgh 156 419 431 William 96 111
HASTINS, William 51
HATFELD, Anne 222 John Gillet Whitely 322
HATTEN, Walter 325
HATTON, Anne 356 Benjamin 459 Margt 356 Walter 267 270 356
HAVETT, William 36
HAWLEY, Abel 295 415 432 Henry 415 432 Robert 31 Sarah 415 432 449

HAYES, Alice 65 Elizabeth 65
HAYS, Christopher 32
HAYSLOP, Betty 314 Hannah 314
   William 314
HAYWARD, William 193
HAZLEUP, George 125
HAZLOP, Ann 41 Charles 41 50
   George 41 William 41
HAZLUP, Elizabeth 50
HEALY, John 48 Rachell 48 Wil-
   liam 48
HEATH, Arody 399 Betsy 454
   Cessey 454 Comfort 213 224
   Edmond 266 Edmund 173 225
   273 319 400 Edmund Jr 225
   Elizabeh 97 Fletcher 224 390
   454 Henry 183 206 209 214 224
   281 294 323 325 339 344 417
   Jacob 97 James 97 Jamimah
   400 Jane 417 Jemyah 340 John
   85 Joseph 97 196 214 215 224
   329 409 417 454 Leah 224
   Major 417 Margaret 80 214 224
   454 Mary 97 Patience 306
   Polly 425 Robert 97 161 Sophia
   214 Tabitha 279 300 417 456
   Teackle 320 393 399 William
   97 399
HEDGE, Elizabeth 81
HEDGES, Thomas 3
HEMMONS, Joseph 343
HENDERSON, Ann 206 Betsy 453
   Bishop 63 Charlotte 453 Charlotte Rebeckah 453 Comfort
   221 George 259 Hannah 106
   Jackey 453 James 450 Jean
   419 Jinny 453 John 43 63 165
   185 257 Joseph 453 Lemuel
   450 Patience 221 Peggy 252
   Rhoda 450 Richard 453 Robert
   63 Sally 453 Samuel 222 323
   371 374 395 400 409 419 440
   452 453 Scarburgh 450 Thomas
   460 William 334 453
   Zorebable 373
HENMAN, Isack 6
HENRY, Elizabeth 330 367 Hugh
   367 Isaac 281 367 James 169
   188 194 200 204 206 208 219
   222 227 228 232 236 239 243
   249 255 257 258 260 263 265
   269 270 274 276 281 285 294

HENRY (continued)
   295 297 298 301 303 315 316
   367 396 Jammes 209 John 53
   184 Mary 243 260 Nancy 367
   Robert Jenkins 184 Sarah Jr
   260 Susannah 367 Tabitha 298
   Thomas 335 William B 367
   William Blair 330
HERBERT, Jane 397 John 171
   Tabitha 171
HERMON, Ursilla Whittington 76
HERRING, Charles 252 Mary 252
   William 142
HERSON, Josiah 285
HEUBANCK, William 12
HEWET, Robert 412
HEWETT, Mary 3 Robert 3
HEWITT, George 153 Robert 2
HEWS, Temperance 156
HICKMAN, Adah 351 Annabeller
   225 Anne 208 366 435 Arthur
   351 Benjamin 12 161 Bridget
   203 311 Catey 423 Christian
   225 Comfort 351 Custis 272
   363 Daniel 397 Edward 126 438
   Elisha 354 Elizabeth 366 Es-
   ther 375 George 126 203 208
   225 302 311 321 438 Hampton
   366 393 435 438 Henry 12 100
   126 Isaiah 303 322F 366 438
   Isaih 435 Jane 2 Jesse 203 308
   311 Joan 2 John 12 271 311
   322 336 461 464 Jos 89 Joseph
   12 100 119 Joshua 225 272
   Kesiah 225 Keziah 225 Knevit
   208 Levin 396 433 Margaret
   Luker 423 Mary 225 Mrs Henry
   126 Mrs Richard 366 Mrs
   Roger 161 Mrs William 12
   Peggy 272 329 377 423 435 466
   Rachel 2 293 Rayth 203
   Rebeckah 435 Richard 12 126
   161 165 172 203 225 311 347
   351 366 397 Richard Jr 232
   Richard Sr 351 Roger 12 161
   Rose 423 Sally 363 423 Sarah
   225 336 Selby 203 279 311 462
   Seymour 438 Solomon 161 203
   Sophia 268 Spencer 374
   Susanna 279 Susannah 423 462
   Susy 363 Thomas 76 209 234
   266 294 302 303 308 322 354

HICKMAN (continued)
366 384 397 398 410 Thomas
Sr 389 William 12 119 133 142
203 225 288 303 333 362 397
398 411 413 William Sr 225
374
HICKMON, Christian 241
HIGGINS, Michael 106
HIGGONS, Robert 13 14
HILL, Arthur 327 328 Christian
128 Dorcus 9 Elisha 208
Elizabeth 46 57 64 328 Esther
275 Francis 39 Hatton 8 Henry
17 144 Hester 22 Huton 9 Isaac
193 272 Jacob 129 Jane 9 17
John 26 Leah 328 Margaret 24
Mary 23 Naomi 157 Nich 25 28
Nicholas 22 23 Patience 23
Prescilla 9 Richard 3 4 9 16 17
23 24 28 46 58 61 246 Robert 8
9 Roger 9 24 Ruth 9 Tabitha 31
34 37 55 57 67 98 William 259
328 350 400 434 447 Zerobable
328 Zorowbable 328
HILTON, Elisha 107 James 63
HINDERSON, Anne 215
HINDLEY, John 325
HINDMAN, Bally 205 Patience
178
HINDMANE, Anne 150
HINMAN, Ann 225 259 285 339
Ann Ritter 274 Anne 146 248
299 339 Argill 69 71 Argol 146
378 Baily 110 245 326 Bal 119
Baly 69 71 79 83 84 Bayley
339 Bayly 90 119 146 225 263
264 378 Bayly Jr 227 Benjamin
146 Bethany 285 Betty 326
Comfort Mary 71 Elizabeth 61
69 71 88 285 384 Esther 71
George 263 339 456 George
Clayton 347 George Cleyton
347 Hannah 285 Jaca 225
James 326 John 69 225 235
285 410 Keziah 347 Leah 285
Levin 225 Major 411 421 438
Margaret 252 339 378 Mary 110
119 146 Moses 162 285 386
410 411 Nancy 456 Nanney 339
Nanny 323 Neome 71 Patience
159 330 Peggy 339 Rachel 285
Ralph 378

HINMAN (continued)
Richard 13 61 69 71 171 206
262 285 Sarah 71 119 346 378
Scarburgh 411 Susanna 222
Tabitha C 347 Thany 346
Thomas 71 146 323 339 419
William 71 324 339 386 395
411 438
HINMON, Ann Ritter 274 Dennis
463 Dennis C 463 George C
463 John 344 Major 430 Nancy
434 Pegey 281 Tabitha 463
William 311
HISLOP, George 12
HITCHENS, Major 149
HITCHINS, Abigail 41 Edward 41
Ezekiel 451 Jarrett 41 Major
41 Mary 41 Rosanna 41
HITCHLNS, Edward 129
HOBRYANT, Leshia 77 Turlo 77
HODCKINS, Ann 2 Anthony 2
Elizabeth 2 Joyce 2
HODGSON, Sarah 63
HODSON, Anthony 24 Hester Ann
144 James Gray 24 John 24
Mary 24
HOFF, Caty 395
HOFFMAN, Andrew 440 James
440
HOGBEN, John 18
HOGGHER, Kindel 129
HOGGHERE, Kendall 129
HOGGSHEAR, Robert 129
HOGSHARE, Thomas 63
HOGSHEAR, Anne 118 Kendall
118 Robert 118 Thomas 118
HOGSHEARE, Kendall 129
HOGSHUR, Thomas 46
HOGSON, Rowland 63
HOLDEN, Ann 446 Anne 276 376
George 113 115 134–137 139
140 142 144 150 163 168–170
180 181 189–191 194 197 206
208 218 222 224 229 231 234
235 245 260 261 263 269 274
276 282 George Jr 232 King
376 Mrs 310 398
HOLDS, Rachel 318 Reubin 318
Susey 318
HOLESTON, Nancy 448
HOLLAND, Ann 281 Benjamin
449 457 John 375 Mary 281

HOLLAND (continued)
Nehemiah 203 Richard 3 William 152 281
HOLLEN, Scarburgh 228
HOLLIDAY, Elizabeth 20 Robert 20
HOLLINGSWORTH, Robert 45
HOLLOCK, John 46
HOLLON, Polly 463
HOLLOWAY, Hezekiah 260
HOLMES, James 105
HOLSHOTT, John 3
HOLSTON, Catey 424 James 343 John 455 Ruth 305 William 175
HOLT, Elijah 454 John 152 208 454 John Jr 228 John Sr 333 340 352 367 Thomas 260 367 William 351 352
HOOK, Ann 103 Betty 103 George 71 Sarah 243 Thomas 71 William 71
HOOTEN, David 133 Ester 67 Esther 133 John 67 Mary 360 Samuel 67
HOOTON, Abraham 66 67 Ester 66 Samuell 66
HOPE, Anabella 429 Anabeller 316 Ann 247 311 Annabella 337 Anne 245 Catherine 53 Charles 374 Comfort 70 Elizabeth 316 George 9 12 20 25 30 31 49 59 70 101 102 118 119 171 174 188 202 234 316 374 George Jr 53 Henry 316 Joanna Custis 59 78 Joanna Mary 78 Johanna 316 Johannah 316 Johannah Custis 70 John 316 337 374 Kendal 323 Kendall 316 Leah 316 337 Lidy 429 Lydia 101 Nancy 316 337 Patience 70 Peggy 316 Rachel 316 Reuben 316 Richard 95 Temperance 30 70 101 119 Thomas 62 70 93 101 118 280 316 William 30 59 70 101 119
HOPKINS, Hanah 23 William 128
HOPMAN, James 247 430 Sinah 258
HORNBY, Esther 71 John 71 93
HORNSBY, Ann 155 238 261 Anne 261 283 Argal 383 Argall 283

HORNSBY (continued)
Argil 278 279 300 Argol 155 243 273 Babel 269 273 279 Bagwell 283 Bagwill 422 Betty 283 Comfort 155 238 261 Eben 324 Ebron 390 Eburn 238 241 261 Edward 390 Eli 238 261 265 324 375 417 435 Elisha 238 324 356 389 390 401 Elizabeth 244 279 383 435 Ester 61 300 Esther 136 155 244 279 Ezekiel 244 Hannah 312 James 155 238 243 244 279 300 383 435 John 136 155 238 243 244 261 269 273 278 279 287 300 341 389 390 John Sr 273 Keziah 273 Laban 261 Laben 238 Leah 283 Levi 244 279 312 Levin 261 Major 283 417 422 Marah 435 Margaret 383 435 Mary 238 241 261 383 Mrs Zorobabel 435 Nancy 422 Naomi 243 Neomy 279 Peggy 283 Rachel 244 273 278 279 Sally 389 Sarah 391 396 Siner 389 Susanna 417 Susannah 273 283 307 Tabitha 244 279 300 William 238 261 389 390 Zerobabel 300 414 Zorobabel 244 278 335 342 356 358 369 391 393 396 435 Zorobable 383
HORSEY, Agnes 179 Elizabeth Revell 188 Isaac 188 Mrs Revil 400 Revell 184 Revil 400 Sarah 44 Smith 455 Stephen 311
HOSIER, Samuel 126
HOTTEN, Walter 372
HOUGH, William 196
HOULSTON, James 67
HOULT, John 326
HOUSTON, Anne 242 Francis 265 275 398 James 86 Joseph 242 Sarah 258 Sarah Wats 278
HOUTTEN, Elizabeth 45 Eve 45 John 45 William 45
HOWARD, Ambros 267 Ambrose 173 Ambross 162 Ann 183 333 Anne 332 Catharine 212 Catron 377 Caziah 377 Daniel 162 183 195 232 377 Elenor 267 Elias 162 Elinor 195 Ezekiel 392

HOWARD (continued)
James 369 378 John 334 John 324 333 348 370 377 386 Keziah 369 377 Leah 377 Margaret 32 Mary 162 212 377 386 Nathaniel 162 277 369 377 Nehemiah 246 324 Patience 162 Polly 348 Solomon 162 183 Susannah 337 Willan 282 William 32 38 49 70
HOWELL, Capt 2 John 172 197 Sarah 172 Thomas 221
HOYNES, Levin 336
HUBANK, Mary 48 Tabitha 48
HUBBARD, William 181
HUCHASON, Mary 72 Steven 72 Susana 72
HUDSON, Anthony 51 59 131 148 James Gray 61 James Grey 47 Levi 360 Margaret 44 Mary 44 Pegg 239 Robert 207 Sarah 149 William 44 51
HUEBANK, Mary 65
HUFF, Joseph 156 325 Rachel 252
HUFFINGTON, Gilbert 177 John 177 Susannah 230
HUFINGTON, Richard 59
HUGGINS, Sarah 367
HUGHBANK, Mary 33 109
HUGHES, Edmund 47 Elizabeth 47 John 47 Joseph 47 95 Thomas 47 William 47 William "Buddle" 270 Woodman 47
HUGHS, Joseph 109 William 66 Woodman 95
HUITT, Mary 8 Micall 8 Robert 8
HUNN, Ann 433 Patience 433
HUNT, Jesse 262 Thomas 149
HUNTINGTON, Samuel 322
HURST, Sarah 59
HURTLEY, Anne 31
HURTLY, Mary 91 William 91
HUSE, Elizabeth 240
HUSK, Dolly 327
HUTCHENSON, Benjamin 301
HUTCHESON, Benjamin 266 307 Margaret 307
HUTCHINSON, Ann 47 Anne 106 Barsheba 106 Benjamin 310 327 Betty 106 Dolley 436

HUTCHINSON (continued)
Edmond 452 Elizabeth 47 49 65 106 126 135 Eunice 327 James 48 166 231 Jessee 369 John 38 47 106 112 147 231 244 279 369 John Jr 328 Leah 435 Levi 369 409 432 Levy 434 Margaret 38 47 280 327 328 Martha 231 Mary 40 47 65 Nancy 231 Peggy 327 380 Rachel 106 Robert 2 13 30 33 34 38 45 47 48 237 304 328 369 Sarah 231 357 369 Stephen 47 65 231 369 Susanna 65 327 Tabey 106 Thomas 48 231 William 327 328
HUTCHISON, James 305 Margaret 273
HUTCHUSON, Robert 201
HUTON, Mary 95
HUTSON, Amy 49 Hannah 370 Ishmael 357 Kelly 357 Levin 370 Raymond 411 Raymond Gorse 357 Robert 162 Scarburgh 357 William 220 230 247 357 397
HUTTEN, George 103
HUTTON, Elizabeth 36 John 36
HYSLIP, Smith 458
HYSLOP, Betsy 407 George 322 374 407 Hannah 348 353 Joice 407 Kendal 448 458 Kendall 448 Leah 448 Molly 407 465 Smith 407 448 William 407
HYSLUP, George 446 George Sr 446 William 446
IDLET, Sarah 71
INGERSON, Catherine 194 276 Samuel 178 194 Tabitha 178
INGOSON, Samuel 276
IREMONGER, Edward 17 Elizabeth 17 Mary 17 Thomas 17 43
IRONMONGER, Betsy 333 Betty 197 Burton 250 Catherine 333 Cornelius 201 210 252 302 333 Daniel 259 Edmund 115 Edward 210 333 379 Esther 214 George 333 379 Jacob 210 John 201 210 265 Major 197 201 241 259 268 285 286 306 313 333 Mary 40 241 259 313 333

IRONMONGER (continued)
Molly 333 Mrs Edward 210
Peggy 333 Philoclear 265 Sally
442 Thomas 40
ISDALE, George 111
ISTALL, John 42
IVY, Susannah 441 Thomas 441
JACKSON, Agnes 110 Ann 109
Archibald 302 Elizabeth 96 98
109 George 385 Henry 110 Jane
10 109 Jean 190 Jenny 302
John 10 98 101 102 109 Jonah
10 Lydia 10 Mary 190 206
Nathaniel 10 Rose 252 Sarah
196 William 109 138 167 169
190 196 206
JACOB, Adah 286 Berry 142 Billy
271 Elizabeh 142 Elizabeth
214 Hancock 142 Henry 441 Is-
sac 13 Mary 142 215 Peggy
441 Robert Clark 142 Susannah
441 Thomas 199 234 247 248
249 252 306 307 320 414 441
Thomas Jr 441 Thomas Sr 441
William 86
JACOBS, John 237 Richard 393
407 Thomas 287 378
JAMES, Able 235 Amey 223 230
Ann 44 David 66 109 138 174
192 220 367 Delight 287 390
Edward 35 Elizabeth 152 161
192 220 287 367 441 465
Euphamy 252 Famy 230 Fanny
223 Hetty 441 Hezekiah 314
315 Jamey 337 Jammy 287
Johannah 223 John 18 72
Jonathan 39 72 Jonna 230
Joseph 72 Joshua 72 155
Laban 220 Lance 145 Leah 287
Levin 465 Margaret 223 230
Mary 72 328 367 441 Nancy
367 441 Patience 462 465
Peggy 230 Rachel 66 155 223
230 Robert 220 248 255 285
287 317 323 335 337 348 367
Sabra 315 Sabrah 314 Sarah 146
220 223 230 247 273 282 323
Spencer 287 337 Stewart 270
Susannah 223 230 465 Thomas
220 223 230 263 301 323 465
Uzeziah 72 William 66 72 150
223 367 422 440 441 462 465

JAMES (continued)
William Sacker 202 220 259
287 317 337 Zadock 331
JAMESON, James 270 Samuel
272 Samuel Heath 270 Sarah
270 Walter 247 270 310 393
JAMISON, Sarah 286
JANNEY, Abel 343
JARGRESS, Rachel 136
JARMAN, William 22 44
JARMINE, Elizabeth 122
JARVIS, Mary 356 Prudence 155
Robert 127 155 William 155
JEFFERY, Patrick 361
JEFFERYS, Joseph 193
JEFFREY, Alexander 243 Francis
243 Marion 243 Pa 354
JEKELL, John 19 Joseph 19
JENIFER, Ann 6 7 10 Col 27
Daniel 6 7 10 16 21 28 30
Jacob 6 Mr 94 St Thomas 21
28 30
JENIFR, Daniel 5
JENKENS, John 108
JENKINS, Ann 14 Elenor 14
Elizabeth 102 240 Francis 38
James 464 John 6 14 46 93 102
139 Margaret 14 Mary 38
Robert 440 460 Thomas 150
440 William 139
JENKINSON, Catherine 73 Com-
fort 97 Custis 97 168 305 324
Elizabeth 37 73 Frances 73 97
James 305 Jesse 73 116 132
Jessey 136 John 73 77 132
Leah 97 Mare 73 Mary 97 Mary
Ann 231 305 Moses 73 Nancy
305 Naomie 97 Neome 73
Peggy 305 Ralph 305 Robert 97
136 198 209 231 249 305 Sally
305 Thomas 32 38 41 43 68 73
78 97 305 Thomas Jr 68 Wel-
thy 97
JEPSON, Henry 134 152
JERMAN, William 52
JESTER, Ann 41 Frances 41
Francis 41 Isaiah 352 James
359 Jedediah 352 Jeptha 148
Margaret 41 148 Mary 41 148
Peggy 352 Richard 41 Samuel
30 41 148 Thomas 41
JESTOR, Samuel 87

KELLAM (continued)
252 278 288 303 306 323 335
William Sr 251 Zerobabel 325
Zorobabel 302 385 391 456
Zorobable 256 257 334
KELLE, Cattarn 57 James 57
Nathaniel 57 Sarah 54 Susanna
57
KELLEY, Charles 440 Griffin 418
Jemima 405 John 464 Joseph
400 Nanny 440 Stephen 460
KELLUM, Comfort 311 Elijah 225
George 421 441 Jessey 431
John 443 Margaret 430 Molley
421 Molly 421 Rosannah 421
Sarah 144 Severn 441 Solomon
421
KELLY, Alice 214 Anne 335
Atharliah 212 Cadey 214
Catharine 212 Catherine 212
Charles 335 Comfort 326
Daniel 73 170 212 303 322 325
David 73 Dennis 73 84 Edmond
212 Edmund 73 136 139
Elizabeth 322 352 434 464 El-
lis 214 Esther 202 214 223
Famey 434 George 73 343 365
Griffin 212 Hannah 384 Henry
326 Hessy 434 Isaiah 335 353
430 Jacob 352 371 415 James
319 Jeremiah 413 John 73 202
212 214 309 323 352 358 365
Joseph 73 183 202 409 434
Joshua 234 Kettey 335 Keziah
347 Leah 223 Levinah 350
Mary 212 323 347 352 Mary
Anne 214 Nancy 352 379 436
Nanny 326 Nicholas 326
Rachel 434 Richard 136 214
323 352 365 421 Sabe 325 Sally
428 Sarah 73 202 212 Scarborough 325 Scarburgh 379
Sophia 335 Stephen 335 Suffia
428 Suffiah 464 Susanna 365
Susannah 214 Tabitha 178 347
Tabitha C 347 Thomas 73 136
309 347 Timothy 106 149 335
363 Warrington 202 William
212 322 335 352
KEMP, James 38 46 50 57 207
Naomi 48

KEMPE, George 70 James 48 53
59 70 Mary 70 Naomi 57 59 70
KENDAL, John 63 323 374
KENDALL, Ann 117 164 Bowden
402 Elizabeth 117 Jabez 128
185 192 303 John 54 77 79 82
103 107 117 128 164 165 185
192 203 224 299 303 333
Joshua 117 128 185 Lemuel 77
114 117 121 131 164 299 Littleton 93 Margaret 192 Mary
117 128 165 Mary Ann 192
Molly 117 Peggy 164 218
Rebeceah 164 Sorrowful Margaret 93 Susanna 164 Susannah
114 Tabitha 77 Theophilus 117
Thomas 192 William 1 10 117
128 139 164 165 185 192 218
279
KENNAHORN, John 143 182 244
William 286 462
KENNET, Susanna 354
KENNIHORN, John 387 Patience
358
KER, Agnes Drummond 400 Ann
403 404 Anne 388 Bridget 270
Catharine 403 Catherine 404
Edward 212 232 234 236 243
244 263 270 275 277 278 287
295 296 306 307 310 311 313
322 324 330 341 356 362 367
372 378 383 388 403 404 439
Elizabeth 403 435 George 374
388 400 403 404 411 423 439
453 455 456 George Corbin 400
Hugh 388 403 404 406 439
Isabel 403 Jacob 376 Jean 403
404 John S 411 414 433 447
452 John Shephard 404 John
Shepherd 374 400 403 465 John
Sheppard 403 Margaret 404
Margratt 311 Mrs Edward 403
404
KERSON, Alexander 134
KILLAHAWN, John 60 Mary 60
Solomon 60 William 60
KILLEY, Joseph 432
KILLMAN, Mathew 316
KILMAN, Abba 448 Betsey 448
Comfort 416 Elizabeth 448
John 448 Mary 448 Samuel 448
Sarah 448 William 448

LEATHERBURY (continued)
Ellenor 5 6 Elliner 294 Ellinor
294 George 5 294 364 398 413
Gilbert 353 John 66 89 150 184
353 460 Mary 60 71 Mrs
Charles 13 66 Patience 18 43
45 294 Peggy 353 Perry 5 43
66 71 87 175 180 268 294 398
431 Rachel 150 Rosey 353
Samuel 399 460 Sarah 184 294
373 William 294 326 364 399
413 423 427 431 446 460
LEATHERMAN, John 171 Sarah
164 Wallop 209
LECAT, Augusten 300 Nathaniel
190
LECATT, Ann Sinah 257 Anne
177 Augustin 33 Augustine 177
245 265 310 437 Charles 151
232 280 Elizabeth 32 33 Esther
232 244 279 John 32 33 45 57
59 138 151 177 John Jr 151
John Sr 30 Joseph 137 151 177
Leven 151 Littleton 125 151
226 246 Major 244 435 Mary 32
33 Nathaniel 140 142 151 160
177 189 216 226 Patience 57
Phillip Alexander 32 Richard
32 Sarah 337 Sarah Scarburgh
253 Shadrack 226 Shadrick 438
Tabitha 33 146 151 Tomasin
33 Tomason 30
LECATTE, Augustine 354 Major
396 Shadrack 325 358
LEE, Anne 148 James 25 30
Richard 96 97 127 William 181
LEGARDE, Monsieur 183
LEGATTE, Littleton 325
LEIGH, John 174 200 214
LEIWS, Josiah 97
LEONARD, Robert 86
LEWIS, 418 Abel 252 405 Agnes
233 Amey 253 Amy 253 Ann 83
Ann Frances 153 Ann Tabitha
253 Anne Tabitha 122 Bettey
319 Betty 211 296 365 410
Comfort 97 122 Crosby 195
Daniel 176 178 296 David 275
Elishe 296 Elizabeth 52 80 97
108 178 260 321 336 337 360
446 Esther 253 Fenn 114 154
George 252 405 Henry 411

LEWIS (continued)
Hetty 296 Isaac 122 210 253
319 336 James 211 343 407
455 Johannah 211 John 16 23
24 28 37 38 42 52 58 67 94 97
114 122 123 178 191 210 211
213 296 299 321 350 365 410
433 437 John Sr 28 Joice 252
380 407 Josiah 252 Joyce 387
Kelly 389 Laban 264 465
Leven 211 Levin 296 343
Liddy 296 Lucresia 28 Lueser
122 Margaret 343 Mary 57 253
296 303 365 434 Matilda 83
Mrs John 365 Nancy 434 465
Phamy 405 Planer William
343 Rachel 296 Richard 28 319
323 336 Ritter 296 331 Robert
28 253 Rodolphus 253 296
Sabrah 296 Samuel 139
Samuell 57 Sarah 211 343
Scarburgh 255 Spencer 303
Stephen 215 233 Tabitha 437
Thomas 98 122 202 210 303
319 William 28 97 100 101 122
124 238 244 253 319 323 336
437
LILESTON, Sarah 448
LILISTON, Thomas 28
LILLASTON, Elijah 348 Jacob
428 Thomas 333 363 Thomas
Sr 363 Tully 363 428 Willet
321 322 363 William 333
LILLESTON, Peggy 295 Sarah
463 Susanna 428 Thomas 308
364
LILLISTON, Ann 197 Annaritta
214 Elijah 170 171 197 389
Elizabeth 389 405 Esther 201
Jacob 197 408 455 John 24 32
171 214 389 Mary 171 Thomas
197 Thomas Jr 274 Willet 201
LILLISTONE, Thomas 315
LINGO, Caleb 255 380 Caty 448
465 David 465 Elizabeth 255
George 448 465 Hannah 155
John 155 255 274 276 374 377
465 Joice 377 Leah 176 380
Leshy 289 Littleton 155 255
Margaret 448 465 Mary 103
Nathaniel 90 Rachel 194 377
465 Ralph 374 Robert 374

LINGO (continued)
Robinson 155 377 **448 465**
Sarah 194 380 Susanna 353
Susy 380 Thomas 380 William
90 155 176 465
LINGOE, Susanna 383
LINSEY, Catherine 102 144
Elizabeth 102 144 Hampton
102 James 102 John 102 144
Margaret 102 144
LINTON, Darby 70 Sarah 133
William 167
LIPPINCOT, Samuel 441
LISLE, Joseph 401
LISNEY, Jane 80 Mary 80 Mrs
Ralph 80 Ralph 68 80
LITCHFIELD, Bettey 308 Comfort 175 Elizabeth 308 Ezekiel
141 175 264 Francis 59 175
222 264 308 Jacob 62 75 77 89
90 97 122 141 222 224 262
Jacob D 61 John 308 Joseph 59
62 89 141 Margaret 15 59 141
Mary 141 308 Mrs William 222
Nancy 308 Sarah 175 Tabitha
141 222 Tabytha 59 William
59 89 141 222 413 Zadock 308
LITTLEHOUSE, Cornelius 62
Dorithy 31 Dorothy 61
Elizabeth 62 Floriana 31 62
Floryana 42 Simon 31 61 William 8 11 31 61 62
LITTLETON, Ann Mary 69 Benjamin 126 Betty 359 Bowman
10 26 85 98 Charles 69 77
Charlotte 240 Comfort 69 240
359 Edmund 69 Elizabeth 10
240 Ester 10 Esther 2 3 George
446 Gertrude 10 21 James 446
Johana 69 John 69 John W 359
John Williams 359 Littleton
359 Margaret 240 Mark 69 76
172 240 337 375 446 Mrs
Nathaniel 26 Nataniel 10
Nathaniel 26 42 Peggy 359
Raner 446 Sarah 10 172 446
Southey 446 Southy 5 6 7 10 21
26 118 Susanna 446 Tabitha 69
Thomas 69 William 69 97 240
375
LIVINGSTONE, Robert 10
LOCKARD, Robert 107

LOGAN, John 374 413 425 437
453 459 Robert 31 36
LOGIN, John 402
LOMBARD, Anne 209 Elizabeth
220 Samuel 209 220
LONG, Coleburn 345 Elizabeth
401 Esther 341 401 John 401
Leannah 401 Levi 430 Margaret 401 Mary 401 Samuel 281
355 356 401 Sarah 401 William
Coleburn 401
LONGO, Elizabeth 95 Isabel 95
James 95 Mary 95
LORD, Fra 7 Thomas 97
LORING, Alice 12 Elizabeth 12
William 12
LOUDFORD, Arthur 3
LOW, Timothy 37
LOWELL, Thomas 280 371
LSYLER, Arthur 63
LUCAR, George 168 Luke 168 176
189 195
LUCAS, Comfort 30 94 Eleanor
177 Elijah 177 357 370
Elizabeth 94 277 Esther 357
Fortune 209 Jabez 140 162 277
397 Joice 377 Levin 124 434
Luck 397 Luke 277 397 Mary
30 94 Nancy 463 Passavell 115
Persevella 124 Rachel 94
Robinson 177 Selby 432
Solomon 124 162 177 385 452
Southy 177 267 Susanna 331
Thomas 30 94 124 133 209
William 30 44 94 124 162 448
William Richard 277 William
Richardson 397 William Sr 44
LUCUST, Elizabeth 421
LUDFORD, Arthyr 3
LUECRAFT, Mary 63
LUIS, William 8
LUKE, John 41
LUKER, Anne 277 Elizabeth 277
John 225 Luke 205 206 213 219
225 226 232 233 235 248 256
266 268 275 277 280 299 320
Mary 225 Peggy 225 Rose 277
Sarah 277 Scarbrough 279
Susanna 277 Susannah 277
LUMBERS, Easther 195 Robert 96
195
LUNDICK, John 371

510

LURSEN, Dorothy 35 50
LURTEN, Betsey 420
LURTON, Betsy 360 Comfort 71
Elizabeth 152 210 Hannah 50
152 158 210 Henry 39 41 50
152 158 179 Jacob 50 70 79 80
94 117 152 158 210 249 250
257 343 356 360 Jacob Sr 250
James 329 368 427 John 39 48
50 85 152 368 407 Laban 368
Labin 402 Lazarus 50 216 Lit-
tleton 140 158 201 216 277 336
341 342 368 Margaret 223 230
Mary 152 158 210 Patience 368
Peggy 230 368 Purnal 402
Rachel 152 210 249 250 Sabra
293 Sally 360 Semer 223
Susanna 152 Tabitha 92 223
368 Thomas 48 50 70 80 158
W 80 William 50 92 William
Polk 356
LYON, John 321 344 Sarah 317
344
MACABE, Rose 66
MACARTY, Darby 109
MACCOLLER, Robert 13
MACCOMB, Elizabeth 13 Esther
13 James 13 John 13
MACCOME, James 36 John 71
Naomi 71 Neome 71
MACCOMES, James 88
MACKANNIE, Wonie 12
MACKARTY, Daniel 11
MACKCOME, Elizabeth 88 James
88
MACKEE, Mary 215 William 215
MACKEEL, John 267
MACKEMY, Anne 152
MACKENNY, Katherine 71 Neall
71
MACKMATH, Elizabeth 406
Fanny 406 Jenny 406 John 406
Sarah 212
MACKWILLIAM, Finley 28
MACKWILLIAN, Ann 15
Elizabeth 15 Fenla 15 Finla 15
16 Margaret 15 Mary 15 16
Overton 15 16 Patience 15 16
Sarah 15 16
MACMATH, Jane 135
MACNAMARRA, John 196
MACOME, Ester 61

MADDOX, Lazrius 58
MADDUX, Thomas 75
MAGRATH, Edward 196
MAHOM, John 323
MAHON, John 247 Margaret 247
Mary 247 Robinson 247 Sarah
247 Sophia 247
MAHOON, Elizabeth 364
MAHORN, Robertson 277 Tabitha
368
MAIDEN, Tabitha 83
MAJOR, Alice 12 Caleb 163 234
Elizabeth 149 Euphamia 244
Euphamla 244 Frederick 261
262 Hannah 195 John 1 4 12
163 174 210 387 Kendall 163
235 Levin 163 Litt Scarburgh
121 Littleton 120 261 262 321
349 Littleton Scarburgh 47 94
95 106 146 161 161 171 179
187 190 192 194 199 213 223
227 228 240 261 304 Mary 4 12
47 50 94 163 Peter 12 47 Phil-
lip 163 Rowles 12 56 121 163
Sarah 321 Thomas 12 William
1 4 6 12 47 50 94
MAKEMIE, Ann 38 70 Betty 34
Ellizabeth 38 Francis 30 31 34
38 John 38 Naomi 30 31 38
Robert 38
MAKEY, Robert 48
MALONE, Rose 204
MANBY, J 228
MANHALL, William 326
MANLOVE, Luke 157
MANNERING, Comfort 122
MAPP, Betsy 366 Betty 268 403
458 Bridget 458 Elizabeth 279
George 458 Hester 458 Housen
Jr 419 Houson Sr 419 Howsen
320 Howson 268 458 Howson Sr
458 John 366 458 Laban 366
Peggy 366 458 Rachel 366
Robins 458 Salley 458 Samuel
419
MARAIN, John 63 Jonathan 63
Joseph 63 Mager 63 Mary 63
MARCEY, Neoma 189
MARCH, Martha 246
MARCHANT, Benjamin 129
Catharine 129 Cathrin 319
Elizabeth 129 Esther 129

MARCHANT (continued)
John 129 319 Margaret 129
Shadrack 129 William 129
Zorobabell 129 Zorowbale 319
MARCY, Catherine 86 John 35
MARINER, Euphamy 421 Richard
299
MARR, William 19
MARRET, John 323 Nimrod 323
Samuel 323
MARRINER, Euphamy 421 George
421 Hastings 421 Jane 13
Levin 421 Major 421 Mary 21
347 Sally 421 Sarah 421 Southy
228 Thomas 21 William 21
MARSHAL, John 135 Mary 135
Peter 322 Thomas 325 Wil-
liam 329
MARSHALL, Annabella 112 164
Beautifila 263 Benjamin 414
426 Betsey 350 Betsy 420 428
Betty 113 Bridget 317 Charles
41 113 229 283 317 Comfort
190 Daniel 107 203 229 263
283 350 428 444 Daniel J 444
Daniel Jenepher 350 428
Easter 465 Elizabeth 203 353
441 Elizabeth Simpson 316 317
Esther 283 413 444 Euphamy
385 Famey 364 Fanney 364
Fanny 364 George 229 263 317
337 411 422 455 Isaac 414 450
James 444 454 Jenefer 353
Jenepher 228 375 385 John 27
32 203 283 353 420 421 444
454 Leah 203 229 444 Levin
203 229 317 362 413 450 Mary
99 112 190 203 353 Nehemiah
324 Patience 228 351 391
Peggy 366 420 Peggy Wise
353 Peter 228 283 350 351 391
Peter Jr 228 Peter Sr 203
Phame 287 Polly 351 391 420
444 465 Rachel 396 Reabeack
422 Rhoda 364 Rhoday 364
Rosannah 317 Roscana 279
Sarah 99 283 287 455 Scarborough 351 Scarburgh 228
Skinner 224 259 283 287 351
444 Solomon 203 229 364 401
415 420 451 Sophia 350 428
Stephen 283 299 343 350 351

MARSHALL (continued)
387 391 413 444 Susanna 287
Tabitha 324 444 451 Thomas 9
72 228 229 283 317 337 338
353 441 William 132 159 203
222 229 244 364 392 401 420
William Jr 345 363 William
Walton 353
MARSY, Alexander 28 Jaen 64
MARTAIN, Betty 288 Comfort 288
Smith 310
MARTAN, Andrew 70
MARTEN, Edward 20
MARTIAL, Ann Mary 100 An-
nabella 100 Charles 100 243
Comfort 100 Daniel 100
Elizabeth 100 John 100 101
208 Mary 100 Mason 191 208
Peter 100 190 Sarah 182 Skin-
ner 253 Solomon 206 William
100
MARTIALL, Daniel 107 147 John
38 Mary 15 William 21
MARTIL, John 191
MARTIN, Andrew 231 368 Betty
373 401 Bridget 49 Charity 206
Comfort 401 Edward 78 112
303 Elizabeth 231 Henry 167
231 267 456 James 253 401
John 37 43 48 341 344 373 399
410 434 454 Luther 312 354
Margaret 205 224 Nancy 448
Peter 205 Polly 254 Richard
106 Ritter 206 Smith 205 342
427 Sophia 299 Susanna 394
425 Thomas 213 William 49
112
MARTING, Andrew 192 Briget 192
Henry 192
MARTINO, Julian 27
MARVILL, John 37 Thomas 37
MASHALL, George 203
MASON, Amey 9 Amy 6 9 Ann
195 Anne 209 Babel 449 Bennet 151 195 209 229 415 Bennett 417 Bridget 229 Daniel
195 Ede 151 Edmund 206 216
229 231 Eleanor 171 195 Elinor
195 Elizabeth 9 Hannah 195
Henry 44 Ishmael 216 Ismael
195 Jacob 229 282 Jeremiah
229 260 John 195

MASON (continued)
Margaret 462 Mary 25 56 145
211 Mary Riley 392 Middleton
138 151 171 177 191 195 Midleton 308 Molly 402 Mrs
Robert 9 Nancy 451 Nanny 229
Nanny Rodgers 360 Peggy 370
Rachel 191 Ritter 342 Robert 6
9 Sally 392 Sarah 52 319
Susanna 392 Susannah 195 229
Temperance 6 9 Thomas 216
229 231 258 451 456 William
38 52 103 162 177 195 370 385
392 451 William Sr 195
Zadock 392 Zorobable 151
MASSEY, Agnis 249 Alexander 28
Ann 185 Anne 265 Atkins 80
461 Atkyns 426 Caleb 415 426
Elizabeth 232 238 251 Esther
238 Isaack 432 Jean 249 John
28 206 232 238 Leah 230 Lit-
tleton 249 Nanney 426 Neomy
249 Polly 377 Sarah 28 230
Stephen 185 249 265 Thomas
28 209 408 426 William 28 238
MASSIE, Alexander 29 Eliner 29
John 28
MASSY, Elizabeth 395 John 395
MATAPANY, 9
MATHEW, John 83
MATHEWS, 388 Anne 331 413
Annie 392 Betty 331 Elias 419
Elizabeth 96 204 Esther 175
Euphamy Atkins 419 Evans
437 George 215 391 413 437
449 George Sr 437 Hannah 211
James 331 John 63 96 323 331
332 392 413 437 Joseph 96 175
185 314 326 370 438 Joseph Jr
215 Mary 331 332 Mrs William
331 Naomi 331 Nehemiah 413
Rebecca 96 153 331 Robins
Kendall 326 Sarah 96 314 357
Scarbrough 331 Staten 331
Staton 331 Thomas 96 331 369
413 Washburn 433 William 83
96 178 181 331 437 438 464
William Sr 369
MATOMPKIN, John 346
MATTHEW, Fletcher 161
MATTHEWS, Anne 218 261 336
Arcady 267 Betsy 449

MATTHEWS (continued)
Betty 246 449 Charles 449
Charles Stockly 296 Comfort
267 Elizabeth 218 Ephaim 336
Ephraim 267 Esther 251 Evans
246 Ezekiel 449 George 192
218 267 336 409 415 449 Han-
nah 218 James 239 258 Jean
218 John 198 243 246 258
Joseph 170 195 209 218 251
265 267 296 311 336 362 395
Joshua 239 Keziah 258 463
Levin 336 Margaret 267 Mary
198 258 296 Meshack 251 309
Naomy 211 Polly 449 Rachel
251 Rebecca 258 311 Robins
Kendall 218 Samuel 258 261
Sarah 251 258 463 Southey 218
242 Southy 209 296 Stayton 258
Tabitha 241 242 258 296
Thomas 193 218 239 246 258
Thomas Stockly 296 William
168 172 195 204 251 296 362
MATTHIS, Jacob 445
MATTS, Ja 6
MAXFIELD, Joseph 129 Mary 129
Stephen 284
MAXWELL, Daniel 197 John 375
MAYS, Midleton 308
MCALLEN, Margaret 258 Rachel
258 Sarah 258
MCBONWELL, 431 Sr 445
MCBRIGHT, Hugh 136 Sabra 136
MCCARTY, Darby 92
MCCLAIN, Fanny 338 John 321
326 Robert 321
MCCLAND, Custis 316
MCCLEAN, Euphamia 243
Euphamy 321 John 321 Robert
243
MCCLENAHAN, Sarah 74
MCCLESTER, Charles 78 John 73
82
MCCLOUD, Custis 188 Elizabeth
188 Peggy 188
MCCOLLOCK, Betsy 439 Wil-
liam 439
MCCOMB, John 119 Naomi 119
MCCORMICK, Patrick 196
MCCREDY, Jemimah 312
MCDANIEL, Prudence 155
MCDOWELL, Patrick 180

MCGAHAN, Charles 111
MCKEE, Nancy 269
MCKEEL, Bonewell 356 357
MCKENNEY, Anne 153
MCKENNY, Catherine 120 Isaac
175
MCLANE, John 344
MCLAUGHLIN, Alenander 270
Alexander 270 James 269 270
Nancy 269 Polly 269 William
269
MCLEAN, John 333 372 374 375
385 413 421 428 438 455 457
MCMASTER, Samuel 376 395
William 394
MCMATH, John 326
MCMILLION, John 166
MCREADY, James 385
MCWILLIAMS, Finley 210 Wil-
liam 250 253 326
MEAD, John 67
MEARS, Abel 261 353 Aby 348
Adah 353 359 Ann Arlington
463 Armstd 460 Armstrit 388
Arthur 464 Asa 388 Bar-
tholomew 11 108 224 304 432
437 Barthomomew 433 Betsy
353 463 Betty 299 464 Caleb
365 376 440 464 Calep 416
Catherine 463 Caty 446 Charity
375 Charles 422 Comfort 348
376 415 457 Coventon 387 437
464 Covington 284 Daniel 267
268 270 Deborah 388 Elisha
261 265 344 348 375 376 378
388 394 414 416 417 422 424
432 444 445 457 Elisha Sr 266
449 Elishe 378 Elizabeth 225
268 353 355 378 416 464
Famey 428 Frances 416 464
Francis 457 George 387 422
Hillary 464 Isaiah 396 James
353 414 416 434 457 464 John
56 261 266 269 270 272 273
299 309 316 321 348 353 354
356 372 378 380 386 388 395
418 422 432 447 449 464
Jonathan 225 231 232 303 323
361 378 432 433 437 Kendall
299 Leah 225 355 418 Levi 267
268 270 375 391 Levin 299 354
417 Lisha 158

MEARS (continued)
Littleton 299 464 Luther 432
457 Margaret 56 266 354 388
416 417 Marget 433 Mary 268
270 366 378 388 440 Mary
Fosque 457 Mecajah 432
Meshack 224 225 418 419
Micajah 440 Milley 422 Moley
422 Molly 353 Nancy 416 418
422 437 Nanny 457 Naomi 299
Nathan 355 Patience 353
Peggy 326 353 378 396 414 422
434 Polly 353 378 Rachel 225
304 396 416 418 Revil 399
Richard 267 268 270 320 353
354 375 378 388 396 415 463
Robert 225 353 416 427 432
437 Rose 354 Rosey 416 Sabra
353 Sally 299 386 388 416 464
Sally Cropper 399 Sarah 225
299 388 Severn 280 299
Shadrack 225 299 345 432
Shadrick 225 Siner 354
Solomon 261 266 388 412 447
Sophia 299 Southy 321 388
Spencer 353 354 416 427 457
464 Susana 225 Susanna 418
Susannah 434 Tabitha 268 269
449 Thomas 56 440 Thomas
Fosque 463 William 60 61 266
267 268 273 346 348 353-355
359 375 378 380 388 394 395
399 415 435 439 457 463 William Jr 359 Zilla 348 Ziporah
432 Zorobabel 353 Zorobable
354
MECOMBE, James 31
MEDCALFE, Isaac 14 John 103
MEERS, Andrew 235 Bartholomew
11 108 143 149 166 190 221
307 Comfort 280 314 Daniel
270 312 Dorothy 36 Easter 307
308 Elijah 143 307 308 403
Elisha 182 238 244 268 308
Elizabeth 11 36 143 149 318
George 235 265 284 314 326
Hillery Bellot Bartholomew
181 John 11 36 50 149 173 182
194 244 248 259 268 284 300
307 308 312 314 John Sr 85
Jonathan 232 235 242 264
Jonothan 318 Kendal 308

MEERS (continued)
Leah 242 318 Levi 270 Lisha
158 Littleton 280 Major 280
Mark 149 235 Mary 11 36 143
147 149 182 308 Meshack 318
Rachel 108 242 318 Richard 11
36 125 143 182 221 248 270
312 Robert 11 36 242 Sabra 173
182 Sabrah 182 Sarah 103 242
400 Shadrach 318 Shadrick 318
Southy 284 308 Tabitha 270
Thomas 149 246 284 Will 265
William 11 36 88 143 161 170
182 252 270 300 308 William
Sr 85 Ziller 314
MEHORN, Margaret 264
MEILL, John 449
MEKEALL, John 87
MELBURN, Drummond 438
MELICHOPS, Elizabeth 145 Mary
145 Naomi 145 Sarah 202
Tabitha 145
MELLICHOP, Nicholas Sr 25
MELLSON, John 43
MELSON, Abigail 108 339 Abigil
434 Adah 322 369 Adra 108
Amey 428 Ann 180 Anne 355
Arcadia 180 Babel 445 Betsey
397 Betty 278 355 434 Bridget
240 332 428 Caleb 439 442
Caty 355 Daniel 108 141 278
384 405 421 422 434 439 442
Easther 332 Edmund 180 338
Elizabeth 108 156 180 241 338
406 Frances 434 463 Francis
339 George 147 180 212 220
322 332 405 Isaac 180 278 457
Issac 355 John 77 108 141 170
180 278 344 John Mackmath
406 Jonathan 434 456 Joseph
108 145 180 Joshua 384 Joyce
241 Kendall 415 Kendle 405
Laney 317 Levin 355 382 413
428 Leviner 301 Mary 108 141
156 339 434 Middleton 68 141
180 255 Mrs Issac 355 Mrs
Solomon 278 Nancy 355 Nanny
413 428 Noah Wyatt 428 Pegg
355 Peter 364 Polly 355
Preeson 347 Rachel 428 Rhody
257 Ritter 400 Sarah 236 256
308 311 332 Shadrick 338 439

MELSON (continued)
Shady 332 Smith 108 141 241
422 424 434 439 440 Smith Jr
397 410 414 Smith Sr 434
Solomon 241 278 397 Sophia
448 Susanna 189 322 332
Tabitha 108 434 439 442 445
William 179 180 191 197 240
322 332
MELTEN, John 97
MELVIN, Alexander 101 Bettey
424 Ephraim 422 George 384
Isaac 450 James 367 417 426
438 John 367 373 455 Mary 328
367 402 Nancy 367 Obadiah
367 Obediah 438 Samuel 327
Smith 312 328 367 Walker 367
William 169
MENDOUM, Elizabeth 308
MERCER, John 222
MERCHANT, John 439
MERCY, Adkins 102 Agnes 198
Atkins 141 Ellizabeth 175 Jane
86 198 John 102 141 143 197
Joshua 143 Leach 141 Leah
141 Littleton 198 Mary 102 141
198 Mrs John 102 Nanny 143
Naomi 197 Neomy 102
Patience 143 Sarah 102
Stephen 198 Thomas 102 141
197 William 102 141 143
MERILL, Comfort 190
MERRIL, Argillus 121 Asenath
426 Elizabeth 146 176 George
426 Isaac 260 John 149 167
Joseph 444 Joshua 157 Levin
167 Martha 121 Mary 426 Max-
ililian 426 Maximilian 426
Rebecca 391 William 121 126
167 255 260 426 William Scott
328 William Sr 328
MERRILL, Asenath 426 Comfort
75 Elizabeth 157 339 Esau 157
Hannah 62 157 Isaac 157 Issac
157 Jacob 72 157 Joseph 339
Leah 157 339 Levin 343
Levinah 157 Mary 157 Nancy
339 Peggy 157 Rachel 157
Rebecca 157 343 Sally 339
Sarah 157 Scarburgh 157
Simpson 157 Thomas 67 75
157 288 Thomas Stockly 62

MERRILL (continued)
William 157 190 339 370 William Scott 370
MERSEY, Ann 314 Thomas 128 William 100
METCAFF, Peggy 428 Thomas 428
METCALF, Anne 255 Charles 255 Elizabeth 163 255 277 381 431 Gordon 255 Isaac 14 21 163 John 48 65 67 160 163 255 384 431 Mark 163 220 223 277 357 384 431 Rachel 255 Samuel 163 213 431 Sarah 48 163 384 431 Tabitha 163 277 384 Thomas 163 213 255 384 410 431 458 Walter 255 William 163 383 431
METCALFE, Ann 17 Elizabeth 17 Isaac 17 35 John 17 48 50 63 68 86 88 89 Samuel 17
MEW, Ann 78 Bridget 78 Lewezer 78 Philip 78
MICHAEL, Adah 264 Adam 92 Adrah 261 Adriana 13 324 Adrians 13 Ann 13 Anne 261 Elizabeth 13 261 Gratiana 13 Joachim 13 146 160 181 261 Joaokim 62 John 13 133 255 261 281 324 Mary 261 Simon 35 261 264 Susanna 181 264 Susannah 261 Symon 13
MICHAELL, Ann 84 Joachim 84 John 84 John Jr 7 Mary 84 Sarah 84 Simon 84 Susanne 84
MIDCALF, Samuel 187 Sarah 463
MIDDLETON, Bridget 60 Catherine 302 Daniel 38 Elenor 38 Elizabeth 463 Gabriell 38 George 3 16 60 147 213 234 272 302 462 463 George Jr 60 George Sr 60 John 38 463 Kendall 424 Major 424 Mary 38 Mrs George 16 Riley 272 389 Tabitha 434 Tamer 260 272 Thomas 38 William 119 147 155 170 191 466 Wise 119 306
MIELLS, Ann 6
MIELS, Ann 6
MIFFLIN, Ann 433 Charles 284 Daniel 128 129 147 178 253 284 324 336 337 387 433

MIFFLIN (continued)
Edward 128 284 Elizabeth Howell Eyre 433 George 284 John 128 Jonathan Walker 433 Mary 129 284 456 Patience 433 Rebecca 433 Samuel 128 129 284 Southy 128 129 284 Warner 284 433
MIKELL, Roger 14
MIKEMIE, Neome 25
MILACHOPS, George 205
MILBOURN, Elijah 376 Joachim 403 Joaikim 376 Joakim 409 Mary 376 Sarah 84
MILBOURNE, Joshua 129 157 Ralph 44
MILBURN, Anne 261 Joachim 261 411 Joakim 413 Joshua 169 Mary 169 Michael 261 Wm 21
MILBURNE, Mary 157
MILBY, Agnes 25 79 Agness 85 Amey 380 Ann 108 Archibald 163 219 Elizabeth 79 85 Frances 111 296 Garrison 69 85 108 Gilbert 300 John 5 42 69 85 108 177 189 204 220 226 245 296 300 411 413 433 440 451 John Jr 41 69 John Sr 69 84 Joseph 5 25 33 37 42 44 Lewcreatia 85 Lukcresha 79 Lukecreshe 79 Mary 79 84 85 108 Miss 296 Mrs John 5 Nanny 198 Nathaniel 79 84 85 108 122 177 261 Patience 69 85 300 456 Peter 66 79 85 177 198 Rosanna 79 85 Sabra 79 85 94 Sabrah 66 Salathiel 69 85 108 111 296 300 Samuel 5 Solomon 300 Tabitha 56 69 85 198 300 William 5 42
MILECHOP, Nicholas 113
MILES, Ann 117 Elizabeth 198 441 Esther 121 George 441 448 Jesse 441 Jessey 441 John 441 Molley 441 Moses 171 Mrs Roger 141 Nancy 441 Parker 441 Patience 49 53 Phillip 414 Rebekah 441 Roger 15 39 141 Rogers 109 Scarburgh 242 247 Stephen 53 Tabitha 441 Tabither 441 Wm 117 138 141 206

MILICHOP, John 113 Nicholas 140
MILICHOPS, Nicholas 145
MILIKEN, Robert 57
MILINER, Noah Wyatt 428
MILLECHOP, Elinor 47 John 47 59 Nicholas 12 20 26 47
MILLECHOPPE, John 30 Mary 30 Nicholas 30 Nicholas Sr 30 Richard 30
MILLECHOPS, George 230 Nicholas 30 36
MILLENER, Betsey 330 Dolly 356 Elizabeth 330 Mary 364 Rachel 330 Robert 330 Smith 330 337 Southy 330 William 330
MILLICHOP, Hannah 167 John 91 Nicholas 91 167
MILLICHOPS, Elizabeth 127 George 207 John 127 Mary 127 Naomi 127 Nicholas 94 127 Tabitha 127
MILLIGAN, Jacaman 362 Jacamen 213 Jacoman 376 John 194 195 234 243 263 376 398 Peggy 376
MILLINER, Amey 317 Anne 317 Betsey 337 Betty 317 James 428 Laney 317 Rachel 317 337 Robert 317 Smith 313 317 369 Southy 317 William 317 337
MILLMAN, Ann 56 Ephraim 304 Nicholas 70 Polly 419
MILLS, Alexander 42 Ann 42 51 53 99 Benjamin 409 438 Edmond 42 Edward 42 53 Elizabeth 42 Hessy 434 Hugh 187 Jesse 434 John 302 Nathan 187 Rebecka 42 Robert 48 58 81 187 Samuel 171 Smith 157 187 Thomas 42 William 39 42 60 187
MILMAN, Ann 178 Anne 130 Elizabeth 178 Ephram 178 Jonathan 178 Mary 178 Nicholas 86 91 176 178 Peter 176 178 Sarah 178 Thomas 178
MILMOND, Betsey 451 Ephraim 451 Kessey 451 Mary 451 Nancy 451 Rachel 451 Tabitha 451

MILNER, Amy 218 Henry 255 Neomi 255 Robert 255 Smith 255 William 255
MINNION, Ann 63 Margaret 63 Owing 63
MINSON, Elizabeth 322 Henry 306 322
MISTER, William 303
MITCALF, Charles 355 Thomas 230
MITCHEL, Daniel 117 James 144
MITCHELL, Ann 117 Mr 196 Mrs William 14 Randle 270 Thomas 13 William 13
MITTCHELL, Brother 50
MONGER, Catharine 418 Cornelius 379 Elizabeth 338 George 330 379 John Major 379 Katron 428 Sally 379 418 Thoman Iron 406
MONTGOMERY, Archibald 295 John 270 271 295 298 354 Patience 295
MOONAH, Alice 204 Daniel 204
MOONEY, Jane 204 John 204 Nicholas 204
MOOR, Ephraim 110 Susana 96 Tabitha 212
MOORE, Agnes 358 Agness 281 Ann 358 Anne 152 Catherine 71 Edward 3 31 53 57 Edward Jr 3 Elizabeth 358 360 Ephraim 110 Ephram 71 James 281 358 John 358 369 371 373-375 390 409-413 419 436 440 457 Joseph 281 358 402 406 Katherine 57 Major 281 Molly 360 Nancy 391 Rebeccah 331 Richard 17 53 Risdon 400 Robert 262 274 280 281 Scarborough 351 Scarburgh 400 Stephen 440 William 281 314 323 360
MORE, Anne 246 Ephraim 185 Isaac Sr 185 Jonathan 268 Joseph 217 Nancy 266 Susannah 309
MOREY, Linsford 235
MORGAN, Arnald 217 Arnold 139 155 162 169 172 200 212 214 255 256 259 267 Betty 331 Comfort 258 Jacob 139 162

PAREMAINE, Jane 9
PARFE, Bryan 23
PARISH, Edward 208 Matthew 107
108 Mr 196
PARK, Arthur 70 Jemima 153
John 70 99 Levina 153 Mary 99
Sarah 99 William 99
PARKE, Henry 17
PARKER, 380 Abigail 65 Abigall
7 Abygall 49 Adah 219 273
Agnes 171 Amey 151 209 Amy
6 9 24 49 65 151 Anderson 24
30 157 174 182 280 287 310
Ann 32 60 64 71 74 101 182
401 428 Anne 119 151 160 340
Bayly 42 Bennet 74 119 Bennit
42 Betsy 402 Betty 64 101 157
174 182 223 271 306 Bridget 20
64 182 Caleb 287 Catharine
310 Catherine 280 400 Charles
7 42 74 82 101 113 119 182 189
225 280 310 331 435 465 Clement 101 197 199 235 243 264
306 312 338 399 418 442 Comfort 29 294 326 Cornelius 118
Dorithy 46 94 Dorothy 61 93
Dorrythea 68 Edward 24 182
234 242 293 Elizabeth 15 29 42
47 49 65 101 196 227 231 233
242 243 311 405 459 465
Elizabeth Deshield 435 Esther
192 202 216 280 Esther Carlisle 423 Euphamy 465
Florence 7 Frances 65 182 342
George 6 7 9 24 25 29 32 35 42
43 47 49 53 65 71 74 80 82 90
101 106 115 119 124 139 151
168 196 202 209 232 234 251
256 271 278 317 338 350 369
393 399 418 423 437 George Jr
42 338 George Matompkin 231
George Sr 25 27 49 52 338
Hancock 118 194 Henry 71 74
82 119 271 378 465 Jacob 350
351 James 338 340 Jemimah
118 John 6 7 9 22 24 26 38 42
49 64 65 88 101 113 114 118
151 157 169 175 182 186 191
192 202 227 242 243 271 280
297 302 306 309–311 316 317
321 342 346 349 350 370 374
378 395 411 438 439 442

PARKER (continued)
John A 351 John Andrews 350
John Jr 20 157 207 431 John R
370 378 429 443 445 455 462
John Riley 235 258 280 459
465 John Sr 24 182 Keziah 118
Leah 60 118 157 444 465
Leven 340 Levin 101 242 Mary
15 49 65 186 216 225 271 293
342 363 Matthew 24 30 157
Matty 302 Michael 342 Molly
280 293 363 423 439 459 Mrs
George Sr 49 Mrs John 65 Mrs
Peter 14 Mrs Phillip 65 Mrs
Sacker 119 Nancy 293 338
Nanny 223 Naomi 31 202
Neomy 192 Patience 340
Peggy 225 280 423 441 Peter
14 15 Philip 59 61 62 74 86
114 121 148 278 Phillip 7 51
65 94 119 242 340 Phillip Jr 61
Polly 435 Prissilla 101 Rachel
151 182 202 Rachell 15
Rebecca 435 441 Richard 74
119 202 271 325 340 353
Robert 9 65 169 179 182 188
225 262 280 306 342 350 399
444 Robert Sr 280 Rosah 352
Rosey 258 273 Rosy 338 Ruth
49 342 429 Sackar 299 303
Sacker 60 64 65 70 73 85 88
118 140 151 166 169 182 186
191 192 194 195 202 227 310
390 437 Sacker Jr 456 Sacker
Sr 456 Samuel 280 413 423 428
Sarah 15 101 157 169 192 218
271 338 341 342 350–352 357
Scarbrough 280 310 Scarburgh
49 245 293 340 Sinah 118 206
Sophah 191 Sophia 227 Sophiah
191 Susanna 65 218 363 Susannah 118 157 168 182 Susey 202
293 Tabitha 55 114 177
Thomas 24 30 76 101 118 157
271 338 350 399 401 436 437
Thomas H 403 441 Thomas
Hall 287 310 441 Thomas
Jacob 441 Thomas Jr 347 384
William 6 14 18 21 22 24 29
31 49 65 66 71 111 116 151 157
163 182 186 191 202 238 242
271 273 297 342 393 396 465

PURNELL (continued)
Hezekiah 192 John 26 27 55 62
194 281 Robert 231 Tabitha 55
PURSE, Gabriel 339
PUSEY, Stephen 460 465 William
454
PYPAR, Issac 72
QUINTON, Abigall 104 Ann 20
Dixcon 104 Philip 86 Phillip
20 40 120 157 449 Phillip Jr
449 Southy 263 Thomas 263
William 449
RACKCLIFFE, Nathaniel Jr 34
RACKLIFF, Charles 1 Elizabeth
1
RAFEL, Lucresey 215
RAFFELD, Sarah 192
RAFIELD, Major 241
RAIFIELD, Comfort 258
RAIN, Betty 175 Samuel 110
RAINE, Samuel 108
RAMSAY, Charles 147
RAMSEY, Ann 204 Barnet 187
Charles 74 Grace 99 Isabel 123
John 318 322 Mary 123 Samuel
198 403 William 198 447
RAMSY, Barnitt 28
RANDALL, Jann 69
RANDEL, William 213
RAPHAEL, Halbert 106
RAPHELL, Hobert 90
RAPHIEL, Halbert 139
RAPHIELD, Custis 319 Holbard
319 Nancy 319 William 319
RAPWELL, Harburt 78
RATCHFIELD, Thomas 125
RATCHFORD, 125
RATCKLIF, Charles 79 Mary 79
RATCLIF, Bridget 14 Elizabeth
14 15 Nathaniel 14 Sarie 14
Whalee 14
RATCLIFFE, George 19 Jemima
139 Nathaniel 19
RATLIF, Charles 115 Waddelo
116 William 116
RATTCLIFE, Charles 15
Elizabeth 15
RAYFIELD, Elizabeth 408 Jenny
369 John 419 Major 408 Mary
408 Peter 369 373 Sarah 369
Sinah 369 Southy 277 William
237 408

READ, Absabeth 337 Ann 56 102
352 Anne 455 Caleb 304 368
407 Charles 304 407 Edmund
328 335 337 438 Elizabeth 304
407 Frances 342 Harry Jr 13
Henry 38 49 51 64 69 89 90 102
110 175 235 352 423 Henry Sr
13 John 13 25 33 49 89 102 226
253 296 304 352 357 369 380
400 414 420 423 438 445 446
449 John Jr 265 John Sr 400
432 Litt 172 Margaret 423
Mary 36 221 Nancy 453
Richard 13 25 89 102 110 114
134 175 223 253 337 438 456
Richard Sr 151 Robert 237
Rose 102 Sarah 34 89 102
Sarah Scarburgh 253 Severn 253
337 455 Smithee 102 Solomon
304 375 415 436 Solomoon 370
Southy 175 235 304 352
Susanna 102 Tabitha 102 134
304 352 368 William 218 253
337 Zorobabel 352 438 452
READE, Baly 267 Henry 19 25
James 25 John 25 Mrs Henry
25 William 25
READY, James M 455
RED, William 182
REDDING, Elizabeth 286
REED, Edmund 218 Henry 229
John 129 179 Sarah 229
REES, Polly 382
REESE, Deere 258 Edward 258
Mary 258 273 Tabitha 258 273
REGGS, Abraham 228 John 228
Joseph 228 Joshua 228
REGS, Rachel 228
REID, John 231 244 303 Solomon
323 William 180
REIDE, Tabitha 96
REMSE, Bennett 3
REVEL, Edward 374 423 John 25
206 227 311 Leah 206 Sally
227 Sarah 311 William 324
REVELL, Agnes 26 179 Ann 47
403 404 Anne 186 Catharine
179 Custis 29 Edward 5 6 14
16 18 19 26 47 113 115 117 150
154 179 188 277 311 435
Elizabeth 26 47 Frances 16 26
29 James 19

525

REVELL (continued)
John 16 26 47 179 188 213 311
435 444 Katherine 188 Leah
213 Mary 186 Mrs Frances 29
Rachel 6 179 Rachell 47
Rebeca 16 Rebecca 179 188
Sarah 47 186 William 311
REVIL, Edward 155 John 277
REVILL, John 311
REW, Absalom 213 260 322 343
427 Beverley 213 Catherine 51
Charles 133 427 Comfort 97
161 213 260 Elizabeth 213 260
427 Frances 260 George 210
John 51 427 Leshe 51 Lisey
296 Nancy 427 Reuben 233 427
Ruben 213 Rubin 260 Sarah
Horsey 427 Sinah 233 338
Southey 83 109 112 114 150
260 Southey Jr 150 Southy 119
120 123 126 127 161 Tamer
260 Thomas 51 Woney 260 427
Wonne 159 210 211 Wonney
213 Wonny 161 162 213 Wony
51
REYLIEE, James 96
RIALLY, Lawrence 6
RICE, Mary 110 William 110
RICHARD, Elizabeth Jr 21
RICHARDS, Alecksander 12
Bridget 153 James 134 135
RICHARDSON, Ann 309 Barsheba
328 Benjamin 158 Betsy 450
Charles 39 92 158 255 309 351
357 375 390 451 Comfort 280
281 Daniel 281 309 340 Edward
417 465 Elizabeth 92 212 280
309 357 394 431 George 39 156
Isaac 417 Jacob 328 370 375
417 James 246 353 John 9 153
156 246 281 309 328 353 394
John Jr 39 Kendal 309 340 464
Kendall 353 429 Kesiah 351
357 Leah 328 Leah Parker 309
Major 431 Margaret 354 Mary
257 328 357 Peggy 394 Peggy
Mears 431 Piwell 39 Rachel
328 329 417 431 Ralph 328 417
Sarah 39 280 Scarbrough 328
Severn 353 Skinner 328
Solomon 257 287 351 357
Susanna 328 346

RICHARDSON (continued)
Tabitha 394 Thomas 39 Wil-
liam 39 280 309 338 340 353
394 431 William Marshall 169
William Martial 100 328
Zerobabel 309 Zorobabel 340
RICHARSON, James 255
RICHE, Mary 200
RICHERSON, Daniel 423 Mary
249 Rachel 377 Solomon 249
250
RICHESON, Benjamin 250 Kendal
276
RICHY, Henry 35
RICKARDS, Ann 190 James 173
Jean 190 Mary 190 Michael
105 190
RICKETS, Elizabeth 35 Ester 35
Mr 62
RIGGAN, Nathan 308
RIGGEN, John 414
RIGGES, John 386
RIGGIN, Joshua 184 Nathaniel 71
Rebecca 331 Stephen 418
RIGGS, Abraham 79 170 245 357
Becky 385 Benjamin 126 Betty
274 Elizabeth 64 Esther 357
George 357 377 Isaac 112 264
267 299 301 Issac 126 James
434 John 127 243 267 301 324
377 Joseph 79 159 377 Joshua
79 159 267 274 301 Leah 357
Margaret 126 Mary 267 357 419
434 Moses 79 Nancy 301
Naomi 126 Rosanna 79 Salady
377 Sarah 274 377 Susana 301
Susanna 285 Susannah 299
Watson 126 136 William 357
RIGHT, Abel 341 Agnes 358 Ann
9 Dennis 454 Elijah 358 Henry
9 Jacob 454 Mary 9 Nancy 454
Rosey 454 Sally 454 William
454
RIGIN, Charity 320 Cherity 320
RIGS, Abraham 119 Joseph 119
Naomi 119 Savage C 403
Savage Crippen 403
RILA, Thomas 16
RILEY, Ann 363 459 Anne Robin-
son 352 Anney 363 Benjamin
74 245 Bennet 262 Betty 271
Elizabeth 119 120 245 271 308

RILEY (continued)
313 363 379 George 443 George
R 380 George Radmond 380
Henry 363 459 John 74 90 262
308 310 321 333 343 352 379
380 392 Larence 24 Lawrence
28 74 Mary 74 95 Mrs Thomas
74 Nancy 465 Ramon 363
Raymond 262 288 371 380
Sarah 28 74 262 379 380 392
Sinah 245 Susanna 459 Susannah 363 Tabitha Robinson 352
Thomas 28 68 73 74 108 119
122 129 141 147 155 169 188
202 207 210 212 214 220-222
224 241 262 296 308 313 338
343 350 363 380 459 465
Thomas Jr 222 Thomas Robin-
son 352 Thomas Sr 262 Wil-
liam 74 126 236 256 262 264
265 306 308 313 380 392 442
William Jr 262 308 310
RILY, Elizabeth 28 John 61
Lawrence 28 Margaret 28 Mary
28 Sarah 18 28 59 Thomas 24
61 Thomas Sr 18 28
RISPASS, Thomas 221
RITE, Mackwilliams 99 Mary 99
William 99
ROACH, Alexander 254 Elizabeth
254 Mary 254 Michael 155
Patience 254 Planner 254
ROADS, John 57 Mary 57
ROBBINS, Ann Starling 75 Diana
75 Elizabeth 75 John 75
Joseph 75 Sarah 75 William 75
ROBERTS, Abel 123 146 147 205
Agnes 186 Ann 284 Arthur 27
29 51 52 65 108 123 274 287
314 315 326 389 430 437 463
Arthur Jr 430 450 Bethulia 29
Comfort 311 Edmund 287 457
Eldred 450 464 Elizabeth 69
120 201 287 450 Frances 29
430 Francis 29 41 50 51 56 79
107 123 146 287 389 430 450
464 Francis Sr 457 Hugh 59 69
71 130 188 241 252 James 457
Joacam 277 Joakim 315 389
John 56 123 146 147 389 430
450 457 Joseph 260 Joshua 389
430 Joyce 52 Katherine 69

ROBERTS (continued)
Margaret 287 Marget 450 Mary
69 71 100 132 252 430 Mary
Bagwell 389 Molly 457 Nancy
315 430 450 464 Patience 227
314 315 464 Peggy 205 464
Peggy Bagwell 464 Rachel 205
457 Rachel James 389 Rachil
James 430 Robert 181 Rose 56
146 147 227 251 Sabra 147 227
251 Samuel 134 Sarah 29 51
127 287 389 430 Sinah 205
Thomas 134 140 158 William
430 450 William S 463 464
William Simkins 463
ROBERTSON, Ann 288 John 79 80
145
ROBESON, Patience 338 Thomas
338
ROBINS, Arthur 7 10 16 18 31 106
139 158 165 206 216 217 252
443 Arthur Sr 420 Barbara 16
25 85 Barbary 15 64 Bodon 85
Bowdoin 98 192 207 219 224
Catherine 148 Easter 85 Edward 26 35 62 72 85 Elizabeth
16 85 Esther 16 Esther Littleton 98 John 10 26 64 85 98
175 309 312 381 John Jr 425
Joseph 127 128 148 Josias 148
Joyce 219 Leah 381 Levi 148
198 Levinah 148 Littleton 85
Margaret 16 31 199 Mark 309
Mary 175 381 Michael 175 265
275 309 317 381 398 Mickel
425 Mrs 10 Polly 425 Sabra 16
Sarah 16 114 148 381 Scarburgh
16 Spencer 309 Susanna 381
425 Thomas 79 85 98 435 Wil-
liam 148 169 175
ROBINSON, Ann 74 Benjamin 73
Edith 7 Elizabeth 6 34 42 74
George 6 James 264 316 321
John 6 Joseph 21 Lawrence 1 2
6 Mary 6 74 Mrs Tully 74
Patience 404 405 431 Sarah 34
42 56 74 Scarburgh 34 74
Susanna 34 42 Tully 20 34 37
38 42 52 56 73 81 West 34 73
William 74
ROBY, Thomas 40
ROCKS, James 464

RODGERS, 191 Abel 166 187 410
Agness 250 Amey 380 456
Amy 423 Ann 250 268 392
Anne 112 187 236 297 Arthur
430 Ayres 465 Babel 211 213
234 250 297 Betsey 423 Betty
392 Clement 456 Csandrah 249
Custis 219 266 330 394 Daniel
117 160 176 249 392 456
Dorothy 297 335 365 Edmund
174 Elizabeth 82 176 186 187
195 219 245 249 250 297 380
392 416 456 Elizabeth Darby
365 Elizabeth Parker 462
Elizabeth Wise 195 Esther 365
Euphamy 465 Finley 295
George 392 Gilbert 297 Hannah
176 456 Hannah Scarburgh 236
Henderson 297 Isaac 213 250
Isaaca 140 Isaack 82 Jacob
136 308 325 329 James 168
173 176 179 181 195 205 209
216 219 221 224 229 232 244
249 280 301 365 385 392 425
427 456 John 87 89 111 160
166 176 186 187 190 214 231
244 249 265 296 297 301 314
328 344 362 369 370 375 380
392 403 415 416 423 424 456
John Jr 139 John Sr 391 Laban
214 219 392 Labin 416 Leavin
250 Levi 314 Levin 303 329
337 357 368 369 369 407 416
437 Major 213 Margaret 213
219 Margret 314 Mary 126 176
206 231 245 250 336 349 365
376 389 462 Mathew 425
Matilda 313 380 Matildah 340
343 Milven 212 Molly 430
Morton 456 Mrs James 425
Mrs John 391 392 Nancy 430
Nanny 265 Naomi 111 Naomy
76 Norwich 186 206 Patience
249 307 Peggy 314 365 392 407
416 Peter 187 244 314 369 417
Polley 314 Polly 236 Richard
65 68 89 187 207 219 247 261
316 365 370 393 463 Richard
Highland 425 Richard Jr 172
201 Robt 187 219 265 297 335
361 410 Ruben 425 Sarah 89
212 297 329 330 385 425 458

RODGERS (continued)
Siner 348 Sisley 65 Smith 245
365 Susannah 314 Thomas 176
195 377 456 Thomas W 436
462 Thomas Wise 195 208 236
380 Tilney 461 West 313 William 29 Z 368 Zerobabel 176
219 235 308 364 Zerobable 296
423 Zerrobabel 174 219 247
249 264 Zerrobable 233
Zorobabel 322 340 343 345 348
368 369 376 380 384 Zorobabel
Jr 364 Zorobabel Sr 364
Zorobable 173 232 259 330 346
357
RODOLPHUS, Widow 1 William
1
ROGERS, Bridget 96 Cazia 59
Comfort 121 Daniel 95 121 125
Daniell 87 94 Eastland 105
Edmund 96 122 Elizabeth 103
225 Gilbert 59 Henry 96 122-
124 Isaac 59 96 103 Jacob 59
89 90 97 105 179 Jean 179
Jeaney 225 John 6-8 11 59 65
66 96 114 121 122 124 205 225
Laban 205 Lawrence 96
Lazarus 59 Leah 152 188
Levin 219 Lydda 190 Mary 7
121 Mathew 94 Micall 89 Mrs
Sollomon 94 Mrs William 90
Nathaniel 121 Newbery 66 Nich
7 Nicholas 8 Peter 8 33 59 96
Rachel 188 Reuben 152 188
Rich 89 Richard 8 33 51 90 94
96 121 122 133 205 Richard Jr
59 60 Richard Sr 121 Robert
205 225 Samuel 96 122-124
Sarah 152 188 189 Sisceley 62
Sisela 59 Sollomon 94 Solomon
59 Sophia 121 Tabitha 59 225
William 8 66 89-91 96 112
William Jr 89 Winney 94
Zerobabel 205 Zorobabel 173
ROGGERS, Peter 47
ROLES, John 324 Jonathan 283
ROLLEY, James 221 222 Tabitha
210 221 William 221 408
ROLLS, Daniel 65 John 14
ROLLY, William 345
ROOKS, James 414
ROOSE, Ellison 126

ROOSE (continued)
James 126 127 John 126 307
ROSE, Allison 84 Eberson 206
Jacob 150 James 150 173 John
84 150 206 215 238 366 Rachel
206 215 Tabitha 150 Thomas
71
ROSS, Absalom 454 459 Andrew
75 Elizabeth 428 454 Esther
454 Ezekiel 162 305 454 Jacob
305 448 459 James 454 459
John 195 Joseph 305 459
Richard 114 Rosey 406 Severn
406 Susanna 459 Tabbe 459
William F 274 276 289 311
315 353 366 William Fraser
268 William T 333
ROUSSALLE, John 26
ROWLES, Anne 160 273 Daniel
45 56 71 76 78 97 121 Daniel
Nickless 105 Daniel Sr 105
Eleanor 105 160 Elizabeth 6 45
173 273 Ellinor 45 Hahcock
Nicholas 216 Hancock 159 160
200 Hancock Nickless 173
Jane 151 160 195 John 5 11 12
14 36 45 48 71 97 105 110 111
134-136 146 151 154 159 160
216 226 273 274 280 301 304
307 John Sr 121 Jonathan 45 51
89 97 102 105 135 274 Major
45 56 71 76 97 105 159 160 172
173 200 Patience 151 160
Phebe 185 Phebee 154 Rachel
151 160 Tabitha 151 159
ROWLEY, Arthur 139 143 148 169
172 235 250 298 340 Comfort
298 299 Grace 143 Henry 298
299 John 139 143 245 Margaret
148 Rachel 148 299 Richard
143 Sarah 143 298 299 William
117 133 143 148 263
ROYAL, Anne 324 Benjamin 210
223 232 287 324 Susanna 256
ROYALL, Ann 347 Benjamin 69
357 Rachel 347
RROSS, John 162
RULE, Agnes 174 Col 316 James
135 140 142 150 168 172 174
188 Margaret 142 160 Peggy
231
RUSS, Mary 311

RUSSEL, Andrew 321 374 Arthur
321 Esther 223 Robert 233
Salathiel 161
RUSSELL, Abel 263 Andrew 211
263 322 Charles 3 Cuthbert 84
Flowerdue 102 George 293 305
340 Isaiah 340 Jemimea 305
John 210 263 Joshua 440
Lavina 233 Mary 211 305
Milby 211 Mrs Samuel 211
Peggy 340 Rachel 211 Robert
171 207 216 340 410 436 438
444 464 Salathiel 210 211
Samuel 211 414 461 Sarah 3
210 223 263 338 340 Solomon
211 305 Thos 373 Upshur 243
RUST, John 10
RUTHERFORD, Ralph 80 92
RYALL, Benjamin 223
RYLAND, Katherine 104
RYLE, Ann 6 Henry 6 Mary 6
RYLEY, John 112 Sarah 35
Thomas 112 125 163 167 178
180 203 210 253
SACHELL, Hennere 49
SACKER, Bridget 20 Comfort 294
Edward 4 Frances 4 Francis 20
SADBERRIE, Christopher 11
Sarah 11
SADBERRY, Lyshia 35
SADLER, Micajah 16 Thomas 76
SALISBURY, Jenny 425 John 425
Sally 425 Thomas 425
SALSBERY, John 98 Mary 98
Sarah 98 William 98
SALTER, Ann 82 Mary 82 Nannie
82 Silvester 82
SAMPELL, Mary 37
SAMPLAR, Andrew 166
SAMSON, Ann 429 Jeptha 87
SAMUELS, Sarah 271 Stockley
271
SANDERS, Andrew 145 Catherine
194 James 139 John 14 83 102
139 Keesier 194 Keziah 438
Mary 69 83 Olinda 83 Rachel
194 Rachell 69 Richard 69 71
125 150 194 358 Samuel 391
438 Sarah 83 Solomon 69
Thomas 39 William 83
SANDFORD, Ann 361 376 412 420
431 Betty 376

SANDFORD (continued)
Elizabeth 420 Esther 420
Green 46 Gyles 46 James 254
John 46 57 69 324 376 412 420
431 452 Kathrine 46 Mary 46
Samuel 21 46 Susanna 46
Thomas 46 324 361 370 376
420
SANDRES, John 420
SANDREWS, Amey 349 Elizabeth
349 John 278 Rachel 243 349
Richard 349 Samuel 349
Thomas 349
SANFORD, Ann 431 Elizabeth 431
John 184 431 Thomas 427 431
SAPPINGTON, Hartly 406
SARAH, Sarah 119
SARE, Jacob 66
SARKER, William 17
SATCHEL, Henry 103 Margaret
117
SATCHELL, Ann 149 Anne 153
314 Bridget 332 Christopher
368 399 401 Elizabeth 149 153
314 Esther 314 Henry 65 89
116 149 153 164 314 Levin 382
Mary 206 305 407 414 Molly
314 Mrs Henry 314 Nancy 458
Rachel 153 217 314 Sarah 149
153 Southey 409 Southy 136
149 153 200 314 322 332 369
371-375 382 385 387 405 410-
412 414 415 428 429 Susan 153
Susannah 314 William 149 365
385 414
SAULSBURY, John 239
SAUNDERS, Catherine 276 James
168 John 168 Keziah 276
Rachel 276
SAVAGE, Abel 63 112 193 205
261 280 303 348 396 419 420
423 428 429 443 451 Abel Jr
419 Abell 43 63 Abigail 80
Adah 271 359 Ann 224 328 393
451 Annabeller 393 Anne 245
250 329 396 Arthur 351 425 439
Babel 348 353 391 Betsey 317
Betsy 419 Betty 250 312 345
Bridget 14 120 Caty 451
Charles 57 64 95 212 340 377
396 430 435 452 Comfort 252
Dorothy 41 212

SAVAGE (continued)
Elizabeth 41 96 112 120 212
249 250 321 328 329 340 393
447 451 Elizabeth Custis 452
Elizabeth Hornsby 396
Elizabeth Rebecca 464 Esther
224 245 250 317 318 Feby 80
Fosque 384 Frances 94 Francis 8 95 120 122 123 143 144
147 149 155 156 182 197 211
212 251 284 312 335 385 390
395 403 407 413 430 444 451
452 457 464 465 Francis Jr 451
Francis Sr 452 Frank 401
George 118 120 322 328 329
359 367 383 385 393 396 435
George Smith 271 359 435
Griffeth 70 96 Griffin 224 245
328 393 409 Griffith 14 112 120
131 250 Jacob 43 63 250 343
351 399 419 443 Jane 451 John
6 41 44 57 63 65 95 120 138
261 312 316 345 362 369 370
379 396 399 401 410 417 419
429 433 443 444 452 John
Smith 425 Jonathan 220 279
Joseph 340 396 435 Katty 420
Kendal 343 353 366 435 Kendall 299 Leah 356 401 410 Littleton 249 257 287 302 310 402
419 Littleton Sr 370 399 Major
205 275 299 302 312 425 Margaret 381 383 396 Mary 8 57 64
70 80 95 109 120 212 228 245
250 271 317 328 329 359 377
382 393 425 435 Mary Ann 41
Matilda 312 Michal 120 Molly
340 Moses 448 Mrs Griffith
120 Mrs John 95 Mrs William
359 Nancy 359 419 443 Nanny
353 419 Nathaniel 420 451
Nelson 249 Parker 63 80 120
140 168 261 342 344 419
Patience 57 70 95 96 118 120
245 246 340 377 381 435 Peggy
205 302 353 377 393 399 401
420 425 435 Peter 287 357 368
420 451 Rachel 138 393
Redegel 120 Redegil 451
Richard 43 57 95 109 120 147
312 319 359 380 382 390 401
433 435 439 451 456

SAVAGE (continued)
Richard Jr 63 Richard R 393
414 435 436 Richard Rodgers
328 Richard Sr 85 Riddagail
285 Roberson 417 Robert 41 43
57 63 64 95 212 252 263 340
351 359 377 382 393 425 435
Robert Jr 382 Robinson 353
372 375 396 414 440 Rose 312
Rowland 8 10 32 57 94 95 120
156 182 189 212 252 266 302
321 353 Rowland Jr 315 Sally
340 344 377 393 419 435 Sarah
41 43 120 131 140 245 249 250
257 305 364 377 393 Scarburgh
120 Severn 357 Severn Eyre
396 Shady 263 Sheabe 280
Sheba 193 Southe 194 Susanna
252 279 353 Susannah 257
Tabitha 120 Tamer 401 Temperance Scarburgh 118 Thomas
6 9 41 44 63 136 205 250 343
399 Thomas Waters 396 W-tt
Griffith 109 William 41 57 63
64 80 120 165 168 199 212 221
223 245 255 261 271 305 317
328 343 348 359 393 396 419
443 447 William Custis 401
William Fletcher 451 William
Hope 245 328 337 359 393
Zorobabel 393
SAVATCH, Richard Sr 85
SAWERS, Tom 107
SAWKILD, Lancelot 17
SAYRES, Benjamin 234
SAYWELL, Richard 9
SCALE, Ann 17 Mary 17
SCANDLIN, Edward 175 James
173 Margaret 173
SCANLON, Oin 45
SCARBOROUGH, Americus 432
Henry 8
SCARBROUGH, Jean 403 William
323
SCARBURGH, Alice 185 186 463
Americus 167 188 189 192 218
240 247 248 265 276 277 286
362 372 397 437 441 456 Ann
32 105 144 210 Anne 187 Ben-
net 32 86 101 108 144 187 210
214 237 462 465 Bennet Jr 114
Bennett 24 60 251 375 416 419

SCARBURGH (continued)
Bradhurst 131 Bridget 443
Brother 50 Catharine 388 Caty
463 Charles 3 5 7 13 20 24 32
51 54 55 60 63 75 90 131 144
169 210 276 313 401 443
Charles Jr 63 90 Comfort 105
313 Dorothy 63 215 216 286
Dorothy Wainhouse 215 216
Edith 55 Edm 88 Edmund 5 11
20 32 38 46 47 50 58 68 90 96
126 172 186 187 215 216 218
240 276 304 313 388 401 443
Edmund Jr 50 440 Edmund
Memore 50 Edmund Memoria
47 Edmund Sr 47 463 Edward K
463 Elizabeth 32 47 50 55 60
131 187 218 240 George 251
373 401 416 454 462 465 Hannah 25 46 72 Henrietta 105
Henry 32 43 47 48 50 58 60 71
74 90 101 105 113 114 118 119
131 144 187 197 210 218 237
243 251 297 369 416 Henry Jr
99 101 Jean 404 John 55 75 90
91 99 111 113 114 131 169 218
276 286 Major 118 Margaret 99
121 144 210 215 Mary 32 47 50
55 60 218 Mary Ann 210 Mary
Cade 56 72 Math 16 Mathew 23
Matilda 50 215 Michaell 50
Michel 63 Michell 47
Mitcheall 84 Mitchel 186 215
Mitchel Jr 150 Mitchell 89 94
218 Mittchell 76 Mrs Henry
105 251 Prosillah 117 Sarah 32
47 50 60 105 131 189 215 218
251 286 416 Tabitha 20 32 37
47 50 60 131 169 187 210 237
Temperance 86 101 Tempernce
70 Ursley 46 William 105 127
185-187 240 319 William M K
463 William Mered K 463
Winefried 187 Winifred 113
Winnefred 74 119
SCOFIELD, Bridget 311 John 311
SCOT, Betsy 462 Day 143
Elizabeth 111 Sally 462 Sarah
83 Thomas 111
SCOTT, Ann 15 16 216 Betsey
462 Catharine 311 404
Catherine 283 400

SHIELD (continued)
Asher 301 Becky 385 Delight
43 48 81 96 115 132 Elizabeth
63 132 Jene 358 John 132 148
236 363 Jonathan 173 Nicholas
236 365 385 Nickolas 318
Nioholas 236 Peter 372 381
401 461 Rachel 363 Reuben
132 140 154 Reubin Taylor 276
Richard 173 358 Ruben 205 236
Sacker 132 140 173 Sarah 132
140 236 309 385 Tabitha 236
William 118 129 William S
381 William Sackar 381 William Sacker 63 132 154
SHILES, Leviner 356
SHIPARD, Jane 49 John 61
SHIPHAM, Agnes 419 Agnis 249
Euphemy Atkins 419 Sarah 336
Susannah 336 William 222 419
William Jr 249
SHIPMAN, William 77 336
SHIPP, Francis 16 Matthew 16
SHIVE, William 3
SHREAVES, Annabella 383 Jacob
383 Levin 383 Molly 383 Stafford 383 Teackle 383 Thomas
383 William 383
SHRIEVES, Teackle 332 William
332
SHRIEVS, Anna 444 Billy 444
Teackle 444 William 444
SICKELS, John 391
SILAVEN, Timothy 109
SILEVANT, Daniel 21 Dorman 21
Mrs Dorman 21
SILL, Ann Ritter 274 Christian
206 240 274 Ester 23 60 66
Esther 91 Gawin 139 Gowen
240 John 95 139 240 274 Mary
273 274 Sarah 95 Will 17 28
William 15 23 34 38 60 91
SILLIVAN, Daniel 454 Susanna
454 William 454
SILVERTHORN, Abey 361 Aby
361 Anne 179 Arthur 179 361
Burton 295 449 Elizabeth 18
179 Esther 332 Henry 361 John
179 361 Joshua 361 Leavin 295
Levin 179 Nancy 361 Sebastian
179 Southey 179 Southy 346
373 Tabitha 295 361 431 432

SILVERTHORN (continued)
Thomas 179 William 361 455
SILVERTHORNE, Ann 295 Arthur
409 Burton 295 John 48 Joshua
409 Mary 48 65 Peggy 449
Sarah 48 Sebastian 37 48 52
Tabitha 48 295
SIMCOCK, John 37 39 Mary 39
Mrs John 39
SIMES, Robert 2
SIMKINS, Ann 43 52 William 52
107 116 156
SIMPKINS, Arthur 227 Mary 227
Patience 227 314 315 Sabra
147 227 251 315 Sabrah 314
William 123 227
SIMPLE, Agnes 177
SIMPLER, Andrew 170
SIMPSON, Ann 126 202 Anne 384
Betsy 460 Charles 384 442
Christopher 201 Comfort 166
202 316 317 343 Drummond
124 164 Elijah 66 201 316 465
Esther 271 George 316 375 431
Grace 335 341 Hancock 236
383 461 John 108 114 123 126
164 174 316 343 375 Laban 166
198 199 201 204 211 225 236
Leah 217 271 316 Margaret 262
400 Mary 126 133 172 202 313
Mary Parker 343 Mrs Southy
316 Mrs William 384 Rachel
164 Rhody 91 Richard 384 S
234 Salathiel 136 188 Samuel
66 166 201 Sarah 67 201 316
Selby 265 316 320 375 460
Sinah 126 Siner 202 Solomon
164 Southey 216 217 242 258
269 272 273 Southy 167–170
172 174 175 178 185 188 192
197 198 202 204 205 208 211
214 220 236 238 248 251 265
272 316 317 330 343 375 384
411 Tabitha 164 384 Thomas
52 91 126 164 202 262 355
William 100 164 262 384
Zophar 127 Zopher 201
SIMSON, Elizabeth 76 John 76
Levin 268 Margaret 76 Mary 76
Patience 49 76 Rachel 76
Samuel 65 67 99 Sarah 67 76
Thomas 76 89 90 99

STATON (continued)
Catharine 211 Catherine 204
Comfort 204 Elizabeth 204
George 204 331 Jacob 204
James 204 463 John 62 463
Joseph 28 53 63 204 323 331
Joseph Jr 34 Kessey 451
Keziah 204 Rebecca 331
Scarbrough 331 Sophia 204
Thomas 204 331 Warrington
169 170 204 451 455
STAYTON, Elizabeth 99 Thomas
99 104
STEAVANS, William 314
STEPHENS, Christopher 167
Elisha 422 459 Elizabeth 167
217 George 167 James 264
John 167 442 Molly 422 Nancy
422 Richard 459 Thomas 264
William 167 441 442
STERLING, Ann Temperance 284
Catherine 284 Elizabeth 449
Harry 368 John 127 213 Mary
350 351 368 Rebecca 368
Richard 37 52 284 368 Sarah
284 Southey 449 Southy 284
William 160 213 284 368 396
STEVENS, Elizabeth 167 George
167 James 140 John 384 Mary
349 384 Molly 412 Rachel 349
Sara 21 Thomas 321 Will 1 10
William 13 19 167 321 383
STEVENSON, Tabithey 226
STEWARD, Andrew 89 286 Daniel
82 Elizabeth 82 286 Martha 82
Sarah 286 Tabitha 82
STEWART, Agnes 146 186
Andrew 60 132 146 304 347 373
Andrews 146 Ann 116 Anne
Snead 229 Benjamin 108 146
158 Charles 347 Daniel 137
Elizabeth 60 116 146 George
146 186 207 208 231 235 236
258 259 265 275 284 287 304
305 317 322 345 347 371 410
James 209 327 347 410 John
146 186 347 Leven 304 305
Levin 146 186 207 230 321 347
363 381 Levin Custis 347
Lishey 146 Mary 218 229 230
345 Mrs Levin 347 Patrick 104
116 144 160 Sabra 146

STEWART (continued)
Sarah 146 186 327 347 Scar-
burgh 218 Ziller 146
STICIKAR, Alice 73 James 73
Jane 73 John 73 Mary 73
Robert 73 Sarah 73
STITH, Griffin 222 331
STOAKLY, Joseph 82
STOCKAM, Rachel 184
STOCKELY, Ann 327 Christopher
54 Peggy 329
STOCKLEY, Alexander 108 153
271 Alexander Jr 168 169 Ann
152 Anne 255 Ayres 154 Betty
154 211 Charles 27 151 152
154 190 Christian 97 127
Christopher 33 97 132 Comfort
108 200 271 Elias 108 134 137
169 Elijah 294 Elizabeth 154
Eyre 114 Francis 30 George
192 Isabel 206 Jane 96 153
John 10 17 30 108 113 152
Joseph 14 28 30 108 133 151–
153 162 170 190 200 271 348
Joseph Sr 200 Kendal 271 Leah
152 153 271 Mary 14 17 27 28
114 200 Mrs William 11 12
Naomi 200 Naomy 128
Nathaniel 140 157 169 200 271
Nehemiah 200 211 261 271 285
294 Rebecca 151 153 Sabra 132
Sarah 30 151–153 157 Thomas
20 29 200 William 11 12 14 19
262 345 346 Woodman 10 14
37
STOCKLFY, Eyre 168
STOCKLY, Airs 310 Alexander 62
107 132 215 220 233 242 245
247 263 265 296 310 311 318
336 348 366 Ann 5 123 124 220
247 310 311 Anne 223 245
Betty 220 Catharine 366
Charles 37 52 53 60 62 88 123
127 147 155 157 211 215 220
310 366 407 408 411 413 422
423 430 440 456 Christopher 42
Comfort 28 220 310 Elijah 245
247 311 Elizabeth 5 60 123 124
233 241 242 Eyre 124 Eyrs 220
Frances 37 Francis 122 123
Hanna 5 Hannah 62 121 Jacob
60 Jane 5 Jemimah 121

STOCKLY (continued)
Jemina 62 John 5 37 62 65 71
107 121 Josenh 265 Joseph 28
29 37 55 60 62 123 132 183 215
220 245 318 366 Joseph Jr 55
63 87 127 Joseph Sr 121 126
Kendal 368 Kendall 279 414
Leah 231 Mary 123 124 146
366 Mrs Nehemiah 310 Nancy
414 449 Naomi 211 245 Naomy
128 Nathaniel 175 189 230
Nehemiah 204 211 220 235 242
245 246 247 258 267 310
Neoma 230 Neomi 62 Neomy
247 Peggy 385 Rachel 215 245
311 Rebecah 247 Rebecca 60
245 311 Rhoda 127 145 Sarah
189 245 247 Tabitha 119 124
241 310 Temperance 121
Thomas 5 29 37 53 55 59 62 88
121 127 145 241 Thomas Jr 55
88 William 5 121 209 219 220
310 385 Woodman 5 37
STOKELEE, Christopher 21
STOKELY, Anna Bella 329 Christopher 29 85 Kendal 305 Peggy
329 Scarburgh 329 William 329
STOKLY, Christian 84 Christopher 84 Isabel 84 Jacob 70
Mary 84
STOT, Sarah 315 Walter 98
STOTT, Amy 40 Anne 239 Bridget
40 239 Daniel 137 Henrietta
239 Henry 33 Joanna 239 John
54 314 315 Jonathan 40 239
Jonathan Dolby 239 Laban 239
Lydia 40 Margaret 40 Mary 227
Sarah 239 314 Susanna 33
STRAFORD, John 26
STRAN, James 194 212 John 281
Sarah 281 Sinah 281 William
281 364 370 400
STRANN, James 161 208 William
332 386 387 410
STRATTON, Ann 37 Elizabeth 14
29 37 Hannah 37 John 11 12 14
29 Mrs John 11
STRIBLING, Christopher 2
STRINGER, Ann 149 Benjamin
204 259 275 289 315 360 384
387 448 Comfort 315 Custis
204 Daniel 138 Elisha 237

STRINGER (continued)
Elishe 221 Elizabeth 143 204
221 231 Fereby 149 315 Ferreby 227 Frances 63 Hillary
368 Hillery 315 Jacob 149 204
360 448 James 329 John 15 16
63 221 231 237 315 360 396
448 450 John Floyd 329 Joynes
204 Mary 221 Peggy 237 Peggy
Smart 329 Rachel 315 360
Sackar 360 Sacker 315 439 460
Sarah 329 Smart 329 Susannah
138 Thomas 40 60 63 82 88 93
108 149 182 204 221 323 324
329 344 William Floyd 329
STRIPE, Abigail 34 Ann 34
Elizabeth 34 John 34 Mary 34
Robert 34 William 34
STUART, Abigale 28 Andrew 28
226 Anna 28 Benjamin 215 226
Daniel 57 Elizabeth 226
George 73 Judith 28 Lizebethy
226 Margaret 28 226 Matilda
226 Nancy 226 Sarah 226 Scar-
burgh 226 Susanna 218
STURGES, Abraham O 438
Elizabeth 168 John 6 Mary 438
Richard 60 William 168
STURGIS, Abigail 254 Abigal 238
Absalom 142 252 274 Absolum
273 Adah 209 238 America 274
Americus 273 Ann 13 Bath-
sheba 159 Bersheba 269 Betty
142 Daniel 13 90 381 Dorothy
Nevill 13 Easter 273 Elizabeth
13 27 90 159 238 Fanney 273
Fanny 273 Isaiah 159 209
Jacob 159 238 251 311 342 375
John 9 13 27 142 158 252 273
428 John Sr 428 Jonathan 13 27
Joshua 158 159 Leurannah 271
Luraner 311 Margaret 271 Mar-
tha 158 159 167 238 Mary 159
260 271 273 Peggy 428 Revel
428 Richard 13 27 31 142 428
Richard Sr 142 Salley 428 Sally
460 Sarah 27 31 142 Susanna
217 Susannah 271 Thomas 440
460 William 117 158 159 209
238 340
STURGUS, Martha 159
SUARBURGH, Mary 20

TAYLOR (continued)
156 203 235 246 247 252 255
308 319 331 365 451 457 465
466 Jemina 130 Jeremiah 128
367 426 464 Jermiah 156 Jesse
246 286 287 Joan 5 John 5 30
33 37 41 45 79 128 130 133 138
142 145 153 155 159 160 165
166 169 173 174 181 198 208
209 227 228 237 253 256 260
275 276 315 316 319 320 326
327 337 340 349 358 362 370
373 374 391 426 455 465
Joseph 130 133 144 156 166
199 289 440 Joshua 56 223 260
296 325 343 357 361 380 382
419 446 448 461 Judith 30 130
Keziah 204 391 Leah 142 305
316 326 340 Leath 286 Leaven
222 228 Leavin 315 Leven 260
Levin 128 134 142 216 283 286
289 357 436 Lezebeth 287 Littleton 193 348 Lizebeth 286
Lyshia 35 Major 227 358 423
455 Margaret 227 282 358 447
464 Mary 26 30 33 39 56 82
114 128 165 227 246 282 286
287 315 450 Mary Ann 461
Mathast 145 Mathew 348 412
Mathias 364 Matthew 460 Matthews 165 Molly 340 363
Moses 276 Mrs Jacob 246 Mrs
John 30 Mrs Thomas 39 Nancy
386 396 436 451 457 464 Nanny
349 375 Naomi 30 56 Naomy
457 Nathan 289 373 Nathaniel
433 Near 421 Nehemiah 135
Nevir 349 Parker 460 Patience
128 165 189 282 326 358 383
Peggy 450 466 Peter 316
Pharaoh 319 Polley 415 441
Polly 276 396 427 457 Purnal
349 Rachel 223 340 371 426
Raymond 465 466 Rebecca 315
331 459 464 Reubin 276
Richard 316 373 Robert 104
138 380 Sackar 396 Sacker 246
253 260 Sally 348 441 460 466
Sam 12 Samuel 23 26 27 44 45
51 56 79 82 87 96 128 145 165
226 326 340 363 364 376 433
441 447 Samuel Sr 340

TAYLOR (continued)
Sarah 35 82 107 118 147 170
223 242 246 288 Savage 440
Scadia 276 Scarburgh 246 457
Selby 349 426 464 Severn 166
349 403 Seymour 349 Shadrack
166 199 246 247 Sidney 441
Sophia 316 348 364 396 453
Sophire 289 Southey 416 Southy
348 Stephen 165 237 253 319
387 Susanna 246 247 296 457
Susannah 195 Susanne 246
Suse 450 Tabitha 142 276 289
326 426 441 464 Tabitha Ewell
416 Teackle 132 165 223 246
247 296 455 457 Teagle 425
Thomas 27 39 45 70 72 95 259
316 335 348 451 Thomas
Teackle 128 281 336 Walter 5
Weltha 289 Whealthy 289 Will
25 William 15 22 33 35 45 51
53 56 82 87 114 142 165 166
199 209 235 256 260 285 289
293 316 319 321 326 336 338
340 348 349 361 363 371 375
378 382 387 396 440 451 William Jr 15 William Mathew
433 William Roley 451 William Wise 332 Winefred 15
Zepheniah 433
TAZEWELL, William 67 77 115
TEACKLE, Abel 454 Ann 393
Anne 229 247 Anne Parker 393
Arthur 248 299 303 325 392 454
Caleb 117 123 246 247 286
Catherine 25 Edwin 392 393
Elizabeth 25 246 247 392
George 349 Harriott 393 James
Justice 392 393 John 25 50 69
89 117 123 199 246 248 300
302 303 320 336 348 389 390
392 393 431 456 John Jr 349
409 435 John Sr 373 374 385
389 390 393 407 408 412 419
436-438 441 461 Joyce 196
Leah 247 Levin 117 177 196
229 247 393 Margaret 25 117
123 199 247 300 335 349 393
394 Mr 65 Mrs Thomas 349
Mrs Upshur 277 Sarah 247
Severn 246 247 Susanna 89 247
Thomas 6 7 13 18 23 25 117

TEACKLE (continued)
135 137 140 144 151 163 177
179 199 215 216 246 247 253
274 299 300 303 304 307 342
348 349 366 Thomas Jr 199
228 Upshur 117 187 199 223
247 271 277 310 William 187
277 300
TEAGLE, Thomas 10
TEMPELLEN, John 80
TENCH, Elizabeth 61
TERNAL, Roger 24
TERNALL, Ann 24 56 John 24
Margaret 24 Robert 61 Roger
24 Thomas 24
TERNON, Roger 12
TERREY, John 10
THATAM, Rachel 293 Tabitha
200
THOMAS, Agnes 206 Ann 279 403
Anne 268 Betty 118 403
Bridget 268 279 403 Elizabeth
279 George 255 268 279 George
Douglas 356 George Jr 206
Harrison 268 445 John 268 279
356 Leven 268 Levin 268 279
327 356 Margaret 112 Marget
445 Mary 279 Morgan 19 Peggy
356 Rosannah 268 Roscana 279
Samuel 24 60 112 Sarah 255
268 279 403 Susanna 445 Wil-
liam 445
THOMPSON, Christophor 117
James 318 434 John 204 378
Robert 16 143
THOMSON, Christopher 27 32
Jemima 132 Joane 31 John 54
104 207 214 215 373 Margaret
464 Mary 104 159 Robert 104
132 Tabitha 373 William 104
159
THORGOOD, Rachel 204
THORN, Joseph 75
THORNBURY, Thomas 31
THORNE, Arthur 36
THORNMAN, Obadiah 264
Obediah 445 Patience 445
Tabitha 264
THORNS, Williams 444
THORNTON, Ann Mary 195 Anne
170 Bridget 125 130 Charles
182 249 275 Comfort 195 239

THORNTON (continued)
David 178 193 Edward 12 34
195 239 296 297 421 429 460
Edward Fiddeman 429 Edward
Sr 195 Esther 195 George 460
Henry 421 Jacaman 193 James
109 125 355 John 125 152 182
195 374 415 421 460 Jonathan
34 96 Joshua 429 Martha 208
Mary 193 421 429 Patience 34
Rachel 153 195 341 421 Rhody
195 Sally 460 Sarah 125 183
193 242 Scarburgh 195 Southy
125 460 Susannah 195 Thomas
34 125 193 208 William 34 125
170 193 343 355 379 460 Wil-
liam Jr 200
THOROWGOOD, Ann 44 Francis
44 Margaret 215 Mitchel 215
Mitchell 218 Pennebruck 215
Sarah Scarburgh 286 Thomas
Scarburgh 215
THORP, Mary 193
THORROWGOOD, Francis 44
THOUNTON, William 464
TIGNAL, Catharine 445 Comfort
288 Dennis 288 394 445 457
Elizabeth 445 Leah 445 Major
288 Mary 288 Moley 422 Nancy
396 Philip 288 299 339 Phillip
445 457 Rachel 445 Rosey 445
Sarah 288 Southy 252 288
Tabitha 166 288 445
TIGNER, Ann 342 Dennis 201 342
Leah 342 Phillip 295 342
Tabitha 212
TIGNOR, Phillip 371
TILER, Jemima 130
TILGHMAN, Joseph 398
TILLINGAST, Nicholas 282
TILLINGHAST, Catherine 282
TILLOTT, James 90 109
TILNAY, Rachel 179
TILNEY, Ann 13 18 Comfort 18
Elizabeth 18 57 114 John 2 4
13 Neomy 278 William 81 100
112 114 252 268 278
TIMBERLAKE, Alice 20
TIMMONS, Sarah 33
TINDELL, Nehemiah 424
TISAKER, William 174
TISDALE, James 109

TRUET, George 21 James 18
TRUETT, Hannan 96
TRUIT, Anne 146 Elias 132 146
   Elizabeth 8 George 8 Henry 8
   James 28 Mary 28
TRUITE, Henry 51
TRUITT, Elias 61 Elishe 61
   Elizabeth 61 Hannah 61 Henry
   61 Mary 78 Sarah 61
TULL, Naomie 74
TULLY, Katherine 33
TUNNEL, Anne 268 Charles 261
   398 Comfort 127 Edmund 156
   Elizabeth 313 392 Esther 313
   Jedday 268 Jediah 390 Joseph
   156 157 167 293 Joseph Sr 383
   Marget 313 Mary 185 193 313
   322 Molly 398 Naomi 156
   Nathan 390 Nathaniel 313
   Rachel 261 383 Rhoda 450
   Sarah 127 313 Scarburgh 82 156
   209 261 Tabitha 398 Washburn
   261 William 185 204 233 313
   398
TUNNELL, Ann 279 403
   Catherine 333 Charles 190
   Comfort 120 190 Edmund 245
   Elias 190 333 403 Elizabeth 96
   190 218 Ezekiel 190 George
   403 457 Isaiah 383 James 383
   403 Jediah 190 John 383
   Joseph 220 440 Joseph Jr 383
   Mary 120 Mrs Nehemiah 447
   Nathaniel 15 23 120 Nathaniell
   10 Nehemiah 378 446 Sarah
   120 127 Scarbrough 333 Scar-
   burgh 103 112 190 267 Thomas
   2 3 Washborn 190 Washbourn
   289 Washbourne 190 Washburn
   267 Washpan 190 William 120
   190 200 William Henry 333
TUNNILL, Edmond 27 Elias 27
   Mary 27 Nathaniel 27
   Scarbrough 27 Washbourn 27
TURLINGTON, Ann 401 Anne 329
   Anne Mary 329 Arthur 401
   Benjamin 154 Catharine 401
   Catherine 401 Comfort 239 401
   Edmond 256 Edmund 119 239
   364 Edmund Sr 364 Elizabeth
   258 Jacob 284 439 James 119
   239 256 277 401

TURLINGTON (continued)
   John 37 347 355 465 Laban 346
   Leah 347 Lishe 256 Mamefield
   37 Mansfield 117 Margaret 329
   401 Mary 37 94 Mrs William
   355 Nancy 396 Peter 37 39 66
   154 329 347 355 Peter Jr 39
   Peter Sr 37 Rachel 347 355
   Sarah 119 154 239 332 342
   Susanna 119 332 Thomas 37
   119 154 239 William 281 329
   345 347 355
TURNAL, Amy 215 Betty 215
   George 215 352 John 215 Mrs
   Robert 339 Nancy 339 Robert
   170 178 294 338 339 Robert Jr
   178 Susanna 339 Thomas 178
   339 372 William 215
TURNALL, Ann 180 Anow Bellow
   73 Robert 122 215 Tabitha 338
   Thomas 73
TURNELL, Betty 217
TURNER, Abel 244 Abraham 199
   221 241 244 Andrew 244 389
   401 432 Atha 395 Betty 440
   Elizabeth 244 George 244 Hil-
   lary 244 Marey 221 Mary 221
   244 Mary Anne 241 Molly 395
   Mrs Richard 244 Rachel 241
   244 Richard 244 Samuel 59-62
   68 Sarah 244 Tabitha 244 288
   401 William 244 414 440 Williams 345
TURPIN, Dennard 383 Denwood
   180 236 William 456
TURPINE, Elizabeth 349 William
   349
TURVIL, Arcadia 79 John 79
TURVILL, John 79
TWARTON, Margaret 47
TWIFOOT, Bartholomew 194
   Bartholomew Jr 194 Daniel 194
   James 194 John 194 Levin 194
   Sarah 194 William 194
TWIFORD, Amey 360 Anne 297
   Bartholomew 113 319 412 Bartholomew Jr 136 Daniel 206
   239 319 379 452 George 319
   358 Hillary 172 James 217 297
   319 323 360 363 412 John 360
   361 439 John O 393 Margaret
   319 Mary 361 Nancy 361

543

WAGGOMAN (continued)
Hezekiah 440 Joseph 278 395
WAIL, William 142
WAINHOUSE, Anne 221 Bridget
172 197 Dorothy 174 188
Elizabeth 221 Fra 18 40 Fran-
cis 37 41 43 52 57 63 172 197
211 221 Margaret 37 63 197
Patience 197 Rose 197 Sarah
156 197 221 William 197 221
WAIR, John 91
WAITE, Diana 38 Joseph 38 Mary
282 Nathaniel 38 William 38
WALE, Elizabeth 51 John 51
Margaret 51 Mary Ester 51
Robert 51 176 185 239 240
Sarah 51 William 51
WALES, John 38
WALFORD, Christian 3 John 3
WALKER, Ann 107 147 168 230
259 434 Annabella 38 Anne 147
Anne Robertson 320 Arcadia
159 Betty 230 436 Comfort 419
Daniel 28 35 38 159 224 259
David 297 Dorothy Wainhouse
286 Elizabeth 31 56 59 68 159
219 408 411 419 434 436 Esther 134 Henry 28 35 219 434
436 Henry Jr 28 Hugh 320 441
James 13 27 28 35 101 259 434
436 James Jr 17 Jane 259 Jean
249 Jemima 159 John 59 75
106 107 115 117 134 136 143
147 173 200 219 224 252 323
409 419 436 John B 408 John
Jr 143 389 410 412 434 John S
434 John Sr 397 409 412 436
Joseph 59 99 132 149 198 206
219 230 262 Joyce 149 Levin
219 320 382 408 417 431 435
436 448 454 Lisey 415 Littleton 149 419 Mary 28 35 59
116 132 149 159 215 Mrs John
434 Mrs Peter 28 Mrs William
419 Nancy 419 436 Naomi 209
233 Nathaniel 31 59 173
Nehemiah 59 111 112 124 132
149 Peter 16 28 35 Rebecca
262 441 Rebecka 429 Robert
219 234 329 412 436 Sabra 269
Sally 306 359 434 436 Sarah
107 147 168 320 Sebella 159

WALKER (continued)
Southy 149 419 Stephen 227 240
Thomas 143 Wiliam Banfield
235 William 219 411 415 419
William B 304 305 314 Wil-
liam Bamfield 259 William
Banfeild 320 William Banfield
205 273 288 295 299
WALLACE, James 456
WALLER, William 1
WALLIS, Ann 34 John 25
Rebekah 441 William 235
WALLOP, Ann 164 Elizabeth 87
George 369 412 413 Izabel 254
James 163 John 8 10 13-15 23
77 79 104 107 113 114 117 125
136 147 163 164 410 412 Mary
254 Parker 164 Peggy 254
Rebeceah 164 Rebecka 8 Sarah
23 77 164 Skiner 289 Skinner
23 87 164 169 171 172 174 182
185 202 205-207 210 220 254
263 297 323 344 Sophia 164
182 William 164 412 446
WALSTON, Thomas 183 William
183
WALTER, Abel 368 Elizabeth 39
Esther 285 John 53 368 Mary
58 Peggy 368 Rachel 285 368
Richard 226 285 368 Sarah 41
Solomon 368 Tabitha 368
Thomas 368 William Henry
335
WALTERS, Leah 340 Thomas
447
WALTHAM, Adah 201 Ann 206
Bridget 29 85 Charleton 29
Charlton 272 Elizabeth 29 33
85 Grace 85 Hester 85 John 29
33 85 201 206 272 306 Peter 29
33 Sarah 272 460 Stephen 29 34
85 272 Teackle 33 218 259 272
283 306 Teakle 29 William
272 306
WALTHAN, Charlton 47 89
Stephen 41 89
WALTHOM, John 225
WALTHUM, Elizabeth 97
WALTON, Edward 452 Elizabeth
452 Esther 452 Job 192 Mary
452 Sakar 452 Sophia 192 William 353 452

WANCHOPE, Henry 144
WANTON, Mary 282 Stephen 282
WAPLES, Samuel 450
WARD, Ann 87 Elizabeth 66 445
461 Golding 458 Isaac 377 Littleton 324 436 458 Mary 377
Michael 65 Sarah 377 Stephen
377 Thomas 43 51 87 William
57 268 282 289 296 345 436
WARDE, Tabitha 69
WARINGTON, Steaven 116
WARNER, Betsy 427 Elizabeth
330 George 370 Isaaac 348
Isaac 369 370 377 386 397 409
412 448 456 Nancy 427 Rachel
204 Sophia 348 William 204
206 237 241 418 464
WARREN, Samuel 283 285 286
Sophia 326
WARRENTON, Sarah 63
WARRINGTON, Abbott 145 202
359 Alexander 40 89 153 198
239 250 298 Ann 85 142 237
260 359 Anne 89 183 239 Arnashai 153 Benjamin 85 256
332 423 Betty 145 202 Bridget
348 Catherine 156 Caty 359
Comfort 183 195 239 246 256
325 359 Edmond 153 237 Edmund 195 Elizabeth 40 133 202
217 239 246 256 285 373 379
386 Ester 434 Esther 239
George 145 256 281 284 285
332 359 457 Jacob 85 237
James 85 144 239 256 344 348
389 447 Jane 100 239 Jemima
153 John 14 40 80 85 131 142
144 183 202 239 256 303 305
341 342 373 386 421 John Burton 386 John Sr 71 Jonathan 85
113 114 142 145 Josephus 239
250 346 Joshua 386 Leah 239
246 Lishe 256 Margaret 85
Marget 250 Mary 40 49 183 237
239 256 332 348 Nancey 285
Nancy 386 Nanney 256 Nanny
256 Peggy 379 386 Polley 273
Rachel 40 85 100 153 183 239
289 379 386 Rachell 40
Rebecca 250 335 359 Rebeckah
250 Rebecker 237 Rhoady 250
Rhoda 250 Sally 239 386

WARRINGTON (continued)
Sarah 85 142 256 332 Shadrack
359 Southy 145 359 Stephen 23
40 85 127 142 144 145 193 202
237 256 373 386 418 431
Steven 14 26 40 Susanna 40
Susy 386 Tabitha 145 256
Teackle 246 359 Thomas 40 85
142 386 Walter 40 45 47 53 90
153 156 194 239 359 William
40 85 100 153 239 346 372 447
William Burton 386
WARRINTON, John Sr 70 Mary 71
Stephen 70
WASHBOURNE, Dorothy 16 John
11 16 28 31 36 38–40 57
Susanna 11
WASHBURNE, Dorithy 68 John 68
Susanna 68
WATERFIELD, Betty 226 Isaac
240 265 353 357 358 Jacob 233
239 364 Susanna 445 William
325 364 414 420 436
WATERS, Abigail 183 Abigall
117 Edward 184 Gabriel 87 96
George 396 Mrs Ricbard 26
Mrs Richard 107 Ricbard 26
Richard 107 183 Spencer 412
459 Thomas 350 438 William
2 183
WATERSON, Rachel 366
WATKINS, Abigail 108
WATKINSON, Abigail 122 Abigal
135 Bridget 246 Cornelius 16
153 257 Dorothy 16 Elizabeth
16 31 263 Levin 153 Peter 16
122 153 Sarah 166 246 Susanna
153 246 Tabitha 153 263
Thomas 153 173
WATSON, Abel 158 215 225 Adah
284 Agnes 257 300 America
387 Americus 275 315 360
Amy 106 147 Ann 52 63 239
277 Arthur 115 284 391 450 452
Barthemy 165 Bartholomew
240 Benjamin 64 80 106 107
115 116 146 158 165 197 201
211 216 259 295 342 Benjamin
Sr 259 Betty 165 362 Bezaleel
161 212 213 224 248 Caleb 295
300 342 Catharine 401
Catherine 401

WATSON (continued)

Comfort 145 153 158 165 221
Custis 257 360 Daniel 44 161
David 33 44 64 65 82 107 144
158 221 275 277 319 Direcktor
165 Directer 116 Director 240
Edmund 106 107 146 156 185
197 211 217 221 227 251 257
300 Elesha 217 Eleshe 217 Eli
239 Elijah 217 221 300 334 378
449 Elizabeth 42 44 64 116 158
259 387 Ephraim 216 217 301
329 343 363 402 412 428 432
437 Esau 165 Esther 191
Euriah 191 Ezekiel 165 201
240 Francis 106 147 George 2
7 Hannah 44 Isaac 387 Israel
330 Jacob 165 240 275 315
James 300 James Tathom 360
Jesse 334 373 Jessy 275
Joanna 33 Johannes 254 406
407 Johannis 360 371 Johennes
255 John 33 42 44 129 158 162
191 217 221 295 300 307 342
362 370 392 415 437 John Mar
428 Joice 116 Joseph 33
Joshua 259 331 Joyce 158 221
Keziah 284 Leah 395 Lender
217 Levi 211 312 Levin 300
Lisha 158 Littleton 158 225
Lucretia 360 Luke 153
Lurcretia 293 Margaret 42 106
147 Martha 44 Mary 33 44 64
158 185 191 221 282 331 389
Meshack 217 282 296 343 345
Mitchel 115 259 275 Mitchell
201 204 Moses 64 115 158 165
201 216 259 Moses Jr 158 Mrs
Bezaleel 224 Neomy 275 279
Newberry 300 Patience 158 221
Patty 240 Peggy 211 259 273
295 309 Perces 161 Peter 33
42 44 52 64 106 147 162 185
191 219 244 251 295 Philender
221 Prieson 293 Priscilla 107
147 251 334 Rachel 165 201
257 397 Reavel 404 Revel 259
Revil 373 Revill 404 Richard
17 Robert 8 10 14 18 28 33 42
60 61 64 65 115 116 146 158
165 192 194 201 221 225 253
259 340 362 Robert Sr 33

WATSON (continued)

Robort 10 Rosey 312 Sacker 201
Sally 295 342 360 454 Sarah 33
44 63 113 144 158 217 221 240
257 300 360 363 Shadrack 185
346 Solomon 158 185 Susan 33
Susana 8 Susanna 33 44 64 428
Susey 363 Tabitha 158 175 217
225 293 360 Thomas 113 175
462 Unice 300 William 211
368 453 Zerobabel 295 428
Zerrobabel 284 Zorobable 257
WATSONE, Robert 8
WATT, Adam 54 163 340 Ann 163
Barbara 111 James 54 163 279
444 John 45 Mason 54 286
Nancy 279 Nehemiah 54 83 111
163 Rachel 279 Scarburgh 163
Susanna 279 Thomas 232 William 54 163 164
WATTS, Adam 83 Ann 49 Anne
297 Capt 79 Charles 131 187
Comfort 131 David 297 369 377
413 460 Dorothy 12 13 Easter
77 Elizabeth 77 95 187 Ester
77 Esther 95 207 369 Henry
237 297 James 83 207 364
Jannat 77 Jannet 77 95 Jannett
12 John 12 24 49 52 53 67 77
78 81 82 92 98 114 131 187 192
225 226 228 233 237 238 246
251 254 256 261 264 267 279
289 295 297 Margaret 210
Margery 12 Mary 49 77 Mr 101
Nehemyah 83 Pricilla 91 Priscilla 77 95 Prisila 82 Rebecca
297 Sarah 77 187 Spencer 413
Tabitha 13 William 77 83 95
97 131 207 237 297 426 461
WATTSON, Abigail 43 Ann 82
Benjamin 40 Daniel 82 David
40 59 Elizabeth 40 41 43 John
40 Mary Bell 40 Moses 40
Peter 40 76 Robert 40 Robert
Jr 41 Susanna 40 82
WAUGH, Betty 124
WEADON, James 2
WEBB, Elizabeth 58 John 58
Joseph 275 Patience 58 Rachel
188 Richard Jr 30 Robert 326
Scarburgh 58 Thomas 58 120
127 130 132 141 146 152 155

WEBB (continued)
159 161 174 182 188 189 192
327 William 188
WELBORN, Ann 280 John 280
WELBOURN, Daniel 52 William
338
WELBOURNE, Thomas 28
WELBURN, Barbara 243 Daniel
224 226 394 395 Drummond
243 432 455 455 Elizabeth 226
Francis 203 226 243 James
226 John 351 Leah 224 226
Mary 203 Rebecca 226 Riley
226 Sabra 459 Thomas 210 243
444 William 243 370 375 411
432 438 452 455 459
WELBURNE, Ann 83 Arcadia 52
99 Barbara 99 Benjamin 37
Dan 85 Daniel 32 52 56 67 71
83 84 87 99 Drummond 400
Elizabeth 83 Francis 56 58 99
167 208 John 400 Mason 83
103 Samuel 56 58 82 83 87 88
99 103 Sarah 83 Thomas 16 23
32 52 99 William 400
WELCH, Bridget 329 Margaret 53
Wally 329 William 266 329
WELFORD, William 118
WELLS, John 161
WELSH, Mary 19 Richard 19
William 280 319
WELTEN, William 83
WESSELLS, Ann 274 275 Arthur
274 Creshe Parks 275 Ephraim
274 275 James 49 54 275 John
275 Rachel 274 Rebecca 275
Rebeccah 275
WESSELS, Elijah 241 Patience
248 Sophia 241
WEST, Abel 155 223 269 273 274
289 296 311 313 376 382 424
462 Abel Sr 349 Abigail 288
Abigal 204 Able 272 Adah 199
200 407 Agnes 182 223 274 424
Agness 203 Alexander 33 34 42
81 91 171 198–200 204 406–408
414 455 Alice 119 Aligal 259
Ann 33 34 94 182 200 259
312–314 366 376 400 424 Ann
Sr 349 Anne 106 188 314 327
399 Anthony 20 33 34 42 56 88
105 179 182 203 273 274 311–

WEST (continued)
131 424 462 Argol Yardly 106
Argoll Yardley 94 Benjamin
259 288 289 321 343 379 388
442 445 Bennony 8 41 Benony
33 34 Betsey 365 Betty 182
259 Bridget 314 365 442
Catherine 33 34 37 462
Cathrine 182 Charles 94 135
136 139 168 188 189 200 294
311 313 348 349 365 376 386
389 393 425 Col 349 Comfort
106 121 182 203 230 288 313
376 406 408 442 462 Edmund
198 375 Edward 110 Elenor 424
Elizabeth 33 45 56 179 189 198
210 230 259 288 313 314 365
406 407 424 442 445 455 Fanny
400 Frances 34 George 12 424
Great John 365 Isaac 200 314
365 424 425 456 Jane 56 Jean
33 179 Jeremiah 313 389 400
John 6 8 9 16 18 25 26 32–34
37 42 56 61 75 81 94 95 97 105
106 146 155 164 179 182 197
199 204 207 223 259 264 273
274 289 307 313 330 365 388
389 400 401 406 407 410 424
425 439 442 445 462 John Jr 25
Jonathan 8 34 37 56 72 80 81
94 188 189 233 314 365 439
Judah 204 Judith 207 Katherine
164 Kendal 365 Kendall 288
Kessey 408 Leah 324 407
Major 182 203 323 402 Margaret 330 424 425 Marget 424
Martha 110 Mary 20 33 34 65
81 179 201 407 Mary Scarburgh
33 Matilda 8 20 33 34 37 42 78
179 313 Nancy 365 Nanney 274
Nanny 204 Parker 199 200 439
442 445 456 Peggy 284 Philip
Parker 198 199 Phillip Parker
200 204 314 331 406 407 Polly
400 Rachel 81 155 204 259 274
376 424 425 Randall 259 388
Randul 259 Revel 424 437 444
Richard 313 376 Salathel 432
Salathiel 410 414 465 Salathiel
Milby 376 Sally 365 Sarah 34
41 73 188 189 200 314 400
Sarah Yardly 106

WEST (continued)
Scarborough 324 Scarburgh 8 33
34 81 83 91 171 182 198 203
406–408 Solomon 73 119
Sophia 240 241 Susanna 274
Susanna Sr 349 Susannah 182
203 424 Tabby 408 Tabitha 442
445 Thomas 288 365 Thorow-
good 365 William 66 110 392
400 Yardly 314 Yearly 314
WESTERHOUSE, Sarah 298 299
WHALE, Rachel 111 William 111
WHALEE, Elizabeth 14
WHALEY, Anne 244 Barbara 136
Esther 244 Solomon 142
Thomas 136
WHALLE, Edward 14
WHALY, John 203
WHARTON, Ann 154 226 Anne
143 Bagwell 297 Bridget 114
120 Charles 31 Daniel 31
Elizabeth 31 154 241 278 297
Francis 31 40 41 100 154
James 143 154 176 226 401
412 John 31 81 105 143 154
181 220 226 227 230 236 241
242 255 257 258 278 297 402
411 413 453 460 Nancy 393
Nanny 227 Polly 247 Revel 114
121 Revell 80 Sarah 31
Susanna 412 Tabitha 226 297
Thomas 31 46 William 207
297 453
WHEALTON, Anne 413 437 Ar-
thur 367 Catherine 56 Elisha
215 374 413 Esther 215 James
215 243 Joyce 154 215
Nehemiah 215 267 304 Rachall
304 Scarburgh 460 Smith 215
Thomas 215 William 154 215
246 289
WHEATLY, Mary 156 Sampson
156 William 156
WHEELDON, Ebenezer 323
WHEELER, John 12
WHEELTON, Arthur 272 444
James 237 272 John 27 169
Joice 432 Joyce 272 Margaret
233 Mary 169 249 Nanne 272
Nehemiah 249 Rhoda 272
Rhody 195 Robert 432
Scarbrough 272

WHEELTON (continued)
Thomas 258 446 William 171
233 249 272
WHELDEN, David 344 379 395
Ebinezer 344
WHELDON, Ebenezer 344
WHELER, Isaac 102
WHELTON, Ann 55 Bridgett 55
Catherine 55 Comfort 55 John
44 55 Mary 55 William 55
WHISHART, Phillip 196
WHITCHARD, Phillip 196
WHITE, Adaniah 154 Adoniah 154
Agnes 273 311 Ambrose 9 Ann
8 233 386 Annabella 358 386
Annobellow 230 Arabella 388
Arthur 407 Benjamin 114 Betty
360 Bridgett 402 Catharine 360
Charity 360 Charles 11 68 89
113 115 141 360 385 Comfort 9
258 Easther 407 Elias 128
Elijah Addison 379 402
Elizabeth 19 115 119 144 188
230 412 Famey 308 Frances
182 Francis 73 Galen 358 386
George 230 311 358 360 386
389 407 George Levie 352
Grace 207 Hancock 118 Hanna
118 Henry 3 4 106 108 113 134
137 140 149 197 200 318 336
Henry Sr 258 Hezekiah 266 294
308 451 Jacob 115 141 155 163
164 200 238 246 268 276 278
327 372 375 384 385 448 459
Jacob Sr 326 Jacobus 338
James 204 407 Jane 8 Joachim
385 Joakim 351 360 384 385
John 3 4 11 46 72 152 165 254
406 407 John Addison 402 John
Jr 11 Joyce 276 384 Laban 232
384 Lawrence 233 Leah 119
123 Levin 258 358 360 372 379
386 388 402 411 412 420 423
424 434 455 Lishey 360
Lucretia 358 386 388 Margaret
448 Mary 89 146 230 245
Michael 344 Mrs Henry 200
Mrs William 119 Nancy 385
Nancy Shield 360 Nathan 156
258 411 Nehemiah 258
Patience 341 Peggy 238 363
Rachel 276 384

WHITE (continued)
Robert 9 238 322 412 Sally 455
Salomy 258 Sarah 11 108 149
153 200 203 230 258 448 Sary
11 Simcock 89 Solomon 123
188 207 339 358 386 Southey
182 258 426 Susa 445 Susanna
238 358 431 Tabitha 89 200
384 Thomas 9 Welthearer 238
Welthia 238 William 10 11 19
32 33 99 104 119 120 122 137
166 178 203 230 245 311 336
337 358 402 406 407 436 440
Wrixom 135 178F 207
WHITFORD, William 71
WHITTINGHAM, Elizabeth 128
WHITTINGTON, Ann 376 387 Ar-
thur 374 376 387 388 Betty 113
Elizabeth 56 128 212 213 376
387 Esther 213 Gartrude 387
George 387 388 Hannah 387
Joshua 212 213 Southey 182
Southy 26 160 169 387 Tabitha
7 William 7 15 56 113 158 212
213
WIAT, Thomas 466
WICHART, James 153
WIDGIN, Mary 9
WIDGION, Ann 273 Viana 273
WIESE, Sarah 168
WILBER, Racher 451
WILIS, Roxe 104
WILKENSON, Jacob 321
WILKERSON, Elizabeth 283 Fan-
ney 376 Gehu 446 Jehu 410
Jehua 376 Jesse 376 381 410
425 Jessey 319 John 381 425
Joshua 319 376 Mary 376 381
410 Polly 425 Susana 446
Thomas 186 288 William 288
WILKINS, Anne 404 405 George
Drummond 404 405 John 68 90
127 141 245 389 438 Nathaniel
67 Thomas 67 Truit 146 Wil-
liam 67
WILKINSON, Elizabeth 133 Han-
nah 323 Jacob 133 201 Levin
322 Mary 128 201 Peter 56
Tabitha 246 Thomas 55 72 133
WILLET, Agnes 310 Ambros 212
220 Ambrose 159 172 220 233
334 Annabellah 284 Anne 212

WILLET (continued)
Betty 212 Catharine 212
Elizabeth 334 John 115 129
139 172 197 212 Jonathan 210
212 303 310 323 440 Margaret
379 Mary 212 Sarah 379 Sinah
212 Thomas 271 334 William
3 24 35 59 212 303 323
WILLETS, William 442
WILLETT, Ambrose 61 89 90
Ann 61 90 Catherine 60 61
Elizabeth 15 61 John 10 61 111
Thomas 412 William 18 25 26
49 61 77
WILLIAM, Custis 434 Isaac 374
Nathaniel 36
WILLIAMS, Alexander 23 Betty
128 Ester 128 Esther 160
Frances 3 Francis 10 Henry 20
21 Isaac 225 248 371 John 3 21
22 73 104 128 160 Jones 39
Margrett 39 Mary 83 Nathaniel
60 Peggy 260 Richard 65
Samuel 11 Sarah 47 Sophia 374
William 11 218 232 235 277
298 321 327 354 376 William
Jr 464
WILLIAMSON, 75 William 24 32
48
WILLIS, Ambrose 153 Bridget
153 458 Custis 353 403 413
414 424 429 436 444 445 448
458 461 464 Daniel 68 153
Henry 68 156 206 Isabella 153
John 40 88 173 John Sr 11
Molly 324 Peggy 323 428 Peter
153 246 Rachel 156 158
Rosanna 246 Sarah 22 27 246
Severn 405 Solomon 279 303
Susanna 246 William 324 Zer-
robabel 246
WILLIT, Ambrose 271 451 Ann
77 Annabeller 225 Betsey
Wise 451 Betsy 451 George
451 Jonathan 305 Nancy 451
Susanna 451
WILLS, Elizabeth 447
WILLSON, Phillip 25 Rebecca 79
Sarah 79 William 12 66 83
WILSA, Joseph 432
WILSON, Eleson 215 Ephraim
414 Levin 184 Rachel 96

WILSON (continued)
Samuel 260 354 376 414
Thomas 37 William 96 119
WIMBERRY, John 82
WIMBPOUGH, Paul 171
WIMBROUGH, Beersheba 254
Elizabeth 356 Esther 382
George 287 John 170 Joseph
254 Patience 254 Rachel 170
Sarah 267 Solomon 209 229
Solomon Lucas 170 Thomas
136 Zorobabel 234
WIMBURY, Rachel 94
WINDER, Andrew 8 Moses 211
WINDOM, George 96 Sissoly 96
WINDOW, Abel 239 277 370 Able
262 Ann 277 287 Babel 239 277
280 Bable 262 Betsy 446 Eli
263 277 Elie 249 Elizabeth 168
239 George 446 Henry 262 337
368 446 James 262 John 72
168 239 262 263 277 287 446
Leah 446 Levi 262 Levin 239
277 299 362 Margaret 319 370
409 Peggy 262 Rachel 362
Robert 262 287 446 Sarah 262
Thomas 143 Violater 278 402
Violetta 263 409 Welthy 262
WISE, Abigail 124 452 Ann C 394
Anne 220 332 452 Barbara 25
Betty 223 Bridget 363 452
Brooks 278 Casey 237 Cassey
312 Charles 332 Drummond
124 Edmund 175 252 306 344
346 353 Elizabeth 16 56 72 245
254 Esther 220 332 391
Ezekiel 124 Frances 65 452
George 65 132 175 312 332 345
391 438 George A 438 455
George Annis 458 George
Douglas 254 Hannah 25 72 245
332 Hannah Scarburgh 56
James 239 245 300 331 343
359 391 Johannas 243 421 452
Johannes 25 343 431 Johannis
124 363 John 5 15 25 34 55 72
90 98 109 118 133 171 197 214
217 237 245 249 278 311 312
325 343 361 365 370 372-374
376 385 394 404 406 409-411
418 425 436 438 450 452 John
Christian 152

WISE (continued)
John Jr 34 65 150 170 217 John
Sr 16 25 65 124 217 332 Joseph
124 Kessey 254 Margaret 214
297 332 Mary 65 148 205 237
245 254 327 332 364 366 Mary
Cade 34 56 72 Matilda 34 55
72 Matthew 124 McKeel 425
Mrs Samuel 315 Mrs Tully
Robinson 254 312 Peggy 249
254 Peter 367 368 376 Rachel
324 370 452 Rebecca 452
Reuben 343 Reubin 361 Sally
Scarbrough 332 Samuel 55 56
72 210 220 315 348 386 455
Sarah 65 152 297 332 385 391
Scarbrough 332 Scarburgh 74
237 Sollomon 452 Solomon 332
352 Spencer 220 Susana 65
Susanna 148 197 245 315 332
418 452 Susannah 182 Tabitha
65 124 312 332 Thomas 55 72
75 90 97 124 135 170 186 210
216 220 245 315 324 Tully 312
321 326 352 365 371 380 423
442 462 Tully P 254 Tully R
217 275 Tully Robinson 138
171 190 206 231 237 249 254
283 306 311 354 William 16 25
34 65 101 133 152 154-156 245
249 318 332 385 391 423 434
464 William Jr 87 216 William Sr 245
WISHARD, Ann 182 Elizabeth 182
Gaeamen 182 Hannah 182
James 182 Joshua 182 Thomas
182 William 182
WISHART, Ann 160 Anne 159
Comfort 128 Elizabeth 159 160
213 George 160 Hannah 77 128
159 160 182 188 235 Jacamen
213 Jacomin 160 James 59 70
77 99 103 111 113 117 126 128
151 155 159 160 235 Jannah
170 Joshua 160 297 327 Mary
70 159 160 Mrs 211 Thomas 70
128 153 159 160 William 160
170 197
WITHERBY, Thomas 46
WITTINGTON, William 26
WOOD, David 140 William 78 80
99

WOOLD, Thomas 137
WOOLDRIDGE, Thomas 353
WORDIE, Alexander 75
WORMSLY, Thomas 62
WREATHWELL, Mary 19 William 19
WRIGHT, Abel 282 285 362 438
Elijah 359 362 456 Elizabeth
362 George 359 362 374 375
430 438 Henry 138 187 355 359
362 393 410 Isaac 359 Jacob
362 Leah 362 Mack Williams
362 Nanny 187 Peggy 359
Rachel 355 359 362 Scarburgh
359 Sinah 362 Susannah 359
Will 23 William 435
WYAT, Diana 16 William 16 123
WYATT, Adah 257 299 437
Andrew 454 Anne 420 Arthur
274 299 389 Esmey 420 George
274 Isma 439 443 455 Ismae
454 Ismael 373 Isme 438 Ismey 401 John 111 274 299 401
438 439 Joshua 274 299 315
321 326 377 380 401 Joyce 274
401 Kendal 274 Kendall 274
299 394 Littleton 108 120 186
236 238 246 353 369 380 383
415 430 Littleton Jr 236 278
282 295 Littleton Sr 323 Margaret 274 Mary 274 299 389
Mrs Joshua 401 Nancy 401
Nanne 274 Peggy 401 Sally 454
Sarah 236 266 Susannah 274
Tamer 401 Thomas 274 389
439 William 108 114 120 186
199 274 323 373 389 401 420
454 William Sr 274
WYLIE, John 39 45
YEO, Hugh 2 3 18 19 Justinian 32
54 74 119 Sary 59 William 18
25 59
YOUNG, Ann 364 431 Annabella
422 Anne 248 329 352 Bagwill
422 Billy 205 Comfort 83 248
379 Elizabeth 155 238 326 422
Ezekiel 100 123 124 173 174
191 205 264 274 281 294 315
316 324 326 329 333 339 364
393 Francis 61 89 100 119 125
191 George 248 276 324 329
362 379 416 433

YOUNG (continued)
George Hope 463 Henry 22 51
James 329 343 373 John
422100 112 119 154 155 180
240 248 323 359 360 364 416
439 443 John Sr 225 Keziah
155 Margaret 248 276 329 362
Mary 122 123 191 276 329 364
422 Mrs Francis 100 Mrs John
119 Nancy 431 Naomi 359
Ommey 421 Patience 248
Peggy 364 Reubin 390 Richard
305 329 340 390 431 Richard Sr
431 Samuel 100 Solomon 248
346 347 Tabitha 122 248 364
Thomas 100 155 274 329 333
364 393 439 William 51 151
170 176 178 194 202 213 215
234 250 264 302 329 333 339
347 354 373 374 377 378 385
392 393 409 410 416 427 434
William Jr 275 276 299 301
305 308 309 316 347 William
Sr 219 223 225 228 230 248 260
267 274-276 279 282 285 288
293 298 299 329 346 362 434
463
YOUNGE, Anne 150 John 150
Patience 150 William 150

www.ingramcontent.com/pod-product-compliance
Lightning Source LLC
Chambersburg PA
CBHW071351290326
41932CB00045B/1422